The Enjoyment
of Music

ALSO BY JOSEPH MACHLIS

Introduction to Contemporary Music, Second Edition

OPERAS IN ENGLISH (*singing versions*)

Beethoven: *Fidelio*

Falla: *Atlantida*

Leoncavallo: *Pagliacci*

Mascagni: *Cavalleria rusticana*

Montemezzi: *L'Amore dei tre re* (The Loves of Three Kings)

Musorgsky: *Boris Godunov*

Poulenc: *Dialogues des Carmélites; La Voix humaine*

Prokofiev: *The Flaming Angel; War and Peace*

Puccini: *La bohème; Il tabarro* (The Cloak); *Tosca*

Tcherepnin: *The Farmer and the Nymph*

Verdi: *Rigoletto; La traviata*

The Enjoyment of Music

An Introduction to Perceptive Listening

Sixth Edition
Chronological

JOSEPH MACHLIS

Professor of Music Emeritus,
Queens College of the City University of New York

WITH

KRISTINE FORNEY

Professor of Music, California State University, Long Beach

W. W. NORTON & COMPANY
New York • London

Acknowledgments

PHOTOGRAPHS:

Paul Klee. *Heroic Strokes of the Bow.* 1938. Colored paste on newspaper on dyed cotton fabric, 28¾ × 10⅞″. Collection, The Museum of Modern Art, New York. Nelson A. Rockefeller Bequest. (p. 115)

Clavichord by Christian Kintzing. Courtesy of The Metropolitan Museum of Art, Purchase, Gift of George Bashlow, Helen C. Lanier, Mr. and Mrs. Jason Berger in honor of Angna Enters, Mrs. Harold Krechmer, Miss Erika D. White, Burt N. Pederson, Risa and David Bernstein, Miss Alice Getty, John Solum, Carroll C. Beverly, and Garry S. Bratman, and The Crosby Brown Collection of Musical Instruments, by exchange, and The Barrington Foundation Inc. Gift, and Rogers Fund, 1986. (1986.239) Photograph by Sheldan Collins. (p. 184)

Henri Matisse. *The Cowboy,* plate 14 from *Jazz.* Paris, Tériad, 1947. Pochoir, printed in color, sheet, 16⅝ × 25⅝″. Collection, The Museum of Modern Art, New York. Gift of the artist. (p. 197)

Vasily Kandinsky. *Painting Number 199.* 1914. Oil on canvas, 64⅛ × 48⅜″. Collection, The Museum of Modern Art, New York. Nelson A. Rockefeller Fund (by exchange). (p. 419)

Louise Nevelson. *Sky Cathedral.* (1958). Assemblage; wood construction painted black, 11′3½″ × 10′1¼″ × 18″. Collection, The Museum of Modern Art, New York. Gift of Mr. and Mrs. Ben Mildwoff. (p. 420)

Georges-Pierre Seurat. *At the "Concert Européen."* 1887–88. Conté crayon, chalk, and gouache on paper, 12¼ × 9⅜″. Collection, The Museum of Modern Art, New York. Lillie P. Bliss Collection. (p. 446)

Robert Motherwell. *Elegy to the Spanish Republic, 108.* (1965–67). Oil on canvas, 6′10″ × 11′6¼″. Collection, The Museum of Modern Art, New York. Charles Mergentime Fund. (p. 491)

Robert Rauschenberg. *First Landing Jump.* 1961. "Combine painting": cloth, metal, leather, etc.; overall, including automobile tire and wooden plank on floor, 7′5⅛″ × 6′ × 8⅞″. Collection, The Museum of Modern Art, New York. Gift of Philip Johnson. (p. 493)

MUSIC:

Arnold Schoenberg, *Pierrot lunaire:* © 1914 by Universal Edition. © Renewed. All rights reserved. Used by permission of European American Music Distributors Corporation, agent for Universal Edition. (pp. 436–37)

TRANSLATIONS:

Excerpt from *Ce Fut en Mai* by Moniot d'Arras, translation by Martin Best. Reprinted by permission of Nimbus Records. (pp. 71–72)

Excerpt from *Le Nozze di Figaro* by W. A. Mozart, translation of the libretto © 1968 by Lionel Salter. Reprinted by kind permission of Deutsche Grammophon GmbH, Hamburg. (pp. 269–75)

Translations of *Erlkönig* by Franz Schubert and *Ich grolle nicht* by Robert Schumann are from *The Ring of Words* by Philip L. Miller. Reprinted by permission of Doubleday & Company, Inc., and Philip L. Miller. (pp. 296–97, p. 300)

Excerpt from *Die Walküre* by Richard Wagner, translation of the libretto © 1967 by William Mann. Reprinted by kind permission of Deutsche Grammophon GmbH, Hamburg. (pp. 378–79)

Excerpt from *La bohème* by Giacomo Puccini, libretto reprinted through the courtesy of Decca International. (pp. 387–90)

Excerpt from *Wozzeck* by Alban Berg, translation of the libretto by Sarah E. Soulsby, London, 1981. Reprinted through the courtesy of London Records, a Division of PolyGram Classics, Inc. (pp. 441–43)

Poetry (*Ancient Voices of Children* by George Crumb) from Federico García Lorca, *Selected Poems.* Copyright 1955 by New Directions Publishing Corporation. Reprinted by permission of New Directions Publishing Corporation. Translation by W. S. Merwin. (p. 513)

Cover illustration by Nenad Jakesevic and Sonja Lamut
Cover design by Mike MacIver

ISBN 0–393–95950–3

W. W. Norton & Company, Inc., 500 Fifth Avenue, New York, N.Y. 10110
W. W. Norton & Company, Ltd., 10 Coptic Street, London WC1A 1PU

3 4 5 6 7 8 9 0

For Earle Fenton Palmer

Contents

PART TWO
MEDIEVAL AND RENAISSANCE MUSIC 55

Unit III: The Middle Ages

Unit IV: The Renaissance

PART SEVEN
THE NINETEENTH CENTURY   279

PART EIGHT
THE TWENTIETH CENTURY   397

Preface

In its chronological version, the sixth edition of *The Enjoyment of Music* offers a newly structured book for those who prefer a chronological ordering. After an introduction to the elements of music, we begin with the Middle Ages and progress historically forward through the contemporary era. As the original philosophy of the book—beginning with the accessible and familiar sounds of the Romantic era—remains a viable one as well, there is also a standard version of the sixth edition that follows my original non-chronological approach.

This new edition represents a major revision as well as a reorganization of material. In the first five editions, the chapters were organized according to individual composers. The chapter on Beethoven, for example, presented various aspects of his creativity—a symphony, a concerto, a piano sonata, a string quartet. In the sixth edition, all these types of pieces are represented, but in divisions organized according to genres. The Classical era is thus subdivided into units entitled The Symphony, Chamber Music, The Concerto, Choral Music, and the like, each containing examples by Haydn, Mozart, and Beethoven. The text itself has not been substantially changed; it is only distributed differently. The biographies—the "story material" of the book—have been retained, as have the direct quotes from letters and writings that were so effective in making each composer come alive. All the same, the new organization constitutes a subtle shift of emphasis from composers' personalities to their works, a shift very much in line with present-day trends in education.

One of the most notable changes in this revision is the addition of Listening Guides that supplement the prose descriptions of the primary repertory. These outline the works in question, presenting their themes and details of their structure, sometimes with approximate timings to assist students in following the specific musical events. It is not necessarily suggested that all pieces be studied in such detail, but the Listening Guides can be effective teaching tools that can facilitate students' comprehension of what they hear.

The section on the elements of music has been slightly reorganized so that more of the basic concepts and building blocks of music are presented in the beginning of the book, while other advanced concepts needed for particular style periods—such as formal structures for the Classical era—have been placed in later chapters. The opening chapters also include new material on musical ensembles—choral groups, orchestra, band, along with a discussion of the role of the conductor. The section on notation that was formerly a part of the elements of music now appears in an Appendix, so that it may be introduced when needed or simply used for reference.

Other unique features of this edition include two new chapters in the twentieth-century music section: one on the American popular scene, including discussion of ragtime, jazz, blues, and musical theater; and one on non-Western music and its influence on the contemporary scene. This revision has also focused attention on social history and the role of the musician in society. This socio-historical focus includes consideration of the role of women in the musical world as performers, composers, teachers, and patrons; two woman composers—Clara Schumann and Thea Musgrave—are represented among the primary repertory of the book.

The book has been completely redesigned so as to take full advantage of the newest technological developments in book production, including the use of a second color for highlighting. Some information has been presented in tabular form for ease in reviewing. This includes, in addition to the Listening Guides, a listing of the principal works of each composer with dates and original titles, which can serve as reference and summary and comparative tables of style traits for consecutive eras, such as Classical-Romantic and Baroque-Classical.

The book formerly came in a long version and a short, to fit courses of differing lengths. In this edition the two have been combined. The primary repertory—equivalent to that of the shorter version—is discussed in detail, together with supplemental examples—formerly only in the long version—that can be substituted for primary examples, studied along with those in class, or used for out-of-class assignments. This arrangement allows the instructor the most flexibility in adjusting the contents of the course to his or her individual requirements.

Whenever possible, operatic scenes studied in class have been made available on videocassettes, which should enliven and enrich the teaching of opera. Throughout this edition, a number of works have been substituted for others: *La Traviata* for *Aida, The Marriage of Figaro* for *Don Giovanni, Die Walkure* for *Tristan und Isolde, The Coronation of Poppea* for *Orfeo.* Several favorite works have made their way into this edition: Palestrina's *Pope Marcellus Mass,* Handel's *Water Music,* Bach's Prelude and Fugue in C minor from Volume I of *The Well-Tempered Clavier,* and Schoenberg's *Pierrot lunaire.* Along with these appear some lesser-known works: Liszt's *Wilde Jagd,* Clara Schumann's *Quatre pièces fugitives,* Quantz's Flute Concerto in G, Joplin's *Treemonisha,* and Messiaen's *Vingt regards sur l'enfant Jésus.* The section on contemporary music has, of course, been updated to include more recent composers such as John Adams and a representative of the younger generation of today, Tobias Picker.

The book has, in the past, presented certain composers as transitional figures between two eras; new examples to this edition include Giovanni Gabrieli bridging the gap between Renaissance and Baroque and Johann Joachim Quantz in an analogous position between the Baroque and Classical eras.

The entirely new package of recordings accompanying this edition is available in three formats—LP, cassette, and compact disk. Careful attention has been given to the choice of recordings, preference going to those that reflect contemporary concepts of performance practice. As a result, the recordings of Medieval and Renaissance music feature historical instruments and choirs of the correct size, while performances of Baroque works accord with present-day scholarship in regard to tempo, dynamics, ensemble size, and other aspects of interpretation.

I am heavily indebted to David Hamilton and Claire Brook for their devoted reading of the manuscript, to Juli Goldfein for her meticulous attention to production details, and to Kristine Forney for her imaginative assistance in revising the text. I hope that the changes introduced in the sixth edition will make this a better book, one that truly enhances our students' enjoyment of music.

Joseph Machlis

Note on Recordings

Sets of recordings containing the music discussed in this book are available from the publisher. The location of each work in the various formats (LP, cassette, and CD) is indicated in the text by the following symbols:

LP

Cassette

CD

(**Note:** longer works often include several CD tracks, to facilitate the location of important internal sections. These track numbers, enclosed in a small box, are indicated in the appropriate Listening Guides either in the text or in the *Listening and Study Guide.*)

Prelude: Listening to Music Today

We are currently experiencing the most radical technological revolution the world has yet known. This age of supertechnology in which we live has touched every aspect of our everyday lives, including when and how we hear music. From the moment we are awakened by our clock radios, our daily activities unfold against a musical background. We listen to music while on the move—on our car stereos, on planes, or with our walkman or diskman while running or biking, and at home for relaxation. We can hardly

Avery Fisher Hall, Lincoln Center, New York, as seen by members of the New York Philharmonic from the stage. (Photo by Norman McGrath)

Bruce Springsteen in concert at the Spectrum, a sports stadium in Philadelphia. (J. Jay/Star File)

avoid it in grocery and department stores, in restaurants, in elevators, in offices—everywhere, music is much in evidence. We can experience music in live concerts—at outdoor festivals, the symphony, the opera, or ballet— or we can hear it at the movies or on television. The advent of MTV (Music Television Video) has revolutionized the way we listen to popular music; now it is a visual experience as well as an aural one. This increased dependency on our eyes—one of our more highly developed senses—makes our ears work less hard, a factor we shall attempt to counteract in this book.

Music media too are rapidly changing. The LP record will be largely unknown to the next generation of music listeners. Cassettes, a relatively recent development, are already being replaced by compact disks, and video disk players will soon be a part of our home stereo systems.

We have learned to accept new sounds in our music experiences, many produced by synthesizers rather than traditional instruments. Much of the music we hear on television, at the movies, and in pop groups is synthetic. These electronic musical instruments can very accurately reproduce the familiar sounds of violins or trumpets, and they can produce totally new timbres and noises for special effects. Composers too have succumbed to the technological revolution—the tools of music composition, formerly a pen, music paper, and perhaps a piano, now more likely include a synthesizer, computer, and laser printer. In short, modern technology has placed at our disposal a wider diversity of music—from every period in history and from every corner of the globe—than has ever before been available.

Given this diversity, we must choose a path of study. In this book, we will focus on the classics of Western art music. Our purpose is to expand the listener's experience through a heightened appreciation of the musical heritage of Europe and its offshoots in America. But no music exists in a vacuum. In discussing the traditions of Western art music, we will touch briefly on popular music, especially blues and jazz, and on the musics of other cultures. The varied musics of Africa and Asia, the worlds of European and American folk music, the remarkable flowering of American jazz in the twentieth century, the vibrant history of popular and theatrical music— each of these is in itself a subject worthy of serious study.

The language of music cannot be translated into the language of words. You cannot deduce the actual sound of a piece from anything written about it; the ultimate meaning lies in the sounds themselves. Unlike popular music, which is intended to be immediately accessible and to speak to its audience without explanation, the world of art music brings us into contact with sounds and concepts that are not always so quickly grasped. What, you might wonder, can be said to prepare the nonmusician to understand and appreciate these sounds? A great deal. We can discuss the social and historical context in which a work was born. We can learn about the characteristic features of the various style periods throughout the history of music, so that we can relate a particular piece or style to parallel developments in literature and the fine arts. We can read about the lives and thoughts of the composers who left us so rich a heritage, and take note about what they said about their art. We can acquaint ourselves with the elements out of which music is made, and discover the plan made by a composer for combining these

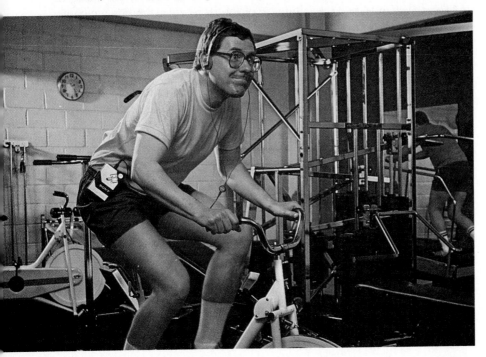

Listening to a favorite tape on his Walkman helps this biker pass the time. (Photo courtesy of Sony Corporation of America)

in any one work. All this knowledge—social, historical, and biographical, technical, and analytical—can be interrelated. What will emerge is a total picture of the work, one that will clarify, in far greater degree than you may have thought possible, the form and meaning of a piece.

There are people who claim they prefer not to know anything about the music they hear, that to intellectualize the listening experience destroys their enjoyment of music. Yet they would never suggest that the best way to enjoy a football game is to know nothing about the rules of the game. A heightened awareness of musical processes and styles brings the listener closer to the sounds, and allows them to hear and comprehend more.

In the course of our discussion we will be building a vocabulary of musical terms that help us understand what the composer tried to communicate. Some of these terms will be familiar to you in another context from which they were borrowed in order to take on a different—perhaps more specific—meaning. Others come from a foreign language, such as the directions for musical expression, tempo, and dynamics which are traditionally given in Italian. We will begin building this vocabulary in the next chapters by breaking music into its constituents, its building blocks—the elements or materials of music. We will then analyze how a composer proceeds to shape a melody, how that melody is fitted with accompanying harmony, how music is organized in time, and how it is structured so as to assume logical, recognizable forms. In doing so we will become cognizant of the basic principles that apply to all styles of music, classical and popular alike, to music from all eras, and beyond that, to other arts as well.

"To understand," said the painter Raphael, "is to equal." When we come to understand a great musical work we grasp the "moment of truth" that gave it birth. For a short time we become, if not the equal of the master who created it, at least worthy to keep the same company. We receive the message of the music, we fathom the intention of the composer. In effect, we listen perceptively—and that is the one sure road to the enjoyment of music.

PART ONE

The Materials of Music

"There are only twelve tones. You must treat them carefully."—PAUL HINDEMITH

Henri Matisse (*1869–1954*) Tristesse du roi, *1952*. (Musée National d'Art Moderne, Paris. Scala/Art Resource)

UNIT I

■

The Elements of Music

1

Melody: Musical Line

"It is the melody which is the charm of music, and it is that which is most difficult to produce. The invention of a fine melody is a work of genius."—JOSEPH HAYDN

Melody is that element of music which makes the widest and most direct appeal. It has been called the soul of music. It is generally what we remember and whistle and hum. We know a good melody when we hear it and we recognize its unique power to move us, although we might be hard put to explain wherein its power lies. The melody is the musical line—or curve if you prefer—that guides our ear through a composition. The melody is the plot, the theme of a musical work, the thread upon which hangs the tale. As Aaron Copland aptly put it, "The melody is generally what the piece is about."

The Nature of Melody

A *melody* is a succession of single tones or pitches perceived by the mind as a unity. Just as we hear the words of a sentence not singly but in relation to the thought as a whole, so too do we perceive the tones of a melody in relation to one another. We derive from them the impression of a beginning, a middle, and an end.

Characteristics of Melody

We can describe three characteristics of any melody: its range, its shape, and the way it moves. A melody goes up and down, its individual tones being higher or lower than one another. By *range* we mean the distance between its lowest and highest tones. A melody may have a narrow, medium, or wide range. *Shape* is determined by the direction a melody takes as it turns upward or downward. This movement can be charted on a kind of line graph that may take the form of an ascending or descending line, an arch, or a wave, to list a few possibilities. *Type of movement* depends upon whether a melody moves stepwise or leaps to a tone several degrees away or farther. Melodies that move principally in stepwise motion are called *conjunct* (joined or connected), while a melody that moves with many leaps is described as *disjunct* (disjointed or disconnected).

These characteristics are illustrated by the examples below.

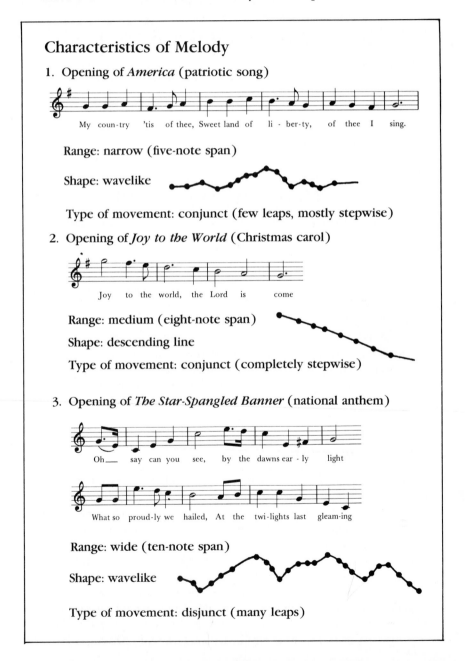

Characteristics of Melody

1. Opening of *America* (patriotic song)

My coun-try 'tis of thee, Sweet land of li - ber-ty, of thee I sing.

Range: narrow (five-note span)

Shape: wavelike

Type of movement: conjunct (few leaps, mostly stepwise)

2. Opening of *Joy to the World* (Christmas carol)

Joy to the world, the Lord is come

Range: medium (eight-note span)

Shape: descending line

Type of movement: conjunct (completely stepwise)

3. Opening of *The Star-Spangled Banner* (national anthem)

Oh— say can you see, by the dawns ear - ly light

What so proud-ly we hailed, At the twi-lights last gleam-ing

Range: wide (ten-note span)

Shape: wavelike

Type of movement: disjunct (many leaps)

The Structure of Melody

We can examine the structure of a melody in much the same way that we analyze the form of a sentence. A sentence can be divided into its component units or phrases; the same is true for a melody. A *phrase* in music, therefore, just as in language, denotes a unit of meaning within a larger structure. The phrase ends in a resting place or *cadence*, which punctuates the music in the same way that a comma or period punctuates a sentence. The cadence may be either inconclusive, leaving the listener with the impression that more is to come, or it may sound final, giving the listener the sense that the melody has reached the end. The cadence, naturally, is where a singer stops to draw breath. Also, a string player will "breathe" at the end of a phrase. If the melody is set to words, the text phrase and the musical phrase will coincide. Many folk and popular tunes consist of four phrases which are set to a four-line poem. The first and third lines of the poem may rhyme, the second and fourth invariably do. This symmetrical type of stanza is reflected in the phrase-and-cadence structure of the melody.

Phrase

Cadence

An example is the well-known American tune, *Amazing Grace*. Its four phrases, both in the poem and the music, are of equal length. Notice that the first and third lines of the stanza rhyme, as do the second and fourth. The first three cadences are inconclusive (incomplete), with an upward inflection like a question at the end of the second phrase. The fourth phrase, with its downward inflection, provides the answer: that is, it gives the listener a sense of finality. One tone serves as home base, around which the melody revolves and to which it ultimately returns.

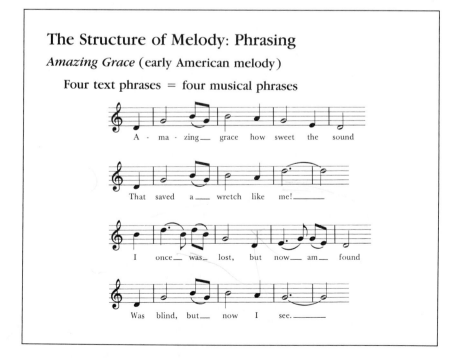

The Structure of Melody: Phrasing

Amazing Grace (early American melody)

Four text phrases = four musical phrases

A melody has to be carefully shaped in order to maintain the listener's interest. What makes a striking effect is the climax, the high point in a melodic line that usually represents the peak of intensity. The climax gives purpose and direction to the melodic line. It creates the impression of crisis met and overcome. The American national anthem, for example, contains a splendid climax in the last phrase on the words "O'er the land of the free." There can be no doubt in anybody's mind that this song is about freedom. Clearly, freedom must be striven for, to judge from the effort we make to get up to the crucial note.

"Melody," wrote the composer Paul Hindemith, "is the element in which the personal characteristics of the composer are most clearly and most obviously revealed." For melody is the essential unit of communication in music: the direct bearer of meaning from composer to listener.

2

Rhythm: Musical Time

"In the beginning was rhythm."—HANS VON BÜLOW

Rhythm—the Greek word for "flow"—is the term we use to refer to the controlled movement of music in time. Since music is an art that exists solely in time, rhythm shapes all the relationships within a composition, down to the minutest detail. Hence the composer Roger Sessions's remark that "an adequate definition of rhythm comes close to defining music itself."

The Nature of Rhythm

It is rhythm that causes people to fall in step when the band plays, to nod or tap with the beat. Rhythm releases our motor reflexes even if we do not respond with actual physical movement. We feel it in ourselves as a kind of ideal motion; we seem to dance without leaving our chairs.

Upon the tick-tock of the clock or any series of noises we hear, we automatically impose a pattern. We hear the sounds as a regular pulsation of strong and weak beats. In other words, we organize our perception of time by means of rhythm. The ancients believed that, in its most general sense, rhythm was the controlling principle of the universe. Certainly, it can be perceived in all the arts. The symmetrical proportions of architecture, the balanced grouping of painting and sculpture, the repeated movements of the dance, the regular meters of poetry— each in its own sphere represents our deep-seated need for rhythmical arrangement. But it is in music, the art of ideal movement, that rhythm finds its richest expression.

In architecture, symmetry and repetition of elements are expressions of rhythm. The Sydney Opera House, Bennelong Point, Sydney Harbor, 1972. (Photo courtesy Australian Tourist Commission)

Meter

If we are to grasp the flow of music through time, time must be organized. Musical time is usually organized in terms of a basic unit of length, known as a *beat*—the regular pulsation to which we may tap our feet. Some beats are stronger than others—these are known as *accented* or *strong* beats. In much of the music we hear, these strong beats occur at regular intervals— every other beat, every third beat, every fourth, and so on—and thus we perceive the beats in groups of two, three, four, or more. These groups are known as *measures* each containing a fixed number of beats. The first beat of the measure generally receives the strongest accent.

Beat

Measure

Meter, therefore, denotes the fixed time patterns within which musical events take place. Within the underlying metrical framework, the rhythm flows freely. Although meter is one of the elements of rhythm, it is possible to draw a subtle distinction between them: rhythm refers to the overall movement of music in time and the control of that movement while meter involves the actual measurement of time. A similar distinction may be drawn in the realm of poetry. For example, the following stanza by Robert Frost is in a simple meter that alternates a strong and weak beat. A metrical reading of this poem will bring out the regular pattern of accented (´) and unaccented (-) syllables:

> The woods are love-ly, dark and deep.
>
> But I have prom-is-es to keep,
>
> And miles to go be-fore I sleep,
>
> And miles to go be-fore I sleep.

When we read rhythmically, on the other hand, we bring out the natural flow of the language within the basic meter, and, more important, the expressive meaning of the words.

Metrical Patterns

Most meters are organized into simple patterns of two, three, or four beats grouped together in a measure. As in poetry, these meters depend on the regular recurrence of accent. Simplest of all is a succession of beats in which *Simple meters* a strong beat alternates with a weak one: ONE-two, ONE-two, or, in marching, LEFT-right, LEFT-right. This pattern of two beats to a measure is known as *duple meter* and occurs in many nursery rhymes and marching songs, as well as in other kinds of music.

Triple meter is another basic pattern in Western music. It consists of three beats to a measure—one strong beat and two weak—and is traditionally associated with such dances as the waltz and the minuet.

Quadruple meter also known as *common time*, contains four beats to the measure, with a primary accent on the first beat and a secondary accent on the third. Although it is sometimes not easy to tell duple and quadruple meter apart, quadruple meter usually has a broader feeling.

Compound meters Meters in which each beat is divided into three (rather than two) are known as *compound meters*. Most frequent among them is *sextuple meter*, with six beats to the measure with a primary accent on the first beat and a secondary accent on the fourth. Marked by a gently flowing effect, this pattern is often found in lullabies and boat songs. The following examples illustrate the four basic patterns:

Examples of Simple and Compound Meters

´ = primary accent
˘ = secondary accent
¯ = unaccented beat

Duple meter: *Twinkle, twinkle little star* (children's song)

Accents: Twin-kle, twin-kle lit-tle star, ¯_____
Meter: 1   2 | 1   2 | 1 2 | 1   2 |

          How I won-der what you are, ¯_____
          1   2| 1   2 | 1   2 | 1   2

Other examples of duple meter:

Yankee Doodle (American Revolutionary War song)

Oh, Susanna (Nineteenth-century American song by Stephen Foster)

Triple meter: *America* (patriotic song)

My coun -try 'tis of thee,
1   2   3 |12 3

Sweet land of li- ber-ty,
1   2 3|12   3

Of thee I sing _____ .
1 2 3| 1   2   3

Other examples of triple meter:

  The Star-Spangled Banner

  Happy Birthday

Quadruple meter: *America, the Beautiful* (patriotic song)

Oh, beau- ti-ful for spa- cious skies,
4 |1   2   3 4 |1 2   3

For am-ber waves of grain _____ ,
4 |1   2   3   4|1   2   3

For pur- ple moun-tain ma- jes-ties
4 |1 2   3   4 |1 2   3

A- bove the fruit-ed plain _____ !
4|1   2   3 4|1   2   3

Other examples of quadruple meter:

  This Land Is Your Land (American folksong)

  Battle Hymn of the Republic (American Civil War song)

  Aura Lee (folksong, same tune as *Love Me Tender*)

Compound (sextuple) meter: *Rock-a-bye Baby* (children's lullaby)

Rock- a-bye ba - by | on the tree-top ____ ,
1   23   456 |1 2 3   4   5   6

When the wind blows __ , the | cra-dle will rock ____
1   2   3   4   5   6 |1 2 3   4   5 6

Other examples of compound (sextuple) meter:

  Greensleeves (English folksong)

  Silent night (Christmas carol)

  Scarborough Fair (American folksong)

Several additional characteristics of meter should be explained. In some cases, a piece will not begin with an accented beat. For example, *America, the Beautiful*, given above under quadruple meter, begins with an *upbeat*, or on the last beat of the measure—in this case on beat 4. (Notice that the

Syncopation

Frost poem cited earlier also begins with a weak beat.) Composers devised a number of ways to keep the recurrent accent from becoming monotonous. They used ever more complex rhythmic patterns within the measure, and learned how to vary the underlying beat in different ways. The most common of these procedures is *syncopation*, a term used to describe a deliberate upsetting of the rhythm through a temporary shifting of the accent to a weak beat or to an *offbeat* (in between the beats). This technique has figured in the music of the masters for centuries, and it is characteristic of the Afro-American dance rhythms out of which jazz developed. The following examples illustrate the technique.

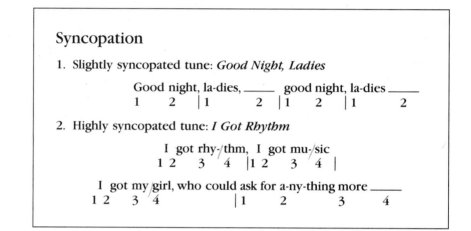

To sum up: music is an art of movement in time. Rhythm, the artistic organization of musical movement, permeates every aspect of the musical process. It binds together the parts within the whole: the notes within the measure, the measures within the phrase.

Time is the crucial dimension in music, and its first law is rhythm.

3

Harmony: Musical Space

"Music, to create harmony, must investigate discord."—PLUTARCH

We are accustomed to hearing melodies against a background of harmony. To the movement of the melody, harmony adds another dimension—depth. Think of harmony as occurring on a vertical plane: it describes the simultaneous happenings in music. Harmony is to music what perspective is to painting—it introduces the impression of musical space. The supporting role of harmony is apparent when a singer is accompanied by a guitar or piano.

Harmony lends a sense of depth to music, as perspective does to painting.
Meindert Hobbema (*1638–1709*) The Avenue, Middelharnis. (Courtesy of the Trustees, The National Gallery, London)

The singer presents the melody while the instrument provides the harmonic background.

Harmony pertains to the movement and relationship of intervals and chords. An *interval* may be defined as the distance—and relationship—between two tones. In the musical scale, the tones are identified either by syllables—*do-re-mi-fa-sol-la-ti-do*—or by numbers—1–2–3–4–5–6–7–8 (1). Thus, the interval *do-re* (1–2) is a second, *do-mi* (1–3) is a third, *do-fa* (1–4) a fourth, *do-sol* (1–5) a fifth, *do-la* (1–6) a sixth, *do-ti* (1–7) a seventh, and from one *do* to the next is an *octave*. The tones of the interval may be sounded in succession or simultaneously.

A *chord* may be defined as a combination of two or more typically three tones that constitutes a single block of harmony. As you see from the example on page 16, melody constitutes the horizontal aspect of music, while harmony, consisting of blocks of tones (the chords), constitutes the vertical.

Interval
Scale

Octave

Chord

The Function of Harmony

Chords have meaning only in relation to other chords: that is, only as each chord leads into the next. Harmony therefore implies movement and progression.

The most common chord in our music is a certain combination of three tones known as a *triad*. Such a chord may be built by combining the first, third, and fifth degrees of the scale: *do-mi-sol*. A triad may be built on the second degree (steps 2–4–6 or *re-fa-la*); on the third degree (steps 3–5–7 or *mi–sol–ti*); and similarly on each of the other degrees of the scale. The triad is a basic formation in our music. In the next example, the melody of *Old MacDonald* is harmonized by triads.

Triad

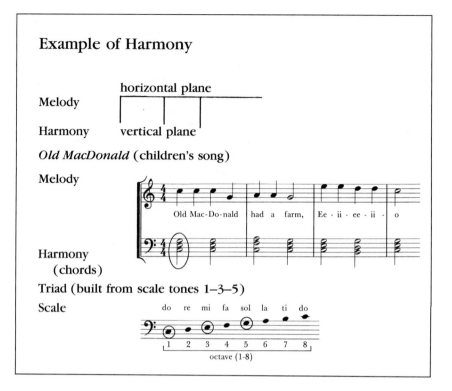

It is apparent that melody and harmony do not function independently of one another. On the contrary, the melody implies the harmony that goes with it, and each constantly influences the other.

Tonality

A system of music must have set procedures for organizing tones into intelligible relationships. One of the first steps in this direction is to select certain tones and arrange them in a family or group. In such a group, one tone assumes greater importance than the rest. This is the first tone of the *Tonic* scale, *do*, also called the *tonic* or keynote, which serves as a home base around which the others revolve and to which they ultimately gravitate. We observed this principle at work earlier with the tune *Amazing Grace* (Chapter 1, page 9). It is this sense of a home base that helps us recognize when a piece of music ends.

The principle of organization around a central tone, the tonic, is called *tonality*. The particular scale chosen as the basis of a piece determines the *Scale* identity of the tonic and the tonality. Two different types of *scale* are commonly found in Western music written between about 1650 and 1900: *major* and *minor*. What characterizes these two types are the intervals upon which they are built. More about the formulation of scales later (see Chapter 16, pages 117–20). For the moment, it is sufficient to offer the following observation concerning the differences usually attributed to major and minor scales: music in major may be thought of as bright while minor sounds more subdued. Some people find that minor sounds sadder than major. Indeed, in the nineteenth century, the minor was regarded as more somber than the major. For this reason, a composer would hardly choose a minor tonality for a triumphal march or grand finale of a piece. For now, we shall regard major and minor as scale types and tonalities, each with its own unique quality of sound.

We will observe later that we make a distinction between notes that belong to a particular scale and tonality and those that do not. The term *diatonic* describes melodies or harmonies that are built from the tones of a major or minor scale; *chromatic* (from the Greek word *chroma* meaning color) describes the full gamut of notes available in the octave.

Diatonic vs. Chromatic

Consonance and Dissonance

Harmonic movement, as we shall see, is generated by motion toward a goal or resolution. This striving for resolution is the dynamic force in our music. It shapes the forward movement, imparting focus and direction. Movement in music receives its maximum impetus from *dissonance*, a combination of tones that sounds discordant, unstable, in need of resolution.

Dissonance introduces the necessary tension into music. Without it, a work would be intolerably dull and insipid. What suspense and conflict are to the drama, dissonance is to music. The resolution of dissonance results in *consonance*, a concordant or agreeable combination of tones that provides a sense of relaxation and fulfillment in music. At their extremes, dissonance can be harsh sounding while consonance is more pleasing to the ear. Each complements the other; both are a necessary part of the artistic whole.

In general, music has grown more dissonant through the ages. It is easy to understand why. A combination of tones that sounded extremely harsh when first introduced began to seem less so as the sound became increasingly familiar. As a result, a later generation of composers had to find ever more dissonant tone combinations in order to create the same tension as their predecessors.

Harmony is a much more sophisticated phenomenon than melody. Historically, it appeared much later, about a thousand years ago, and its real development took place only in the West. The music of the Orient to this day is largely melodic. Indeed, we may consider the great achievement of Western music to be harmony (hearing in depth), even as in painting it is perspective (seeing in depth). Our harmonic system has advanced steadily over the past ten centuries. Today it is adjusting to new needs. These constitute the latest chapter in man's age-old attempt to impose order upon the raw material of sound—to organize tones in such a way that they will manifest a unifying idea, a selective imagination, a reasoning will.

4

Musical Texture

"Ours is an age of texture."—GEORGE DYSON

In writings on music we encounter frequent references to its fabric or *texture*. Such comparisons between music and cloth are not as unreasonable as may at first appear, since the melodic lines may be thought of as so many threads that make up the musical fabric. This fabric may be one of several types: monophonic, polyphonic, or homophonic.

Types of Texture

Monophonic

The simplest texture is *monophonic* or single-voice texture. ("Voice" refers to an individual part or line, even when we speak of instrumental music— an allusion to the fact that all music stems from vocal origins.) Here the melody is heard without either a harmonic accompaniment or other vocal lines. Attention is focused on the single line. All music up to about a thousand years ago of which we have any knowledge was monophonic.

To this day the music of the Oriental world—of China, Japan, India, Java, Bali, and the Arab nations, for example—is largely monophonic. The melody may be accompanied by a variety of rhythm and percussion instruments that embellish it, but there is no third dimension of depth or perspective that harmony alone confers upon a melody.

Polyphonic

When two or more melodic lines are combined, we have a *polyphonic* or many-voiced texture. Here the music derives its expressive power and its interest from the interplay of several lines. Polyphonic texture is based on counterpoint. This term comes from the Latin *punctus contra punctus*, "point against point" or "note against note"—that is to say, one musical line

Counterpoint

against the other. *Counterpoint* is the art of combining in a single texture two or more simultaneous melodic lines, each with a rhythmic life of its own.

It was a little over a thousand years ago that European musicians hit upon the device of combining two or more lines simultaneously. At this point Western art music parted company from that of the monophonic Orient. There ensued a magnificent flowering of polyphonic art that came to its high point in the fifteenth and sixteenth centuries. This development of counterpoint took place at a time when composers were mainly preoccupied with sacred choral music, which, for the most part, is many-voiced.

In the third type of texture a single voice takes over the melodic interest while the accompanying voices surrender their individuality and become blocks of harmony, the chords that support, color, and enhance the principal

Homophonic

part. Here we have a single-melody-with-chords or *homophonic* texture. Again the listener's interest is directed to a single line, but this line, unlike the melody of Oriental music, is conceived in relation to a harmonic background. Homophonic texture is heard when a pianist plays a melody in the right hand while the left sounds the chords, or when the singer or violinist carries the tune against a harmonic accompaniment on the piano. Homophonic texture, then, is based on harmony, just as polyphonic texture is based on counterpoint.

We have said that melody is the horizontal aspect of music while harmony is the vertical. The comparison with the warp and woof of a fabric consequently has real validity. The horizontal threads, the melodies, are held together by the vertical threads, the harmonies. Out of their interaction comes a weave that may be light or heavy, coarse or fine.

A composition need not use one texture or another exclusively. For example, a symphonic movement may present a theme against a homophonic texture. Later in the movement, however, the texture is apt to become increasingly contrapuntal. So, too, in a homophonic piece the composer may enhance the effect of the principal melody through an interesting play of counterthemes and counterrhythms in the accompanying parts.

Contrapuntal Devices

When several independent lines are combined, composers try to give unity and shape to the texture. A basic procedure for achieving this end is *imitation*, in which a theme or motive is presented in one voice and then restated in another. While the imitating voice restates the theme, the first voice continues with counterpoint. Thus a polyphonic texture is achieved. We have spoken of the vertical and horizontal threads in musical texture. To these imitation adds a third, the diagonal (see the music example on page 20).

Imitation

The length of the imitation may be brief or may last the entire work. In the latter case, we have a strict type of composition known as a *canon*. (The name comes from the Greek word for "law" or "order.") The simplest and most popular form of canon is a *round*, in which each voice enters in succession with the same melody. A round is a perpetual canon for singing voices; commonly known examples include the childrens' songs *Row, Row, Row Your Boat* and *Frère Jacques* (Brother John).

Canon and round

Contrapuntal writing is marked by a number of devices that have flourished for centuries. *Inversion* is a technique that turns the melody upside down; that is, it follows the same intervals but in the opposite direction. Where the melody originally moved up by a third, the inverted version moves down by a third. *Retrograde* refers to a statement of the melody backwards, beginning with its last note and proceeding to its first. These two techniques can be combined in the *retrograde inversion* of a melody: upside down and backwards. *Augmentation* calls for the melody to be presented in longer time values, often twice as slow as the original. Think of it as augmenting or increasing the time it takes to play the melody. The opposite technique is called *diminution* in which the melody is presented in short time values, thus diminishing the time it takes to be played. These devices are illustrated below with a theme from the Sonata for Violin and Piano by César Franck.

Inversion

Retrograde

Retrograde inversion
Augmentation

Diminution

Musical Texture and the Listener

Different types of texture require different types of listening. Monophonic music—the simplest type, since it has only a single melodic line—hardly figures in the music of the West at present. Homophonic music poses no special problems to music lovers of today. They are able to differentiate between the principal melody and its attendant harmonies, and to follow the interrelation of the two. They are helped in this by the fact that most of the music they have heard since their childhood consists of melody and chords.

The case is different with polyphonic music, which is not apt to appeal to those who listen with half an ear. Here we must be aware of the independent lines as they flow alongside one another, each in its own rhythm. This requires much greater concentration on our part. Only by dint of repeated hearings do we learn to follow the individual voices and to separate each within the contrapuntal web.

Examples of Musical Texture

Monophonic—one melodic line, no accompaniment

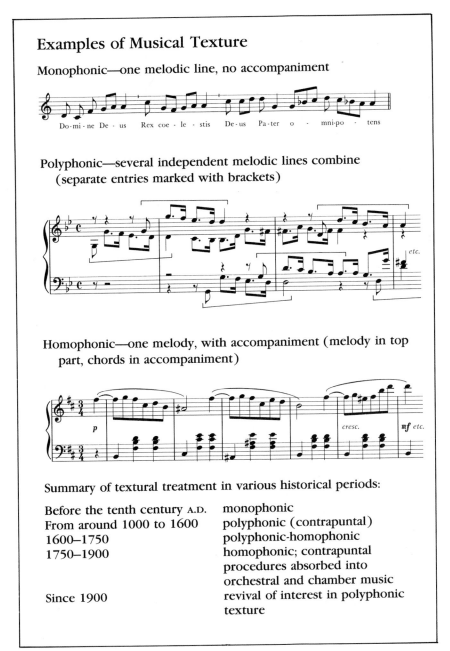

Do-mi - ne De - us   Rex coe - le - stis   De - us Pa - ter o - mni-po - tens

Polyphonic—several independent melodic lines combine
(separate entries marked with brackets)

Homophonic—one melody, with accompaniment (melody in top
part, chords in accompaniment)

Summary of textural treatment in various historical periods:

Before the tenth century A.D.   monophonic
From around 1000 to 1600   polyphonic (contrapuntal)
1600–1750   polyphonic-homophonic
1750–1900   homophonic; contrapuntal
                                procedures absorbed into
                                orchestral and chamber music
Since 1900   revival of interest in polyphonic
                                texture

5

Musical Form

"The principal function of form is to advance our understanding. It is the organization of a piece which helps the listener to keep the idea in mind, to follow its development, its growth, its elaboration, its fate."
—ARNOLD SCHOENBERG

Form is that quality in a work of art which presents to the mind of the beholder an impression of conscious choice and judicious arrangement. Form represents clarity and order in art. It shows itself in the selection of certain details and rejection of others. Form is manifest too in the relationship of the parts to the whole. It helps us to grasp the work of art as a unity. It can be as potent a source of beauty as the content itself.

Whether in the domestic arts—the setting of a table, the weaving of a basket—or in the loftier ones, a balance is required between unity and variety, between symmetry and asymmetry, activity and repose. Nor is this balance confined to art. Nature has embodied it in the forms of plant and animal life and in what mankind likes to think of as her supreme handiwork—the human form.

Structure and Design in Music

Repetition and contrast

Our lives are composed of sameness and differentness: certain details are repeated again and again, others are new. Music mirrors this dualism. Its basic law of structure is *repetition and contrast*—unity and variety. Repetition fixes the material in our minds and ministers to our need for the familiar. Contrast sustains our interest and feeds our love of change. From the interaction of the familiar and the new, the repeated elements and the contrasting ones, result the lineaments of musical form. These are to be found in every type of musical organism, from the nursery rhyme to the symphony.

Variation

One further principle of form that falls between repetition and contrast is *variation*, where some aspects of the music are altered but recognizable. We hear this formal technique when we listen to a new arrangement of a well-known popular song. The tune is recognizable, but many features of the known version may be changed.

The principle of form is embodied in a variety of musical structures. These utilize procedures worked out by generations of composers. No matter how diverse, they are based in one way or another on repetition and contrast. The forms, however, are not fixed molds into which composers pour their material. What gives a piece of music its aliveness is the fact that it adapts a general plan to its own requirements. All faces have two eyes, a nose, and a mouth. In each face, though, these features are found in a wholly individual combination. The forms that students in composition follow are ready-made formulas set up for their guidance. The forms of the masters are living organisms in which external organization is delicately adjusted to inner content. No two symphonies of Haydn or Mozart, no two sonatas of Beethoven are exactly alike. Each is a fresh and unique solution to the problem of fashioning musical material into a logical and coherent form.

Two-Part and Three-Part Form

The principles of form may be illustrated through two of the most basic and common patterns in music. Two-part or *binary form* is based on a statement and a departure, without a return to the opening section. Three-part or *ternary form*, on the other hand, extends the idea of statement and departure by bringing back the first section. Formal patterns can be simply outlined: binary form as **A-B** and ternary form as **A-B-A,** as illustrated in the following chart.

Binary form

Ternary Form

Binary and Ternary Form

Binary form: *Yankee Doodle*

Statement—**A**

Yan-kee Doo-dle went to town, a - ri - ding on a po - ny,

Stuck a fea-ther in his cap and called it ma - ca - ro - ni.

Departure—**B**

Yan - kee Doo-dle keep it up, Yan - kee Doo-dle dan - dy,

Mind the mu-sic and the step and with the girls be han-dy.

Ternary form: *Twinkle, Twinkle Little Star*

Statement—**A**

Twin-kle, twin-kle lit - tle star, How I won-der what you are.

Contrast (Departure)—**B**

Up a - bove the world so high, Like a dia-mond in the sky!

Repetition—**A**

Twin-kle, twin-kle lit - tle star, How I won-der what you are.

*Left: The facade of St. Paul's Cathedral in London (1675–1710), designed by Sir Christopher Wren, illustrates that three-part (**A-B-A**) form is as appealing to the eye as it is to the ear. Right: The Trylon and Perisphere, symbol of New York's World's Fair of 1939, is a visual realization of binary (**A-B**) form.* (The Bettmann Archive)

Both two-part and three-part forms are common in short pieces such as songs and dances. With its attractive symmetry and its balancing of the outer sections against the contrasting middle one, three-part form constitutes a simple, clear-cut formation that is a favorite in architecture and painting as well as music.

The Building Blocks of Form

Theme

When a melodic idea is used as a building block in the construction of a musical work, it is known as a *theme*. The theme is the first in a series of musical situations, all of which must grow out of the basic idea as naturally as does the plant from the seed. The process of spinning out a theme, of weaving and reweaving threads of which it is composed, is the essence of musical thinking. This process of expansion has its parallel in prose writing, where an idea stated at the beginning of a paragraph is embroidered and enlarged upon until all its aspects appear in view. Each sentence leads smoothly into the one that follows. In similar fashion, every measure in a musical work takes up where the one before left off and brings us inexorably to the next.

Thematic development

The most tightly knit kind of expansion in Western music is known as *thematic development.* To develop a theme means to unfold its latent energies, to search out its capacities for growth and bring them to fruition. Thematic development is one of the most important techniques in musical composition, demanding of the composer imagination, master craftsmanship, and intellectual power.

In the process of development, certain procedures have proved to be particularly effective. The simplest is repetition, which may be either exact or varied; or the idea may be restated at another pitch. Such a restatement at a higher or lower pitch level is known as a *sequence*. The original idea may also be varied in regard to melody, harmony, rhythm, or other elements that we have not yet discussed, such as loudness or softness, tempo, or particular instrumental sound. It may be attended by expansion or contraction of the note lengths as well as by bold and frequent changes of tonality.

Sequence

A basic technique in thematic development is the breaking up of the theme into its constituent motives. A *motive* is the smallest fragment of a theme that forms a melodic-rhythmic unit. Motives are the cells of musical growth. Through fragmentation of themes, through repeating and varying motives and combining them in ever fresh patterns, the composer imparts to the musical organism the quality of dynamic evolution and growth.

Motive

These musical building blocks can be seen in action even in simple songs, such as the popular national tune *America*. In this piece, the opening three-note motive ("My country") is repeated in sequence almost immediately at a different pitch level on the words "Sweet land of." A fine example of a sequence occurs later in the piece: the musical motive set to the words "Land where our fathers died" is repeated beginning on a slightly lower note for the words "Land of the pilgrim's pride."

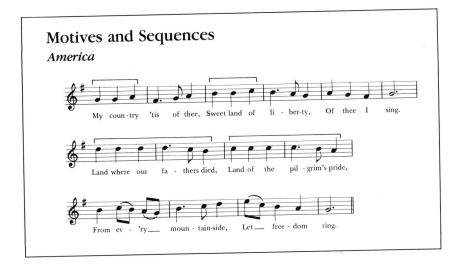

Motives and Sequences
America

In subsequent chapters we shall examine the great forms of Western music. No matter how imposing their dimensions, they all show the principle of repetition and contrast, of unity and variety, that we have traced here. In all its manifestations our music displays the striving for organic form that binds together the individual tones within a phrase, the phrases within a section, the sections within a *movement* (a complete, comparatively independent division of a large-scale work), and the movements within a work

Movement

as a whole; even as, in a novel, the individual words are bound together in phrases, sentences, paragraphs, sections, chapters, and parts.

It has been said that architecture is frozen music. By the same token, music is floating architecture. Form is the structural principle in music. It distributes the areas of activity and repose, tension and relaxation, light and shade, and integrates the multitudinous details, large and small, into the spacious structures that are the glory of Western music

6

Tempo and Dynamics

"The whole duty of a conductor is comprised in his ability to indicate the right tempo."—RICHARD WAGNER

The Pace of Music

Tempo

Meter tells us how many beats there are in the measure, but it does not tell us whether these beats occur slowly or rapidly. The *tempo*, by which we mean the rate of speed, the pace of the music, provides the answer to this vital question. Consequently, the flow of music in time involves both meter and tempo.

Tempo carries emotional implications. We hurry our speech in moments of agitation. Our bodies press forward in eagerness, hold back in lassitude. Vigor and gaiety are associated with a brisk gait as surely as despair demands a slow one. In an art of movement such as music, the rate of movement is of prime importance. We respond to musical tempo physically and psychologically. Our pulse, our breathing, our entire being adjusts to the rate of movement and to the feeling engendered thereby on the conscious and subconscious levels.

Because of the close connection between tempo and mood, tempo markings indicate the character of the music as well as the pace. The tempo terms are generally given in Italian, as in the following list:

solemn (very, very slow)	*grave*
broad (very slow)	*largo*
quite slow	*adagio*
a walking pace	*andante*
moderate	*moderato*
fast (cheerful)	*allegro*
lively	*vivace*
very fast	*presto*

Frequently encountered too are modifying adverbs such as *molto* (very), *meno* (less), *poco* (a little), and *non troppo* (not too much).

Of great importance are the terms indicating a change of tempo. The principal ones are *accelerando* (getting faster) and *ritardando* (holding back, getting slower); *a tempo* (in time) indicates a return to the original pace.

Loudness and Softness

Dynamics denote the degree of loudness or softness at which the music is played. In this area, as in that of tempo, certain responses seem to be rooted in the nature of our emotions. Mystery and fear call for a whisper, even as jubilation and vigorous activity go with full resonance.

Dynamics

The principal dynamic indications are:

very soft	*pianissimo* (*pp*)
soft	*piano* (*p*)
moderately soft	*mezzo piano* (*mp*)
moderately loud	*mezzo forte* (*mf*)
loud	*forte* (*f*)
very loud	*fortissimo* (*ff*)

Of special importance are the directions to change the dynamics. Such changes are indicated by words or signs. Among the commonest are:

growing louder	*crescendo* (━━━━)
growing softer	*decrescendo or diminuendo* (━━━━)
sudden stress	*sforzando* (*sf*), "forcing"—accent on a single note or chord

Dynamic contrasts in music are analagous to light and shade in painting. **Rembrandt van Rijn** (*1606–69*) Les disciples d'Emmaus. (*Musée Jacquemart-André, Paris*)

As the orchestra increased in size and precision, composers extended the
range of dynamic markings in both directions, so that we find *ppp* and *fff*.
Ultimately four and even five *p*'s or *f*'s were used.

Tempo and Dynamics as Elements of Musical Expression

The markings for tempo and dynamics contribute to the expressive content
of a piece of music. These so-called expression marks steadily increased in
number during the late eighteenth and nineteenth centuries, as composers
tried to indicate their intentions ever more precisely. In this regard it is
instructive to compare a page of a Handel score (early eighteenth century)
with one of Mahler on the facing page (late nineteenth century).

   Crescendo and diminuendo are among the important expressive effects
available to the composer. Through the gradual swelling and diminishing
of the tone volume, the illusion of distance enters music. As orchestral style
developed, composers quickly learned to take advantage of this effect.

A page from the score of
The Royal Fireworks
Music *by* **George
Frideric Handel.** (Note
the absence of expression
marks.)

*A page from the score of **Gustav Mahler's** Symphony No. 2.* (Observe the profusion of expression marks.)

UNIT II

■

Musical Instruments and Ensembles

7

Musical Instruments I

"With these artificial voices we sing in a manner such as our natural voices would never permit."—JOHN REDFIELD

Properties of Musical Sound

Pitch

Any musical sound can be described in terms of four qualities or properties: pitch, duration, volume, and timbre. By *pitch* we mean the location of a tone in the musical scale in relation to high or low. The pitch is determined by the rate of vibration, which to a large extent depends on the length of the vibrating body. Other conditions being equal, the shorter a string or column of air, the more rapidly it vibrates and the higher the pitch. The longer a string or column of air, the fewer the vibrations per second and the lower the pitch. The width, thickness, density, and tension of the vibrating body also affect the outcome. *Duration* depends on the length of time over which the vibration is maintained. We hear tones as being not only high or low but also short or long. *Volume* (dynamics) depends on the degree of force of the vibrations as a result of which the tone strikes us as being loud or soft.

Duration

Volume

Timbre

The fourth property of sound is tone color or *timbre*. (The word retains its French pronunciation, *tám'br.*) This is what makes a note on the trumpet sound altogether different from the same note played on a violin or a flute. Timbre is influenced by a number of factors, such as the size, shape, and proportions of the instrument, the material of which it is made, and the manner in which vibration is set up.

30

The composer has available two basic mediums—human voices and musical instruments. (An *instrument* is a mechanism that is able to generate musical vibrations and launch them into the air.) One may write for either or both, according to one's purpose. When writing for a group of instruments, the composer will try to make each instrument do the things for which it is best suited, taking into account its capacities and limitations. There are, to begin with, the limits of each instrument's range—the distance from its lowest to its highest tone, beyond which it cannot go. There are also the limits of dynamics—the degree of softness or loudness beyond which it cannot be played. There are technical peculiarities native to its low, middle, and high registers, as a result of which a certain combination of notes may be executed more easily on one instrument than on another. (By *register*, we mean a specific area in the range of an instrument or voice, such as low, middle, or high.) These and a host of similar considerations determine the composer's choices.

Instrument

Register

The Voice as a Model for Instrumental Sound

The human voice is perhaps the most natural of all musical instruments, and clearly one of the earliest. Each person's voice has a particular quality or character and range. The standard designations for vocal ranges, from highest to lowest, are *soprano, mezzo-soprano*, and *alto* (short for *contralto*) for female voices, *tenor, baritone,* and *bass* for male voices.

Vocal ranges

In earlier eras, social and religious customs severely restricted women's participation in public musical events. Thus, young boys and occasionally adult males with soprano—or alto-range voices sang female roles in church music and on the stage. In the sixteenth century, women singers came into prominence in the realm of secular music. Tenors were most often featured as soloists in early opera; the lower male voices, baritone and bass, became popular as solo voices in the eighteenth century.

Throughout the ages, the human voice has served as a model for instrument builders and players, who have sought to transfer its lyric beauty and expressiveness to their instruments. Critics today still praise a violinist or a cellist for having a "singing tone" and Chopin taught his piano pupils that "everything must be made to sing."

String Instruments

The string family includes two types of instruments: those that are bowed and those that are plucked. The bowed string family has four members: violin, viola, violoncello, and double bass, each with four strings that are set vibrating by drawing a bow across them. The hair of the bow is rubbed with rosin so that it will "grip" the strings. The bow is held in the right hand while the left hand is used to *stop* the string by pressing a finger down at a particular point, thereby leaving a certain portion of the string free to vibrate. By stopping the string at another point, the violinist changes the length of the vibrating portion, and with it the rate of vibration and the pitch.

Violinist Itzhak Perlman (Photo Julian Kreeger)

Yo-Yo-Ma, cellist. (Photo © Martha Swope)

Violin

Viola

Cello

Double Bass

Double-bass player Gary Karr

The *violin* was brought to its present form by the brilliant instrument *Violin* makers who flourished in Italy from around 1600 to 1750. Most famous among them were the Amati and Guarneri families—in these dynasties the secrets of the craft were transmitted from father to son—and the master builder of them all, Antonio Stradivari (c. 1644–1737).

Pre-eminent in lyric melody, the violin is also capable of brilliance and dramatic effect, of subtle nuances from soft to loud, of the utmost rhythmic precision and great agility in rapid passages. It has an extremely wide range.

The *viola* is somewhat larger than the violin, and is lower in range. Its *Viola* strings are longer, thicker, heavier. The tone is husky in the low register, somber and penetrating in the high. The viola is an effective melody instrument, and often serves as a foil for the more brilliant violin by playing a secondary melody. It usually fills in the harmony, or may *double* another part, that is, reinforce it by playing the same notes an octave higher or lower.

The *violoncello*, popularly known as *cello*, is lower in range than the *Violoncello* viola and is notable for its lyric quality, which takes on a dark resonance in the low register. Cellos often carry the melody, they enrich the sonority with their full-throated songfulness, they accentuate the rhythm, and together with the basses, they supply the foundation for the harmony of the string choir.

The *double bass*, known also as *contrabass* or *bass viol*, is the lowest *Double bass* in range of the string section. Accordingly, it plays the bass part—that is, the foundation of the harmony. Its deep indistinct tones come into focus when they are played an octave higher (doubled), usually by the cello.

These four string instruments constitute the string section of the orchestra, which has come to be known as "the heart of the orchestra." This term indicates the versatility and importance of this section.

The string instruments are pre-eminent in playing *legato* (smooth and *Special effects* connected), though they are capable too of the opposite quality of tone, *staccato* (short and detached). A special effect, *pizzicato* (plucked), is executed by the performer's plucking the string with a finger instead of using the bow. *Vibrato* denotes a throbbing effect achieved by a rapid wrist-and-finger movement on the string that slightly alters the pitch. In *glissando* a finger of the left hand slides along the string while the right hand draws the bow, thereby sounding all the pitches of the scale. *Tremolo*, the rapid repetition of a tone through a quick up-and-down movement of the bow, is associated in the popular mind with suspense and excitement. No less important is the *trill*, a rapid alternation between a tone and the one above it. *Double-stopping* involves playing two strings simultaneously; when three or four strings are played simultaneously, it is called *triple-* or *quadruple-stopping*. Thereby the members of the violin family, essentially melodic instruments, became capable of harmony. The *mute* is a small attachment that fits over the bridge, muffling (and changing) the sound. *Harmonics* are crystalline tones in the very high register. They are produced by lightly touching the sring at certain points while the bow is drawn across the string.

Two plucked string instruments, the harp and the guitar, are in common use. The *harp* is one of the oldest of musical instruments. Its plucked strings *Harp* produce an ethereal tone that sounds lovely, both alone and in combination with other instruments. The pedals are used to tighten the strings, hence to raise the pitch. Chords on the harp are frequently played in broken form—that is, the tones are sounded one after another instead of simultaneously. From this technique comes the term *arpeggio* which means a broken chord (*arpa* is the Italian for harp). Arpeggios occur in a variety of forms on many instruments.

Guitar   The *guitar*, too, is an old instrument, dating back at least to the Middle Ages. It has always been widely used as a solo instrument, and is associated today with folk and popular music as well as classical styles. The standard acoustical guitar (as opposed to electric) is made of wood, has a fretted fingerboard and six nylon strings, which are plucked with the fingers of the right hand or with a pick.

Woodwind Instruments

In woodwind instruments, the tone is produced by a column of air vibrating within a pipe that has little holes along its length. When one or another of these holes is opened or closed, the length of the vibrating air column within the pipe is changed. The woodwind instruments are capable of remarkable agility by means of an intricate mechanism of keys arranged to suit the natural position of the fingers.

The woodwinds are a less homogeneous group than the strings. Nowadays they are not necessarily made of wood, and they represent several methods of setting up vibration: by blowing across a mouth hole (flute family); by blowing into a mouthpiece that has a single reed (clarinet and saxophone families); or by blowing into a mouthpiece fitted with a double reed (oboe and bassoon families). They do, however, have one important feature in common: the holes in their pipes. In addition, their timbres are such that composers think of them and write for them as a group.

Flute   The *flute* is the soprano voice of the woodwind choir. Its timbre ranges from the poetic to the brilliant. Its tone is cool and velvety in the expressive low register, and smooth in the middle. In the upper part of the range the timbre is bright, birdlike, and stands out against the orchestral mass. The present-day flute, made of a silver alloy rather than wood, is a cylindrical tube that is held horizontally. It is closed at one end. The player's lips are used to blow across a mouth hole cut in the side of the pipe at the other end. The flute is much prized as a melody instrument and offers the performer complete freedom in playing rapid repeated notes, scales, and trills.

Piccolo   The *piccolo* (from the Italian *flauto piccolo*, "little flute") has a piercing tone that produces the highest notes in the orchestra. In its upper register it takes on a shrillness that is easily heard even when the orchestra is playing fortissimo. Composers are more and more often making use of the limpid singing quality of its lower register.

Oboe   The *oboe* is made of wood. Its mouthpiece is a double reed consisting of two slips of cane bound together so as to leave between them an extremely small passage for air. Oboe timbre is generally described as plaintive, nasal,

James Galway, flute virtuoso. (Photo by Brian Davis)

Heinz Holliger playing the oboe.

Richard Stoltzman playing the clarinet in Carnegie Hall.

Bernard Garfield, principal bassoonist of The Philadelphia Orchestra.

reedy. The instrument is associated with pastoral effects and with nostalgic moods. The pitch of the oboe is not readily subject to change, for which reason it is chosen to sound the tuning note for the other instruments of the orchestra.

English horn

The *English horn* is an alto oboe. Its wooden tube is wider and longer than that of the oboe and ends in a pear-shaped opening called a *bell*, which largely accounts for its soft, somewhat mournful timbre. The instrument is not well named, for it is neither English nor a horn. Its expressive, gently poignant tone has made it a favorite with composers.

Clarinet

The *clarinet* has a single reed, a small flexible piece of cane fastened against its chisel-shaped mouthpiece. The instrument possesses a beautiful liquid tone, as well as a remarkably wide range from low to high and from soft to loud. Almost as agile as the flute, it has an easy command of rapid scales, trills, and repeated notes.

Bass clarinet

The *bass clarinet* is one octave lower in range than the clarinet. Its rich singing tone, flexibility, and wide dynamic range make it an invaluable member of the orchestral community.

Bassoon

The *bassoon* is a double-reed instrument. Its tone is weighty and thick in the low register, dry and sonorous in the middle, reedy and intense in the upper. Capable of a hollow-sounding staccato and wide leaps that create a humorous effect, it is at the same time a highly expressive instrument.

Contrabassoon

The *contrabassoon*, known also as *double bassoon*, produces the lowest tone in the orchestra. Its function in the woodwind section may be compared to that of the double bass among the strings, in that it supplies a foundation for the harmony.

Saxophone

The *saxophone* is of more recent origin, having been invented by the Belgian Adolphe Sax in 1840. It was created by combining the features of several other instruments—the single reed of the clarinet, the conical tube of the oboe, and the metal body of the brass instruments. The saxophone blends well with either woodwinds or brass. In the 1920s it became the characteristic instrument of the jazz band.

8

Musical Instruments II

"Lucidity is the first purpose of color in music."—ARNOLD SCHOENBERG

Brass Instruments

The principal instruments of the brass family are the trumpet, French horn, trombone, and tuba. These instruments have cup-shaped mouthpieces (except for the horn, whose mouthpiece is shaped like a funnel). The tube flares at the end into a bell. The column of air within the tube is set vibrating by the tightly stretched lips of the player, which act as a kind of double reed. To go from one pitch to another involves not only mechanical means, such as a slide or valves, but also variation in the pressure of the lips and breath. This demands great muscular control. Wind instrument players often speak about their *embouchure* referring to the entire oral mechanism of lips, lower facial muscles, and jaws.

Trumpets and horns were widely used in the ancient world. The earliest instruments were fashioned from the horns and tusks of animals, which at a later stage of civilization were reproduced in metal. They were used chiefly in religious ceremonies and for military signals. Their tone was on the terrifying side, as is evidenced by what happened to the Biblical walls of Jericho.

The *trumpet*, highest in pitch of the brass choir, possesses a firm, brilliant timbre that lends radiance to the orchestral mass. It is associated with martial pomp and vigor. Played softly, the instrument commands a lovely round tone. The muted trumpet is much used; the mute, a pear-shaped device of metal or cardboard, is inserted in the bell, achieving a bright, buzzy sound. Jazz trumpet players have experimented with various kinds of mutes to produce different timbres, and these are gradually finding their way into the symphony orchestra.

Trumpet

The *French horn*—generally referred to simply as *horn*—is descended from the ancient hunting horn. Its golden resonance lends itself to a variety of uses: it can be mysteriously remote in soft passages, and nobly sonorous in loud. The timbre of the horn blends equally well with woodwinds, brass, and strings, for which reason it serves as the connecting link among them. Although capable of considerable agility, the horn is at its best in sustained utterance; for sheer majesty, nothing rivals the sound of several horns intoning a broadly flowing theme in unison. The muted horn has a poetic faraway sound. Horn players often "stop" their instrument by plugging the bell with their hand; the result has an ominous rasping quality.

French horn

The *trombone*—the Italian word means "large trumpet"—has a grand sonorousness that combines the brilliance of the trumpet with the majesty of the horn, but in the tenor range. In place of valves it has a movable U-shaped slide that alters the length of the vibrating air column in the tube. Composers use the trombone to achieve effects of nobility and grandeur.

Trombone

The *tuba* is the bass instrument of the brass choir. Like the string bass and contrabassoon, it furnishes the foundation for the harmonic fabric. The tuba adds body to the orchestral tone, and a dark resonance ranging from velvety softness to a rumbling growl.

Tuba

Other brass instruments are used in concert and marching bands. Among these is the *cornet* which has a rounder but less brilliant sound than the trumpet. In the early twentieth century, the cornet was very popular in concert bands; today, however, the trumpet has replaced it in virtually all ensembles. The *bugle* evolved from the military or field trumpet of early times; it has a powerful tone that carries in the open air. Since it is not equipped with valves, it is able to sound only certain tones of the scale, which accounts for the familiar pattern of duty calls in the army. The *flue-*

Other brass instruments

Trumpeter Wynton Marsalis.
(Photo by Marcus Devoe)

Steven Johns playing the tuba. (Photo by
Jane Hamborsky)

*Barry Tuckwell plays the French
horn.* (Photo by Richard Holt/
EMI, Ltd.)

Christian Lindberg, trombonist

gelhorn, much used in jazz and commercial music, is really a valved bugle with a wide bell. The *baritone* and its relative, the *euphonium,* are tenor-range instruments whose shapes resemble the tuba, while the *sousaphone* is an adaptation of the tuba designed by the American bandmaster John Philip Sousa. It features a forward bell and is coiled to rest over the player's shoulder while marching.

Percussion Instruments

The percussion family comprises a variety of instruments that are made to sound by striking or shaking. Some are made of metal or wood. In others, such as the drums, vibration is set up by striking a stretched skin.

The percussion section of the orchestra is sometimes referred to as "the battery." Its members accentuate the rhythm, generate excitement at the climaxes, and inject splashes of color into the orchestral sound. Like seasoning in food, they are most effective when used sparingly.

The percussion instruments fall into two categories: those capable of being tuned to definite pitches, and those that produce a single sound in the borderland between music and noise (instruments of indefinite pitch). In the former class are the *kettledrums,* or *timpani,* which are generally used in sets of two or three. The kettledrum is a hemispheric copper shell across which is stretched a "head" of plastic or calfskin held in place by a metal ring. A pedal mechanism enables the player to change the tension of the head, and with it the pitch. The instrument is played with two padded sticks, which may be either soft or hard. Its dynamic range extends from a mysterious rumble to a thunderous roll. The muffled drum frequently figures in passages that seek to evoke an atmosphere of mystery or mourning. The *glockenspiel* (German for "set of bells") consists of a series of horizontal tuned steel bars of various sizes. The player strikes these with mallets, producing a bright metallic sound. The *celesta* which in appearance resembles a miniature upright piano, is a kind of glockenspiel that is operated by a keyboard: the steel plates are struck by small hammers and produce a sound like a music box. The *xylophone* consists of tuned blocks of wood laid out in the shape of a keyboard. Struck with mallets with hard heads, the instrument produces a dry, crisp timbre. The *marimba* is a more mellow xylophone of African and Latin-American origin. The *vibraphone* combines the principle of the glockenspiel with resonators, each containing revolving disks operated by electric motors. Its highly unusual tone is marked by an exaggerated vibrato, which can be controlled by changing the speed of the motor. This instrument is featured in jazz combinations, and has been used by a number of contemporary composers. *Chimes* or *tubular bells* consist of a set of tuned metal tubes of various lengths suspended from a frame and struck with a hammer. They are frequently called upon to simulate church bells.

Pitched percussion instruments

In the other group are the percussion instruments that do not produce a definite pitch. The *side drum* or *snare drum* is a small cylindrical drum with two heads stretched over a shell of metal. It is played with two drumsticks and owes its brilliant tone to the vibrations of the lower head against taut snares (strings). The *tenor drum* is larger in size, with a wooden shell,

Unpitched percussion instruments

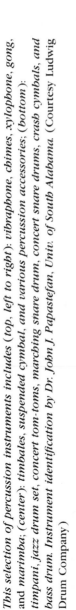

This selection of percussion instruments includes (top, left to right): vibraphone, chimes, xylophone, gong, and marimba; (center): timbales, suspended cymbal, and various percussion accessories; (bottom): timpani, jazz drum set, concert tom-toms, marching snare drum, concert snare drums, crash cymbals, and bass drum. Instrument identification by Dr. John J. Papastefan, Univ. of South Alabama. (Courtesy Ludwig Drum Company)

and has no snares. The *bass drum*, played with a large soft-headed stick, produces a low heavy sound. The *tom-tom* is a name given to American Indian or Oriental drums of indefinite pitch. The *tambourine* is a small round drum with "jingles"—little metal plates—inserted in its rim. It is played by striking the drum with the fingers or elbow, by shaking, or by passing the hand over the jingles. The tambourine is much used in the folk dances of Italy. *Castanets* are widely used in Spain. They consist of little wooden clappers moved by the player's thumb and forefinger. The *triangle* is a slender rod of steel bent in the shape of a triangle. It is open at the upper end and, when struck with a steel beater, gives off a bright tinkling sound. *Cymbals* are two large circular brass plates of equal size. When struck sidewise against each other, they produce a shattering sound. The *gong*, or *tam-tam*, is a broad circular disk of metal, suspended in a frame so as to hang freely. When struck with a heavy drumstick, it produces a deep roar.

Other Instruments

Besides the instruments just discussed, several others, especially those of the keyboard family, are frequently heard in solo and ensemble performances.

The *piano* was originally known as the *pianoforte*, Italian for "soft-loud,"   *Piano* which indicates its wide dynamic range and its capacity for nuance. Its strings are struck with hammers controlled by a keyboard mechanism. The piano cannot sustain tone as well as the string and wind instruments, but in the hands of a fine performer it is capable of producing a singing melody. Each string (except in the highest register) is covered by a damper that stops the sound when the finger releases the key. There are three pedals. If the one on the right is pressed down, all the dampers are raised, so that the strings continue to vibrate, producing that luminous haze of sound which the great piano composers used to such advantage. The pedal on the left shifts the hammers to reduce the area of impact on the strings, thereby inhibiting the volume of sound; hence it is known as the "soft pedal." The middle pedal (missing on upright pianos) is the sustaining pedal, which sustains only the tones held down at the moment the pedal is depressed. The piano is pre-eminent for brilliant scales, arpeggios, and trills, rapid passages, and octaves. It has a wide range from lowest to highest pitch, spanning eighty-eight keys or semitones.

The *organ*, once regarded as "the king of instruments," is a wind instru-   *Organ* ment; air is fed to its pipes by mechanical means. The pipes are controlled by two or more keyboards and a set of pedals. Gradations in the volume of tone are made possible on the modern organ by means of swell boxes. The organ possesses a multicolored sonority that is capable of filling a huge space. Electrically amplified keyboards, capable of imitating pipe organs and other timbres, are commonplace today. A number of sound production methods have been explored, including vibrating metal reeds, oscillators, and, most recently, digital waveform synthesis.

The instruments described in this chapter and in the previous one form a vivid and diversified group. To the composer, performers, and listener alike, they offer an endless variety of colors and shades of expression.

Misha Dichter at the piano. (Photo by J. Henry Fair)

Performing on the modern Holtkamp Organ at Furman University, Greenville, South Carolina. (Photo courtesy H. Neil Gillespie)

9
Musical Ensembles

Choral Groups

By choral music, we mean music performed by many voices in a chorus or choir. A *chorus* is a fairly large body of singers who perform together; their music is usually sung in several parts. A chorus most often consists of both men and women, but the term can also refer to a men's chorus or a women's chorus. A *choir* is traditionally a smaller group, often connected with a church. The standard voice parts in both chorus and choir correspond to the voice ranges explained earlier: sopranos, altos, tenors, and basses.

Chorus

Choir

In early times, choral music was often performed without accompaniment. This singing style is known as *a cappella* (meaning "in the church style"). The organ eventually became coupled with the choir in church music, and by the eighteenth century, the orchestra had established itself as a partner of the chorus.

a cappella

There are many smaller, specialized vocal ensembles as well, such as a madrigal choir, chamber chorus, or glee club. The *madrigal choir* might perform a cappella secular works, known as *partsongs*, and a *glee club* often performs popular music and college songs, along with more serious works. The designation *chamber choir* refers to a small group of up to twenty-four singers, usually performing a cappella or with piano accompaniment.

Other choral groups

A recent photograph of the renowned West-minster Choir with their conductor, Joseph Flummerfelt. (Photo courtesy Westminster Choir College, Princeton, N.J.)

The Tokyo String Quartet (Peter Oundjian, Kikuei Ikeda, violins; Sadao Harada, viola; and Kazuhide Isomura, cello) enjoys an international reputation. (Photograph by Christian Steiner)

Chamber Ensembles

Chamber music is ensemble music for up to about ten players, with one player to a part, as distinct from orchestral music, in which a single instrumental part is performed by anywhere from two to eighteen players. The essential trait of chamber music is its intimacy; its natural setting is the home.

Many of the standard chamber music ensembles depend on string players. Most common is the string quartet, consisting of two violins, viola, and cello. Other popular combinations are the duo sonata, the piano trio and quartet, the string quintet, as well as larger groups—sextet, septet, and octet. Winds too have standard chamber combinations, especially woodwind and brass quintets. These ensembles are outlined on the facing page.

The Orchestra

Instruments have traditionally been grouped into several large standard ensembles. Most popular among these are the orchestra, which has varied in size and makeup throughout its history but features strings as its core; and the band, a generic name that has been applied to concert bands and to marching and military bands, as well as to jazz and rock bands. Although they play different musical styles, all these bands consist largely of winds and percussion, omitting strings almost entirely.

From the twenty-piece group of the Baroque era and the forty-odd instruments of the Classical orchestra, the modern orchestra has grown into an ensemble of more than a hundred players. The performers are divided into the four instrumental families we have studied, and approximately two-thirds of the orchestra consists of string players. In large cities, orchestral musicians give full time to rehearsal and performance. The list on page 47 shows the distribution of instruments typical of a large orchestra today.

Standard Chamber Ensembles

DUO SONATA	Solo instrument and piano		

TRIO

String trio	Violin 1	or	Violin
	Violin 2		Viola
	Cello		Cello

Piano trio	Piano
	Violin
	Cello

QUARTETS

String quartet	Violin 1
	Violin 2
	Viola
	Cello

Piano quartet	Piano
	Violin
	Viola
	Cello

QUINTETS

String quintet	Violin 1	or	Violin 1
	Violin 2	(more rarely)	Violin 2
	Viola 1		Viola
	Viola 2		Cello 1
	Cello		Cello 2

Piano quintet	Violin 1	
	Violin 2	
	Viola	} string quartet
	Cello	
	Piano	

Woodwind quintet	Flute
	Oboe
	Clarinet
	French horn (not a woodwind instrument)
	Bassoon

Brass quintet	Trumpet 1
	Trumpet 2
	French horn
	Trombone
	Tuba

(*Above*) *The Boston
Symphony Orchestra
with its conductor Seiji
Ozawa.* (Photograph by
Christian Steiner)
(*Below*) *The seating
plan of the orchestra.*

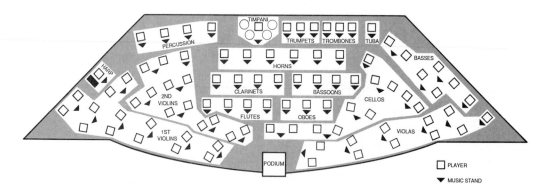

The instruments of the orchestra are arranged so as to secure the best balance of tone. Most of the strings are near the front, as are the gentle woodwinds. Brass and percussion are at the back. A characteristic seating plan for the Boston Symphony Orchestra is shown above; this arrangement varies from one orchestra to another.

Typical Distribution of Orchestral Instruments

Strings	18 first violins divided into two or more groups
	15 second violins
	12 violas
	12 cellos
	9 double basses
	1–2 harps, when needed
Woodwinds	3 flutes, 1 piccolo
	3 oboes, 1 English horn
	3 clarinets, 1 bass clarinet
	3 bassoons, 1 double bassoon
Brass	4–6 French horns
	4 trumpets
	3 trombones
	1 tuba
Percussion	5 players
	1 timpani player (2–4 timpani)
	2–4 on other instruments

The Band

The band is a much-loved American tradition, be it a concert, marching, military, or jazz ensemble. The earliest wind and percussion groups were used for military purposes. Musicians accompanied soldiers to war, playing their brass and percussion instruments from horseback to spur the troops on to victory, and their fifes and drums from among the ranks of the foot soldiers. Concert wind groups originated in the Middle Ages. In northern Europe, a wind band of three to five musicians played each evening, often from the high tower of a local church or city hall. From these traditions grew the military bands of the French Revolution and American Civil War. One American bandmaster, John Philip Sousa (1854–1932), achieved world fame with his band and the repertory of marches that he wrote for it.

Today the *concert band*, an ensemble ranging anywhere from forty to eighty members or more, is an established institution in most secondary schools, colleges, and universities and in many communities as well. Modern composers like to write for this ensemble since it traditionally plays new compositions. The *marching band*, best known in the United States, is a popular group for entertainment at sports events and parades. Besides its core of winds and percussion, this group often includes a spectacular display of drum majors/majorettes, flag twirlers, and the like. The precise instru-

Concert band

Marching band

A performance by the Wind Symphony of California State University, Long Beach, Larry Curtis conducting. (Photo courtesy CSULB Photographic Services)

Jazz band   mentation of *jazz bands* depends on the particular music being played, but generally includes a reed section made up of clarinets and saxophones of various sizes, a brass section of trumpets and trombones, and a rhythm section of percussion, piano, and strings, especially double bass and electric guitar.

The Role of the Conductor

When they are playing, musicians think about meter in order to keep "in time." Large ensembles, such as an orchestra, band, or chorus, need the assistance of a conductor in order to play or sing together; the conductor beats the meter with the right hand in a prescribed pattern that all the musicians in the group understand. These conducting patterns, shown in the diagrams below, further emphasize the strong and weak beats of the measure: beat 1, the strongest in any meter, is always given a *downbeat*, or a downward motion by the conductor; a secondary accent is shown by a change of direction; and the last beat of the measure, a weak beat, is always an upbeat or upward motion, thereby leaving the right hand ready for the downbeat of the next measure.

Basic Conducting Patterns

Duple Meter	Triple Meter	Quadruple Meter	Sextuple Meter
↓ ↑ ↓ ↑	↓ → ↑ ↓ → ↑	↓ ← → ↑ ↓ ← → ↑	↓ ← ← → → ↑
1 2 1 2	1 2 3 1 2 3	1 2 3 4 1 2 3 4	1 2 3 4 5 6

Jesús López-Cobos
conducting the Cincinnati
Symphony Orchestra.
(Photo Mark Alexander)

Britten's Young Person's Guide to the Orchestra

A helpful introduction to the orchestra is Benjamin Britten's *Young Person's Guide to the Orchestra*, which was written expressly for the purpose of illustrating the timbre of each orchestral instrument. The work, composed in 1946, is subtitled *Variations and Fugue on a Theme by Purcell* and is based on a dance tune by Henry Purcell (1659–95), the great composer of the English Baroque.

Britten's plan was to introduce the sound of the entire orchestra playing together, then the sonorities of each instrumental family as a family—woodwinds, brass, strings, percussion—and then to repeat the statement by the full orchestra. Once the listener has the theme well in mind, the composer features each instrument in the order of highest to lowest in range within each family. With this section, we encounter variations of the theme, each presented by a new instrument and with differing accompanying instruments. (See Listening Guide 1 for the order of instruments.) Finally, the work closes with a grand *fugue*, a polyphonic form popular in the Baroque era (1600–1750), which is also based on Purcell's theme. Just as in the variations, the fugue presents its subject, or theme, in rapid order in each instrument.

The modern orchestra, with its amplitude of tonal resources, its range of dynamics, and its infinite variety of color, offers a memorable experience both to the musician and the music lover. There is good reason for the widespread conviction that it is one of the wonders of our musical culture.

Listening Guide 1

BRITTEN: *Young Person's Guide to the Orchestra*
(*Variations and Fugue on a Theme by Purcell*)

Date: 1946

Theme: Based on a dance from Henry Purcell's incidental music to the play *Abdelzar* (*The Moor's Revenge*)

Form: Theme and variations, followed by a fugue

I. THEME: 8 measures in D minor, stated six times to illustrate the instrumental families of the orchestra:

1. entire orchestra
2. woodwinds
3. brass
4. strings
5. percussion
6. entire orchestra

II. VARIATIONS: 13 short variations, each illustrating a different instrument or family of instruments:

	Variations	Solo Instrument	Accompanying Instruments
Woodwinds	1	flutes, piccolo	violins, harp, triangle
	2	oboes	strings and timpani
	3	clarinets	strings and tuba
	4	bassoons	strings and snare drum
Strings	5	violins	brass and bass drum
	6	violas	woodwinds and brass
	7	cellos	clarinets, violas, harp
	8	double basses	woodwinds and tambourine
	9	harp	strings, gong, and cymbal
Brass	10	French horns	strings, harp, and timpani
	11	trumpets	strings and snare drum
	12	trombones, tuba	woodwinds and high brass
Percussion	13	percussion	strings

(Order of introduction: timpani, bass drum and cymbals, timpani, tambourine and triangle, timpani, snare drum and wood block, timpani, castanets and gong, timpani, whip, whole percussion section)

III. FUGUE: subject based on a fragment of the Purcell theme, played in imitatio
instrument of the orchestra in same order as in variations:

Woodwinds: piccolo
                     flutes
                     oboes
                     clarinets
                     bassoons
Strings: first violins
                     second violins
                     violas
                     cellos
                     double basses
                     harp
Brass: French horns
                     trumpets
                     trombones, tuba
Percussion: percussion

Full orchestra at end

TRANSITION I

■

Hearing Musical Styles

"A good style should show no sign of effort. What is written should seem a happy accident."—SOMERSET MAUGHAM

The Concept of Style

Style may be defined as the characteristic manner of presentation in any art. The word may refer to the element of flexibility that shapes each type of art work to its function. We distinguish between the style of a novel and that of an essay, between the style of a cathedral and that of a palace. The word may also indicate the creator's personal manner of expression—the distinctive flavor that sets one artist apart from all others. Thus we speak of the style of Dickens or Thackeray, of Raphael or Michelangelo, of Wagner or Brahms. In a larger sense we often identify style with national culture, as when we speak of French, Italian, or German style; or with an entire civilization, as when we contrast the musical style of the West with that of the Orient.

It is the difference in the treatment of the elements of music that makes one musical work sound very different from another, the music of another culture widely divergent from ours. We have seen that a violin and a piano have individual qualities of sound and unique capabilities, and that one melody, with its characteristic ups and downs, does not sound just like another. But it is differing concepts of how to combine the elements of music that produces varying musical styles.

Musical Styles in History

Since all the arts change from one age to the next, one very important use of the word "style" is in connection with the various historical periods. Here the concept of style enables us to draw the proper connection between the artists and their time, so that the art work is placed in its socio-historical frame. No matter how greatly the artists of a particular era may vary in personality and outlook, when seen in the perspective of time they turn out to have certain qualities in common. The age has put its stamp upon all.

Because of this we can tell at once that a work of art—whether music, poetry, painting, or architecture—dates from the Middle Ages or the Renaissance, from the eighteenth century or the nineteenth. The style of a period, then, is the total art language of all its artists as they react to the artistic, political, economic, religious, and philosophical forces that shape their environment.

Scholars will always disagree as to precisely when one style period ends and the next begins. Each period leads by imperceptible degrees into the following one, dates and labels being merely convenient signposts. The following outline shows the main style periods in the history of Western music. Each represents a conception of form and technique, an ideal of beauty, a manner of expression and performance attuned to the cultural climate of the period—in a word, a style! (The dates, naturally, are approximate.)

350–600 A.D.	Period of the Church Fathers
600–850	Early Middle Ages—Gregorian Chant
850–1150	Romanesque period—Development of the staff in musical notation, about 1000
1150–1450	Gothic period
1450–1600	Renaissance
1600–1750	Baroque period
1725–1775	Rococo period
1750–1825	Classical period
1820–1900	Romantic period
1890–1915	Post-Romantic period—including Impressionism
1910–	Twentieth century

MEDIEVAL (handwritten)

memorize (handwritten)

PART TWO

Medieval and Renaissance Music

"Music was originally discreet, seemly, simple, masculine, and of good morals. Have not the moderns rendered it lascivious beyond measure?"—JACOB OF LIÈGE

Sandro Botticelli (*1445–1510*) Adoration of the Magi (National Gallery of Art, Washington. Andrew W. Mellon Collection.)

UNIT III

The Middle Ages

10

The Culture of the Middle Ages

*"Nothing is more characteristic of human nature than to be soothed
by sweet modes and stirred up by their opposites. Infants, youths, and
old people as well are so naturally attuned to musical modes by a
kind of spontaneous feeling that no age is without delight in sweet
song."*—BOETHIUS (c. 480–524)

The relics of the ancient civilizations—Sumer, Babylonia, Egypt—bear witness to a flourishing musical art. In the antique world, religious myth and tradition ascribed divine powers to music. The walls of Thebes rose and those of Jericho fell to the sound of music. David played his lyre to cure the melancholy of Saul. In the temple at Jerusalem the Levites, who were the musicians, "being arrayed in fine linen, having cymbals and psalteries and harps, stood at the east of the altar, and with them an hundred and twenty priests with trumpets."

Only a few fragments have descended to us of the music of antiquity. The centuries have forever silenced the sounds that echoed through the Athenian amphitheater and the Roman circus. Those sounds and the attitudes they reflected, in Greece and throughout the Mediterranean world, formed the subsoil out of which flowered the music of later ages. They became part of the heritage of the West.

The Middle Ages extended over the thousand-year period between the fall of Rome, commonly set at A.D. 476 and the flowering of the culture of the modern world. The first half of this millennium, from around 500 to 1000 and often referred to as the Dark Ages, should not be viewed as a period of decline, but rather of ascent, during which Christianity triumphed

Feudalism

The monastic influence

over paganism throughout Europe. In this society all power flowed from the king, with the benign approval of the Church and its bishops. The two centers of power, Church and state, were bound to clash, and the struggle between them shaped the next chapter of European history. The concept of a strong, centralized government as the ultimate dispenser of law and order found its embodiment in Charlemagne (742–814), the legendary emperor of the Franks in whose domains Roman, Frankish, and Teutonic elements intermingled. This progressive monarch, who regretted until his dying day that he did not know how to write—he regarded the ability as a talent he simply did not possess—encouraged education and left behind him an ideal of social justice that illumined the "darkness" of the early Medieval world.

The culture of this period was largely shaped by the rise of monasteries. It was the monks who preserved the learning of the ancient world and transmitted it, through their manuscripts, to European scholars. In their desire to enhance the church service, they extensively cultivated music. Because of their efforts, the art music of the Middle Ages was largely religious. Women too played a role in the preservation of knowledge and in music for the church, for one of the important societal roles of women in this era was as a nun. One woman stands out in particular, Hildegard of Bingen, abbess of an abbey in a small town in West Germany. She is remembered today for her writings on natural history, medicine, and for her poetry and music for special services of the church. During this period, too, the Church consolidated its political power to such a degree that the Pope could challenge the supremacy of kings and even dictate to them.

Polyphony emerged as a stylistic factor of prime importance in Western music at about the same time that European painting began to reflect the science of perspective. **Giotto** (*c. 1267–1337*) Lamentation. (Arena Chapel, Padua. Scala/Art Resource)

The Virgin, seen as the sweetly-loving Mother of God, in this detail of a statue from the Ile-de-France, c. 1200, by an unknown artist. (Museum of Fine Arts, Boston. William Francis Warden Fund)

The High Middle Ages, from around 1000 to 1400, witnessed the building of the great cathedrals and the founding of universities throughout Europe. Cities emerged as centers of art and culture, and with them came the townsman, the bourgeois, who was destined to play an ever expanding role in civic life. National literatures developed and played their part in shaping the languages of Europe: the *Chanson de Roland* in France, Dante's *Divine Comedy* (1307) in Italy, Chaucer's *Canterbury Tales* (1386) in England. These literary landmarks have their counterparts in painting with Giotto's frescoes for the Arena chapel in Padua (1306), Duccio's panels for Siena (1308), and Orcagna's *Last Judgment* for Florence (c. 1355).

Although feudal society was male-dominated, idealizing as it did the figure of the fearless warrior, women's status was raised by the universal cult of Mary, the mother of Christ, and was further enhanced by the concepts of chivalry that sprang out of the age of knighthood. In the songs of the court minstrels—the troubadours and trouvères—woman was adored with a fervor that laid the foundation for our concept of romantic love. This poetic attitude found its perfect symbol in the image of the faithful knight who worshiped his lady from afar and was inspired by her to deeds of daring and self-sacrifice.

The age of knighthood

The Middle Ages, in brief, encompassed a period of enormous ferment and change. Out of its stirrings, faint at first but with increasing clarity and strength, emerged the profile of what we today know as Western civilization.

11

Mass and Motet in the Middle Ages

*"When God saw that many men were lazy, and gave themselves only
with difficulty to spiritual reading, He wished to make it easy for
them, and added the melody to the Prophet's words, that all being
rejoiced by the charm of the music, should sing hymns to Him with
gladness."*—ST. JOHN CHRYSOSTOM (345–407)

The early music of the Christian Church was shaped by Greek, Hebrew, and Syrian influences. It became necessary in time to assemble the ever growing body of music into an organized liturgy. The task extended over several generations but is traditionally associated with the name of Pope Gregory the Great, who reigned from 590 to 604.

Gregorian chant

Like the music of the Greeks and Hebrews from which it descended, *Gregorian chant* (also known as *plainchant* or *plainsong*) consists of a single-line melody. In other words, it is monophonic in texture and does not know the third dimension of harmony and counterpoint. Its freely flowing vocal line is subtly attuned to the inflections of the Latin text. Gregorian melody is generally free from regular accent. Its unmeasured flow embodies what may be called prose rhythm in music, or free-verse rhythm, as distinguished from metrical-poetry rhythm such as we find in the regularly accented measures of duple or triple meter.

The Gregorian melodies, numbering more than three thousand, formed a body of anonymous music whose roots reached deep into the spiritual life of the people. In melodic style, Gregorian chant avoids wide leaps and dynamic contrasts. Its gentle rise and fall constitute a kind of disembodied musical speech, "a prayer on pitch." Free from the shackles of regular phrase structure, the continuous, undulating vocal line is the counterpart in sound of the sinuous traceries of Romanesque art and architecture.

At first the Gregorian chants were handed down orally from one generation to the next. As the number of chants increased, singers needed to be reminded of the general outlines of the different melodies. Thus came into being *neumes*, little ascending and descending signs that were first written above the words to suggest the contour of the melody, and which developed into a musical notation with square notes on a four-line staff (see page 62).

Neumes

As far as the setting of text is concerned, the melodies fall into three main classes: *syllabic*, that is, one note to each syllable of text; *neumatic*, generally with groups of two to four notes to a syllable; and *melismatic*, with a single text syllable extending over longer groups of notes. The melismatic style, descended from the rhapsodic improvisations of the Orient, became a prominent feature of Gregorian chant and exerted a strong influence on subsequent Western music.

Text settings

60

Decorative manuscript page from the Hunterian Psalter (c. 1175) depicting King David tuning his harp, surrounded by his musicians playing bells, rebec, fiddle, triple-duct flute, hammer psaltery, and hurdy-gurdy. (Ms. Hunter 229. Courtesy the Librarian of Glasgow University Library)

From Gregorian chant to the Baroque era, Western music used a variety of scale patterns or *modes*—including not only the major and minor modes, but also several did not have as strong a sense of gravitation to a tonic note as marks our modern major-minor system. *Modes*

The modes served as the basis for European art music for a thousand years. With the development of polyphony, or many-voiced music, a harmonic system evolved, based on modes. The adjective *modal* consequently refers to the type of melody and harmony that prevailed in the early and later Middle Ages. It is frequently used in opposition to *tonal*, which refers to the harmony based on the major-minor tonality that came later.

The Mass

The Mass is the most solemn ritual of the Roman Catholic Church. It constitutes a re-enactment of the sacrifice of Christ. The name is derived from the Latin *missa*, "dismissal" (of the congregation at the end of the service).

The aggregation of prayers that make up the Mass fall into two categories:

Proper and Ordinary

those that vary from day to day throughout the church year dependent upon the particular feast celebrated, the *Proper*; and those that remain the same in every Mass, the *Ordinary*. (A chart of the organization of the Mass with the individual movements of the Proper and Ordinary appears in Chapter 14, page 91.) The liturgy, which reached its present form about nine hundred years ago, is supported by Gregorian melodies for each item of the ceremony. In this way, Gregorian chant was central to the celebration of the Mass, which was and remains today the most important service in the Catholic Church.

A Gregorian Melody: Haec dies

Gradual

A fine example of Gregorian chant is *Haec dies*, the Gradual from the solemn Mass for Easter Day. *Gradual* is the name of the fourth item of the Proper or variable part of the Mass. Derived from the Latin word for steps (because the melody may have been sung from the steps of the altar), the term was applied to the singing of portions of a Psalm in a musically elaborate, melismatic style. The Gradual is performed in a responsorial manner, that is, as a series of interchanges between soloist and chorus in which one answers the other. The solo passage is known as a *verse*, the choral answer is the *respond*. The Gradual therefore involves the contrast between two dissimilar bodies of sound, and is monophonic in texture.

Haec dies opens with a brief introductory passage for a soloist. The choral response occupies the first half of the melody. The second half is given over to the verse of the soloist, which is followed by a brief choral conclusion. (See Listening Guide 2 for the text, which is drawn from two Psalms.) The melody moves by step or small leap within a narrow range and consists of a series of tiny motives that grow like cells and expand in a natural process of variation. Striking is the way in which certain key words are extended over a series of notes. This melismatic treatment brings into prominence such important words as *Dominus* (Lord) or *exsultemus* (we will rejoice), setting them apart from the others.

Melismatic setting

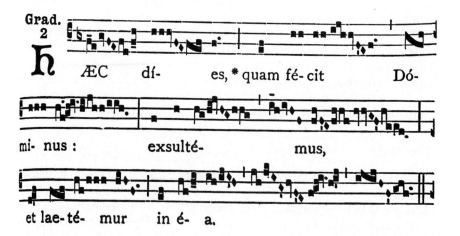

The opening of the chant, Haec dies, *in Gregorian notation.*

The Rise of Polyphony: The Notre Dame School

Towards the end of the Romanesque period (c. 850–1150) began the single most important development in the history of Western music: the emergence of polyphony. (You will remember that *polyphony* combines two or more simultaneous melodic lines.) This occurred at about the same time that European painting began developing the science of perspective. Thus hearing and seeing in depth came into European culture together.

Once several melodic lines proceeded simultaneously, the flexible prose rhythms of single-line music disappeared. Polyphony contributed to the increased use of regular meters that enabled the different voices to keep together. This music had to be written down in a way that would indicate precisely the rhythm and the pitch, which necessitated a more exact notational system not unlike the one in use today. (For an explanation of our modern notational system, see Appendix I, Musical Notation.)

With the development of exact notation, music took a long step from being an art of improvisation and oral tradition to one that was carefully planned and preserved. The period of anonymous creation drew to a close and the individual composer began to be recognized.

Development of notation

This development took shape during the Gothic era (c. 1150–1450), a period that witnessed the rise of the cathedrals with their choirs and organs. The learned musicians, for the most part monks and priests, mastered the art of constructing extended musical works through the various devices of counterpoint discussed earlier (Chapter 4, pages 19–21). Their prime interest at this point was in the structural combining of musical elements,

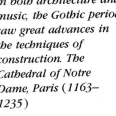

In both architecture and music, the Gothic period saw great advances in the techniques of construction. The Cathedral of Notre Dame, Paris (1163–1235)

which explains the derivation of the word "composer" from the Latin *com-ponere* "to put together." The creative musician of the late Gothic period thought of himself primarily as a master builder.

Organum

The earliest kind of polyphonic music was called *organum*. This developed when the custom arose of adding to the Gregorian melody a second voice that ran parallel to the plainchant at the interval of a fifth or fourth above or below.

The way was now open for the development of a polyphonic art in which the individual voices moved with ever greater independence, not only in parallel but also in contrary motion. In the forefront of this development were the composers whose center was the Cathedral of Notre Dame in Paris

Notre Dame school
Léonin

during the twelfth and thirteenth centuries. Their leader, Léonin, is the first composer of polyphonic music whose name is known to us. He lived in the latter part of the twelfth century and appears to have won considerable fame.

It was self-evident to the Medieval mind that the new must be founded on the old. Therefore the composer of organum based his piece on a pre-existing Gregorian chant. While the tenor sang the melody in enormously long notes, the upper voice moved freely and rapidly above it. This is known as *organal style*. In such a setting, the chant was no longer recognizable as a melody. Its presence was symbolic, anchoring the new in the old, inspiring and guiding the added voice.

A contrasting style in Notre Dame organum set the original chant in a faster moving, rhythmic version that paralleled the movement of the freshly

Discant style

composed upper voice. This is known as *discant style*, as distinguished from organal style. Both could occur in contrasting sections of the same piece.

An Example of Organum: Haec dies

The organum *Haec dies*, is based on the same Gregorian melody that we just studied. Here, however, it appears in extremely long notes in the lower voice while the upper presents the newly composed organal part. The long notes of the Gregorian melody were often supported by the organ, as in the performance that you will hear. The upper part is written for a high male voice, a countertenor or male alto. (See Listening Guide 2 for the text.)

This too is a Gradual for Easter. The solo sections are answered by choral ones. The organal style sections alternate with those in discant styles, which are more rhythmic, with fixed patterns of long and short notes repeated or varied. Already European music was on its way to the metrical patterns that were to make Western rhythms so accessible to the ear.

A fragment of Gregorian chant might also be used for the basis of a short composition that was sung to one or two words or a single syllable. Such

Clausula

a piece was known as a *clausula*. The organum *Haec dies* includes such a passage, which gives the effect of being freely improvised.

As *Haec dies* clearly shows, the Gregorian melodies are remarkable for their gentle flow, their organic unity, and the way they shape themselves to the natural inflections of the Latin text. Our richest legacy from the period of pure monophonic music, they nourished more than a thousand years of European music.

The Early Medieval Motet

While Léonin limited himself to polyphony in two parts, his successor Pérotin extended the technique by writing for three and four voices. He is remembered today as the foremost member of a school that laid the foundation for a magnificent flowering of polyphonic art. Toward the end of Pérotin's life, clerics began composing new texts for the previously textless upper voices of organum. The addition of these texts resulted in the *motet*, the most important form of early polyphonic music. This term is applied loosely to a vocal composition, sacred or secular, which may or may not have had instrumental accompaniment.

Pérotin

The early motet illustrates how Medieval composers based their own works on what had been handed down from the past. They selected a fragment of Gregorian chant and, keeping the notes intact, gave them precise rhythmic values, usually of very long notes that contrasted with the more active movement of the other parts. This served as the structural skeleton of the piece, and became known as the *cantus firmus* (fixed melody), to which composers added one, two, or three countermelodies of their own. (A *countermelody* is a melody heard against another.) The cantus firmus therefore served as a point of departure, and could be repeated as many times as necessary to fill out the length of the piece. The part containing the cantus firmus was called the *tenor*, from the Latin *tenere* (to hold), so called because the tenor "held" the long notes. (It should be noted that terms such as tenor, countertenor, alto, and bass did not signify specific ranges until a later time.) The second, third, and fourth parts were known respectively as *duplum*, *triplum*, and *quadruplum*. However, nomenclature in the Middle Ages was far from standardized. Different names were used at different times and places.

Early motet

Cantus firmus

The term "motet" derives from the French *mot* (word), referring to the words that were added to the vocal lines. The duplum and triplum might present two different Latin texts at the same time; or one might have Latin words while another French. In this way a sacred text might be combined with a quite secular—even racy—one. The basic Gregorian theme, hidden among the voices, fused these disparate elements into a unity—if not in the listener's ear, at least in the composer's mind.

An Anonymous Motet: O mitissima—Virgo—Haec dies

Like the two examples that preceded it, our next is based on the Gregorian chant *Haec dies*, which is now heard in a motet for three voices, each with a different text. (The title of such a piece gives the opening words of all three parts.) The Gregorian melody in the bottom part is set to only two words, *Haec dies*, which are stretched out to such lengths that the syllables lose all verbal meaning and function simply as sound. This part, instead of being sung, could be played on a vielle (the Medieval ancestor of the violin). The interchange of vocal and instrumental music has persisted into our own time, where a popular song may be taken over by an instrumental work, or a symphonic theme can become a popular song.

This anonymous thirteenth-century motet is found in two versions in different manuscripts. In one, all three voices are in Latin, the upper two presenting two different poems in praise of the Virgin Mary. This is the version you will hear, which appears in Listening Guide 2. In another, the top voice sings a love song in French.

The opening and closing sounds as well as the cadences—resting places that punctuate the music—are based on open fifths and octaves, which have a hollow sound to our ears. Yet these intervals must have delighted Medieval ears, as they did composers of the modern era such as Debussy, who, as we shall see, loved the Medieval sound and tried to recapture it.

The motet is in triple meter, which to Medieval listeners symbolized the perfection of the Trinity. Its rhythm is based on an alternation of long and short notes sung at a rather lively tempo. Music has clearly come a long way from the slow, circuitous movement of Léonin's time. The two upper voices move in similar rhythm; they lie in the same range and cross each other in a lively interchange. The bottom voice, on the other hand, unfolds a repeated rhythmic pattern based on the notes of the chant, in the order long-long-short-long. A repetition of a musical pattern—melodic, rhythmic, or harmonic—is commonly known as an *ostinato*. Since all three voices move to light, fluent rhythms, the overall effect is of a vivacity that belies the supplicating Latin text.

Listening Guide 2   1A/1   I/1/1

Chant, Organum, and the Motet
1 A. Gregorian chant: *Haec dies*
Text: Psalms 118:24 and 106:1
Chant type: Gradual, from Proper
Occasion: Easter Sunday
Performance: Responsorial (solo and chorus)
Style: Elaborate and melismatic (melisma on "Domino")

Do - mi - no, _____

Performance	Text	Translation
Solo intonation	Haec dies,	This is the day
Choral response	quam fecit Dominus exsultemus et laetemur in ea.	which the Lord hath made; we will rejoice and be glad of it.
Solo verse	Confitemini Domino, quoniam bonus: quoniam in saeculum misericordia	O give thanks to the Lord, for he is good: for his mercy endureth
Chorus	ejus.	forever.

2 **B. Organum: *Haec dies* (excerpt)**

Date: c. 1175

Composer: Notre Dame School of Paris, in style of Léonin

Voices/Text: 2–voice, both with *Haec dies*

Characteristics: Alternates organal and discant style

Upper voice—freely composed, rhythmic, fast moving

Lower voice—contains *Haec dies* chant

Organal style—chant in long notes in lower voice

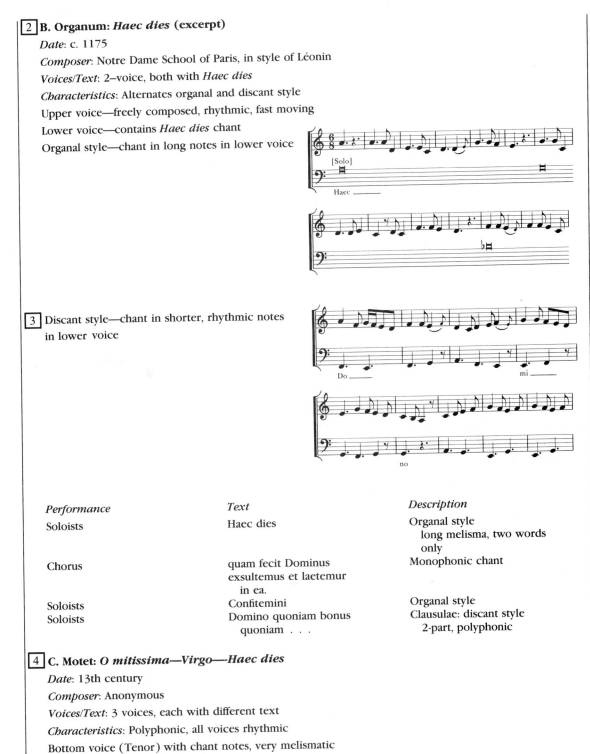

3 Discant style—chant in shorter, rhythmic notes
in lower voice

Performance	Text	Description
Soloists	Haec dies	Organal style long melisma, two words only
Chorus	quam fecit Dominus exsultemus et laetemur in ea.	Monophonic chant
Soloists	Confitemini	Organal style
Soloists	Domino quoniam bonus quoniam . . .	Clausulae: discant style 2-part, polyphonic

4 **C. Motet: *O mitissima—Virgo—Haec dies***

Date: 13th century

Composer: Anonymous

Voices/Text: 3 voices, each with different text

Characteristics: Polyphonic, all voices rhythmic

Bottom voice (Tenor) with chant notes, very melismatic
on two words only (*Haec dies*)

TOP VOICE:

O mitissima Virgo Maria,	O sweetest Virgin Mary,
Posce tuum filium,	beg thy son
Ut nobis auxilium	to give us help
Det et remedium	and resources
Contra demonum	against the Demon's
Fallibiles astucias	deceptions and
Et horum nequicias.	their iniquities.

MIDDLE VOICE:

Virgo virginum,	Virgin of virgins,
Lumen luminum,	light of lights,
Reformatrix hominum,	reformer of men,
Que portasti Dominum,	who bore the Lord,
Per te Maria,	through thee, Mary
Detur venia,	let grace be given
Angelo nunciante,	as the Angel announced:
Virgo es post et ante.	Thou art a Virgin before and after.

BOTTOM VOICE: (played instrumentally)

Haec dies	This is the day . . .

Motet opening: ostinato pattern bracketed (long-long-short-long)

12

Secular Music in the Middle Ages

"There are many new things in music that will appear altogether plausible to our descendents."—JEAN DE MURIS (1319)

Alongside the learned or art music of the cathedrals and choir schools there sprang up a popular literature of songs and dances that reflected every aspect of Medieval life. The earliest secular songs that have been preserved were set to Latin texts, which suggests their origin in university towns rather than in the villages. Typical are the student or Goliard songs of the period, many with lewd texts, which express the seize-the-moment philosophy that has always inspired youthful poets. Both poetry and music celebrate the joys of the bottle, the impermanence of love, the beauty of springtime, and the cruelty of fate. Seven hundred years later the German composer Carl Orff resurrected their spirit in his *Carmina burana*.

Goliard songs

Jongleurs, Troubadours, and Trouvères

The *jongleurs* emerged as a class of musicians who wandered among the courts and towns. These were versatile entertainers who played instruments, sang and danced, juggled and showed tricks along with animal acts, and performed plays. In an age that had no newspapers, they regaled their audience with gossip and news. These actor-singers were viewed as little better than vagabonds and thus lived on the fringe of society.

On an altogether different social level were the poet-musicians who flourished at the various courts of Europe. The *troubadours* were Medieval poet-musicians who lived in Provence, the region roughly equivalent to southern France, while the *trouvères* were active in the provinces to the north. Both terms mean the same thing—finders or inventors, implying that these musicians presented original material, as distinguished from the Church musicians who based their art on melodies that had been handed down from the past. Troubadours and trouvères flourished in aristocratic circles, numbering kings and princes among their ranks; but an artist of more humble birth might be accepted among them if his talent warranted it. They either sang their music themselves or entrusted its performance to a minstrel. In Germany they were known as *minnesingers* or singers of courtly love.

Secular music became an integral part of Medieval court life, supplying the necessary accompaniment for dancing, dinner, and after-dinner entertainment. It was indispensable in the ceremonies that welcomed visiting dignitaries, at tournaments and civic processions; military music supported campaigns, strengthened the spirit of warriors departing on the Crusades, and greeted them upon their return. Among the royal minstrels were Alfonso

Roles of secular music

Heinrich von Meissen, called "Frauenlob" or champion of ladies, is exalted by musicians playing drum, flute, shawm, fiddles, psaltery, and bagpipe. Frauenlob was a minnesinger (singer of courtly love), the German counterpart of the troubadour. (Heidelberg University Library)

the Wise of Spain and Richard the Lion-Hearted of England, whose mother, the legendary Eleanor of Aquitaine, presided over a famous court of poet-musicians. Whether in France or Germany, England or Spain, the aristocratic singers were creating a literature that would exert a profound influence upon European culture.

Courtly poetry   The poems of the troubadour and trouvère repertory ranged from simple ballads to love songs, political and moral ditties, war songs, laments, and dance songs. They exalted the virtues prized by the age of chivalry—valor, honor, nobility of character, devotion to an ideal, and the quest for perfect love. Like so many of our popular songs today, many of them dealt with the subject of unrequited passion. The object of the poet's desire was generally unattainable, either because of her exalted rank or because she was already wed to another. This poetry, in short, dealt with love in its most idealized form. Significantly, the songs in praise of the Virgin Mary were cast in the same style and language, sometimes even to the same melodies, as served to express love of a more worldly kind.

Moniot d'Arras: Ce fut en mai

Moniot d'Arras (Fl. 1213–39), one of the last trouvères, was a monk in the abbey of St. Vaast. His work in his native Arras marked the end of the trouvère tradition. Characteristic is his love song *Ce fut en mai* (It happened in May). The poem tells of an unhappy lover who finds solace in religious feeling. (See Listening Guide 3.) The music is folklike and charming, and makes no attempt to express the unhappiness described in the text. The song is monophonic in texture, consisting of a single line of melody heard against an accompaniment that was improvised. In our recording the accompaniment is played on a psaltery, a dulcimer, and a vielle. The *psaltery* was a Medieval folk instrument like our zither, consisting of a soundbox over which were stretched four or five melody strings and a larger number of accompanimental strings; these were plucked. The *dulcimer* resembled the psaltery, but its strings, instead of being plucked, were struck with little hammers. And the *vielle,* as you may remember, was an ancestor of the violin.

The poem consists of five stanzas, with an elaborate rhyme scheme; the melody unfolds in two short sections, each of which is repeated. The overall musical form is *strophic,* meaning the same melody is repeated with every stanza of the poem. A brief instrumental interlude is repeated between the stanzas. The use of a poem based on stanzas dictates the repetition of a musical section. When only one or two lines were repeated at the end of each stanza, the repetition took shape as a musical refrain. Thus, music responded to the fixed forms of poetry in the most natural manner, creating an intimate relationship between the words and music.

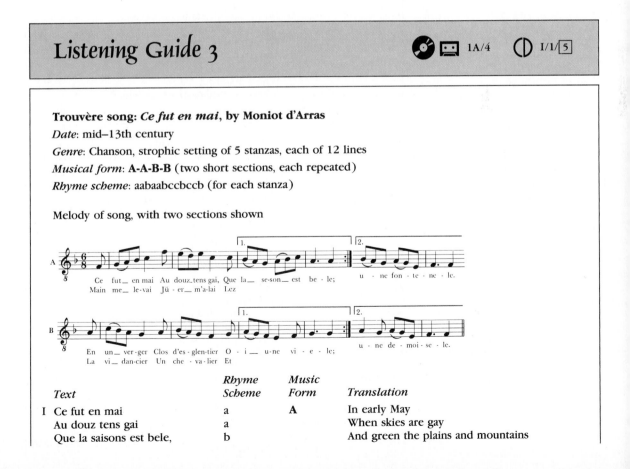

Listening Guide 3

1A/4   I/1/5

Trouvère song: *Ce fut en mai,* by Moniot d'Arras

Date: mid–13th century

Genre: Chanson, strophic setting of 5 stanzas, each of 12 lines

Musical form: **A-A-B-B** (two short sections, each repeated)

Rhyme scheme: aabaabccbccb (for each stanza)

Melody of song, with two sections shown

Text	Rhyme Scheme	Music Form	Translation
I Ce fut en mai	a	**A**	In early May
Au douz tens gai	a		When skies are gay
Que la saisons est bele,	b		And green the plains and mountains

Main me levai,	a	A	At break of day
Jöer m'alai,	a		I rose to play
Lez une fontenele.	b		Beside a little fountain
En un vergier	c	B	In garden close
Clos d'aiglentier	c		Where shone the rose
Oi une viele;	b		I heard a fiddle played, then:
La vi dancier	c	B	A handsome knight
Un chevalier	c		That charmed my sight
Et une damoisele.	b		Was dancing with a maiden.
II Cors orent gent	a	A	Both fair of face,
Et avenant,	a		They turned with grace
Et molt très bien dançoient;	b		To tread their Maytime measure;
En acolant	a	A	The flowering place,
Et en baisant	a		Their close embrace,
Molt biau se deduisoient.	b		Their kisses brought them pleasure.
Au chief du tor,	c	B	Yet shortly they
En un destor,	c		Had slipped away
Doi et doi s'en aloient;	b		And strolled among the bowers;
Le jeu d'amor	c	B	To ease their heart
Desus la flor	c		Each played the part
A lor plaisir faisoient.	b		In love's games on the flowers.
III J'alai avant,	a	A	I crept ahead
Molt redoutant	a		All chill with dread
Que nus d'aus ne me voie	b		Lest someone there should see me,
Maz et pensant	a	A	Bemused and sad
Et desirrant	a		Because I had
D'avoir ausi grant joie.	b		No joy like theirs to please me.
Lors vi lever	c	B	Then one of those
Un de lor per	c		I'd seen there, rose
De si loing com j'estoie	b		And from afar off speaking
Por apeler	c	B	He questioned me
Et demander	c		Who I might be
Qui sui ni que queroie.	b		And what I came there seeking.
IV J'alai vers aus,	a	A	I stepped their way
Dis lor mes maus,	a		To sadly say
Que une dame amoie,	b		How long I'd loved a lady
A cui loiaus	a	A	Whom, all my days
Sanz estre faus	a		My heart obeys
Tot mon vivant seroie,	b		Full faithfully and steady,
Por cui plus trai	c	B	Though still I bore
Peine et esmai	c		A grief so sore
Que dire ne porroie.	b		In losing one so lovely
Et bien le sai,	c	B	That surely I
Que je morrai,	c		Would come to die
S'ele ne mi ravoie.	b		Unless she deigned to love me.
V Tot belement	a	A	With wisdom rare,
Et doucement	a		With tactful air,
Chascuns d'aus me ravoie.	b		They counselled and relieved me;
Et dient tant	a	A	They said their prayer
Que Dieus briement	a		Was God might spare
M'envoit de celi joie	b		Some joy in love that grieved me
Por qui je sent	c	B	Where all my gain
Paine et torment:	c		Was loss and pain
Et je lor en redoie	b		So I, in turn, extended
Merci molt grant	c	B	My thanks sincere
Et en plorant	c		With many a tear
A Dé les comandoie.	b		And them to God commended.

Tr. by MARTIN BEST

Guillaume de Machaut and the French Ars Nova

The breakup of the feudal social structure brought with it new concepts of life, art, and beauty. This ferment was reflected in the musical style that made its appearance at the beginning of the fourteenth century in France and somewhat later in Italy, known as *Ars Nova* (new art). The music of the French Ars Nova shows greater refinement than the *Ars Antiqua* (old art), which it displaced. Writers such as Petrarch, Boccaccio, and Chaucer were turning from the divine comedy to the human; painters would soon begin to discover the beauties of nature and the attractiveness of the human form. So, too, composers turned increasingly from religious to secular themes. The Ars Nova encompassed developments in rhythm, meter, harmony, and counterpoint that transformed the art.

Its outstanding figure was the French composer-poet Guillaume de Machaut (c. 1300–77). He took holy orders at an early age, became secretary to John of Luxembourg, King of Bohemia, and was active at the court of Charles, Duke of Normandy, who subsequently became King of France. He spent his old age as a canon of Rheims, admired as the greatest musician of the time.

Machaut's double career as cleric and courtier impelled him to both religious and secular music. His poetry reveals him as a proponent of the ideals of Medieval chivalry—a romantic who, like Sir Thomas Malory in his lament for King Arthur, exalted the moral and social code of an age that was already finished.

Machaut: Hareu! hareu! le feu—Helas!—Obediens

The secular motet came to full flower in the art of Machaut. He expanded the form of the preceding century to incorporate the new developments made possible by the Ars Nova, especially the greater variety and flexibility of rhythm. Characteristic is the motet *Hareu! hareu! le feu/Helas! ou sera pris confors/Obediens usque ad mortem*. Since the three simultaneous parts have different texts, the listener is obviously expected to follow the general idea rather than the individual words. The top voice, the triplum, sings a poem on a favorite theme of fourteenth-century verse—the suffering of the lover who is consumed by his desire. At the same time, the middle voice, the duplum, sings a fifteen-line poem in a similar vein. (See Listening Guide 4 for the texts.)

The texts

The tenor is taken from a plainsong Gradual that refers to Christ, but Machaut chooses only the section that goes with the words *obediens usque ad mortem* (obedient even unto death), a sentiment appropriate to the chivalric love described in the other poems. The notes of this cantus firmus are arranged in a rhythmic pattern that is repeated again and again.

This procedure identifies *Hareu! hareu! le feu* as an *isorhythmic motet* (*iso* means "the same"), based on a repeating rhythm or an *ostinato*. The cantus firmus was probably played on an instrument, such as the slide trumpet (an early type of trumpet, with a single slide rather than a double, like today's trombone).

Isorhythmic motet

The upper two voices move at a much faster rate, in a compound meter we could call 6/8 time. Though they occupy the same range, the triplum generally stays at the top of that range, the duplum near the bottom. Such a highly stylized art may lack the directly emotional expressiveness of some later music, but its delight in structural sophistication tells us something important about the society for which it was created.

Listening Guide 4   1A/5   I/1/6

MACHAUT: *Hareu! hareu! le feu—Helas!— Obediens*

Date: mid–14th-century

Genre: Isorhythmic motet, 3-voiced

Text: 3 different texts (2 French, 1 Latin)

Form: Based on rhythmic ostinato pattern: short-long-long-long-short. Repetitions of ostinato: 6 in very long notes, 6 in diminution (half as long)

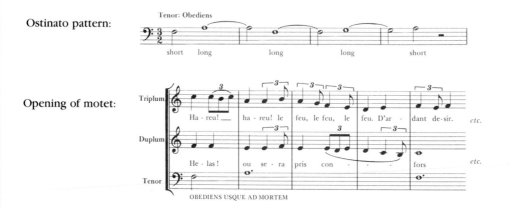

Ostinato pattern:

Opening of motet:

TRIPLUM VOICE

Form	Text	Rhyme Scheme	Translation
Long note ostinato			
1	Hareu! hareu! le feu, le feu, le feu	a	Help! Help! Fire! Fire! Fire!
	D'ardant desir, qu'einc si ardant ne fu,	a	My heart is on fire with burning desire
	Qu'en mon cuer a espris et soustenu	a	Such as was never seen before.
2	Amours, et s'a la joie retenu	a	Love, having started it, fans the flames,
	D'espoir qui doit attemprer telle ardure.	b	Withholding all hope of joy which might put out such a blaze.
	Las! se le feu qui ensement l'art dure,	b	Alas, if this fire keeps on burning,
3	Mes cuers sera tous bruis et esteins,	c	My heart, already blackened and shrivelled.

	Qui de ce feu est ja nercis et teins,	c	Will be burnt to ashes.
	Pour ce qu'il est fins, loyaus et certeins;	c	For it is true, loyal, and sincere.
4	Si que j'espoir que deviez yert, eins	c	I expect I shall be mad with grief
	Que bonne Amour de merci l'asseure	b	Before gentle Love consoles it
	Par la vertu d'esperance seure.	b	With sound hope.
5	Car pour li seul, qui endure mal meint;	d	It alone, suffering much Hardship,
	Pitié deffaut, ou toute biauté meint;	d	Is devoid of Pity, abode of all beauty.
	Durtés y regne et Dangiers y remeint,	d	Instead, Harshness rules over it and Haughtiness flourishes.
6	Desdeins y vit et Loyautez s'i feint	d	Disdain dwells there, while Loyalty is a rare visitor
	Et Amours n'a de li ne de moy cure.	b	And Love pays no heed to it or to me.
	Joie le het, ma dame li est dure,	b	Joy hates it, and my lady is cruel to it.

Diminution of ostinato

1	Et, pour croistre mes dolereus meschiés,	e	To complete my sad misfortune,
2	Met dedens moy Amours, qui est mes chiés,	e	Love, my sovereign lord,
3	Un desespoir qui si mal entechiés	e	Fills me with such bitter despair
4	Est quietous biens a de moy esrachiés,	e	That I am left penniless,
5	Et en tous cas mon corps si desnature	b	And so wasted in body
6	Qu'il me convient morir malgré Nature.	b	That I shall surely die before my time.

DUPLUM VOICE

Long note ostinato

1	Helas! ou sera pris confors	a	Alas, where can I find consolation
	Pour moy qui ne vail nés que mors?	a	Who am as good as dead?
2	Quant riens garentir ne me puet	b	When my one salvation
3	Fors ma dame chiere qui wet	b	Is my dear lady,
	Qu'en desespoir muire, sans plus,	c	Who gladly lets me die in despair,
4	Pour ce que je l'aim plus que nulz,	c	Simply because I love her as no other could.
5	Et Souvenir pour enasprir	d	And Memory, in order to keep
	L'ardour de mon triste desir	d	My unhappy desire alive,
6	Me moustre adés sa grant bonté	e	Reminds me all the while of her great goodness.

Diminution of ostinato

1	Et sa fine vraie biauté	e	And her delicate beauty,
2	Qui doublement me fait ardoir.	f	Thereby making me want her all the more.
3	Einssi sans cuer et sans espoir.	f	Deprived thus of heart and hope
4	Ne puis pas vivre longuement,	g	I cannot live for long.
5	N'en feu cuers humeins nullement	g	No man's heart can long survive
6	Ne puet longue duree avoir.	h	When once aflame.

The English Carol

Burden

The English carol took shape as a Medieval strophic song, with a *refrain* or a repeated section of music and text that was called a *burden*. It originated as a dance-song in a lively rhythm, with an English or Latin text on a religious subject, especially one associated with Christmas. We still today sing Christmas carols. The subject might also be a particular event or occasion. The carol was in polyphonic texture, for two or three voices. From earliest times English partsongs had favored vocal lines that moved in parallel thirds and sixths, at a time when vocal polyphony on the Continent featured open fifths and octaves. As a result, the English carol had a remarkably "modern" sound in comparison with its French or Italian counterpart.

An Anonymous Carol: Deo gratias, Anglia

S1A/1

S1/1

The anonymous carol *Deo gratias, Anglia,* popularly known as the Agincourt carol, celebrated the victory of the English King Henry V over the French at Agincourt in 1415. It was a victory of the English archers, who with unerring aim shot their arrows at the eyes of their heavily armored foes. The battle took place as the age of knighthood was drawing to a close. Shakespeare immortalized the battle in the ringing lines that conclude the King's exhortation to his nobles just before they fought (*The Life of Henry the Fifth,* Act IV, scene 3):

We few, we happy few, we band of brothers;
For he today that sheds his blood with me
Shall be my brother; be he ne'er so vile,
This day shall gentle his condition;
And gentlemen in England now abed
Shall think themselves accursed they were not here;
And hold their manhoods cheap whiles any speaks
That fought with us upon Saint Crispin's day.

This victory song, in a lilting triple meter, had six verses or stanzas of text, of which our recording presents three. These are sung in old English, with the refrain or burden in Latin: *Deo gratias, Anglia, redde pro victoria* ("England, give thanks to God for the victory.") The verses are set for two voices, the burden for three. In our recording, voices are doubled by wind instruments, especially the cornetto, an early instrument consisting of a wooden tube with fingerholes and a cup-shaped mouthpiece (see page 79). Percussion instruments were added as well to give the requisite martial sound.

Early Instruments and Instrumental Music

The fourteenth century witnessed a steady growth in the scope and importance of instrumental music. Though the central role in art music was still reserved for vocal works, instruments gradually found more and more uses. As we have seen, they could play a supporting role in vocal music,

Three mounted trumpeters sound the attack of a fortress, from Le livre de la déstruction de Troyes, *1467.* (Paris, Bibliothèque Nationale)

doubling or accompanying the singers. Instrumental arrangements of vocal works grew increasingly popular. In dance music, where rhythm was the prime consideration, instruments found early and abiding employment.

The "learned" vocal music of church and court was routinely written down, in part because its complexity made it difficult to remember, in part so that it could be carried from one place to another and even preserved for future generations. Much instrumental music, on the other hand, was improvised, like jazz, and never written down at all. (If it were not for recordings, we would know very little about jazz of the past—and, indeed, we only know indirectly what jazz was like before it was recorded.) We can therefore only speculate about the extent and variety of the instrumental repertory during the late Middle Ages. But our speculation can be guided by an ever growing body of knowledge. Some of the instruments themselves survive, in museums and private collections. Paintings and sculpture contain many representations of instruments—not always reliable in detail, but informative about their use and playing technique. Historical documents, such as court payrolls, tell us about the size and makeup of musical establishments. From these—and from such instrumental music as does survive—scholars have in recent years reconstructed a remarkable body of information about Medieval and Renaissance instruments.

Improvisational nature

These old instruments were more limited in range and volume than their modern counterparts; yet today we have abandoned the notion that they were nothing more than primitive versions of their descendants. It has become increasingly clear that these instruments were perfectly suited to the purposes of the societies that devised them. There were no large concert halls to be filled; there was no need for the smoothly blended colors of the symphony orchestra. More delicate timbres were cultivated, and also saltier, more raucous ones; in fact, instruments were divided into "indoor" and "outdoor" categories.

In those days, too, each individual instrument was a unique handcrafted item. The kind of standardization we take for granted today, the result of mass production, simply did not exist. No doubt this was one reason why composers do not seem to have been much concerned about which particular instruments were used in the performance of their music. In fact, the surviving sources of Medieval music contain no instrumental indications; it is only with the late Renaissance that such things begin to be specified.

But there is also another reason—the essentially contrapuntal nature of most Medieval and Renaissance music. Counterpoint, we saw, was an art of line rather than color; of unfolding horizontal voices rather than vertical chordal masses. What was important to composers of the time was not the specific color, but that each line stand out. Otherwise, instruments were regarded as pretty much interchangeable.

The revival of early music has burgeoned in recent decades, as scholars and performers have endeavored to reconstruct the appropriate performing conditions. A growing number of ensembles specialize in this repertory, and their members have mastered the playing techniques of old instruments. Their concerts and recordings have made the public aware of the sound of old instruments to a degree that was undreamed of fifty years ago. What was once considered esoteric or "scholarly" has now become the regular fare of many music lovers.

In our recorded performances of Medieval vocal music, we have already encountered a number of instruments from the period. Although a complete survey is naturally beyond the compass of a book such as this, let us briefly mention some of the principal types.

String instruments

Early instruments fall into the same categories as modern ones—that is, strings, winds, brass, percussion, and keyboard. String instruments further divide into plucked and bowed instruments. The elaborate concert *harp* of today has ancestors going back to antiquity, in many shapes and sizes. Instruments with frets, like the guitar, are also very ancient; the *lute*, with a more rounded body than the guitar, is of Middle Eastern origin and apparently reached Europe around the thirteenth century. It has been brilliantly revived in the twentieth century by artists such as Julian Bream.

Playing on strings with a bow seems also to have come from the East. There were two principal types of bowed instruments in the Middle Ages: the pear-shaped *rebec* and the *vielle* or fiddle, whose figure-eight body proclaims it the ancestor of the violin. The rebec was particularly associated with popular song and dance, while the vielle was primarily cultivated by the privileged classes.

Wind instruments

Among the woodwinds, today's flute inherits a long tradition, although in earlier times it was made of wood rather than metal, and lacked the

The Virgin surrounded by angel musicians performing the motet Ave Regina caelorum *by Walter Frye, the English composer. Accompanying instruments include (counterclockwise from top left): shawm, harp, portative organ, lute, vielle, recorders, and hammer dulcimer.* Mary, Queen of Heaven, *by the* **Master of the St. Lucy Legend,** *c. 1485.* (National Gallery of Art, Washington. Samuel H. Kress Collection)

modern system of keys. There was also another type of flute, with a whistle mouthpiece, played vertically, known as the *recorder*; its tone is more delicate and breathy than that of the transverse or horizontally played flute. Made in many sizes, the recorder remained in use until the eighteenth century, and has been widely revived in our own day. The other principal family of winds, you will recall, uses reeds to produce the sound. The *shawm*, the ancestor of the oboe, came in a variety of sizes, and still survives in many folk traditions of Europe, Africa, and Asia, retaining its loud nasal tone. Less raucous were instruments in which the reed was covered by a reed-cap, such as the *crumhorn*.

Medieval "brass" instruments were not always made from brass; other metals, ivory, horn, and wood were also used. The *cornetto* developed from the traditional cow horn, but was made of wood; its fingerholes made possible the playing of scales (valves for brass instruments were not invented until the nineteenth century). Another early device for filling in all the scale tones was the slide, as in the trombone; in the Middle Ages, besides the *sackbut*,

"Brass" instruments

the ancestor of the trombone, there was also a type of *slide trumpet*, mentioned earlier. Medieval *trumpets* were not always coiled in the modern fashion, and could be as much as six feet long—impressive to see as well as to hear at court ceremonials.

Keyboard instruments

Several types and sizes of organ were already in use in the Middle Ages. There were large ones, requiring a team of men to pump their giant bellows and often several more to manipulate the cumbersome slider mechanisms that opened and closed the pipes. At the other end of the scale were *portative* and *positive* organs, miniatures with keyboards and a few ranks of pipes. One type of small organ, the *regal* took its name from one of the reedy stops of the larger organs.

A fifteenth-century ancestor of the piano was the *clavichord*, in which a keyboard was used to set strings in vibration; its very gentle tone was suitable only for private practice and intimate settings. Soon the harpsichord—and later the piano—would achieve greater carrying power, without superseding the charm of the smaller instrument.

Percussion instruments

Ample evidence indicates that many kinds of percussion instruments were common in the Middle Ages and Renaissance; what we do not know is precisely how they were used musically. Here, modern performers are very much on their own. The small drums known as *nakers*, which usually came in pairs, are mentioned in Marco Polo's account of his travels in Asia. The *tabor* was a larger, cylindrical drum, while the *tambourine* is still used today in Spanish and Italian music.

Now we shall turn to an example of instrumental dance music from this period. Characteristic of the fragmentary state in which this type of music has been handed down to us is the fact that the composer is unknown to us.

An Anonymous Dance: Saltarello

Professional instrumentalists of the Middle Ages must have been both skilled and sophisticated, since historical evidence indicates that their earnings were often quite high. However, many of them did not read or write musical notation—they didn't need to, for most of their music-making was improvised; consequently little of their music has survived. This particular Saltarello dates from the fourteenth century, when it was among several tunes added to the end of a large manuscript of Italian vocal music.

The saltarello is a lively Italian "jumping dance." This early example consists of short sections of varying lengths, alternating in the pattern **a-b-a-c-a-c-a.** Each section has two alternate endings, one a step above the other. These were known as "open" and "closed"; the open ending leads back to a repetition, while the closed finishes that section and prepares the next. Each new section uses melodic figures from the preceding one. This chainlike construction obviously permits additional repetitions should the dancers have energy for more.

The wild, piercing sound of the shawm (used as the solo instrument in our recording) seems quite appropriate for this energetic, even frenetic dance. Aside from the melody, everything about this performance is conjectural, resting upon the educated guesses of a knowledgeable and sensitive scholar-musician: the tempo, the phrasing, the *embellishment* or melodic decoration of the written music, the rhythmic backing by nakers, tabor, and tambourine, the addition of a sustained single note (known as a *drone*, a common feature of folk music around the world) here played on a trumpet. But the results are musically convincing, breathing fresh life into music of which only the skeleton has survived the ravages of time.

Listening Guide 5

1A/7　　　I/1/7

Saltarello (Anonymous)

Date: 14th century, Italian

Form: Sectional, with repeats; A section as refrain; much embellishment on melodic lines

Instrumentation used in recording: Shawm (loud, double-reed instrument), sustaining (drone) instrument, and percussion

Character: Fast and lively, leaping dance

7 **A section** (called *prima pars*, or first part), played twice (recording takes second ending each time)

Prima pars.

8 **B section** (*secunda pars*), short section played twice

Secunda pars.

A section, played twice

9 **C section** (*tertia pars*), short section, played twice (high note is held longer than indicated)

Tertia pars.

A section, played twice, much embellishment

C section, played twice

A section, played twice, much embellishment, ends on long, high note

UNIT IV

◼

The Renaissance

13

The Renaissance Spirit

". . . we here in the West have in the last two hundred years recovered the excellence of good letters and brought back the study of the disciples after they had long remained as if extinguished. The sustained industry of many learned men has led to such success that today this our age can be compared to the most learned times that ever were."—LOYS LE ROY (1575)

The Renaissance (c. 1450–1600) is one of the most beautiful if misleading names in the history of culture: beautiful because it implies an awakening of intellectual awareness, misleading because it suggests a sudden rebirth of learning and art after the presumed stagnation of the Middle Ages. History moves continuously rather than by leaps and bounds. The Renaissance was the next phase of a cultural process that, under the leadership of the Church, the universities, and princely courts, had begun long before.

The Arts in the Renaissance

Philosophical developments

What the Renaissance does mark is the passing of European society from an exclusively religious orientation to a more secular one; from an age of unquestioning faith and mysticism to one of belief in reason and scientific inquiry. The focus of human destiny was seen to be life on earth rather than in the hereafter. There was a new reliance on the evidence of the senses rather than on tradition and authority. Implied was a new confidence in people's ability to solve their problems and rationally order their world. This awakening found its symbol in the culture of Greek and Roman antiquity. Renaissance society discovered the summit of human wisdom not only in the Church fathers and saints, as their ancestors had done, but also in Homer and Virgil and the ancient philosophers.

82

The Renaissance painter preferred realism to allegory and psychological characterizations to stylized stereotypes. These characteristics are exemplified in Madonna and St. Anne *by* **Leonardo da Vinci** (*1452–1519*) (© Photo P.M.N., The Louvre, Paris)

Historical developments   Historians used to date the Renaissance from the fall of Constantinople to the Turks in 1453 and the emigration of Greek scholars to the West. Today, we recognize that there are no such clear demarcations in history. But a series of momentous circumstances around this time help to set off the new era from the old. The introduction of gunpowder signaled the eventual end of the age of knighthood. The development of the compass made possible the voyages of discovery that opened up a new world and demolished old superstitions. The revival of ancient letters was associated with the humanists, and was spurred by the introduction of printing. This revival had its counterpart in architecture, painting, and sculpture. If the Romanesque found its grand architectural form in the monastery and the Gothic in the cathedral, the Renaissance lavished its constructive energy upon palace and château. The gloomy fortified castles of the Medieval barons gave way to spacious edifices that displayed the harmonious proportions of the classical style. (The term *classical* in this context refers to the culture of the Ancient Greeks and Romans, whose art embodied the ideals of order, stability, and balanced proportions.) In effect, Renaissance architecture embodied the striving for a gracious and reasoned existence that was the great gesture of the age.

Artistic developments   So, too, the elongated saints and martyrs of Medieval painting and sculpture were replaced by the David of Donatello and the gentle Madonnas of Leonardo. Even where artists retained a religious atmosphere, the Mother of Sorrows and the symbols of grief gave way to smiling madonnas—often posed for by very secular ladies—and dimpled cherubs. The human form, denied for centuries, was revealed as a thing of beauty; also as an object of anatomical study. Nature entered painting along with the nude, and with it an intense preoccupation with the laws of perspective and composition.

The human form, denied for centuries, was revealed in the Renaissance as a thing of beauty. David *by* **Donatello** (*c. 1386–1466*). (Alinari/Art Resources)

Medieval painting had presented life as an allegory; the Renaissance preferred realism. The Medieval painters posed their figures frontally, impersonally; the Renaissance developed psychological characterization and the art of portraiture. Medieval painting dealt in types; the Renaissance concerned itself with individuals. Space in Medieval painting was organized in a succession of planes over which the eye traveled as over a series of episodes. The Renaissance created unified space and the simultaneous seeing of the whole. It discovered the landscape, created the illusion of distance, and opened up endless vistas upon the physical loveliness of the world.

The Renaissance came to flower in the nation that stood closest to the classical Roman culture. Understandably the great names we associate with its painting and sculpture are predominantly Italian: Donatello (c. 1386–1466), Masaccio (1401–28), Botticelli (c. 1445–1510), Leonardo da Vinci (1452–1519), Michelangelo (1475–1564), Raphael (1483–1520), and Titian (1488–1576). With masters who lived in the second half of the century, such as Tintoretto (1518–94) and Veronese (1528–88), we approach the world of the early Baroque. From the multicolored tapestry of Renaissance life emerge figures that have captured the imagination of the world: Lorenzo de' Medici and Ludovico Sforza, Lucrezia Borgia and Isabella d'Este. Few centuries can match the sixteenth for its galaxy of great names. The list includes Erasmus (1466–1536) and Martin Luther (1483–1546), Machiavelli (1469–1527) and Galileo (1564–1642), Rabelais (1494?–1553) and Cervantes (1547–1616), Marlowe (1564–93) and Shakespeare (1564–1616). *Intellectual developments*

The Renaissance marks the birth of modern European temper and of Western society as we have come to know it. In that turbulent time was shaped the moral and cultural climate we still inhabit.

The Musician in Renaissance Society

The painting and poetry of the Renaissance abound in references to music. Nothing more clearly attests to the vast importance of the arts in the cultural life of the time. The pageantry of the Renaissance unfolded to a momentous musical accompaniment. Throwing off its Medieval mysticism, music moved toward clarity, simplicity, and a frankly sensuous appeal.

Musicians of the sixteenth century were supported by the chief institutions of their society—the Church, city, and state; royal and aristocratic courts. As the influence of the art spread, professional possibilities widened. Musicians could find employment as choirmasters, singers, organists, instrumentalists, copyists, composers, teachers, instrument builders, music printers, and publishers. There was a corresponding growth in the basic musical institutions: church choirs and schools, publishing houses, civic wind bands. So too were there increased opportunities for apprentices to study with master singers, players, and instrument builders. *Musicians as professionals*

The rise of the merchant class brought with it a new group of patrons of music. This development was paralleled by the emergence, among the cultivated middle and upper classes, of the amateur musician. When, in the early sixteenth century, the system for printing type was made available to music, printed music books became available—and affordable. This in turn

The painting and poetry of the Renaissance abound in references to music making. A painting by **Jacopo Tintoretto** (1518–94), The Muses In Concert. (Scala/Art Resource)

made possible the rise of the great publishing houses, such as Attaingnant in Paris or Susato in Antwerp. As a result, there was a dramatic upsurge of musical literacy.

Renaissance Musical Style

The vocal forms of the sixteenth century were marked by smoothly gliding melodies conceived entirely in relation to the voice. The Renaissance *A cappella music* achieved an exquisite appreciation of *a cappella* music. (You will recall that this term refers to a vocal work without instrumental accompaniment.) The sixteenth century has come to be regarded as the golden age of the a cappella style. Its polyphony was based on a principle called *continuous imitation*. The motives wandered from vocal line to vocal line within the texture, the voices imitating one another so that the same theme or motive was heard now in the soprano or alto, now in the tenor or bass. There resulted a close-knit musical fabric capable of the most subtle and varied effects.

Most church music was written in a cappella style. Secular music, on the other hand, was divided between purely vocal works and those in which the singers were supported by instruments. The period also saw the growth of solo instrumental music, especially for lute and the keyboard instruments. In the matter of harmony, the Renaissance leaned toward fuller chords. There was a turning away from the parallel fifths and octaves favored by Medieval composers to the more euphonious thirds and sixths; also a greater use of dissonance was linked to the text. The expressive device of *word* *Word painting* *painting*, or musically pictorializing words from the text, was much favored:

an unexpected, harsh dissonance might coincide with the word "death" or an ascending line might lead up to the word "heavens" or "stars."

Polyphonic writing offered the composer many possibilities, such as the use of a cantus firmus (fixed melody) as a basis for elaborate ornamentation in the other voices. Triple meter had been especially attractive to the Medieval mind because it symbolized the perfection of the Trinity. The new era, much less preoccupied with religious symbolism, showed a greater interest in duple meter. *Cantus firmus*

The composers of the Flemish school were pre-eminent in European music from around 1450 to the end of the sixteenth century. They came from the southern Lowlands, which is now Belgium, and from the adjoining provinces of northern France and Burgundy. In their number were several who wrote their names large in the history of music.

14

Renaissance Sacred Music

"He who does honor and reverence to music is commonly a man of worth, sound of soul, by nature loving things lofty." —PIERRE DE RONSARD to FRANCIS II (1560)

Music played a prominent part in the ritual of the Church. There were several types of music for church services in addition to the monophonic Gregorian chant, such as polyphonic settings of the Mass, motets, hymns, and Magnificats. (A *Magnificat* is a canticle in honor of the Virgin.) These were normally based on counterpoint and, especially in the early sixteenth century, on pre-existent music. Such works were sung by professional singers, usually churchmen, trained from childhood in the choir schools.

The Renaissance Motet

The Renaissance motet now became a sacred form with a single Latin text, for use in the Mass and other religious services. Motets in praise of the Virgin Mary were extremely popular, because of the many brotherhoods of laymen all over Europe devoted to Marian worship. These works were in three or four voices, sometimes based on a chant or other cantus firmus. Until this point the voices had been equal in importance. Now the interest shifted to the top voice or melody, with the lower parts serving as a background and sometimes played on instruments.

Dufay: Alma redemptoris mater

Guillaume Dufay (1397?–1474) was one of the earliest composers of the Burgundian School to make his career in Italy, where he spent his formative years. He was also active at the court of Philip the Good, Duke of Burgundy (1419–67), which for several decades rivaled that of the kings of France in the brilliance of its art. He spent his last years in his native Cambrai in northern France, where he continued to compose up to his death.

In the music of Dufay and his Burgundian colleagues, the rhythmic complexities of fourteenth-century music were abandoned in favor of an uncomplicated, more accessible style. The meandering vocal lines of the past were replaced by well-defined melodies and clear-cut rhythms, with something of the charm of folksong. Harmony grew simpler and more consonant, foreshadowing a language based on triads and sense of key. Eventually, Dufay expanded the standard musical texture from three voices to four.

Dufay's style is well exemplified in his Latin motet *Alma redemptoris mater* for three voices on a text praising the Virgin Mary. (In such works, some or all of the voices may be played on instruments as well). Several important characteristics distinguish his music from that of earlier times. To begin with, the cantus firmus, drawn from a Gregorian chant, has been elevated to the highest part, where the listener can easily hear it. Instead of being a mystical symbol, it is now a graceful melody that delights the ear. As a result, this voice dominates the others. Also, instead of following the sacred chant slavishly, Dufay adapts it both rhythmically and melodically to his own expressive purpose. Equally significant, Dufay has replaced the open fifths and octaves that impart so stark a color to Medieval music with the gentler thirds and sixths. As a result, he seems to have moved a considerable distance away from Machaut's archaic sound.

Guillaume Dufay (left) and fellow-composer Gilles Binchois. Miniature from a fifteenth-century manuscript.

Dufay's motet opens with an extended melisma on the first vowel of *Alma*. (See Listening Guide 6.) Throughout the piece, single words are sustained for series of notes. When words are dissolved in music this way, the composer is obviously using the text merely as scaffolding. Dufay's prime concern is the flow of the melodic lines.

The motet is in triple meter and in several sections. It opens in three-part harmony, but toward the end the sopranos divide to make four voice parts. In effect, harmony is moving toward the four-part structure that will become the standard, in which each of the four voices—soprano, alto, tenor, bass—occupies its respective register instead of crowding the others in the same range. This means, too, that the separate voices can take on greater independence, with an attendant broadening of the musical space.

Listening Guide 6

1A/6   I/1/10

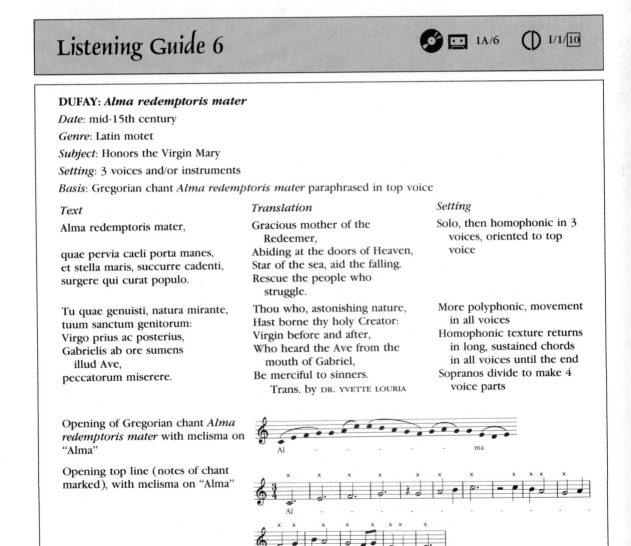

DUFAY: *Alma redemptoris mater*

Date: mid-15th century

Genre: Latin motet

Subject: Honors the Virgin Mary

Setting: 3 voices and/or instruments

Basis: Gregorian chant *Alma redemptoris mater* paraphrased in top voice

Text	Translation	Setting
Alma redemptoris mater,	Gracious mother of the Redeemer,	Solo, then homophonic in 3 voices, oriented to top voice
quae pervia caeli porta manes, et stella maris, succurre cadenti, surgere qui curat populo.	Abiding at the doors of Heaven, Star of the sea, aid the falling. Rescue the people who struggle.	
Tu quae genuisti, natura mirante, tuum sanctum genitorum: Virgo prius ac posterius, Gabrielis ab ore sumens illud Ave, peccatorum miserere.	Thou who, astonishing nature, Hast borne thy holy Creator: Virgin before and after, Who heard the Ave from the mouth of Gabriel, Be merciful to sinners.	More polyphonic, movement in all voices Homophonic texture returns in long, sustained chords in all voices until the end Sopranos divide to make 4 voice parts
	Trans. by DR. YVETTE LOURIA	

Opening of Gregorian chant *Alma redemptoris mater* with melisma on "Alma"

Opening top line (notes of chant marked), with melisma on "Alma"

An engraving from the late sixteenth century of singers and instrumentalists performing the Mass. A Religious Service *by* **Collaert** *after* **Stradanus.** (The Metropolitan Museum of Art, Whittlesey Fund)

The Early Renaissance Mass

Sections of the Mass

With the rise of polyphony, composers concentrated their musical settings on the invariable portion of the Mass that was sung daily, known as the Ordinary. Thus came into prominence the five sections known as the musical setting of the Mass: Kyrie, Gloria, Credo, Sanctus, and Agnus Dei. (Today these sections of the Mass are recited or sung in the language of the country—the vernacular.) The opening section, the Kyrie—a prayer for mercy—dates from the early centuries of Christianity, as its original Greek text attests. It is an A-B-A form that consists of nine invocations: three of "Kyrie eleison" (Lord, have mercy), three of "Christe eleison" (Christ, have mercy), and again three of "Kyrie eleison." There follows the Gloria (Glory to God in the highest). This is a joyful hymn of praise which is omitted in the penitential seasons, Advent and Lent. The third movement is the confession of faith, Credo (I believe in one God, the Father Almighty). It includes also the *Et incarnatus est* (And He became flesh), the *Crucifixus* (He was crucified), and the *Et resurrexit* (And He rose again). Fourth is the Sanctus (Holy, Holy, Holy), which concludes with the *Hosanna* (Hosanna in the highest) and the *Benedictus* (Blessed is He who comes in the name of the Lord), after which the *Hosanna* is repeated as a kind of refrain. The fifth and last part, the Agnus Dei (Lamb of God, who takes away the sins of the world), is sung three times. Twice it concludes with "Miserere nobis" (Have mercy on us), and the third time with the prayer "Dona nobis pacem" (Grant us peace). A summary of the order of the Mass, with its Proper and Ordinary movements, follows. (Remember that we studied an example of a Gradual for Easter Sunday, *Haec dies*.)

Movements and Order of the Mass

Proper	Ordinary
Introit	
	Kyrie
	Gloria
Collect	
Epistle	
Gradual	
Alleluia (or Tract)	
Evangelium	
	Credo
Offertory	
Secret	
Preface	
	Sanctus
Canon	
	Agnus Dei
Communion	
Post-Communion	
Ite missa est	

Like the motet, the polyphonic setting of the Mass was usually based on a fragment of Gregorian chant. This became the cantus firmus that served as the foundation of the work, supporting the florid patterns that the other voices wove around it. When used in all the movements of a Mass, the Gregorian cantus firmus helped to weld the work into a unity. It provided composers with a fixed element that they could embellish with all the resources of their artistry.

Of the Masses for special services the most important is the Mass for the Dead, the Requiem, which is sung at funerals and memorial services. The name comes from the opening verse "Requiem aeternam dona eis, Domine" (Rest eternal grant unto them, O Lord). Included are prayers in keeping with the solemnity of the occasion, among them the awesome evocation of the Last Judgment, *Dies irae* (Day of Wrath).

Requiem

The history of the Mass as an art form extends over the better part of eight hundred years. In that time it garnered for itself some of the greatest music ever written.

Josquin Desprez: Agnus Dei, from Missa La sol fa re mi

"He is the master of the notes. They have to do as he bids them; other composers have to do as the notes will."—MARTIN LUTHER

With the Franco-Flemish master Josquin Desprez (c. 1440–1521), the transition is complete from the anonymous composer of the Middle Ages, through

Josquin Desprez

the shadowy figures of the late Gothic, to the highly individual artist of the Renaissance. He is the first musician, as one historian put it, "who impresses us as having genius."

Josquin studied with the Flemish master Johannes Ockeghem, who exerted a powerful influence on several generations of composers. Josquin's varied career led him to Italy, where he served at several ducal courts—especially those of Galeazzo Sforza, Duke of Milan, and Ercole d'Este, Duke of Ferrara—as well as at the Sistine Chapel in Rome. During his stay in Italy his northern art absorbed the classical virtues of balance and moderation, the sense of harmonious proportion and lucid form that found their archetype in the radiant art of Raphael. After leaving the Papal Chapel he returned to France. His last appointment was as a canon at the collegiate church of Condé, where he was buried in the choir of this church.

The older generation of musicians had been preoccupied with solving the technical problems of counterpoint—problems that fit the intellectual climate of the waning Middle Ages. Josquin appeared at a time when the humanizing influences of the Renaissance were wafting through Europe. The contrapuntal ingenuity that he inherited from Ockeghem he was able to harness to a higher end—the expression of emotion. His music is rich in feeling, in serenely beautiful melody and expressive harmony. Its clarity of structure and humanism bespeak the spirit of the Renaissance.

Josquin composed at least seventeen complete settings of the Mass. He used a variety of techniques, basing the music on pre-existent models, both monophonic and polyphonic. The *La sol fa re mi* Mass, written while he was in Italy, is for four voices. It is based on the five-note figure in the title, (A G F D E), which serves as an ostinato that pervades the work.

A rather humorous story is the generally accepted explanation for this ostinato. It seems that Josquin's patron, Cardinal Ascanio Sforza, temporarily financially strapped, put off the composer's requests for payment with a reassuring "Lascia fare a me" (Leave it to me). Whereupon Josquin's friend, the Renaissance poet Serafino d'Aquila, translated the remark into its musical equivalent and incorporated it into a sonnet addressed to the composer. This five-note ostinato is heard again and again in all the movements of the Mass.

The Agnus Dei text is in three sections, as is Josquin's setting; in this work, the first and last sections are the same, giving the movement an **A-B-A** form. (See Listening Guide 7 for the text and analysis.) The outside sections are for four voices while the middle one is for two. The tenor presents the ostinato over and over again at various pitch levels. In our recording the basic motive is also heard on the sackbut (an early trombone).

One has only to examine the score to be dazzled by Josquin's mastery of contrapuntal technique. Yet despite the wizardry behind it, his piece sounds so simple in its flow and so natural. This is truly the art that conceals art.

Listening Guide 7

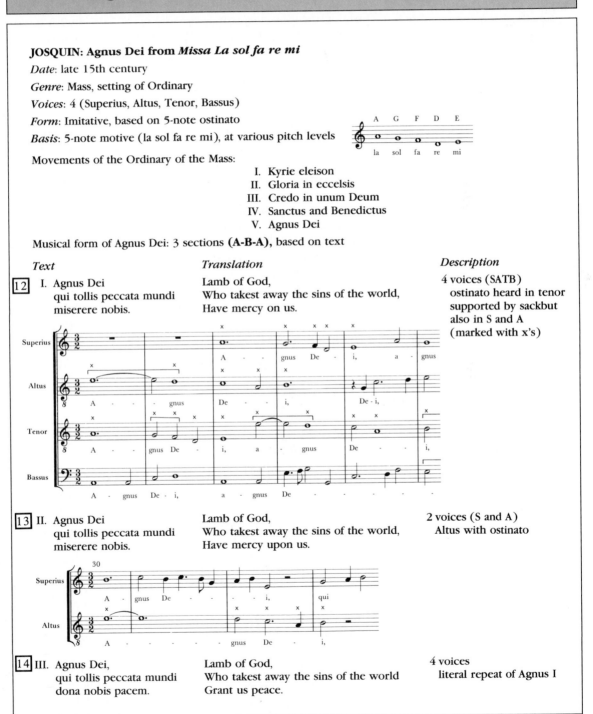

JOSQUIN: Agnus Dei from *Missa La sol fa re mi*

Date: late 15th century

Genre: Mass, setting of Ordinary

Voices: 4 (Superius, Altus, Tenor, Bassus)

Form: Imitative, based on 5-note ostinato

Basis: 5-note motive (la sol fa re mi), at various pitch levels

Movements of the Ordinary of the Mass:

    I. Kyrie eleison
   II. Gloria in eccelsis
  III. Credo in unum Deum
  IV. Sanctus and Benedictus
   V. Agnus Dei

Musical form of Agnus Dei: 3 sections **(A-B-A)**, based on text

Text	*Translation*	*Description*

12 I. Agnus Dei
    qui tollis peccata mundi
    miserere nobis.
	Lamb of God,
	Who takest away the sins of the world,
	Have mercy on us.
		4 voices (SATB)
		ostinato heard in tenor
		supported by sackbut
		also in S and A
		(marked with x's)

| **13** II. Agnus Dei
    qui tollis peccata mundi
    miserere nobis. | Lamb of God,
Who takest away the sins of the world,
Have mercy upon us. | 2 voices (S and A)
Altus with ostinato |

| **14** III. Agnus Dei,
    qui tollis peccata mundi
    dona nobis pacem. | Lamb of God,
Who takest away the sins of the world
Grant us peace. | 4 voices
literal repeat of Agnus I |

The High Renaissance Mass

Counter Reformation

After the revolt of Martin Luther (1483–1546) the desire for a return to true Christian piety brought about a reform movement in the Catholic Church. This movement became part of the Counter-Reformation whereby the Church strove to recapture the minds of its people. Among its manifestations were the activities of Franciscans and Dominicans among the poor; the founding of the Society of Jesus (Jesuits) by St. Ignatius Loyola (1491–1556); and the deliberations of the Council of Trent, which extended—with some interruptions—from 1545 to 1563.

Council of Trent

In its desire to regulate every aspect of religious discipline, the Council took up the matter of church music. The cardinals were much concerned over the corruption of the traditional chant by the singers, who added all manner of embellishments to the Gregorian melodies. They objected to the use of instruments other than the organ in religious services, to the practice of incorporating popular songs in Masses, to the secular spirit that was invading sacred music, and to the generally irreverent attitude of church musicians. They pointed out that in polyphonic settings of the Mass the sacred text was made unintelligible by the overelaborate contrapuntal texture. Certain zealots advocated abolishing counterpoint altogether and returning to Gregorian chant, but there were many music lovers among the cardinals who opposed so drastic a step. The committee assigned to deal with the problem contented itself with issuing general recommendations for a more dignified service. The authorities favored a pure vocal style that would respect the integrity of the sacred texts, that would avoid virtuosity and encourage piety.

Palestrina: Gloria from Pope Marcellus Mass

"I have held nothing more desirable than that what is sung throughout the year, according to the season, should be more agreeable to the ear by virtue of its vocal beauty."

Giovanni Pierluigi, called da Palestrina after his birthplace (c. 1525–94), met the need for a reformed church music in so exemplary a fashion that for posterity he has remained *the* Catholic composer. He served as organist and choirmaster at various churches including that of St. Peter's in Rome. His patron, Pope Julius III (r. 1550–1555), appointed him a member of the Sistine Chapel choir even though, as a married man, he was ineligible for the semiecclesiastical post. He was dismissed by a later pope but ultimately returned to St. Peter's, where he spent the last twenty-three years of his life. Palestrina's music gives voice to the religiosity of the Counter-Reformation, its transports and its visions. The contemplative beauty of his music does not exclude intense emotion; but this is emotion directed to an act of faith.

A true Italian, Palestrina was surpassingly sensitive to the needs of the human voice. It was from this vantage point that he viewed his function as a church composer. It was his good fortune to live not only at a time when

A contemporary engraving which depicts Palestrina presenting his earliest printed work to Pope Julius III.

the art of music had progressed far enough for him to achieve this goal, but also within a historical situation that made it necessary for him to do so.

Palestrina wrote over a hundred Masses, of which the most famous is the Mass for Pope Marcellus, successor to Julius III. It is popularly believed that this Mass was written to satisfy the new strict demands placed on polyphonic church music by the Council of Trent. Since the pontifical choir sang without instrumental accompaniment at this time, the *Pope Marcellus Mass* was probably performed a cappella. It was written for six voice parts—soprano, alto, two tenors, and two basses, a typical setting for the all-male church choirs of the time. The highest voice was sung by boy sopranos or male falsettists, the alto part by male altos or countertenors (tenors with very high voices), and the lower parts were distributed among the normal ranges of the male voice.

The Gloria from the *Pope Marcellus Mass* exhibits the salient characteristics of Palestrina's conservative style. As was typical, the work begins with a monophonic intonation of the opening line "Gloria in excelsis Deo" (Glory be to God in the highest), followed by a carefully constructed polyphonic setting of the remaining text. Notable is the way Palestrina balances the harmonic and polyphonic elements of his art so that the words of the sacred text are clear and audible, an effect desired by the Council of Trent. (See Listening Guide 8 for the text and anaylsis.)

Palestrina's style incarnates the pure a cappella ideal of vocal polyphony, in which the individual voice fulfills its destiny through submergence in the group. His music remains an apt symbol of the greatness art can aspire to when it subserves a profound moral conviction.

Listening Guide 8

💿📼 1A/10   ◐ I/1/18

PALESTRINA: Gloria, from _Pope Marcellus Mass_

Date: published 1567

Genre: Mass, setting of Ordinary

Voices: 6 (SATTBB); Frequent textural changes, reduction
of voices

Opening of "Gloria," showing 4 voice parts (of six), in clear word declamation

Text	Translation	Voices
18 Gloria in excelsis Deo	Glory be to God on high,	1
et in terra pax hominibus	And on earth peace to men	4
bonae voluntatis.	of goodwill.	4
Laudamus te,	We praise Thee,	4
Benedicimus te.	We bless Thee.	4
Adoramus te.	We adore Thee.	3
Glorificamus te.	We glorify Thee.	4
Gratias agimus tibi propter	We give Thee thanks for	5
magnam gloriam tuam.	Thy great glory.	3
Domine Deus, Rex caelestis,	Lord God, heavenly King,	4
Deus Pater omnipotens.	God the Father Almighty.	3
Domini Fili	O Lord, the only-begotten Son,	4
unigenite, Jesus Christe.	Jesus Christ.	6/5
Domine Deus, Agnus Dei,	Lord God, Lamb of God,	3
Filius Patris.	Son of the Father.	6
Qui tollis	Thou that takest	4
peccata mundi,	away the sins of the world	4
miserere nobis.	have mercy on us,	4
	have mercy on us,	5

19 Qui tollis peccata mundi,
   suscipe deprecationem nostrum.
	Thou that takest away the sins
	   of the world, receive our prayer.
		5/4

Qui sedes ad dexteram Patris,	Thou that sittest at the right hand,	3
miserere nobis.	of the Father, have mercy on us.	3
Quoniam tu solus sanctus.	For thou alone art holy.	4
Tu solus Dominus.	Thou only art the Lord.	4
Tu solus Altissimus.	Thou alone art most high.	4
Jesu Christe, cum Sancto Spiritu	Jesus Christ, along with the Holy Ghost	6/3/4
in gloria Dei Patris.	in the glory of God the Father	5
Amen.	Amen.	6

The English Anthem

In the years after Henry VIII broke away from Rome in 1534 to establish the Church of England or Anglican Church, English replaced Latin as the accepted language of the service. Composers developed two types of Anglican church music—the service and the anthem. The *service* denoted music for the unchanging Morning and Evening Prayers and for Communion. The *anthem* was a devotional work similar to the motet of the Catholic Church, and was written in two different forms: a *verse anthem* was for solo voices with a choral refrain, and a *full anthem* was for choir throughout.

Service

Anthem

Tomkins: When David Heard That Absalom Was Slain

Thomas Tomkins (1572–1656) was one of the most important composers of the Anglican Church. He was active at Worcester Cathedral and at London, where he was Gentleman in Ordinary of the Chapel Royal. *When David Heard That Absalom Was Slain* is a full anthem in polyphonic style for five voices, based on the Biblical account of David's lament over the death of his son Absalom, who had risen against him. Tomkins's piece, published in 1622, plays on the interval of a half step that was frequently found in laments, but derives its euphonious quality from the English tradition of harmonizing in thirds. The music is in a freely flowing contrapuntal style with interchanges between the voices. Tomkins uses very little text and repeats again and again such key words as "he wept" or "Absalom, my son," as well as the underlying idea, "Would God I had died for thee." This deeply moving anthem illustrates the richness of the English choral tradition.

 S1A/3
S1/6

15

Renaissance Secular Music

"I am not pleased with the Courtier if he be not also a musician, and besides his understanding and cunning (in singing) upon the book, have skill in like manner on sundry instruments."—BALDASSARE CASTIGLIONE (1528)

Music in Court and City Life

The secular music of the Renaissance was intended for both the professional and the amateur. Court festivities included music performed by professionals for the entertainment of noble guests and dignitaries. With the rise of the middle class, music making in the home became increasingly popular. Most middle- and upper-class homes had a lute (a plucked-string instrument with a rounded body) or a keyboard instrument, and the study of music was considered part of the proper upbringing for a young lady or—in lesser degree—gentleman. Women began to play a prominent part in the performance of music both in the home and at court. During the later sixteenth century in Italy, a number of professional women singers achieved great fame. In addition, dances provided a popular outlet for music at all levels of society.

Amateur music making

From the union of poetry and music came two important secular forms: the chanson and the madrigal. In both of these, music was used to enhance the poetry of such major literary figures as Petrarch and Pierre de Ronsard. In this domain the intricate verse forms of French and Italian poetry helped to shape the ensuing musical forms.

The Burgundian Chanson

The fifteenth-century *chanson* was the characteristic genre at the court of the dukes of Burgundy and the kings of France, who were great patrons of the arts. It was usually for three voices, with one or both lower voices played by instruments. Chansons were set to the courtly love poetry of the French Renaissance, the poems being in the form of a *rondeau*, a *ballade*, or a *virelai*. These fixed forms established the character of the setting and the repetition of sections. If there was a recurrent refrain of one or two lines, this naturally was reflected in the music.

Text forms

Ockeghem: L'autre d'antan

Johannes Ockeghem (c. 1410–97) was born in Flanders. He became a singer at the Church of Our Lady in Antwerp, then entered the service of Charles I, Duke of Bourbon. He ultimately joined the French court, where he served for many years. His settings of the Mass include a Requiem; he also wrote motets and about twenty chansons in fixed forms.

Music played an increasingly important role in the celebrations of sixteenth-century nobility. The Wedding at Cana *by* **Paolo Veronese** (*1528–88*). (The Louvre, Paris)

His chanson *L'autre d'antan* (The Other Year) is in a more popular style of poetry than many of the court chansons. This informal love song tells in a simple, direct manner how the lover was first vanquished, then spurned. The fair one's glance that pierced his defenses was "forged in Milan"—a reference to the town that forged the best armor and swords. One line from the chanson, "Puis apres nostre amour cessa" (And then our love ended), echoes a sentiment that resounds through popular poetry down to our day.

The work utilizes one of the most widespread poetic forms of the late fifteenth century, the rondeau. This example has a six-line refrain for the opening stanza. The first half of the refrain ends the second stanza, the opening line is heard twice in the course of the third stanza, and the entire refrain returns as the fourth and last stanza. The musical form accommodates itself to this intricate scheme, consisting of two sections that are repeated according to the repetition in the poem. (See Listening Guide 9 for the text and musical structure.)

Ockeghem's chanson is based on imitative counterpoint and the setting is mostly by syllable, with some melismas near the end of phrases. In this recording, two parts are sung, and the bottom one is played on a bowed string instrument. The two voices in this chanson sing in the same range, with much crisscrossing of parts. The music is in a much older style than we heard in the selections from Palestrina and Tomkins, as is indicated by the hollow-sounding cadences on intervals of the fifth and octave rather than on the more euphonious third.

Listening Guide 9

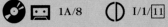

OCKEGHEM: *L'autre d'antan*

Date: late 15th century

Genre: Burgundian chanson, 3 voices

Poem: Anonymous rondeau

Musical form: two sections, **A** and **B** repeated as follows:
A-B-a-A-a-b-A-B (capital letters = refrain text)

	Text	Rhyme Scheme	Musical Form	Translation
Refrain	*L'autre d'antan, l'autrier passa,*	a	A	*The other year, the other day, she passed by*
	Et en passant me trespercha	a		*And, in passing, pierced me through*
	D'ung regard forgié a Melan	b		*With a glance forged in Milan*
	Qui me mist en l'arriere ban,	b a	B	*That knocked me into the rear ranks*
	Tant malvais brassin me brassa.	a		*So rude a blow she dealt me.*
	L'autre d'antan, l'autrier passa.			*The other year, the other day, she passed by.*
	Par tel fachon me fricassa	a	a	She destroyed me so thoroughly
	Que de ses gaiges me cassa;	a		That she dismissed me from her troops;
Partial Refrain	Mais, par Dieu, elle fist son dan.	b		But, by God, she did her damage.
	L'autre d'antan, l'autrier passa,	a	A	*The other year, the other day, she passed by*
	Et en passant me trespercha	a		*And, in passing, pierced me through*
	D'un regard forgié a Melan.	b		*With a glance forged in Milan.*
	Puis après nostre amour cessa,	a	a	And then our love ended,
	Car, oncques puis qu'elle dansa	a		For, ever since she did her dance,
	L'autre d'antan, l'autre d'antan	b		The other year, the other year,
	Je n'eus ne bon jour ne bon an,	b	b	I've had neither good day nor good year,
	Tout de mal enuy amassa.	a		So much bad luck has piled up.
	L'autre d'antan, l'autrier passa.	a		*The other year, the other day, she passed.*
Refrain	*L'autre d'antan, l'autrier passa,*	a	A	*The other year, the other day, she passed by*
	Et en passant me trespercha	a		*And, in passing, pierced me through*
	D'ung regard forgié a Melan	b		*With a glance forged in Milan*
	Qui me mist en l'arriere ban,	b	B	*That knocked me into the rear ranks*
	Tant malvais brassin me brassa.	a		*So rude a blow she dealt me.*
	L'autre d'antan, l'autrier passa.	a		*The other year, the other day, she passed by.*

Trans. by HOWARD GAREY

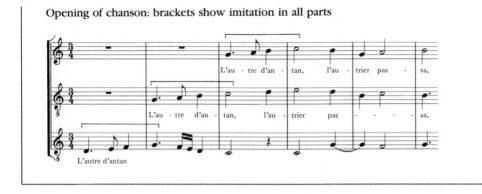

Opening of chanson: brackets show imitation in all parts

The Later Chanson

The Flemish tradition culminates in the towering figure of Roland de Lassus (c. 1532–94). A citizen of the world (he was equally well known in Italy as Orlando di Lasso), Lassus absorbed into his art the main currents of Renaissance music—the elegance and wit of the French, the profundity and rich detail of the Netherlanders, the sensuous beauty of the Italians. The greater part of his career was spent at the court of the Dukes of Bavaria in Munich, whence his fame spread all over Europe.

Roland de Lassus

His works number over two thousand, from impetuous love songs (some with texts almost too explicit for the concert hall) to noble Masses, motets, and the profoundly felt *Penitential Psalms*. In his panoramic view of life, as in his feeling for vivid detail, Lassus elicits comparison with another great Fleming—the painter Pieter Brueghel (c. 1525–69). His music is compounded of passion, tenderness, brilliance, humor, and—at the last—mysticism.

Lassus is one of the masters of the French chanson, which he handled with a freedom and fluency that made it—alongside the Italian and English madrigal—one of the more attractive genres of the Renaissance. The use of short lyric poems of a secular nature, in the language of the composer instead of in Church Latin, inevitably brought with it a closer relationship between words and music, in a larger sense between music and life.

Lassus wrote about a hundred and fifty chansons, most of them on the verses of such famous French poets as Pierre de Ronsard and Clément Marot. The texts cover a wide range of emotions from amorous to bawdy to religious.

Lassus: Bon jour mon coeur

The chanson *Bon jour mon coeur*, on a poem by Ronsard, has the lover greeting his beloved with a series of endearments. (See text in Listening Guide 10.) It is set for the four voices that were becoming basic in vocal music—soprano, alto, tenor, bass. The chanson opens in a chordal or homophonic style that seems quite simple but is marked by many subtleties in the treatment of the text. For example, the opening lines alternate between

Roland de Lassus is shown at the keyboard leading his chamber ensemble in St. George's Hall at the court of Albrecht V in Munich. Along with three choirboys, about fifteen instrumentalists, playing a variety of winds and strings, encircle him. From a miniature by **Hans Mielich** (*1516– 73*). (Munich, Bayerische Staatsbibliothek)

phrases of two and three measures, with the chords on the first words giving way to contrapuntal style on such emotional epithets as "ma douce vie" (my sweet life) and "ma chère amie" (my dear friend). In addition, the chordal setting of one note to a syllable is stretched out to short melismas on the key words "vie" and "amie." Lassus makes the text clear by having all the voices sing the same syllable at the same time. This declamatory manner brings into relief the passages in which he moves from chordal to contrapuntal texture.

The art of Lassus incarnates the verve and splendor of the Renaissance, and well merits the judgment carved on his tomb: "Here lies that Lassus who refreshes the weariness of the world, and whose harmony resolves its discord."

Listening Guide 10

1B/2 I/1/20

LASSUS: *Bon jour mon coeur*

Date: mid-16th century

Genre: French chanson, 4 voices

Poem: 9-line poem (aabccbbbb) by Pierre de Ronsard

Musical style: free form, homophonic texture

Text	*Translation*
Bon jour mon coeur, bon jour ma douce vie.	Good day my heart, good day my sweet life.
Bon jour mon oeil, bon jour ma chère amie.	Good day my eye, good day my dear friend.
Hé bon jour ma toute belle,	ah, good day, my beauty,
Ma mignardise, bon jour,	my darling one, good day,
Mes délices, mon amour.	my delight, my love.
Mon doux printemps, ma douce fleur nouvelle,	My sweet spring, my sweet fresh flower,
Mon doux plaisir, ma douce columbelle,	My sweet pleasure, my sweet young dove,
Mon passereau, ma gente tourterelle,	My sparrow, my gentle turtle dove,
Bon jour, ma douce rebelle.	good day, my sweet rebel.

"Bon jour mon coeur"	"Bon jour ma douce vie"
2 measures	3 measures
completely chordal	more movement
long notes	arched line

Opening of chanson, illustrating 2- and 3-measure phrases

Instrumental Dance Music

The sixteenth century witnessed a remarkable flowering of instrumental dance music. With the advent of music publishing, printed dance music became readily available for solo instruments as well as small ensembles. Venice, Paris, and Antwerp took the lead as centers of the new publishing

In this miniature, accompaniment is provided for an aristocratic group dancing a ronde in a garden by three "loud" wind instruments. (Bibliothèque Nationale, Paris)

industry. The dances were often fashioned from vocal works such as madrigals and chansons, which were published in simplified four-part versions that were played instead of sung.

The instruments to be used in these dance arrangements were left unspecified. As often as not they were determined by the circumstances surrounding the performance. Outdoor performances called for "loud" instruments such as the shawm (medieval oboe) and sackbut (medieval trombone). For stately occasions, on the other hand, "soft" instruments such as recorders and bowed strings were preferred. Although percussion parts were not written out in Renaissance music, the evidence suggests that they were improvised at the performance.

Dance types   A number of dance types became popular during the sixteenth century, several of which survived into the Baroque era. The stately court dance known as the *pavane* often served as the first number of a set and was followed by one or more quicker dances, especially the Italian *saltarello* (hopping dance) and the French *galliard* (a more vigorous version of the saltarello). The *allemande* or German dance, in moderate duple time, retained its popularity throughout the time of Bach and was adapted into the Baroque dance suite. Less courtly was the *ronde* or round dance, a lively romp associated with the outdoors in which the participants formed a circle.

Susato: Three Dances

One of the most popular dance collections of the sixteenth century was published in Antwerp in 1551 by Tielman Susato (c. 1515–67), a music printer who was also a prolific composer and instrumentalist. His collection, called *Danserye*, was described on its title page as "very cheerful and fit to play on all musical instruments." It contained pavanes, galliards, *basses danses* (an older version of the pavane), as well as allemandes, rondes, and *branles* (a quick dance of the follow-the-leader type). Many of the dances in Susato's collection were drawn from vocal models, these being identified above the music. One of the loveliest of the pavanes is *Mille regretz* (A Thousand Regrets), based on a widely known chanson of the same name by Josquin Desprez. The dance unfolds in three sections, each of which is repeated. The performance you will hear features four recorders of varying size—soprano, alto, tenor, and bass—with finger cymbals used to emphasize the beat. When a section is repeated, the principal recorder freely ornaments the top part. Like its chanson model, this piece has an unusual harmonic character. It is neither in major nor minor but in one of the Medieval modes— the Phrygian—that was then going out of fashion. The use of this mode imparts to the music a charmingly archaic atmosphere.

Pavane

The pavane is followed by two rondes, each in two-part form with repeated sections. In our performance these feature "soft" instruments. The first ronde is introduced by a drum, followed by a high recorder in the upper part and a regal or reed organ in the bass. The middle parts are filled in by various other recorders at each repetition. The second ronde, based on a chanson entitled *Mon amy* (My Friend), is performed at a slower tempo on bowed string instruments of the *viola da gamba* type. This Renaissance instrument had six or more strings and was fretted, like a guitar. Gambas were held between the legs like a cello. (Indeed, *gamba* is the Italian word for leg.) The strings are accompanied by a harpsichord and lute that support the harmonies. This set of dances closes with a restatement of the first ronde minus the repeats, a procedure we will observe again in the minuet-and-trio movements of the Classical era. (See Listening Guide on page 106.)

Two rondes

It was through dance pieces such as these that Renaissance composers explored the possibilities of purely instrumental forms. From these humble beginnings sprang the imposing structures of Western instrumental music.

The Italian Madrigal

In the madrigal the Renaissance found one of its chief forms of secular music. The sixteenth-century *madrigal* was an aristocratic form of poetry-and-music that came to flower at the small Italian courts, where it was a favorite diversion of cultivated amateurs. The text was a short poem of lyric or reflective character, rarely longer than twelve lines, marked by elegance of diction and refinement of sentiment. Conspicuous in it were the affecting words for weeping, sighing, trembling, dying that the Italian madrigalists learned to set with such a wealth of expression. Love and unsatisfied desire were by no means the only topics of the madrigal. Included, too, were humor and satire, political themes, scenes and incidents of city and country life, with the result that the Italian madrigal literature of the sixteenth century presents a vivid panorama of Renaissance thought and feeling.

Listening Guide II

1B/1   I/1/[15]

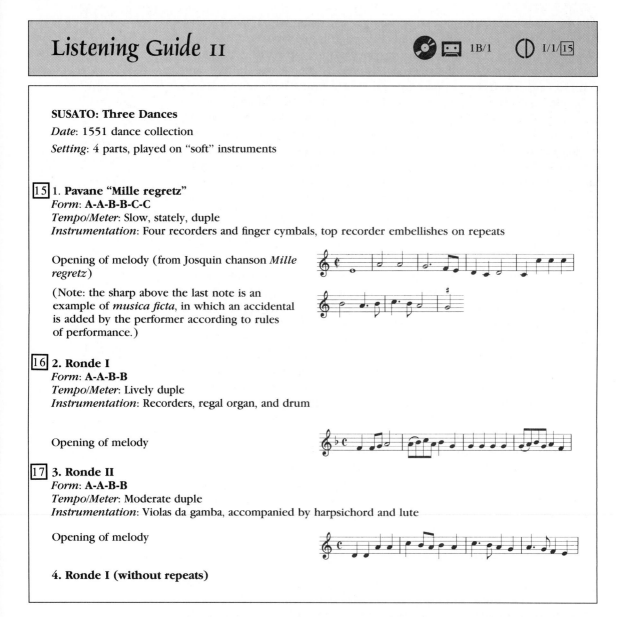

SUSATO: Three Dances

Date: 1551 dance collection

Setting: 4 parts, played on "soft" instruments

[15] **1. Pavane "Mille regretz"**
Form: **A-A-B-B-C-C**
Tempo/Meter: Slow, stately, duple
Instrumentation: Four recorders and finger cymbals, top recorder embellishes on repeats

Opening of melody (from Josquin chanson *Mille regretz*)

(Note: the sharp above the last note is an example of *musica ficta*, in which an accidental is added by the performer according to rules of performance.)

[16] **2. Ronde I**
Form: **A-A-B-B**
Tempo/Meter: Lively duple
Instrumentation: Recorders, regal organ, and drum

Opening of melody

[17] **3. Ronde II**
Form: **A-A-B-B**
Tempo/Meter: Moderate duple
Instrumentation: Violas da gamba, accompanied by harpsichord and lute

Opening of melody

4. Ronde I (without repeats)

Instruments participated, duplicating or even substituting for the voices. Sometimes only the top part was sung while the other lines were played on instruments. During the first period of the Renaissance madrigal—the second quarter of the sixteenth century—the composer's chief concern was to give pleasure to the performers, often amateurs, without much thought to virtuosic display. In the middle phase (c. 1550–80), the Renaissance madrigal became a conscious art form directed toward the listener.

The final phase of the Italian madrigal (1580–1620) extended beyond the late Renaissance into the world of the Baroque. The form became the

In this highly stylized, sixteenth-century painting, four aristocratic singers perform from part books in an imaginary landscape. The couple in back are beating time, as was customary. Concert in the Open Air. *Anonymous* (Italian School). (Bourges, Musée de Berry)

direct expression of the composer's personality and feelings. Certain traits were carried to the point of mannerism: rich chromatic harmony, dramatic declamation, vocal virtuosity, and vivid depiction in music of emotional words.

Monteverdi: Ohimè! se tanto amate

It was in the art of Claudio Monteverdi (1567–1643) that the late Renaissance madrigal came to full flower. We shall discuss his music later in connection with the Baroque. Suffice it here to say that he published eight books of madrigals between 1587 and 1634. These consequently span the transition from Renaissance to Baroque.

Ohimè! se tanto amate, from Monteverdi's *Fourth Book of Madrigals* (1603), a superb example of his style, is a setting for five voices of a poem by Guarini. The words are in the courtly manner of much madrigal poetry, both tongue-in-cheek and exaggeratedly romantic in their subtle suggestions of sexual desire. Notable is the way Monteverdi uses the conventional "sigh" motive based on the descending interval of a third, and plays on it with the key word "Ohimè!"—the unhappy lover's "Alas!"—against a harmonic background now consonant, now dissonant. This motive becomes the unifying element of the piece. (See Listening Guide 12 for the text.)

Other basic words in the text are set in an equally telling manner. The phrase "S'io moro" (If I die) is set for three voices instead of five to suggest the ebbing strength of the dying lover, but upon its return is carried by all five voices. "Languido e doloroso" (languid and sad) calls forth an ascending chromatic scale with a harsh dissonance to bring out the sadness in "doloroso." And in the witty wordplay of the final line Monteverdi makes the lover sigh "a thousand times." This vivid depiction of the text through music, known as word painting, was a hallmark of the Italian madrigal. This is music of amorous dalliance, as elegant as the courtly lifestyle out of which it sprang.

Listening Guide 12   1B/3   I/1/21

Monteverdi: *Ohimè! se tanto amate*

Date: published 1603, *Fourth Book of Madrigals*

Genre: Italian madrigal, 5 voices (SSATB)

Poem: 8-line madrigal (aabcbcdd) by Battista Guarini

Text

Ohimè! se tanto amate
di sentir dir *ohimè*, deh, perché fate
chi dice *ohimè* morire?
S'io moro, un sol potrete
languido e doloroso *ohimè* sentire;
Ma se, cor mio, volete
che vita abbia' da voi, e voi da me,
avrete mille e mille dolci *ohimè*.

Translation

Alas, if you so love
to hear me say alas, then why do you slay
the one who says it?
If I die, you will hear only
a single, languid, sorrowful alas;
but if, my love, you wish
to let me live and wish to live for me,
you will have a thousand times a sweet alas.

Opening of madrigal, showing "sighs" of falling thirds on "ohimè" (alas)

Harsh dissonances, set to "e doloroso"
(and sorrowful)

Repetitions of "mill'e mille dolc'ohimè"
(sweet alas thousands and thousands of
times)

The English Madrigal

Just as English poets took over the Italian sonnet, so the composers of England adopted the Italian madrigal and developed it into a native art form. All the brilliance of the Elizabethan age is reflected in the school of madrigalists who flourished in the late sixteenth century during the reign of Elizabeth I (1558–1603) and on into the reign of James I (1603–25). Among the most important figures were Thomas Morley (1557–1603), John Wilbye (1574–1638), Thomas Weelkes (c. 1575–1623), and Orlando Gibbons (1583–1625).

The first collection of Italian madrigals published in England appeared in 1588 and was called *Musica transalpina*—Music from beyond the Alps. The madrigals were "Englished"—that is, the texts were translated. In their own madrigals the English composers preferred simpler texts. New, humorous madrigal types were cultivated, some with refrains of nonsense syllables such as *fa la la*.

Farmer: Fair Phyllis

John Farmer was active in the 1590s in Dublin, where he was organist and Master of the Children at Christ Church. In 1599 he moved to London, and published his only collection of four-part madrigals. One of these, *Fair Phyllis*, attained great popularity. He died in 1601.

Fair Phyllis is characteristic of the English madrigal in its pastoral text and gay mood. Typical are the repeated sections, the fragments of contrapuntal imitation that overlap and obscure the underlying meter, the changes from homophonic to polyphonic texture, and the cadences on the weaker pulse of the measure. The last line of the poem is set to chords, with a change to triple meter.

The English composers took over the word painting of the Italians. For example, he opening line, "Fair Phyllis I saw sitting alone," is sung by a single voice. (See Listening Guide 13 for the text.) So too the statement that Phyllis's lover wandered up and down is rendered musically by a downward movement of the notes which is repeated at various pitch levels and imitated in all the parts.

The Renaissance madrigal impelled composers to develop new techniques of combining music and poetry. In doing so it prepared the way for one of the most influential forms of Western music—the opera.

Listening Guide 13

 1B/5

FARMER: *Fair Phyllis*

Date: published 1599

Genre: English madrigal, 4 voices

Poem: 6 lines (ababcc), 11 syllables each

Musical style: polyphonic, with varied textures

Text

Fair Phyllis I saw sitting all alone
Feeding her flock near to the mountain side
The shepherds knew not whither she was gone
But after her lover Amyntas hied
Up and down he wandered whilst she was missing
When he found her, oh then they fell a kissing

Word-painting examples:

"Fair Phyllis I saw sitting all alone"—sung by soprano alone

"up and down"—descending line, repeated in all parts imitatively

TRANSITION II

■

From Renaissance to Baroque

"The (Venetian) church of St. Mark was . . . so full of people that one could not move a step . . . a new platform was built for the singers, adjoining . . . there was a portable organ, in addition to the two famous organs of the church, and the other instruments made the most excellent music, in which the best singers and players that can be found in this region took part."—F. SANSOVINO (1604)

Polychoral Music in Venice

Venice was a major seaport in the sixteenth century and enjoyed a unique position at the crossroads of trade with the East. Its magnificent Basilica of St. Mark, famous throughout Europe as a specimen of Byzantine architecture,

Venetian painters captured the splendid pageantry of their city in their canvases. Singers and instrumentalists took part in this religious ceremony. **Gentile Bellini** (*c. 1429–1507*), Procession in Piazza San Marco (Accademia, Venice)

This drawing by **Giovanni Antonio Canal** (*1697–1768*), *called "Canaletto," shows singers crammed into a pulpit at St. Mark's, reading from a large choirbook.* (Hamburg, Kunsthalle)

was the musical center for an impressive line of choirmasters and organists. The chief characteristic of the Venetian School was *polychoral* singing, involving the use of two or three choirs that either answered each other antiphonally, making possible all kinds of echo effects, or sang together. (*Antiphonal* performance suggests groups singing in alternation, and then together.) This antiphonal style was furthered by the fact that two organs were installed in St. Mark's, with a choir at each organ and also at other points in the basilica. The element of space thus became a factor in music, rather like the stereophonic listening of our day. The result was an interplay of sound that was heightened by the use of strings and winds, a sound that found its counterpart in the dazzling colors and tumultuous scenes of the Venetian painters.

Antiphonal style

Giovanni Gabrieli: Plaudite, psallite

The Venetian tradition, which influenced composers all over Europe, reached its high point in the works of Giovanni Gabrieli (c. 1557–1612), who fully exploited the possibilities of multiple choirs. The use of such large forces drew him away from the subtle complexities of the old contrapuntal tradition to a broad homophonic style. Once the composition was based on chords, he was able to make words more understandable by having all the voices unite on the same syllable at the same time.

Dynamic contrast

Gabrieli was the first composer to indicate the dynamics in instrumental music and to take full advantage of the dynamic contrasts possible between a string and wind group, as in his famous *Sonata pian' e forte* (soft and loud). He was also one of the first to specify which instruments were to play a particular piece, wherefore he has been hailed in some books of music history as the "Father of Orchestration." In any case, he achieved a sonorous balance between voices and instruments that was without precedent in his time.

S1A/2

S1/5

The polychoral motet *Plaudite, psallite* (Oh clap your hands and sing), from the *Symphoniae sacrae* (Sacred Symphonies) published in 1597, is in Gabrieli's grandest manner. Written for three four-voice choirs and organ, the motet in our recording is performed with brass instruments doubling the voices. Here contrasts in dynamics are based not on crescendo and diminuendo but on the difference in sound between a larger and smaller group (what will be identified in our discussion of the Baroque as *terraced dynamics*).

The text is a mosaic of lines drawn principally from Psalm 47 and from St. Paul's Letter to the Ephesians. This motet, in duple meter, changes to triple on the Alleluias that recur four times as a kind of refrain. The choirs both alternate in antiphonal singing and join forces with the brass in mighty outpourings of polychoral sound. It is likely that this work was intended for performance on Ascension, one of the highest Christian feast days.

This music, belonging as it does to the final decades of the sixteenth century, leaves behind it the world of the Renaissance. The splendor of its sound brings us into the next great style period—the Baroque.

PART THREE

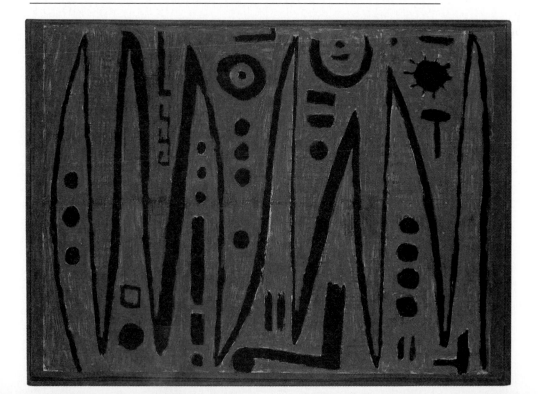

More Materials of Music

"In any narrative—epic, dramatic, or musical—every word or tone should be like a soldier marching towards the one, common, final goal: conquest of the material. The way the artist makes every phrase of his story such a soldier, serving to unfold it, to support its structure and development, to build plot and counterplot, to distribute light and shade, to point incessantly and lead up gradually to the climax—in short, the way every fragment is impregnated with its mission towards the whole, makes up this delicate and so essential objective which we call FORM."—ERNST TOCH

Paul Klee (*1879–1940*) Heroic Strokes of the Bow. (Collection, The Museum of Modern Art, New York. Nelson A. Rockefeller Bequest)

UNIT V

■

The Organization of
Musical Sounds

16

Tonality, Key, and Scale

*"All music is nothing more than a succession of impulses that
converge towards a definite point of repose."*—IGOR STRAVINSKY

At the beginning of this book we discussed various elements of music. Now
that we have had occasion to hear how these are combined in a number of
works, we are ready to consider the materials of music on a more advanced
level.

In Chapter 3 we described our perceptions of harmony in terms of
tonality, a principle of organization whereby we hear a piece of music in
relation to a central tone, the tonic, and according to a *scale* or group of
notes that is either major or minor. When we listen to a composition in the
key of C major we hear a piece built around the central tone C, the major
scale on C, and the harmonies formed from that scale.

By a *key*, then, we mean a group of related tones with a common center   *Key*
or tonic. These tones revolve around the central tone, the tonic or keynote,
to which they ultimately gravitate. This "loyalty to the tonic" is fostered in
us by much of the music we hear. It is the unifying force in the *do-re-mi-
fa-sol-la-ti-do* scale we discussed earlier.

Tonality, needless to say, resides in our minds rather than in the tones
themselves. It underlies the whole system of relationships among tones as
embodied in keys, scales, and the harmonies based on those, such relationships converging upon the "definite point of repose" mentioned in the
statement above by Stravinsky. Specifically, tonality refers to those relationships as they were manifest in Western music from around 1600 to 1900.

117

The Miracle of the Octave

A string of a certain length, when set in motion, vibrates at a certain rate per second and produces a certain pitch. Given the same conditions, a string half as long will vibrate twice as fast and sound an octave higher. A string twice as long will vibrate half as fast and sound an octave lower. When we sound two tones other than the octave together, such as C–D or C–F, the ear hears two distinctly different tones. But when we strike an octave such as C–C or D–D, the ear recognizes a very strong similarity between the two tones. Indeed, if one were not listening carefully one would almost believe that a single tone was being sounded. This "miracle of the octave" was observed at an early stage in all musical cultures, with the result that the octave became the basic interval in music. (An interval, we saw, is the distance and relationship between two tones.)

The method of dividing the octave determines the scales and the characters of a musical system. It is precisely in this particular that one system differs from another. In Western music the octave is divided into twelve equal intervals. The fact is apparent from the look of the piano keyboard, where counting from any tone to its octave we find twelve keys—seven

Half steps and whole steps

white and five black. These twelve tones are a half tone (*semitone*) apart. That is, from C to C sharp is a half step, as is from C sharp to D. The half step is the smallest unit of distance in our musical system. From C to D is a distance of two half steps, or a whole step.

Chromatic scale

The twelve semitones into which Western music divides the octave constitute what is known as the *chromatic scale*. They are duplicated in higher and lower octaves. No matter how vast and intricate a musical work, it is made up of the twelve basic tones and their higher and lower duplications. Hence the statement of the composer Paul Hindemith quoted at the beginning of this book: "There are only twelve tones. You must treat them carefully."

On the keyboard, you will note that the black keys are named in relation to their white-key neighbors. When the black key between C and D is thought of as a semitone higher than C, it is known as C sharp (♯). When the same key is thought of as a semitone lower than D, it is called D flat (♭). Thus D sharp is the same tone as E flat, F sharp is the same tone as G flat, and G sharp is the same tone as A flat. Which of these names is used depends upon the scale and key in which a particular sharp or flat appears.

The Major Scale

We have noted that a *scale* (from the Italian *scala*, "ladder") is a series of tones arranged in consecutive order, ascending or descending. Specifically, a scale presents the tones of a key.

Much of Western art music is based on two contrasting scales, the *major* and the *minor*. These consist of seven different tones, with the octave *do* added at the end of the series. The major scale has the familiar *do-re-mi-fa-sol-la-ti-do* pattern already mentioned. If you play the white keys on the

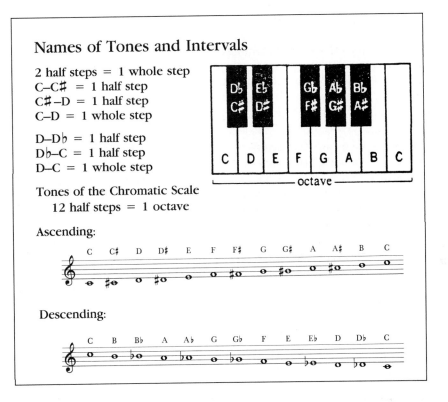

Names of Tones and Intervals

2 half steps = 1 whole step
C–C♯ = 1 half step
C♯–D = 1 half step
C–D = 1 whole step

D–D♭ = 1 half step
D♭–C = 1 half step
D–C = 1 whole step

Tones of the Chromatic Scale
   12 half steps = 1 octave

Ascending:

Descending:

piano from C to C you will hear this series. Let us examine it a little more closely.

We notice that there is no black key on the piano between E–F (*mi-fa*) and B–C (*ti-do*). These tones, therefore, are a half step apart, while the others are a whole step apart. Consequently, when we sing the *do-re-mi-fa-sol-la-ti-do* sequence we are measuring off a pattern of eight tones that are each a whole step apart except tones 3–4 (*mi-fa*) and 7–8 (*ti-do*). (The succession of intervals that form a major scale are summarized on the table below.) You will find it instructive to sing this scale, trying to distinguish between the half- and whole-step distances as you sing.

This scale implies certain relationships based upon tension and resolution. We have already indicated one of the most important of these—the thrust of the seventh tone to the eighth (*ti* seeking to be resolved to *do*). There are others: if we sing *do-re* we are left with a sense of incompleteness that is resolved when *re* moves back to *do*; *fa* gravitates to *mi*; *la* descends to *sol*.

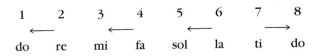

1	2	3	4	5	6	7	8
do	re	mi	fa	sol	la	ti	do

Most important of all, the major scale defines the two poles of traditional harmony: the *do* or tonic, the point of ultimate rest; and the *sol* or dominant, representative of the active harmony. Tonic going to dominant and returning to tonic becomes a basic progression of harmony. It will also serve, we shall find, as a basic principle of form.

The Minor Scale

Whether the major scale begins on C, D, E, or any other tone, it follows the same pattern in the arrangement of the whole and half steps. Such a pattern **Mode** is known as a *mode*. Thus all the major scales exemplify the major mode of arranging whole and half steps.

The *minor mode* complements and serves as a foil to the major. It differs from the major primarily in that its third degree is lowered a half step; that is, the scale of C minor has an E flat instead of E. The minor is pronouncedly different from the major in mood and coloring. *Minor*, the Latin word for

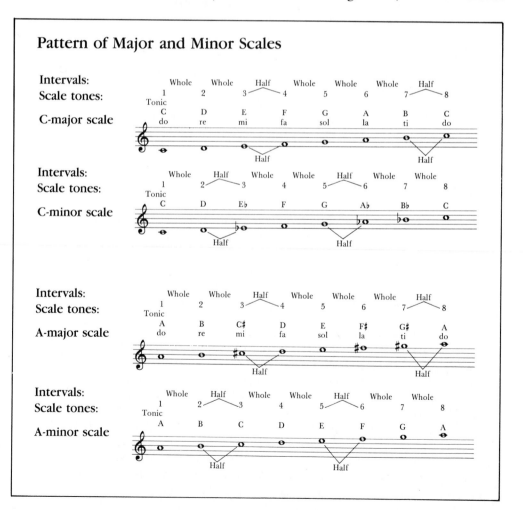

Pattern of Major and Minor Scales

"smaller," refers to the fact that the distinguishing interval C–E♭ is smaller than the corresponding interval C–E in the major ("larger") scale.

Like the major, the pattern of the minor scale, given in the table on p. 120, may begin on any of the twelve tones of the octave. In each case, there will be a different group of seven tones out of twelve; that is, each scale will include a different number of sharps or flats. This gives us twelve keys according to the major mode and twelve keys according to the minor mode.

Chromaticism

When seven tones out of twelve are selected to form a major or minor key, the other five become extraneous in relation to that key and its tonic note. They enter the composition only occasionally, mainly to embellish the melody or harmony. In order for a piece to sound firmly rooted in a key, seven notes of the key should prevail. If the five foreign tones become too prominent in the melody and harmony, the relationship to the key center is weakened and the key feeling becomes ambiguous. The distinction between the tones that do not belong within the key area and those that do is expressed in the contrasting terms "chromatic" and "diatonic." *Chromatic* refers to the twelve-tone scale, including all the semitones of the octave, whereas *diatonic* refers to music based on the seven tones of a major or minor scale, and to harmonies that are firmly rooted in the key.

Chromatic

Diatonic

We can best associate chromatic music with the Romantic era. Composers such as Liszt and Wagner indefatigably explored the possibilities of chromaticism, which surcharged their music with emotion. In contrast, music of the Classical era, that of Josef Haydn, Wolfgang Amadeus Mozart, and Ludwig van Beethoven, tends to be diatonic, centering around a keynote and its closely related harmonies.

17

The Major-Minor System

"Form follows function."—LOUIS SULLIVAN

Transposition

Suppose a certain melody begins on G. If you felt that the song lay a little too high for your voice, you might begin on F instead of G and shift all the tones of the melody one step lower. Someone else might find that the song was too low. That person could begin on A and sing each tone of the melody one step higher than it was written. That act of shifting all the tones of a musical composition a uniform distance to a different level of pitch is called *transposition.*

When we transpose a piece we shift it to another key. We change the level of pitch, the keynote, and the number of sharps or flats. But the melody line remains the same because the pattern of its whole and half steps has been retained in the new key. That is why the same song can be published in various keys for soprano, alto, tenor, or bass.

Choice of key　　　Why does a composer choose one key rather than another? In former times external factors strongly influenced this choice. Up to around the year 1815, for example, the brass instruments were not able to change keys as readily as they are now. In writing for string instruments composers considered the fact that certain effects, such as playing on the open strings, could be achieved in one key but not in another. Several nineteenth-century composers seemed to associate a certain emotional atmosphere or color with various keys.

Modulation

If a piece of music can be played in one key as in another, why not put all music in the key of C and be done with it? Because the contrast between keys and the movement from one key to another is an essential element of musical structure. We have seen that the tones of the key form a group of "seven out of twelve," which imparts coherence and focus to the music. But this closed group may be opened up, in which case we are shifted— either gently or abruptly—to another area centering on another keynote. Such a change gives us a heightened sense of activity. It is an expressive gesture of prime importance.

The process of passing from one key to another is known as *modulation*. There is no way to describe in words something that can be experienced only in the domain of sound. Suffice it to say that the composer has available a number of ways of modulating whereby the listener is "lifted" from one tonal area to another. As the composer Arnold Schoenberg put it, "Modulation is like a change of scenery."

The twelve major and twelve minor keys may be compared to so many rooms in a house, with the modulations equivalent to corridors leading from one to the other. We shall see that modulation was a common practice of the Baroque and was refined as a formal procedure in the Classical era. The eighteenth-century composer as a rule established the home key, shaped the passage of modulation—the "corridor'—in a clear-cut manner, and usually passed to a key area that was not too far away from the starting point. There resulted a spaciousness of structure that was the musical counterpart of the rolling sentences of the eighteenth-century novel and the balanced facades of eighteenth-century architecture.

Nineteenth-century Romanticism, on the other hand, demanded a whipping-up of emotions, an intensifying of all musical processes. In the Romantic era modulations were more frequent and abrupt. There came into being a hyperemotional music that wandered restlessly from key to key in accord with the need for excitement of the mid- and late-Romantic era.

Active and Rest Chords

Just as melodies have inherent active and rest poles, so do the harmonies built around these tones. The three-note chord or *triad*, built on the first scale tone, is known as the I chord or the *tonic* and serves as a point of rest. But rest only has meaning in relation to activity. The chord of rest is counterposed to other chords, which are active. The active chords seek to be completed, or *resolved* in the rest chord. This striving for resolution is the dynamic force in our music. It shapes the forward movement, imparting to it direction and goal.

Triad

Tonic

The fifth scale step, the *dominant*, is the chief representative of the active principle. We therefore obtain two focal points: the active triad, the V chord, which seeks to be resolved to the restful tonic chord. The triad built on the fourth scale step (*fa*) is known as the *subdominant* (meaning below the dominant). The movement from the subdominant to the tonic (IV to I) is familiar from the chords traditionally associated with the "Amen" sung at the close of many hymns.

Dominant

Subdominant

These three triads, the basic ones of our system, suffice to harmonize many a tune. The Christmas carol *Silent Night* illustrates the use of these chords.

Silent night! I _____	Holy night! I _____	All is calm, V_____	all is bright, I_____
Round yon Virgin IV_____	Mother and Child! I_____	Holy Infant, so IV_____	tender and mild, I_____
Sleep in heavenly V_____	peace, I_____	Sleep in heavenly I ____ V_____	peace. I_____

The Key as a Form-Building Element

By marking off an area in musical space with a fixed center, the key provides the framework within which musical growth and development take place. The three main harmonies of the key—tonic (I), dominant (V), and subdominant (IV)—become the focal points over which melodies and chord progressions unfold. In brief, the key is the neighborhood inhabited by a tune and its harmonies. Thus the key becomes a prime factor for musical unity.

At the same time the contrast between keys may further the cause of variety. Composers pitted one key against another, thereby achieving a dramatic opposition between them. They began by establishing the home key. Presently they modulated to a related key, generally that of the dominant (for example, from C major to G major, or from G major to D major). In so doing they created a tension, since the dominant key was unstable com-pared to the tonic. This tension required resolution, which was provided by the return to the home key.

The progression or movement from home key to contrasting key and back outlined the basic musical pattern of statement-departure-return. The home key was the anchor, the safe harbor; the foreign key represented adventure. The home key was the symbol of unity; the foreign key ensured variety and contrast.

PART FOUR

The Baroque Era

"Provided only that we abstain from receiving anything as true which is not so, there can be nothing so remote that we cannot reach it, nor so obscure that we cannot discover it."—RENÉ DESCARTES

Peter Paul Rubens (*1577–1640*). The Garden of Love. (Museo del Prado, Madrid)

UNIT VI

∎

The Baroque and the Arts

18

The Baroque Spirit

"I do not know what I may appear to the world; but to myself I seem to have been only like a boy playing on the seashore, and diverting myself in now and then finding a smoother pebble or a prettier shell than ordinary, whilst the great ocean of truth lay all undiscovered before me."—SIR ISAAC NEWTON (1642–1727)

The period of the Baroque stretched across a turbulent century and a half of European history. It opened shortly before the year 1600, a convenient signpost that need not be taken too literally, and may be regarded as having come to a close with the death of Bach in 1750.

The term "baroque" was probably derived from the Portuguese *barroco*, a pearl of irregular shape much used in the jewelry of the time. The century and a half of Baroque art divides itself into three fifty-year periods: early, middle, and late Baroque. Since public interest until recently concentrated on the late phase, many came to think of Bach and Handel as the first great composers. Viewed against the total panorama of their era, these masters are seen rather to have been the heirs of an old and surpassingly rich tradition.

The period 1600–1750 was a time of change and adventure. The conquest of the New World stirred the imagination and filled the coffers of the Old. The middle classes gathered wealth and power in their struggle against the aristocracy. Empires clashed for mastery of the world. Appalling poverty and wasteful luxury, magnificent idealism and savage oppression—against contradictions such as these unfolded the pomp and splendor of Baroque art: an art bold of gesture and conception—vigorous, decorative, monumental.

The bold and vigorous Baroque style was foreshadowed in this dramatic drawing by **Michelangelo** *(1474–1564), Studies for the Libyan Sibyl. (The Metropolitan Museum of Art, Purchase, 1924, John Pulitzer Bequest)*

Baroque art   The transition from the classically minded Renaissance to the Baroque was foreshadowed in the art of Michelangelo (1475–1564). His turbulent figures, their torsos twisted in struggle, reflect the Baroque love of the dramatic. In like fashion the Venetian school of painters—Titian, Tintoretto, Veronese—captured the dynamic spirit of the new age. Their crowded canvases are ablaze with color and movement. They glory in the tension of opposing masses. They dramatize the diagonal.

Politics   The Baroque was the era of absolute monarchy. Rulers throughout Europe took as their model the splendor of the French court at Versailles. Louis XIV's famous "I am the State" summed up a way of life in which all art and culture served the cult of the ruler. Courts large and small maintained elaborate musical establishments including opera troupes, chapel choirs, and orchestras. Baroque opera, the favorite diversion of the aristocracy, aimed at a lofty pathos that left no room for the frailties of ordinary people. It centered on the gods and heroes of antiquity, in whom the occupants of the royal box and their courtiers found a flattering likeness of themselves.

Scientific frontiers   The Baroque was also an age of reason. Adventurers more bold than the conquistadors set forth upon the uncharted sea of knowledge. The findings of Kepler, Galileo, and Copernicus in physics and astronomy, of Descartes in mathematics and Spinoza in philosophy were so many milestones in the intellectual history of Europe. Harvey explained the circulation of the blood. Newton's theory of gravitation revealed a universe based upon law and order. The philosopher Locke expressed the confidence of a brave new age when he wrote, "To love truth for truth's sake is the principal part of human perfection in this world."

Excluded from the salons of the aristocracy, the middle classes created a culture of their own. Their music making centered on the home, the church, and the university group (known as *collegium musicum*). For them came into being the comic opera which, like the prose novel, was filled with keen and witty observation of life. For them painting forsook its grandiose themes and turned to intimate scenes of bourgeois life. The leaders of the Dutch school—Vermeer, Frans Hals, Ruysdael—embodied the vitality of a new burgher art that reached its high point in Rembrandt (1606–69), a master whose insights penetrated the recesses of the soul. Under the leadership of merchant princes and financiers, the culture of the city came to rival that

The art of **Jan Vermeer** (*1632–75*) *turned to intimate scenes of bourgeois life.* The Artist and His Studio. (Kunsthistorisches Museum, Vienna)

The rapturous mysticism of the Counter-Reformation found expression in the eerie landscapes of **El Greco** (*1541–1614*). View of Toledo (The Metropolitan Museum of Art, Bequest of Mrs. H. O. Havemeyer, 1929. The H. O. Havemeyer Collection)

of the palace. These new connoisseurs vied with the court in their love of splendor, responding to the sensuous beauty of brocade and velvet, marble and jewels and precious metals. This aspect of the Baroque finds expression in the painting of Peter Paul Rubens (1577–1640), whose canvases exude a driving energy, a reveling in life. His voluptuous nudes established the seventeenth-century ideal of feminine beauty.

Religion   The Baroque was an intensely devout period. Religion was a rallying cry on some of the bloodiest battlefields in history. The Protestant camp included England, Scandinavia, Holland, and the north German cities, all citadels of the rising middle class. On the Catholic side were the two powerful dynasties, Hapsburg and Bourbon, who fought one another no less fiercely than they did their Protestant foes. After decades of struggle, the might of the Spanish-Hapsburg empire was broken. France emerged as the leading state on the Continent; Germany was in ruins; England rose to world power. Europe was ready to advance to the stage of modern industrial society.

The theatricality of the Baroque is brilliantly manifested in this sculpture by **Gianlorenzo Bernini** (*1598–1680*), Apollo and Daphne.

Protestant culture was rooted in the Bible. John Milton (1608–74) in *Paradise Lost* produced the poetic epic of Protestantism, even as Dante three and a half centuries earlier had produced that of the Catholic in *The Divine Comedy.* The Catholic world tried to retrieve the losses inflicted by Luther's secession. The Counter-Reformation mobilized all the forces of the church militant. Its rapturous mysticism found expression in the canvases of El Greco (1541–1614). His eerie landscapes, bathed in an unearthly light, are creations of a visionary mind that distorts the real in its search for a reality beyond. Baroque theatricalism and pathos came to fullness in the sculptor Gianlorenzo Bernini (1598–1680). His famous *Apollo and Daphne* captures in marble all the restlessness and dramatic quality of the Baroque.

Between the conflicting currents of absolute monarchy and rising bourgeois power, Reformation and Counter-Reformation, the Baroque fashioned its grandiose art. Alien to its spirit were restraint and detachment. Rather it achieved its ends through violent opposition of forces, lavish creativity, and emotional abandon. With these went the capacity to organize a thousand details into an overpowering whole.

Artists played a variety of roles in Baroque society. They might be ambassadors and intimates of princes, as were Rubens and Van Dyck; or priests, as was Vivaldi; or political leaders, like Milton. They functioned under royal or princely patronage, as did Corneille and Racine; or, like Bach, were in the employ of a church or a free city. To the aristocrats whom they served they might be little more than purveyors of elegant entertainment. Yet, beneath the obsequious manner and fawning dedications demanded by the age, there was often to be found a spirit that dared to probe all existing knowledge and shape new worlds; a voice addressing itself to those who truly listened—a voice that was indeed "the trumpet of a prophecy."

The role of the artist

19

Main Currents in Baroque Music

"The end of all good music is to affect the soul."—CLAUDIO MONTEVERDI

Origins of the Monodic Style

With the transition from Renaissance to Baroque came a momentous change: the shifting of interest from a texture of several independent parts to music in which a single melody predominated; that is, from polyphonic to homophonic texture. The new style, which originated in vocal music, was *Monody* named *monody*—literally, "one song," music for one singer with instrumental accompaniment. (Monody is not to be confused with monophony, which is an unaccompanied vocal line; see page 18). The year 1600 is associated with the emergence of the monodic style. Like many such milestones, the date merely indicates the coming to light of a process that was long preparing.

The Camerata The victory of the monodic style was achieved by a group of Florentine writers, artists, and musicians known as the Camerata, a name derived from the Italian word for salon. Among them were Vincenzo Galilei, father of the astronomer Galileo Galilei, and the composers Jacopo Peri and Giulio

A contemporary engraving by **Bernardo Buontalenti** *depicts the composer Jacopo Peri in one of his own stage works (c. 1589).*

Caccini. The members of the Camerata were aristocratic humanists. Their aim was to resurrect the musical-dramatic art of ancient Greece. Since almost nothing was known of ancient music, the Camerata instead came forth with an idea that was very much alive.

This idea was that music must heighten the emotional power of the text. "I endeavored," wrote Caccini in 1602, "the imitation of the conceit of the words, seeking out the chords more or less passionate according to the meaning." Thus came into being what its inventors regarded as the *stile rappresentativo* (representational style), consisting of a vocal line that moved freely over a foundation of simple chords.

Stile rappresentativo

The Camerata appeared at a time when it became necessary for music to free itself from the complexities of counterpoint. The year 1600, like the year 1900, bristled with discussions about *le nuove musiche*—"the new music"—and what its adherents proudly named "the expressive style." They soon realized that this representational style could be applied not only to a poem but to an entire drama. In this way they were led to what many regard as the single most important achievement of Baroque music—the invention of the opera.

Origins of the opera

New Harmonic Structures

The melody-and-chords of the new music was far removed from the intricate interweaving of voices in the old. Since musicians were familiar with the basic harmony, it was unnecessary to write the chords out in full. Instead, the composer put a numeral, indicating the chord required, above or below the bass note. For example, the figure 6 under a bass note indicated a chord whose root lay a sixth above the note. The application of this principle on a large scale resulted in "the most successful system of musical shorthand ever devised"—the *figured bass* or *thorough-bass* (from *basso continuo*, a continuous bass, "thorough" being the old form of "through"). The actual filling in and elaboration of the harmony was left to the performer.

Figured bass

So important was this practice for a century and a half that the Baroque is often referred to as the period of thorough-bass. The figured bass required at least two players: one to perform the bass line on a sustaining instrument— cello or bassoon—and the other to fill in or "realize" the chords on an instrument capable of harmony, such as a harpsichord or organ, a guitar or lute. At a time when printing was an involved and costly process, it was a boon to composers to be able to present their music in abbreviated fashion, knowing that the performers would fill in the necessary details.

Thorough-bass instruments

The Baroque witnessed one of the most significant changes in all music history: the transition from the Medieval church modes to major-minor tonality. As music turned from vocal counterpoint to instrumental harmony, it demanded a simplification of the harmonic system. The various church modes gave way to two standard scales: major and minor. With the establishment of major-minor tonality, the thrust to the keynote or tonic became the most powerful force in music.

Major-minor tonality

Now each chord could assume its function in relation to the key center.

The thorough-bass instrument looming above the harpsichord testifies to the importance of the basso continuo practice in Baroque performance. A wash drawing by **Giuseppe Zocchi** (*1711–69*), Concerto.

Tonic and dominant

Composers of the Baroque soon learned to exploit the opposition between the chord of rest, the I (tonic), and the active chord, the V (dominant). So, too, the movement from home key to contrasting key and back became an important element in the shaping of musical structure. Composers developed larger forms of instrumental music than had ever been known before.

Important in this transition was a major technical advance. Due to a curious quirk of nature, keyboard instruments tuned according to the scientific laws of acoustics (first discovered by the ancient Greek philosopher Pythagoras) give a pure sound in some keys but increasingly out-of-tune intervals in others. As instrumental music acquired greater prominence, it became more and more important to be able to play in all the keys; thus a variety of tuning systems were developed. In the seventeenth century, a discovery was made: by slightly mistuning the intervals within the octave—and thereby spreading the discrepancy evenly among all the tones—it became possible to play in every major and minor key without unpleasant results. This tuning adjust-

Equal temperament

ment is known as *equal temperament*. It increased the range of harmonic possibilities available to the composer. Although we are uncertain which of the many temperaments or tuning systems was preferred by Johann Sebastian Bach, he demonstrated that he could write in every one of the twelve major and twelve minor keys. The result, *The Well-Tempered Clavier*, is a two-volume collection, each containing twenty-four preludes and fugues, or one in every possible key. Equal temperament eventually transformed the major-minor system, making it a completely flexible medium of expression.

The growing harmonic sense brought about a freer handling of dissonance. Baroque musicians used dissonant chords for emotional intensity and color. In the setting of poetry the composer heightened the impact of an expressive word through dissonance. Such harmonic freedom could not fail to shock the conservatives. The Italian theorist Artusi, writing in 1600 *On the Imperfections of Modern Music*—an attack on Monteverdi and his fellow innovators—rails against those musicians who "are harsh to the ear, offending rather than delighting it," and who "think it within their power to corrupt, spoil, and ruin the good old rules."

The major-minor system expressed a new dynamic culture. By dividing the world of sound into definite areas and regulating the movement from one to the other, composers were able to mirror the exciting interplay of forces in the world about them.

Use of dissonance

notes that sound harsh together

Rhythm in Baroque Music

The Baroque, with its fondness for energetic movement, demanded a vigorous rhythm based on the regular recurrence of accent. The bass part became the carrier of the new rhythm. Its relentless beat is an arresting trait in many compositions of the Baroque. This steady pulsation, once under way, never slackens or deviates until the goal is reached. It imparts to Baroque music its unflagging drive, producing the same effect of turbulent yet controlled motion that animates Baroque painting, sculpture, and architecture.

Composers became ever more aware of the capacity of the instruments for rhythm. They found that a striking dance rhythm could serve as the basis for an extended piece, vocal or instrumental. In a time when courtiers

The Residenz, home of the Prince-Bishop of Würzburg, is the masterful work of architect **Balthazar Neumann** *(1687–1753). The accumulation of sculptural ornaments, such as the sinuously curved gables and ornate window frames, identify it as a superb example of secular Baroque architecture.*

listened to music primarily for entertainment, composers dressed up a good part of their material in dance rhythms. Many a dance piece served to make palatable a profounder discourse. In effect, rhythm pervaded the musical conception of the Baroque and helped it capture the movement and drive of a vibrant era.

Continuous Melody

The elaborate scrollwork of Baroque architecture bears witness to an abundance of energy that would not leave an inch of space undecorated. Its musical counterpart is to be found in one of the main elements of Baroque style—the principle of continuous expansion. A movement based on a single affection or mood will start off with a striking musical figure that unfolds through a process of ceaseless spinning out. We shall see that in this regard the music of the Baroque differs from that of the Classical era, with its balanced phrases and cadences. It is constantly in motion, in the act of becoming. When its energy is spent, the work comes to an end.

In vocal music the melody of the Baroque was imbued with the desire always to heighten the impact of the words. Wide leaps and the use of chromatic tones helped create a noble melody whose spacious curves outlined a style of grand expressiveness and pathos.

Terraced Dynamics

Baroque music does not know the constant fluctuation of volume that marks later styles. The music moves at a fairly constant level of sonority. A passage uniformly loud will be followed by one uniformly soft, creating the effect of light and shade. The shift from one level to the other, known as *terraced dynamics*, is a characteristic feature of the Baroque style.

For greater volume of tone, Baroque composers wrote for a larger number of players rather than directing each instrument to play louder; as a means of expression within a passage they found their main source of dynamic expression in the contrast between a soft passage and a loud—that is, between the two terraces of sound rather than in the crescendos of later styles. Each passage became an area of solid color set off against the next. This conception shapes the structure of the music, endowing it with a monumental simplicity.

It follows that Baroque composers were much more sparing of expression marks than those who came after. The music of the period carries little else than an occasional *forte* or *piano*, leaving it to the player to supply whatever else may be necessary.

The Rise of the Virtuoso Musician

The heightened interest in instruments in the Baroque era went hand in hand with the need to master their technique. There followed a dramatic rise in the standards of playing, which paralleled the design improvements introduced by the great builders of instruments in Italy and Germany. This in turn made it possible for composers to write works that demanded a more advanced playing technique. Out of this development came the challenging harpsichord sonatas of Domenico Scarlatti and the virtuosic violin works of Arcangelo Corelli, to name only two masters of the period.

The emergence of instrumental virtuosity had its counterpart in the vocal sphere. The rise of opera saw the development of a phenomenal vocal technique that has never been surpassed. At this time, too, women began to enter the ranks as professional musicians, both as composers and performers. In Italy, Barbara Strozzi (1619–64) enjoyed a successful career as a singer before turning her efforts to composing, and a trio of women singers from Ferrara in northern Italy were known throughout Europe not only for "the timbre and training of their voices but in the design of exquisite passages of embellishment."

The advance in vocal virtuosity was much encouraged by the rise of the *castrato*, the artificial male soprano or alto who dominated the operatic scene of the early eighteenth century. Such singers were castrated during their boyhood in order to preserve the soprano or alto register of their voices for the rest of their lives. What resulted, after years of training, was an incredibly agile voice of enormous range, powered by breath control the like of which singers today cannot even begin to approach. The castrato's voice combined the power of the male with the brilliance of the upper register. Strange as it may seem to us, Baroque audiences associated it with heroic male roles. The era of the French Revolution witnessed the decline and eventual abolition of a custom so incompatible with human dignity. When castrato roles are performed today, they are usually sung in lower register by a tenor or baritone, or in the original register by a woman singer in male costume.

The castrato

Improvisation

Improvisation played a prominent part in the musical practice of the Baroque. The realizing of the thorough-bass would have been impossible if musicians of the period had not been ready to "think with their fingers." A church organist was expected as a matter of course to be able to improvise an intricate contrapuntal piece. The ability in this regard of great organists such as Bach and Handel was legendary. This abandonment to the inspiration of the moment suited the rhapsodic temper of the Baroque, and even influenced the art of composition. Many passages in the solo keyboard repertory of the time, with their abrupt changes of mood, bear the mark of extemporaneous speech.

Improvisation functioned in Baroque music in another way. Singers and players added their own embellishments to what was written down (as is the custom today in jazz). This was their creative contribution to the work. The practice was so widespread that Baroque music sounded quite different in performance from what it looked like on paper.

The Doctrine of the Affections

With "man the measure of all things," there was much speculation concerning the passions and affections, by which were meant the deep-lying forces that determine our emotional life. It was realized that these are peculiarly responsive to music. The *doctrine of the affections* related primarily to the union of music and poetry, where the mental state was made explicit by the text. The Baroque inherited from the Renaissance an impressive technique of *tone* or word painting, in which the music vividly mirrored the words. Ideas of movement and direction—stepping, running, leaping, ascending, descending—were represented graphically through the movement of the melody and rhythm. Bach exhorted his pupils to "play the chorale according to the meaning of the words." He associated the idea of resurrection with a rising line. The sorrow of the Crucifixion was symbolized by a bass line that might descend stepwise along the chromatic scale.

This supremacy of music shows itself in two traits that strike the listener in hearing the vocal literature of the Baroque. We have already encountered both. In the first place, lines, phrases, and individual words are repeated over and over again in order to allow room for the necessary musical expansion. This practice springs from the realization that music communicates more slowly than words and needs more time in which to establish its meaning. In the second place, a single syllable will be extended to accommodate all the notes of an expressive melodic line, so that the word is stretched beyond recognition, or treated melismatically. Thus, the music born of words ends by swallowing up the element that gave it birth.

In instrumental music the practice took root of building a piece on a single mood or "affection." This was established at the outset by a striking musical subject out of which grew the entire composition. In this way composers discovered the imperious gesture that opens a piece of Baroque music, establishing a tension and pathos that pervade the whole movement.

The Composer and Patron

The Baroque was a period of international culture. National styles existed—without nationalism. Jean-Baptiste Lully, an Italian, created the French lyric tragedy. Handel, a German, gave England the oratorio. There was free interchange among national cultures. The sensuous beauty of Italian melody, the pointed precision of French dance rhythm, the luxuriance of German counterpoint, the freshness of English choral song—these nourished an all-European art that absorbed the best of each.

Baroque composers were employed by courts, towns, churches, or opera houses. They were in direct contact with their public. Most likely they were their own musical interpreters, which made the contact even closer. They frequently created their compositions for specific occasions—a royal wedding or a religious service, for example—and for immediate use: in a word, for communication. They began by writing for a particular time and place, but they ended by creating for the ages.

■

Vocal Music of the Baroque

20

Baroque Opera

The Components of Opera

An *opera* is a drama that is sung. It combines the resources of vocal and instrumental music—soloists, ensembles, chorus, orchestra, and sometimes ballet—with poetry and drama, acting and pantomime, scenery and costumes. To weld the diverse elements into a unity is a problem that has exercised some of the best minds in the history of music.

Explanations necessary to plot and action are generally presented in a kind of musical declamation known as *recitative*. This disjunct vocal style, which grew out of the earliest monodies of the Florentine Camerata, imitates the natural inflections of speech; its rhythm is curved to the rhythm of the language. Instead of a purely musical line, recitative is often characterized by a rapid patter and "talky" repetition of the same note; also by rapid question-and-answer dialogue that builds dramatic tension in the theater. In time, two styles of recitative became standard: *secco*, which features a sparse accompaniment and moves with great freedom, and *accompagnato*, which is accompanied by various instruments and thus moves more evenly.

Recitative

Recitative gives way at the lyric moments to the *aria* (Italian for "air"), which releases through melody the emotional tension accumulated in the course of action. The aria is a song, generally of a highly emotional kind. It is what audiences wait for, what they cheer, what they remember. An aria, because of its beauty, can be effective even when removed from its context. Many arias are familiar to multitudes who have never heard the operas from which they are excerpted. One formal convention that developed early in

Aria Big moment

139

the genre's history is the *da capo aria*, a ternary or **A-B-A** form that brought back the first section with improvised embellishments by the soloist.

Ensembles

An opera may contain ensemble numbers—trios, quartets, quintets, sextets, septets—in which the characters pour out their respective feelings. The chorus is used in conjunction with solo voices or it may function independently. It may comment and reflect upon the action in the manner of the chorus in Greek tragedy. Or it may be integrated into the action.

The orchestra too supports the action of the opera, setting the appropriate mood for different scenes. An opera usually begins with an instrumental number, known as the *overture*, which may introduce melodies from arias to come. Each act of the opera normally has an orchestral introduction, and interludes may occur between scenes as well.

Libretto

The opera composer works with a *librettist*, who writes the text of the work, creating characters and plot with some dramatic insight and fashioning situations that justify the use of music. The *libretto*, or text of the opera, must be devised so as to give the composer an opportunity for diverse numbers—arias, recitatives, duets, ensembles, choruses, interludes—that have become the traditional features of this art form.

Early Opera in Italy

An outgrowth of Renaissance theatrical traditions and the musical experiments of the Florentine Camerata, early opera lent itself to the lavish spectacles and scenic displays that graced royal weddings and similar ceremonial occasions. *Orfeo* (1607) and *Arianna* (1608) were composed by the first great master of the new genre, Claudio Monteverdi (1567–1643), in whom the dramatic spirit of the Baroque found its true spokesman. It was in his operas that the innovations of the Florentine Camerata reached artistic maturity.

Claudio Monteverdi: His Life and Music

"The modern composer builds upon the foundation of truth."

Claudio Monteverdi

Monteverdi spent twelve fruitful years at the court of the Duke of Mantua. In 1613 he was appointed choirmaster of St. Mark's in Venice, and retained that post until his death thirty years later. Into his operas and ballets, madrigals and religious works he injected an emotional intensity that was new to music. The new-born lyric drama of the Florentines he welded into a coherent musical form and tightened their shapeless recitative into an expressive line imbued with drama. He originated what he called the *stile concitato* (agitated style) to express the hidden tremors of the soul, introducing such novel sound-effects as the string tremolo and pizzicato as symbols of passion. Monteverdi aspired above all to make his music express the emotional content of poetry. "The text," he declared, "should be the master of the music, not the servant."

Principal Works

Operas, including *Orfeo* (1607), *Arianna* (1608, music lost), *Il ritorno d'Ulisse* (The Return of Ulysses, 1640), *L'incoronazione di Poppea* (The Coronation of Poppea, 1642); other dramatic music includes ballets and *Combattimento di Tancredi e Clorinda* (The Combat of Tancredi and Clorinda, 1624)

Secular vocal music, including 9 books of madrigals, scherzi musicali, canzonettas

Sacred vocal music, including Vespers (1610), Masses, Magnificats, madrigali spirituali, motets, and psalms

Monteverdi used dissonance and instrumental color for dramatic expressiveness, atmosphere, and suspense. He emphasized the contrast between characters by abrupt changes of key. He held that rhythm is bound up with emotion. A master of polyphonic writing, he retained in his choruses the great contrapuntal tradition of the past. There resulted a noble art, full of pathos and rooted in the verities of human nature. The characters in his music dramas were neither puppets nor abstractions, but men and women who gave vent to their joys and sorrows through song. When his patron, the Duke of Mantua, suggested a libretto on a mythological subject of the kind fashionable at the time—a dialogue of the winds—the composer protested: "How shall I be able to imitate the speaking of the winds that do not speak; and how shall I be able to move the affections by such means? Arianna was moving because she was a woman, and likewise Orfeo was moving because he was a man and not a wind. The harmonies imitate human beings, not the noise of winds, the bleating of sheep, the neighing of horses."

Monteverdi: The Coronation of Poppea

Although the earliest operas derived their plots from Greek mythology, Monteverdi's *The Coronation of Poppea*, a late work from his Venetian period, instead turned to history. By this time the first public opera houses had been opened in Venice. Opera was moving out of the palace to become a widely cultivated form of popular entertainment. In the early court operas Monteverdi used a heterogeneous orchestra consisting of whatever instruments happened to be available. But in writing for a theater whose repertory would include works by other composers, he adhered to—and helped evolve—a more standardized ensemble.

The enduring popularity of Monteverdi's final opera is attested to by the fact that the composer Pietro Francesco Cavalli (1602–76) himself oversaw productions of the work in Rome, featuring some revisions he made to the last act. It is with his reworkings that the opera is performed today.

The libretto for *The Coronation of Poppea* by Giovanni Busenello was based on an episode in Roman history. The Emperor, Nero, plots to depose his wife, Ottavia, in order to marry his mistress, the courtesan Poppea. His advisor, the philosopher Seneca, who in bygone years had been Nero's tutor, views this decision as an affront to the state and voices his objection. For this he is condemned to death. Once he is out of the way, Poppea triumphs and is crowned Empress of Rome.

The action called for a varied cast of characters spread across the social spectrum from Emperor to commoners, with vivid characterization of the main personages and dramatic confrontations between them. The opera treats powerful emotions that find expression in recitatives and arias, choruses and passages in arioso style (between aria and recitative). Also effective is Monteverdi's use of the "agitated style," in movements interspersed with *Ritornello* instrumental sinfonias and ritornelli. (A *ritornello*, a term allied to our word return, originally denoted an instrumental passage heard at the beginning and end of an aria, but came to mean a passage that returned again and again in the manner of a refrain.) Also, Monteverdi established the love duet as an essential feature of the opera both in the first act and at the end.

The characters in this historic drama are hardly admirable. Nero (a castrato role) is a spoiled, self-indulgent playboy; his wife Ottavia plots to poison her rival; his mistress Poppea is calculating and ambitious; and Seneca, despite his courage in opposing the Emperor, is pompous and self-seeking. What gives them all their humanity is the moving music in which Monteverdi has clothed their emotions.

In the final scene of the opera Nero achieves his purpose and leads Poppea to the throne. The finale is introduced by an energetic sinfonia of martial character in which short motives are exchanged among the instruments *Sinfonia* antiphonally or in a dialogue. (A *sinfonia* is a short instrumental work whose primary function is to facilitate scene changes.) When the consuls and tribunes arrive to salute Poppea, we hear a chorus for tenors and basses with much imitation between the two lines. (For the complete text, see Listening Guide 14.)

A second Sinfonia quietly sets the scene for the final love duet between Nero and Poppea, which closes the opera. In the duet, the opening section returns after the middle part, which is repeated, giving a pattern of **A-B-B-A** that foreshadows the da capo or **A-B-A** aria that was to dominate opera *Ground bass* later on. The opening section unfolds over a four-note *ground bass* that is carried by various instruments, such as lute, harp, and harpsichord. The term ground bass refers to a short phrase repeated over and over in the lower voice while the upper voices pursue their independent course. With each repetition, some aspect of the melody, harmony, or rhythm is changed. The lovers' voices intermingle in a tender dialogue, with melismatic treatment of the emotional phrase "pur t'annodo" (let me enfold you). Notable is Monteverdi's affective use of dissonance on such words as "pena" (grieving) and "moro" (death). The lovers hope that their union will put an end to all contention.

Listening Guide 14

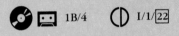

1B/4   I/1/22

MONTEVERDI: *The Coronation of Poppea*, Act III, scene 7

Date: 1642

Genre: Opera, Italian

Basis: Roman history

Characters: Nero, Emperor of Rome
Poppea, his mistress, soon to be Empress
Ottavia, wife of Nero, to be deposed
Seneca, sage and advisor to Nero
Consuls and Tribunes

Act III, scene 7: Coronation Scene

22 Sinfonia—Orchestra introduction, martial in character for entrance of Consuls and Tribunes

23 Chorus—Consuls and Tribunes, crowning of Poppea

Text	*Translation*	*Description*
A te, a te sovrana augusta	O hail to thee our empress, our ruler	Two-part writing, imitative, recitative-like
con il consenso universal di Roma indiadedian la chioma.	By our unanimous consent, and that of all Romans, Now with this crown, we crown thee.	
A te l'Asia, a te l'Africa s'atterra,	Now shall Asia, now shall Africa be humble before thee.	fanfare-like passage
a te l'Europa e'l mar che cinge e serra	And now let Europe, and all the seas which belong to	dance-like meter, melodic
quest'imperio felice	This most fortunate empire	
hora consacra e dona	Offer and consecrate in honor,	"agitated" style used
questa del mondo imperial corona.	this the crown of the mighty Roman empire.	

[handwritten margin notes: "imitat poly", "vocal line", "WORD-PAINTING", "POLITICAL FORMAL", "now you can top for1", "ha ha ha ha", "(CROWN) MELIZMA", "CO BO O O O O O O NA"]

Example from chorus, with dancelike meter and imitation between two voices and melisma on "corona" (crown)

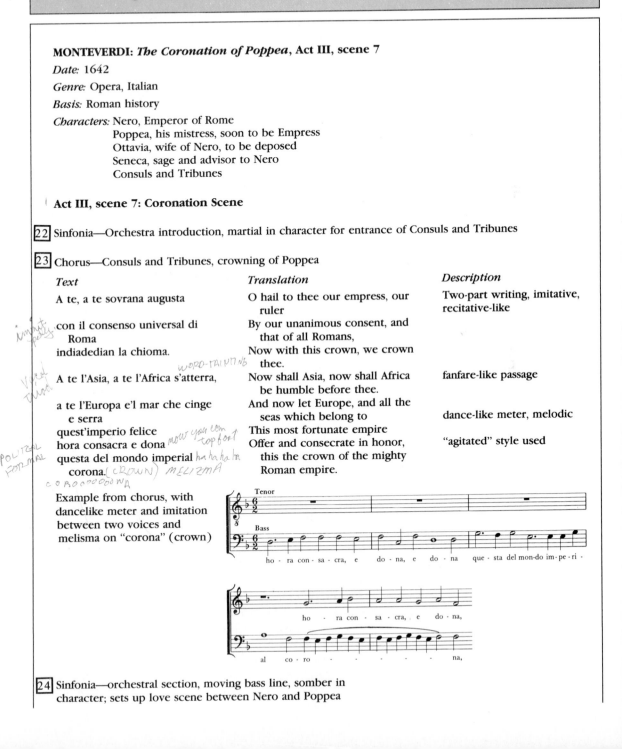

24 Sinfonia—orchestral section, moving bass line, somber in character; sets up love scene between Nero and Poppea

25 Duet—Nero and Poppea
Form: **A-B-B-A, A** section with four-note ground bass

Text	*Translation*	*Description*
A Pur ti miro pur ti stringo	I adore you, I embrace you,	Four-note ground bass in
pur ti godo pur t'annodo	I desire you, I enchain you,	opening
più non peno più non moro	no more grieving, no more sorrow,	Imitation between two voices
o mia vita o mio tesoro.	O my dearest, o my beloved.	
26 B Io son tua speme mia	I am yours o my love,	Middle section, free bass
dillò di l'idol mio,	tell me so, you are mine,	Short motives imitated
tu sei pur si mio ben,	mine alone, o my love.	Entire middle section repeated
si mio cor, mia vita, si.	Feel my heart, see my love, see.	
B Io son tua, *etc.*	I am yours, *etc.*	Repeat
A Pur ti miro, *etc.*	I adore you, *etc.*	Repeat of opening

ARIA *THRU DISSONANCE*

Opening of duet (ground bass shown in brackets)

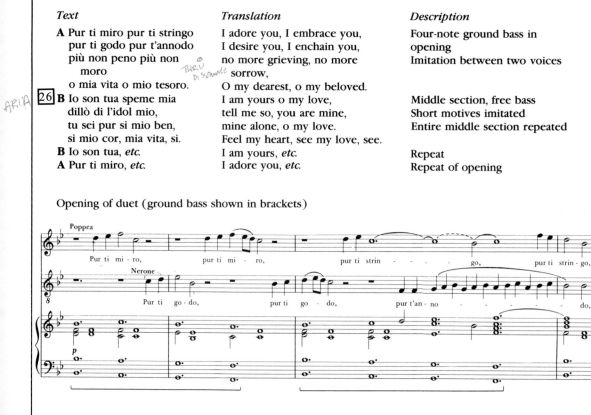

Example showing dissonances from duet on word "peno"

When an art form genuinely mirrors the soul of a nation, its history manifests a striking unity of outlook and achievement. From Monteverdi the heritage descends through two hundred and fifty years of Italian opera to Giuseppe Verdi. In *The Coronation of Poppea*, written when the master was seventy-five, we hear the throb of passion, the profoundly human quality that echoes in more familiar guise in the soaring phrases of Verdi's masterpieces. Monteverdi was indeed—as his contemporaries called him—a "prophet of music."

Opera in England

During the reigns of the first two Stuart kings, James I (r. 1603–25) and
Charles I (r. 1625–49), the English masque emerged into prominence. This
was a type of aristocratic entertainment that combined vocal and instrumental music, with poetry and dance. Many masques were presented privately in the homes of the nobility. The best-known example is Milton's
Comus, with music by Henry Lawes, which was produced in 1634.

The masque

In the period of the Commonwealth that followed (1649–60), stage plays
were forbidden; the Puritans regarded the theater as an invention of the
devil. However, a play set to music could be passed off as a "concert." The
"semi-operas" that flourished during the rule of Oliver Cromwell (1653–
58) were essentially plays with a liberal mixture of solo songs, ensembles,
and choral numbers interspersed with instrumental pieces. Since the dramatic tradition in England was much stronger than the operatic, it was
inevitable that in these works the spoken word took precedence over the
sung. However, in the 1680s, an important step toward opera was taken
when John Blow presented his *Venus and Adonis,* which was sung throughout. This paved the way for the first great English opera, *Dido and Aeneas,*
by Blow's pupil Henry Purcell.

Henry Purcell: His Life and Music

> *"As Poetry is the harmony of Words, so Musick is that of Notes; and as
> Poetry is a Rise above Prose and Oratory, so is Musick the exaltation
> of Poetry."*

Henry Purcell (1659–95) occupies a special niche in the annals of his
country. He was last in the illustrious line that, stretching back to pre-Tudor
times, won for England a foremost position among the musically creative
nations. With his death the ascendancy came to an end. Until the rise of a
native school of composers almost two hundred years later, he remained
for his countrymen the symbol of an eminence they had lost.

Henry Purcell

Purcell's brief career unfolded at the court of Charles II (1660–85),
extending through the turbulent reign of James II (1685–88) into the period
of William and Mary (1689–1702). He held various posts as singer, organist,
and composer. Purcell's works cover a wide range, from the massive contrapuntal choruses of the religious anthems and the odes in honor of his
royal masters.

Yet this national artist realized that England's music must be part of the
European tradition. It was his historic role to assimilate the achievements
of the Continent—the dynamic instrumental style, the movement toward
major-minor tonality, the recitative and aria of Italian opera, and the pointed
rhythms of the French—and to acclimate these to his native land.

Purcell's court odes and religious anthems hit off the tone of solemn
ceremonial in an open-air music of great breadth and power. His instrumental
music ranks with the finest achievements of the middle Baroque. His songs
display the charm of his lyricism no less than his gift for setting the English
language. In the domain of the theater he produced, besides a quantity of

Principal Works

Dramatic music, including *Dido and Aeneas* (1689) and *The Fairy Queen* (1692); incidental music for plays

Sacred vocal music, including a Magnificat, Te Deum, and anthems

Secular vocal music, including court odes and welcome songs

Instrumental music, including fantasias, sonatas, marches, overtures, In nomines; harpsichord suites and dances

music for plays, what many of his countrymen still regard as the peak of English opera.

Purcell: Dido and Aeneas

Presented in 1689 "at Mr. Josias Priest's boarding school at Chelsy by young Gentlewomen . . . to a select audience of their parents and friends," *Dido and Aeneas* achieved a level of pathos for which there was no precedent in England. A school production imposed obvious limitations, to which Purcell's genius adapted itself in extraordinary fashion. Each character is projected in a few telling strokes. The mood of each scene is established with the utmost economy. The libretto by Nahum Tate, one of the drearier poets laureate of England, provided Purcell—despite some inferior rhymes—with a serviceable framework. As in all school productions, this one had to present ample opportunities for choral singing and dancing. The opera took about an hour. Within that span, Purcell created a work of incredible concentration and power.

He based the work on an episode in Virgil's *Aeneid*, the epic poem that traces the adventures of the hero Aeneas after the fall of Troy. Both Purcell and his librettist could assume that their audience was thoroughly familiar with Virgil's classic. They could therefore compress the plot and suggest rather than fill in the details. Aeneas and his men are shipwrecked on the shores of Carthage. Dido, the Carthagenian Queen, falls in love with him; he returns her affection. But he cannot forget that the gods have commanded him to continue his journey until he reaches Italy; it is his "manifest destiny" to be the founder of Rome. Much as he hates to hurt the Queen, he knows that he must depart; she too ultimately realizes that she must let him go. She prepares to meet her fate in the moving lament that is the culminating point of the opera, "When I am laid in earth." (For the text, see Listening Guide 15.) In Virgil's poem Dido mounts the funeral pyre, whose flames light the way for Aeneas's ships as they sail out of the harbor.

Following the brief recitative "Thy hand, Belinda," Dido's lament unfolds over a five-measure *ground bass* or ostinato that descends along the chromatic scale, always a symbol of grief in Baroque music. Purcell ended with a final chorus based on a four-line stanza in the pattern **A-A-B-B.** Notice, in the last line, the repeated melodic "sigh" of a descending half step on the

Listening Guide 15

1B/6   I/1/28

PURCELL: *Dido and Aeneas*, end of Act III

Date: 1689

Genre: opera

28 Recitative: "Thy hand, Belinda," sung by Dido;

Text: Thy hand, Belinda, darkness shades me,
  On thy bosom let me rest,
  More I wou'd but death invades me,
  Death is now a welcome guest.

Introduces lament aria; sung over sparse accompaniment
Aria: "When I am laid in earth," Dido's lament

Basis: ground bass, 5-measure pattern in slow triple meter, descending chromatic scale, repeated eleven times

29 Opening of aria,
with two statements
of ground bass

Statements of Ground Bass	*Setting*
1	Instrumental introduction
2	When I am laid in earth, may my wrongs
3	create no trouble in thy breast.
4	When I am laid . . .
5	create no trouble . . .
6	Remember me, remember me, but ah
7	forget my fate, remember me, but ah forget my
8	fate. Remember me . . .
9	forget my fate . . .
10	Instrumental closing
11	Instrumental closing

30 Final chorus: "With drooping wings"
    Poetic form: Quatrain (aabb)
    Musical style: Imitative polyphony for first three lines; homophonic for last line of text

Example showing polyphony
and repeated melodic "sigh"
of descending second on word "soft"

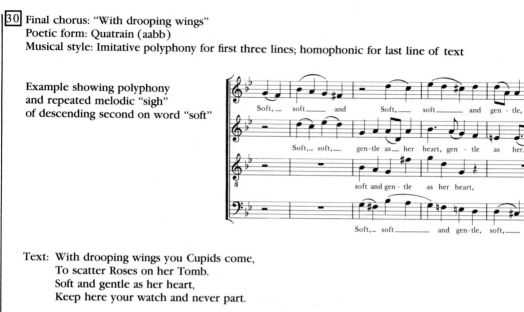

Text: With drooping wings you Cupids come,
       To scatter Roses on her Tomb.
       Soft and gentle as her heart,
       Keep here your watch and never part.

word "soft," an emotional effect much in evidence in the madrigals of Monteverdi and his followers.

In *Dido and Aeneas* Purcell struck the true tone of lyric drama. He might have established opera had he lived twenty years longer. As it was, his masterpiece had no progeny. It remained as unique a phenomenon in history as the wonderful musician whom his contemporaries called "the British Orpheus."

Late Baroque Opera

Opera in the late Baroque found its master in George Frideric Handel, who, although German by birth, dominated the operatic scene in London during the first decades of the eighteenth century. This was the London of the Hanoverian Kings George I (r. 1714–27) and II (r. 1727–60). It was their taste that he managed to please, and their aristocrats whom, as an opera impresario, he had to win over.

Handel was in every sense an international figure. His art united the beautiful vocal melody of the Italian school with the stately gestures of the French style and the contrapuntal genius of the Germans. To these elements he added the majestic choral tradition of the English. The result was perfectly suited to the London scene. We will discuss his life and career in detail in a later chapter. Suffice it here to introduce an aria that well exemplifies the operatic art of the late Baroque.

Handel: "V'adoro" from Julius Caesar

Handel's dramatic works were in the new vein of *opera seria*, or serious Italian opera, that projected heroic or tragic subjects. His opera about Julius Caesar, written in 1724, is one of his finest. The action takes place in the

The title page of Julius Caesar, *published in London in 1724.*

period when Caesar and his legions conquer Egypt. Cleopatra, engaged in a struggle against her brother Ptolemy, who is her rival for the throne, succeeds in captivating the conqueror. (The subject was subsequently treated, in somewhat more intellectual fashion, by George Bernard Shaw.) The libretto freely departs from historical fact but this does not seem to have disturbed either Handel or his listeners.

In the second act Cleopatra, eager to conquer Caesar with her beauty, enchants him with her love song. The "single affection" on which her aria is based is established by the opening words, "V'adoro" (I adore you). Handel's orchestral background creates the proper atmosphere for a romantic encounter. Besides the usual oboes and strings, bassoons and harp, it includes bass viol and bass lute to carry the continuo (bass line).

S1A/7

S1/17

Cleopatra's aria, an **A-B-A** or da capo form, unfolds in a long-breathed Largo in triple time. There is much repetition of text, which consists of a four-line stanza. The first two lines are set to the **A** section, which ends with a cadence in F. Cleopatra's mention of her sad heart calls for a change of mood; the middle section begins in D minor. (This key is the *relative minor* of F major, so called because both share the same key signature of one flat.) At the end of this **B** section Handel, instead of proceeding immediately with the repetition of the first part, interjects a line of recitative on the part of the enraptured Caesar: "Not even the Thunderer in heaven has a melody to rival so sweet a song!" The repetition of the **A** section gave the soprano an opportunity for embellishing the melody with trills, runs, grace notes, and similar ornaments. These were not written down by Handel but were added by the singer in accordance with the performance practice of the Baroque.

Julius Caesar has been revived in recent years with great success. Its music rises above the conventions of late Baroque opera to speak to our own time.

21

Bach and the Baroque Cantata

The Baroque inherited the great vocal polyphony of the sixteenth century. At the same time composers pursued a new interest in solo song accompanied by instruments, and in dramatic musical declamation. Out of the fusion of all these came a new Baroque form—the cantata.

The *cantata* (from the Italian *cantare*, "to sing"—that is, a piece to be sung) is a work for vocalists, chorus, and instrumentalists based on a poetic narrative of a lyric or dramatic nature. It is generally short and intimate, consisting of several movements including recitatives, arias, and ensemble numbers.

Cantatas, however, might be based on either secular or sacred themes. In the Lutheran tradition, to which the late Baroque composer Johann Sebastian Bach belonged, the sacred cantata was an integral part of the service, related, along with the sermon and prayers that followed it, to the Gospel for the day. Every Sunday of the church year required its own cantata. With extra works for holidays and special occasions, an annual cycle came to about sixty cantatas. Bach composed four or five such cycles, from which only two hundred works have come down to us. By the second quarter of the eighteenth century, the German cantata had absorbed the recitative, aria, and duet of the opera; the pomp of the French operatic overture; and the dynamic instrumental style of the Italians. These elements were unified by the all-embracing presence of the Lutheran chorale.

The Lutheran Chorale

A *chorale* is a hymn tune, specifically one associated with German Protestantism. The chorales served as the battle hymns of the Reformation. Their sturdy contours bear the stamp of an heroic age.

As one of his reforms, Martin Luther required that the congregation participate in the service. To this end, he inaugurated services in German rather than Latin, and allotted an important role to congregational singing. "I wish," he wrote, "to make German psalms for the people, that is to say sacred hymns, so that the word of God may dwell among the people also by means of song."

Luther and his fellow reformers created the first chorales. They adapted a number of tunes from Gregorian chant, others from popular sources and from secular art music. Originally sung in unison, these hymns soon were written in four-part harmony to be sung by the choir. The melody was put in the soprano, where all could hear it and join in singing. In this way, the chorales greatly strengthened the trend to clear-cut melody supported by chords (homophonic texture).

In the elaborate vocal works that appeared in the Protestant church service, the chorale served as a unifying thread. When at the close of an extended work the chorale unfolded in simple four-part harmony, its granitic strength reflected the faith of a nation. One may imagine the impact upon a congregation attuned to its message. The chorale nourished centuries of German music and came to full flower in the art of Bach.

Johann Sebastian Bach

> *"The aim and final reason of all music should be nothing else but the Glory of God and the refreshment of the spirit."*

Johann Sebastian Bach (1685–1750) was heir to the polyphonic art of the past. He is the culminating figure of Baroque music and one of the titans in the history of the art.

Johann Sebastian Bach

His Life

Bach was born at Eisenach in Germany, of a family that had supplied musicians to the churches and town bands of the region for upwards of a century and a half. Left an orphan at the age of ten, he was raised in the town of Ohrdruf by an older brother, an organist who prepared him for the family vocation. From the first he displayed inexhaustible curiosity concerning every aspect of his art. "I had to work hard," he reported in later years, adding with considerably less accuracy, "Anyone who works as hard will get just as far."

His professional career began when he was eighteen with his appointment as organist at a church in Arnstadt. The certificate of appointment admonishes the young man to be true, faithful, and obedient to "our Noble and Most Gracious Count and Master . . . to conduct yourself in all things toward God, High Authority, and your superiors as befits an honorable servant and organist." High Authority soon had cause to reprove the new organist "for having made many curious *variationes* in the chorale and mingled many strange tones in it, and for the fact that the Congregation has been confused by it." The church elders were inquiring shortly after "by what right he recently caused a strange maiden to be invited into the choir loft and let her make music there." The maiden seems to have been his cousin Maria Barbara, whom he married in 1707.

Early years

After a year at a church in Mühlhausen, Bach—at twenty-three—received his first important post: court organist and chamber musician to the Duke of Weimar. His nine years at the ducal court (1708–17) were spent in the service of a ruler whose leaning toward religious music accorded with his own. The Weimar period saw the rise of his fame as an organ virtuoso and the production of many of his most important works for that instrument.

The Weimar period

Disappointed because the Duke had failed to promote him, Bach decided to accept an offer from the Prince of Anhalt-Cöthen. He needed his master's permission to take another post. This the irascible Duke refused to give. The musician stood up for his rights; whereupon, as the court chronicle relates, "on November 6, the former music director and court organist Bach

The Cöthen period

was placed under arrest in the County Judge's place of detention for too stubbornly forcing the issue of his dismissal and finally on December 2 was freed from arrest with notice of his unfavorable discharge."

At Cöthen, Bach served a prince partial to chamber music. In his five years there (1717–23) he produced suites, concertos, sonatas for various instruments, and a wealth of keyboard music; also the six concerti grossi dedicated to the Margrave of Brandenburg. The Cöthen period was saddened by the death of Maria Barbara in 1720. The composer subsequently married Anna Magdalena, a young singer in whom he found a loyal and understanding mate. Of his twenty children—seven of the first marriage and thirteen of the second—half did not survive infancy. One son died in his twenties, another was mentally deficient. Four others became leading composers of the next generation: Wilhelm Friedemann and Carl Philipp Emanuel, sons of Maria Barbara; and Anna Magdalena's sons Johann Christoph and Johann Christian.

The Leipzig years

Bach was thirty-eight when he was appointed to one of the most important posts in Germany, that of Cantor of St. Thomas's in Leipzig. The cantor taught at the choir school of that name, which trained the choristers of the city's principal churches (he was responsible for nonmusical subjects too); and served as music director, composer, choirmaster, and organist of St. Thomas's Church. Several candidates were considered before him, among them the

A contemporary engraving of St. Thomas Church in Leipzig, where Bach worked from 1723 to the end of his life.

then much more famous composer Georg Philipp Telemann (1681–1767), who declined the offer. As one member of the town council reported, "Since the best man could not be obtained, lesser ones would have to be accepted." It was in this spirit that Leipzig received the greatest of her cantors.

Bach's twenty-seven years in Leipzig (1723–50) saw the production of stupendous works. The clue to his inner, spiritual life must be sought in his music. It had no counterpart in an outwardly uneventful existence divided between the cares of a large family, the pleasures of a sober circle of friends, the chores of a busy professional life, and the endless squabbles with a host of officials of town, school, and church who never conceded that they were dealing with anything more than a competent choirmaster. The city fathers were impressed but also disquieted by the dramaticism of his religious music. Besides, like most officials they were out to save money and not averse to lopping off certain rights and fees that Bach felt belonged to him. Despite his complaints, he remained in Leipzig. With the years the Council learned to put up with their obstinate cantor. After all, he was the greatest organist in Germany.

The routine of his life was enlivened by frequent professional journeys, when he was asked to test and inaugurate new organs. His last and most interesting expedition, in 1747, was to the court of Frederick the Great at Potsdam, where his son Carl Philipp Emanuel served as accompanist to the flute-playing monarch. Frederick on the memorable evening announced to his courtiers with some excitement, "Gentlemen, old Bach has arrived." He led the composer through the palace, showing him the new pianos that were beginning to replace the harpsichord. Upon Bach's invitation the King gave him a theme on which he improvised one of his astonishing fugues. After his return to Leipzig he further elaborated on the royal theme, added a trio sonata, and dispatched *The Musical Offering* to "a Monarch whose greatness and power, as in all the sciences of war and peace, so especially in music everyone must admire and revere."

The prodigious labors of a lifetime took their tolls; his eyesight failed. After an apoplectic stroke he was stricken with blindness. He persisted in his final task, the revising of eighteen chorale preludes for the organ. The dying master dictated to a son-in-law the last of these, *Before Thy Throne, My God, I Stand*.

His Music

The artist in Bach was driven to conquer all realms of musical thought. His position in history is that of one who consummated existing forms rather than one who originated new ones. His sheer mastery of the techniques of composition has never been equaled. With this went incomparable profundity of thought and feeling and the capacity to realize to the full all the possibilities inherent in a given musical situation.

Bach epitomized the great religious artist. He considered music to be "a harmonious euphony to the Glory of God." And the glory of God was the central issue of man's existence. His music issued in the first instance from the Lutheran hymn tunes known as chorales. Through these, the most learned

Principal Works

Sacred vocal works, including over 200 church cantatas; 7 motets; Magnificat (1723); *St. John Passion* (1724); *St. Matthew Passion* (1727); *Christmas Oratorio* (1734); Mass in B minor (1749)

Secular vocal works, including over 20 cantatas

Orchestral music, including 4 Orchestral Suites, 6 *Brandenburg Concertos*, concertos for 1 and 2 violins, for 1, 2, 3, and 4 harpsichords

Chamber music, including 6 sonatas and partitas for unaccompanied violin, 6 sonatas for violin and harpsichord, 6 suites for cello, *The Musical Offering* (1747), flute sonatas, viola da gamba sonatas

Keyboard music, including 2 volumes of *Das wohltemperirte Clavier* (The Well-Tempered Clavier, 1722, 1742), 6 *English Suites* (c.1722), 6 *French Suites* (c. 1722), *Chromatic Fantasy and Fugue* (c. 1720), *Italian Concerto* (1735), *Goldberg Variations* (1741–42), *The Art of the Fugue* (c. 1745–50), suites, fugues, capriccios, concertos, inventions, sinfonias

Organ music, including over 150 chorale preludes, toccatas, fantasias, preludes, fugues, passacaglias

composer of the age was united to the living current of popular melody, to become the spokesman of a faith.

Organ music   The prime medium for Bach's talents was the organ. In his own lifetime he was known primarily as a virtuoso organist, only Handel being placed in his class. When complimented on his playing he would answer disarmingly, "There is nothing remarkable about it. All you have to do is hit the right notes at the right time and the instrument plays itself."

Keyboard music   In the field of keyboard music his most important work is *The Well-Tempered Clavier*. The forty-eight preludes and fugues in these two volumes have been called the pianist's Old Testament (the New being Beethoven's sonatas). Of the sonatas for various instruments, a special interest is attached to the six for unaccompanied violin. The master created for the four strings of the violin an intricate polyphonic structure that wrests from the instrument forms and textures of which one would never have suspected it capable. The *Brandenburg Concertos* present various instrumental combinations pitted against one another. The four Suites for Orchestra are appealingly lyrical. (See page 179 for a discussion of the suite.)

Religious music   The two-hundred-odd cantatas that have come down to us form the centerpiece of Bach's religious music. They constitute a personal document of transcendent spirituality; they project his vision of life and death. The drama of the Crucifixion inspired Bach to plenary eloquence. His Passions are epics of the Protestant faith.

B-minor mass   The Mass in B minor occupied Bach for a good part of the Leipzig period.

The first two movements, the Kyrie and Gloria, were written in 1733 and dedicated to Friedrich Augustus, Elector of Saxony. The greatest of Protestant composers turned to a Catholic monarch in the hope of being named composer to the Saxon court, a title that would strengthen him in his squabbles with the Leipzig authorities. The honorary title was eventually granted. To the Kyrie and Gloria originally sent to the Elector "as an insignificant example of that knowledge which I have achieved in music" he later added the other three movements required by Catholic usage, the Credo, Sanctus, and Agnus Dei. The dimensions of this mightiest of Masses make it unfit for liturgical use. It has found a home in the concert hall.

In his final years the master, increasingly withdrawn from the world, fastened his gaze upon the innermost secrets of his art. *The Musical Offering*, in which he elaborated the theme of Frederick the Great, runs the gamut of contrapuntal writing. The work culminates in an astounding six-voice fugue. Bach's last opus, *The Art of the Fugue*, constitutes his final summation of the processes of musical thought. There is symbolism in the fact that he did not live to finish this encyclopedic work.

Last works

Bach: Cantata No. 80, A Mighty Fortress Is Our God

Bach's cantatas are generally laid out in anywhere from five to eight movements, of which the first, last, and usually one middle movement are choral numbers. These are normally fashioned from a chorale tune in one of various ways, ranging from simple hymnlike settings to elaborate choral fugues. Interspersed with the choruses are solo arias and recitatives, some of which may also be based on a chorale melody or its text. Bach's lyricism found its purest expression in his arias. These are elaborate movements with ornate vocal lines and expressive instrumental accompaniments. Many are in the da capo aria form of Italian opera (A-B-A), in which the contrasting middle section is followed by an ornamented repetition of the first part. Others follow less clear-cut patterns. The aria is introduced by a recitative, which may be either *secco* (supported only by an organ or harpsichord) or *accompagnato* (accompanied by the orchestra).

The orchestral accompaniments abound in striking motives that combine contrapuntally with the vocal line to create the proper mood for the text and illustrate its meaning. In many cases the aria is conceived as a kind of duet between the voice and a solo instrument—violin, flute, oboe, or the like—so that a single instrumental color prevails throughout the piece. This accorded with the doctrine of the "single affection." Bach's orchestra included several instruments popular in the eighteenth century that have not survived the twentieth. The *oboe d'amore* was a mezzo-soprano instrument pitched somewhat below the ordinary oboe, with the pear-shaped bell of the English horn. The "amore" (Italian for love) probably referred to its sound, which was sweeter than that of other oboes. It was invented around 1720 and Bach, one of the most progressive musicians of his day, introduced it into his music a few years later. The *taille* was a tenor oboe. The *oboe da caccia* (*caccia* is the Italian word for the chase or hunt) was probably an alto oboe built in the shape of a curved hunting horn, with an expanding

An illustration from **J. G. Walther's** Music Dictionary (*1732*) *showing the disposition of an orchestra in a cantata performance.*

bell or, more frequently, a pear-shaped bell that gave the sound an outdoor quality.

In the cantata *A Mighty Fortress Is Our God*, Bach was treading on hallowed ground. Martin Luther's chorale of that name, for which the founder of Lutheranism probably composed the music as well as the words, is a centerpiece of Protestant hymnology. Luther's words and melody are used in the first, second, fifth, and last movements. The rest of the text is by Bach's favorite librettist, Salomo Franck.

Bach took it for granted that the devout congregation of St. Thomas's Church knew Luther's chorale by heart. A majestic melody of imposing directness, it is today a familiar, Protestant hymn tune. Except for an occasional leap, the melody moves stepwise along the scale. It is presented in nine phrases that parallel the nine lines of each stanza of Luther's poem (the first two phrases are repeated for lines three and four of the poem. See Listening Guide 16).

First movement

The cantata opens with a choral fugue in D, in which each line of text receives its own fugal treatment. That is, the musical phrase is announced by one voice and imitated in turn by the other three. Each phrase is an embellished version of the original chorale tune. The trumpets and drums we hear in this movement were added after the master's death by his son

Wilhelm Friedemann, who strove to enhance the pomp and splendor of the sound.

The second number depicts Christ's struggle against the forces of evil. Strings in unison set up a leaping figure over a running bass. (We say that instruments are playing *in unison* when they are all playing the same notes.) There follows a duet for soprano and bass in D major; the combination of the soprano's variation on the original tune, the florid counterpoint of the bass, and the assured stride of the great chorale makes one of Bach's most vivid musical pictures.

A note of pathos enters the third number, a recitative and *arioso* (a short aria-like passage) for bass in B minor and F-sharp minor. The vocal line unfolds over chromatic harmonies that in Bach's mind were associated with grief; he uses the most unstable chords in his vocabulary. The pace of the accompaniment picks up in the arioso, which is based on a three-measure phrase whose stepwise movement soon gives way to wide leaps. It is immediately repeated a step higher, in a rising sequence that gives a sense of intensification.

The fourth movement is an aria for soprano in B minor whose basic "affection" was an image dear to the visionary in Bach: the soul in rapturous communion with its Maker. The serenely flowing melody, in a pastoral 12/8 meter, is first announced by the instruments playing the continuo, and unwinds in long graceful phrases. The continuo rounds off the piece with the same melody that introduced it.

Fifth is a spanking Allegro in which the orchestra creates the proper framework for the battle between good and evil, with running sixteenth notes played in unison by oboes and violins. Luther's chorale, sung in unison by all the voices in a marchlike 6/8 meter, takes on a quality of unconquerable strength.

There follows a recitative and arioso for tenor in B minor and D major. Characteristic of Baroque vocal writing are the roulades or groups of rapid notes that decorate the vocal line, especially the one that exhorts the faithful to "go forth joyfully to do battle!"

The seventh movement is a duet for alto and tenor, in the course of which we hear the sound of the oboe da caccia. The mood is pastoral, the tonality a bright G major. A canon unfolds in which the violin imitates the oboe a measure later. The two voices follow their own version of the canon, the tenor following the alto a measure behind, while the instruments engage in a more florid canon of their own. Such is Bach's mastery of the art of counterpoint that all these devices, of a complexity that staggers the imagination, unfold with the greatest ease in the service of his expressive purpose.

The final number rounds off the cantata with the chorale sung in D major by full chorus and orchestra. We now hear Luther's melody in Bach's four-part harmonization, each vocal line doubled by instruments. The great melody of the chorale stands revealed in all its simplicity and grandeur.

Bach's spirit animated not only the nineteenth century but, in even more fruitful manner, the twentieth. We see him today not only as a consummate artist who brought new meanings to music, but as one of the giants of Western culture.

Listening Guide 16

💿 📼 2B/2   ◐ I/2/10

BACH: Cantata No. 80, *A Mighty Fortress Is Our God* (*Ein Feste Burg ist unser Gott*)

Date: 1724, Revised for the Feast of the Reformation

Form: Eight movements, for chorus, soloists, and orchestra

Basis: Chorale (hymn) tune by Martin Luther

OVERALL STRUCTURE

Movement	Medium	Use of Chorale Tune
1. Choral fugue	Chorus and orchestra	Embellished chorale
2. Aria, Duet	Soprano and bass	Soprano line only
3. Recitative/arioso	Bass solo	
4. Aria	Soprano solo	
5. Chorale	Chorus and orchestra	Unison chorale
6. Recitative/Arioso	Tenor solo	
7. Aria, Duet	Alto and tenor	
8. Chorale	Chorus and orchestra	Four-part chorale

[handwritten annotations: "= Lutheran's words"; "Solo voice w/ orch accomp"; "Solo voice / orch dissonant"]

Original chorale tune by Luther

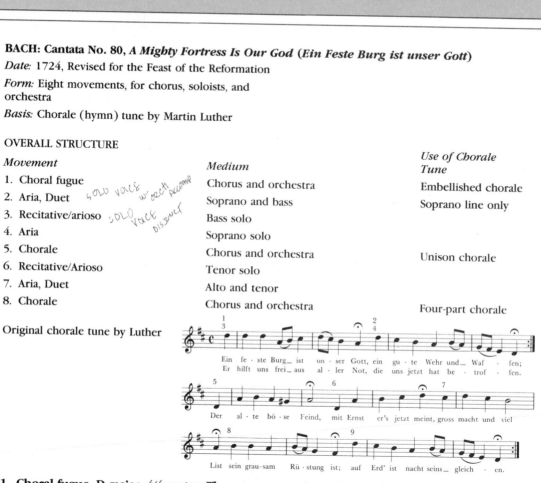

Ein fe - ste Burg_ ist un - ser Gott, ein gu - te Wehr und_ Waf - fen;
Er hilft uns frei_ aus al - ler Not, die uns jetzt hat be - trof - fen.

Der al - te bö - se Feind, mit Ernst er's jetzt meint, gross macht und viel

List sein grau-sam Rü - stung ist; auf Erd' ist nacht seins_ gleich - en.

1. Choral fugue, D major, 4/4 meter. Three trumpets, timpani, two oboes, first and second violins, violas, and continuo (cellos, basses, organ).

First Sung by	Text	Translation
Tenors	Ein feste Burg ist unser Gott	A mighty fortress is our God,
Sopranos	ein' gute Wehr und Waffen;	A good defense and weapon;
Tenors	er hilft uns frei aus aller Not,	He helps free us from all the troubles
Sopranos	die uns jetzt hat betroffen.	That have now befallen us.
Basses	Der alte böse Feind,	Our ever evil foe,
Altos	mit Ernst er's jetzt meint,	In earnest plots against us,
Sopranos	gross Macht und viel List	With great strength and cunning
Tenors	sein grausam Rüstung ist,	He prepares his dreadful plans.
Tenors	auf Erd' ist nicht seins gleichen.	Earth holds none like him.

Opening melody in tenors, with notes of chorale marked

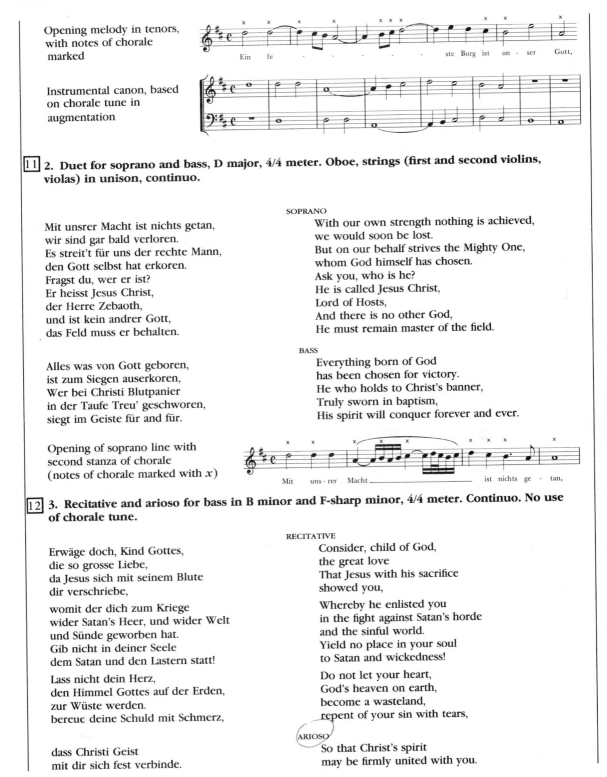

Instrumental canon, based on chorale tune in augmentation

11 **2. Duet for soprano and bass, D major, 4/4 meter. Oboe, strings (first and second violins, violas) in unison, continuo.**

SOPRANO

Mit unsrer Macht ist nichts getan,	With our own strength nothing is achieved,
wir sind gar bald verloren.	we would soon be lost.
Es streit't für uns der rechte Mann,	But on our behalf strives the Mighty One,
den Gott selbst hat erkoren.	whom God himself has chosen.
Fragst du, wer er ist?	Ask you, who is he?
Er heisst Jesus Christ,	He is called Jesus Christ,
der Herre Zebaoth,	Lord of Hosts,
und ist kein andrer Gott,	And there is no other God,
das Feld muss er behalten.	He must remain master of the field.

BASS

Alles was von Gott geboren,	Everything born of God
ist zum Siegen auserkoren,	has been chosen for victory.
Wer bei Christi Blutpanier	He who holds to Christ's banner,
in der Taufe Treu' geschworen,	Truly sworn in baptism,
siegt im Geiste für and für.	His spirit will conquer forever and ever.

Opening of soprano line with second stanza of chorale (notes of chorale marked with *x*)

Mit uns-rer Macht _____ ist nichts ge - tan,

12 **3. Recitative and arioso for bass in B minor and F-sharp minor, 4/4 meter. Continuo. No use of chorale tune.**

RECITATIVE

Erwäge doch, Kind Gottes,	Consider, child of God,
die so grosse Liebe,	the great love
da Jesus sich mit seinem Blute	That Jesus with his sacrifice
dir verschriebe,	showed you,
womit der dich zum Kriege	Whereby he enlisted you
wider Satan's Heer, und wider Welt	in the fight against Satan's horde
und Sünde geworben hat.	and the sinful world.
Gib nicht in deiner Seele	Yield no place in your soul
dem Satan und den Lastern statt!	to Satan and wickedness!
Lass nicht dein Herz,	Do not let your heart,
den Himmel Gottes auf der Erden,	God's heaven on earth,
zur Wüste werden.	become a wasteland,
bereue deine Schuld mit Schmerz,	repent of your sin with tears,

ARIOSO

dass Christi Geist	So that Christ's spirit
mit dir sich fest verbinde.	may be firmly united with you.

Melody of bass arioso, becoming
chromatic and disjunct

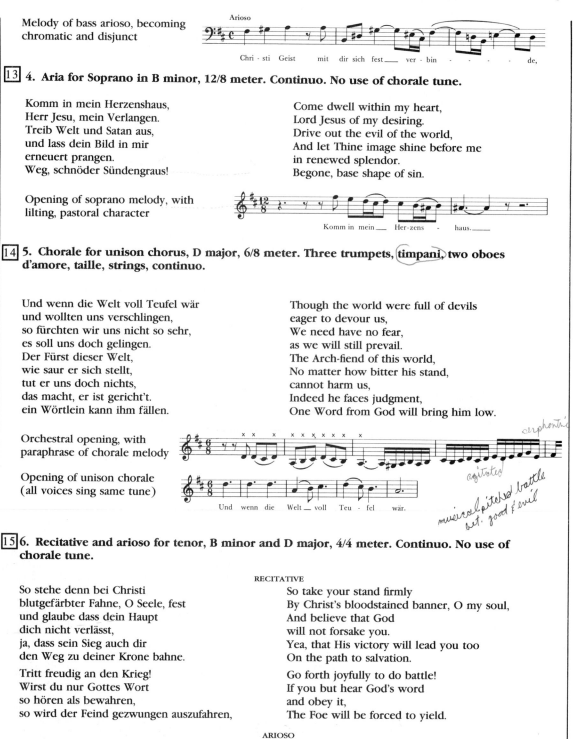

Chri-sti Geist mit dir sich fest___ ver-bin - - - - de,

13 **4. Aria for Soprano in B minor, 12/8 meter. Continuo. No use of chorale tune.**

Komm in mein Herzenshaus,	Come dwell within my heart,
Herr Jesu, mein Verlangen.	Lord Jesus of my desiring.
Treib Welt und Satan aus,	Drive out the evil of the world,
und lass dein Bild in mir	And let Thine image shine before me
erneuert prangen.	in renewed splendor.
Weg, schnöder Sündengraus!	Begone, base shape of sin.

Opening of soprano melody, with
lilting, pastoral character

Komm in mein___ Her-zens - haus.___

14 **5. Chorale for unison chorus, D major, 6/8 meter. Three trumpets, timpani, two oboes d'amore, taille, strings, continuo.**

Und wenn die Welt voll Teufel wär	Though the world were full of devils
und wollten uns verschlingen,	eager to devour us,
so fürchten wir uns nicht so sehr,	We need have no fear,
es soll uns doch gelingen.	as we will still prevail.
Der Fürst dieser Welt,	The Arch-fiend of this world,
wie saur er sich stellt,	No matter how bitter his stand,
tut er uns doch nichts,	cannot harm us,
das macht, er ist gericht't.	Indeed he faces judgment,
ein Wörtlein kann ihm fällen.	One Word from God will bring him low.

Orchestral opening, with
paraphrase of chorale melody

Opening of unison chorale
(all voices sing same tune)

Und wenn die Welt___ voll Teu - fel wär.

15 **6. Recitative and arioso for tenor, B minor and D major, 4/4 meter. Continuo. No use of chorale tune.**

RECITATIVE

So stehe denn bei Christi	So take your stand firmly
blutgefärbter Fahne, O Seele, fest	By Christ's bloodstained banner, O my soul,
und glaube dass dein Haupt	And believe that God
dich nicht verlässt,	will not forsake you.
ja, dass sein Sieg auch dir	Yea, that His victory will lead you too
den Weg zu deiner Krone bahne.	On the path to salvation.
Tritt freudig an den Krieg!	Go forth joyfully to do battle!
Wirst du nur Gottes Wort	If you but hear God's word
so hören als bewahren,	and obey it,
so wird der Feind gezwungen auszufahren,	The Foe will be forced to yield.

ARIOSO

dein Heiland bleibt dein Heil,	Your Savior remains your salvation.
dein Heiland bleibt dein Hort.	Your Savior remains your refuge.

Rapid notes on "Tritt freudig an
die Krieg" (Go forth
joyfully to do battle)

16 **7. Duet for alto and tenor, G major, 3/4 meter. Oboe da caccia, violin, continuo. No use of
chorale tune.**

Wie selig sind doch die,	How blessed are they
die Gott im Munde tragen,	whose words praise God,
doch selger ist das Herz,	yet more blessed is he
das ihn im Glauben trägt.	who bears Him in his heart.
Es bleibet unbesiegt	He remains unvanquished
und kann die Feinde schlagen	and can defeat his foes,
und wird zuletzt gekrönt,	And is finally crowned
wenn es den Tod erlegt.	when Death comes to fetch him.

Opening canon between
oboe da caccia and violin
in triple meter

17 **8. Chorale, D major, 4/4 meter. Full chorus and orchestra.**

Das Wort, sie sollen lassen stahn	Now let the Word of God abide
und kein Dank dazu haben.	without further thought.
Er ist bei uns wohl auf dem Plan	He is firmly on our side
mit seinem Geist und Gaben.	with His spirit and strength.
Nehmen sie uns den Leib,	Though they deprive us of life,
Gut, Ehr, Kind und Weib,	Wealth, honor, child and wife,
lass fahren dahin,	we will not complain,
sie habens kein Gewinn;	It will avail them nothing
das Reich muss uns doch bleiben.	For God's kingdom must prevail.

Opening of hymnlike setting
of chorale, in four voices
(instruments doubling
voices) and continuo

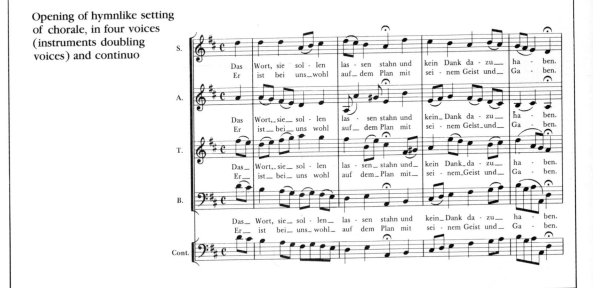

Handel and the Baroque Oratorio

The Oratorio

The *oratorio,* one of the great Baroque vocal forms, descended from the religious play-with-music of the Counter-Reformation. It took its name from the Italian word for a place of prayer. The first oratorios were sacred operas, and were produced as opera. However, toward the middle of the seventeenth century, the oratorio shed the trappings of the stage and developed its own characteristics as a large-scale musical work for solo voices, chorus, and orchestra, based as a rule on a biblical story and imbued with religious feeling. It was performed in a church or hall without scenery, costumes, or acting. The action usually unfolded with the help of a narrator, in a series of recitatives and arias, ensemble numbers such as duets and trios, and choruses. The role of the chorus was often emphasized. Bach's Passions represent a special type of oratorio, focusing on the final events of Christ's life. More typical of the genre are the oratorios of George Frideric Handel, perhaps the consummate master of this vocal form.

George Frideric Handel

"Milord, I should be sorry if I only entertained them. I wished to make them better."

If Bach represents the subjective mysticism of the late Baroque, Handel incarnates its worldly pomp. Born in the same year, the two giants of the age never met. The Cantor of Leipzig had little point of contact with a composer who from the first was cut out for an international career. Handel's natural habitat was the opera house. He was at home amid the intrigues of court life. A magnificent adventurer, he gambled for fame and fortune in a feverish struggle to impose his will upon the world, and dominated the musical life of a nation for a century after his death.

George Frideric Handel

His Life

The early operas

Handel was born in 1685 at Halle in Germany, in what was then the kingdom of Saxony, the son of a prosperous barber-surgeon who did not regard music as a suitable profession for a young man of the middle class. His father's death left him free to follow his bent. After a year at the University of Halle the ambitious youth went to Hamburg, where he gravitated to the opera house and entered the orchestra as a second violinist. He soon absorbed the Italian operatic style that reigned in Hamburg. His first opera, *Almira,* was written when he was twenty, and it created a furor.

162

Handel's thoughts turned to Italy. Only there, he felt, would he master the operatic art. He reached Rome shortly before his twenty-second birthday; the three years he spent in Italy unfolded against a splendid background peopled by music-loving princes and cardinals. His first operas were received enthusiastically, and at the age of twenty-five he was appointed conductor to the Elector of Hanover.

He received the equivalent of fifteen hundred dollars a year at a time when Bach at Weimar was paid eighty. A visit to London in the autumn of 1710 brought him for the first time to the city that was to be his home for well-nigh fifty turbulent years. *Rinaldo*, written in a fortnight, conquered the English public with its fresh, tender melodies. A year later Handel obtained another leave and returned to London, this time for good. With the *Birthday Ode for Queen Anne* and the Te Deum (Hymn of Thanksgiving) for the Peace of Utrecht he entered upon the writing of large-scale works for great public occasions, following in the footsteps of Purcell. Anne rewarded him with a pension, whereupon nothing would make him go back to his Hanoverian master. By an unforeseen turn of events his master came to him. Anne died and the Elector ascended the throne of England as George I. The monarch was vexed with his truant composer; but he loved music more than protocol, and soon restored him to favor.

The move to London

Handel's opportunity came with the founding in 1720 of the Royal Academy of Music. The enterprise, launched for the purpose of presenting Italian opera, was backed by a group of wealthy peers headed by the King. Handel was appointed one of the musical directors and at thirty-five found himself occupying a key position in the artistic life of England. For the next eight years he was active in producing and directing his operas as well as writing them. To this period belongs *Julius Caesar*, from which comes the aria we studied in the chapter on Baroque opera. Handel's crowded life passed at a far remove from the solitude typical of later composers' approach to the creative process. He produced his works in bursts of inspiration that kept him chained to his desk for days at a time. He would turn out an opera in from two to three weeks.

Opera in London

Handel functioned in a theater riddled with the worst features of the star system. When the celebrated soprano Cuzzoni refused to sing an aria as he directed, Handel, a giant of a man, seized her around the waist and threatened to drop her out of a window if she would not obey. The rivalry between Cuzzoni and the great singer Faustina Bordoni culminated in a hair-pulling match on the stage, accompanied by the smashing of scenery and fistfights throughout the house. A rivalry no less fierce developed between Handel and his associate in directing the Academy, the composer Giovanni Bononcini. The supposition that genius resided in one or the other, which brought to the arena of art the psychology of the prize ring, appealed strongly to the fashionable hangers-on of the Royal Academy. Associated with opposing political parties, Bononcini was the protégé of the Tory Duchess of Marlborough, whereupon Handel, whose interest in British politics was—to say the least—limited, became *the* Whig composer. The feud was immortalized in a jingle that made the rounds of the coffee houses.

*Handel's house on Brook
Street, London. Watercolor
signed "L.M."* (Mr. Gerald
Coke)

Some say that Signor Bononcini
Compared to Handel is a ninny;
Whilst others say that to him Handel
Is hardly fit to hold a candle.
Strange that such difference should be
'Twixt Tweedledum and Tweedledee.

The rise of ballad opera

It was amid such distractions that Handel's operas—he produced forty in a period of thirty years—came into being. Some were written too hastily, in others he obviously accommodated himself to the needs of the box office; yet all bear the imprint of genius. Despite his productivity the Royal Academy tottered to its ruin, its treasury depleted by the extravagance of the peers, its morale sapped by mismanagement and dissension. The final blow was administered in 1728 by the sensational success of John Gay's *The Beggar's Opera*. Sung in the vernacular (English, in this case), its tunes related to the experience of the audience, this humorous ballad opera was the answer of middle-class England to the gods and heroes of the aristocratic opera seria. Ironically, even a bit of Handel's *Rinaldo* found its way into the score.

It should have been apparent to the composer-impresario that a new era had dawned; but, refusing to read the omens, Handel invested thousands in the New Royal Academy of Music. Again a succession of operas rolled from his pen, among them *Orlando*, "the boldest of his works." But not even Handel's colossal powers could indefinitely sustain the pace. He was fifty-two when he crashed. "This infernal flesh," as he called it, succumbed to a paralytic stroke. Desperate and grievously ill, he acknowledged defeat and went abroad to recover his health. His enemies gloated: the giant was finished.

They underestimated his powers of recovery. He came back to resume the battle. It took five more expensive failures to make him realize that opera seria in London was finished. At this lowest point in his fortunes there opened, by chance, the road that was to lead him from opera in Italian to oratorio in English, from ruin to immortality. Many years before, in 1720, he had written a masque entitled *Haman and Mordecai*, on a text by Pope adapted from Racine's *Esther*. He subsequently decided to bring this "sacred opera" before the public. When the Bishop of London forbade the representation of biblical characters in a theater, Handel hit upon a way out. "There will be no acting upon the Stage," he announced in the advertisement, "but the house will be fitted up in a decent manner, for the audience." In this way London heard its first Handelian oratorio.

He could not remain indifferent to the advantages of a type of entertainment that dispensed with costly foreign singers and lavish scenery. *Deborah* and *Athalia* had been composed in 1733. The next six years witnessed his final struggle on behalf of opera seria. Then, in 1739, there followed two of his greatest oratorios, *Saul* and *Israel in Egypt*, both composed within the space of a little over three months. Many dark moments still lay ahead. He had to find his way to a new middle-class public. That indomitable will never faltered. *Messiah, Samson, Semele, Joseph and His Brethren, Hercules, Belshazzar*, although they did not conquer at once, were received sufficiently well to encourage him to continue on his course. Finally, with *Judas Maccabaeus*, the tide turned. The British public responded to the imagery of the Old Testament. The suppression of the last Stuart rebellion created the proper atmosphere for Handel's heroic tone. He kept largely to biblical subjects in the final group of oratorios (1748–52)—*Alexander Balus, Joshua, Susanna, Solomon, Jephtha*—an astonishing list for a man in his sixties. With these the master brought his work to a close.

The Handelian oratorio

There remained to face one final enemy—blindness. But even this blow did not reduce him to inactivity. Like Milton and Bach, he dictated his last works, which were mainly revisions of earlier ones. He continued to appear in public, conducting the oratorios and displaying his legendary powers on the organ.

The final years

In 1759, shortly after his seventy-fourth birthday, Handel began his usual oratorio season, conducting ten major works in little over a month to packed houses. *Messiah* closed the series. He collapsed in the theater at the end of the performance and died some days later. The nation he had served for half a century accorded him its highest honor. "Last night about Eight O'clock the remains of the late great Mr. Handel were deposited at the foot of the Duke of Argyll's Monument in Westminster Abbey. . . . There was almost the greatest Concourse of People of all Ranks ever seen upon such, or indeed upon any other Occasion."

His Music

Himself sprung from the middle class, Handel made his career in the land where the middle class first came to power. A vast social change is symbolized by his turning from court opera to oratorio. In so doing, he became one of

Principal Works

Operas (over 40), including *Almira* (1705), *Rinaldo* (1711), *Giulio Cesare* (Julius Caesar, 1724), *Orlando* (1733)

Oratorios, including *Esther* (1718), *Alexander's Feast* (1736), *Israel in Egypt* (1739), *Messiah* (1742), *Samson* (1743), *Belshazzar* (1745), *Judas Maccabaeus* (1747), *Solomon* (1749), *Jephtha* (1752); other sacred vocal music includes *Ode for the Birthday of Queen Anne* (c. 1713), *Acis and Galatea* (masque, 1718), *Ode for St. Cecilia's Day* (1739), Utrecht Te Deum (1713), anthems, Latin church music

Secular vocal music, including solo and duo cantatas; arias

Orchestral music, including the 12 Concerti Grossi, Op. 6 (1739), *Water Music* (1717), *Royal Fireworks Music* (1749); concertos for oboe, organ, horn

Chamber music, including solo and trio sonatas

Keyboard music, including harpsichord suites, fugues, preludes, airs, dances

the architects of the new bourgeois culture and a creator of the modern mass public.

The oratorios

The oratorios of Handel are choral dramas of overpowering vitality and grandeur. Vast murals, they are conceived in epic style. Their soaring arias and dramatic recitatives, stupendous fugues and double choruses consummate the splendor of the Baroque. With the instinct of the born leader he gauged the need of his adopted country, and created in the oratorio an art form steeped in the atmosphere of the Old Testament, ideally suited to the taste of England's middle class.

Handel made the chorus—the people—the center of the drama. Freed from the rapid pace imposed by stage action, he expanded to vast dimensions each scene and emotion. The chorus now touches off the action, now reflects upon it. As in Greek tragedy, it serves both as protagonist and ideal spectator. The characters are drawn larger than life-size. Saul, Joshua, Deborah, Judas Maccabaeus, Samson are archetypes of human nature, creatures of destiny, majestic in defeat as in victory.

Handel's rhythm has the powerful drive of the Baroque. One must hear one of his choruses to realize what momentum can be achieved with a simple 4/4 time. He leaned to diatonic harmony even as Bach's more searching idiom favored the chromatic. His melody, rich in mood and feeling, unfolds in great majestic arches. His thinking is based on massive pillars of sound—the chords—within which the voices interweave. Rooted in the world of the theater, Handel made use of tone color for atmosphere and dramatic expression.

Handel: Messiah

"For the Relief of the Prisoners in the several Gaols, and for the Support of Mercer's Hospital in Stephen's-street and of the Charitable Infirmary on the

Inn's Quay, on Monday the 12th of April, will be performed at the Musick Hall in Fishamble-Street, *Mr. Handel's new Grand Oratorio, called the Messiah* in which the Gentlemen of the Choirs of both Cathedrals will assist, with some Concertos on the Organ, by Mr. Handel." In this fashion Dublin was apprised in the spring of 1742 of the launching of one of the world's most widely loved works.

The music was written down in twenty-four days, Handel working as one possessed. His servant found him, after the completion of the "Hallelujah Chorus," with tears streaming from his eyes. "I did think I did see all Heaven before me, and the Great God Himself!" Upon finishing *Messiah*, the master went on without a pause to *Samson*, the first part of which was ready two weeks later. Truly it was an age of giants.

With its massive choruses, tuneful recitatives, and broadly flowing arias *Messiah* has come to represent the Handelian oratorio in the public mind. Actually it is not typical of the oratorios as a whole. Many are imbued with dramatic conflict, while *Messiah* is cast in a mood of lyric contemplation.

The libretto is a compilation of verses from the Bible. The first part treats of the prophecy of the coming of Christ and His birth; the second of His suffering, death, and the spread of His doctrine; and the third of the redemption of the world through faith. The verses are drawn from various prophets of the Old Testament, especially from Isaiah, from the Psalms, the Evangelists, and Paul.

Handel's original orchestration was extraordinarily modest and clear in texture. He wrote mainly for strings and continuo; oboes and bassoons were employed to strengthen the choral parts. Trumpets and drums were reserved for special numbers.

The Overture—called "Sinfony" in the score—opens the Christmas section with a Grave (slow, solemn) in a somber E minor. The strings project an "affection" of intense pathos. Handel here returned to the *French overture* that had been developed a century earlier by the master of Baroque opera in France, Jean-Baptiste Lully. This form consisted of two sections: a slow introduction in pompous style with dotted rhythms (this is often repeated), followed by an Allegro in imitative style on a short, striking subject. Handel's stately opening section leads into a sturdy fugue in three voices. In Baroque fashion, the brisk rhythm persists without a letup until the brief return to the opening's slow dotted rhythm.

Part I

French overture

The recitative "Comfort ye, my people" underlines the consolatory sense of the words by replacing the E minor of the overture with E major. This tenor arioso unfolds over one of those broadly flowing accompaniments of which Handel knew the secret. At the end, the arioso style is replaced by simple recitative.

There follows the aria "Ev'ry valley shall be exalted," which contains several examples of Baroque word painting. In this and later arias, at the end of the vocal part, there is usually a place for the soloist to improvise a cadenza. Handel broadens the architecture of his arias by orchestral introductions and ritornelli.

The first chorus, "And the glory of the Lord," is a vigorous Allegro in A major with much repetition of text. The vision of divine glory fires Handel's

A performance of Handel's Messiah, *1784. From a contemporary engraving.*

imagination to a spacious choral fresco in which an exciting contrapuntal texture alternates with towering chords. The forward stride of the bass never slackens. Highly dramatic is the grand pause before the end.

One of the highlights of the score is the chorus, "For unto us a Child is born." The theme, taken from one of the master's Italian duets, is of Handelian sturdiness. Powered by the unflagging rhythmic energy of the Baroque, harmonic and contrapuntal elements are fused into a stalwart unity. There is joyously florid expansion on the word "born." Unforgettable is the pomp and glory at "Wonderful Counselor . . ." The words peal forth in earth-shaking jubilation, yet with what economy of means the effect is achieved.

Part II
The climax of the work comes in the second part, the Easter section, with the "Hallelujah Chorus." The musical investiture of the key word (Hallelujah) is one of those strokes of genius that resound through the ages. The drums beat, the trumpets resound. This music sings of a victorious Lord, and His host is an army with banners.

Part III
The third part, the Redemption section, opens with "I know that my Redeemer liveth," a serene expression of faith that is one of the great Handel arias. When the soprano voice ascends stepwise on the statement "For now is Christ risen from the dead," reaching the high point on "risen," there is established unassailably the idea of redemption that is the ultimate message of Handel's oratorio.

Messiah was meant to be an "Entertainment," as its librettist described it. That is, it was intended for the commercial concert hall by a bankrupt impresario-composer eager to recoup his losses. That so exalted a conception could take shape in such circumstances testifies to the nature of the age whence it issued—and to the stature of the master whom Beethoven called "the greatest of us all."

Listening Guide 17

2A/1   1/2/1

HANDEL: *Messiah*

Date: 1742

Genre: Oratorio (English), in three parts

PART ONE: CHRISTMAS SECTION

1 1. Overture

Form: French overture, two parts (slow, fast), first repeated: **A-A-B**

Orchestra: strings, two oboes, and two bassoons

A: Grave, E minor, played twice; stately, dotted rhythms

Opening melody

2 **B:** Allegro moderato, E minor, fugue in three voices, polyphonic

Opening subject introduced by oboes and first violins

PART TWO: EASTER SECTION

3 44. "Hallelujah Chorus," Allegro Four-part chorus (SATB), with homophonic refrain on "Hallelujah" alternating with polyphony

Opening of chorus, with refrain in homophonic style

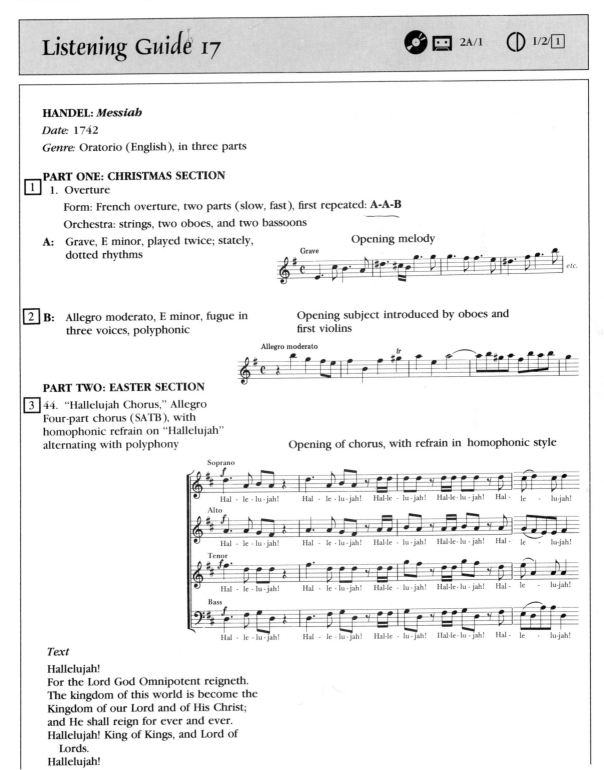

Text

Hallelujah!
For the Lord God Omnipotent reigneth.
The kingdom of this world is become the
Kingdom of our Lord and of His Christ;
and He shall reign for ever and ever.
Hallelujah! King of Kings, and Lord of
   Lords.
Hallelujah!

PART THREE: REDEMPTION SECTION

45. "I know that my Redeemer liveth," soprano aria;
Larghetto; two sections (A, B), with
recurring refrain

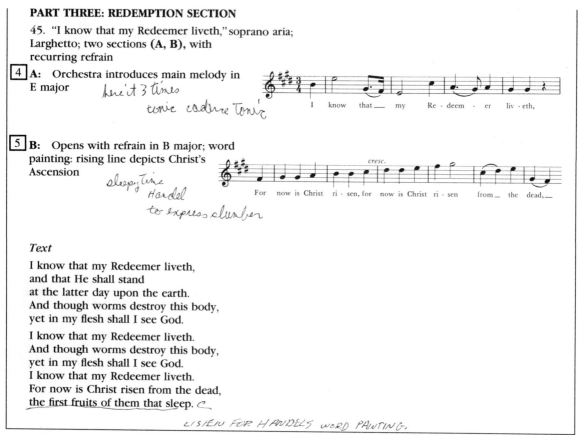

4 A: Orchestra introduces main melody in
E major   *here it 3 times*
tonic cadence tonic

I know that ___ my   Re - deem - er   liv - eth,

5 B: Opens with refrain in B major; word
painting: rising line depicts Christ's
Ascension   *sleepy time*
Handel
to express slumber

cresc.

For now is Christ ri - sen, for now is Christ ri - sen from ___ the dead, ___

Text

I know that my Redeemer liveth,
and that He shall stand
at the latter day upon the earth.
And though worms destroy this body,
yet in my flesh shall I see God.

I know that my Redeemer liveth.
And though worms destroy this body,
yet in my flesh shall I see God.
I know that my Redeemer liveth.
For now is Christ risen from the dead,
the first fruits of them that sleep.

LISTEN FOR HANDEL'S WORD PAINTING.
CONJUNCT ASCENDING VOCAL LINE.

UNIT VIII

■

Instrumental Music of the Baroque

23

The Baroque Concerto — *early 18th century as 1st standardized genre of orchestral music*

The Rise of Instrumental Music

The Baroque was the first period in history in which instrumental music was comparable in importance to vocal. The growing interest in this branch of the art stimulated the development of new instruments and the perfection of old. Playing techniques grew more fluent, and great virtuosos appeared—Bach and Handel at the organ, Corelli and Tartini on the violin.

On the whole, composers still thought in terms of line, so that a string instrument, a woodwind, and a brass might be assigned to play the same line in the counterpoint. Besides, since a movement was based upon a single affection, the same instrumental color might be allowed to prevail throughout, as opposed to the practice we will observe in the Classical and Romantic periods, when color was constantly changed. Much music was still performed by whatever instruments happened to be available at a particular time and place. At the same time, composers—especially in the late Baroque—chose instruments more and more for their color. As their specifications became more precise, the art of orchestration was born.

In recent years, a new drive for authenticity has made the original sounds of eighteenth-century music familiar to us even as it has revived Medieval and Renaissance instruments. Recorders and wooden flutes, restored violins with gut strings, the refractory but mellower-toned valveless brass instruments are heard again, and the Baroque orchestra has recovered not only its scale, but also its transparent tone quality. The gentler voices of the authentic instruments balance more comfortably in counterpoint. Naturally, they are not completely suitable for our largest concert halls, but they have proved especially effective on recordings, and many versions are now available of Bach's *Brandenburg Concertos,* for example, played on eighteenth-century instruments.

Concerto Types

No less important than the principle of unity in Baroque music was that of contrast. This found expression in the *concerto*, an instrumental form based on the opposition between two dissimilar masses of sound. (The Latin verb *concertare* means "to contend with," "to view with." The *concertante* style is based on this principle.)

Solo concerto

Baroque composers produced two types of concerto: the solo concerto and the concerto grosso. That for solo instrument and an accompanying instrumental group became an important medium for experimentation in sonority and instrumental virtuosity. The violin concerto was the most important variety of solo concerto. It usually consisted of three movements, in the sequence allegro-adagio-allegro, and prepared the way for the violin concerto of the Classic and Romantic periods. The *concerto grosso* was

Concerto grosso

based on the opposition between a small group of instruments and a larger group.

The concerto embodied what one writer of the time called "the fire and fury of the Italian style." Of the many Italian masters of the concerto, Vivaldi was the greatest and most prolific.

Antonio Vivaldi: His Life and Music

"Above all, he was possessed by music." —MARC PINCHERLE

For many years interest in the Baroque centered on Bach and Handel to such an extent that other masters were neglected. None suffered more in this regard than Antonio Vivaldi (1678–1741), who has been rediscovered in the twentieth century.

Antonio Vivaldi

Antonio Vivaldi was born in Venice, the son of a violinist. He was ordained in the Church in his twenties, and came to be known as "the red priest," an epithet which in that distant age referred to nothing more than the color of his hair. For the greater part of his career Vivaldi was *maestro de' concerti* at the most important of the four music schools for which Venice was famous. These were attached to charitable institutions of a religious nature that the city maintained for the upbringing of orphaned girls, and they played a vital role in the musical life of the Venetians. Much of Vivaldi's output was written for the concerts at the Conservatorio del'Ospedale della Pietà, which attracted visitors from all over Europe. Judging by the music that Vivaldi wrote for them, the young ladies were expert performers.

In addition to his position in Venice, Vivaldi spent time in other Italian cities, especially in conjunction with his work as an opera composer. The end of his life is mysterious; a contemporary Venetian account states that "the Abbé Don Antonio Vivaldi, greatly esteemed for his compositions and concertos, in his day made more than fifty thousand ducats, but as a result of excessive extravagance he died poor in Vienna." He was buried in a pauper's grave, and to save expense his funeral was given "only a small peal of bells."

In Concert in a Girl's School, **Francesco Guardi** (*1712–93*) *depicts a Venetian entertainment featuring an orchestra of young ladies* (*upper left*). *The school might well have been the one at which Vivaldi was music master.* (Munich, Alte Pinakothek; Photo Joachim Blauel-Artothek)

Principal Works

Orchestral music, over 230 violin concertos including *Le quattro stagioni* (The Four Seasons, Op. 8, nos. 1–4, c. 1725); other solo concertos (bassoon, cello, oboe, flute, recorder), double concertos, ensemble concertos, sinfonias

Chamber music, including sonatas for violin, cello, flute; trio sonatas

Vocal music, including oratorios (*Juditha triumphans*, 1716), mass movements (Gloria), Magnificat, psalms, hymns, motets; secular vocal music, including solo cantatas and operas

Vivaldi was active during a period that was of crucial importance in the exploration of the new instrumental style—a style in which the instruments were liberated from their earlier bondage to vocal music. His novel use of rapid scale passages, extended arpeggios, and contrasting registers contributed decisively to the development of violin style and technique. In his love of brilliant color, Vivaldi was a true son of Venice. He also played a leading part in the history of the concerto, exploiting with vast effectiveness the contrast in sonority between large and small groups of players.

As the list on page 173 indicates, Vivaldi was amazingly prolific, even for that prolific era. Much of his music is still unknown. Only with the publication of his complete works—a project begun in 1947 and still not finished—will it be possible to evaluate fully the achievement of this strikingly original musician.

Vivaldi: "Spring" from The Four Seasons

Perhaps Vivaldi's best-known work is *The Four Seasons*, a group of four violin concertos. We have spoken of the fondness for word painting that shows itself in Baroque vocal works, where the music is meant to portray the action described by the words. In *The Four Seasons*, Vivaldi applies this principle to instrumental music. Each of the concertos is accompanied by a poem, presumably written by the composer, describing the joys of that particular season. Each line of the poem is printed above a certain passage in the score; the music at that point mirrors, as graphically as possible, the action described.

Vivaldi finds ways to depict the pleasures of the hunt and the baying of dogs in "Autumn," or teeth chattering from the cold and people slipping on the ice in "Winter." When they fall down, the music descends; when they pick themselves up and proceed on their way, it moves upward. Yet although the pictorial image influences the shape of the musical motive, once stated, the motive is treated in a purely musical way. In short, it becomes music.

First movement   Of the four concertos, "Spring" (*La Primavera*) is the least graphic; it evokes mood and atmosphere rather than specific actions. The solo violin is accompanied by an orchestra consisting of first and second violins, violas, and cellos, with the basso continuo realized (improvised from the figured bass) on harpsichord or organ. The poem is a sonnet whose first two quatrains are distributed throughout the first movement, an Allegro in E major. (See Listening Guide 18 for the text.)

Both poem and music evoke the birds' joyous welcome to spring and the gentle murmur of streams, followed by thunder and lightning. The image of birdcalls takes shape in staccato notes, trills, and running scales; the storm is portrayed by shuddering repeated notes answered by quickly ascending scales. Throughout, an orchestral refrain (ritornello) returns again and again in alternation with the solo section. Ultimately, "the little birds return to their melodious warbling" and we return to the home key of E. A florid passage for the soloist leads to the final ritornello.

Second movement   In the second movement, a Largo in 3/4, Vivaldi evokes an image of the goatherd who sleeps "in a pleasant field of flowers" with his faithful dog by his side. Over the bass line of the violas, which sound an ostinato rhythm of an eighth note followed by a quarter on the second beat of each measure, he wrote, "The dog who barks." This dog clearly has a sense of rhythm. The solo violin unfolds a tender, melancholy melody in the noblest Baroque style.

Third movement   The Finale, an Allegro, is marked "Rustic Dance." Nymphs and shepherds dance in the fields as the music suggests the drone sound of bagpipes. Ritornelli and solo passages alternate in bringing the work to a happy conclusion.

Vivaldi's art flowered from a noble tradition. His dynamic conceptions pointed to the future. How strange that he had to wait until the middle of the twentieth century to come into his own.

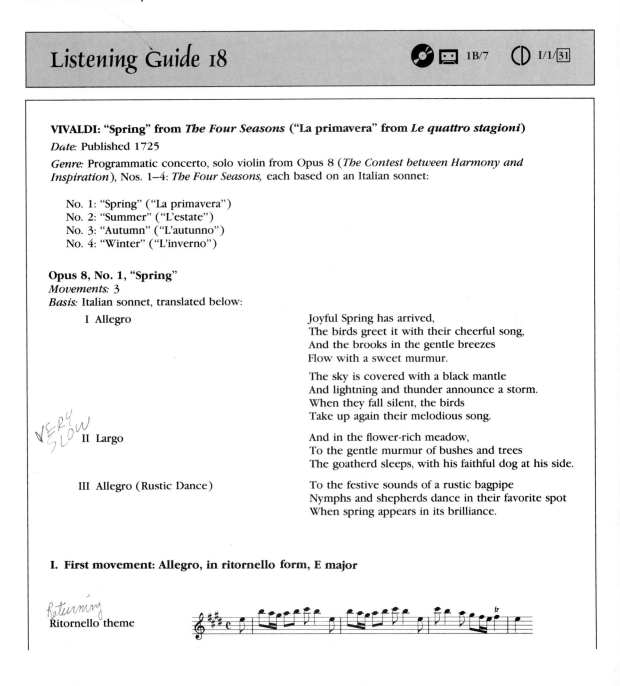

Listening Guide 18

⊙ ▭ 1B/7   ◖ I/1/31

VIVALDI: "Spring" from *The Four Seasons* ("La primavera" from *Le quattro stagioni*)

Date: Published 1725

Genre: Programmatic concerto, solo violin from Opus 8 (*The Contest between Harmony and Inspiration*), Nos. 1–4: *The Four Seasons,* each based on an Italian sonnet:

No. 1: "Spring" ("La primavera")
No. 2: "Summer" ("L'estate")
No. 3: "Autumn" ("L'autunno")
No. 4: "Winter" ("L'inverno")

Opus 8, No. 1, "Spring"
Movements: 3
Basis: Italian sonnet, translated below:

I Allegro	Joyful Spring has arrived, The birds greet it with their cheerful song, And the brooks in the gentle breezes Flow with a sweet murmur.
	The sky is covered with a black mantle And lightning and thunder announce a storm. When they fall silent, the birds Take up again their melodious song.
II Largo *[VERY SLOW]*	And in the flower-rich meadow, To the gentle murmur of bushes and trees The goatherd sleeps, with his faithful dog at his side.
III Allegro (Rustic Dance)	To the festive sounds of a rustic bagpipe Nymphs and shepherds dance in their favorite spot When spring appears in its brilliance.

I. First movement: Allegro, in ritornello form, E major

[Returning]
Ritornello theme

	Time	*Program*	*Description*
31	0:00	Spring	Ritornello 1, in E major
	0:31	Birds	Solo 1
			Birdlike trills and high running scales
32	1:04	Spring	Ritornello 2
	1:11	Murmuring brooks	Solo 2
			Whispering figures like water flowing
	1:33	Spring	Ritornello 3
	1:41	Thunder and lightning	Solo 3, modulates
			Repeated notes, fast ascending scales
33	2:06	Spring	Ritornello 4, in relative minor (C sharp)
	2:14	Birds	Solo 4
	2:30		Trills and repeated notes
			Ritornello 5, returns to E major
	2:41		Solo 5
			Florid running passage
34	2:54		Ritornello 6, closing tutti

35 **II. Second movement: Largo, 3/4 meter, C-sharp minor. Orchestration reduced; for solo violin, two violins, and viola**

Opening of movement, with solo violin, slow and melodious, representing the sleeping goatherd ("Il capraro che dorme"); viola, with insistent rhythm, representing the dog barking ("Il cane che grida")

36 **III. Third movement: Danza Pastorale (Rustic dance), Allegro, E major. Lilting, compound meter, in ritornello form**

Opening of movement, with dance tune (ritornello) in upper strings; sustained notes (like bagpipe drone) in lower strings

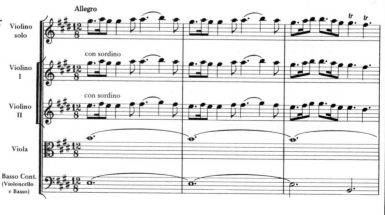

Bach: Brandenburg Concerto *No. 2*

During his six years as court composer at Cöthen, Bach served a prince who favored chamber music. This, accordingly, was a period richly productive of chamber works. In 1717 Bach had occasion to play before a royal visitor, Margrave Christian of Brandenburg, son of the Great Elector. The prince was so impressed that he asked the composer to write some works for his orchestra. Several years later Bach sent him the six pieces that have become known as the *Brandenburg Concertos*, with a dedication in flowery French that begged His Royal Highness "not to judge their imperfection by the strictness of that fine and delicate taste which all the world knows You have for musical works; but rather to take into consideration the profound respect and the most humble obedience to which they are meant to bear witness." It is not known how the Margrave responded to the concertos that have immortalized his name.

In these pieces Bach captured the spirit of the concerto grosso, in which two groups vie with each other in sonorous flights of fancy. The second of the set, in F major, has long been a favorite, probably because of the brilliant trumpet part. The solo group—the *concertino*—consists of trumpet, flute, oboe, and violin, all of them instruments in the high register. The accompanying group—the *tutti* or *ripieno* (Italian for full)—includes first and second violins, violas, and double basses. The basso continuo is played by cello and harpsichord.

The opening movement of *Brandenburg Concerto* No. 2 is a sturdy Allegro, bright and assertive. The broad, simple outlines of its architecture depend on well-defined areas of light and shade—the alternation of the tutti and the solo group. The virile tone of the opening derives from the disposition of the parts. Flute, oboe, and violin play the recurring or ripieno theme in unison with the first violin of the accompanying group, while the trumpet outlines the tonic triad. The contrapuntal lines unfold in a continuous, seamless texture, powered by a rhythmic drive that never flags from beginning to end. The movement modulates freely from the home key of F major to the neighboring major and minor keys. When its energies have been fully expended, it returns to F for a vigorous cadence.

The slow movement, an Andante in D minor, is a soulful colloquy among solo violin, oboe, and flute. Each in turn enters with the theme. This moving Andante is informed with all the noble pathos of the Baroque. Third and last is an Allegro assai (very fast), in which trumpet, oboe, violin, and flute enter successively with the jaunty subject of a four-voiced fugue. After much interchange in the nature of a lively conversation among four equals, the movement reaches its destination with the final pronouncement of the subject by the trumpet.

First movement

 S1B/4

S1/24

Second and third movements

24

Other Baroque
Instrumental Forms

Sonata, Passacaglia, and Overture

Chamber sonata

Church sonata

The sonata was widely cultivated throughout the Baroque. In its early stages, it consisted of either a movement in several sections, or several movements that contrasted in tempo and texture. A distinction was drawn between the *sonata da camera* or *chamber sonata*, which was usually a suite of stylized dances intended for performance in the home, and the *sonata da chiesa* or *church sonata*. This was more serious in tone and more contrapuntal in texture. Its four movements, arranged in the sequence slow-fast-slow-fast, were supposed to make little use of dance rhythms. In practice the two types somewhat overlapped. Many church sonatas ended with one or more dancelike movements, while many chamber sonatas opened with an impressive introductory movement in the church-sonata style.

Trio Sonata

Sonatas were written for one to six or eight instruments. The favorite combination for such works was two violins and continuo. Because of the three printed staffs in the music, such compositions came to be known as *trio sonatas*. Yet the title is misleading, because it refers to the number of parts rather than to the number of players. As we saw, the basso continuo needed two performers—a cellist (or bass viol player or bassoonist) to play the bass line, and a harpsichordist or organist to realize the harmonies indicated by the figures. Thus it takes four players to perform a trio sonata.

Passacaglia

Chaconne

One of the most majestic forms of Baroque music is the *passacaglia*, which utilizes the principle of the ground bass. A melody is introduced alone in the bass, usually four or eight bars long, in a stately triple meter. The theme is repeated again and again, serving as the foundation for a set of continuous variations that exploit all the resources of polyphonic art. A related type is the *chaconne*, in which the variations are based not on a melody but on a succession of harmonies repeated over and over. Passacaglia and chaconne exemplify the Baroque urge toward abundant variation and embellishment of a musical idea, and that desire to make "much out of little" which is the essence of the creative act.

Overtures, French and Italian

The operatic overture was an important genre of large-scale orchestral music. Two types were popular during this period. The French overture, of which we heard an example in Handel's *Messiah*, generally followed the pattern slow-fast. Its fast section was in the loosely fugal style known as fugato. The *Italian overture* consisted of three sections: fast-slow-fast. The opening section was not in fugal style; the middle section was lyrical; there followed a vivacious, dancelike finale. This pattern, expanded into three separate movements, was later adopted by the concerto grosso and the solo concerto. In addition, we shall see that the opera overture of the Baroque was one of the ancestors of the symphony of later eras.

The Baroque Suite

The suite of the Baroque era consisted of a series of varied dance movements, all in the same key. It was a natural outgrowth of earlier dance traditions that paired dances of contrasting tempos and character (a typical pair from the Renaissance was pavane-galliard, the first slow and stately, the second quick and lively). The suite presented an international galaxy of dance types: the German *allemande*, in duple meter at a moderate tempo; the French *courante*, in triple meter at a moderate tempo; the Spanish *sarabande*, a stately dance in triple meter; and the English *jig* (gigue), in a lively 6/8 or 6/4. These had begun as popular dances, but by the time of the late Baroque they had left the ballroom far behind and become abstract types of art music. Between the slow sarabande and fast gigue might be inserted a variety of optional numbers of a graceful song or dance type such as the minuet, the *gavotte*, the lively *bourrée* or the *passepied*. These dances of peasant origin introduced a refreshing earthiness into their more formal surroundings. The suite sometimes also incorporated the operatic overture, as well as a variety of other brief pieces with attractive titles.

The standard form of the pieces in the suite was a highly developed binary structure (**A-B**) consisting of two sections of approximately equal length, each being rounded off by a cadence. The first part usually moved from the home key (tonic) to a contrasting key (dominant), while the B part made the corresponding move back. Both parts used closely related or even identical material. The form was made apparent to the ear by the modulation and the full stop at the end of the first part. As a rule, each part was repeated, giving an **A-A-B-B** structure.

The essential element of the suite was dance rhythm, with its imagery of physical movement. It offered composers an elegant entertainment based on popular rhythms that could be transmuted into art.

Handel: Water Music

The two suites of Handel, the *Water Music* and the *Royal Fireworks Music*, are as memorable a contribution to the genre as are the four orchestral suites of Bach. The *Water Music* was surely played (but probably not first composed) for a royal party on the Thames in London on July 17, 1717. Two days later the *Daily Courant* reported: "On Wednesday Evening, at about 8, the King took Water at Whitehall in an open Barge, and went up the River towards Chelsea. Many other Barges with Persons of Quality attended, and so great a Number of Boats, that the whole River in a manner was cover'd; a City Company's Barge was employ'd for the Musick, wherein were 50 Instruments of all sorts, who play'd all the Way from Lambeth (while the Barges drove with the Tide without Rowing, as far as Chelsea) the finest Symphonies, compos'd express for this Occasion, by Mr. Handel; which his Majesty liked so well, that he caus'd it to be plaid over three times in going and returning."

The twenty-two numbers of the *Water Music* were performed without continuo instruments, as it was not possible to bring a harpsichord aboard

In this imaginary depiction of Handel's Water Music, *the composer is seen perched on the edge of the front barge with King George I on his left; in the second barge, musicians seem to be playing Handel's work.* (The Bettmann Archive)

the barge. The conditions of an outdoor performance, in which the music would have to contend with the breeze on the river, bird calls, and similar noises, impelled Handel to a music that unfolded in sweeping lines, marked by lively rhythms and catchy melodies. This accorded well with the broad, virile style Handel had made his own.

The *Water Music* opens with a French overture and includes a variety of dance numbers, among them minuets in graceful 3/4 time, bourrées in fast 4/4, and hornpipes in lively triple meter. Occasional echo effects exemplify the terraced dynamics of the Baroque. In these varied numbers Handel combined the Italian string style of Corelli with the rhythmic vivacity of the French and the songfulness of Purcell to produce an amalgam imprinted with his own robust personality and perfectly suited to the taste of an English audience ruled by a German king.

S1A/4

S1/8

The work is divided into three suites, of which the first, in F major, is the most popular. We will study Nos. 3, 5, and 6 of this suite.

No. 3

The third number is an **A-B-A** form. Handel underlines the contrast between the **A** and **B** sections in a number of ways that show how a composer can create contrast:

1. Key. The **A** section is in F major, the **B** part in the relative minor, D minor.
2. Orchestration. The **A** section pits two horns against strings and double reeds; the **B** section omits the horns.
3. Texture. The **A** section is homophonic, with one instrumental group

answering the other; the **B** section is in a contrapuntal style, with one voice imitating the other.

4. Meter. The **A** section is in 3/4 time, the **B** section in 4/4.
5. Tempo. The **A** section is a vigorous Allegro, the **B** section a more relaxed Andante.
6. Mood. The **A** section is bright and assertive, the **B** section quietly lyrical.
7. Melody. The **A** section is based on repeated-note figures, the **B** section avoids them.

No. 5 is an Air, which to the Baroque meant an expressive, singing melody. *No. 5*
This little piece in binary form exemplifies the easy tunefulness that endeared Handel to the London public.

No. 6, a Minuet and Trio, opens with a duet between first and second *No. 6*
horn, in which the first presents a fanfare outlining the F major chord and the second imitates it two measures later. The fanfare then becomes the theme played by the entire group. Section **A** is a two-part dance form, as is Section **B**. The contrast between them is underlined by a change of mode, Section **A** being in F major while Section **B** is in F minor. The **A** section is repeated without the introductory fanfare.

More than two and a half centuries after it was written, Handel's *Water Music* is still a favorite with the public. One has only to hear a few measures of it to understand why.

25

Baroque Keyboard Music

Keyboard Instruments

The three important keyboard instruments of the Baroque were the organ, the harpsichord, and the clavichord. The Baroque organ had a pure, trans- *Organ*
parent tone. Its stops let the voices stand out clearly so that the ear could follow the counterpoint. The colors of the various stops constrasted sharply; but although the tone was penetrating, it was not harsh because the wind pressure was low. Through the use of two keyboards it was possible to achieve terraced dynamics, or even levels of soft and loud.

The *harpsichord* too was capable of producing different sonorities be- *Harpsichord*
cause of its two keyboards. The instrument differed from the piano in two important respects. First, its strings were plucked by quills instead of being struck with hammers. The resultant tone was bright and silvery, but it could not be sustained like the tone of the piano. There had to be continual movement in the sound: trills, embellishments of all kinds, chords broken up into arpeggio patterns, and the like. Second, the pressure of the fingers

The Compenius organ at Frederiksborg Castle, Denmark, dates from the early seventeenth century.

on the keys varied the tone only slightly on the harpsichord, whereas the piano has a wide range of dynamics. The harpsichord was therefore incapable of the crescendo and decrescendo that we will see as an essential feature of Classic-Romantic music. But it was an ideal medium for contrapuntal music, for it brought out the inner voices with luminous clarity. It was immensely popular during the Baroque as a solo instrument. In addition, the harpsichord was indispensable in the realization of the thorough-bass, and was the mainstay of the ensemble in chamber music and at the opera house.

Clavichord

The *clavichord* was a favorite instrument for the home. Its sound is produced by the action of a hammer in contact with a string as long as a note is depressed. This allowed for some unique expressive effects not available on the harpsichord. However, by the end of the eighteenth century both clavichord and harpsichord had been supplanted in public favor by the piano. The word *clavier* was used in Germany as the term for keyboard instruments, including harpsichord, clavichord, and organ. Whether a certain piece was intended for one rather than the other must often be gathered from the style rather than the title.

Keyboard Forms

The keyboard forms of the Baroque fell into two categories: free forms based on harmony, with a strong element of improvisation, such as the prelude,

A two-manual harpsichord by Jan Couchet of Antwerp, made in about 1650. (Metropolitan Museum of Art, The Crosby Brown Collection of Musical Instruments, 1889. Photograph by Sheldon Collins)

toccata, fantasia, and chorale prelude; and stricter forms based on counterpoint, such as the fugue and the invention. Bach's keyboard music shows his mastery of both types.

A *prelude* is a fairly short piece based on the continuous expansion of a melodic or rhythmic figure. The prelude originated in improvisation on the lute and keyboard instruments. In the late Baroque it served to introduce a group of dance pieces or a fugue. Since its texture was for the most part homophonic, it made an effective contrast with the contrapuntal texture of the fugue that followed it.

Prelude

The Baroque *toccata* (from the Italian *toccare*, "to touch," referring to the keys) was a composition for organ or harpsichord that exploited the resources of the keyboard in a glittering display of chords, arpeggios, and scale passages. It was free and rhapsodic in form, marked by passages in a harmonic style alternating with fugal sections. In the hands of the north German organists the toccata became a virtuoso piece of monumental proportions, either as an independent work or as companion piece to a fugue.

Toccata

A *fantasia* was, as its name implies, a fantasy piece of large dimensions in the style of a rapturous improvisation, marked by a truly Baroque wealth of detail, freedom of expression, and virtuosic brilliance. Like the toccata, it often served as introductory piece to a fugue. Bach's magnificant Fantasia and Fugue in G minor for organ juxtaposes great chordal masses of sound with passages of melodious counterpoint.

Fantasia

This German clavichord by Christian Kintzing, dated 1763, offered an amazing range of tonal variety. (Metropolitan Museum of Art)

Chorale prelude

Church organists, in announcing the chorale to be sung by the congregation, fell into the practice of embellishing the traditional melodies. There grew up a body of instrumental art—*chorale prelude* and *chorale variations*—in which organ virtuosity of the highest level was imbued with the spirit of inspired improvisation.

Invention

An *invention*—the word signifies an ingenious idea—is a short piece for the keyboard in contrapuntal style. The title is known to pianists from Bach's collection of fifteen inventions in two voices and a like number in three. His purpose in the inventions, he wrote, was "upright instruction wherein the lovers of the clavier, and especially those desirous of learning, are shown a clear way not alone to have good *inventiones* but to develop the same well."

The Fugue and Its Devices

From the art and science of counterpoint issued one of the most exciting types of Baroque music, the fugue. The name is derived from *fuga*, the Latin for "flight," implying a flight of fancy, or possibly the flight of the theme from one voice to the other. A *fugue* is a contrapuntal composition in which a theme or subject of strongly marked character pervades the entire fabric, entering now in one voice, now in another. The fugue consequently is based on the principle of imitation. The subject constitutes the unifying idea, the focal point of interest in the contrapuntal web.

Fugal voices

A fugue may be written for a group of instruments; for a solo instrument such as organ, harpsichord, or even violin; for several solo voices or for full chorus. Whether the fugue is vocal or instrumental, the several lines are called voices, which indicates the origin of the type. In vocal and orchestral fugues each line is articulated by another performer or group of performers. In fugues for keyboard instruments the ten fingers—on the organ, the feet as well—manage the complex interweaving of the voices.

The *subject* or theme is stated alone at the outset in one of the voices—soprano, alto, tenor, or bass. It is then imitated in another voice—this is the *answer*—while the first continues with a *countersubject* or countertheme. Depending on the number of voices in the fugue, the subject will then appear in a third voice and be answered in the fourth, with the other voices usually weaving a free contrapuntal texture against these. (If a fugue is in three voices there is, naturally, no second answer.) When the theme has been presented in each voice once, the first section of the fugue, the Exposition, is at an end. The Exposition may be restated, in which case the voices will enter in a different order. From then on the fugue alternates between sections that feature the entrance of the subject and less weighty interludes known as *episodes*, which serve as areas of relaxation.

Subject

Answer
Countersubject

Episodes

The subject of the fugue is stated in the home key, the tonic. The answer is given in a related key, that of the dominant, which lies five tones above the tonic. There may be modulation to foreign keys in the course of the fugue, which builds up tension against the return home. The Baroque fugue thus embodied the contrast between home and contrasting keys that was one of the basic principles of the new major-minor system.

Key relationships

As the fugue unfolds, there must be not only a sustaining of interest but the sense of mounting urgency that is proper to an extended art work. Each recurrence of the theme reveals new facets of its nature. The composer manipulates the subject as pure musical material in the same way that the sculptor molds his clay. Especially effective is *stretto*, in which the theme is imitated in close succession. The effect is one of voices crowding upon each other, creating a heightening of tension that brings the fugue to its climax. The final statement of the subject, generally in a decisive manner, brings the fugue to an end.

Stretto

The fugue is based on a single affection expressed by the subject that dominates the piece. Episodes and transitional passages are usually woven from its motives or from those of the countersubject. There results a remarkable unity of texture and atmosphere. Another factor for unity is the unfaltering rhythmic beat. The only section of the fugue that follows a set order is the Exposition. Once that is done with, the further course of the fugue is bound only by the composer's fancy. Caprice, exuberance, surprise—all receive free play within the supple framework of this form.

Fugal technique reached unsurpassable heights at the hands of Bach and Handel. In the Classic-Romantic period the fugue was somewhat neglected, although we will observe that fugal writing became an integral part of the composer's technique. Passages in fugal style occur in many a symphony, quartet, and sonata, often in the Development section. Such an imitative passage inserted in a nonfugal piece is known as a *fugato*. It affords the composer the excitement of fugal writing without the responsibilities.

Fugato

The fugue, then, is a rather free form based on imitative counterpoint, that combined the composer's technical skill with imagination, feeling, and exuberant ornamentation. There resulted a type of musical art that may well be accounted one of the supreme achievements of the Baroque.

Bach: Prelude and Fugue in C minor, from The Well-Tempered Clavier, Book I

In Chapter 19 we described *The Well-Tempered Clavier* as the celebrated work that circumnavigated the tonal globe, a journey made possible by the new system of equal temperament for tuning keyboard instruments. It was this system, you will remember, that made it possible to play in all the keys. The first volume, completed in 1722 during the years Bach worked in Cöthen, contains a prelude and fugue in each of the twelve major and twelve minor keys. The second volume, also containing twenty-four preludes and fugues, appeared twenty years later.

The Prelude and Fugue in C minor is No. 2 in the first volume of *The Well-Tempered Clavier*. The Prelude is a "perpetual-motion" type of piece based on running sixteenth notes in both hands that never let up, outlining a single chord in each measure. We associate emotion in music with a beautiful melody. This Prelude shows how deeply moving a series of harmonies can be. The music modulates from C minor to the relative major, E-flat major, then returns to the home key. Notable is the utter unity of mood, the "single affection" that gives this piece its unflagging momentum.

The fugue, in three voices, is based on one of those short, incisive themes for which Bach had a special affinity. First presented by the alto voice in the home key of C minor, it is answered by the soprano in G minor, key of the dominant. There are two countersubjects that serve to shed new light on the subject, whose successive entries are separated by episodes woven out of the basic idea. (See Listening Guide 19.) As in the Prelude, the music is pervaded by a total unity of mood powered by unflagging rhythm. It is this quality that gives the fugue its relentless drive and inevitability. When the piece finally reaches the C-major chord at the end, we are left with the sense of a journey completed, an action happily consummated.

Listening Guide 19

2B/1   I/2/6

BACH: Prelude and Fugue in C minor, from *The Well-Tempered Clavier*, Book I

Date: 1722

6 0:00 **Prelude**: Free, improvisatory-style piece
Establishes key of C minor
Begins Allegro with fast repeated sixteenth-note pattern through various harmonies
Ends with cadenza-like passage

Fugue: 3-voiced (SAB), with two-measure subject
Features many episodes with fragments of subject

Subject

Code for line graph:

Subject/Answer:
Countersubject 1:
Countersubject 2:
Episode:

7 1:45 EXPOSITION:

episode 1   episode 2

S
A
B

Measure	1	3	5	7	9
Key	c	G		c	

episode 3   episode 4

8 2:15 S
A
B

Measure	11	13	15	17	20
Key	E♭	(relative major)	G		c

episode 5   cadential extension

9 2:49 S
A   free
B   free

Measure	23	26	29
Key		c	c

Domenico Scarlatti

Domenico Scarlatti: Sonata in D, K. 491

Born in the same year as Bach and Handel, Domenico Scarlatti (1685–1757) was one of the most original spirits in the history of music. He left his native Italy in his middle thirties to take a post at the court of Portugal. When his pupil, the Infanta of Portugal, married the heir to the Spanish throne, the composer followed her to Madrid, where he spent the last twenty-eight years of his life.

Scarlatti's genius was subtly attuned to the harpsichord. His art was rooted in Baroque tradition. At the same time it looked forward to the Classical style to come. Scarlatti's fame rests upon his over five hundred sonatas, of which only thirty were published by the composer himself under the unassuming title of *Esercizi per gravicembalo*—exercises or diversions for harpsichord. The Scarlattian sonata is a one-movement binary form. As in the binary dance movements discussed earlier, the first part modulates from home to related key, the second marks the return. At the end of the second part, he presents the final section of the first part transposed back to the tonic. His sonatas thus bear the seed of the sonata-allegro form that was about to come into being. The brilliant runs and scale passages, crossing of hands, contrasts of low and high register, double notes, repeated notes, trills, and arpeggio figures, managed with inimitable grace and ingenuity, established the composer as one of the creators of the true keyboard idiom.

S1B/5

S1/27

Scarlatti's Sonata in D, K. 491, is an ingratiating example of his style. (The K. followed by a numeral refers to the chronological list of Scarlatti's works that was compiled by the harpsichordist Ralph Kirkpatrick in order to make it easier to identify a particular piece.) This one exemplifies the binary structure basic to Scarlatti's sonatas. He indicated that the two parts were to be repeated, but in performance nowadays they seldom are. (After all, the movement from the home key to the dominant key is much more familiar in our time than it was in his.)

The Sonata in D is based on two themes and a closing passage that display all the grace and charm of the masters' writing. In the first part the music moves from the home key to the contrasting key of A major, which lies a fifth above. The second part traces the movement back. Trills, rapid scales, and arpeggios that demand nimble fingers add excitement and brilliance to the sound. In every measure this delightful piece proclaims its true domain: the Rococo.

In the past few decades Domenico Scarlatti has come into his own. He stands revealed as an artist of boundless imagination whose fastidious taste led him to a superb sense of style.

To the Age of Enlightenment

The Rococo and the Age of Sensibility

As famous as Louis XIV's "I am the State" is his successor's "After me, the deluge." In the reigns of the two Louis, which lasted for more than a hundred years, the old regime passed from high noon to twilight. The gilded minority at the top of the social pyramid exchanged the goal of power for that of pleasure. Art moved from the monumentality of the Baroque to the caprice of the Rococo.

The Rococo

The word derives from the French *rocaille*, a shell, suggesting the decorative scroll-and-shell-work characteristic of the style. The Rococo took shape as a reaction from the grandiose gesture of the Baroque. Its elegant prettiness is familiar to us from the Dresden china shepherdesses, the gilt mirrors, and graceful curves of the Louis XV style. Out of the disintegrating world of the Baroque came an art of subtle allure centered on the salon and the boudoir—a miniature, ornate art aimed at the enchantment of the senses and predicated upon the attractive doctrine that the first law is to enjoy oneself.

The greatest painter of the French Rococo was Jean Antoine Watteau (1685–1721). To the dream-world of love and gallantry that furnished the themes of his art, Watteau brought the insights and the techniques of his Flemish heritage. His counterpart in music was François Couperin (1668–1733), who—although he spoke the language of the Rococo—was rooted in the illustrious past. He was one of a family of distinguished musicians and the greatest of the French school of clavecinists. (The harpsichord is known in French as *clavecin*.) His art crystallizes the miniature world of the Rococo and the attributes of Gallic genius—wit, refinement, clarity, and precision. Its goal is to charm, to delight, to entertain.

François Couperin

The desire to systematize all knowledge that characterized the Enlightenment made itself felt also on the musical scene. Jean-Philippe Rameau (1683–1764), the foremost French composer of the eighteenth century, tried to establish a rational foundation for the harmonic practice of his time.

Jean-Philippe Rameau

189

Jean Antoine Watteau (*1684–1721*), *with his dream-world of love and gallantry, was the artistic counterpart of François Couperin.* La Gamme d'Amour (*The Gamut of Love*). (The National Gallery, London)

His theoretical works, such as the *Treatise on Harmony* (1722), set forth concepts that furnished the point of departure for modern musical theory.

Rameau's operas have not maintained themselves on the stage. He is remembered today for his instrumental compositions. Listening to his charming miniatures, one understands why the greatest composer of modern France, Claude Debussy, remarked: "French music aims first of all to give pleasure. Couperin, Rameau—these are true Frenchmen!"

The Rococo witnessed as profound a change in taste as has ever occurred in the history of music. In turning to a polished entertainment music, composers embraced a new ideal of beauty. Elaborate polyphonic texture yielded to a single melody line with a simple chordal accompaniment, much the same way that the contrapuntal complexities of late Renaissance music gave way to the early Baroque ideal of monody. It is surely true that history repeats itself. This age desired its music above all to be simple and not devoid of natural feeling. Thus was born the "sensitive" style of the *Empfindsamkeit* and the Age of Sensibility—an age that saw the first stirrings of that responsiveness to emotion that was to come to full flower with Romanticism.

Empfindsamkeit

The gallant style reached its apex in Germany in the mid-eighteenth century, a period that saw the activity of Bach's four composer sons—Wilhelm Friedemann, Carl Philipp Emanuel, Johann Christoph, and Johann Christian. They and their contemporaries consummated that revolution in taste which caused Bach's music to be neglected after his death.

The gallant style

This musical revolution saw the expansion of the major instrumental genres of the sonata, the new directions of the concerto, and the enrichment of symphonic styles with elements drawn from the operatic aria and overture, from the tunes and rhythms of Italian comic opera. To the charm of the gallant style they added the emotional urgency of a world in ferment. From all this was born a new thing—the idiom of the Classical sonata cycle, which we will discuss in a later chapter. The new art form was the collective achievement of several generations of musicians who were active in Italy, France, and Germany throughout the pre-Classical period (c. 1740–75).

C.P.E. Bach

One of the outstanding figures of the late Rococo was Carl Philipp Emanuel Bach (1714–88), the second son of Johann Sebastian. He deepened the emotional content of the abstract instrumental forms and played a decisive role in the creation of the modern piano idiom. His dramatic sonata style exerted a powerful influence upon the masters of the Classical era—Haydn, Mozart, and Beethoven. And his theoretical treatise, the *Essay on the True Art of Playing Keyboard Instruments* (1753–62), throws much light on the musical practice of the mid-eighteenth century.

Johann Christian Bach

Of major importance too was Johann Christian Bach (1735–82), the youngest son of the great Cantor. Johann Christian at nineteen went to Italy, where he converted to Catholicism and to the Italian ideal of suavely beautiful melody. Known as the "London Bach"—a good part of his artistic career unfolded in that city—he was a prolific composer of operas in the Italian manner and exerted a strong influence on Mozart.

Quantz: Flute Concerto in G

Among the international composers of this era was Johann Joachim Quantz (1697–1773), court composer and flute instructor to Frederick the Great. Through his treatise *On Playing the Flute* (1752), which was as much a compendium of applied aesthetics as an instruction manual for mastering the instrument, Quantz exerted considerable influence on the musical thinking of his age.

Although musical nationalism did not become a potent force until the nineteenth century, musicians in the eighteenth century were already beginning to be aware of the problem of national styles. The dominant trend of the time was toward an international style, a view that Quantz advocated. "Every one must agree," he wrote, "that a style blended and mixed together from the good elements of both French and Italian styles will certainly be more universal and more pleasing."

At the same time he was a spokesman for the Rococo and the Age of Sensibility. His generation understood that Bach and Handel had carried polyphonic art as far as it could go, and that the time had come to explore

In The Flute Concert *by the nineteenth century painter,* **Adolph von Menzel,** *Frederick the Great is seen playing the flute to the accompaniment of a small chamber orchestra with Carl Philipp Emanuel Bach at the harpsichord.* (Nationalgalerie, Berlin)

simpler paths. In their enthusiasm they naturally underestimated the achievement of their forebears. "Earlier composers," Quantz declared, "occupied themselves too much with musical artifices, and pushed their use so far that they almost neglected the most essential part of music, that which is intended to move and please."

S1B/6

S1/29

Quantz's trio sonatas and concertos show the simple, clear-cut forms of the new age, with light-hearted Rococo-style melodies in the fast movements and "sensitive," more German-style melodies in the slow movements. His most popular work today is the Flute Concerto in G major, whose first movement foreshadows the concerto form of the upcoming Classical era, but in a simpler version. It is based on a single theme that is first heard in the home key of G, then in D major, thus establishing the tonic-dominant relationship that was to become basic to the form. Quantz embellishes his theme with the birdlike trills and rapid scales, which come so naturally to the flute. This buoyant Allegro is followed by an arioso marked Mesto (sad) in G minor that reflects the pre-romantic melancholy of the Age of Sensibility, and a spirited finale marked Allegro vivace in the home key of G major.

The decades that comprised the aftermath of the Baroque witnessed the birth of that whole new manner of thinking which came to fruition in the Classical symphony, concerto, and sonata. The composers who led music through this change are assured of an honorable place in the history of their art.

The Changing Opera

The vast social changes taking shape in the eighteenth century were bound to be reflected in the lyric theater. Baroque opera, geared to an era of absolute monarchy, had no place in the changing scene. Increasingly its pretensions were satirized by men of letters all over Europe. The defeat of opera seria in London by *The Beggar's Opera* in 1728 had its counterpart in Paris a quarter of a century later. In 1752 a troupe of Italian singers presented in the French capital a soon-to-be-famous comic opera *La serva padrona* (The Servant Mistress) by Giovanni Battista Pergolesi (1710–36). Immediately there ensued the "War of the Buffoons" between those who favored the traditional French court opera and those who saw in the Italian comic opera, called *opera buffa,* a new realistic art. The former camp was headed by the King, Madame de Pompadour, and the aristocracy; the latter by the Queen and the Encyclopedists—Rousseau, d'Alembert, Diderot—who hailed the comic form for its expressive melody and natural sentiment, and because it had thrown off what they regarded as the outmoded "fetters of counterpoint." In the larger sense, the War of the Buffoons was a contest between the rising bourgeois art and a dying aristocratic art.

"War of the Buffoons"

Rousseau put his theories into practice in his opéra comique, *Le devin du village* (The Village Soothsayer, 1752). The versatile philosopher-humanist was a limited composer. But his little operatic piece, with its fresh melodies, its pastoral background, and its fund of feeling, gave impetus to the trend toward simplicity and naturalness, qualities that were to take a central place in the new middle-class art.

Gluck: Orpheus and Eurydice

It was a German-born composer trained in Italy and writing for the Imperial Court in Vienna who brought lyric tragedy into harmony with the thought and feeling of a new era. Christoph Willibald Gluck (1714–87) found his way to a style that met the new need for dramatic truth and expressiveness. "I have striven to restrict music to its true office of serving poetry by means of expression and by following the situations of the story, without interrupting the action or stifling it with a useless superfluity of ornaments." How well he realized the aesthetic needs of the new age: "Simplicity, truth, and naturalness are the great principles of beauty in all forms of art."

Christoph Willibald Gluck

This conviction was embodied in his works written for the Imperial theatre at Vienna, notably *Orpheus and Eurydice* (1762) and *Alceste* (1767), both of which were collaborations with the poet Raniero Calzibigi. There followed the lyric dramas with which he conquered the Paris Opéra, the most important being the two based on Homeric legend—*Iphigenia in Aulos,* (1774) and *Iphigenia in Taurus* (1778). In these works he successfully fused a number of elements: the monumental choral scenes and dances that had always been a feature of French lyric tragedy, the animated ensembles of comic opera, the verve and dynamism of the new instrumental style in Italy and Germany, and the broadly arching vocal line that was part of Europe's

Orpheus, sung by Marilyn Horne, is shown leading Eurydice out of the nether regions in Act III of the Metropolitan Opera production of Gluck's masterpiece. (Copyright © Beth Bergman, 1983)

operatic heritage. The result was a music drama whose dramatic truth and expressiveness profoundly affected the course of operatic history.

There can be no better introduction to Gluck's art than to listen, with libretto, to the complete recording of *Orpheus*. In the original version of the opera the male role was sung by a castrato. When Gluck revised the work for the Paris production he altered the role of Orpheus from contralto to tenor (a change much more in line with modern conceptions of music drama). A half century later his great admirer Hector Berlioz prepared a third version. Eager that his friend, the famous Pauline Viardot, sing Orpheus, Berlioz restored the role to the contralto register, but retained other innovations of Gluck's Paris version. It is in this version that the opera is often performed today.

Overwhelmed with grief at the death of his beloved wife, Orpheus arouses the pity of the god Amore, who permits him to descend to Hades to find his beloved and lead her back to the land of the living. The god of love imposes only one condition; Orpheus must not turn to look at her until he has recrossed the river Styx.

S1B/7

S1/33

In Act III Orpheus leads his wife out of the nether regions. He urges her on, eager to recross the Styx, but she, increasingly agitated by the fact that he has not looked at her, becomes convinced that he no longer loves her. Orpheus naturally cannot disclose the reason for his strange behavior. Finally, unable to bear her reproaches, he impetuously turns around, whereupon the god's decree comes to pass: she dies, and Orpheus sings "J'ai perdu mon Euridice" (I have lost my Eurydice), a lament that became one of the famous arias of the eighteenth century. Orpheus's outpouring of grief moves not only the audience but also the god Amor, who restores Eurydice to life and a happy ending.

Gluck rose above the miniature world of the Rococo by combining several

A Comparison of Baroque and Classical Styles

Baroque (c. 1600–1750)	*Classical* (c. 1750–1825)
Monteverdi, Purcell, Scarlatti, Corelli, Vivaldi, Handel, Bach	Haydn, Mozart, Beethoven, Schubert
Continuous melody with wide leaps, chromatic tones for emotional effect	Symmetrical melody in balanced phrases and cadences; tuneful, diatonic, with narrow leaps
Single rhythm dominates; steady energetic pulse; freer in vocal music	Dance rhythms favored; regularly recurring accents
Chromatic harmony for expressive effect; major-minor system established with brief excursions to other keys	Diatonic harmony favored; tonic-dominant relationship expanded, becomes basis for large-scale form
Polyphonic texture predominates, linear-horizontal dimension	Homophonic textures; chordal-vertical dimension
Instrumental genres: Fugue, concerto grosso, trio sonata, suite, chaconne, prelude, passacaglia	Symphony, solo concerto, solo sonata, string quartet, and other chamber music ensembles
Opera, oratorio, cantata	Opera, Mass, solo song
Binary form predominant	Ternary form predominant; sonata-allegro form developed
	Secular music dominant
Religious music dominant	Continuously changing dynamics through crescendo and decrescendo
Terraced (contrasting) dynamics	Changing tone colors from one section to the next
Continuous tone color throughout one movement	Orchestra standardized into four choirs. Introduction of clarinet, trombone; rise of piano to prominence
String orchestra, with added woodwinds; organ and harpsichord in use	Improvisation largely limited to cadenzas in concertos
Improvisation expected; harmonies realized from figured bass	Emotional balance and restraint
Single affection; emotional exuberance and theatrical gesture	

units into one well-rounded section. What sustains his work, besides its fund of melody, is his sense of dramatic characterization and that sure intuition for what will be effective in the theater that makes the true opera composer.

PART FIVE

More Materials
of Form

Henri Matisse (*1869–1954*) The Cowboy *from* Jazz. (Paris, Teriade, 1947. Collection, The Museum of Modern Art, New York. Gift of the artist.)

UNIT IX

■

Focus on Form

26

The Development of Musical Themes

"I alter some things, eliminate and try again until I am satisfied. Then begins the mental working out of this material in its breadth, its narrowness, its height and depth."—LUDWIG VAN BEEETHOVEN

Thinking, whether in words or tones, demands continuity and sequence. Every thought must flow out of the one before and lead logically into the next. In this way is created a sense of steady progression toward a goal. If we were to join the beginning of one sentence to the end of another, it would not make any more sense than if we united the first phrase of one melody and the second of another. On the contrary, an impression of cause and effect, of natural flow and continuity, must prevade the whole musical fabric.

We saw that when a musical idea is used as a building block in the construction of a composition, it is called a *theme*. We also saw that a musical expansion of this theme is known as *thematic development* and that, conversely, a theme can be fragmented by dividing it into its constituent motives, a *motive* being its smallest melodic unit. A motive can grow, as a germ cell multiplies, into an expansive melody, or it can be treated in *sequence*, that is, repeated at a higher or lower level.

Thematic development is generally too complex a technique to appear to advantage in short lyric pieces, songs, or dances. In such compositions a simple contrast between sections and a modest expansion within each section supplies the necessary continuity. By the same token, thematic development finds its proper frame in the large forms of music. To those forms it imparts an epic-dramatic quality, along with the clarity, coherence, and logic that are the indispensable attributes of this most advanced type of musical thinking.

An example from the well-known opening of Beethoven's Symphony No. 5, which we shall study later, illustrates the thematic development of a four-note motive that is repeated in sequence one step lower, and that grows into a theme.

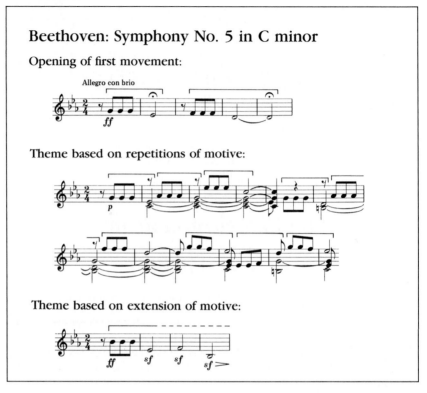

Beethoven: Symphony No. 5 in C minor

Opening of first movement:

Theme based on repetitions of motive:

Theme based on extension of motive:

27

The Sonata Cycle

"The history of the sonata is the history of an attempt to cope with one of the most singular problems ever presented to the mind of man, and its solution is one of the most successful achievements of his artistic instincts."—HUBERT PARRY

All music has form, some of it simple, some of it complex. In some cases the form is dictated by considerations outside music, such as a text or an accompanying program, as we observed in *The Four Seasons* by Vivaldi. We have already discussed two of the simplest forms: two-part or binary **(A-B)** and three-part or ternary **(A-B-A).**

Form is especially important in *absolute* or *pure* music, where there is no story or text to hold the music together. Here the story is the music itself; its shape, consequently, is of primary concern for both the composer and the listener. Large-scale works have an overall form that shapes the relations of the several movements and the various tempos in which those are cast. In addition, each movement has an internal form that binds its different sections into one artistic whole.

The term *sonata* comes from the Italian *suonare*, "to sound," indicating a piece to be sounded on instruments, as distinct from *cantata*, a piece to be sung. A sonata (as the Classical masters Haydn, Mozart, and their successors understood the term) is an instrumental work consisting of a series of three or four contrasting movements. For the purposes of this study, we refer to such a compositional structure as a *sonata cycle*. The name sonata is used specifically for a chamber piece intended for one or two instruments. However, other types of instrumental works are also examples of the sonata cycle. If more than two players are involved, the work is called, as the case may be, a trio, quartet, quintet, sextet, septet, octet, or nonet. A sonata cycle for solo instrument and orchestra is called a concerto; a sonata cycle for the whole orchestra, a symphony. The sonata, clearly, accounts for a large part of the instrumental music we hear.

The First Movement

The most highly organized and characteristic movement of those making up the sonata cycle is the opening one, which is usually in a fast tempo such as Allegro. This is written in what is variously known as *first-movement form*, *sonata-allegro form*, or simply, *sonata form* (We will use the term *sonata-allegro* to describe this form.) A movement in sonata-allegro form is based on two assumptions. The first is that a musical movement takes on direction and goal if, after establishing itself in the home key, it modulates to another area and ultimately returns to the home key. We may therefore regard sonata form as a drama between two contrasting key areas. The "plot"—that is, the action and the tension—derives from this contrast, thus providing the framework for a statement, a departure, and a return.

Sonata-allegro form

Second is the assumption that a theme may have its latent energies released through the development of its constitutent motives. Most useful for this purpose is a brief, incisive theme, one that has momentum and tension, and that promises more than it reveals at first sight. The themes will be stated or "exposed" in the first section; developed in the second, and restated or "recapitulated" in the third.

The opening section of sonata-allegro form, the *Exposition* or Statement, generally sets forth the two opposing keys and their respective themes. (A theme may consist of several related ideas, in which case we speak of it as a *theme group*.) The first theme and its expansion establish the home key or tonic. A transition or *bridge* leads into a contrasting key; in other words, the function of the bridge is to modulate. The second theme and its expansion establish the contrasting key. A closing section or *codetta* rounds off the Exposition in the contasting key. In the Classical sonata form, the Exposition

Exposition (Statement)

is repeated. The adventurous quality of the Exposition derives in no small measure from the fact that it brings us from the home key to the contrasting key.

Development

The *Development* wanders further through a series of foreign keys, building up tension against the inevitable return home. Temperature is kept at fever pitch through frequent modulations, resulting in a sense of breathless activity and excitement.

At the same time the composer proceeds to reveal the potentialities of the themes by breaking them into their component motives, recombining them into fresh patterns, and releasing their latent energies, their explosive force. Conflict and action are the essence of drama. In the Development, the conflict erupts, the action reaches maximum intensity. The protagonists of the drama are hurled one against another; their worlds collide. Emotion is transformed into motion. The theme may be modified or varied, expanded or contracted, combined with other motives or with new material. If the sonata is for orchestra—that is, a symphony—a fragment of the theme may be presented by one group of instruments and imitated by another. Now it appears in the upper register, now deep in the bass. Each measure seems to grow out of the preceding by an inescapable law of cause and effect. Each adds to the drive and the momentum.

Recapitulation
(Restatement)

When the developmental surge has run its course, the tension abates. A bridge passage leads back to the tonic. The beginning of the third section, the *Recapitulation* or Restatement, is in a sense the psychological climax of sonata form, just as the peak of many a journey is the return home. The first theme appears as we first heard it, in the tonic, proclaiming the victory of unity over variety, of continuity over change.

The Recapitulation follows the general path of the Exposition, restating the first and second themes more or less in their original form, but with the wealth of additional meaning that these have taken on in the course of their wanderings. Most important of all, in the Recapitulation the opposing elements are reconciled, the home key emerges triumphant. For this reason, the third section differs in one important detail from the Exposition: the composer now remains in the tonic for the second theme, which was originally in a contrasting key. In other words, although the second theme and its expansion unfold in substantially the same way as before, we now hear this material transposed into the home key. There follows the final pro-

Coda

nouncement, the *coda*, in the home key. This is fashioned from material previously heard in the codetta, to which new matter is sometimes added. The coda rounds off the movement with a vigorous final cadence.

The procedure just described is summed up in the chart at the top of the next page. The main features outlined there are present in one shape or another in innumerable sonata-allegro movements, yet no two are exactly alike in their disposition of the material. Each constitutes a unique solution of the problem in terms of character, mood, and relation of forces, for the true artist—and it is the artist's work alone that endures—shapes the form according to the specific content; so that what looks on paper like a fixed plan becomes, when transformed into living sound, a supple framework for infinite variety.

Summary of Sonata-Allegro Form

Exposition (*or Statement*)	*Development*	*Recapitulation* (*or Restatement*)
[Slow introduction—optional] First theme (or theme group) and its expansion in tonic ↓	Builds up tension against the return to tonic by	First theme (or theme group) and its expansion in tonic ↓
Bridge—modulates to a contrasting key ↓	1. Frequent modulation to foreign keys	Bridge (rarely modulates) ↓
Second theme (or theme group) and its expansion in contrasting key ↓	2. Fragmentation and manipulation of themes and motives ↓	Second theme (or theme group) and its expansion transposed to tonic ↓
Codetta. Cadence in contrasting key (Exposition repeated)	Transition back to tonic	Coda. Cadence in tonic

A dramatist creates opposing personalities as the chief characters of a work. So, too, the composer achieves a vivid contrast between the musical ideas that form the basis of a movement. The opposition between two themes may be underlined in a number of ways: through a contrast in dynamics—loud against soft; in register—low against high; in timbre—strings against winds, one instrumental combination against another; in rhythm and tempo—an animated pattern against one that is sustained; in tone production—legato against staccato; in type of melody—an active melody line with wide range and leaps against one that moves quietly along the scale; in type of harmony—consonance against dissonance, diatonic chords against chromatic; in type of accompaniment—quietly moving chords against extended arpeggios. Not all of these may appear in a given work. One contrast, however, is required, being the basis of the form: the contrast of key. And the opposition may be further intensified by putting one theme in the major and the other in minor.

The Second Movement

The second is most often the slow movement of the sonata cycle, offering a contrast to the Allegro that preceded it. If so, it will be a songful movement that gives the composer an opportunity to present the purely lyrical aspect of the musical art. It is often an Andante or Adagio in **A-B-A** form or a theme and variations.

We saw that repetition is a basic element of musical structure. This being

Theme and Variations

so, composers devised ways of varying an idea when they restated it. Variation is an important procedure that is to be found in every species of music. But there is one type of piece in which it constitutes the ruling principle—the *theme and variations*, which frequently serves as the second movement of a sonata or symphony. The theme is stated at the outset, so that the audience will know the basic idea that serves as the point of departure. The melody may be of the composer's invention or may be borrowed from another, as in the case of Britten's *Variations and Fugue on a Theme by Purcell* (see page 50). The theme is apt to be a small two- or three-part form, simple in character to allow room for elaboration. There follows a series of variations in which certain features of the original idea are retained while others are altered. Each variation sets forth the idea with some new modification—one might say in a new disguise—through which the listener glimpses something of the original theme.

To the process of variation the composer brings all the techniques of musical embellishment. To begin with, the melody may be varied by the addition or omission of notes or by shifting the melody to another key.

Melodic variation

Melodic variation is a favorite procedure in a jazz group, where the solo player embellishes a popular tune with a series of arabesques.

Harmonic variation

In harmonic variation the chords that accompany a melody are replaced by others, perhaps shifting from major to minor mode. Or the melody may be entirely omitted, the variation being based on the harmonic skeleton. The type of accompaniment may be changed or the melody may be shifted to a lower register with new harmonies sounding above it.

Rhythmic variation

So too the rhythm, meter, and tempo may be varied, with interesting changes in the nature of the tune. This may take on the guise of a waltz, a polka, a minuet, a march. The texture may be enriched by interweaving the melody with new themes. Or the original theme may itself become an accompaniment for a new melody. By combining these methods with changes in dynamics and tone color, the expressive content of the theme may be changed, so that it is presented now as a funeral march, now as a serenade, folk dance, caprice, or boat song. This type of character variation was especially in favor in the nineteenth century.

The theme and variations challenges the composer's inventiveness and makes possible a high degree of unity in diversity. One therefore understands why variation form has attracted composers for more than three hundred years, both as an independent piece and as one of the movements of a sonata.

The Third Movement

Minuet and trio

In the Classical symphony, the third movement almost invariably is a *minuet and trio*. The minuet originated in the French court in the mid-seventeenth century; its stately 3/4 time embodied the ideal of grace of an aristocratic age. In the eighteenth century the minuet was taken over into the sonata, where it served as the third movement.

Since dance music lends itself to symmetrical construction, we often find in a minuet a clear-cut structure based on phrases of four and eight measures. (All the same, we shall see that the minuets of Haydn and Mozart reveal an abundance of nonsymmetrical phrases.) In tempo the minuet ranges from stateliness to a lively pace and whimsical character. As a matter of fact, certain of Haydn's minuets are closer in spirit to the village green than to the palace ballroom.

The custom prevailed of presenting two dances as a group, the first being repeated at the end of the second (**A-B-A**). The one in the middle was originally arranged for only three instruments; hence the name trio, which persisted even after the customary setting for three was abandoned. The trio as a rule is lighter in texture and quieter of gait. Frequently woodwind tone figures prominently in this section, creating an out-of-doors atmosphere that lends it a special charm. At the end of the trio we find da capo or D.C. ("from the beginning"), signifying that the first section is to be played over again. Minuet-trio-minuet is a symmetrical three-part structure in which each part in turn is a small two-part or three-part form.

This structure is elaborated through repetition of the subsections, a procedure that the composer indicates with a *repeat sign* (:‖:). However, when the minuet returns after the trio the repeat signs are customarily ignored. A codetta may round off each section.

Minuet (A)	Trio (B)	Minuet (A)
‖:a:‖:b-a:‖	‖:c:‖:d-c:‖	a - b - a
or	or	or
‖:a:‖:b:‖	‖:c:‖:d:‖	a - b

In the nineteenth-century symphony the minuet will be displaced by the *scherzo*. This is generally the third movement, occasionally the second, and is usually in 3/4 time. Like the minuet, it is a three-part form (scherzo-trio-scherzo), the first section being repeated after the middle part. But it differs from the minuet in its faster pace and vigorous rhythm. The scherzo—Italian for "jest'—is marked by abrupt changes of mood ranging from the humorous or the whimsical to the mysterious and even demonic. In the hands of Beethoven the scherzo became a movement of great rhythmic drive.

Scherzo

The Fourth Movement

The Classical sonata often ended with a *rondo*, which is a lively movement suffused with the spirit of the dance. Its distinguishing characteristic is the recurrence of a central idea—the rondo theme—in alternation with contrasting elements. Its symmetrical sections create a balanced architecture that is satisfying aesthetically and easy to grasp. In its simplest form, **A-B-A-B-A,** the rondo is an extension of three-part form. If there are two contrasting themes the sections may follow an **A-B-A-C-A** or similar pattern.

The true rondo as developed by the Classical masters was more ambitious in scope. Typical was the formation **A-B-A-C-A-B-A.** Because the theme is to be heard over and over again it must be catchy and relaxing. The rondo figured in eighteenth- and nineteenth-century music both as an independent

Rondo

piece and as a member of the sonata cycle. While eighteenth-century composers were fond of using a rondo for the fourth movement, we will observe that symphonists in the nineteenth century as often as not cast the finale in the shape of a sonata-allegro whose spacious dimensions served to balance the first movement.

The Sonata Cycle as a Whole

The four-movement cycle of the Classical masters, as found in their symphonies, sonatas, string quartets, and various types of chamber music, became the vehicle for their most important instrumental music. The following outline sums up the common practice of the Classic-Romantic era. It will be helpful provided you remember that it is no more than a general scheme and does not necessarily apply to all works of this kind.

The Classical masters of the sonata thought of the four movements of the cycle as self-contained entities connected by key. First, third, and fourth movements were in the home key, with the second movement in a contrasting key. The nineteenth century sought a more obvious connection between movements—a thematic connection. This need was met by *cyclical structure* in which a theme from the earlier movements appeared in the later ones as a kind of motto or unifying thread.

The sonata cycle satisfied the composers' need for an extended instrumental work of an abstract nature. It mobilized the contrasts of key and mode inherent in the major-minor system. With its fusion of sensuous, emotional, and intellectual elements, its intermingling of lyric contemplation and action, the sonata cycle may justly claim to be one of the most ingenious art forms ever devised.

Sonata Cycle: General Scheme

Movement	Character	Form	Tempo
First	Epic-dramatic	Sonata-allegro	Allegro
Second	Slow and lyrical	Theme and variations Sonata form, or **A-B-A**	Andante, Adagio, Largo
Third	Dancelike Minuet (18th century) Scherzo (19th century)	Minuet and trio Scherzo and trio	Allegretto Allegro
Fourth	Lively, "happy ending" (18th century) Epic-dramatic with triumphal ending (19th century)	Sonata-allegro Sonata-rondo Theme and variations	Allegro, Vivace, Presto

PART SIX

Eighteenth-Century Classicism

"When a nation brings its innermost nature to consummate expression in arts and letters we speak of its classic period. Classicism stands for experience, for spiritual and human maturity which has deep roots in the cultural soil of the nation, for the mastery of the means of expression in technique and form, and for a definite conception of the world and of life; the final compression of the artistic values of a people."—PAUL HENRY LANG

Francesco Guardi (*1712–93*) Fantastic Landscape. (The Metropolitan Museum of Art, Gift of Julia A. Berwind, 1953)

UNIT X

◼

The Classical Spirit

(Handwritten margin notes: 1800's incredibly romantic; 20th century everything breaks down)

28

Classicism in the Arts

"Tis more to guide, than spur the Muse's steed;
Restrain his fury, than provoke his speed;
The winged courser, like a gen'rous horse,
Shows most true mettle when you check his course."—ALEXANDER POPE

Historians observe that style in art moves between two poles, the classic and the romantic. Both the classic artist and the romantic strive to express significant emotions, and to achieve that expression within beautiful forms. Where they differ is in their point of view. The classical spirit seeks order, poise, and serenity as surely as the romantic longs for strangeness, wonder, and ecstasy. Classic artists are apt to be more objective in their approach to art and to life. They try to view life sanely and "to see it whole." The romantics, on the other hand, are apt to be intensely subjective, and view the world in terms of their personal feelings. The German philosopher Friedrich Nietzsche, in his writings on art, dramatized the contrast between the two through the symbol of Apollo, Greek god of light and measure, as opposed to Dionysus, god of passion and intoxication. Classic and romantic ideals have alternated and even existed side by side from the beginning of time, for they correspond to two basic impulses in human nature: on the one hand, the need for moderation, the desire to have emotion purged and controlled; on the other, the desire for uninhibited emotional expression, the longing for the unknown and the unattainable.

Specifically, the classic and romantic labels are attached to two important periods in European art. The Classical era held the stage in the last quarter of the eighteenth century and the early decades of the nineteenth.

The dictionary defines Classicism in two ways: in general terms, as pertaining to the highest order of excellence in literature and art; specifically, pertaining to the culture of the ancient Greeks and Romans. Implicit in the

210

The Temple of Athena Nike, Athens, c. 427–423 B.C. The art of ancient Greece embodied the ideals of order, stability, and harmonious proportions.

Classical attitude is the notion that supreme excellence has been reached in the past and may be attained again through adherence to tradition.

Being part of a tradition implies a relationship to things outside oneself. Classical artists neither glory in nor emphasize their apartness from others. Artists regard neither their individuality nor their personal experience as the primary material of their art. For them the work of art exists in its own right rather than as an extension of their egos. Where Romantics are inclined to regard art primarily as a means of self-expression, Classicists stress its powers as a means of communication. Their attention is directed to clarity of thought and beauty of form. For the extremely personal utterance of the Romantics, Classicists substitute symbols of universal validity. Classicism upholds the control and the discipline of art. This wholeness of view encourages the qualities of order, stability, and harmonious proportion that we associate with the Classical style.

Enlightened despotism

The art of the eighteenth century bears the imprint of the spacious palaces and formal gardens, with their balanced proportions and finely wrought detail, that formed the setting for enlightened despotism. In the middle of the century, Louis XV presided over the extravagant fetes in Versailles (although he foresaw the deluge). Frederick the Great ruled in Prussia, Maria Theresa in Austria, Catherine the Great in Russia. In such a society the ruling class enjoyed its power through hereditary right. The past was revered, tradition was prized, and the status quo upheld no matter what the cost.

Yet disruptive forces were gathering beneath the glittering surface. The American Revolution dealt a shattering blow to the doctrine of the divine right of kings. And before the century had ended, Europe was convulsed by the French Revolution. The Classical era therefore witnessed both the twilight of the old regime and the dawn of a new political-economic alignment in Europe—specifically, the transfer of power from the aristocracy to the middle class, whose wealth was based on a rapidly expanding capitalism, on mines and factories, steam power and railroads. This shift was made possible by the Industrial Revolution, which gathered momentum in the mid-eighteenth century with a series of important inventions, from Watt's steam engine and Hargreaves's spinning jenny in the 1760s to Cartwright's power loom in 1785 and Eli Whitney's cotton gin in 1793.

Bourgeois revolution

These decades saw significant advances in science. Benjamin Franklin discovered electricity in 1752, Priestley discovered oxygen in 1774, Jenner perfected vaccination in 1796, Laplace advanced his mechanistic view of the universe, and Volta invented the voltaic pile in 1800. There were important events in intellectual life, such as the publication of Winckelmann's *History of Ancient Art* (1764), the French *Encyclopédie* (1751–52), and the first edition of the *Encyclopaedia Britannica* (1771).

The intellectual climate of the Classical era, consequently, was nourished by two opposing streams. On the one hand Classical art captured the exquisite refinement of a way of life that was drawing to a close. On the other it caught the first intimations of a new way of life that was struggling to be born. The eighteenth century has been called the Age of Reason; but the opponents of the established order, the philosophers who created the French *Encyclopédie* and the Enlightenment—Voltaire, Rousseau, and their comrades—

Intellectual dualism

Eighteenth-century Classicism drew its inspiration from the art and culture of ancient Greece. A painting by **Jacques-Louis David** (*1748–1825*), The Death of Socrates. (The Metropolitan Museum of Art. Wolfe Fund, 1931. Catherine Lorillard Wolfe Collection)

also invoked reason for the purpose of attacking the existing order. Therewith these spokesmen for the rising middle class became the prophets of the approaching upheaval.

Classical ideals

Whereas the Romantics idealized the Middle Ages, to eighteenth-century thinkers the Medieval period represented a thousand years of barbarism— the Dark Ages. The term *Gothic* represented everything that was opposed to what they regarded as rational and cultivated. Their ideal was the civilization of ancient Greece and Rome. To the Gothic cathedral, with its stained-glass windows, its bizarre gargoyles, its ribbed columns soaring heavenward in passionate mysticism, they opposed the Greek temple, a thing of beauty, unity and proportion, lightness and grace.

Yet here too the revival of interest in Classical antiquity meant different things to the opposing camps. The aristocrats and their spokesmen exalted Hellenism as the symbol of a rational, objective attitude that guarded one against becoming too deeply involved with the issues of life. They saw the ancient gods, kings, and heroes as a reflection of themselves—themselves ennobled, transfigured. But to the protagonists of the middle class, Greece and Rome represented city-states that had rebelled against tyrants and thrown off despotism. It was in this spirit that the foremost painter of revolutionary France, Jacques Louis David, decked his canvases with the symbols of Athenian and Roman democracy. In this spirit, too, Thomas Jefferson patterned both the Capitol and the University of Virginia after Greek and Roman temples, thereby giving strength to the Classic revival in this country, which made Ionic, Doric, and Corinthian columns an indispensable feature of our public buildings well into the twentieth century.

The Classical point of view held sway in English letters to such an extent that the mid-eighteenth century is known as the Augustan Age (after the

Thomas Jefferson's design for the library of the University of Virginia at Charlottesville reflects his admiration for the pure beauty of the Roman temple form.

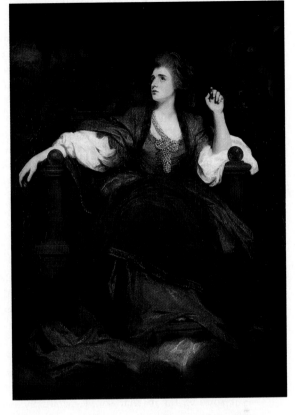

Sir Joshua Reynolds (*1723–92*) *invested his subjects with qualities borrowed from the noble past.* Mrs. Siddons as the Tragic Muse (*1784*). (Henry E. Huntington Library and Art Gallery, San Marino, Cal.)

Roman emperor Augustus, patron of the poet Virgil). Its arbiter was Samuel Johnson, whose position of leadership in literature was as undisputed as was that of his friend Sir Joshua Reynolds in painting. Both men upheld a highly formal, aristocratic type of art. Yet within the formal stream of Augustan Classicism we become aware of a current of tender sentiment that is an early sign of the Romantic spirit. The novels of Samuel Richardson, Henry Fielding, Laurence Sterne, and Tobias Smollett were suffused with homely bourgeois sentiment, as were the poems of Thomas Gray, Oliver Goldsmith, and William Cowper. For the Age of Reason was also, curiously, the Age of Sensibility, and the sensibility steadily broadens into a trend toward the Romantic.

The Augustan Age

Thus it is that the Age of Reason begins to give way to the Age of Romance considerably earlier than is commonly supposed. In the 1760s there already appeared a number of works—such as Percy's *Reliques of Ancient English Poetry*—that clearly indicate the new interest in a romantic medievalism. In the same decade Rousseau, the "father of Romanticism," produced some of his most significant writings. His celebrated declaration, "Man is born free and everywhere he is in chains," epitomizes the temper of the time. So too the first outcropping of the Romantic spirit in Germany, the movement known as *Sturm und Drang* (Storm and Stress), took shape in the 1770s, when it produced two characteristic works by its most significant young writers—the *Sorrows of Werther* by Goethe and *The Robbers* by Schiller. (Goethe, we shall see, became a favorite lyric poet of the Romantic com-

The Age of Sensibility

Sturm und Drang

posers.) By the end of the century the atmosphere had completely changed. The two most important English poets of the late eighteenth century— Robert Burns and William Blake—stand entirely outside the Classical stream, as does the greatest end-of-the-century painter, the Spaniard Goya, whose passionate realism anticipates a later age.

Eighteenth-century Classicism, then, mirrored the unique moment in history when the old world was dying and the new was in process of being born. From the meeting of two historic forces emerged an art of noble simplicity whose achievement in music constitutes one of the pinnacles of Western culture.

The Artist under Patronage

The culture of the eighteenth century was under the patronage of an aristocracy for whom the arts were a necessary adornment of life. Art was part of the elaborate ritual that surrounded the existence of princes. The center of art life was the palace and the privileged minority residing therein. In these high places great emphasis was placed on elegance of manner and beauty of style.

Eighteenth-century artists, consequently, functioned under the system of aristocratic patronage. The social functions at court created a steady demand for new works that they had to supply. It is true that in point of social status they were little better than servants, but this was not quite as depressing as it sounds, for in that society virtually everybody was a servant of the prince save other princes. The patronage system gave artists economic security and a social framework within which they could function. It offered important advantages to the great artists who successfully adjusted to its requirements, as the career of Haydn richly shows. On the other hand, Mozart's tragic end illustrates how heavy was the penalty exacted from those unable to make that adjustment.

Women too found a place as musicians under the patronage system. In Italy and France, professional female singers achieved prominence in opera and in court ballets. Some found a place within aristocratic circles as singers, instrumentalists, and music teachers, offering private lessons to members of the nobility and bourgeoisie. With the growth of the music trades, especially music printing and publishing, women found more opportunities open to them. Important also was the rise of amateur music making, which allowed women of the middle as well as upper classes an outlet for their talents.

At this time music was beginning to move from palace to public concert hall. The rise of the public concert gave composers a new platform where they could appear as performer or conductor of their works. Haydn and Beethoven conducted their symphonies at concerts, Mozart and Beethoven played their piano concertos. Their audience came to hear their new works, unlike ours, which is mainly interested in the music of the past and generally avoids contemporary works. The eagerness of eighteenth-century audiences for new music could not but stimulate composers to be as productive as possible.

29

Classicism in Music

*"Ought not the musician, quite as much as the poet and painter, to
study nature? In nature he can study man, its noblest creature."*—
JOHANN FRIEDRICH REICHARDT (1774)

The Classical period in music (c. 1750–1825) centers on the achievements
of the four masters of the Viennese school—Haydn, Mozart, Beethoven, and
Schubert—and their contemporaries. Their art reached its flowering in a
time of great musical experimentation and discovery, when musicians were
confronted by three challenging problems: first, to explore to the full the
possibilities offered by the major-minor system; second, to perfect a large
form of absolute instrumental music that would mobilize those possibilities
to the fullest degree; and third, having found this ideal form in the sonata
cycle, to differentiate between its various types—the solo and duo sonata,
trio, quartet, and other kinds of chamber music, the concerto, and the
symphony.

The Viennese school

If by Classicism we mean strict adherence to traditional forms we certainly
cannot apply the term blanketly to the composers of the Viennese school.
They experimented boldly and ceaselessly with the materials at their disposal.
An enormous distance separates Haydn's early symphonies and string quartets from his later ones; the same is true of Mozart, Beethoven, and Schubert.
Nor can we call these masters Classical if we mean that they—like the poets
and painters of the mid-eighteenth century—subordinated emotional expression to accepted "rules" of form. The slow movements of Haydn and
Mozart are filled with expression of the profoundest kind. What could be
more impassioned than Beethoven's music, or more suffused with lyric
tenderness than Schubert's?

It should not surprise us, therefore, that Romantic elements abound in
the music of Haydn, Mozart, and Beethoven, especially in their late works.
As for Schubert, although his symphonies and chamber music fall within the
Classical orbit, his songs and piano pieces, which we will take up later in
this book, stamp him a Romantic.

In consequence, the term Classicism applies to the art of the four Viennese
masters in only one—but that one perhaps the most important—of its meanings: "as pertaining to the highest order of excellence." They and their
contemporaries solved the problems presented to them so brilliantly that
their symphonies and concertos, piano sonatas, duo sonatas, trios, string
quartets, and similar works remained as unsurpassable models for all who
came after.

Elements of Classical Style

The music of the Viennese masters is notable for its elegant, singable melodies. These were usually based on symmetrical four-bar phrases marked

Symmetrical melody

215

off by clear-cut cadences, so that they were immediately perceptible to the ear. Classical melody sang even when it was intended for instruments. It moved stepwise or by narrow leaps within a narrow range, and it was firmly rooted in the key. Clarity was helped by repetition and the frequent use of sequence—that is, the repetition of a pattern at a higher or lower pitch. These and kindred devices made for symmetrical, balanced structures that were readily accessible to the listener.

Equally clear were the harmonies that sustained these melodies. The chords were firmly rooted in the key, and did not change so rapidly as to be confusing. The chords underlined the balanced symmetry of phrases and cadences; they formed vertical columns of sound over which the melody unfolded freely and easily.

Diatonic harmony

The harmony of the Classical period was based on the seven tones of the major or minor scale; in other words, it was largely *diatonic*. This circumstance gives the music of Haydn, Mozart, and Beethoven its freshness, its resilience, its sense of being rooted in the key.

Rhythmic regularity

Melody and harmony were powered by strong flexible rhythms that moved at a steady tempo, setting up expectations that were sure to be fulfilled. Much of the music was in one of the four basic meters—2/4, 3/4, 4/4, or 6/8. If a piece began in a certain rhythm, it was apt to stay there until it was over. Classical rhythm worked closely with melody and harmony to make clear the symmetrical phrase-and-cadence structure of the piece. Out of the interaction of these three basic elements came musical structures that delighted the ear without mystifying it.

The form unfolded in clearly shaped sections that established the home key, moved to a contrasting but closely related key or keys, and returned to the home key. There resulted the beautifully molded, architectural forms of the Classical style, amply fulfilling the listener's need for both unity and variety.

Folk elements

Despite its aristocratic elegance, Classical music absorbed a variety of folk and popular elements. This influence makes itself felt not only in the German dances and waltzes of the Viennese masters but also in their songs and in the Allegros and rondos of their symphonies, concertos, string quartets, and sonatas. How often the rondo finale of a Haydn or Mozart symphony has all the verve and lightheartedness of a popular dance, and what charm this adds to the movement!

Instrumental Music in the Classical Period

Classical orchestra

The Classical masters established the orchestra as we know it today. They based the ensemble on the blending of the four instrumental groups. The heart of this orchestra was the string choir. Woodwinds, used with great imagination, ably seconded the strings. The brass sustained the harmonies and contributed body to the tone mass, while the timpani supplied rhythmic life and vitality. The eighteenth-century orchestra numbered from thirty to forty players. The volume of sound was still largely considered in relation to the salon rather than the concert hall. (It was toward the end of the

Le concert, *by Augustin de St. Aubin (1736–1807), illustrates the informal seating of the orchestra when music was primarily performed in the salon.* (The Metropolitan Museum of Art, Harris Brisbane Dick Fund, 1933)

Classical period that musical life began to move from the one to the other.) The orchestra of Haydn and Mozart lent itself to delicate nuances in which each timbre stood out radiantly. They created a dynamic style of orchestral writing in which all the instruments participated actively. The interchange and imitation of themes among the various instrumental groups assumed the excitement of a witty conversation. The Classical orchestra brought to absolute music a number of effects long familiar in the opera house. The gradual crescendo and decrescendo established themselves as staples of the new symphonic style. Hardly less conspicuous were the abrupt alterations of soft and loud, sudden accents, dramatic pauses, the use of tremolo and pizzicato. These and similar devices of operatic music added drama and tension to the Classical orchestral style.

The central place in Classical instrumental music was taken by the symphony. This grew rapidly in dimension and significance until, with the final works of Mozart and Haydn, it became the most important type of absolute music. Important, too, was the concerto, which combined a virtuoso part for the featured player with the resources of the orchestra. Piano and violin concertos were the chief types, although other solo instruments were not neglected.

Chamber music enjoyed a great flowering in the Classical era. Especially popular was the string quartet as well as other small combinations that lent themselves ideally to music making in the home. Widely cultivated was a type of composition that stood midway between chamber music and symphony, known as *divertimento*. The title fixes the character of this category of music as sociable diversion or entertainment. Closely related were the *serenade*, the *notturno* (night piece), and the *cassation* (a term of obscure origin probably referring to something in the streets or out-of-doors). Contemporary accounts tell of groups of street musicians who performed these

Classical forms

works—for strings, winds, or both—outside the homes of the wealthy or in a quiet square before an appreciative audience of their fellow townsmen.

At this time, too, the piano came into favor, gradually supplanting the harpsichord and clavichord as an instrument for the home. Its more powerful tone also made it popular in the concert hall, although it must be remembered that the piano of the late eighteenth century was less powerful than its modern equivalent. The piano sonata became the most ambitious form of solo music, in which composers worked out new conceptions of keyboard style and sonata structure, creating a rich literature for both the amateur and the virtuoso.

Vocal Music in the Classical Period

Classical opera

The opera house was a center of experimentation in the Classical era. Opera was the most important branch of musical entertainment and the one that reached the widest public. The music was the point of departure and imposed its forms on the drama. Each scene was a closed musical unit. There was the greatest possible distinction between the rapid patter of recitative and the lyric curve of aria. The voice reigned supreme, yet the orchestra displayed all the vivacity of the Classical instrumental style.

Opera buffa

A significant development was the rise of Italian comic opera (*opera buffa*), which adapted certain features of serious opera and in turn influenced the latter. Far from being an escapist form of entertainment, comic opera was directly related to the life of the time. Its emphasis was on the affairs of "little people," on swift action, pointed situations, spontaneous emotion, and sharpness of characterization. From its cradle in Italy, Classical opera buffa spread all over Europe, steadily expanding its scope until it culminated in the works of the greatest musical dramatist of the eighteenth century—Mozart.

Church music

As a center of music making, the Church retained its importance alongside opera house and aristocratic salon. Whereas the first half of the century had seen the high point of Protestant music in the art of Bach and his contemporaries, the Catholic countries now assumed first place, especially the Hapsburg domains. The masters of the Viennese Classical school produced a great deal of Catholic church music: Masses, vespers, litanies, and the like. They did as composers have always done: they used the living idiom of their day (an idiom based on opera and symphony) to express their faith in God and man.

Classicism, to sum up, achieved the final synthesis of the intellectual currents of eighteenth-century life. The Classical masters struck a perfect balance between emotion and intellect, heart and mind. We have made reference to Nietzsche's distinction between the Dionysian and the Appollonian. The Classical spirit finds a fit symbol in the god of light, whose harmonious proportions so eloquently proclaim the cult of ideal beauty.

UNIT XI

Classical Chamber Music

30

Eighteenth-Century Chamber Music Style

"No other form of music can delight our senses with such exquisite beauty of sound, or display so clearly to our intelligence the intricacies and adventures of its design."—SIR WILLIAM HENRY HADOW

The Chamber Music Style

Chamber music, as we have seen, is music for small ensembles (two to about ten players) with one player to the part. It is so named for its suitability for performance in a small chamber or salon. In the intimate domain of chamber music, each instrument is expected to assert itself to the full, but the style of playing differs from that of the solo virtuoso. Where virtuosos are encouraged to exalt their own personalities, chamber music players function as part of a team.

The Classical era saw the golden age of chamber music. Haydn and Mozart, Beethoven, and Schubert established the true chamber music style, which is the nature of a friendly conversation among equals. The central position in Classical chamber music was held by the *string quartet*, which, we have seen, consists of two violins (a first and a second), viola, and cello. Other favored combinations were the duo sonata—piano and violin, or piano and cello; the trio—piano, violin, and cello; and the quintet, usually a combination of string or wind instruments, or a string quartet and solo instrument such as the piano or clarinet. The age produced, too, some memorable examples of chamber music for larger groups—sextets, septets, and octets.

Small chamber groups

219

By the early 1800s, when **Carl Heinrich Arnold** (*1798–1874*) *made this drawing of* A String Quartet at Spohr's House, *chamber music-making at home was exceedingly popular.*

The Movements of the String Quartet

The string quartet presents a special challenge both to composer and listener. To begin with, a small ensemble of string instruments lacks the contrasting tone colors of woodwinds and brass. This circumstance stimulates the composer to overcome the lack by every means possible.

First movement

In its general structure the string quartet follows the four-movement scheme of the sonata cycle. The first movement is usually an Allegro in sonata-allegro form. The musical texture is woven out of the themes and their motives, and the composer aims to distribute the material among the four instruments so as to achieve equality among them. Haydn favored a dense musical texture based on the continual expansion and development of motives, while Mozart was apt to be more lyrical and relaxed. Beethoven's first movements are motivic, like Haydn's, and show a great expansion of the form. Schubert further expanded the architecture by adding the element of pure song that was his special gift.

Second movement

The second movement is generally slow and lyrical, and apt to be a theme and variations or an **A-B-A** form. The tempo is andante or adagio, the accent is on beauty of melody, and a single line is apt to predominate rather than the continual interplay that characterized the first movement.

Third movement

Third is the dance movement, which is in triple meter. This, in the Classical era, was a graceful minuet and trio in moderate tempo. The minuet was repeated after the trio, giving an **A-B-A** form. Haydn's minuets tended to be folk-like in character, Mozart's were more elegant and closer to the character of the court dance. Beethoven substituted the impetuous scherzo, a presto or allegro molto instead of the earlier allegretto or allegro moderato.

Fourth is a fast movement, either a sonata-allegro or a rondo form, with a single melody predominating. In this finale folk-dance elements frequently come to the fore.

Fourth movement

Because the string quartet was addressed to a small group of cultivated music lovers, composers did not need here the expansive gestures of the great public forms of music such as the symphony or concerto. They could therefore entrust to the string quartet their most private thoughts. In consequence, the final string quartets of Haydn, Mozart, and Beethoven contain some of their most profound utterances, and are justly prized as constituting one of the high points of their art.

The description of the four movements of the classical string quartet applies equally to the other types of chamber music. The composer adjusts the material to the particular combination of instruments chosen, but the underlying structure is more or less the same.

31

Wolfgang Amadeus Mozart

"People make a mistake who think that my art has come easily to me. Nobody has devoted so much time and thought to composition as I. There is not a famous master whose music I have not studied over and over."

Something of the miraculous hovers about the music of Mozart (1756–91). One sees how it is put together, where it is bound, and how it gets there; but its beauty of sound and perfection of style, its poignancy and grace defy analysis and beggar description. For one moment in the history of music all opposites were reconciled, all tensions resolved. That luminous moment was Mozart.

Wolfgang Amadeus Mozart

His Life

Wolfgang Amadeus Mozart was born in Salzburg, Austria, son of Leopold Mozart, an esteemed composer-violinist attached to the court of the Archbishop of Salzburg. He began his career as the most extraordinarily gifted child in the history of music. He first started to compose before he was five, and performed at the court of the Empress Maria Theresa at the age of six. The following year his ambitious father organized a grand tour that included Paris, London, and Munich. By the time he was thirteen the boy had written sonatas, concertos, symphonies, religious works, and several operas.

He reached manhood having attained a mastery of all forms of his art. The speed and sureness of his creative power, unrivaled by any other composer, is best described by himself: "Though it be long, the work is complete and finished in my mind. I take out of the bag of my memory what has previously been collected into it. For this reason the committing to paper is done quickly enough. For everything is already finished, and it rarely differs on paper from what it was in my imagination. At this work I can therefore allow myself to be disturbed. Whatever may be going on about me, I write and even talk."

From patronage to free artist

Mozart's relations with his patron, Hieronymus von Colloredo, Prince-Archbishop of Salzburg, were most unhappy. The high-spirited young artist rebelled against the social restrictions imposed by the patronage system. At length he could endure his position no longer. He quarreled with the Archbishop, was dismissed, and at twenty-five established himself in Vienna to pursue the career of a free artist, while he sought an official appointment. Ten years remained to him. These were spent in a tragic struggle to achieve financial security and to find again the lost serenity of his childhood. Worldly success depended on the protection of the court. But the Emperor Joseph II—who referred to him as "a decided talent"—either passed him by in favor of lesser men such as Antonio Salieri or, when he finally took Mozart into his service, assigned him to tasks unworthy of his genius, such as composing dances for the court balls. Of his remuneration for this work Mozart remarked with bitterness, "Too much for what I do, too little for what I could do."

Marriage to Constanze

In 1782 he married Constanze Weber, against his father's wishes. The step signaled Mozart's liberation from the close ties that had bound him to the well-meaning but domineering parent who strove so futilely to ensure the happiness of the son. Constanze brought her husband neither the strength of character nor the wealth that might have protected him from a struggle with the world for which he was singularly unequipped. She was an undistinguished woman to whom Mozart, despite occasional lapses, was strongly attached. It was not till many years after his death that she appears to have realized, from the adulation of the world, the stature of her husband.

The da Ponte operas

With the opera *The Marriage of Figaro*, written in 1786 on a libretto by Lorenzo da Ponte, Mozart reached the peak of his career. He was commissioned to do another work for the Prague Opera the following year. With da Ponte again as librettist he produced *Don Giovanni*. But the opera baffled the public. His vogue had passed. The composer whom we regard as the epitome of clarity and grace was, in the view of the frivolous audience of his time, difficult to understand. His music, it was said, had to be heard several times in order to be grasped. What better proof of its inaccessibility? In truth, Mozart was entering regions beyond the aristocratic entertainment level of the day. He was straining toward an intensity of utterance that was new in the world. Of *Don Giovanni* Joseph II declared, "The opera is heavenly, perhaps more beautiful than *Figaro*. But no food for the teeth of my Viennese." Upon which Mozart commented, "Then give them time to chew it." One publisher advised him to write in a more popular style. "In that case I can make no more by my pen," he answered. "I had better starve and die at once."

His final years were spent in growing want. The frequent appeals to his friends for aid mirror his despair and helplessness. He describes himself as "always hovering between hope and anxiety." He speaks of the black thoughts that he must "repel by a tremendous effort." The love of life that had sustained him through earlier disappointments began to desert him. Again and again he embarked on endeavors that seemed to promise a solution to all his difficulties, only to return empty-handed.

Late operas

In the last year of his life, after a falling off in his production, he nerved himself to the final effort. For the popular Viennese theater he wrote *The Magic Flute*, on a libretto by the actor-impresario-poet Emanuel Schikaneder. Then a flurry of hope sent him off to Prague for the coronation of the new Emperor, Leopold II, as King of Bohemia. The festival opera he had composed for this event, *The Clemency of Titus*, failed to impress a court exhausted by the protracted ceremonies of the coronation. Mozart returned to Vienna broken in body and spirit. With a kind of fevered desperation he turned to his last task, the Requiem. It had been commissioned by a music-loving count who fancied himself a composer and intended to pass off the work as his own. Mozart in his overwrought state became obsessed with the notion that this Mass for the Dead was intended for himself and that he would not live to finish it. A tragic race with time began as he whipped his faculties to this masterwork steeped in visions of death.

He was cheered in his last days by the growing popularity of *The Magic Flute*. The gravely ill composer, watch in hand, would follow the performance in his mind. "Now the first act is over. . . . Now comes the aria of the Queen of Night. . . ." His premonition concerning the Requiem came true. He failed rapidly while in the midst of the work. His favorite pupil, Süssmayr, completed the Mass from the master's sketches, with some additions of his own.

Mozart died in 1791, shortly before his thirty-sixth birthday. In view of his debts he was given "the poorest class of funeral." His friends followed to the city gates; but the weather being inclement, they turned back, leaving the hearse to proceed alone. "Thus, without a note of music, forsaken by all he held dear, the remains of this prince of harmony were committed to the earth—not even in a grave of his own but in the common paupers' grave."

His Music

Mozart is pre-eminent for the inexhaustible wealth of his melodic ideas. His melodies are simple, elegant, and songful. He had a fondness for moderately chromatic harmonies, especially in the development sections of his sonata forms. A born man of the theater, he infused a sense of drama into his instrumental forms, particularly through contrasts of mood ranging from the ebullient to the tragic. His richly colorful orchestration is notable for its limpid quality as well as for the freedom of the part writing and the careful interweaving of the instrumental lines.

It has been said that Mozart taught the instruments to sing. Indeed he led them to the great vocal art of the past. The peasant touch is missing from his music, which draws its inspiration neither from folksong nor nature. Because of the mastery with which everything is carried out, the most complex operations of the musical mind are made to appear effortless. This deceptive simplicity is indeed the art that conceals art.

Principal Works

Orchestral music, including some 40 symphonies (late symphonies: No. 35, *Haffner*, 1782; No. 36, *Linz*, 1783; No. 38, *Prague*, 1786; No. 39, 40, and 41, *Jupiter*, all from 1788); cassations, divertimentos, serenades (K. 525, *Eine kleine Nachtmusik*, 1787), marches and dances

Concertos, including 5 for violin and 27 for piano; concertos for clarinet, oboe, French horn, bassoon, flute, and flute and harp

Operas, including *Idomeneo* (1781), *Die Entführung aus dem Serail* (The Abduction from the Seraglio, 1782), *Le nozze di Figaro* (The Marriage of Figaro, 1786), *Don Giovanni* (1787), *Così fan tutte* (1790), *Die Zauberflöte* (The Magic Flute, 1791).

Choral music, including 18 masses, the Requiem, K. 626 (incomplete, 1791), and other liturgical music

Chamber music, including 23 string quartets; string quintets; clarinet quintet; oboe quartet; flute quartet; piano trios and quartets, violin and piano sonatas; wind serenades and divertimentos

Keyboard music, including 17 piano sonatas, and Fantasia in C minor (K. 475, 1785)

Secular vocal music

The Salzburg years saw the completion of a quantity of social music— *Chamber music*
divertimentos and serenades of great variety. In chamber music he favored
the string quartet. His works in this form range in expression from the
buoyantly songful to the austerely tragic. The last ten quartets rank with
the finest specimens in the literature, among them being the set of six
dedicated to Haydn, his "most celebrated and very dear friend." Worthy
companions to these are the string quintets, in which he invariably used
two violas, and the enchanting Quintet for Clarinet and Strings.

One of the outstanding pianists of his time, Mozart wrote copiously for *Piano pieces*
his favorite instrument. Among his finest solo works are the Fantasia in C
minor, K. 475 and the Sonata in C minor, K. 457. (The K followed by a
number refers to the catalogue of Mozart's works by Ludwig Koechel, who
enumerated them all in what he took to be the order of their composition.)
Mozart led the way in developing one important form: the concerto for
piano and orchestra. He wrote more than twenty works for this medium,
which established the piano concerto as one of the important types of the
Classical era.

The more than forty symphonies—their exact number has not been de- *Symphonies*
termined—that extend across his career tend toward ever greater richness
of orchestration, freedom of part writing, and depth of emotion. The most
important are the six written in the final decade of his life. With these works
the symphony achieves its position as the most weighty form of abstract
music. In an age when composers produced their works almost exclusively
on commission, it is significant that Mozart's last three symphonies were
probably never performed during his lifetime: he seems to have written
them for no specific occasion but from inner necessity.

But the central current in Mozart's art that nourished all the others was
opera. Here were embodied his joy in life, his melancholy, all the impulses
of his many-faceted personality. None has ever surpassed his power to de-
lineate character in music or his lyric gift, so delicately molded to the curve
of the human voice. His orchestra, although it never obtrudes upon the
voice, becomes the magical framework within which the action unfolds.

Mozart: Eine kleine Nachtmusik, *K. 525*

Mozartian elegance and delicacy of touch are embodied in this serenade for
strings, whose title means "A Little Night Music." Probably the work was
intended for a double string quartet supported by a bass. The version we
know has four movements—compact, intimate, and beautifully propor-
tioned; originally there were five.

The opening movement is a sonata-allegro form in 4/4 time in G major. *First movement*
As was customary in music of this type, the first movement has a marchlike
character, as if the musicians were being introduced to the audience. The
first theme ascends rapidly to its peak, then turns downward at the same
rate. The second theme, with the downward curve of its opening measure,
presents a graceful contrast to the upward-leaping character of the first idea.
A delightful closing theme rounds off the Exposition. As befits the character

Second movement

of a serenade, which is less serious than a symphony or concerto, the Development section is brief. The Recapitulation follows the course of the Exposition, and expands the closing theme into a vigorous coda. (See Listening Guide 20 for themes and an analysis of all four movements.)

Second is the Romanza, an eighteenth-century Andante that maintains the balance between lyricism and a pleasant reserve. The key is C major, the meter duple; symmetrical sections are arranged in an **A-B-A-C-A** or rondo structure. The **A** theme is utterly gracious, a mood that is maintained by the **B** theme. The **C** theme is darker in tone, centers about **C** minor, and is heard against a restless background of quick notes. The primacy of the C major tonality is re-established with the return of the **A** theme.

Third movement

The Minuet and Trio is an Allegretto in G major, marked by regular four-bar structure and repeated sections. It opens in a bright, decisive manner. The Trio presents a lovely contrast with a soaring curve of truly Mozartian melody; the Minuet returns, presented without repeats.

Fourth movement

The rondo finale, a sprightly Allegro, in the home key of G, alternates with an idea in the key of the dominant, D major. Here, too, there is a contrast of direction. The downward "dip" in the first measure of this tune stands out against the upward-skipping character of the principal theme. We have here a perfect example of the Classical rondo finale, bright, jovial, and—a trait inseparable from this master—stamped with an aristocratic refinement.

In the music of Mozart subjective emotion is elevated to the plane of the universal. The restlessness and the longing are exorcised by the ideal loveliness of Apollonian art. Mozart is one of the supreme artists of all time; the voice of pure beauty in music, and probably the most sheerly musical composer that ever lived.

Listening Guide 20   4A/1   I/4/1

Mozart: *Eine kleine Nachtmusik*, K. 525

Date: 1787

Medium: Double string quartet or chamber orchestra

Movements: 4

I. First movement: Allegro, sonata-allegro form, 4/4 meter, G major

EXPOSITION

1 0:00   Theme 1—aggressive, ascending "rocket" theme, symmetrical phrasing, in G major

2 0:48   Theme 2—graceful, contrasting theme, less hurried, in key of dominant, D major

| 1:00 | Closing theme—insistent, repetitive character |

Repeat of Exposition

| **3** | 3:05 | DEVELOPMENT |
Short, begins in D major, manipulates Theme 1, modulates, and prepares for Recapitulation in G major

RECAPITULATION
4	3:38	Theme 1, in G major
5	4:20	Theme 2, in G major
	4:33	Closing theme, leads to
	5:03	Coda

II. Second movement: Romanza, Andante, rondo (A-B-A-C-A) form, duple meter, C major

| **6** | 0:00 | A section—lyrical, serene melody |

7	1:53	B section—more rhythmic movement, but in mood of A section
8	2:53	A section heard again
9	3:21	C section—in C minor, active rhythmic accompaniment
10	4:12	A section—in tonic of C major

III. Third movement: Minuet and Trio, Allegretto, 3/4 meter, G major, regular 4-measure phrases

| **11** | 0:00 | Minuet theme—in accented triple meter, decisive, two sections, each repeated |

| **12** | 0:57 | Trio theme—more lyrical and connected; two sections, each repeated |

| **13** | 1:45 | Minuet returns, with repeats |

IV. Fourth movement: Allegro, 4/4 meter, G major Rondo-like form, two main themes in alternation

| **14** | | Theme A—merry, quick-paced theme, symmetrical 4-measure phrases in G major, which are repeated |

| **15** | | Theme B—begins with downward leap, opposite in character to A theme, in D major |

34

Joseph Haydn

"I have only just learned in my old age how to use the wind instruments, and now that I do understand them I must leave the world."

The long career of Joseph Haydn (1732–1809) spanned the decades when the Classical style was being formed. He imprinted upon it the stamp of his personality, and made a contribution to his art—especially the symphony and string quartet—that in scope and significance was second to none.

His Life

Joseph Haydn

He was born in Rahrau, a village in lower Austria, son of a wheelwright. Folksong and dance were his natural heritage. The beauty of his voice secured him a place as chorister in St. Stephen's Cathedral in Vienna, where he remained until he was sixteen. With the breaking of his voice his time at the choir school came to an end. He then established himself in an attic in Vienna, managed to obtain a dilapidated harpsichord, and set himself to master his craft. He eked out a living through teaching and accompanying, and often joined the roving bands of musicians who performed in the streets. In this way the popular Viennese idiom entered his style along with the folk idiom he had absorbed in childhood.

Before long, Haydn attracted the notice of the music-loving aristocracy of Vienna, and was invited to the country house of a nobleman who maintained a small group of musicians. His next patron kept a small orchestra, so that he was able to experiment with more ample resources. In 1761, when he was twenty-nine, he entered the service of the Esterházys, a family of enormously wealthy Hungarian princes famous for their patronage of the arts. He remained in their service for almost thirty years—that is, for the greater part of his creative career.

Esterházy patronage

The palace of the Esterházys was one of the most splendid in Europe, and music played a central part in the constant round of festivities there. The musical establishment under Haydn's direction included an orchestra, an opera company, a marionette theater, and a chapel. The agreement between prince and composer sheds light on the social status of the eighteenth-century artist. Haydn is required to abstain "from undue familiarity and from vulgarity in eating, drinking, and conversation." He is charged to act uprightly and to influence his subordinates "to preserve such harmony as is becoming in them, remembering how displeasing any discord or dispute would be to His Serene Highness. . . . It is especially to be observed that when the orchestra shall be summoned to perform before company the said Joseph Heyden shall take care that he and all the members of his orchestra do follow the instructions given and appear in white stockings, white linen, powdered, and with a pigtail or tie-wig."

A recent photograph of the Esterházy palace at Fertód, Hungary. (© Ibusz Hungarian Travel Co.)

Haydn's life is the classic example of the patronage system operating at its best. Though he chafed occasionally at the restrictions imposed on him by court life, he inhabited a world that questioned neither the supremacy of princes nor the spectacle of a great artist in a servant's uniform. His final estimate of his position in the Esterházy household was that the advantages outweighed the disadvantages. "My Prince was always satisfied with my works. I not only had the encouragement of constant approval but as conductor of an orchestra I could make experiments, observe what produced an effect and what weakened it, and was thus in a position to improve, alter, make additions or omissions, and be as bold as I pleased. I was cut off from the world, there was no one to confuse or torment me, and I was forced to become *original*."

Later years

Haydn had married when still a young man, but did not get on with his wife. They ultimately separated, and he found consolation elsewhere. By the time he reached middle age his music had brought him fame throughout Europe. After the Prince's death he made two visits to England (1791–92, 1794–95), where he conducted his works with phenomenal success. He returned to his native Austria laden with honor, financially well off.

When he was seventy-six a memorable performance of his oratorio *The Creation* was organized in his honor by the leading musicians of Vienna and members of the aristocracy. At the words "And there was light"—who that has heard it can forget the grandeur of the C-major chord on the word "light"?—the old man was deeply stirred. Pointing upward he exclaimed, "It came from there!"

He died a year later, revered by his countrymen and acknowledged throughout Europe as the premier musician of his time.

His Music

It was Haydn's historic role to help perfect the new instrumental language of the late eighteenth century. His terse, angular themes lent themselves readily to motivic development. Significant too, in his symphonies of the 1790s, was his expansion of the size and resources of the orchestra through greater emphasis on the brass, clarinets, and percussion. It was in his expressive harmony, structural logic, and endlessly varied moods that the mature Classical idiom seemed to be fully realized for the first time.

Principal Works

Orchestral music, including over 100 symphonies (6 *Paris Symphonies*, Nos. 82–87, 1785–86; 12 *London* or *Salomon Symphonies*, Nos. 93–104, 1791–95); concertos for violin, cello, harpsichord, and trumpet

Chamber music, including some 68 string quartets, piano trios, and divertimentos

Sacred vocal music, including 14 masses (*Mass in Time of War*, 1796; *Lord Nelson Mass*, 1798); oratorios, including *Die sieben letzten Worte* (The Seven Last Words of Christ, 1796), *Die Schöpfung* (The Creation, 1798), and *Die Jahreszeiten* (The Seasons, 1801)

Dramatic music, including 14 operas

Keyboard music, including about 40 sonatas
Songs, including folksong arrangements; secular choral music

String quartets

As we mentioned earlier, the string quartet occupied a central position in Haydn's art; his works are today an indispensable part of the repertory. One understands Mozart's remark, "It was from Haydn that I first learned the true way to compose quartets."

Symphonies

Like the quartets, the symphonies—over a hundred in number—extend across the whole of Haydn's career. Especially popular are the twelve written in the 1790s, in two sets of six, for his appearances in England. Known as the *London* or *Salomon Symphonies* after the London impresario who commissioned them, they abound in effects that the public associates with later composers: syncopation, sudden crescendos and accents, dramatic contrasts of soft and loud, daring modulations, and an imaginative color scheme in which each choir of instruments plays its allotted part. Of Haydn's symphonies it may be said, as it has been of his quartets, that they are the spiritual birthplace of Beethoven.

Church music

Haydn was also a prolific composer of church music. His fourteen Masses form the chief item in this category. The prevailing cheerfulness of these works reflects a trusting faith undisturbed by inner torment or doubt. "At the thought of God," he said, "my heart leaps for joy and I cannot help my music doing the same." Among his oratorios, *The Creation* attained a popularity second only to that of Handel's *Messiah*. Haydn followed it with another work based on English literature—*The Seasons* on a text drawn from James Thomson's celebrated poem. Completed when the composer was on the threshold of seventy, it was his last major composition.

Haydn's tonal imagery was basically instrumental in character. Yet he recognized that a good melody must be rooted in the nature of the human voice. "If you want to know whether you have written anything worth preserving," he counseled, "sing it to yourself without any accompaniment." His ceaseless experimenting with form should dispel the notion that the Classicist adheres to tradition. On the contrary, he chafed against the arbitrary restrictions of the theorists. "What is the good of such rules? Art is free and should be fettered by no such mechanical regulations." So, too, when his attention was called to an unconventional passage in a string quartet of Mozart's, he retorted, "If Mozart wrote it so he must have had a good reason."

Haydn: Symphony No. 104 (London)

Haydn's last symphony is regarded by many as his greatest. The solemn introduction, marked Adagio, opens in D minor with a fanfare-like motive announced in unison by the whole orchestra. The atmosphere is one of "strangeness and wonder." The movement proper, an Allegro in sonata form, is launched by an irresistible tune that has all the energy and verve of Haydn's mature style. This theme and those that follow are shaped out of a few basic intervals in such a way that, despite the variety of the ideas, they all hang together. There results the effortless continuity that constitutes the essence of the high Classical style. Instead of introducing a lyrical second theme, Haydn repeats his opening theme in the new key. This monothematic technique is a hallmark of Haydn's mature style, and underscores an important point about sonata-allegro form. Many people think it is based on the opposition between two themes. Clearly, in Haydn's mind the opposition is between two keys. (See Listening Guide 21 for analysis.)

First movement

The second movement is an Andante that has been well described as a perfect example of Viennese grace and warmth. The form is a free amalgam of **A-B-A** with the spirit of theme and variation. The movement is notable for the way it modulates to faraway keys, and for the wealth of imagination behind its variation technique.

Second movement

Third is a Minuet and Trio—that is, an **A-B-A** form—in Haydn's most exuberant manner. The main theme consists of two symmetrical four-bar phrases that are announced forte and immediately repeated pianissimo. It is fascinating to observe how Haydn upsets the four-bar symmetry of the Classical minuet by sneaking in a six-bar phrase every now and then. Characteristic, in the codetta that rounds off this section, is the syncopated accent followed by an abrupt pause. Perhaps no other composer in history understood so well the value of a sudden silence in music. The effect is unfailingly dramatic. The Trio, in the contrasting key of B-flat major, is within itself an **a-b-a** form, to which Haydn adds an exquisite passage modulating back to the home key of D. Brass, timpani, and clarinets are silent during this more lyrical episode.

Third movement

The finale is an Allegro spiritoso in duple meter. The theme has the high spirits that Haydn derived from his heritage of Croatian folksong and dance. The effect of folk dance is heightened by the low D, which is sustained as a pedal point (sustained pitch) by horns and cellos. This kind of drone bass has always been a feature of European folk instruments, whether of the bagpipe or accordion variety. The music moves at a whirlwind pace through a shapely sonata-allegro form. An energetic cadence in the home key of D ends this enchanting work that captures, for Haydn's aristocratic listeners, all the verve and humor of the folk.

Fourth movement

Listening Guide 21   3A/1   I/3/1

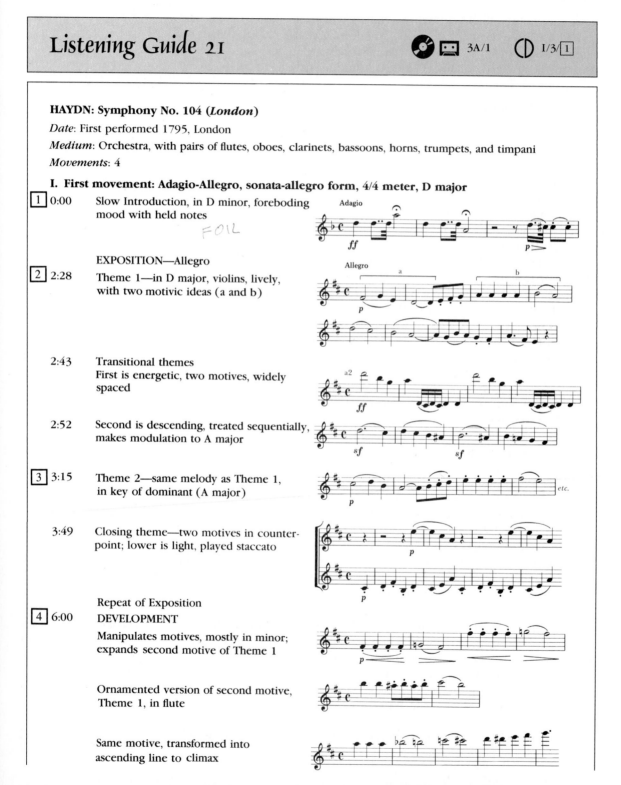

HAYDN: Symphony No. 104 (London)

Date: First performed 1795, London

Medium: Orchestra, with pairs of flutes, oboes, clarinets, bassoons, horns, trumpets, and timpani

Movements: 4

I. First movement: Adagio-Allegro, sonata-allegro form, 4/4 meter, D major

1	0:00	Slow Introduction, in D minor, foreboding mood with held notes
2	2:28	EXPOSITION—Allegro Theme 1—in D major, violins, lively, with two motivic ideas (a and b)
	2:43	Transitional themes First is energetic, two motives, widely spaced
	2:52	Second is descending, treated sequentially, makes modulation to A major
3	3:15	Theme 2—same melody as Theme 1, in key of dominant (A major)
	3:49	Closing theme—two motives in counterpoint; lower is light, played staccato
4	6:00	Repeat of Exposition DEVELOPMENT Manipulates motives, mostly in minor; expands second motive of Theme 1
		Ornamented version of second motive, Theme 1, in flute
		Same motive, transformed into ascending line to climax

RECAPITULATION

5 7:08   Theme 1—returns in D major in oboe
line, with added countermelody in flute

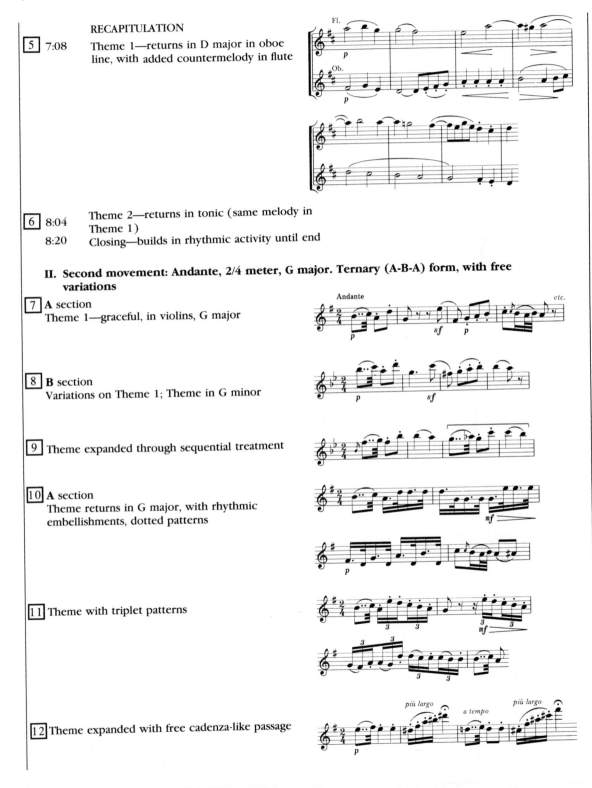

6 8:04   Theme 2—returns in tonic (same melody in
Theme 1)
8:20   Closing—builds in rhythmic activity until end

II. Second movement: Andante, 2/4 meter, G major. Ternary (A-B-A) form, with free variations

7 **A section**
Theme 1—graceful, in violins, G major

8 **B section**
Variations on Theme 1; Theme in G minor

9 Theme expanded through sequential treatment

10 **A section**
Theme returns in G major, with rhythmic
embellishments, dotted patterns

11 Theme with triplet patterns

12 Theme expanded with free cadenza-like passage

III. Third movement: Menuetto, Allegro, 3/4 meter, D major, three-part form: (Minuet-Trio-Minuet)

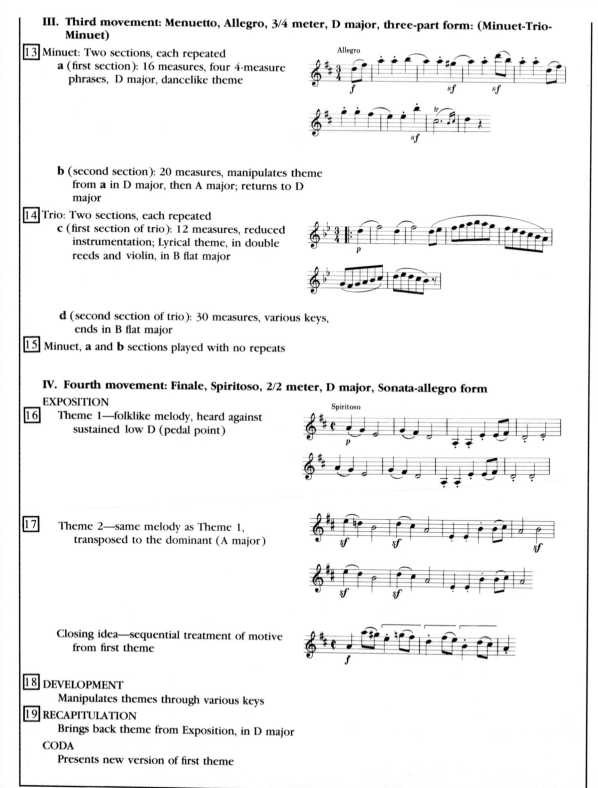

13 Minuet: Two sections, each repeated
  a (first section): 16 measures, four 4-measure phrases, D major, dancelike theme

  b (second section): 20 measures, manipulates theme from **a** in D major, then A major; returns to D major

14 Trio: Two sections, each repeated
  c (first section of trio): 12 measures, reduced instrumentation; Lyrical theme, in double reeds and violin, in B flat major

  d (second section of trio): 30 measures, various keys, ends in B flat major

15 Minuet, **a** and **b** sections played with no repeats

IV. Fourth movement: Finale, Spiritoso, 2/2 meter, D major, Sonata-allegro form

EXPOSITION

16 Theme 1—folklike melody, heard against sustained low D (pedal point)

17 Theme 2—same melody as Theme 1, transposed to the dominant (A major)

Closing idea—sequential treatment of motive from first theme

18 DEVELOPMENT
  Manipulates themes through various keys

19 RECAPITULATION
  Brings back theme from Exposition, in D major

  CODA
  Presents new version of first theme

35

Ludwig van Beethoven

"Freedom above all!"

Beethoven (1770–1827) belonged to the generation that received the full impact of the French Revolution. He created the music of a heroic age and, in accents never to be forgotten, proclaimed its faith in the power of man to shape his destiny.

His Life

Beethoven was born in Germany, in the city of Bonn in the Rhineland, where his father and grandfather were singers at the court of the local prince, the Elector Max Friedrich. The family situation was unhappy, the father being addicted to drink, and Ludwig at an early age was forced to take over the support of his mother and two younger brothers. At eleven and a half he was assistant organist in the court chapel and a year later he became harpsichordist in the court orchestra. A visit to Vienna in his seventeenth year enabled him to play for Mozart. The youth improvised so brilliantly on a theme given him by the master that the latter remarked to his friends, "Keep an eye on him—he will make a noise in the world some day."

Arrangements were made some years later for him to study with Haydn in Vienna at the Elector's expense. He left his native town when he was twenty-two, never to return. Unfortunately, the relationship between pupil and teacher left much to be desired. The aging Haydn was ruffled by the young man's volcanic temperament and independence of spirit. Beethoven worked with other masters, the most academic of whom declared that "he has learned nothing and will never do anything in decent style."

Meanwhile his powers as a pianist took the music-loving aristocracy by storm. He was welcomed in the great houses of Vienna by the powerful patrons whose names appear in the dedications of his works—Prince Lichnowsky, Prince Lobkowitz, Count Razumovsky, and the rest. To this "princely rabble," as he called them, the young genius came—in an era of revolution—as a passionate rebel, forcing them to receive him as an equal and friend. "It is good to move among the aristocracy," he observed, "but it is first necessary to make them respect you."

Beethoven functioned under a modified form of the patronage system. He was not attached to the court of a prince. Instead, the music-loving aristocrats of Vienna helped him in various ways—by paying him handsomely for lessons, or through gifts. He was also aided by the emergence of a middle-class public and the growth of concert life and music publishing. At the age of thirty-one he was able to write, "I have six or seven publishers for each of my works and could have more if I chose. No more bargaining. I name my terms and they pay." A youthful exuberance pervades the first decade of his career, an almost arrogant consciousness of his strength. "Power is

Ludwig van Beethoven

The rebel

241

*Beethoven's work room,
drawn three days after the
composer's death by* **J. N.
Höchle.**

Deafness

the morality of men who stand out from the mass, and it is also mine!" Thus spoke the individualist in the new era of individualism.

Then, as the young eagle was spreading his wings, fate struck in a vulnerable spot: he began to lose his hearing. His helplessness in the face of this affliction dealt a shattering blow to his pride. "Ah, how could I possibly admit an infirmity in the one sense that should have been more perfect in me than in others. A sense I once possessed in highest perfection. Oh I cannot do it!" As his deafness closed in on him—the first symptoms appeared when he was in his late twenties—it became the symbol of his terrible sense of apartness from other men, of all the defiance and insecurity and hunger for love that had rent him for as long as he could remember. Upon the mistaken advice of his doctors he retired in 1802 to a summer resort outside Vienna called Heiligenstadt. A titanic struggle shook him, between the destructive forces in his soul and his desire to live and create. It was one of those searing experiences that either break a man or leave him stronger. "But little more and I would have put an end to my life. Only art it was that withheld me. Ah, it seemed impossible to leave the world until I had produced all that I felt called upon to produce, and so I endured this wretched existence."

It was slowly borne in on him that art must henceforth give him the happiness life withheld. Only through creation could he attain the victory of which fate had threatened to rob him. The will to struggle asserted itself; he fought his way back to health. "I am resolved to rise superior to every obstacle. With whom need I be afraid of measuring my strength? I will take Fate by the throat. It shall not overcome me. Oh how beautiful it is to be alive—would that I could live a thousand times!" He had stumbled on an idea that was to play a decisive part in nineteenth-century thought: the concept of art as refuge, as compensation for the shortcomings of reality—art as the ultimate victory over life.

Having conquered the chaos within himself, he came to believe that man could conquer chaos. This became the epic theme of his music: the progression from despair to conflict, from conflict to serenity, from serenity to triumph and joy. The revelation that had come to him through suffering was a welcome message to the world that was struggling to be born. He became the major prophet of the nineteenth century, the architect of its heroic vision of life. "I am the Bacchus who presses out the glorious wine for mankind. Whoever truly understands my music is freed thereby from the miseries that others carry about in them."

The remainder of his career was spent in an unremitting effort to subjugate the elements of his art to the expressive ideal he had set himself. Fellow musicians and critics might carp at the daring of his thoughts, but his growing public, especially among the younger generation, responded to the powerful thrust of his music. His life was outwardly uneventful. There were the interminable quarrels with associates and friends—he grew increasingly suspicious and irritable, especially in his last years, when he became totally deaf. There were the complicated dealings with his publishers, in which he displayed an impressive shrewdness; his turbulent love affairs (he never married); his high-handed interference in the affairs of his brothers; his tortured relationship with his nephew Carl, an ordinary young man upon whom he fastened a tyrannical affection. All these framed an inner life of extraordinary intensity, an unceasing spiritual development that opened up new domains to tonal art.

The final years

Biographers and painters have made familiar the squat, sturdy figure—he was five foot four, the same height as that other conqueror of the age, Napoleon—walking hatless through the environs of Vienna, the bulging brow furrowed in thought, stopping now and again to jot down an idea in his sketchbook; an idea that, because he was forever deprived of its sonorous beauty, he envisioned all the more vividly in his mind. A ride in an open carriage in inclement weather brought on an attack of dropsy that proved fatal. He died in his fifty-seventh year, famous and revered.

His Music

Beethoven is the supreme architect in music. His genius found expression in the structural type of thinking embodied in the sonata and symphony. The sketchbooks in which he worked out his ideas show how gradually they reached their final shape: "I carry my thoughts within me long," he wrote, "often very long before I write them down. As I know what I want, the fundamental idea never deserts me. It mounts, it grows in stature. I hear, I see the picture in its whole extent standing all of a piece before my spirit, and there remains for me only the task of writing it down."

His compositional activity fell into three periods. The first reflected the Classical elements he inherited from Haydn and Mozart. The middle period saw the appearance of characteristics more closely associated with the nine-

Three periods

Principal Works

Orchestral music, including nine symphonies: No. 1 (1800); No. 2 (1802); No. 3, *Eroica* (1803); No. 4 (1806); No. 5 (1808); No. 6, *Pastoral* (1808); No. 7 (1812); No. 8 (1812); No. 9, *Choral* (1824); Overtures, including *Leonore* (Nos. 1, 2, 3) and *Egmont*, and incidental music

Concertos, including 5 for piano (No. 5, *Emperor,* 1809), 1 for violin (1806), and 1 triple concerto (piano, violin, and cello, 1804)

Chamber music, including string quartets (Op. 18, Nos. 1–6, 1798–1800), piano trios, quartets, 1 quintet; violin and cello sonatas; serenades and wind chamber music

32 piano sonatas, including Op. 13, *Pathétique* (1806), Op. 27, No. 2, *Moonlight* (1801), Op. 53, *Waldstein* (1804), Op. 57, *Appassionata* (1805)

1 opera (*Fidelio,* 1805)

Choral music, including *Missa Solemnis* (1823)

Songs, including song cycle *An die ferne Geliebte* (To the Distant Beloved, 1816)

teenth century: strong dynamic contrasts, explosive accents, and longer movements. He expanded the dimensions of the first movement, especially the coda, and like Haydn and Mozart made the Development section the dynamic center of the form. In his hands the slow movement acquired a hymnic character, the embodiment of Beethovenian pathos. The scherzo became a movement of rhythmic energy ranging from "cosmic laughter" to mystery and wonder. His goal throughout was powerful expression rather than elegance. He enlarged the finale into a movement comparable in size and scope to the first, and ended the symphony on a note of triumph.

In his third period—the years of the final piano sonatas and string quartets—he found his way to more chromatic harmonies and developed a skeletal language from which all nonessentials were rigidly pared away. This was a language far transcending his time. To someone who asked him if one of his more advanced quartets was music, he replied, "Not for you. For a later time."

Symphonies   In the symphony Beethoven found the ideal medium wherein to address mankind. His nine symphonies are spiritual dramas of universal appeal. Their sweep and tumultuous affirmation of life mark them a pinnacle of the rising democratic art. They are conceived on a scale too grand for the aristocratic salon; they demand the amplitude of the concert hall.

The first two symphonies stand closest to the two classical masters who preceded him; with his Third Symphony, the *Eroica*, Beethoven achieved his mature style. The work was originally dedicated to Napoleon, first consul of the Republic, in whom he saw incarnated the spirit of revolution and the freedom of man. When the news came that Napoleon had proclaimed himself Emperor, Beethoven was disenchanted. "He too is just like any other! Now he will trample on the rights of man and serve nothing but his own ambition." The embittered composer tore up the dedicatory page of the just completed work and renamed it "Heroic Symphony to celebrate the memory of a great man."

The Fifth Symphony has fixed itself in the popular mind as the archetype of all that a symphony is. The Seventh rivals it in universal appeal. The Ninth, the *Choral Symphony*, strikes the searching tone of Beethoven's last period. Its finale, in which vocal soloists and chorus join with the orchestra, contains the famous line, "Be embraced, ye millions!" The choral movement is a setting of Schiller's *Ode to Joy*, a ringing prophecy of the time when "all men shall be brothers." In these works there sounds the rhetoric of the new century.

Piano concertos

The concerto offered Beethoven a congenial public form in which he combined virtuosity with symphonic architecture. His five piano concertos went hand in hand with—and in turn encouraged—the rising popularity of the instrument. The piano occupied a central position in Beethoven's art.

Piano sonatas

His thirty-two sonatas are an indispensable part of its literature, whether for the amateur pianist or concert artist. We have already suggested that they are aptly called the pianist's New Testament (the Old being *The Well-Tempered Clavier* of Bach).

String quartets

He wrote much chamber music, the string quartet being closest to his heart. The six quartets of Opus 18 are the first in a series that extended throughout the whole of his career. His supreme achievements in this area are the last five quartets, which, together with the *Grand Fugue*, Op. 133, occupied the final years of his life. In these, as in the last five piano sonatas, the master's gaze is focused within, encompassing depths that music never before had plumbed.

Vocal music

Although his most important victories were won in the instrumental field, Beethoven enriched the main types of vocal music. Of his songs the best known is the cycle of six, *An die ferne Geliebte* (To the Distant Beloved). His sole opera *Fidelio* centers on wifely devotion, human freedom, and the defeat of those who would destroy it. Although the pious Haydn considered him an atheist, he hymned "Nature's God" through the traditional form of religious music. The *Missa solemnis* (Solemn Mass) ranks in importance with the Ninth Symphony and the final quartets. The work transcends the limits of any specific creed or dogma. Above the Kyrie of the Mass he wrote a sentence that applies to the whole of his music: "From the heart . . . may it find its way to the heart."

His creative activity, extending over a span of thirty-five years, bears witness to a ceaseless striving after perfection. "I feel as if I had written scarcely more than a few notes," he remarked at the end of his career. And a year before his death: "I hope still to bring a few great works into the world." Despite his faith in his destiny he knew the humility of the truly great. "The real artist has no pride. Unfortunately he sees that his art has no limits, he feels obscurely how far he is from the goal. And while he is perhaps being admired by others, he mourns the fact that he has not yet reached the point to which his better genius, like a distant sun, ever beckons him."

Beethoven: Symphony No. 5 in C minor

First movement

The most popular of all symphonies, Beethoven's Symphony No. 5 in C minor, Opus 67, is also the most concentrated expression of the frame of mind and spirit that we have come to call Beethovenian. The first movement, marked Allegro con brio (lively, with vigor), springs out of the rhythmic idea of "three shorts and a long" that dominates the symphony. It is the most compact and commanding gesture in the whole symphonic literature. Out of this motive flowers the first theme, which is a repetition, at different levels of the scale and with altered intervals, of the germinating rhythm. The power of the movement springs from the almost terrifying single-mindedness with which this idea is pursued. It is rhythm, torrential yet superbly controlled, that is the generating force behind this "storm and stress." Beethoven here achieved a vehemence that was new in music.

We reach an area of relaxation with the lyric second theme. Yet even here the headlong course of the movement does not slacken. As the violins, clarinet, and flute sound the gentle melody in turn, the basic rhythm of "three shorts and a long" persists in the cellos and double basses. Characteristic of Beethoven's style are the powerful crescendos and the abrupt contrasts between soft and loud.

This sonata-allegro is dramatic, peremptory, compact. (See Listening Guide 22 for analysis.) It ends with an extended coda in which the basic rhythm reveals a new fund of explosive energy.

Second movement

Beethovenian serenity and strength imbue the second movement, Andante con moto (at a going pace, with movement). The key is A flat; the form, a theme and variations, with two melodic ideas. In the course of the movement Beethoven brings all the procedures of variation—changes in melodic outline, harmony, rhythm, tempo, dynamics, register, key, mode, and type of accompaniment—to bear upon his two themes.

Third movement

Third in the cycle of movements is the Scherzo, which returns to the somber C minor that is the home key of the work. From the depths of the bass rises a characteristic subject, a rocket theme introduced by cellos and double basses. The Trio shifts to C major, presenting a gruff, humorous motive. Then the Scherzo returns in a modified version, with changed orchestration, and is followed by a transitional passage in which the basic rhythm of the first movement—"three shorts and a long"—is tapped out mysteriously by the timpani. There is a steady accumulation of tension until the orchestra, in a blaze of light, surges into the triumphal Allegro in C major. Three instruments here appear for the first time in the symphonies of the Classical Viennese school—piccolo, double bassoon, and trombone, lending brilliance and body to the orchestral sound.

Fourth movement

The fourth movement is a monumental sonata form in which two themes in C major are opposed to one in G. The Development is marked by dynamic rhythm and free modulation. Then—an amazing stroke!—Beethoven brings back the "three shorts and a long" as they appeared in the third movement. This return of material from an earlier movement gives the symphony its cyclical form. The symphonic stream at the very end becomes an overwhelming torrent as the tonic chord—source and goal of all activity—is hurled forth by the orchestra again and again.

Listening Guide 22

4B   I/4/33

BEETHOVEN: Symphony No. 5 in C minor, Op. 67

Date: 1807–08

Movements: 4

I. First movement: Allegro con brio, 2/4 meter, C minor. Sonata-allegro form

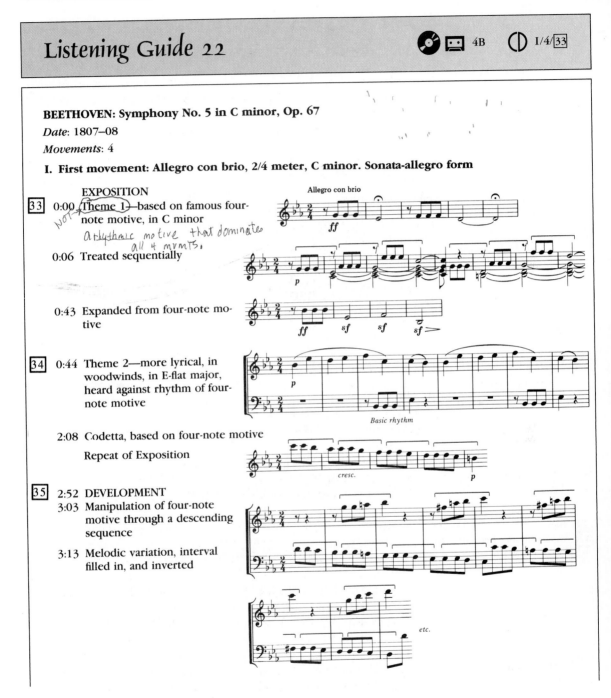

EXPOSITION

33   0:00 Theme 1—based on famous four-
note motive, in C minor

NOT A rhythmic motive that dominates all 4 mvmts.

0:06 Treated sequentially

0:43 Expanded from four-note motive

34   0:44 Theme 2—more lyrical, in
woodwinds, in E-flat major,
heard against rhythm of four-
note motive

2:08 Codetta, based on four-note motive

Repeat of Exposition

35   2:52 DEVELOPMENT
3:03 Manipulation of four-note
motive through a descending
sequence

3:13 Melodic variation, interval
filled in, and inverted

4:12 Expansion through repetition

RECAPITULATION
36 Theme 1—in C minor, brief oboe solo
37 Theme 2—returns in C major

38 CODA—extended treatment of four-note motive

II. Second movement: Andante con moto, 3/8 meter, A-flat major. Theme and variation form, with two themes.

39 0:00 Theme 1—broad, flowing melody, heard in low strings

40 0:51 Theme 2—upward thrusting four-note motive

Examples of variations on Theme 1

41 1:55 Embellished with running sixteenth notes

42 3:50 Embellished with thirty-second notes

43 5:04 Melody exchanged between woodwind instruments

44 6:36 Melody shifted to minor, more disjunct

45 8:09 CODA, marked Più mosso (faster), in bassoon

III. Third movement: Scherzo, 3/4 meter, C minor Scherzo and Trio form

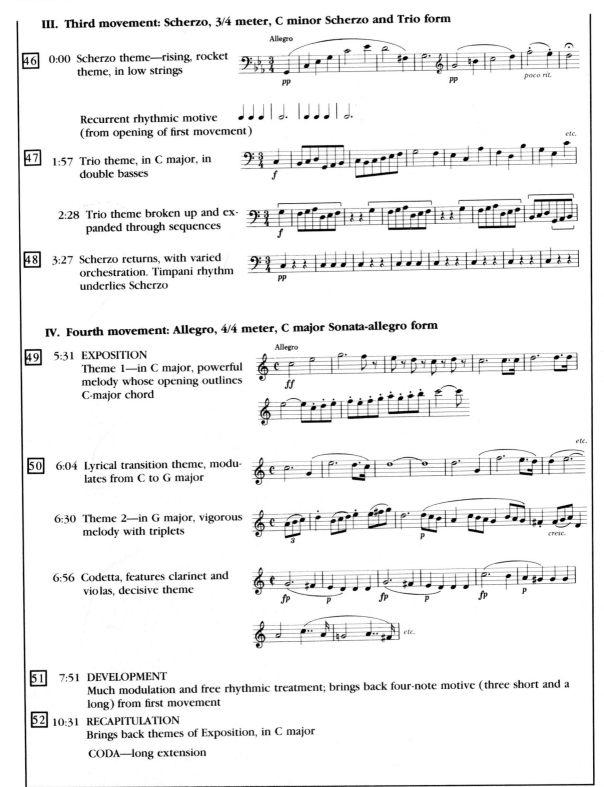

46 0:00 Scherzo theme—rising, rocket theme, in low strings

Recurrent rhythmic motive (from opening of first movement)

47 1:57 Trio theme, in C major, in double basses

2:28 Trio theme broken up and expanded through sequences

48 3:27 Scherzo returns, with varied orchestration. Timpani rhythm underlies Scherzo

IV. Fourth movement: Allegro, 4/4 meter, C major Sonata-allegro form

49 5:31 EXPOSITION
Theme 1—in C major, powerful melody whose opening outlines C-major chord

50 6:04 Lyrical transition theme, modulates from C to G major

6:30 Theme 2—in G major, vigorous melody with triplets

6:56 Codetta, features clarinet and violas, decisive theme

51 7:51 DEVELOPMENT
Much modulation and free rhythmic treatment; brings back four-note motive (three short and a long) from first movement

52 10:31 RECAPITULATION
Brings back themes of Exposition, in C major

CODA—long extension

UNIT XIII

■

The Eighteenth-Century Concerto and Sonata

36

The Classical Concerto

The Movements of the Concerto

In the Baroque era, we saw that the word *concerto* implied a mixing together of two disparate elements, such as a soloist and orchestra or a solo group and orchestra. The Classical era shifted the emphasis to the concerto for solo instrument—especially piano or violin—and orchestra.

Cadenza The three movements of the Classical concerto follow the traditional pattern fast-slow-fast already established. A characteristic feature of the concerto is the *cadenza*, a fanciful solo passage in the manner of an improvisation that is interpolated into the movement. The cadenza came out of a time when improvisation was an important element in art music, as it still is today in jazz. Taken over into the solo concerto, the cadenza made a dramatic effect: the orchestra fell silent and the soloist launched into a free play of fantasy on one or more themes of the movement.

First movement The concerto begins in sonata-allegro form, the first section being a double Exposition. That is, the orchestra announces the two contrasting themes but remains in the tonic key, then the soloist takes over the themes, with modulation to the dominant key for the second theme. The Development section gives the soloist ample opportunity for virtuoso display. The Recapitulation remains in the tonic key, with a cadenza toward the end of the movement in the style of a brilliant improvisation, and a coda brings the movement to a close with a strong affirmation of the home key.

Second movement Second is the slow lyrical movement, generally an Andante, Adagio, or Largo, which features the soloist in poetic, songlike melody. This movement is often in a key that lies close to the tonic but contrasts with it, such as the key a fourth above. Thus, if the first movement is in C major, the second might very well be in F major, four steps above.

Third movement

The finale is generally an Allegro molto (very fast) or Presto, usually shorter than the first movement, often in rondo form or in a rondo that has taken over some developmental features of sonata-allegro form. This movement may contain a cadenza of its own that calls for virtuoso playing and brings the piece to an exciting end.

Summary of Concerto Form

First movement:	Double Exposition Form
Exposition 1:	Orchestra, in tonic
	Theme 1
	Theme 2
Exposition 2:	Soloist with orchestra
	Theme 1, in tonic
	Theme 2, in dominant
Development:	Varied treatment of themes by soloist and orchestra
Recapitulation:	Theme 1 and 2, in tonic, orchestra and soloist
Cadenza:	Soloist
Coda:	Orchestra and soloist, in tonic
Second movement:	Slow, lyrical, in **A-B-A** or theme and variations form, in key closely related to tonic
Third movement:	Fast sonata or rondo form, in tonic

Mozart: Piano Concerto in C major, K. 467

Mozart, we saw, played a crucial role in the development of the piano concerto. His concertos were written primarily as display pieces for his own public performances. They abound in the brilliant flourishes and ceremonious gestures characteristic of eighteenth-century social music.

First movement

The sunny Piano Concerto in C major, K. 467 (1785), belongs to one of Mozart's most productive periods. The first movement is an Allegro maestoso whose opening pages show how richly Mozart's instrumental art was nourished by the opera house; the principal theme could have come straight out of a scene in an opera buffa. More important, its first two measures constitute a motive that is wonderfully capable of growth and development. (See the analysis in Listening Guide 23.) In connection with this movement we may speak of a theme group rather than a single theme.

Mozart, in his concertos, uses the sonata-allegro form with infinite variety; no two first movements are alike. Since this particular movement is fashioned out of flowing melodies, the result is an unusually spacious form. The orchestra presents the thematic material, which is then repeated by the soloist—in short, a double Exposition. The virtuoso figuration in the piano part is heard against broadly spun phrases in the strings or woodwinds.

The Recapitulation opens with the strings playing the main theme in the home key, followed immediately by the second idea. Where are the subsidiary themes we heard in the Exposition? It turns out that Mozart is saving them for the coda, which rounds out the movement with all the courtly grace of the eighteenth century and prepares the way for the cadenza. We unfortunately do not possess Mozart's cadenza; it is a wise artist who makes his own as short as possible. The basic motive returns in the final measures. One might have expected so bright an Allegro to have a brilliant ending. Mozart surprises us. The movement ends like one of those opera buffa scenes in which the characters tiptoe off stage.

Second movement

The second movement is a serenely flowing Andante in F. Its gentle poignancy explains why nineteenth-century composers such as Chopin and Tchaikovsky worshiped Mozart above all others. After a middle section that stresses D minor, the melody returns in the remote key of A-flat major—a procedure closer to the Romantic mind than the Classical. Mozart does not repeat the theme literally; he varies it with fanciful embellishments. The movement finds its way back to the home key, and the coda rounds it off with a pianissimo ending.

Third movement

The gay finale is a rondo in C major, marked Allegro vivace assai (very fast and lively), that opens with a tune straight out of opera buffa. In its vivacity and good humor, this movement typifies the Classical rondo finale. But at this time the rondo was absorbing certain features of sonata-allegro form, especially the dynamic movement from key to key and—most important of all—the development of themes and motives. There resulted a form that may be considered a sonata-rondo, of which this Allegro is an excellent example.

The filigree work on the piano demands nimble fingers. Clearly Mozart enjoyed displaying his prowess as a pianist. There is much lively interplay between piano and orchestra, both of which—after a brief cadenza that ushers in the final appearance of the theme—share in the brilliant C-major ending.

Listening Guide 23

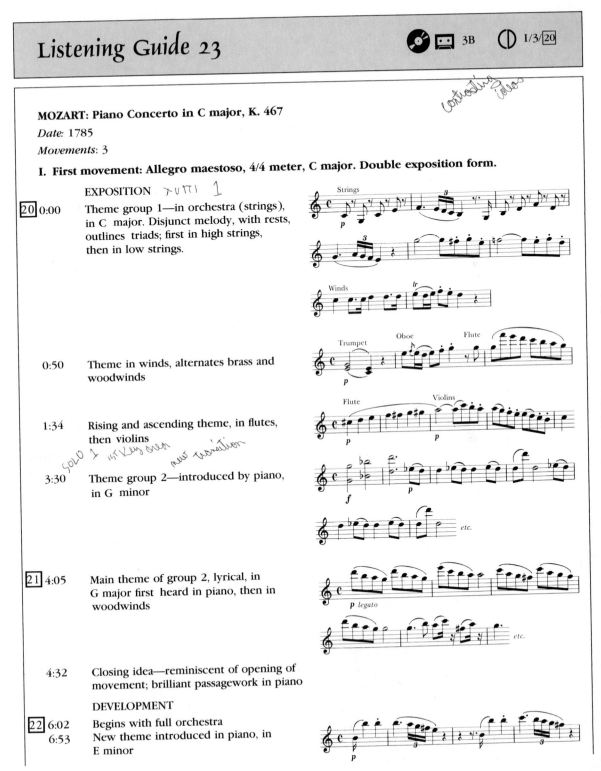

MOZART: Piano Concerto in C major, K. 467

Date: 1785

Movements: 3

I. First movement: Allegro maestoso, 4/4 meter, C major. Double exposition form.

EXPOSITION

20 0:00 Theme group 1—in orchestra (strings), in C major. Disjunct melody, with rests, outlines triads; first in high strings, then in low strings.

0:50 Theme in winds, alternates brass and woodwinds

1:34 Rising and ascending theme, in flutes, then violins

3:30 Theme group 2—introduced by piano, in G minor

21 4:05 Main theme of group 2, lyrical, in G major first heard in piano, then in woodwinds

4:32 Closing idea—reminiscent of opening of movement; brilliant passagework in piano

DEVELOPMENT

22 6:02 Begins with full orchestra
6:53 New theme introduced in piano, in E minor

7:09 Figurations in piano, lyrical melodies in strings and woodwinds

RECAPITULATION *Tutti 3*

23 8:25 Theme group 1—opening idea, in orchestra, in C major

Transition, piano figurations

24 9:35 Theme group 2—in piano, in C major

Closing idea—based on opening theme, in C major

25 12:02 Cadenza—improvised by piano, no accompaniment leads into brief orchestral coda

II. Second movement: Andante, 4/4 meter, F major. Ternary (A-B-A) form

Like eine kleine nacht musik

26 0:00 A section—underlying rhythmic pulse in triplets; muted middle-range strings, with plucked cellos and basses

Violin II and Violas

Cello and Basses — pizzicato

Theme—muted violins, 3-measure phrases

Theme repeated in piano statement, against pizzicato strings

27 2:09 B section—in D minor, in piano, with strings accompanying more chromatic, disjunct lines

4:13 A section—melody returns in A-flat major, in piano, varied from opening, ends in F major

Tutti 4 for Clarinet solo

III. Third movement: Allegro vivace assai, 2/4 meter, C major. Rondo form.

29 0:00 A theme—light, bouncy tune, introduced in strings, in C major

Allegro vivace assai

Theme heard in piano, then in strings and woodwinds, with piano figurations

30 1:37 B theme—in G major, in woodwinds and horns, taken over by piano

Developmental section—more chromatic, piano runs

31 2:47 A theme—in piano, then full orchestra, C major; motives exchanged between piano and woodwinds

32 5:10 B theme—returns in C major, in piano, light character; piano runs lead to hold on G major chord

33 6:03 Cadenza—solo piano

34 7:01 A theme—first in piano, then strings; piano has fast runs to final three closing chords

Beethoven: Piano Concerto No. 5 in E-flat major (Emperor)

The name *Emperor* that attached itself to Beethoven's last piano concerto was not given by him. To the Viennese the word suggested all that was noble and great. The work is truly an emperor among concertos, but it hardly needs so conservative a label to affirm its greatness. Beethoven had completed six of his symphonies by the time he wrote this concerto. He here achieved a remarkable fusion of concerto style and symphonic form, projecting the tensions between piano and orchestra within a truly imposing architecture.

S2B/1

S2/23

The Classical concerto, we saw, began with a long orchestral passage that built up suspense against the entrance of the soloist. In this concerto, Beethoven brings in the piano at once, creating thereby a dramatic confrontation between piano and orchestra. The *Emperor Concerto* opens with a majestic pronouncement of the three chords that served as the pillars of Classical harmonic architecture—the tonic (I), subdominant (IV), and dominant (V). Each chord in turn is announced by the orchestra and expanded on the piano in a cadenza-like passage consisting of arpeggios, trills, broken octaves, and rapid scales. After this spectacular introduction, the orchestra sets forth the principal themes of the movement in a spacious Exposition.

First movement

The piano enters boldly with an ascending chromatic scale followed by a trill. The themes take on a different quality when they are set forth by the piano in this second Exposition. At the end of the Development section, Beethoven prepares for the Recapitulation by repeating the procedure he used at the beginning of the piece. The orchestra announces the three basic chords, each of which is expanded on the piano in a new cadenza-like passage. Again we hear an ascending chromatic scale, and the Recapitulation begins with the main idea in the home key. The subsidiary ideas are heard as before, but shifted to new keys.

In the Classical concerto the orchestra was supposed to pause at a certain point and leave the soloist free to improvise a cadenza. Beethoven, in this work, opened a new chapter in the history of the piano concerto by writing out the cadenza. In other words, the time had passed when the composer could depend on the performer's ability to improvise a cadenza at the performance. Henceforth composers (with a few exceptions) followed Beethoven's example and wrote out the cadenza in advance.

The slow movement is another example of what came to be called, in Beethoven literature, the "hymnic Adagio:" a movement of profound serenity, inner strength, and depth of feeling. It is in an **A-B-A** or three-part form. The movement ends with a shadowy pianissimo that covers a daring modulation. Out of it, like an upsurge of light, emerges the final movement, an energetic rondo.

Second and third movements

The *Emperor* was a milestone in the history of the piano concerto. In it Beethoven looked beyond his time to the future. Since its full realization demands artistry of the higest order, it still poses a challenge to the concert pianist today.

37

The Classical Sonata

The Movements of the Sonata

We saw in an earlier chapter that the sonata, as Haydn, Mozart, and their successors understood the term, was an instrumental work consisting of a series of contrasting movements for one or two instruments. The movements were three or four in number (sometimes two), and followed the basic sonata-cycle we described in our discussion of string quartet, symphony, and concerto.

In the Classical era the sonata became an important genre for amateurs in the home, as well as for composers appearing in concerts as performers of their own music. The late eighteenth century favored the sonata for piano solo as well as sonatas for violin or cello and piano. These at first presented the piano as the major instrument with the string instrument acting as accompaniment. Mozart and Beethoven changed this approach. In their duo sonatas the two instruments are treated as equal partners.

Beethoven: Piano Sonata in C minor, Op. 13 (Pathétique)

Unlike the case of the *Emperor Concerto*, the title of the Piano Sonata in C minor, Opus 13—*Pathétique*—was Beethoven's own. Certainly the quality of Beethovenian pathos is manifest from the first chords of the slow introduction. Marked Grave (solemn), this celebrated opening has something fantasy-like about it, as if Beethoven had captured here the passionate intensity that so affected his listeners when he improvised at the keyboard.

Striking, too, are the contrasts between forte and piano. This type of contrast, an essential feature of Beethoven's dynamism, is used with maximum effectiveness a little further on when it is combined with a change of register: fortissimo chords in the bass are contrasted with a softly expressive melody in the treble. All in all this introduction, written on the threshold of the nineteenth century (1798), speaks a powerful language new to piano music. It ends with a descending chromatic scale and the instruction "Attacca subito l'Allegro" (attack the Allegro immediately).

Introduction

First movement

The movement proper, marked Allegro di molto e con brio (very fast and with vigor), opens in the home key—C minor—with an impetuous idea that climbs to its peak and descends, while the left hand maintains the rumble of a sustained tremolo in the bass. Beethoven uses the resources of the instrument most imaginatively: contrasts in dynamics and register, the brilliance of rapid scale passages, the excitement of tremolo, and the power of a slowly gathering crescendo allied with a gradual climb in pitch. Very dramatic, just before the end of the movement, is a brief reminder of the slow introduction, followed by a precipitous cadence in the home key.

Second movement

The second movement is the famous Adagio cantabile (slow and songful) which shows off the piano's ability to sing. Like the slow movement of the

Emperor Concerto, this "hymnic adagio" combines an introspective character with the quality of strength that Beethoven made his own.

The final movement is a Rondo, to whose principal theme the C-minor tonality imparts a darker coloring that sets it apart from the usually cheerful rondo-finales of Haydn and Mozart. (See Listening Guide 24 for analysis). The frame is spacious; within it, lyric episodes alternate with dramatic.

The *Pathétique* has been a favorite for generations. In the hands of a great artist it stands revealed as one of Beethoven's most personal sonatas.

Third movement

Listening Guide 24

4A/5   1/4/16

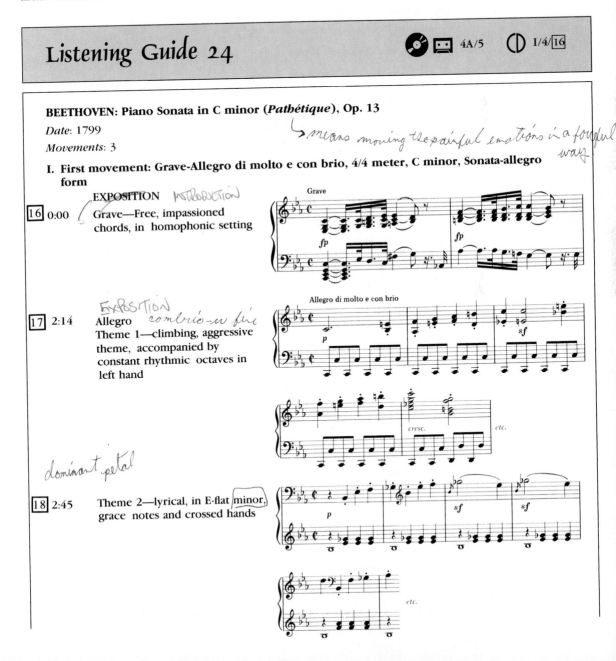

BEETHOVEN: Piano Sonata in C minor (*Pathétique*), Op. 13

Date: 1799

Movements: 3

→ means moving the painful emotions in a forceful way [handwritten]

I. First movement: Grave-Allegro di molto e con brio, 4/4 meter, C minor, Sonata-allegro form

16 0:00   **EXPOSITION** INTRODUCTION [handwritten]
Grave—Free, impassioned chords, in homophonic setting

17 2:14   EXPOSITION [handwritten]
Allegro con brio—w fire [handwritten]
Theme 1—climbing, aggressive theme, accompanied by constant rhythmic octaves in left hand

dominant pedal [handwritten]

18 2:45   Theme 2—lyrical, in E-flat minor, grace notes and crossed hands

[handwritten: TIC In Eb no's then repeat of Expo.]

[handwritten: X = SLOW INTRO]
[handwritten: Y = ALLEGRO]

3:15   Theme 3—in E-flat major, builds to crescendo

3:34   Codetta—closes Exposition with ideas from opening Allegro and then the Grave

[handwritten: RETURN OF INTRO]

DEVELOPMENT

[19] 6:25   Combines opening Allegro and Grave themes

Allegro molto e con brio

RECAPITULATION

[20] 7:09   Themes 1, 2, and 3 return in C minor

8:37   Grave returns, leading to Coda (Allegro), like opening

II. Second movement: Adagio cantabile, 2/4 meter, A-flat major. Rondo form (A-B-A-C-A)

[21] 0:00   A section—lyrical melody, first in middle range, then repeated up an octave

Adagio cantabile

[22] 1:13   B section—contrasting lyrical melody, modulating

[23] 2:10   A section returns in A-flat major

[24] 2:45   C section—more dramatic, with triplet figures, accents, and arpeggios

[25] 3:30   A section—returns in A-flat major

III. Third movement: Allegro, duple meter, C minor. Rondo form (A-B-A-C-A-B-A)

[26] 0:00   A section—quick-paced melody in C minor, its recurrence the basis for the movement

Allegro

[27] 0:20   B section—modulates to E-flat major, melody moves up and down scale; then slower, chordal section, leading to exchange of motive between right and left hands

[28] 1:15   A section—in C minor

[29] 1:34   C section—modulates to A-flat major, with disjunct theme and syncopated rhythms, motivic exchange between hands

[30] 2:29   A section—in C minor

[31] 2:44   B section—in C major

[32] 3:33   A section—in C minor, final statement

An eighteenth-century engraving dated 1773, showing a typical violin-piano duo, with a woman at the keyboard. (Paris, Bibliothèque Nationale)

Mozart: Sonata for Violin and Piano in E-flat, K. 302

During the Classical period the violin achieved great popularity as an instrument for chamber music, especially in duo sonatas. Mozart himself played the violin and was partial to it; his sonatas for violin and piano—more than thirty—extend throughout his career.

    Characteristic is the Sonata in E-flat major, K. 302. It has one unusual feature: it is in two movements. The first, an Allegro in sonata-allegro form, is based on two strongly contrasting ideas. An arresting theme based on descending arpeggios that outline the tonic chord is counterposed to a sprightly legato melody based on a repeated-note motive. This motive is repeated at different pitches—that is, in sequence. It is announced by the violin, then the piano takes it over.

First movement

    Second is a Rondo that differs from the usual Rondo finale of the Classical period in that it is a reflective movement, marked Andante grazioso (fairly slow, graceful) rather than a lively Allegro. The first theme begins with a single note in the melody that is heard six times while the harmonies underneath it change. Announced by the piano, it is taken over by the violin. This basic idea alternates with two other themes in the pattern **A-B-A-C-A-B-C-A.** The movement shows a balanced structure based on symmetrical four-measure phrases. Of special interest is the manner in which contrasting sections wander through a variety of keys. Striking too is Mozart's way of varying each repetition of the main theme through changing rhythms, ornaments in the violin part, and triplet patterns.

Second movement

UNIT XIV

◼

Choral Music and Opera in the Classical Era

38

Mass, Requiem, and Oratorio

The late eighteenth century inherited a rich tradition of choral music from the Baroque. Among the principal forms of choral art were the Mass and Requiem. A *Mass*, you will recall, is a musical setting of the most solemn service of the Roman Catholic Church and a *Requiem* is a musical setting of the Mass for the Dead. Both types were originally intended to be performed in church. By the nineteenth century they had found a much larger audience in the concert hall.

The blending of many voices in a large space such as a church or cathedral could not fail to be an uplifting experience. For this reason both the Catholic and Protestant church were patrons of music throughout the ages. The two choral works to be studied in this chapter show how the masters of the Classical Viennese school responded to the great tradition of religious choral music.

Important too was the *oratorio*, which we have encountered as a genre made popular by Handel in such works as *Messiah*. Haydn wrote two oratorios—*The Creation* and *The Seasons*, which attained enormous popularity throughout the nineteenth century and helped build the new mass public.

Haydn: Credo, from Mass in D minor (Lord Nelson)

Haydn's Mass in D minor (*Lord Nelson*) is not directly connected with the great Admiral. Haydn was finishing the work as Horatio Nelson destroyed the French fleet in the harbor of Abukir, Egypt, on August 1, 1798. The news of England's victory brought great rejoicing in Austria, since the Emperor's sister, Marie Antoinette, had been a victim of the French Revolution. Haydn first called the work "Mass in a time of anxiety," which suggests how involved his country was in the distant war. Two years later it was performed in the presence of Lord Nelson, at that time a guest of the Esterházys, and came to be known by his name.

Scored for three high trumpets and timpani, solo organ and strings, four vocal soloists (soprano, alto, tenor, bass) and a four-part chorus, the Mass is notable for its heroic tone and freshness of invention. It has become one of Haydn's most frequently performed works. His biographer, H. C. Robbins Landon, calls it "Haydn's greatest symphony."

We shall study the Credo, which has one of the longest texts among the movements of the Mass. (When Stravinsky, a century and a half later, was asked why the Credo of his Mass was so long, he answered, "There is much to believe.") This movement begins as an Allegro con spirito in duple meter, in G major, for full chorus. It is cast in the style of a *canon*, in which one vocal line imitates another at a fixed distance throughout a movement. In this case Haydn pairs sopranos and tenors against altos and basses, who imitate the two higher voices a measure later at the interval of a fifth. It takes a master to handle so intricate a procedure with such grace and ease. (For the full text of this movement see Listening Guide 25.)

Canon

The *Et incarnatus est de Spiritu Sancto* (And was made flesh by the Holy Ghost) is a lovely Largo in G major, in triple time, for soprano, tenor, alto, and baritone soloists, with full chorus. Here the sopranos carry the main line, with repetition of text throughout. This homophonic texture in the chorus is integrated with a tightly knit, polyphonic passage for the quartet of soloists. Thus the two types of texture are brought into an artistic unity. Notice the descending vocal line with which Haydn sets the saddest phrase of the text, *Crucifixus etiam pro nobis* (He was also crucified for us).

The *Et resurrexit* (And He rose again), a Vivace for solo soprano and chorus, begins with an upward-leaping figure in the orchestra whose joy is mirrored in the voices. The chorus unfolds a homophonic texture against an extremely active orchestral background. The soprano soloist enters toward the end with a florid, melismatic expansion of the final word, "Amen." The chorus takes over the expansion of "Amen," and brings the Credo to a powerful conclusion. How masterful is Haydn's way of introducing high trumpets and drums at strategic points to give the movement a sense of glory.

Listening Guide 25

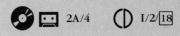

2A/4   I/2/18

HAYDN: Credo from *Lord Nelson Mass* "NO DOUBT ABOUT IT" EMD.
Date: 1798

Medium: Four soloists, four-part chorus, strings, three trumpets, and timpani
Genre: Mass, setting of Ordinary
THREE MAIN SECTIONS OF CREDO

18 I. "Credo in unum Deum," Allegro con spirito

Text	*Translation*	*Description*
Credo in unum Deum, Patrem omnipontem, factorem coeli et terrae, visibilium omnium et invisibilium omnium, et ex Patre natum omnia saecula. Deum de Deo, lumen de lumine, Deum verum de Deo vero, genitum, non factum, consubstantialem Patri, per quem omnia facta sunt: Qui propter nos homines et propter nostram salutem descendit de coelis.	I believe in one God, the Father almighty, maker of heaven and earth, and of all things visible and invisible. And in one Lord Jesus Christ, the only begotten son of God, born of the Father before all ages; God of God, Light of Light, true son of God; begotten, not made; of one being with the Father, by whom all things were made. Who for us men, and for our salvation, came down from heaven.	Choral canon, imitative voices paired (ST, AB)

Repetition of final phrase of text, ending in unison homophonic statement |

Opening canon in chorus,
showing voice pairings (ST,
AB)

19 II. "Et incarnatus est," Largo

Et incarnatus est de Spiritu sancto ex Maria virgine, et homo factus est. Crucifixus etiam pro nobis sub Pontio Pilato, passus et sepultus est.	And was incarnate by the Holy Ghost, of the Virgin Mary; and was made man. He was crucified for us, suffered under Pontius Pilate, and was buried.	Soprano solo, followed by choral setting, closing with SATB soloists, alternating with chorus

Opening of melodious soprano
solo

20│ **III. "Et resurrexit," Vivace**

| Et resurrexit tertia die secundum Scripturas, et ascendit la coelum, sedet ad dexteram Patria. Et iteram venturus est cum gloria judicare vives et mortuos; Cuius regni non erit finis. Et in Spiritum Sanctum, Dominum et vivicantem. Qui cum Patre et Filio simul adoratur et conglorificatur, qui locutus est per Prophetas, et unam sanctum catholicam et apostolicam Ecclesiam. Confiteor unum baptisma in remissionem peccatorum. Et expecto resurrectionem peccatorum. Et expecto resurrectionem mortuorum, et vitam venturi saeculi. Amen. | And on the third day He rose again from the dead according to the Scriptures; and he ascended into heaven. He sitteth at the right hand of the Father; and he shall come again to judge the living and the dead; and his kingdom shall have no end. And in the Holy Spirit, the Lord and Giver of life, who with the Father and Son is worshipped and glorified; who spoke by the prophets. And in one holy, Catholic, and apostolic church. I acknowledge one Baptism for the remission of sins, and I look for the resurrection of the dead, and the life of the world to come. Amen. | Chorus, homophonic setting against active orchestral writing

Choral declamation

Soprano solo, ornamented Choral closing and Amen |

Homophonic setting of chorus at opening

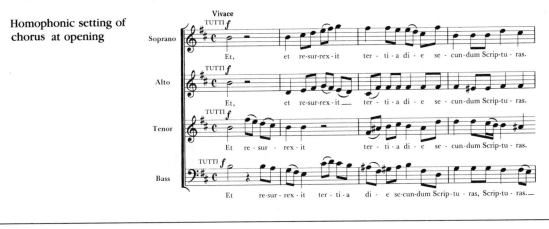

Mozart: Dies irae *from the Requiem*

Mozart's last composition, the Requiem, quickly established itself as one of the masterpieces of the Classical Viennese school. Its most dramatic section is the vision of Judgment Day presented by the *Dies irae* (Day of Wrath). The text came from a Latin poem by a thirteenth-century friar, Thomas of Celano, who was associated with St. Francis of Assisi. In a movement of indescribable power, Mozart captures the terror contained in the words "Day of Wrath, day of mourning, that will destroy the world to ashes, according to the prophecy of David and the Sybil." The movement is in D minor, the same key that Haydn used seven years later for his *Lord Nelson Mass.*

Mozart's score calls for an orchestra consisting of two basset horns (alto clarinets much used in the eighteenth century), two bassoons, two trumpets,

S2A/4

S2/15

three trombones, strings, organ, timpani, four soloists (soprano, alto, tenor, bass) and a four-part chorus.

With its headlong running notes and shattering accents, the *Dies irae* unfolds an awesome canvas. On the words "Quantus tremor est futurus" (What trembling there will be), the singers imitate the trembling, first the bass alone, then the other voices. The cadence is abrupt and powerful.

There follows the *Tuba mirum* (The trumpet flings its wondrous sound). (In ancient Rome *tuba* referred to a trumpet.) Wondrous indeed is the trombone solo that accompanies the opening section for the bass soloist, presently joined by the tenor, who continues with an Andante in B-flat major on the text "Mors stupebit et natura" (Death and nature are stupefied when mankind rushes forward to answer the summons to Judgment.)

The final chorus, *Rex tremendae majestatis* (King of tremendous majesty) vividly projects the sense of the words. A majestic Moderato in 4/4 time, this number opens with an outcry of the full chorus. Dotted rhythms and syncopated chords in the orchestra impart to the music an overwhelming urgency, and lead up steadily to the final plea, which is sung softly: "Salva me, fons pietatis" (Save me, fount of pity!).

There is grandeur in this music. One can only feel sad that its creator never knew how much his Requiem would ultimately mean to the world.

39

Classical Opera

"I had always placed a certain confidence in opera, hoping that from it will rise . . . tragedy in a nobler form."—JOHANN VON SCHILLER

Opera seria

The opera of the eighteenth century accurately reflected the society out of which it sprang. The prevalent form was *opera seria*, "serious" or tragic Italian opera, a highly formalized genre inherited from the Baroque that occupied itself mainly with the affairs of kings and heroes drawn from the legends of Greek antiquity. Its rigid conventions were shaped by the poet Pietro Metastasio (1698–1782), whose librettos were set again and again throughout the century. Opera seria consisted mainly of a series of recitatives and arias that were specifically designed to display the virtuosity of star singers. It spoke to a society dominated by the tastes and needs of the aristocracy.

However, new winds were blowing in the second half of the century. Increasingly the need was felt for simplicity and naturalness, for an opera more realistically attuned to human emotion. One impulse toward reform came from the operas of Christoph Willibald Gluck, whose achievement in

In this anonymous eighteenth-century watercolor, Haydn is thought to be at the harpischord while conducting an opera performance at Esterházy. (Theatermuseum, Munich)

this regard we have already recounted. Another derived from the popular comic opera that flourished in every country of Europe. Known in England as *ballad opera*, in Germany as *Singspiel*, in France as *opéra comique*, and in Italy as *opera buffa*, comic opera was the answer of the rising middle class to the aristocratic form it would inevitably supplant. It differed from opera seria in several basic respects. It was sung in the language of the audience rather than in Italian, which was the official language of international opera. It presented lively, down-to-earth plots rather than the remote concerns of gods and mythological heroes. It featured exciting ensembles at the end of each act in which all the characters participated instead of the solo arias that were the norm in the older opera. And it abounded in farcical situations, humorous dialogue, popular tunes, and the impertinent remarks of the buffo, the traditional character derived from the theater of buffoons, who spoke to the audience with a wink and a nod, and in a bass voice, which brought a new sound into a theater hitherto dominated by the artificial soprano of the castrato.

Comic opera

As the Age of Revolution approached, comic opera became an important social force whose lively wit delighted even the aristocrats it satirized.

Mozart: The Marriage of Figaro

Mozart found his ideal librettist in Lorenzo da Ponte (1749–1838), an Italian-Jewish adventurer and poet whose dramatic vitality was akin to his own.

da Ponte

"The Count discovers the Page." Detail of an illustration from the first Paris edition of Beaumarchais's comedy Le Mariage de Figaro, *engraved by* **Jean-Baptiste Liénard,** *1785.*

One of the picturesque figures of the age, Da Ponte ultimately emigrated to America, operated a grocery store and sold illicit liquor on the side, taught Italian at Columbia College, was one of the first impresarios to bring Italian opera to New York, and wrote a fascinating book of memoirs. Seven years older than Mozart, he survived him by almost half a century, and died without ever suspecting that he would be remembered only because of his association with one far greater than himself. Their collaboration produced, in addition to *The Marriage of Figaro, Don Giovanni,* and *Così fan tutte.*

Da Ponte adapted his libretto for *The Marriage of Figaro* from the play by Pierre-Augustin Caron de Beaumarchais (1732–99), which was truly revolutionary in that it satirized the upper classes and allowed Figaro, the clever and impudent valet of Count Almaviva, consistently to outwit his master. When Louis XVI read the manuscript, he pronounced it detestable and unfit to be seen. It was the liberal friends of Marie Antoinette who persuaded the King to revoke his veto and saw to it that the play was produced. Hapsburg Vienna was even more conservative than Bourbon Paris: the play was forbidden there. But what could not be spoken could be sung. Mozart's opera was produced at the Imperial Court Theater in May 1786, and brought him the greatest success of his life.

Da Ponte used all the traditional devices of bedroom farce. Characters are disguised as each other, fall prey to all sorts of misunderstandings, and are caught in compromising situations they barely manage to wriggle out of. He cut some of Beaumarchais's complications and, as court poet to Emperor Joseph II, was clever enough to know that he must soften the political satire sufficiently to make it palatable.

Although *The Marriage of Figaro* came out of the rich tradition of popular comic opera, Mozart's genius lifted the genre to another dimension. In place of the stereotyped characters of opera buffa he created real human beings who come alive through his music, so that we can identify with their emotions. The Count is a likable philanderer, the Countess is noble in her suffering. Her maid, Susanna, is pert and endlessly resourceful in resisting the advances of her master. Figaro is equally resourceful in foiling the schemes of the Count. And the Countess's page, Cherubino, is irresistible in his boyish ardor and innocence.

In Classical opera the part of a young man was often sung by a soprano or alto wearing trousers. In Mozart's opera the soprano voice is ideally suited to Cherubino's romantic idealism. His aria in Act I, "Non so più," establishes his character as a young man in love with love. "I no longer know who I am or what I'm doing," he sings. "Every woman I see makes me blush and

Act I

A slightly earlier moment between Susanna and Cherubino from a recent performance of The Marriage of Figaro *by the New York City Opera.* (Photo © by Martha Swope)

tremble." (For the Italian-English text and analysis of the aria see Listening Guide 26.)

Cherubino's aria is followed by recitative, which we know is the rapid-fire, talky kind of singing whose main function it is to advance the plot. Eighteenth-century audiences accepted this change of texture and orchestration just as we today accept, in a Broadway musical, the change from song to spoken dialogue.

The action moves rapidly, with overtones of farce. Cherubino has sung his love song to the Countess in Susanna's room. When the Count arrives to ask Susanna to meet him that night in the garden, Cherubino hides behind a huge armchair. At this point the music master Basilio, a gossip if ever there was one, arrives looking for the Count, who tries to hide behind the chair. Susanna adroitly places herself between the Count and Cherubino, so that the page is able to slip in front of the chair and curl up in it. Ever resourceful, she manages to cover him with a tablecloth (in some productions, a dressing gown). With both the front and back of the armchair occupied, Susanna berates Basilio as a gossip and panderer. At this point the Count reveals his presence by planting himself in front of the chair.

Susanna is aghast that the Count has been discovered in her room. The Count, having overheard Basilio's statement that Cherubino adores the Countess, is angry with the young man. And Basilio thoroughly enjoys the rumpus he has stirred up. The action stops as the three join in a trio in which each of them expresses his or her emotion. There is quick exchange among the three voices and much repetiton of text. The extended structure of this trio is related to sonata form. No one ever equaled Mozart's ability to reconcile the demands of a dramatic situation with the requirements of absolute musical form.

The Count pulls the tablecloth from the chair and discovers Cherubino. Furious at finding the youth in Susanna's room, he vows to banish him from the castle. At this point Figaro arrives with a group of peasants whom he has told that the Count has decided to abolish the "right of the first night," the hated feudal privilege that gave the lord of the manor the right to deflower every young woman in his domain. In their gratitude the peasants have come to serenade their master, singing, "His great kindness preserves the purity of a bride for the one she loves." Figaro, delighted to have forced the Count's hand, announces his impending marriage to Susanna, and the Count plays along by accepting the tributes of the crowd.

Figaro intercedes for the page with his master, whereupon the Count relents, appoints Cherubino to a captain's post in his regiment, and leaves with Basilio. The complications in the next three acts lead to a happy ending. The Count is reconciled with his wife, and Figaro wins his beloved Susanna.

Two centuries have passed since Mozart's characters first strutted across a stage. They live on in the opera houses of the world, lifted above time and fashion by the genius of their creator.

Listening Guide 26

 2A/5   I/2/21

MOZART: *The Marriage of Figaro* (*Le nozze di Figaro*)

Date: 1786

Genre: Opera buffa (comic opera)

Librettist: Lorenzo da Ponte

Basis: Play by Beaumarchais

Principal characters:
Figaro, servant to Count Almaviva
Susanna, maid to Countess Almaviva
Cherubino, page
Count Almaviva
Countess Almaviva
~~Doctor Bartolo~~ *BASILIO*
Marcellina, his housekeeper

Act I, #6: Aria, Cherubino

Form: **A-B-A-C,** followed by recitative

A—quick rhythms (in E-flat)

A

♪ Non so   più co-sa son, co-sa fac-cio,

B—more lyrical (in B-flat)

So   lo ai   no-mi d'a-mor di di-let-to,

A—returns (in E-flat)

C—begins quietly, then builds
(in E-flat, modulates)

Par-lo d'a-mor ve-glian - do,

Cherubino *just a kid (puberty)*

[21] Non so più cosa son, cosa faccio, *A*
or di foco, ora sono di ghiaccio,
ogni donna cangiar di colore,
ogni donna mi fa palpitar.
Solo ai nomi d'amor, di diletto, *B*
mi si turba, mi s'altera il petto,
e a parlare mi sforza d'amore
un desio ch'io non posso spiegar. *A*
Parlo d'amor vegliando, *C*
parlo d'amor sognando,
all'acqua, all'ombra, ai monti,
ai fiori, all'erbe, ai fonti,
all'eco, all'aria, ai venti,
che il suon de' vani accenti
portano via con sè.
E se non ho chi m'oda.
parlo d'amor con me!   *prima*

I don't know what I am, what I'm doing;
first I seem to be burning, then freezing;
every woman makes me change colour,
every woman I see makes me shake.
Just the words 'love' and 'pleasure'
bring confusion; my breast swells in terror
yet am I compelled to speak of love
by a force which I cannot explain.
I speak of love while waking,
I speak of love while dreaming,
to the water, to shadows, to mountains,
to the flowers, the grass and the fountains,
to the echo, to the air, to the winds
which carry the idle words
away with them.
And if there is no one to listen,
I speak of love to myself!

music starting / stopping, just like a teen. alteration in moods

(Seeing the Count in the distance, Cherubino hides behind the chair.)

22 Ah! Son perduto!   I'm done for!

Susanna

Che timor . . . il Conte! Misera me!   I'm afraid . . . the Count! Poor me!

(tries to conceal Cherubino)

Count Almaviva (*entering*)

Susanna, tu mi sembri agitata   Susanna, you seem to be agitated
e confusa.   and confused.

Susanna

Signor, io chiedo scusa,   My lord, I beg your pardon,
ma, se mai qui sorpresa,   but . . . indeed . . . the surprise . . .
per carità, partite.   I implore you, please go.

Count (*sits down on the chair and takes Susanna's hand; she draws it forcibly away*)

Un momento, e ti lascio.   One moment, then I'll leave.
Odi.   Listen.

Susanna

Non odo nulla.   I don't want to hear anything.

Count

Due parole: tu sai che ambasciatore a Londra Just a couple of words: you know that the king
il re mi dichiarò;   has named me ambassador to London;
e di condur meco Figaro destinai.   I had intended to take Figaro with me.

Susanna

Signor, se osassi—   My lord, if I may dare—

Count (*rising*)

Parla, parla, mia cara,   Speak, speak, my dear,
e con quel dritto ch'oggi prendi su me,   and with that right you have of me today,
finche tu vivi chiedi, imponi, prescrivi.   as long as you live you may ask, demand,
                                                  prescribe.

Susanna

Lasciatemi, signor,   Let me go, my lord,
dritti non prendo,   I have no rights,
non ne vò, non ne intendo.   I do not want them, nor claim them.
Oh me infelice!   Oh what misery!

Count

Ah no, Susanna, io ti vò far felice!   Ah no, Susanna, I want to make you happy!
Tu ben sai quanto io t'amo;   You well know how much I love you;
a te Basilio tutto già disse.   Basilio has told you that already.
Or senti, se per pochi momenti   Now listen, if you would meet me
meco in giardin, sull'imbrunir del giorno,   briefly in the garden at dusk,
ah, per questo favore io pagherei . . .   ah, for this favour I would pay . . .

Basilio (*outside the door*)

È uscito poco fa.   He went out just now.

Count

Chi parla?   Whose voice is that?

Susanna

O Dei!   Oh, heavens!

Count

Esci, ed alcun non entri.   Go, and let no one come in.

Susanna

Ch'io vi lascio qui solo?   And leave you here alone?

Da madama sarà, vado a cercarlo.

Basilio (*outside*)
He'll be with my lady, I'll go and find him.

Qui dietro mi porrò.

Count
I'll get behind here.

(*points to the chair*)

Non vi celate.

Susanna
No, don't hide.

Taci, e cerca ch'ei parta.

Count
Hush, and try to make him go.

Ohimè! che fate?

Susanna
Oh dear! What are you doing?

(*The Count is about to hide behind the chair; Susanna steps between him and the page. The Count pushes her gently away. She draws back; meanwhile the page slips round to the front of the chair and hops in with his feet drawn up. Susanna rearranges the dress to cover him.*)

Susanna, il ciel vi salvi!
Avreste a caso veduto il Conte?

Basilio
Heaven bless you, Susanna!
Have you seen his lordship by any chance?

E cosa deve fare meco il Conte?

Susanna
And what should his lordship be doing here
    with me?

Animo, uscite.

Come now, be gone!

Aspettate, sentite, Figaro di lui cerca.

Basilio
But listen, Figaro is looking for him.

Oh cielo!
Ei cera chi, dopo voi, più l'odia.

Susanna
(*aside*) Oh dear!
Then he's looking for the one man who,
    after yourself, hates him most!

Vediam come mi serve.

Count (*aside*)
Now we'll see how he serves me.

Io non ho mai nella moral sentito,
ch'uno ch'ami la moglie odii il marito.

Basilio
I have never heard it preached
that one who loves the wife should hate the
    husband.

Per dir che il Conte v'ama.

That's a way of saying that the Count loves you.

Sortite, vil ministro dell'altrui sfrenatezza:
io non ho d'uopo della vostra morale,
del Conte, del suo amor!

Susanna
Get out, vile minister of others' lechery!
I have no need of your preaching,
nor of the Count or his lovemaking!

Non c'è alcun male.
Ha ciascun i suoi gusti.
Io mi credea che preferir
doveste per amante,
come fan tutte quante,
un Signor liberal, prudente e saggio,
a un giovinastro, a un paggio.

Basilio
No offence meant.
Everyone to their own taste.
I thought you would have preferred
as your lover,
as all other women would,
a lord who's liberal, prudent, and wise,
to a raw youth, a mere page.

A Cherubino?

Susanna
To Cherubino?

A Cherubino! Cherubin d'amore,
ch'oggi sul far del giorno
passeggiava qui intorno per entrar.

Basilio
To Cherubino! Love's little cherub,
who early today
was hanging about here waiting to come in.

Uom maligno, un'impostura è
    questa.

Susanna
You insinuating wretch, that's a lie.

E un maligno con voi
chi ha gli occhi in testa?
E quella canzonetta,
ditemi in confidenza,
Io sono amico,
ed altrui nulla dico,
è per voi, per madama?

Basilio
Do you call it an insinuation
to have eyes in one's head?
And that little ditty,
tell me confidentially
as a friend,
and I will tell no one else,
was it written for you or my lady?

Chi diavol gliel'ha detto?

Susanna (*aside*)
Who the devil told him about that?

A proposito, figlia, istruitelo meglio.

Basilio
By the way, my child, you must teach him
    better,

Egli la guarda a tavola sì spesso,
e con tale immodestia,
che s'il Conte s'accorge—
e sul tal punto, sapete, egli è una bestia—

At table he gazes at her so often
and so wantonly,
that if the Count noticed it—
on that subject, as you know, he's quite wild—

Scellerato! e perchè andate voi
tai menzogne spargendo?

Susanna
You wretch! Why do you go around
spreading such lies?

Io! che ingiustizia!
Quel che compro io vendo,
a quel che tutti dicono,
Io non aggiungo un pelo.

Basilio
I! How unfair!
That which I buy I sell,
and to what is common knowledge
I add not a tittle.

Come! che dicon tutti?

Count (*emerging from his hiding-place*)
Indeed! And what is common knowledge?

Oh bella!

Basilio (*aside*)
How wonderful!

Oh cielo!

Susanna (*aside*)
Oh heavens!

Act I, #7: Terzetta (Trio): Count, Basilio, and Susanna

Form: sonata-type structure, with development and recapitulation

Style: quick exchange between voices; much text repetition; each character with own emotional
    commentary

The Count—angry

Basilio and the Count—comforting Susanna
who has fainted

[23] Cosa sento! Tosto andate,
    E scacciate il seduttor!

Count
I heard it all! Go at once
throw the seducer out!

In mal punto son qui giunto;
Perdonate, o mio signor.

Che ruina! me meschina!
Son'oppressa dal terror!

Tosto andate, andate . . .

In mal punto . . .

⎡ Che ruina!

⎢ . . . son qui giunto; . . .

⎢ . . . e scacciate . . .
⎣ . . . il seduttor.

. . . perdonate, . . .
⎡ . . . o mio signor.

⎣ Me meschina!

Me meschina!
Son oppressa dal terror,

Ah! già svien la poverina!
Come, oh Dio! le batte il cor.

Pian, pianin, su questo seggio—

Dove sono? Cosa veggio?
Che insolenza! andate fuor.

Siamo qui per aiutarvi, . . .

⎡ . . . è sicuro il vostro onor.

⎣ . . . non turbarti, o mio tesor.

Ah, del paggio, quel ch'ho detto,
era solo un mio sospetto.

E un'insidia, una perfidia,
non credete all'impostor.

Parta, parta il damerino, . . .

Poverino!

. . . parta, parta il damerino.

Basilio
    I have come at an unfortunate moment;
    forgive me, my lord.

Susanna (*nearly fainting*) *(pretend)*
    What a catastrophe! I am ruined! *petal point*
    Terror grips my heart!

Count
    Go at once, go . . .

Basilio
    I have come . . .

Susanna
    What a catastrophe!

Basilio
    . . . at an unfortunate moment

Count
    . . . and throw . . .
    . . . the seducer out.

Basilio
    . . . forgive me, . . .
    . . . o my lord.

Susanna
    I am ruined!
    I am ruined!
    Terror grips my heart.

Basilio, Count (*supporting Susanna*)
    Ah! The poor girl's fainted!
    O God, how her heart is beating. *P*

Basilio
    Gently, gently on to the chair—
(*taking her to the chair*)

Susanna (*coming to*)
    Where am I? What's this I see?
    What insolence! Leave this room.

Basilio, Count
    We're here to help you, . . .

Basilio
    . . . your virtue is safe.

Count
    . . . do not worry, sweetheart.

Basilio
    What I was saying about the page
    was only my own suspicion.

Susanna
    It was a nasty insinuation,
    do not believe the liar.

Count
    The young fop must go, . . .

Susanna, Basilio
    Poor boy!

Count
    . . . the young fop must go.

Transition to Susi. when she wakes up

Susanna, Basilio

Poverino!   Poor boy!

Count

Poverino! poverino!   Poor boy! Poor boy!
ma da me sorpreso ancor!   But I caught him yet again!

Susanna

Come?   How!

Basilio

Che?   What?

Susanna

Che?   What?

Basilio

Come?   How?

Susanna, Basilio

Come? che?   How? What?

Count

Da tua cugina,   At your cousin's house
l'uscio ier trovai rinchiuso,   I found the door shut yesterday.
picchio, m'apre Barbarina,   I knocked and Barbarina opened it
paurosa, fuor dell'uso.   much more timidly than usual.
Io, dal muso insospettito,   My suspicions aroused by her expression,
guardo, cerco in ogni sito,   I had a good look around
ed alzando pian, pianino,   and, very gently lifting
il tappeto al tavolino,   the cloth upon the table,
vedo il paggio.   I found the page.

(*imitating his own action with the dress over the chair, he reveals the page*)

Ah, cosa veggio?   Ah, what do I see?

Susanna

Ah! crude stelle!   Ah! wicked fate!

Basilio

Ah! meglio ancora!   Ah! Better still!

Count

24 Onestissima signora, . . .   Most virtuous lady, . . .

Susanna

Accader non può di peggio.   Nothing worse could happen!

Count

. . . or capisco come va!   . . . now I see what's happening!

Susanna

Giusti Dei, che mai sarà!   Merciful heaven, whatever will happen?

Basilio

Così fan tutte . . .   They're all the same . . .

Susanna

Giusti Dei! che mai sarà!   Merciful heaven! Whatever will happen!
Accader non può di peggio,   Nothing worse could happen!
ah no! ah no!   ah no! ah no!

Basilio

. . . le belle,   . . . the fair sex,
non c'è alcuna novità,   there's nothing new about it,
così fan tutte.   they're all the same.

Or capisco come va,
onestissima signora!

Count
Now I see what's happening,
most virtuous lady!

Ah, del paggio quel che ho detto,
era solo un mio sospetto.

Basilio
What I was saying about the page
was only my own suspicion.

[handwritten: TWIST SARCASTIC]

Accader non può di peggio, *ecc.*

Susanna
Nothing worse could happen, *etc.*

Onestissima signora, *ecc.*

Count
Most virtuous lady, *etc.*

Così fan tutte, *ecc.*

Basilio
They're all the same, *etc.*

Tr. by LIONEL SALTER

TRANSITION IV

From Classicism to Romanticism

"I am very greatly obliged by the diploma of honorary membership you so kindly sent me. May it be the reward of my devotion to the art of music to be wholly worthy of such a distinction one day. In order to give musical expression to my sincere gratitude as well, I shall take the liberty before long of presenting your honorable Society with one of my symphonies in score."—FRANZ SCHUBERT

Schubert: Unfinished Symphony

Although we will discuss the songs of Franz Schubert (1797–1828) in connection with the Romantic era, his symphonies, as well as his chamber music, pronounce him the heir of the Viennese Classical tradition. In his handling of large forms and in his radiant orchestral sonorities, Schubert clearly follows directly in the line of development from Haydn, Mozart, and even Beethoven, who, like Schubert, spanned the two eras as a transitional figure.

S2B/2

S2/34

The name *Unfinished* that has attached itself to Schubert's Symphony No. 8 in B minor is unfortunate, suggesting as it does that the composer was snatched away by death before he could complete it. Actually the work was written in 1822, when Schubert was twenty-five years old, and was sent to the Styrian Musical Society of Graz in fulfillment of the promise made in a letter (see the quotation above). He completed two movements and sketched the opening measures of a scherzo. Given his facility, a work was no sooner conceived than written down. Why he never completed this one has never been convincingly answered.

This symphony displays Schubert's gift of melody, his radiant orchestral sound, and his power of making the instruments sing. The wonder is all the greater when we remember that Schubert never heard his finest symphonic scores. His Symphony No. 8 was first performed in Vienna thirty-seven years after his death.

First movement

The first movement is an Allegro moderato, based on three ideas. The first, an introductory theme, establishes the home key with a simple but

A Comparison of Classical and Romantic Styles

Classical (c. 1750–1825)	Romantic (c. 1820–1900)
Haydn, Mozart, Beethoven, Schubert	Beethoven, Schubert, Mendelssohn, Schumann, Chopin, Liszt, Berlioz, Brahms, Tchaikovsky, Strauss
Symmetrical melody in balanced phrases and cadences; tuneful; diatonic, with narrow leaps	Expansive, singing melodies; wide ranging; more varied, with chromatic inflections
Clear rhythmically, with regularly recurring accents; dance rhythms favored	Rhythmic diversity and elasticity; tempo rubato
Diatonic harmony favored; tonic-dominant relationships expanded, become basis for large-scale forms	Increasing chromaticism; expanded concepts of tonality
Homophonic textures; horizontal perspective	Homophony, turning to increased polyphony in later years of era
Symphony, solo concerto, solo sonata, string quartet	Same large forms, including one-movement symphonic poem; solo piano works
Opera, mass, solo song	Same vocal forms, adding works for solo voice/orchestra
Ternary form predominant; sonata-allegro form developed; absolute forms preferred	Expansion of forms and interest in continuous forms as well as miniature programmatic forms
Secular music dominant; aristocratic audience	Secular music dominant; middle-class audience
Continuously changing dynamics through crescendo and decrescendo	Widely ranging dynamics for expressive purposes
Changing tone colors between sections of works	Continual change and blend of tone colors; experiments with new instruments and unusual ranges
String orchestra with woodwinds and some brass; 30 to 40-member orchestra; rise of piano to prominence	Introduction of new instruments (tuba, English horn, saxophone); much larger orchestras; piano dominates as solo instrument
Improvisation largely limited to cadenzas in concertos	Increased virtuosity and expression; composers specify more in scores
Emotional restraint and balance	Emotions, mood, atmosphere emphasized; interest in the bizarre and macabre

memorable statement in the low strings. This is followed by a broadly curved melody typical of Schubert's genius, given out by oboe and clarinet. After a modulation from B minor to G major, a great lyric subject is "sung" by the cellos against a syncopated accompaniment.

Here Schubert deviates from the Classical sonata-allegro procedure by beginning the fragmentation and development of the lyric second theme in the Exposition. The Development section is remarkable for its dramatic intensity and momentum. The Recapitulation restates the material of the first section. The second theme returns in the D major, and the coda brings back the introductory theme, so that the movement ends in the home key with the idea out of which it flowered.

Second movement   The second movement, an Andante con moto in E major, is an abbreviated sonata form, lacking a true development section. It too exudes the subtle color changes and long-breathed melodies for which Schubert is so well known.

The creator of this music passed his uneventful life in the city of Beethoven; too diffident to approach the great man, he worshiped from afar. He could not know that of all the composers of his time, his name alone would be linked to that of his idol. They who far surpassed him in fame and worldly success are long forgotten. Today we speak of the four masters of the Viennese Classical school: Haydn, Mozart, Beethoven—and Schubert.

PART SEVEN

The Nineteenth-Century

"Music is the most romantic of all the arts—one might almost say, the only genuinely romantic one—for its sole subject is the infinite. Music discloses to man an unknown realm, a world in which he leaves behind all definite feelings to surrender himself to an inexpressible longing."—E.T.A. HOFFMANN
(1776–1822)

J.M.W. Turner (*1775–1851*) Slave Ship (*Slavers Throwing Overboard the Dead and Dying, Typhoon Coming On*) (Henry Lillie Pierce Fund. Courtesy, Museum of Fine Arts, Boston)

UNIT XV

■

The Romantic Movement

40

The Spirit of Romanticism

"Romanticism is beauty without bounds—the beautiful infinite."—JEAN
PAUL RICHTER (1763–1825)

The Romantic era, stemming out of the social and political upheavals that
followed in the wake of the French Revolution, came to the fore in the
second quarter of the nineteenth century.

French Revolution

The French Revolution was the outcome of momentous social forces. It
signaled the transfer of power from a hereditary feudal-agricultural aristocracy to the middle class, whose position depended on commerce and industry. As in the case of the American Revolution, this upheaval heralded
a social order shaped by the technological advances of the Industrial Revolution. The new society, based on free enterprise, emphasized the individual
as never before. The slogan "Liberty, Equality, Fraternity" inspired hopes
and visions to which few artists failed to respond. Sympathy for the oppressed,
interest in simple folk and in children, faith in mankind and its destiny—all
these, so intimately associated with the time, point to the democratic character of the Romantic movement.

Whereas the eighteenth century had found inspiration in the art of ancient
Greece, the Romantics discovered the so-called Dark Ages. King Arthur and
Siegfried, fairy tale and medieval saga usurped the place formerly held by
the gods and heroes of antiquity. The Romantics became intensely aware
of nature, but nature as a backdrop for the inner conflicts of man. When the
heroine of a Romantic novel felt sad, it rained.

281

Revolutionary ardor was one of the mainsprings of the Romantic period, as can be seen in this massive sculptural group by **François Rude** *(1784–1855), La Marseillaise (The Departure of the Volunteers of 1792).* Arc de Triomphe, Paris.

Romantic poets

The Romantic poets rebelled against the conventional form and matter of their Classical predecessors; they leaned toward the fanciful, the picturesque, and the passionate. In Germany a group of young writers created a new kind of lyric poetry that culminated in the art of Heinrich Heine; he became one of the favorite poets of Romantic composers. A similar movement in France was led by Victor Hugo, its greatest prose writer, and Alphonse de Lamartine, its greatest poet. In England the revolt against the formalism of the Classical age numbered among its adherents a line of lyric poets such as Gray, Cowper and Burns, Wordsworth and Coleridge, Byron, Shelley, and Keats. The new spirit of individualism expressed itself in the Romantic artists' sense of uniqueness, their heightened awareness of themselves as individuals apart from all others. "I am different from all the men I have seen," proclaimed Jean Jacques Rousseau. "If I am not better, at least I am different."

Thus, one of the prime traits of the Romantic arts was their emphasis on an intensely emotional type of expression. It has been well said that with Romanticism the pronoun "I" made its appearance in poetry. The new age found expression in the passionate lyricism of such lines as Shelley's—

> Oh! lift me as a wave, a leaf, a cloud!
> I fall upon the thorns of life! I bleed!

or Keats's—

> When I have fears that I may cease to be
> Before my pen has gleaned my teeming brain . . .

Sympathy for the oppressed underscored the essentially democratic character of the Romantic movement. **Honoré Daumier** (*1808–79*) The Third-Class Carriage. (The Metropolitan Museum of Art, Bequest of Mrs. H. O. Havemeyer, 1929. The H. O. Havemeyer Collection)

The newly won freedom of the artist proved to be a mixed blessing. Confronted by a philistine world indifferent to artistic and cultural values, artists felt more and more cut off. A new type emerged—the artist as bohemian, the rejected dreamer who starved in an attic and through peculiarities of dress and behavior "shocked the bourgeois." Eternal longing, regret for the lost happiness of childhood, an indefinable discontent that gnawed at the soul—these were the ingredients of the Romantic mood. Yet the artist's pessimism was not without its basis in external reality. It became apparent that the high hopes fostered by the Revolution were not to be realized overnight. Despite the brave slogans, all people were not yet equal or free. Inevitably optimism gave way to doubt and disenchantment—"the illness of the century."

This malaise was reflected in the arts of the time. Hugo dedicated *Les Misérables* "to the unhappy ones of the earth." The nineteenth-century novel found its great theme in the conflict between the individual and society. Jean Valjean and Heathcliff, Madame Bovary and Anna Karenina, Oliver Twist, Tess of the d'Urbervilles, and the Karamazovs—a varied company rises from those impassioned pages to point up the frustrations and guilts of the nineteenth-century world.

Hardly less persuasive was the art of those who sought escape. Some glamorized the past, as did Walter Scott and Alexandre Dumas. Longing for far-off lands inspired the exotic scenes that glow on the canvases of J.M.W. Turner and Eugène Delacroix. The Romantic poets and painters loved the picturesque and the fantastic. Theirs was a world of "strangeness and wonder": the eerie landscape we encounter in the writings of Coleridge, Hawthorne, or Poe.

Romantic painters

The nineteenth-century longing for far-off lands inspired such exotic scenes as the painting Femmes d'Alger *by* **Eugène Delacroix** *(1798–1863).* (The Louvre, Paris)

Romanticism, in fine, dominated the artistic output of the nineteenth century. It gave its name to a movement and an era, and created a multitude of colorful works that still hold millions in thrall.

41

Romanticism in Music

"Music is the melody whose text is the world."—SCHOPENHAUER

Great changes in the moral, political, and social climate of an epoch seek to be expressed also in the art of that epoch. But they cannot be unless the new age places in the artist's hand the means of giving expression to new ideas. This was precisely the achievement of the Romantic movement in music—that it gave composers the means of expressing what the age demanded of them.

The Industrial Revolution brought with it not only cheaper and more responsive instruments, but important improvements in wind instruments that strongly influenced the sound of Romantic music. For example, the addition of valves to brass instruments made them much more maneuverable, so that composers like Wagner and Tchaikovsky could assign melodies to the horn that would have been unplayable in the time of Haydn and Mozart. Several new wind instruments were developed as well, including the tuba and the saxophone. So too, as a result of improved manufacturing techniques, the piano acquired a cast-iron frame and thicker strings that gave it a deeper and more brilliant tone. If an impassioned piano work by Liszt sounds different from a sonata of Mozart, it is not only because Liszt's time demanded of him a different kind of expression, but also because it put at his disposal a piano capable of effects that were neither available nor necessary in the earlier period.

Improved instruments

Secondly, the gradual democratization of society brought with it a broadening of educational opportunities. New conservatories were established in the chief cities of Europe that trained more and better musicians than formerly. As a result, nineteenth-century composers could count on instrumental performers whose skill was considerably more advanced than in former times. As music moved from palace and church to the public concert hall, orchestras increased in size and efficiency, and gave composers a means of expression more varied and colorful than they had ever had before. This naturally had a direct influence upon the sound. For example, where most eighteenth-century music ranged in dynamic level only from piano (soft)

The public concert hall

The nineteenth-century orchestra offered the composer new instruments and a larger ensemble. Contemporary woodcut of an orchestral concert at the Covent Garden Theater, London, 1846.

to forte (loud), the dynamic range of the orchestra in the nineteenth century was far greater. Now came into fashion the heaven-storming crescendos, the violent contrasts of loud and soft that lend such drama to the music of the Romantics. As orchestral music became more and more important, the technique of writing for orchestra—that is, orchestration—became almost an art in itself. At last the musician had a palette comparable to the painter's, and used it as the painter did—to conjure up sensuous beauty and enchantment, to create mood and atmosphere, to suggest nature scenes and calm or stormy seascapes.

Increased expressiveness   The desire for direct communication led composers to use a large number of expressive terms intended to serve as clues to the mood of the music, with the result that a highly characteristic vocabulary sprang up. Among the directions frequently encountered in nineteenth-century scores are *dolce* (sweetly), *cantabile* (songful), *dolente* (weeping), *mesto* (sad), *maestoso* (majestic), *gioioso* (joyous), *con amore* (with love, tenderly), *con fuoco* (with fire), *con passione, espressivo, pastorale, agitato, misterioso, lamentoso, trionfale*. These suggest not only the character of the music but the frame of mind behind it.

Use of folklore   The interest in folklore and the rising tide of nationalism impelled Romantic musicians to make use of the folk songs and dances of their native lands. As a result, a number of national idioms—Hungarian, Polish, Russian, Bohemian, Scandinavian—came to the fore and opened up new areas to European music, greatly enriching its melody, harmony, and rhythm.

Exoticism

Nineteenth-century exoticism manifested itself, first, as a longing of the northern nations for the warmth and color of the south; second, as a longing of the West for the fairy-tale splendors of the Orient. The former impulse found expression in the works of German, French, and Russian composers who turned for inspiration to Italy and Spain. The long list includes several well-known works by Russian composers, such as Tchaikovsky's *Capriccio italien* and Rimsky-Korsakov's *Capriccio on Spanish Themes*. The German contribution includes Mendelssohn's *Italian Symphony*. Among the French works are Chabrier's *España* and Lalo's *Symphonie espagnole*. The masterpiece in this category is Bizet's *Carmen*, which we shall study later.

The glamour of the East was brought to international prominence by the Russian national school. The fairy-tale background of Asia pervades Russian music. Rimsky-Korsakov's orchestrally resplendent *Scheherazade*, Alexander Borodin's opera *Prince Igor*, and Ippolitov-Ivanov's *Caucasian Sketches* are among the many Orientally inspired works that found favor throughout the world. A number of French and Italian composers also utilized exotic themes: Saint-Saëns in *Samson and Delilah*, Verdi in *Aïda*, and Puccini in his operas *Madama Butterfly* and *Turandot*. As we will see later, it was not until the twentieth century that the musical idioms of these distant cultures permeated Western styles to any great extent.

The Royal Pavilion at Brighton (1815–18), built for the prince regent, later George IV, by **John Nash** *(1752–1835), is a confection of Islamic domes, minarets, and screens that reflect the nineteenth-century longing for the exotic splendors of the Orient.*

Romantic Style Traits

Even when written for instruments, Romantic melody was easy to sing and hum. The nineteenth century above all was the period when musicians tried to make their instruments "sing." It is no accident that the themes from Romantic symphonies, concertos, and other instrumental works have been transformed into popular songs, for Romantic melody was marked by a lyricism that gave it an immediate emotional appeal, as is evidenced by the enduring popularity of the tunes of Schubert, Chopin, Verdi, among others. Through innumerable songs and operas as well as instrumental pieces, Romantic melody appealed to a wider audience than had ever existed before.

Singable melody

Nineteenth-century music strove for a harmony that was highly emotional and expressive. Under the impact of the Romantic movement, composers such as Richard Wagner sought combinations of pitches more dissonant than their forebears had been used to.

Expressive harmony

The composers of the nineteenth century gradually expanded the instrumental forms they had inherited from the eighteenth. These musicians needed more time to say what they had to say. A symphony of Haydn or Mozart is apt to take about twenty minutes; one by Tchaikovsky, Brahms, or Dvořák lasts at least twice that long. As public concert life developed, the symphony became the most important form of orchestral music, comparable to the most spacious form in Romantic literature—the novel. As a result, nineteenth-century composers approached the writing of a symphony with greater deliberation—some would say trepidation—than their predecessors. Where Haydn wrote more than a hundred symphonies and Mozart more than forty, Schubert, Bruckner, and Dvořák (following the example

Expanded forms

of Beethoven) wrote nine; Tchaikovsky, six; Schumann and Brahms, four; César Franck, one. As the Romantics well realized, it was not easy to write a symphony after Beethoven. New orchestral forms emerged as well, including the one-movement symphonic poem, the choral symphony, and works for solo voice with orchestra.

Music in the nineteenth century drew steadily closer to literature and painting—that is, to elements that lay outside the realm of sound. The connection with Romantic poetry and drama is most obvious, of course, in the case of music with words. However, even in their purely orchestral music the Romantic composers responded to the mood of the time and captured with remarkable vividness the emotional atmosphere that surrounded nineteenth-century poetry and painting.

The result of all these tendencies was to make Romanticism as potent a force in music as it was in the other arts. Nineteenth-century music was linked to dreams and passions, to profound meditations on life and death, human destiny, God and nature, pride in one's country, desire for freedom, the political struggles of the age, and the ultimate triumph of good over evil. These intellectual and emotional associations, nurtured by the Romantic movement, enabled music to achieve a commanding position in the nineteenth century as a moral force, a vision of human greatness, and a direct link between the artist's inner life and the outside world.

The Musician in Nineteenth-Century Society

The emergence of a new kind of democratic society could not but affect the conditions governing the lives of composers and performers. Concert life began to center on the public concert hall as well as the salons of the aristocracy and upper middle class. Where eighteenth-century musicians had functioned under the system of aristocratic patronage and based their careers upon the favor of royal courts or the nobility, nineteenth-century musicians were supported by the new middle-class public. Musicians of the eighteenth century had been a kind of glorified servant class who ministered to the needs of a public high above them in social rank. In the nineteenth century, however, musicians met their audience as equals. Indeed, as solo performers began to dominate the concert hall, whether as pianists, violinists, or conductors, they were "stars" who were idolized by audiences. Mendelssohn, Liszt, and Paganini were welcomed into the great homes of their time in quite a different way than had been the case with Haydn and Mozart half a century earlier.

Ascendancy of the soloist

Music thrived in the private home and in the civic life of most cities and towns as well. Permanent orchestras and singing societies abounded, printed music was readily available at a cost affordable to many, and music journals kept the public informed about musical activities and new works.

With this expansion of musical life, composers and performing artists were called upon to assume new roles as educators. Felix Mendelssohn, active as composer, pianist, and conductor, used his immense prestige to found and direct the Leipzig Conservatory, whose course of training became

An evening of string quartet music at the Berlin house of Bettina von Arnim, featuring Joseph Joachim as first violinist. Water color by **Johann Carl Arnold**, *c. 1855.* (Freies Deutsches Hochstift, Goethemuseum, Frankfurt [Main] Photo: Ursula Edelmann)

a model for music schools all over Europe and America. The Russian composer-pianist Anton Rubinstein performed a similar role as founder of the St. Petersburg (now Leningrad) Conservatory. Robert Schumann became a widely read critic. Franz Liszt was not only active as a composer and conductor but was also the greatest pianist of his time. In later life he taught extensively and raised up a generation of great concert pianists. Richard Wagner directed his own theater at Bayreuth and was thus instrumental in educating the new public to understand his music dramas. Composers everywhere were active in organizing concerts and music festivals, and thus played a leading role in educating the new mass public.

Women in Music

Standard histories of music have largely excluded consideration of the role of women as composers and performers; this circumstance results from insufficient attention to social considerations of the time, including the educational opportunities, the hierarchy of the social classes, and the economics of the music professions. Recent scholarship supports the contributions of women to music through the eras—although rarely as leaders in innovative changes of style.

The society of the nineteenth century saw sizable numbers of women make careers as professional musicians. This was possible through the broadening of educational opportunities that included the establishment of public conservatories whose doors were open to women; in such schools, women could receive training as singers, instrumentalists, and even as composers. Likewise, the rise of the piano as the favored chamber instrument—both solo and with voice or instruments—provided women of the middle and upper classes with a performance outlet that was socially acceptable. There was one area in which women's talents received full expression—the lyric theater. As opera singers, they performed major roles in dramatic works for the stage.

Composition, on the other hand, proved to be largely a man's province. The generally accepted view held by men that women lacked creativity in the arts drove some nineteenth-century women to pursue literary careers under male pseudonyms: George Eliot, George Sand, and Daniel Stern, to name three. However, despite the social pressures against them, a few women defied the conventions of their time and made a name for themselves as composers. We shall discuss the work of one of the best known of these pioneers: the pianist-composer Clara Schumann.

Women also exerted an important influence as patrons of music or through their friendships with composers. George Sand played an important part in the career of Chopin, as did Carolyne Sayn-Wittgenstein in that of Liszt. Nadejda von Meck is remembered as the woman who supported Tchaikovsky in the early years of his career and made it possible for him to compose. Also, several women of the upper class became known as the hostesses of musical salons where composers could gather to perform and discuss their music. One such musical center was in the home of the Mendelssohn family, where Fanny Mendelssohn, a respected performer and composer herself, hosted concerts that featured works by her more famous brother, Felix.

All in all, women made steady strides toward professional expertise throughout the nineteenth century, and thereby laid the foundation for their achievements in the twentieth.

UNIT XVI

◼

The Nineteenth-Century Art Song

42

The Romantic Song

"Out of my great sorrows I make my little songs."—HEINRICH HEINE

The art song met the nineteenth-century need for intimate personal expression. Coming into prominence in the early decades of the century, the art song emerged as a particularly attractive example of the new lyricism.

Types of Song Structure

We distinguish between two main types of song structure. We are already familiar with one of these, *strophic form*, in which the same melody is repeated with every stanza, or strophe, of the poem. This formation, which occurs very frequently in folk and popular song, permits no real closeness between words and music. Instead it sets up a general atmosphere that accommodates itself equally well to all the stanzas. The first may tell of the lover's expectancy, the second of his joy at seeing his beloved, the third of her father's harshness in separating them, and the fourth of her sad death, all these being sung to the same tune.

Strophic form

The other song type is what the Germans call *durchkomponiert*, or "through-composed"—that is, composed from beginning to end, without repetitions of whole sections. Here the music follows the story line, changing with each stanza according to the text. This makes it possible for the composer to mirror every shade of meaning in the words.

Through-composed form

There is also an intermediate type that combines features of the other two. The same melody may be repeated for two or three stanzas, with new material introduced when the poem requires it, generally at the climax. This, in other words, is a *modified strophic form*.

Modified strophic form

292

The immense popularity of the Romantic art song was due in part to the emergence of the piano as the universal household instrument. A lithograph by **Achille Devéria** *(1800–57),* In the Salon. *(Germanische Nationalmuseum, Nürnberg)*

The Lied

Despite the prominence of song throughout the ages, the art song as we know it today was a product of the Romantic era. It was created by the union of poetry and music in the early nineteenth century. Among the great Romantic masters of the art song were Franz Schubert, Robert Schumann, Johannes Brahms, and Hugo Wolf. The new genre thus came to be known throughout Europe by the German word for song—*Lied* (plural, *Lieder*). A Lied is a solo vocal song with piano accompaniment. Some composers wrote groups of Lieder that were unified by some narrative thread or a descriptive theme; such a group is known as a *song cycle*.

Song cycle

The Lied depended for its flowering on the upsurge of lyric poetry that marked the rise of German Romanticism. Goethe (1749–1832) and Heine (1797–1856) are the two leading figures among a group of poets who, like Wordsworth and Byron, Shelley and Keats in English literature, cultivated a subjective mode of expression through the short lyric poem. The Lied brought to flower the desire of the Romantic era for the union of music and poetry, ranging from tender sentiment to dramatic balladry. Its favorite themes were love and longing, the beauty of nature, and the transience of human happiness.

The triumph of the Romantic art song was made possible by the emergence of the piano as the universal household instrument of the nineteenth century. The piano accompaniment translated the poetic images into musical equivalents. Voice and piano together created a short lyric form charged with feeling, suited alike for amateurs and artists, for the home as for the concert room. Within a short time the Lied achieved immense popularity and made a durable contribution to world art.

43

Franz Schubert

Franz Schubert

"When I wished to sing of love it turned to sorrow. And when I wished to sing of sorrow it was transformed for me into love."

In the popular mind Franz Schubert's life has become a romantic symbol of the artist's fate. He suffered poverty and was neglected during his lifetime. He died young. And after his death he was enshrined among the immortals.

His Life

Franz Schubert (1797–1828) was born in a suburb of Vienna, the son of a schoolmaster. The boy learned the violin from his father, piano from an elder brother; his beautiful soprano voice gained him admittance to the imperial chapel and school where the court singers were trained. His teachers were fully astonished at the musicality of the shy, dreamy lad. One of them remarked that Franz seemed to learn "straight from Heaven."

His school days over, young Schubert tried to follow in his father's footsteps, but he was not cut out for the routine of the classroom. He found escape in the solitude of his attic, immersing himself in the lyric poets who were the first voices of German Romanticism. As one of his friends said, "Everything he touched turned to song." The music came to him with miraculous spontaneity. *Erlkönig*, set to a poem by Goethe, was written in a few hours when he was a teenager. It is one of his greatest songs.

Schubert's talent for friendship attracted a little band of followers. Their appreciation of his genius comforted him for the neglect of the world. With their encouragement Schubert, not yet twenty, broke with the drudgery of his father's school. In the eleven years that were left him he occupied no official position (although he occasionally made halfhearted attempts to obtain one). He lived with one or another of his friends in a mixture of poverty and camaraderie, hope and despair. And steadily, with an almost self-devouring intensity, the music poured from the bespectacled young man. "How do you compose?" he was asked. "I finish one piece," was the answer, "and begin the next."

Schubert was singularly unable to stand up to the world. Songs that in time sold in the hundreds of thousands he surrendered literally for the price of a meal. As the years passed, the buoyancy of youth gave way to a sense of loneliness, the tragic loneliness of the Romantic artist. "No one feels another's grief," he wrote, "no one understands another's joy. People imagine that they can reach one another. In reality they only pass each other by." Yet he comprehended—and in this he was the Romantic—that his very suffering must open to his art new layers of awareness. "My music is the product of my talent and my misery. And that which I have written in my greatest distress is what the world seems to like best."

In this unfinished oil sketch of a "Schubertiade," Moritz von Schwind (1804–71) shows Schubert seated at the piano. Next to him is the singer Johann Michael Vogl, who introduced many of Schubert's songs to the Viennese public. (Vienna, Schubert-Museum)

He still yielded to flurries of optimism when success appeared to lie within his grasp, but eventually there came to him an intimation that the struggle had been decided against him. "It seems to me at times that I no longer belong to this world." This was the emotional climate of the magnificent song cycle *Winterreise* (Winter Journey), in which he struck a note of somber lyricism new to music. The long, dark journey—was it not the symbol of his own life? Overcoming his discouragement, he embarked on his last effort. To the earlier masterpieces was added, in that final year, an amazing list that includes the Mass in E flat, the String Quintet in C, the three posthumous piano sonatas, and thirteen of his finest songs.

Despite the magnitude of these achievements, he made arrangements to study counterpoint. "I see now how much I still have to learn." Ill with typhus, he managed to correct the proofs of the last part of *Winterreise*. The sense of defeat accompanied him through the final delirium: he fancied that he was being buried alive. "Do I not deserve a place above the ground?" His last wish was to be buried near the master he worshiped above all others—Beethoven.

He was thirty-one years old when he died in 1828. His possessions consisted of his clothing, his bedding, and "a pile of old music valued at ten florins": his unpublished manuscripts. In the memorable words of Sir George Grove, "There never has been one like him, and there never will be another."

His Music

Schubert stood at the confluence of the Classic and Romantic eras. His symphonies, as we saw, are Classical in their clear form, their dramatic

1) Identify the source of the following quote:
   "With drooping wings you Cupids come,
   To scatter Roses on her Tomb."

Discuss the composition: composer, date, genre, distinguishing features of the work.
[Bring in Doctrine of the Affections, ground bass, melisma, word painting.]

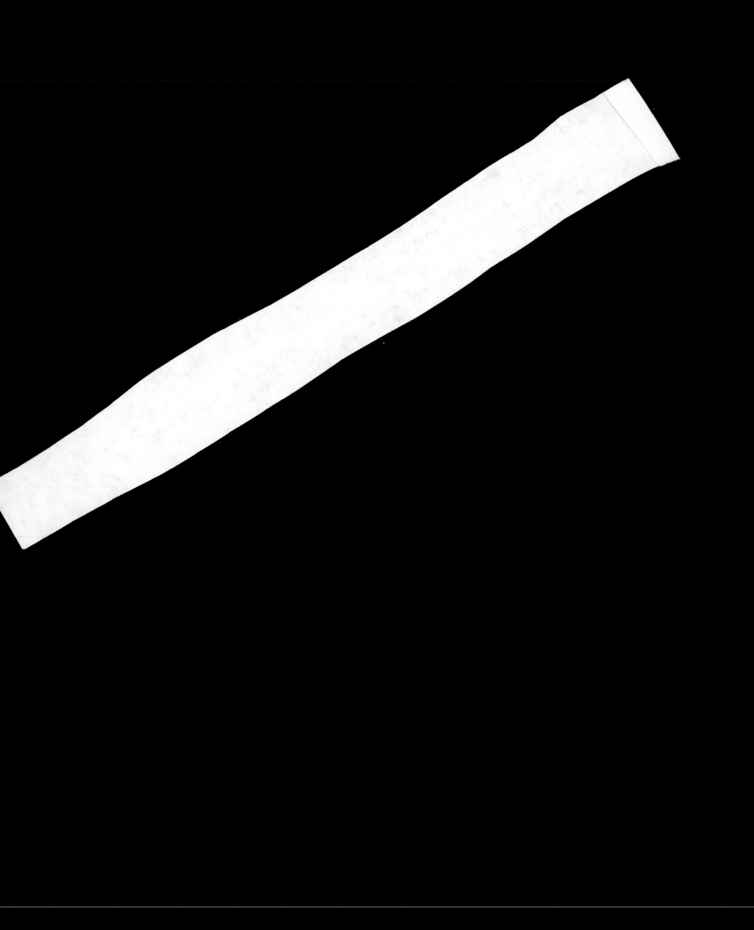

Principal Works

More than 600 Lieder, including 3 song cycles, among them *Die schöne Müllerin* (The Lovely Maid of the Mill, 1823) and *Winterreise* (Winter's Journey, 1827)

8 symphonies, including the *Unfinished* (No. 8, 1822)

Chamber music, including 15 string quartets; 1 string quintet; 2 piano trios and the *Trout Quintet*; 1 octet; various sonatas

Piano sonatas, dances, and character pieces

Choral music, including 7 masses, other liturgical pieces, and partsongs

Operas and incidental music for dramas

momentum, and continuity. But in his Lieder and piano pieces he was wholly the Romantic. The melodies have a tenderness, a quality of longing that match the Romantic quality of the poetry to which they are set. This magical lyricism impelled the composer Franz Liszt to call him "the most poetic musician that ever was."

Chamber music was Schubert's birthright as a Viennese. To the tradition of intimate social music he brought his own inwardness of spirit. His string quartets, the *Trout Quintet*, the two piano trios, and the transcendent Quintet in C bear the true Schubertian stamp. They end the line of Viennese Classicism.

Chamber music

In the Impromptus and *Moments musicaux* (Musical Moments), the piano sings the new lyricism. Here spontaneity and the charm of the unexpected take their place as elements of Romantic art. His piano sonatas were neglected for years, but have now found their rightful place in the repertory. Schubert, whose lyric imagination needed room in which to unfold, expanded the Classical sonata form he inherited from his predecessors.

Piano works

Finally there are the songs, more than six hundred of them. Many were written down at white heat, sometimes five, six, seven in a single morning. Of special interest are the accompaniments: a measure or two, and the music conjures up the rustling brook, the dilapidated hurdy-gurdy, or the lark "at heaven's gate." Certain of his melodies achieve the universality of folksong. Their eloquence and freshness of feeling have never been surpassed. A special place is occupied by two superb song cycles—*Die schöne Müllerin* (The Lovely Maid of the Mill) and *Winterreise*, both on poems of Wilhelm Müller.

Songs

Schubert: Erlkönig

This masterpiece of Schubert's youth (1815) captures the Romantic "strangeness and wonder" of Goethe's celebrated ballad. *Erlkönig* (The Erlking) is based on the legend that whoever is touched by the King of the Elves must die.

The eerie atmosphere of the poem is established by the piano part. Galloping triplets are heard against a rumbling figure in the bass. This motive, so Romantic in tone, pervades the song and imparts to it an astonishing unity. The poem has four characters: the narrator, the father, the child, and the seductive Elf (see Listening Guide 27).

The characters are vividly differentiated through changes in the melody, harmony, rhythm, and type of accompaniment. The child's terror is suggested by clashing dissonance and a high range. The father, allaying his son's fears, is represented by a more rounded vocal line, sung in a low range. As for the Erlking, his cajoling is given in suavely melodious phrases.

The song is through-composed; the music follows the unfolding of the narrative with a steady rise in tension—and pitch—that builds to the climax. Abruptly the obsessive triplet rhythm lets up, slowing down as horse and rider reach home. "In his arms the child"—a dramatic pause precedes the two final words—"was dead."

The thing seems strangely simple, inevitable. The doing of it by a marvelous boy of eighteen was a milestone in the history of Romanticism.

Listening Guide 27   5A/1   II/1/1

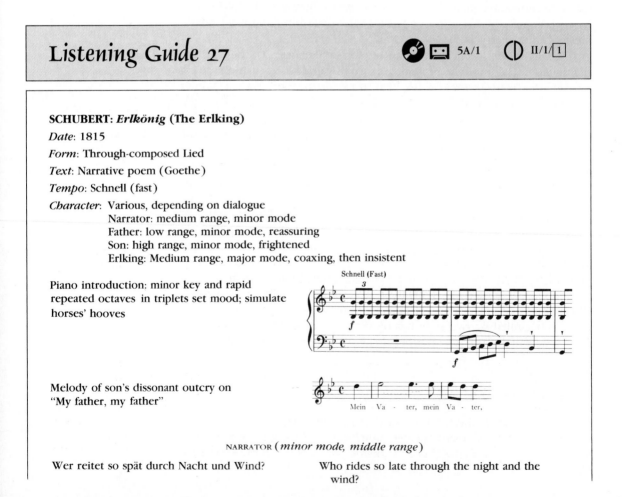

SCHUBERT: *Erlkönig* **(The Erlking)**

Date: 1815

Form: Through-composed Lied

Text: Narrative poem (Goethe)

Tempo: Schnell (fast)

Character: Various, depending on dialogue
        Narrator: medium range, minor mode
        Father: low range, minor mode, reassuring
        Son: high range, minor mode, frightened
        Erlking: Medium range, major mode, coaxing, then insistent

Piano introduction: minor key and rapid repeated octaves in triplets set mood; simulate horses' hooves

Schnell (Fast)

Melody of son's dissonant outcry on "My father, my father"

Mein Va - ter, mein Va - ter,

NARRATOR (*minor mode, middle range*)

Wer reitet so spät durch Nacht und Wind?   Who rides so late through the night and the wind?

Es ist der Vater mit seinem Kind; / It is the father with his child;
er hat den Knaben wohl in dem Arm, / he folds the boy close in his arms,
er fasst ihn sicher, er hält ihn warm. / he clasps him securely, he holds him warmly.

FATHER (*low range*)

"Mein Sohn, was birgst du so bang dein Gesicht?" / "My son, why hide your face so anxiously?"

SON (*high range*)

"Siehst, Vater, du den Erlkönig nicht? / "Father, don't you see the Erlking?
den Erlenkönig mit Kron' und Schweif?" / The Erlking with his crown and his train?"

FATHER (*low range*)

"Mein Sohn, es ist ein Nebelstreif." / "My son, it is a streak of mist."

ERLKING (*major mode, melodic*)

"Du liebes Kind, komm, geh mit mir! / "Dear child, come, go with me!
gar schöne Spiele spiel' ich mit dir; / I'll play the prettiest games with you.
manch bunte Blumen sind an dem Strand; / Many colored flowers grow along the shore,
meine Mutter hat manch' gülden Gewand." / My mother has many golden garments."

SON (*high range, frightened*)

"Mein Vater, mein Vater, und hörest du nicht, / "My father, my father, and don't you hear
was Erlenkönig mir leise verspricht?" / The Erlking whispering promises to me?"

FATHER (*low range, calming*)

"Sei ruhig, bleibe ruhig, mein Kind; / "Be quiet, stay quiet, my child;
in dürren Blättern säuselt der Wind." / The wind is rustling in the dead leaves."

ERLKING (*major mode, cajoling*)

"Willst, feiner Knabe, du mit mir gehn? / "My handsome boy, will you come with me?
meine Töchter sollen dich warten schön; / My daughters shall wait upon you;
mein Töchter führen den nächtlichen Reihn / my daughters lead off in the dance every night,
und wiegen und tanzen und singen dich ein." / and cradle and dance and sing you to sleep."

SON (*high range, outcry*)

"Mein Vater, mein Vater, und siehst du nicht dort / "My father, my father, and don't you see there
Erlkönigs Töchter am düstern Ort? / The Erlking's daughters in the shadows?"

FATHER (*low range, reassuring*)

"Mein Sohn, mein Sohn, ich seh' es genau, / "My son, my son, I see it clearly;
es scheinen die alten Weiden so grau." / The old willows look so gray."

ERLKING (*gay, then insistent*)

"Ich liebe dich, mich reizt deine schöne Gestalt, / "I love you, your beautiful figure delights me!
und bist du nicht willig, so brauch' ich Gewalt." / And if you're not willing, then I shall use force!"

SON (*high range, terrified*)

"Mein Vater, mein Vater, jetzt fasst er mich an! / "My father, my father, now he is taking hold of me!

Erlkönig hat mir ein Leids gethan!" / The Erlking has hurt me!"

NARRATOR (*middle register, speechlike*)

Dem Vater grauset's, er reitet geschwind, / The father shudders, he rides swiftly on;
er hält in Armen das ächzende Kind, / He holds in his arms the groaning child,
erreicht den Hof mit Müh' und Noth: / He reaches the courtyard weary and anxious;
in seinen Armen das Kind war todt. / In his arms the child was dead.

Tr. by PHILIP L. MILLER

44

Robert Schumann

"Music is to me the perfect expression of the soul."

Robert Schumann

The turbulence of German Romanticism, its fantasy and subjective emotion, found their voice in Robert Schumann. His music is German to the core, yet he is no local figure. He rose above the national to make his contribution to world culture.

His Life

Robert Schumann (1810–56) was born in Zwickau, a town in northwestern Germany, son of a bookseller whose love of literature was reflected in the boy. At his mother's insistence he undertook the study of law, first at the University of Leipzig, then at Heidelberg. The youth daydreamed at the piano, steeped himself in Goethe and Byron, and attended an occasional lecture. His aversion to the law kept pace with his passion for music; it was his ambition to become a pianist. At last he won his mother's consent and returned to Leipzig to study with Friedrich Wieck, one of the foremost pedagogues of the day.

The young man practiced intensively to make up for his late start. Sadly, physical difficulties with the fingers of his right hand ended his hopes as a pianist. He then turned his interest to composing, and in a burst of creative energy produced, while still in his twenties, his most important works for piano.

He was engaged concurrently in an important literary venture. With a group of like-minded enthusiasts he founded the journal *Die Neue Zeitschrift für Musik* (The New Journal for Music). Under his direction the periodical became one of the most important music journals in Europe.

The hectic quality of this decade was intensified by his courtship of the gifted pianist Clara Wieck. When he first came to study with her father she was an eleven-year-old prodigy. She was about sixteen when Robert realized he loved her. Friedrich Wieck's opposition to their marriage bordered on the psychopathic. Clara was the supreme achievement of his life and he refused to surrender her to another. At length, since she was not yet of age, the couple was forced to appeal to the courts against Wieck. The marriage took place in 1840, when Clara was twenty-one and Robert thirty. This was his "year of song," when he produced over a hundred of the Lieder that represent his lyric gift at its purest.

The two artists settled in Leipzig, pursuing their careers side by side. Clara became the foremost interpreter of Robert's piano works and in the ensuing decade contributed substantially to the spread of his fame. Yet neither her love nor that of their children could ward off his increasing withdrawal from the world. Moodiness and nervous exhaustion culminated, in 1844, in a severe breakdown. The doctors counseled a change of scene. The couple moved to Dresden, where he seemingly made a full recovery. But the periods of depression returned ever more frequently.

In 1850 Schumann was appointed music director at Düsseldorf. But he was ill-suited for public life and was forced to relinquish the post. During a tour of Holland, where Clara and he were warmly received, he began to complain of "unnatural noises" in his head. His last letter to the violinist Joseph Joachim, two weeks before the final breakdown, is a farewell to his art. "The music is silent now . . . I will close. Already it grows dark."

He fell prey to auditory hallucinations. Once he rose in the middle of the night to write down a theme that he imagined had been brought him by the spirits of Schubert and Mendelssohn. It was his last melody. A week later, in a fit of melancholia, he threw himself into the Rhine River. He was rescued by fishermen and placed in a private asylum near Bonn. He died two years later at the age of forty-six.

His Music

In the emotional exuberance, fantasy, and whimsy of his music Schumann is the true Romantic. His piano pieces brim over with impassioned melody, novel changes of harmony, and vigorous rhythms. The titles are characteristic: *Fantasiestücke* (Fantasy Pieces), Romances, *Scenes from Childhood*. He often attached literary meanings to his music, and was especially fond of cycles of short pieces connected by a literary theme or musical motto.

As a composer of Lieder he ranks second only to Schubert. His favorite theme is love, particularly from a woman's point of view. His favored poet was Heine, for whom he had an affinity like Schubert's for Goethe. Notable are several song cycles, the best known of which are *Dichterliebe* on poems of Heine, and *Frauenliebe und Leben* on poems of Chamisso.

Principal Works

More than 300 Lieder, including song cycles *Frauenliebe und Leben* (A Woman's Love and Life, 1840) and *Dichterliebe* (A Poet's Love, 1840)

Orchestral music, including 4 symphonies and 1 piano concerto (A minor, 1841/45)

Chamber music, including 3 string quartets, 1 piano quintet, 1 piano quartet; piano trios; sonatas

Piano music including 3 sonatas; numerous miniatures and collections including *Papillons* (Butterflies, 1831), *Carnaval* (1835), and *Kinderszenen* (Scenes from Childhood, 1838); large works including *Symphonic Etudes* (1835–37), and Fantasy in C (1836–38)

1 opera; incidental music

Choral music

Thoroughly Romantic in feeling are the four symphonies. These works, especially the first and fourth, communicate a lyric freshness that has kept them alive. Typical of the essence of German Romanticism is the opening of the *Spring Symphony*, his first. "Could you infuse into the orchestra," he wrote the conductor, "a kind of longing for spring? At the entrance of the trumpets I should like them to sound as from on high, like a call to awakening."

Schumann: Ich grolle nicht

The introspective side of Schumann's lyricism predominates in what is probably his most powerful love song, from the *Dichterliebe* cycle. Heine's lines fired the composer to a Lied of brooding intensity (see Listening Guide 28

Listening Guide 28   5B/1   II/2/1

SCHUMANN: *Ich grolle nicht* (I bear no grudge)

Date: 1840, from song cycle *Dichterliebe*

Form: 2-part, each beginning with same text and music

Text: Heine poem

Tempo: Nicht zu schnell (not too fast)

Character: Dramatic love song

Opening (and refrain)

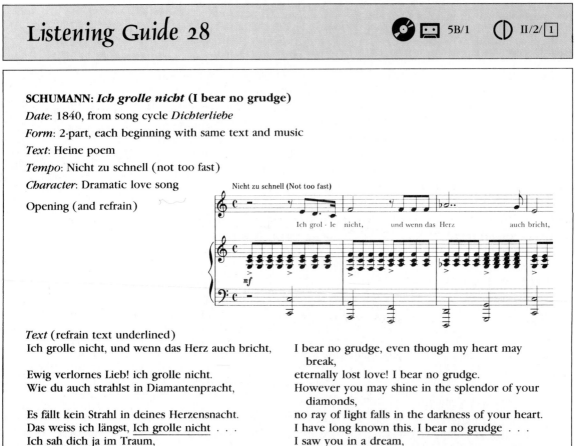

Text (refrain text underlined)

Ich grolle nicht, und wenn das Herz auch bricht,

Ewig verlornes Lieb! ich grolle nicht.
Wie du auch strahlst in Diamantenpracht,

Es fällt kein Strahl in deines Herzensnacht.
Das weiss ich längst, Ich grolle nicht . . .
Ich sah dich ja im Traum,
Und sah die Nacht in deines Herzens Raum,
Und sah die Schlang', die dir am Herzen frisst,
Ich sah, mein Lieb, wie sehr du elend bist.
Ich grolle nicht, ich grolle nicht.

I bear no grudge, even though my heart may break,
eternally lost love! I bear no grudge.
However you may shine in the splendor of your diamonds,
no ray of light falls in the darkness of your heart.
I have long known this. I bear no grudge . . .
I saw you in a dream,
and saw the night within the void of your heart,
and saw the serpent that is eating your heart—
I saw, my love, how very miserable you are.
I bear no grudge, I bear no grudge.

Tr. by PHILIP L. MILLER

for the text). The soaring melody becomes a kind of graph that follows sensitively the rise and fall of emotion. Sustained dissonances in the accompaniment build harmonic and psychological tension. The song falls into two halves, both of which begin identically.

Ich grolle nicht stands between the strophic song and the through-composed type. Schumann repeats material from the first half of the song in the second, and also introduces new material that builds relentlessly to the tragic chords of the climax: "And saw the snake that eats your heart . . ."

45

Johannes Brahms

"It is not hard to compose, but it is wonderfully hard to let the superfluous notes fall under the table."

An austere, high-minded musician, Johannes Brahms created an art dedicated to the purity of the Classical style. His veneration for the past and his mastery of musical architecture brought him closer to the spirit of Beethoven than any of his contemporaries.

Johannes Brahms

His Life

Johannes Brahms (1833–97) was born in Hamburg, son of a double-bass player whose love of music was greater than his attainments. As a youth of ten Johannes helped increase the family income by playing the piano in the dance halls of the slum district where he grew up. By the time he was twenty he had acquired sufficient reputation as a pianist to accompany the Hungarian violinist Eduard Reményi on a concert tour.

His first compositions made an impression on Joseph Joachim, leading violinist of the day, who made it possible for Brahms to visit Robert Schumann at Düsseldorf. Schumann recognized in the shy young composer a future leader of the circle dedicated to absolute music. In his role as music critic, Schumann published in his journal the famous essay entitled "New Paths," in which he named the twenty-year-old "young eagle" as one who "was called forth to give us the highest ideal expression of our time." Brahms awoke to find himself famous.

Robert and Clara Schumann took the fair-haired youth into their home. Their friendship opened up new horizons for him. Five months later came the tragedy of Schumann's mental collapse. With a tenderness and strength he had not suspected in himself, he tided Clara over the ordeal of Robert's illness.

Robert lingered for two years while Johannes was shaken by the great love of his life. Fourteen years his senior and the mother of seven children, Clara Schumann appeared to young Brahms as the ideal of womanly and artistic achievement. What had begun as filial devotion ripened into romantic passion. "You have taught me," he wrote her, "to marvel at the nature of love, affection, and self-denial. I can do nothing but think of you." At the same time he was torn by feelings of guilt, for he loved and revered Robert Schumann, his friend and benefactor, above all others. He thought of suicide and spoke of himself, as one may at twenty-two, as "a man for whom nothing is left."

This conflict was resolved the following year by Schumann's death, but another conflict took its place. Now that Clara was no longer the unattainable ideal, Brahms was faced with the choice between love and freedom. Time and again in the course of his life he was torn between the two, with the decision always going to freedom. His ardor subsided into a lifelong friendship. Two decades later he could still write her, "I love you more than myself and more than anybody and anything on earth."

Ultimately, he settled in Vienna, which remained the center of his activities for the next thirty-five years. In the stronghold of the Classical masters he found a favorable soil for his art, his northern seriousness refined by the grace and congeniality of the South. The time was ripe for him. His fame filled the world and he became the acknowledged heir of the Viennese masters.

This exacting artist had a curiously dual nature. He could be morose and withdrawn, yet he loved rough humor. A bohemian at heart, he craved bourgeois respectability. Behind a rough exterior he hid the tenderness that found expression in his music. Although he complained of loneliness and on occasion fell in love, he was unable to accept the responsibility of a sustained relationship. His motto was *Free—but happy!* "It would be as difficult for me to marry," he explained, "as to write an opera. But after the first experience I should probably undertake a second!"

Just as in early manhood his mother's death had impelled him to complete *A German Requiem*, so the final illness of Clara Schumann in 1896 gave rise to the *Four Serious Songs*. Her death profoundly affected the composer, already ill with cancer. He died ten months later, at the age of sixty-four, and was buried not far from Beethoven and Schubert.

His Music

Brahms was a traditionalist. His aim was to show that new and important things could still be said in the tradition of the Classical masters. In this he differed from avowed innovators such as Berlioz, Liszt, and Wagner.

Orchestral music   Brahms's four symphonies are unsurpassed in the late Romantic period for breadth of conception and design, yet their forms draw upon those of earlier eras. Among his other orchestral works, the *Variations on a Theme by Haydn* and his two concert overtures are frequently heard. In the two

Principal Works

Orchestral music, including 4 symphonies (1876, 1877, 1883, 1884–85), *Variations on a Theme by Haydn* (1873), 2 overtures (*Academic Festival*, 1880; *Tragic*, 1886), and 4 concertos (2 for piano, 1858, 1881; 1 for violin, 1878; 1 double concerto for violin and cello, 1887)

Chamber music, including string quartets, quintets, sextets; piano trios, quartets, and 1 quintet; clarinet quintet; and sonatas (violin, cello, clarinet/viola)

Piano music, including sonatas, character pieces, dances, and variation sets (on a theme by Handel, 1861; on a theme by Paganini, 1862–63)

Choral music, including *A German Requiem* (1868), *Alto Rhapsody* (1869), and partsongs

Lieder, including *Four Serious Songs* (1896) and folksong arrangements

piano concertos and the violin concerto, the solo instrument is integrated into a full-scale symphonic structure.

In greater degree than any of his contemporaries Brahms captured the tone of intimate communion that is the essence of chamber-music style. He is an important figure too in piano music. His three sonatas are works of his youth. His two variation sets, on themes by Handel and Paganini, represent his top achievement in this field. The Romantic in Brahms also found expression in short lyric pieces: the Rhapsodies, Ballades, Capriccios, and lyrical meditations known as Intermezzi are among the treasures of the literature. On a more popular level are the *Hungarian Rhapsodies* and the set of sixteen Waltzes for piano duet. *Chamber music*

As a song writer Brahms stands in the direct line of succession to Schubert and Schumann. His output includes about two hundred solo songs and an almost equal number for two, three, and four voices. The favorite themes are love, nature, death. We will study his finest choral work, *A German Requiem*, written to texts from the Bible he selected himself. A song of acceptance of death, this work more than any other spread his fame during his lifetime. *Vocal music*

The nationalist in Brahms—he spoke of himself as *echt deutsch* (truly German)—inspired his arrangements of German folk and children's songs as well as the popular tone of many of his art songs. In his waltzes he paid tribute to the popular dance of his beloved Vienna, but he knew he was too much the north German to capture the real Viennese flavor. When he gave his autograph to Johann Strauss's daughter—composers customarily inscribed a few bars of their music—he wrote the opening measures of the *Blue Danube Waltz* and noted beneath it, "Not, alas, by Johannes Brahms."

Brahms: Vergebliches Ständchen

S3A/4

S3/10

The extrovert side of Brahms's personality—robust, delighting in broad humor—is to be observed in *Vergebliches Ständchen* (Futile Serenade, 1877–79?). It is his version of a lusty folksong from the lower Rhineland.

The four stanzas call forth a modified strophic form. Following a short introduction, the melody outlines the common triads and moves in an animated 3/4 time, achieving the simplicity and naturalness of the folk mood. The opening phrase contains the same little motive repeated three times, each time from a lower note—or in sequence.

The relationship of folksong to the dance is underlined by the regularity of structure: four measures to the phrase, four phrases to the stanza. Yet Brahms introduces a charming asymmetry: the usual four-bar phrase is extended for two bars by repeating the words "mach' mir auf" (let me in). This extension is repeated in every stanza; the momentary waywardness sets off the symmetry of the rest.

Charming too is the sudden change of color at the third stanza. The melody takes on a plaintive tone as the lover beseeches: "The night is so cold, so icy the wind." This is achieved by a change from major to minor. The lively accompaniment keeps the song moving and creates an admirable frame for the spirited dialogue. Here is the thoroughly German aspect of Brahms—the soil from which flowered the more cultivated blossoms of his art.

Unit XVII

■

The Nineteenth-Century Piano Piece

46

The Piano in the Nineteenth Century

"Provided one can feel the music, one can also make the pianoforte sing."—LUDWIG VAN BEETHOVEN

The rise in popularity of the piano was an important factor in shaping the musical culture of the Romantic era. All over Europe and America the instrument became a mainstay of music in the home. It proved especially attractive to the amateur because, unlike the string and wind instruments, it was capable of playing melody and harmony together. The piano thus played a crucial role in the taste and experience of the new mass public.

Hardly less important was the rise of the piano recital. At first the performer was also the composer; Mozart and Beethoven introduced their own piano concertos to the public, Franz Liszt first presented his *Hungarian Rhapsodies* as did Paganini his thrilling violin pieces. With the rise of the concert industry, however, a class of virtuoso performers arose whose only function it was to dazzle audiences by playing music others had written.

At the same time a series of crucial technical improvements led to the development of the modern concert grand. By the opening of the twentieth century the piano recital had come to occupy a central position on the musical scene. A long line of spectacular virtuosos stretched from Ignacy Jan Paderewski, Josef Hofmann, and Josef Lhevinne, to mention only a few, to Artur Rubinstein and Vladimir Horowitz in our own time.

The modern piano

305

A rather ornate grand piano made by Johann Georg Groeber of Innsbruck, Austria, in about 1810. (Yale University Collection of Musical Instruments)

The Short Lyric Piano Piece

The short lyric piano piece was the instrumental equivalent of the song in its projection of lyric and dramatic moods within a compact frame. Among the terms most frequently used as titles are *bagatelle* (literally, "trifle"), *impromptu* ("on the spur of the moment"), *intermezzo* (interlude), *nocturne* (night song), *novelette* (short story), *moment musical, song without words, album leaf, prelude, romance, capriccio* (caprice); and, of larger dimensions, the *rhapsody* and *ballade*. In the dance category are the *waltz, mazurka, polka, écossaise* (Scottish dance), *polonaise* (Polish dance), *march,* and *country dance*. Composers also used titles of a fanciful and descriptive nature. Typical are Schumann's *In the Night, Soaring*, and *Whims*; Liszt's *Forest Murmurs* and *Fireflies*. The nineteenth-century masters of the short piano piece—Schubert, Chopin and Liszt, Mendelssohn, Schumann and Brahms, among others—showed inexhaustible ingenuity in exploring the technical resources of the instrument and its capacities for lyric-dramatic expression.

47

Frédéric François Chopin

"My life . . . an episode without a beginning and with a sad end."

In the annals of his century, Frédéric François Chopin (1810–49) is known as the "poet of the piano." The title is a valid one. His art, issuing from the heart of Romanticism, constitutes the golden age of that instrument.

Frédéric François Chopin

His Life

Chopin, the national composer of Poland, was half French. His father had emigrated to Warsaw, where he married a lady-in-waiting to a countess and taught French to the sons of the nobility. Frédéric, who displayed his musical gift in childhood, was educated at the newly founded Conservatory of Warsaw. His student years were climaxed by a mild infatuation with a young singer, Constantia Gladkowska, who inspired him with sighs and tears in the best nineteenth-century manner. "It was with thoughts of this beautiful creature that I composed the Adagio of my new concerto." The concerto was the one in F minor. Frédéric was nineteen.

When the young artist set forth to make a name in the world, his comrades sang a farewell cantata in his honor. Frédéric wept, convinced he would never see his homeland again. In Vienna the news reached him that Warsaw had risen in revolt against the Tsar. Gloomy visions tormented him; he saw his family and friends massacred. He left Vienna in the summer. On reaching Stuttgart he learned that the Polish capital had been captured by the Russians. The tidings precipitated a torrent of grief, and the flaming defiance that found expression in the *Revolutionary Etude.*

In September 1831, the young man reached Paris, where he spent the rest of his career. Paris in the 1830s was the center of the new Romanticism. The circle in which Chopin moved included as brilliant a galaxy of artists as ever gathered anywhere. Among the musicians were Liszt and Berlioz, Rossini and Meyerbeer. The literary figures included Victor Hugo, Balzac, Lamartine, George Sand, de Musset, and Alexandre Dumas. Heinrich Heine was his friend, as was the painter Delacroix. Although Chopin was a man of emotions rather than ideas, he could not but be stimulated by his contact with the leading intellectuals of France.

Through Liszt he met Mme. Aurore Dudevant, "the lady with the somber eye," known to the world as the novelist George Sand. She was thirty-four, Chopin twenty-eight when the famous friendship began. Mme. Sand was brilliant and domineering; her need to dominate found its counterpart in Chopin's need to be ruled. She left a memorable account of this fastidious artist at work: "His creative power was spontaneous, miraculous. It came to him without effort or warning. . . . But then began the most heartrending labor I have ever witnessed. It was a series of attempts, of fits of irresolution and impatience to recover certain details. He would shut himself in his room for days, pacing up and down, breaking his pens, repeating and modifying one bar a hundred times. . . ."

For the next eight years Chopin spent his summers at Mme. Sand's chateau at Nohant, where she entertained the cream of France's intelligentsia. These were productive years for him, although his health grew progressively worse and his relationship with Mme. Sand ran its course from love to conflict, from jealousy to hostility. They parted in bitterness.

According to his friend Liszt, "Chopin felt and often repeated that in breaking this long affection, this powerful bond, he had broken his life." Chopin's creative energy, which had lost its momentum in his middle thirties, came to an end. The "illness of the century," the lonely despair of the Romantic artist, pervades his last letters. "What has become of my art?" he writes during a visit to Scotland. "And my heart, where have I wasted it? I scarce remember any more how they sing at home. That world slips away from me somehow. I forget. I have no strength. If I rise a little I fall again, lower than ever."

He returned to Paris suffering from tuberculosis and died some months later, at the age of thirty-nine. His funeral was his greatest triumph. Princesses and artists joined to pay him homage. Meyerbeer, Berlioz, and Delacroix were among the mourners. George Sand stayed away. His heart was returned to Poland, the rest of him remained in Paris. And on his grave a friendly hand scattered a gobletful of Polish earth.

His Music

Chopin was one of the most original artists of the Romantic era. His idiom is so entirely his own there is no mistaking it for any other. He was the only master of the first rank whose creative life centered about the piano. From the first, his imagination was wedded to the keyboard, to create a universe within that narrow frame. His genius transformed even the limitations of the instrument into sources of beauty. (The prime limitation is the piano's inability to sustain tone for any length of time.) Chopin overcame these with such ingenuity that to him as much as to any individual is due the

Modern piano style

modern piano style. The widely spaced chords in the bass, sustained by pedal, set up masses of tone that wreathe the melody in enchantment. "Everything must be made to sing," he told his pupils. The delicate ornaments

Principal Works

Piano and orchestra, including 2 piano concertos

Piano music, including 4 Ballades, Fantasy in F minor (1841), *Berceuse* (1844), *Barcarolle* (1846), 3 sonatas, preludes, études, mazurkas, nocturnes, waltzes, polonaises, impromptus, scherzos, rondos, marches, and variations

Chamber music, all including piano; songs

in his music—trills, grace notes, runs of gossamer lightness—seem magically to prolong the single tones. And all this generally lies so well for the hand that the music seems almost to play itself.

It is remarkable that so many of his works have remained in the pianist's repertory. His Nocturnes—night songs, as the name implies—are tinged with varying shades of melancholy. The Preludes are visionary fragments; some are only a page in length, several consist of two or three lines. The Etudes crown the literature of the study piece. Here piano technique is transformed into poetry. The Impromptus are fanciful, capricious, yet they have a curious rightness about them. The Waltzes capture the brilliance and coquetry of the salon. The Mazurkas, derived from a Polish peasant dance, evoke the idealized landscape of his youth.

Small forms

Among the larger forms are the four Ballades. These are epic poems of spacious structure, like sagas related by a bard. The Polonaises revive the stately processional dance in which Poland's nobles were wont to hail their kings. The Fantasy in F minor and the dramatic Scherzos reveal the composer at the summit of his art.

Larger forms

Chopin's style emerged fully formed when he was twenty. It was not the result of an extended intellectual development, as was the case with masters like Beethoven or Wagner. In this he was the true lyricist, along with his contemporaries Schumann and Mendelssohn. All three died young, and all three reached their peak through the spontaneous lyricism of youth. In them the first period of Romanticism found its finest expression.

Chopin: Polonaise in A flat

The heroic side of Chopin's art shows itself in the most popular of his Polonaises, the one in A flat, Opus 53 (1842). The introduction establishes a dramatic mood against which is set the opening dance theme, a proud and chivalric melody in a stately triple meter. The octaves for the left hand in the following section approach the limits of what the piano can do. The emotional temperature drops perceptibly after the octave episode, which is Chopin's way of building up tension against the return of the theme that rounds off the ternary form. A coda (Italian for "tail"), a concluding section appended to a form, closes the work. In the hands of a virtuoso this Polonaise takes on surpassing brilliance; it is the epitome of the grand style. (See outline of the work in Listening Guide 29.)

Important here, as in all of Chopin's music, is the *tempo rubato*—the "robbed time" (better, "borrowed time") that is so characteristic of Romantic style. In tempo rubato, certain liberties can be taken with the rhythm without upsetting the basic beat. As Chopin taught it, the accompaniment—say the left hand—was played in strict time while above it the right-hand style might hesitate a little here or hurry forward there. In either case, the "borrowing" had to be repaid before the end of the phrase. Rubato, like any seasoning, has to be used sparingly. But when it is done well it imparts to the music a waywardness, a quality of caprice that can be enchanting. And it remains an essential ingredient of the true Chopin style.

Tempo rubato
> ESSENTIAL INGREDIENT TO CHOPIN'S STYLE

Listening Guide 29

6A/1   II/1/30

CHOPIN: Polonaise in A flat, Op. 53

Date: 1842

Form: **A-B-A′**, with introduction

Genre: Polonaise, a stately triple-meter Polish dance

Tempo: Alla Polacca e maestoso (like a polonaise and majestic). Use of rubato tempo

30 0:00 INTRODUCTION
    Dramatic mood established, fast ascending lines builds into main theme of **A**

31 0:31 SECTION **A**
    Stately dancelike theme, in tonic key (A-flat major); repeated in louder statement, in octaves

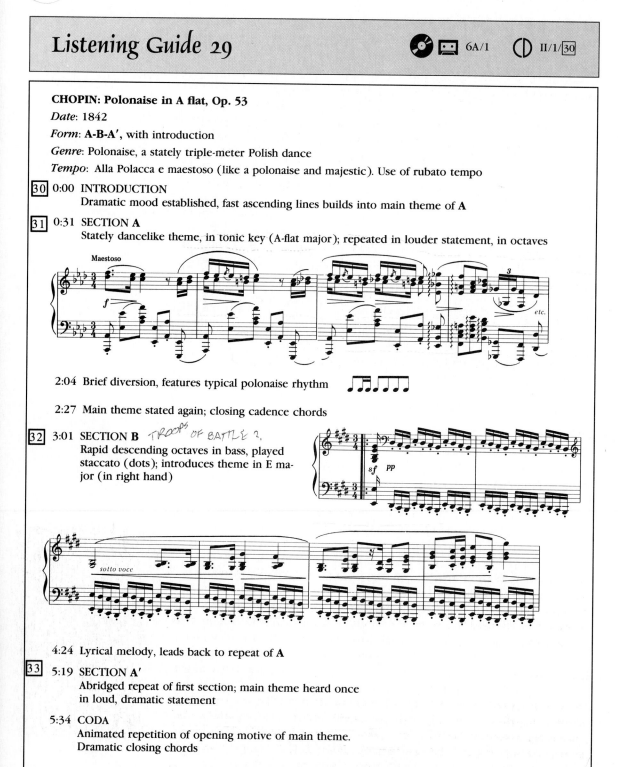

2:04 Brief diversion, features typical polonaise rhythm

2:27 Main theme stated again; closing cadence chords

32 3:01 SECTION **B** *TROOPS OF BATTLE ?.*
    Rapid descending octaves in bass, played
    staccato (dots); introduces theme in E ma-
    jor (in right hand)

4:24 Lyrical melody, leads back to repeat of **A**

33 5:19 SECTION **A′**
    Abridged repeat of first section; main theme heard once
    in loud, dramatic statement

5:34 CODA
    Animated repetition of opening motive of main theme.
    Dramatic closing chords

Chopin: Prelude in E minor

The Prelude in E minor, Opus 28, No. 4 (1839) reveals Chopin's uncanny power to achieve the utmost expressiveness with the simplest means. The melody hardly moves, unfolding in sustained tones over a succession of chords that change very subtly, usually one note at a time:

S3B/1

S3/7

The music creates a gently mournful mood that is the essence of Romanticism. Tension gathers slowly; there is something inevitable about the rise to the climax, where the melody, advancing in bold leaps, takes on the character of a passionate outcry that subsides to a sorrowful pianissimo ending. Rarely has so much been said in a single page. Schumann did not exaggerate when he said of the Preludes, "In each piece we find in his own hand, 'Frédéric Chopin wrote it!' He is the boldest, the proudest poet of his time."

His countrymen have enshrined Chopin as the national composer of Poland. Withal he is a spokesman of European culture. It is not without significance that despite his homesickness he spent the whole of his adult life in Paris. Thus Poland was idealized in his imagination as the symbol of that unappeasable longing which every Romantic artist carries in his heart: the longing for the lost land of happiness that may never be found again. Heine, himself an expatriate, divined this when he wrote that Chopin is "neither a Pole, a Frenchman, nor a German. He reveals a higher origin. He comes from the land of Mozart, Raphael, Goethe. His true country is the land of poetry."

48

Franz Liszt

"Sorrowful and great is the artist's destiny."

As composer and conductor, teacher, and organizer of musical events, Franz Liszt (1811–86) occupied a central position in the artistic life of the nineteenth century. Yet this fabulously successful artist did not escape the Romantic melancholy. "To die and die young—" he once exclaimed, "—what happiness!"

His Life

Liszt was born in Hungary, son of a steward in the employ of a wealthy family. A stipend from a group of Hungarian noblemen enabled him to pursue his musical studies in Paris. There he came under the spell of French Romanticism, with whose leaders—Victor Hugo, Delacroix, George Sand, and the composer Hector Berlioz—he formed close friendships.

Franz Liszt

An imaginary gathering painted by **Joseph Dannhauser** *in 1840 shows Liszt at the piano with Marie D'Agoult at his feet. Seated behind him are George Sand and Alexandre Dumas père. Standing are Victor Hugo, Paganini, and Rossini. Looking out upon this improbable assemblage is a marble bust of Beethoven.*

The appearance in Paris of the sensational violinist Paganini in 1831 made Liszt aware of the possibilities of virtuoso playing. The new music public required spectacular soloists. Liszt met the need. He was one of the greatest of pianists—and showmen. An actor to his fingertips, he possessed the personal magnetism of which legends are made. Instead of sitting with his back to the audience or facing it, as had been the custom hitherto, he introduced the more effective arrangement that prevails today. It showed off his chiseled profile. He crouched over the keys, he thundered, he caressed. Countesses swooned. Ladies less exalted fought for his snuffbox and tore his handkerchief to shreds. Liszt encouraged these antics as a necessary part of the legend. But behind the facade was a true musician.

Inseparable from the legend of the pianist was that of the lover. Liszt never married. His path for the better part of fifty years led through a thicket of sighs, tears, and threats of suicide.

Important in his intellectual development was his relationship with Countess Marie d'Agoult, who wrote novels under the name of Daniel Stern. They eloped to an idyllic interlude in Switzerland that lasted for a number of years. Of their three children, Cosima subsequently became the wife of composer Richard Wagner. Liszt and the Countess parted in bitterness. She later satirized him in her novels.

He withdrew from the concert stage at the height of his fame in order to devote himself to composing. In 1848 he settled in Weimar, where he became court conductor to the Grand Duke. The Weimar period (1848–61) saw the production of his chief orchestral works. As director of the ducal opera house he was in a position to mold public taste. He used his influence unremittingly on behalf of the "Music of the Future," as he and

Wagner named the type of music that they, along with Berlioz, advocated. At Weimar Liszt directed the first performances of Wagner's *Lohengrin*, Berlioz's *Benvenuto Cellini*, and many other contemporary works.

The Weimar period also saw his association with the woman who most decisively influenced his life. Princess Carolyne Sayn-Wittgenstein, wife of a powerful nobleman at the court of the Tsar, fell in love with Liszt during his last concert tour of Russia. Shortly thereafter she came to Weimar to unite her life with his. For years their home, the Altenburg, was a center of artistic activity. A woman of domineering will and intellect, the Princess assisted Liszt in his later literary efforts. These include a book on Gypsy music and a *Life of Chopin*. Both are eloquent but inaccurate.

In his last years Liszt sought peace by entering the Church. He took minor orders and was known as Abbé Liszt. This was the period of his major religious compositions. At seventy-five he was received with enthusiasm in England, which had always been reluctant to recognize him as a composer. He journeyed to Bayreuth to visit the widowed Cosima and died during the festival of Wagner's works, naming with his last breath the masterpiece of the "Music of the Future"—Wagner's opera *Tristan und Isolde*.

His Music

Liszt's goal was pure lyric expression, the projecting of a state of soul through what he called "the mysterious language of tone." To give his lyricism free scope he created the symphonic poem. Here, as in his symphonies and concertos, he based his music on the technique of *thematic transformation*. By varying the melodic outline, harmony, or rhythm of a theme, by shifting it from soft to loud, from slow to fast, from low to high register, from strings to woodwinds or brass, he found it possible to transform its character so that it might suggest romantic love in one section, a pastoral scene in another, tension and conflict in a third, and triumph in the last.

Thematic transformation

Liszt was one of the creators of modern piano technique. The best of his piano pieces, like his songs, are in the vein of true Romantic lyricism. Characteristic are the colorful *Hungarian Rhapsodies* and the vastly popular

Piano pieces

Principal Works

Orchestral music, including symphonic poems (*Les Préludes*, 1848); *Dante Symphony* (1856), *Faust Symphony* (1857), 2 piano concertos; *Totentanz* (for piano and orchestra, 1849)

Piano music, including *Transcendental Etudes* (1851), Sonata (B minor, 1853), *Hungarian Rhapsodies*, nocturnes, waltzes, ballades, polonaises, and other character pieces; numerous transcriptions of orchestral and opera works for piano

Choral music, including masses, oratorios, psalms, cantatas, and secular partsongs

1 opera; songs with piano

Liebestraum (Love Dream, c. 1850). In a class apart are his chief works for the piano, the Sonata in B minor and the two piano concertos that date from the 1850s. Here is the Liszt of impassioned rhetoric, the contemporary in every sense of Victor Hugo, Byron, and Delacroix.

Liszt: Wilde Jagd (*Wild Hunt*)

From the beginning of his career Liszt was fascinated by the technical possibilities of the piano. Like Chopin he was drawn to the étude or study piece, in which a composer confronted a single technical problem. Like Chopin, too, he transformed the étude from a dry exercise into a poetic mood piece. In his Twelve Transcendental Etudes, completed in 1838 and revised thirteen years later, the master did what the title implies. He transcended the limitations of the keyboard and even transformed those limitations into sources of tonal beauty.

Typical is the eighth étude, *Wilde Jagd*, which shows off Liszt's reckless virtuosity, his imaginative use of contrast between the low and high registers of the piano, his dramatic exploitation of massed chords, his fondness for irregular rhythmic accentuations. Marked Presto furioso (very fast and furious) and martellato (hammered), *Wilde Jagd* opens fortississimo (*fff*). The form is a loose **A-B-A** in which the drama of the opening is contrasted with a calmer melody based on parallel chords that suggest distant hunting horns. (See Listening Guide 30 for an analysis.) Dear to Romantic poets and painters was the image of the supernatural hunt, which Liszt here evokes with the flair for pianistic virtuosity that was his alone.

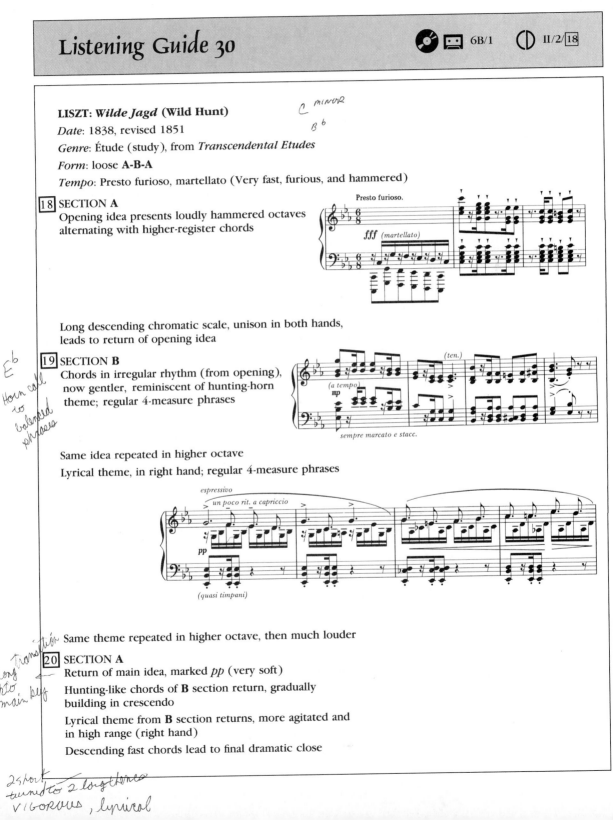

Listening Guide 30

6B/1   II/2/18

LISZT: *Wilde Jagd* (Wild Hunt)   *C minor   B♭*

Date: 1838, revised 1851

Genre: Étude (study), from *Transcendental Etudes*

Form: loose **A-B-A**

Tempo: Presto furioso, martellato (Very fast, furious, and hammered)

18 SECTION A
Opening idea presents loudly hammered octaves
alternating with higher-register chords

Long descending chromatic scale, unison in both hands,
leads to return of opening idea

E♭ Horn call to balanced phrases

19 SECTION B
Chords in irregular rhythm (from opening),
now gentler, reminiscent of hunting-horn
theme; regular 4-measure phrases

Same idea repeated in higher octave

Lyrical theme, in right hand; regular 4-measure phrases

long transition back to main idea

Same theme repeated in higher octave, then much louder

20 SECTION A
Return of main idea, marked *pp* (very soft)

Hunting-like chords of **B** section return, gradually
building in crescendo

Lyrical theme from **B** section returns, more agitated and
in high range (right hand)

Descending fast chords lead to final dramatic close

*2 short turned to 2 long tones
VIGOROUS, lyrical*

49

More Romantic Piano Music

Clara Schumann: Her Life and Music

Clara Schumann

> *"The superiority which characterizes the artist as a pianist is matched by her compositions. A unique mixture of authentic masculine seriousness and intellectual rigor together with feminine emotion and amiability is reflected in the works of Clara Schumann."*—ANONYMOUS REVIEWER, Breslauer Zeitung, 23 December, 1877

Clara Schumann (1819–96) is universally regarded as one of the most distinguished woman musicians of the nineteenth century. She was admired throughout Europe as a leading pianist of her time, but the world in which she lived was not prepared to acknowledge that a woman could be an outstanding composer. Hence her considerable creative gifts were not recognized or encouraged during her lifetime.

We have touched upon Clara Schumann's life in our discussion of Robert Schumann and Johannes Brahms. Her close association with two great composers put her in the center of the musical life of her time. From her earliest years she had the clearest possible conception of her goals as an artist, and the strength of character to realize them. When she faced the first great crisis in her life, the violent opposition of Friedrich Wieck, her father and teacher, to her marriage to Robert, she had the courage to defy him. She then faced the problems of a woman torn between the demands of an exacting career and her responsibilities as a wife and mother. She bore Robert seven children (an eighth died in infancy), yet she managed throughout those years to maintain her position as one of the outstanding concert artists of Europe. Liszt admired her playing for its "complete technical mastery, depth, and sincerity of feeling." Her position was made more difficult by the fact that during her lifetime she was much more famous than her husband. The disparity in their reputations might have led to serious strains between them, were it not for the fact that from the first she dedicated her talents to the propagation of his music. She gave the first performance of all his important works and also became known as a leading interpreter of the music of Brahms and Chopin.

Given Robert's shifting moods and frequent depressions, her task as his wife was not an easy one. She sustained him with her love and loyalty even though in the end she was not able to stave off his breakdown. After his death she had to concertize in order to support herself and her children. Now she in turn was sustained by Brahms's devotion. But the memory of Robert cast too heavy a shadow for them to be able to find a happy ending. As we saw, their love was transformed into a lifelong friendship.

Clara had the talent, the training, and the background that many composers would envy, but from the beginning of her career she accepted without

Principal Works

Solo piano music, including dances, caprices, romances, scherzos, impromptus, character pieces (*Quatre pièces fugitives*, Op. 15, 1845), variations (including one on a theme by Robert Schumann, 1854), cadenzas for Mozart and Beethoven piano concertos

1 piano concerto with orchestra or quintet (1837)

Chamber music, including 1 piano trio (1846) and 3 Romances for violin and piano (1855–56)

Lieder, with texts by Burns, Rückert, Heine, Geibel, Rollet, and Lyser

question the attitude of her time toward a woman composer. At twenty she confided to her diary, "I once believed that I possessed creative talent, but I have given up this idea; a woman must not desire to compose—there has never yet been one able to do it. Should I expect to be the one? To believe this would be arrogant, something which my father once, in former days, induced me to do."

Robert was sympathetic to her creative efforts, but he too accepted the attitude of the time. "Clara has composed a series of small pieces," he wrote in their joint diary, "which show a musical and tender ingenuity such as she never attained before. But to have children, and a husband who is always living in the realm of imagination, does not go together with composing. She cannot work at it regularly, and I am often disturbed to think how many profound ideas are lost because she cannot work them out."

Clara's output runs to twenty-three opuses, mostly songs and piano pieces—polonaises, valses romantiques, romances, and similar pieces. There are two large-scale works—a piano concerto and a trio for piano and strings, several virtuoso pieces, and a gesture of homage—a set of *Variations on a Theme by Robert Schumann*.

Clara Schumann: Quatre pièces fugitives

These four short pieces (1845) well illustrate Clara's affinity for the short lyric form. As might be expected from a great pianist, she had a natural command of the piano idiom. This set of unrelated works was composed over a period of several years and was dedicated to her half-sister, Marie Wieck, who, at age thirteen, was just embarking on a concert career. The third piece of the group, marked Andante espressivo, follows a clear-cut three-part (**A-B-A**) structure, with marked contrast between the **A** and **B** sections. The opening section presents a slow, heartfelt melody, somber in character. The middle part is more animated and moves with faster notes, after which the music returns to the slow, sad melody of the first part. (For analysis, see Listening Guide 31.) The mood of intimate lyricism falls well

Listening Guide 31

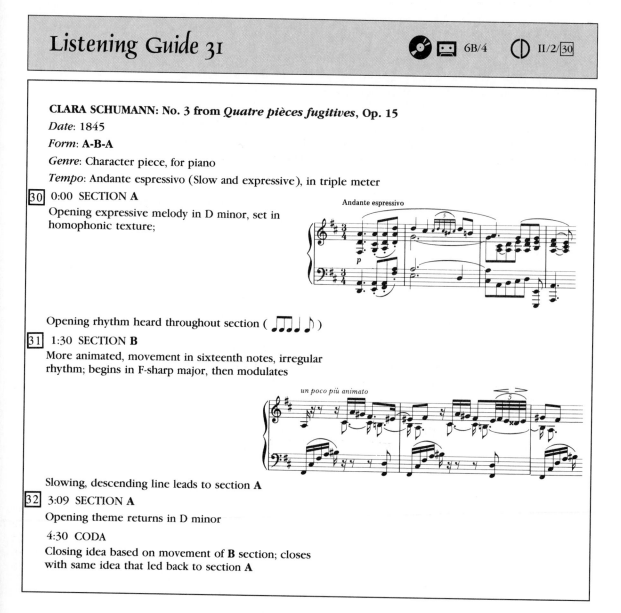

6B/4   II/2/30

CLARA SCHUMANN: No. 3 from *Quatre pièces fugitives*, Op. 15

Date: 1845

Form: **A-B-A**

Genre: Character piece, for piano

Tempo: Andante espressivo (Slow and expressive), in triple meter

30 0:00 SECTION **A**

Opening expressive melody in D minor, set in
homophonic texture;

Opening rhythm heard throughout section (♩♫♩♪)

31 1:30 SECTION **B**

More animated, movement in sixteenth notes, irregular
rhythm; begins in F-sharp major, then modulates

Slowing, descending line leads to section **A**

32 3:09 SECTION **A**

Opening theme returns in D minor

4:30 CODA

Closing idea based on movement of **B** section; closes
with same idea that led back to section **A**

within the Romantic style. This is the finely wrought work of one who well
deserves the praise the world has at last accorded her.

Robert Schumann: "Eusebius" and "Florestan" from Carnaval

Carnaval (1835) is a splendid example of Schumann's interest in creating
a series of piano miniatures held together by a central idea: the pianistic
counterpart of the song cycle. He called the work *Scènes mignonnes sur*

quatre notes (Little Scenes on Four Notes). The cycle consists of twenty short pieces with fanciful titles.

In the music criticism he wrote for his journal, he often cast an article in the form of a dialogue or short story. He would draw the characters from among his own circle of friends, to whom he gave—as he wrote in his diary—"more beautiful, more suitable names." Thus Clara became Chiarina, and her father Friedrich Wieck was transformed into Magister Raro. He himself signed his essays with one of two pen names representing the dual sides of his nature: Eusebius was dreamy and thoughtful, Florestan was vigorous and impulsive. In his diary he called them his "best friends." All these characters came together in *Carnaval*, each holding the center of the stage for a brief spell before giving way to the next. By including Eusebius and Florestan among them, Schumann was able to create two musical self-portraits.

"Eusebius," marked Adagio, opens with a haunting melody in a most unusual rhythm—seven notes to a measure. Four symmetrical phrases, each four measures long, are arranged in the pattern **A-A-B-A.** The melody is then repeated in a more elaborate form, with added notes an octave higher and fuller harmonies in the bass in the form of arpeggios. In this exquisite little tone poem Schumann gives us an idealized portrait of the Romantic dreamer.

In contrast, "Florestan" is marked Passionato and is in a vigorous 3/4 meter. The melody ranges widely across the keyboard, its brusque phrases alternating with adagio passages in which Schumann refers back to an early work of his named *Papillons* (Butterflies). There was obviously a connection in his mind, but he chose not to reveal it.

As a piano composer Schumann, like Chopin, has his own sound, so that a piece by him is instantly recognizable as his. This is the mark of a true master.

UNIT XVIII

■

Romantic Program Music

50

The Nature of Program Music

". . . The renewal of music through its inner connection with poetry."—FRANZ LISZT

Program music is instrumental music endowed with literary or pictorial associations; the nature of these associations is indicated by the title of the piece or by an explanatory note—the "program"—supplied by the composer. Program music, we saw earlier, is distinguished from *absolute* or *pure music*, which consists of musical patterns that have no literary or pictorial meanings.

This literary-inspired genre was of special importance in a period like the nineteenth century when musicians became sharply conscious of the connection between their art and the world about them. It helped them to bring music closer to poetry and painting, and to relate their work to the moral and political issues of their time. It also helped them to approach the forms of absolute music in a new way. All the same, the distinction between absolute and program music is not as rigid as many supposed. A work called Symphony No. 1 or Third String Quartet falls into the former category. Yet the composer in the course of writing it may very well have had in mind specific images and associations that he has not seen fit to divulge. Beethoven, whom we saw as the master of absolute music, confessed to a friend, "I have always a picture in my thoughts when I am composing, and work to it." Conversely, a piece entitled *Romeo and Juliet Overture* comes under the heading of program music. Yet if we were not told the title, we would listen to it as a piece of absolute music. What concerns us ultimately is the destiny not of the lovers but of the themes.

Varieties of Program Music

A primary impulse toward program music derived from the opera house, where the overture was a rousing orchestral piece in one movement designed to serve as an introduction to an opera (or a play). Many operatic overtures achieved independent popularity as concert pieces. This pointed the way to a new type of overture not associated with an opera: a single-movement concert piece for orchestra, based on a striking literary idea, such as Tchaikovsky's *Romeo and Juliet*. This type of composition, the *concert overture*, might be descriptive, like Mendelssohn's *The Hebrides (Fingal's Cave)*; or it could embody a patriotic idea, as does Tchaikovsky's *1812 Overture*.

The concert overture

An engaging species of program music is the kind written for plays; this *incidental music* generally consists of an overture and a series of pieces to be performed between the acts and during the important scenes. Nineteenth-century composers produced a number of works of this type that were notable for tone painting (instrumental pictorialization), characterization, and theater atmosphere.

Incidental music

The most successful pieces of incidental music were generally arranged into suites, a number of which became vastly popular. We will study Mendelssohn's music for Shakespeare's *A Midsummer Night's Dream*, one of the most successful works in this category. Hardly less appealing are the two suites from Bizet's music for Alphonse Daudet's play *L'Arlésienne* (The Woman of Arles) and the two from Grieg's music for Henrik Ibsen's poetic drama *Peer Gynt*. Incidental music is still used today, and has spawned two very important offshoots: film music, which plays an important role in, as Aaron Copland put it, "warning the screen," and background music for television drama.

The impulse toward program music was so strong that it invaded even the hallowed form of absolute music—the symphony. Thus came into being the *program symphony*, a multimovement orchestral work. The best-known examples are three program symphonies of Berlioz—*Symphonie fantastique, Harold in Italy, Romeo and Juliet*—and two of Liszt, the *Faust* and *Dante* symphonies.

The program symphony

As the nineteenth century wore on, the need was felt more and more for a large form of orchestral music that would serve the Romantic era as well as the symphony had served the Classical. Toward the middle of the century the long-awaited step was taken with the creation of the *symphonic poem*. This was the nineteenth century's one original contribution to the large forms. It was the achievement of Franz Liszt, who first used the term in 1848. His *Les Préludes* is among the best-known examples of this type of music.

The symphonic poem

A symphonic poem is a piece of program music for orchestra, in one movement, which in the course of contrasting sections develops a poetic idea, suggests a scene, or creates a mood. It differs from the concert overture in one important respect: whereas the concert overture generally retains one of the traditional Classical forms, the symphonic poem is much freer in its structure. The symphonic poem (also called *tone poem*) gave composers the canvas they needed for a big single-movement form. It became the most widely cultivated type of orchestral program music through the second half of the century.

The varieties of program music just described—concert overture, incidental music, program symphony, and symphonic poem—comprise one of the striking manifestations of nineteenth-century Romanticism. This type of music emphasized the descriptive element; it impelled composers to try to express specific feelings; and it proclaimed the direct relationship of music to life.

51

Felix Mendelssohn

"People often complain that music is too ambiguous; that what they should think when they hear it is so unclear, whereas everyone understands words. With me it is exactly the opposite, and not only with regard to an entire speech but also with individual words. These too seem to me so ambiguous, so vague, so easily misunderstood in comparison to genuine music, which fills the soul with a thousand things better than words."

Felix Mendelssohn

Felix Mendelssohn stands out in the roster of musicians for the fortunate circumstances that attended his career: he was born to wealth; he found personal happiness; and he was the idol of a vast public, not only in his German homeland, but also in England.

His Life

Felix Mendelssohn (1809–47) was the grandson of Moses Mendelssohn, the Jewish philosopher who expounded Plato to the eighteenth century. His father was an art-loving banker; his mother read Homer in the original Greek. They joined the Protestant faith when Felix was still a child. The Mendelssohn home was a meeting place for the wit and intellect of Berlin. The garden house, seating several hundred guests, was the scene of memorable musicales where an orchestra under the boy's direction performed his numerous compositions. Here, when he was seventeen, his Overture to *A Midsummer Night's Dream* was presented to an enraptured audience. Felix was not the only musician in the household: his sister Fanny was a gifted pianist and composer of songs (some of which were published under her brother's name).

The youth's education was thorough and well rounded. He visited the venerable poet Goethe at Weimar and attended the philospher Hegel's lectures at the University of Berlin. He worshiped Bach, Mozart, and Beethoven. In 1829 the twenty-year-old enthusiast organized a performance of Bach's *St. Matthew Passion*, which had lain neglected since the death of its composer. The event proved to be a turning point in the nineteenth-century revival of that master.

Mendelssohn's misfortune was that he excelled in a number of roles—as pianist, conductor, organizer of musical events, and educator. For the last fifteen years of his life his composing was carried on amid the distractions of a public career that taxed his energies and caused his early death. At twenty-six he was conductor of the Gewandhaus Orchestra at Leipzig, which he transformed into the finest in Europe. He was summoned to Berlin by Frederick William IV, King of Prussia, to carry out that monarch's plans for an Academy of Music. Later he founded the Conservatory of Leipzig, which raised the standards for the training of musicians. He made ten visits to England, where his appearances elicited a frenzy of enthusiasm. All this in addition to directing one or another of the provincial festivals that formed the backbone of musical life in Germany. Mendelssohn composed with a speed and facility that invite comparison with Mozart or Schubert, but he seldom allowed himself the inner repose that might have imparted profundity to much of his music.

The happiness he found in the company of his wife and children was shattered, in 1847, by a severe blow—the death of his sister Fanny, to whom he was deeply attached. Six months later, at the age of thirty-eight, he succumbed to a stroke. Huge throngs followed his funeral bier. Condolences came from all over Europe. A world figure had died.

His Music

Mendelssohn was dedicated to a mission: to preserve the tradition of the Classical forms in an age that was turning from them. His fastidious craftsmanship links him to the great tradition. But it should not be supposed that he was untouched by Romanticism. In his early works he is the ardent poet of nature, a landscape painter of gossamer brush. Tenderness and manly

Principal Works

Orchestral music, including 5 symphonies (No. 3, *Scotch*, 1842; No. 4, *Italian*, 1833; No. 5, *Reformation*, 1832); concert overtures (*A Midsummer Night's Dream*, 1843; *The Hebrides or Fingal's Cave*, 1830); 2 piano concertos, 1 violin concerto (1844)

Dramatic music, including 1 opera and incidental music for 6 plays (*A Midsummer Night's Dream*, 1843)

Choral music, including 2 oratorios (*St. Paul*, 1836; *Elijah*, 1846), cantatas, motets, anthems, and partsongs

Chamber music, including 6 string quartets, 2 string quintets, piano quartets, 1 octet, and various sonatas

Piano music, including *Songs Without Words* (8 sets, 1829–45); sonatas, fugues, fantasias

Organ music; solo vocal music; transcriptions and arrangements of Bach, Handel, Mozart, and Beethoven

fervor breathe from his music, and a gentle melancholy that is very much of the age.

Of his symphonies the best known are the Third, the *Scotch*, and the Fourth, the *Italian*—mementos of his youthful travels. Both works were begun in 1830, when he was twenty-one. The Concerto for Violin and Orchestra (1844) retains its position as one of the most popular ever written. The Octet for Strings, which he wrote when he was sixteen, is much admired, as are the *Songs Without Words* (1829–45), eight sets of short piano pieces. Mendelssohn was a prolific writer for the voice. The oratorio *Elijah* represents the peak of his achievement in this category.

In England Mendelssohn was admired as no composer had been since Handel and Haydn. The first edition of Grove's Dictionary, which appeared in 1880, devoted its longest article to him—sixty-eight pages. Bach received eight.

Mendelssohn: A Midsummer Night's Dream

The Overture to Shakespeare's fairy play *A Midsummer Night's Dream* is in Mendelssohn's happiest vein. The mood of elfin enchantment that the seventeen-year-old composer achieved here was to return again and again in his later music, but nowhere more felicitously. Four prolonged chords in the woodwinds and horns open the portals to the realm of the fairy king Oberon and his queen, Titania. The fairy music is introduced by the violins

Some years before Mendelssohn wrote the incidental music for A Midsummer Night's Dream, **Henry Fusili** (*1741–1825*) *created this fanciful canvas entitled* Titania and Bottom, *c. 1790.* (London, Tate Gallery/Art Resource)

in a high register, very lively and very softly, and staccato (short and detached). An energetic transition leads into the second theme, which represents the young lovers in the play. It is a lyrical idea, smooth and flowing,
that provides an effective contrast with the fairy music. Third is the noisy
dance of the clowns, which is played fortissimo in an energetic rhythm with
wide leaps in the melody to underline its boisterous character. Its last four
notes suggest the "hee-haw" of a donkey, since in the play a magic spell
fastens an ass's head on Puck the Weaver.

These three basic ideas are presented in the first section, developed in
a middle section, and restated in the last section—in short, it is in sonata-
allegro form.

A coda concludes the piece on a note of quiet farewell. As the youthful
composer explained, "After everything has been satisfactorily settled and
the principal players have joyfully left the stage, the elves follow them, bless
the house, and disappear with the dawn. So ends the play, and my overture
too."

In 1842 King Frederick William decided on a production of Shakespeare's
comedy at the royal theater and suggested to Mendelssohn that he write
incidental music for the play. Several of the pieces—the Scherzo, Nocturne,
and the Wedding March—have achieved worldwide popularity and are frequently performed together with the Overture as a suite.

The Nocturne (night song) is heard while the two pairs of lovers, lost
in the enchanted wood, sleep. Here Mendelssohn is the poet of nature. The
beauty of the forest is evoked by the French horn in a serenely tender
melody.

Mendelssohn has always been extremely popular with the public. His
elegant workmanship, melodious charm, and refinement of feeling are qualities that wear well through the ages.

Listening Guide 32   🎵 📼 5A/4   ◐ II/1/[12]

MENDELSSOHN: *A Midsummer Night's Dream*, Overture

Date: ~~1843~~ *1826*

Genre: Orchestral overture, ~~from incidental music to play~~ *wrote it first, 17 yrs later, 1843*

Program: Based on Shakespeare's play, *A Midsummer Night's Dream*; plot centers on four groups of
characters: courtly party (Theseus and Hippolyta); four young lovers; the fairies (Oberon and Titania,
as King and Queen); and the clownish tradesmen. Action focuses on pairs of lovers from all groups and
transformations brought on by mischievous Puck.

Form: Sonata-allegro form, three main sections:
    Exposition—three main themes introduced
    Development—varies themes
    Recapitulation—main themes return
    Coda—closing

Time	Program	Musical Description
[12] 0:00	Introduction to realm of the fairies	Four long chords in winds

EXPOSITION: Allegro di molto

0:25   Fairy theme   1. Soft, lively, high violins playing staccato

1:08   Transitional theme   Loud, energetic, descending, then ascending line

13 2:11   Young lovers' theme   2. Lyrical, expressive melody in violins

3:03   Clowns' theme; magic spell   3. Rhythmic theme, disjunct; wide leap
        places ass's head on Bottom   reminiscent of donkey's heehaw
        the Weaver

DEVELOPMENT

14 3:47   Fairy music developed; exchanged between strings
                                            in imitation

5:57   Realm of fairies returns   Four chords in winds

RECAPITULATION (RETURN)

15 6:22   Fairy music   1. Like opening, light staccato strings
    7:05   Lovers' theme   2. Lyrical melody
    7:56   Clowns' theme   3. Active, disjunct

CODA

16 9:22   Extension of clowns' theme and heehaw
                                            Transitional theme from Exposition heard slower

11:16   Realm of fairies   Four closing chords, like opening

52

Hector Berlioz

"To render my works properly requires a combination of extreme precision and irresistible verve, a regulated vehemence, a dreamy tenderness, and an almost morbid melancholy."

Hector Berlioz described the prevailing characteristics of his music as passionate expression, intense ardor, rhythmic animation, and unexpected turns. The flamboyance of Victor Hugo's poetry and the dramatic intensity of Eugène Delacroix's painting found their counterpart in Berlioz's music. He was the first great exponent of musical romanticism in France.

Hector Berlioz. Portrait by **Gustave Courbet** (*1819–77*).

His Life

Hector Berlioz (1803–69) was born in France in a small town near Grenoble. His father, a well-to-do physician, expected him to follow in his footsteps, and at eighteen Hector was dispatched to the medical school in Paris. The Conservatory and the Opéra, however, exercised an infinitely greater attraction than the dissecting room. The following year the fiery youth made a decision that horrified his upper middle-class family: he gave up medicine for music.

The Romantic revolution was brewing in Paris. Berlioz, along with Victor Hugo and Delacroix, found himself in the camp of "young France." Having been cut off by his parents, he gave lessons, sang in a theater chorus, and turned to various musical chores. He fell under the spell of Beethoven; hardly less powerful was the impact of Shakespeare, to whose art he was introduced by a visiting English troupe. For the actress whose Ophelia and Juliet excited the admiration of the Parisians, young Berlioz conceived an overwhelming passion. In his *Memoirs*, which read like a Romantic novel, he describes his infatuation for Harriet Smithson: "I became obsessed by an intense, overpowering sense of sadness. I could not sleep, I could not work, and I spent my time wandering aimlessly about Paris and its environs."

In 1830 he was awarded the coveted Prix de Rome, which gave him an opportunity to live and work in the Eternal City. That year also saw the composition of what has remained his most celebrated work, the *Symphonie fantastique*. Upon his return from Rome a hectic courtship of Miss Smithson ensued. There were strenuous objections on the part of both their families and violent scenes, during one of which the excitable Hector attempted suicide. He was revived. They were married.

Now that the unattainable ideal had become his wife, his ardor cooled. It was Shakespeare he had loved rather than Harriet, and in time he sought the ideal elsewhere. All the same, the first years of his marriage were the most fruitful of his life. By the time he was forty he had produced most of the works on which his fame rests.

In the latter part of his life he conducted his music in all the capitals of Europe. But Paris resisted him to the end. His last major work was the opera *Béatrice et Bénédict*, on his own libretto after Shakespeare's *Much Ado About Nothing*. After this effort the flame was spent, and for the last seven years of his life the embittered master wrote no more. He died at sixty-six, tormented to the end. "Some day," wrote Richard Wagner, "a grateful France will raise a proud monument on his tomb." The prophecy has been fulfilled.

His Music

Berlioz was one of the boldest innovators of the nineteenth century. His approach to music was wholly individual, his sense of sound unique. From the start he had an affinity—where orchestral music was concerned—for the vividly dramatic or pictorial program.

His works exemplify the favorite literary influences of the Romantic period. *The Damnation of Faust* was inspired by Goethe; *Harold in Italy*, a program symphony with viola solo and *The Corsair*, an overture, are after Byron. Shakespeare is the source for the overture *King Lear* and for the dramatic symphony *Romeo and Juliet*.

Berlioz's most important opera, *The Trojans* on his own libretto based on Virgil, has been successfully revived in recent years. His sacred vocal works, including the Requiem and the Te Deum, are often conceived on a grandiose scale. This love of huge orchestral and choral forces represents only one aspect of Berlioz's personality. No less characteristic is the tenderness that finds expression in the oratorio *L'enfance du Christ*, which we shall study later; the fine-spun lyricism that wells up in his songs; the sensibility that fills his orchestra with Gallic clarity and grace.

It was in the domain of orchestration that Berlioz's genius asserted itself most fully. His daring originality in handling the instruments opened up a new world of Romantic sonority. His scores, calling for a larger orchestra

Principal Works

Orchestral music, including overtures: *Waverley* (1828), *Rob Roy* (1831), *Le roi Lear* (King Lear, 1831), and program symphonies: *Symphonie fantastique* (1830), *Harold en Italie* (Harold in Italy, 1834), and *Roméo et Juliette* (1839)

Choral music, including a Requiem mass (1837), Te Deum (Hymn of Praise, 1849), *La damnation de Faust* (The Damnation of Faust, 1846), and the oratorio *L'enfance du Christ* (The Childhood of Christ, 1854)

3 operas, including *Les Troyens* (The Trojans, 1858) and *Béatrice et Bénédict* (1862)

9 solo vocal works with orchestra

Writings on music, including a treatise on orchestration (1834/55)

than had ever been used before, abound in novel effects and discoveries that served as models to all who came after him. Indeed, the conductor Felix Weingartner called Berlioz "the creator of the modern orchestra."

Berlioz: Symphonie fantastique

Berlioz's best-known symphony was written at the height of his infatuation with Harriet Smithson, when he was twenty-seven years old. It is hardly to be believed that this remarkable "novel in tones" was conceived by a young man only three years after the death of Beethoven. Extraordinary is the fact that he not only attached a program to a symphony, but that he drew the program from his personal life. "A young musician of morbid sensibility and ardent imagination in a paroxysm of lovesick despair has poisoned himself with opium. The drug, too weak to kill, plunges him into a heavy sleep accompanied by strange visions. . . . The beloved one herself becomes for him a melody, a recurrent theme [*idée fixe*] that haunts him everywhere."

Idée fixe

The "fixed idea" that symbolizes the beloved—the basic theme of the symphony—is subjected to variation in harmony, rhythm, meter, and tempo; dynamics, register, and instrumental color. These transformations take on literary as well as musical significance. Thus the basic motive, recurring by virtue of the literary program, becomes a musical thread unifying five movements that are diverse in mood and character. (See Listening Guide 33 for theme and analysis.)

I. "Reveries, Passions." "He remembers the weariness of soul, the indefinable yearning he knew before meeting his beloved. Then, the volcanic love with which she at once inspired him, his delirious suffering . . . his religious consolation." The Allegro section introduces a soaring melody— the fixed idea. At the climax of the movement the fixed idea is recapitulated fortissimo by full orchestra.

First movement

II. "A Ball." "Amid the tumult and excitement of a brilliant ball he glimpses the loved one again." The dance movement is in ternary or three-part form. In the middle section the fixed idea reappears in waltz time.

Second movement

III. "Scene in the Fields." "On a summer evening in the country he hears two shepherds piping. The pastoral duet, the quiet surroundings . . . all unite to fill his heart with a long absent calm. But *she* appears again. His heart contracts. Painful forebodings fill his soul. . . ." The composer described his aim in the pastoral movement as a mood "of sorrowful loneliness."

Third movement

IV. "March to the Scaffold." "He dreams that he has killed his beloved, that he has been condemned to die and is being led to the scaffold. . . . At the very end the fixed idea reappears for an instant, like a last thought of love interrupted by the fall of the axe." This diabolical march movement exemplifies the nineteenth-century love of the fantastic. The theme of the beloved appears at the very end, on the clarinet, and is cut off by a grim fortissimo chord.

Fourth movement

V. "Dream of a Witches' Sabbath." "He sees himself at a witches' sabbath surrounded by a host of fearsome specters who have gathered for his funeral. Unearthly sounds, groans, shrieks of laughter. . . ." The melody of his be-

Fifth movement

Francisco Goya (*1746–1828*) *anticipated the passionate intensity of Berlioz's music in this painting of the* Witches' Sabbath, *c. 1819–23.* (Museo del Prado, Madrid)

loved is heard, but it has lost its noble and reserved character. It has become a vulgar tune, trivial and grotesque. It is she who comes to the infernal orgy. A howl of joy greets her arrival. She joins the diabolical dance. Bells toll for the dead. A burlesque of the *Dies Irae*. Dance of the witches. The dance and the *Dies Irae* combined."

This final movement opens with a Larghetto (not quite as slow as largo). Berlioz here exploits an infernal spirit that nourished a century of satanic operas, ballets, and symphonic poems. The infernal mood is heightened with the introduction of the traditional religious chant *Dies irae* (Day of Wrath) from the ancient Mass for the Dead. The movement reaches its climax when this well-known melody, now in shorter note values, is combined with the Witches' Dance. This passage leads to a rousingly theatrical ending for a theatrical subject.

There is a bigness of line and gesture about the music of Berlioz, an overflow of vitality and inventiveness. He is one of the major prophets of the Romantic era.

Listening Guide 33   5A/3   II/1/7

BERLIOZ: *Symphonie fantastique*

Date: 1830

Genre: Program symphony, 5 movements

Program: A lovesick artist in an opium trance is haunted by a vision of his beloved, which becomes an *idée fixe* (fixed idea).

idée fixe (Passionate, but noble and sdy)
→ Harriet Smithson (performed Shakespearian pp

I. "Reveries, Passions"

Largo, Allegro agitato e appassionato assai (lively, agitated, and very impassioned). Introduces the main theme, the fixed idea

II. "A Ball"

Valse Allegro non troppo (Waltz, not too fast), triple meter dance, **A-B-A** form

III. "Scene in the Fields"

Adagio, in 6/8 meter, **A-B-A** form

IV. "March to the Scaffold" (Listening Guide in *Listening and Study Guide*)

Allegretto non troppo *BAD OPIUM TRIP* here guiliteme blade and headplop
Duple meter march in minor mode

V. "Dream of a Witches' Sabbath"

Time	Description
7 0:00	Larghetto—very soft muted strings evoke infernal atmosphere; chromatic scales in strings, low brass, and high woodwinds evoke "unearthly sounds, groans, shrieks of laughter"
8 1:36	Allegro—fixed idea in high clarinet in transformed version with trills and grace notes ("a vulgar tune, trivial and grotesque")
2:46	Dance tune forecast by its opening motive in strings
3:08	Bells chime ("Bells toll for the dead")
9 3:34	Chant tune *Dies irae* sounded in tubas and bassoons, first slow, then twice as fast in the brass
4:05	"Burlesque of the *Dies irae*" in strings and woodwinds in irregular rhythm
10 5:25	"Dance of the Witches" ("Ronde du Sabbat")— begins in low strings with driving rhythm; contrapuntal fabric as tune is passed to other instruments
11 8:12	"The dance and the *Dies irae* combined"

Dies irae (day of wrath) (mass of the dead) Funeral rite — *Catholics were shocked*

ITALY, POLAND, BOHEMIA > AUSTRIAN POWER

NATIONALISM = desire from political oppression cultural identity

53

Richard Strauss

*"I work very long on melodies. The important thing is not the
beginning of the melody but its continuation, its development into a
fully completed artistic form."*

Richard Strauss

Among the composers who inherited the symphonic poem of Liszt, Richard
Strauss (1865–1949) occupied a leading place. Although he lived well into
the twentieth century, the symphonic poems he wrote during the last years
of the nineteenth century came out of and belong to the Romantic tradition.

His Life

Strauss was born in Munich. His father was a virtuoso horn player who
belonged to the court orchestra. His mother was the daughter of a successful
Munich brewer. In this solid middle-class environment, made familiar to
American readers by the novels of Thomas Mann, a high value was placed
on music and money. These remained Strauss's twin passions throughout
his life.

His first works were in the Classical forms. At twenty-one he found his
true style in the writing of vivid program music, setting himself to develop
what he called "the poetic, the expressive in music." *Macbeth*, his first
symphonic poem, was followed by *Don Juan*, an extraordinary achievement
for a young man of twenty-four. Then came the series of symphonic poems
that blazed his name throughout the civilized world: *Death and Transfiguration, Till Eulenspiegel's Merry Pranks, Thus Spake Zarathustra, Don
Quixote, A Hero's Life.*

In the early years of the twentieth century Strauss conquered the operatic
stage with *Salome, Elektra,* and *Der Rosenkavalier* (The Cavalier of the
Rose). The international triumph of the last-named on the eve of the First
World War marked the summit of his career. He collected unprecedented
fees and royalties for his scores. Strauss was eager to dispel the romantic
notion that the artist is better off starving in a garret. On the contrary, he
insisted that "worry alone is enough to kill a sensitive man, and all thoroughly
artistic natures are sensitive."

Strauss's collaboration with Hugo von Hofmannsthal, the librettist of *Elektra* and *Der Rosenkavalier,* continued until the latter's death in 1929. By
this time, new conceptions of modernism had come to the fore; the onetime bad boy of music, now entrenched as a conservative, was inevitably
left behind. The coming to power of the Nazis in 1933 confronted Strauss
with a challenge and an opportunity. He was by no means reactionary in
his political thinking; his daughter-in-law was Jewish, and the cosmopolitan
circles in which he traveled were not susceptible to Hitler's ideology. Hence
the challenge to speak out against the Third Reich—or to leave Germany
as Thomas Mann, Hindemith, and other intellectuals were doing. On the

other hand the new regime was courting men of arts and letters. Strauss saw the road open to supreme power, and took the opportunity. In 1933, on the threshold of seventy, he was elevated to the official hierarchy as president of the Reichsmusikkammer (State Chamber of Music). His reign was brief and uneasy. He declined to support the move to ban Mendelssohn's music from Teutonic ears. His opera *Die schweigsame Frau* was withdrawn after its premier because the librettist, Stefan Zweig, was non-Aryan; whereupon Strauss resigned.

The war's end found the eighty-one-year-old composer the victim of a curious irony. He was living in near poverty because the huge sums owing him for performances of his works in England and America had been impounded as war reparations. He was permitted to return to his villa at Garmisch, in the Bavarian Alps. To his friends Strauss explained that he had remained in Nazi Germany because someone had to protect culture from Hitler's barbarians. Perhaps he even believed it.

There were speeches at the Bavarian Academy of Arts on the occasion of his eighty-fifth birthday. Shortly thereafter he died.

His Music

Strauss carried to its extreme limit the nineteenth-century appetite for story-and-picture music. His symphonic poems are a treasury of orchestral discoveries. In some he anticipates modern sound effects—the clatter of pots and pans, the bleating of sheep, the gabble of geese, hoofbeats, wind, thunder, storm. Much more important, these works are packed with movement and gesture, with the sound and fury of an imperious temperament.

Strauss's operas continue to be widely performed. *Salome*, to Oscar Wilde's famous play, and *Elektra*, based on Hofmannsthal's version of the Greek tragedy, are long one-act operas. Swiftly paced, moving relentlessly to their climaxes, they are superb theater. *Der Rosenkavalier* has a wealth of sensuous lyricism and some entrancing waltzes. There comes a time, alas, when the opera seems a trifle long. It is a sign that one's youth is over.

Principal Works

Orchestral music: symphonic poems including *Macbeth* (1888), *Don Juan* (1888–89), *Tod und Verklärung* (Death and Transfiguration, 1889) *Till Eulenspiegels lustige Streiche* (Till Eulenspiegel's Merry Pranks, 1895), *Also sprach Zarathustra* (Thus Spake Zarathustra, 1896), *Don Quixote* (1897), and *Ein Heldenleben* (A Hero's Life, 1898); 2 symphonies (*Domestic*, 1903; *Alpine*, 1915); 3 concertos (2 for horn, 1 for oboe)

15 operas, including *Salome* (1906), *Elektra* (1909), *Der Rosenkavalier* (The Cavalier of the Rose, 1911), and *Die schweigsame Frau* (The Silent Woman, 1935)

Choral works, with and without orchestra; chamber works

Strauss: Don Juan

S4A/1
S4/ 1

The figure of Don Juan has attracted artists for hundreds of years, from Molière in the seventeenth century to Bernard Shaw in the twentieth. It is a mistake to regard the Don as a great lover. Actually he is incapable of love; what drives him is the need for conquest. Oblivious of other human beings, he cannot relate to anyone outside himself. This condemns him to the loneliness that is his real punishment, a loneliness he forever seeks to escape. Strauss, on the score of his symphonic poem, quoted excerpts from *Don Juan* by the Austrian Romantic poet Nicolaus Lenau (1802–50). Lenau's Don seeks the ideal woman, hoping through her to enjoy all women. Because he cannot find her he reels from one to another, eaten by boredom and satiety. In a duel with the son of a man he has killed he drops his sword and lets his enemy kill him, thus ending a life that has brought him only self-disgust.

Strauss's symphonic poem suggests the fiery ardor with which Don Juan pursues his ideal. Marked Allegro molto con brio (very fast, with vigor), the piece opens with one of those upward-sweeping gestures of which Strauss knew the secret. We hear the theme of Don Juan, a brusque, impetuous melody whose tension is underlined by dotted rhythms, wide leaps, and wide range. In dramatic contrast are the three themes that represent his romantic longing and search for fulfillment, culminating in a love song sung by the oboe "in a sustained and expressive manner." It is followed by a gallant tune on the horns that evokes the chivalric side of his nature, and an idea marked giocoso (playful) suggesting a scene of merrymaking.

Strauss weaves a colorful fabric out of his themes, pitting one against the other, combining and transforming them. The final buildup expatiates on both themes of the Don in a section notable for its sweep and passion. An ominous silence, and the epilogue unfolds briefly in shuddering tremolos in the strings that descend from high to low register and lead to the pianissimo ending. Don Juan's hectic life is over.

A world figure, Strauss dominated his era as few artists have done. He may have suspected toward the end that the world had been too much with him. "We are all of us children of our time," he said, "and can never leap over its shadows." He was one of the major artists of our century.

54

The Rise of Musical Nationalism

"I grew up in a quiet spot and was saturated from earliest childhood with the wonderful beauty of Russian popular song. I am therefore passionately devoted to every expression of the Russian spirit. In short, I am a Russian through and through!"—PETER ILYICH TCHAIKOVSKY

In giving voice to their personal views of life, artists also express the hopes and dreams of the group with which they are identified. It is this identification, seeping through from the most profound layers of the unconscious, that makes Shakespeare and Dickens so English, Dostoevsky so Russian, Proust so French.

In nineteenth-century Europe, political conditions encouraged the growth of nationalism to such a degree that it became a decisive force within the Romantic movement. National tensions on the Continent—the pride of the conquering nations and the struggle for freedom of the suppressed ones—gave rise to emotions that found an ideal expression in music.

The rise of nationalism is reflected in this heroic painting by **Jacques Louis David** (*1748–1825*), *titled* Napoleon at St. Bernard (Musée National de Château de Versailles)

335

The Romantic composers expressed their nationalism in a number of ways. Several based their music on the songs and dances of their people: Chopin in his Mazurkas, Liszt in his *Hungarian Rhapsodies*, Dvořák in the *Slavonic Dances*, Grieg in the *Norwegian Dances*. A number wrote dramatic works based on folklore or the life of the peasantry. Examples are the German folk opera *Der Freischütz* by Carl Maria von Weber, the Czech national opera *The Bartered Bride* by Bedřich Smetana, as well as the Russian fairy-tale operas and ballets of Tchaikovsky and Rimsky-Korsakov. Some wrote symphonic poems and operas celebrating the exploits of a national hero, a historic event, or the scenic beauty of their country. Tchaikovsky's *1812 Overture* and Smetana's *The Moldau* exemplify this trend, as does the glorification of the gods and heroes of German myth and legend in Richard Wagner's music dramas, especially *The Ring of the Nibelung*, a vast epic centering about the life and death of Siegfried.

The political implications of musical nationalism were not lost upon the authorities. Verdi's operas had to be altered again and again to suit the Austrian censor. Sibelius's tone poem *Finlandia* with its rousing trumpet calls was forbidden by the tsarist police when Finland was demanding her independence at the turn of the century. During World War II the Nazis forbade the playing of *The Moldau* in Prague and of Chopin's Polonaises in Warsaw because of the powerful symbolism residing in these works.

Nationalism added to the language of European music a variety of national idioms of great charm and vivacity. By associating music with the love of homeland, nationalism enabled composers to give expression to the cherished aspirations of millions of people. In short, national consciousness pervaded every aspect of the European spirit in the nineteenth century. The Romantic movement is unthinkable without it.

A Czech Nationalist: Bedřich Smetana

"I try to write only as I feel in myself."

Bedřich Smetana

The Czech national school of composers was founded by Bedřich Smetana (1824–84). As in the case of several nationalist composers, Smetana's career unfolded against a background of political agitation. Bohemia stirred restlessly under Austrian rule, caught up in a surge of nationalist fervor that culminated in the uprisings of 1848. Young Smetana aligned himself with the patriotic cause. After the revolution was crushed, the atmosphere in Prague was oppressive for those suspected of sympathy with the nationalists. In 1856 Smetana accepted a post as conductor in Sweden.

On his return to Bohemia five years later, he resumed his career as a national artist and worked for the establishment of a theater in Prague where the performances would be given in the native tongue. Of his eight operas on patriotic themes, several are still performed today. One—*The Bartered Bride*—attained worldwide fame. Hardly less important in the establishing

Principal Works

8 operas, including *The Bartered Bride* (1866)

Orchestral music, including *Má vlast* (My Country), cycle of 6 symphonic poems (No. 2 is *The Moldau* or *Vltava*, 1874)

Chamber and keyboard works; choral music and songs

of Smetana's reputation was the cycle of six symphonic poems entitled *My Country*, which occupied him from 1874 to 1879. These works are steeped in the beauty of Bohemia's countryside, the rhythm of her folksongs and dances, the pomp and pageantry of her legends. Best known of the series is the second, *The Moldau*, Smetana's finest achievement in the field of orchestral music.

Smetana: The Moldau

In this tone poem the famous river becomes a poetic symbol of the beloved homeland. (For the text of Smetana's program, see Listening Guide 34.) The music suggests the rippling streams that flow through the Bohemian forest to form the mighty river. A hunting scene is evoked by French horns and trumpets, and a peasant wedding in the lilting measures of a folk dance. The mood changes to one of enchantment as nymphs emerge from their fairy-tale haunts to hold their nightly revels. Finally, as the Moldau approaches Prague, it flows past castles and fortresses that remind the poet of his country's vanished glory.

The Moldau ("Vlatava" in Czechoslovakia) flows in majestic peace through Prague.

Listening Guide 34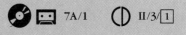

SMETANA: *The Moldau*

Date: 1874

Genre: Symphonic poem, from cycle *Má vlast*

Tempo: Allegro commodo non agitato (fast not agitated)

Program: Scenes along the river Moldau in Bohemia

Smetana's program: "Two springs pour forth in the shade of the Bohemian forest, one warm and gushing, the other cold and peaceful. Coming through Bohemia's valleys, it grows into a mighty stream. Through the thick woods it flows as the gay sounds of the hunt and the notes of the hunter's horn are heard ever closer. It flows through grass-grown pastures and lowlands where a wedding feast is being celebrated with song and dance. At night, wood and water nymphs revel in its sparkling waves. Reflected on its surface are fortresses and castles—witnesses of bygone days of knightly splendor and the vanished glory of martial times. The Moldau swirls through the St. John Rapids, finally flowing on in majestic peace toward Prague and welcomed by historic Vysehrad. Then it vanishes far beyond the poet's gaze."

Time	Program	Description
1 0:00	Source of river, two springs	Rippling figures in flute, then added clarinets; plucked string accompaniment
	Stream broadens	Rippling figure moves to low strings
2 1:03	River theme	Stepwise melody in violins, minor mode, rippling in low strings. Repeated

Allegro commodo non agitato

p dolce — *sf* — *p* — *dim.*

3 2:48	Hunting scene	Fanfare in French horns and trumpets. Rippling continues (in strings). Dies down to gently rocking motion

f

4 3:39	Peasant dance	Repeated notes in strings lead to rustic folk tune, staccato in strings and woodwinds. Closes with repeated single note in strings

L'istesso tempo, ma moderato

mf

5 5:15	Nymphs in moonlight	Mysterious, long notes in double reeds. Rippling figures in flutes; muted string theme with harp, punctuated by French horn. Brass crescendo, fanfare

dolcissimo

6	7:59	River theme	Like beginning, strings in minor, then shift to major (raised third scale step)
7	8:50	St. John's Rapids	Brass and woodwinds exchange an agitated dialogue, build to climax, die out
	10:03	River theme	Full orchestra, loudest statement
8	10:32	Ancient castle (near river mouth)	Brass hymnlike tune, slow, then accelerates
	11:24	River dies away	Strings slow down, loose momentum. Two forceful closing chords

Other Nationalists

Antonín Dvořák (1841–1904) stands alongside Bedřich Smetana as a founder of the Czech national school. His art too was rooted in the songs and dances of Bohemia. The spontaneity and melodiousness of his music assured its popularity. When the last decade of the century arrived, Dvořák was famous throughout Europe.

Dvořák

In 1892 he was invited to become director of the National Conservatory of Music in New York City. His stay in the United States was fruitful. Out of it came his most popular work, the Symphony "From the New World."

Coming to the United States as one of the leading nationalists of Europe, Dvořák tried to influence his American pupils toward a native art. One of his students was Henry T. Burleigh, the black baritone and arranger of spirituals. The melodies he heard from Burleigh strengthened his conviction that American composers would find themselves only when they had thrown off their European past and drew inspiration from the Indian, Negro, and cowboy songs of their own country. The rich harvest of modern American works based on folklore proves his point.

To the international music public, Edvard Grieg (1843–1907) came to represent "the voice of Norway." The nationalist movement of which his music was an expression had a political background. The struggle for independence from Sweden came to a head during the last quarter of the nineteenth century. This cause, to which Grieg was devoted with all his heart, was crowned with success not long before his final illness. His songs and piano pieces attained enormous popularity during his lifetime, and are still current. To the concert public he is best known for his Piano Concerto and the incidental music for *Peer Gynt*.

Grieg

As in the case of Smetana and Grieg, the career of Jean Sibelius (1865–1957) unfolded against a struggle for national independence. In the final decades of the nineteenth century, Finland tried to free itself from the yoke of tsarist Russia. Out of this ferment flowered the art of Sibelius, which served

Sibelius

notice to the world that his country—musically—had come of age. During the 1890s he produced a series of symphonic poems that captured the spirit of Finnish legends and myths. Best known of these is *Finlandia* (1899), which occupies the same position in Finland as *The Moldau* does in Czechoslovakia.

The Mighty Five

It was Mikhail Ivanovich Glinka (1804–57) who laid the foundation for the Russian national school. His dream of a Russian music was taken over by a group of young musicians whom an admiring critic named "The Mighty Five." Their leader was Mily Balakirev (1837–1910), a self-taught composer who persuaded his four disciples—Alexander Borodin (1833–87), César Cui (1835–1918), Nikolai Rimsky-Korsakov (1844–1908) and Modest Musorgsky (1839–81)—that they would have to free themselves from the influence of German symphony, Italian opera, and French ballet if they wanted to express the Russian soul. Their colleague Peter Ilyich Tchaikovsky (1840–93) was more amenable to European influences.

Tchaikovsky and Musorgsky are now recognized as Russia's greatest composers. Of the others, Cui and Balakirev are all but forgotten outside their native land. The works of Glinka, Borodin, and Rimsky-Korsakov, on the other hand, are still very much with us.

The English nationalists

Late in the century musical nationalism came to England in the works of Sir Edward Elgar (1857–1934), Frederick Delius (1862–1934), and their followers. Spain produced three important nationalists in Isaac Albéniz (1860–1909), Enrique Granados (1867–1916), and Manuel de Falla (1876–1946). America's contribution to musical nationalism, relatively late in flowering, will be discussed in later chapters.

Absolute Forms

55

The Romantic Symphony

"A great symphony is a man-made Mississippi down which we irresistibly flow from the instant of our leave-taking to a long foreseen destination."—AARON COPLAND

During the Classical period, the symphony established itself as the most exalted form of absolute orchestral music. The three Viennese masters—Haydn, Mozart, and Beethoven—carried it to its highest level of significance and formal beauty. They bequeathed to the composers of the Romantic era a flexible art form that could be brought into harmony with the emotional needs of the new age.

In the course of its development the symphony steadily gained greater weight and importance. By now music had moved from palace to public concert hall, and the orchestra had very much increased in size, as had the symphony. The nineteenth-century symphonists were not as prolific as their forbears had been. Their works grew steadily longer and more expansive. Mendelssohn, Schumann, Brahms, Tchaikovsky, each wrote fewer than seven symphonies. All of these were in the domain of absolute music, while Liszt and Berlioz cultivated the program symphony.

The Nature of the Symphony

We know well the standard four-movement symphony form that was the legacy of the Classical masters. In the hands of Romantic composers, the symphony takes on new proportions. The number and tempo scheme of the movements is not religiously followed; Tchaikovsky, for example, closes his Sixth Symphony, the *Pathétique*, with a long and expressive slow movement and Beethoven pushed the cycle to five movements in his Sixth Symphony, the *Pastoral.*

First movement   First movements generally retain the basic elements of sonata-allegro form. The most dramatic movement of the Romantic cycle, the first, might draw out the slow introduction and oftens features a long and expressive Development section that ventures into distant keys and transforms themes into something the ear hears as entirely new.

Second movement   The second movement of the Romantic symphony may retain its slow and lyrical nature; the range of moods presented, however, spans the emotional spectrum from whimsical and playful to tragic and passionate. This movement is frequently in a loose three-part form, but may also fall into the theme and variations mold.

Third in the cycle is the strongly rhythmic and impetuous scherzo, with overtones of humor, surprise, whimsy, or folk dance. In mood it may be *Third movement*   anything from elfin lightness to demonic energy. The tempo marking—generally Allegro, Allegro molto, or Vivace—indicates a lively pace. Scherzo form generally follows the **A-B-A** structure of the minuet and trio. In some symphonies, such as Beethoven's Ninth, the scherzo comes second in the cycle.

The fourth and last member of the Romantic symphony cycle is of a *Fourth movement*   dimension and character designed to balance the first movement. The work may draw to a close on a note of triumph or pathos. Frequently, this movement is a spirited Allegro in sonata-allegro form. We shall see, however, that some composers experimented with fourth movement forms. Brahms's Fourth Symphony, for example, turns to the noble Baroque passacaglia (a work based on a melodic or harmonic ostinato) for its closing movement.

The nineteenth-century symphony holds a place of honor in the output of the Romantic era. It retains its hold on the public, and remains one of the striking manifestations of the spirit of musical Romanticism.

56

Two Romantic Symphonists

Mendelssohn: Symphony No. 4 (Italian)

> *"The Italian Symphony* is getting on well. It is becoming the merriest piece I have yet composed."

The *Italian Symphony* dates from the "grand tour" that Mendelssohn undertook in his early twenties, in the course of which he visited England, Scotland, Italy, and France. Like most visitors from northern Europe he was enchanted by Italy, its sunny skies and exuberant people. He recorded his impressions in one of his most widely loved works, the first version of which occupied him from 1831 to 1833. Despite the success of the symphony, it failed to satisfy him; he kept revising the piece for a number of years.

First movement

The first movement is a dynamic Allegro vivace (fast and lively) whose headlong pace never slackens. Its main theme is a dancelike tune of boundless energy. The drive and vigor of this music are not to be resisted. The strings are clearly the heart of Mendelssohn's orchestra; woodwinds and brass are set off against them with capital effect. The orchestral sound is transparent—everything is clear and bright, with much staccato in the graceful manner associated with this composer. The second theme, a less active, gracious melody in the woodwinds, contrasts with the first. A codetta rounds off the opening section of the movement, the Exposition. Mendelssohn, in accordance with earlier Classical procedure, indicates that this is to be repeated.

The Development refashions both themes into fresh patterns and introduces a striking new motive that is bandied about by various instruments.

An exciting crescendo leads into the final section of the movement, the Recapitulation. The material is restated in shortened form. The coda is marked Più animato poco a poco (more animated, little by little) and provides a fitting climax to this truly sunny Allegro. (For an analysis of this movement and those that follow it, see Listening Guide 35.)

The Symphony

Multimovement work for orchestra
4 movements standard: fast–slow–moderate dance–fast

Standard Symphony Form

I. First movement: Allegro
   Sonata-allegro form
     Slow introduction (optional)
     Exposition
       Theme 1—rhythmic
       Theme 2—lyrical
       Codetta or Closing Theme
     Development—fragmentation or expansion of themes
     Recapitulation (Restatement)
       Theme 1
       Theme 2
     Coda
II. Second movement
     Slow, lyrical
     Sonata-allegro form, **A-B-A,** or theme and variations form
III. Third movement
     Triple meter, dance movement (Minuet or Scherzo)
     Sectional, with repeats
IV. Fourth movement
     Allegro or Presto, shorter and lighter than first
     movement, various forms possible

Second movement   Second is an Andante con moto (moderately slow, with motion). The form is a modified sonata-allegro, consisting of an Exposition and Recapitulation without a Development—what is known as a *sonatina* (little sonata). In this Andante Mendelssohn reveals his gift for lyricism of a subdued, somewhat elegiac cast.

Third movement   The third movement of the *Italian Symphony* is lyrical in nature and stands closer to the minuet of the Classical symphony than to the more boisterous Scherzo of the Romantic era The broad string melody of the opening section contrasts with the middle section, or Trio, which features wind instruments. The prominence of horn sound imparts to this music a suggestion of the outdoors.

Fourth movement   The final movement is a Presto based on the popular Italian "jumping dance" known as the *saltarello,* characterized by triplets in a rapid 4/4 time. The movement evokes a scene of tumultuous merrymaking, with crowds dancing wildly in the streets. Of special note are the slowly gathering crescendos that propel the music forward. Beyond that it combines the Classical impulse toward clarity of form with the Romantic fondness for picturesque mood and atmosphere.

Listening Guide 35

5B/2   II/1/17

MENDELSSOHN: *Italian Symphony*

Date: 1833

Movements: 4

I. First movement: Allegro vivace, sonata-allegro form, 6/8 meter, A major

EXPOSITION (to be repeated)
17 Theme 1—dancelike, energetic theme in A major

18 Theme 2—gracious melody in woodwinds

Closing—based on Theme 1

19 DEVELOPMENT
Introduction of new motive, then expanded

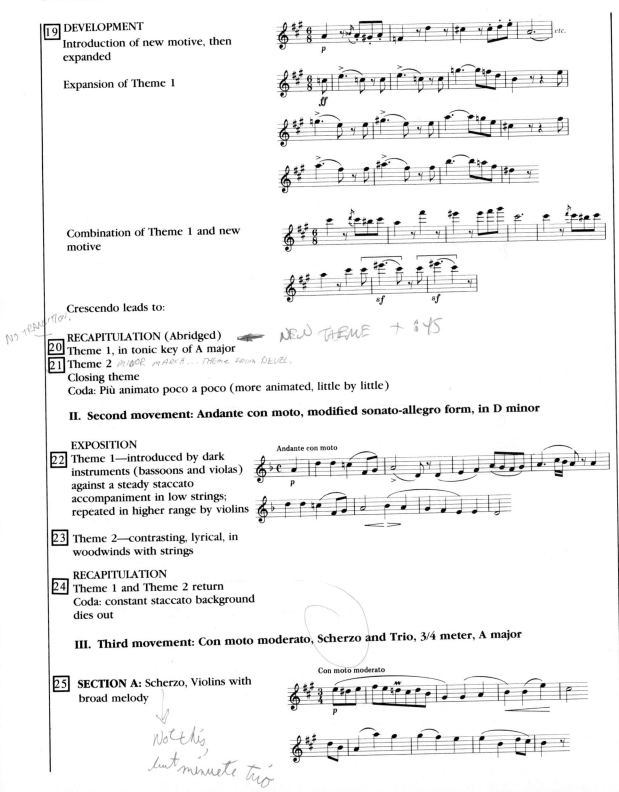

Expansion of Theme 1

Combination of Theme 1 and new motive

Crescendo leads to:

NO TRANSITION.

RECAPITULATION (Abridged)   ← *NEW THEME + p.45*
20 Theme 1, in tonic key of A major
21 Theme 2   *MINOR MARCH... THEME FROM DEVEL.*
Closing theme
Coda: Più animato poco a poco (more animated, little by little)

II. Second movement: Andante con moto, modified sonato-allegro form, in D minor

EXPOSITION
22 Theme 1—introduced by dark instruments (bassoons and violas) against a steady staccato accompaniment in low strings; repeated in higher range by violins

23 Theme 2—contrasting, lyrical, in woodwinds with strings

RECAPITULATION
24 Theme 1 and Theme 2 return
Coda: constant staccato background dies out

III. Third movement: Con moto moderato, Scherzo and Trio, 3/4 meter, A major

25 **SECTION A:** Scherzo, Violins with broad melody

Not this, but minuete trio

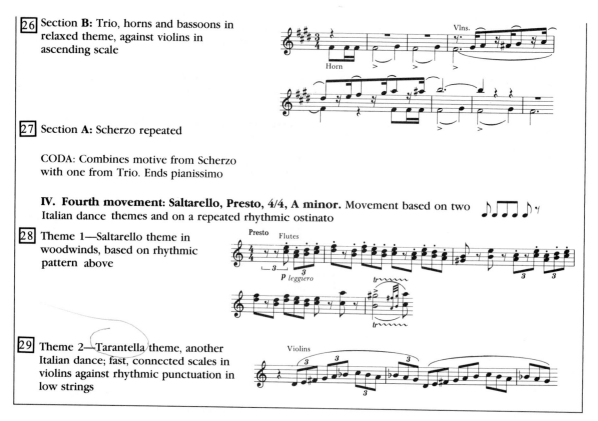

26 Section **B:** Trio, horns and bassoons in relaxed theme, against violins in ascending scale

27 Section **A:** Scherzo repeated

CODA: Combines motive from Scherzo with one from Trio. Ends pianissimo

IV. Fourth movement: Saltarello, Presto, 4/4, A minor. Movement based on two Italian dance themes and on a repeated rhythmic ostinato

28 Theme 1—Saltarello theme in woodwinds, based on rhythmic pattern above

29 Theme 2—Tarantella theme, another Italian dance; fast, connected scales in violins against rhythmic punctuation in low strings

Brahms: Symphony No. 4

Brahms was fond of saying that it was no laughing matter to compose a symphony after Beethoven. "You have no idea," he told a friend, "how the likes of us feel when we hear the tramp of a giant like him behind us." He therefore did not attempt the symphonic form until he was past forty and at the height of his powers.

S3A/5

S3/12

The Fourth is notable for its tone of autumnal resignation and the beauty of its themes. The first movement, marked Allegro non troppo (not too fast), opens with a long-breathed, heartfelt melody that can only be described as Brahmsian. Wide leaps give it a distinctive character and a feeling of enormous strength. Second is an Andante moderato (moderately slow) that presents one of Brahms's loveliest tunes, in the mood of gentle resignation that marked the master's maturity. Third is the Scherzo, an Allegro giocoso (fast and playful) that is full of high spirits and boundless vigor.

For the culminating movement of his final symphony Brahms turned to a form that flourished in the age of Bach and earlier, the passacaglia. His choice of an archaic form indicates his strong identification with the past.

Passacaglia A *passacaglia*, as mentioned earlier, is a composition in moderately slow triple meter based on a short melody which is repeated over and over again as the basis for continuous variation in the other voices. In the passacaglias of earlier eras this melody was usually in the bass part while the other voices flowed freely about it. Brahms departs from this procedure by having the wind instruments announce the eight-measure theme above the harmonies that accompany it. Thereupon he spreads it throughout the musical texture so that it appears now in the upper register, now in the lower or hidden among the other voices, but always present in one guise or another. Using this comparatively simple tune as a point of departure, he constructs a monumental movement marked Allegro energico e passionato (an energetic and impassioned Allegro). The constant repetition of the basic melody supplies the element of unity, while the orchestral voices keep changing around it in a series of thirty strict variations on the tune, followed by a coda. Brahms deploys all the resources of his imagination to build a musical structure marked by a steadily mounting tension that is maintained all the way to the powerful ending. The ear is continually challenged by the shifting moods, the mind is fascinated by the technical mastery with which all this is accompanied. Most important of all, our emotions are stirred by the magnificent canvas that unfolds before us.

57

The Romantic Concerto

"We are so made that we can derive intense enjoyment only from a contrast."—SIGMUND FREUD

The Nature of the Concerto

The Romantic concerto is, in its dimensions, comparable to the symphony. Retaining its three-movement structure, the Romantic cycle presents a dramatic Allegro, usually in sonata form, followed by a lyrical slow movement and a brilliant finale.

Double exposition

The elaborate structure of the Classical double exposition is treated with more freedom by Romantic composers. The solo instrument may not wait for an orchestral exposition to make its first statement, and the cadenza, normally played at the close of the Recapitulation and before the Coda, may occur earlier as a part of the Development.

Second movements continue to deliver lyrical melodies, often in a loosely structured three-part form. The brilliant finales of the Romantic concerto bring the dramatic tension between soloist and orchestra, analogous to that between protagonist and chorus in Greek tragedy, to a head. The soloist is often featured again in a flashy cadenza that closes the concerto cycle.

In this contemporary woodcut from the 1870s, the noted virtuoso Hans von Bülow is seen performing a piano concerto with orchestra in New York City.

Virtuosity in the Nineteenth Century

The roots of the Romantic concerto stretched back to the late eighteenth century. Mozart and Beethoven, both formidable pianists, performed their concertos in public; these works delighted and dazzled their audiences. The concerto thus had to be a "grateful" vehicle that enabled performing artists to exhibit their gifts as well as the capacities of the instrument. This element of technical display, combined with appealing melodies, has helped to make the concerto one of the most widely appreciated types of concert music.

As the concert industry developed, ever greater emphasis was placed upon the virtuoso soloist. Technical brilliance became a more and more important element of concerto style. Nineteenth-century performers such as Paganini and Liszt carried virtuosity to new heights. This development kept pace with the increase in the size and resources of the symphony orchestra. The Romantic concerto took shape as one of the most favored genres of the age. Mendelssohn, Chopin, Liszt, Schumann, Brahms, and Tchaikovsky all contributed to its literature. Their concertos continue to delight audiences all over the world, alongside those of Haydn, Mozart, and Beethoven.

58

Two Romantic Concertos

Schumann: Piano Concerto in A minor

In 1841 Schumann composed a *Phantasie for Piano and Orchestra* which ultimately became the first movement of his celebrated Piano Concerto. He added the second and third movements in 1845.

First movement

The first movement, a spacious Allegro affetuoso (fast and with feeling) opens with a brief but dramatic Introduction, followed by the main theme, a haunting melody of great tenderness and an inward quality typical of Schumann. The second theme of the movement is not a new idea at all, but an imaginative transformation of the first theme. A Development section features some interesting transformations of the theme, which lead to the Recapitulation. The cadenza, Schumann's own, is both emotional and introspective. This Allegro achieves a nice balance between lyrical and virtuoso elements.

Second movement

Second is an Intermezzo (Interlude) marked Andantino grazioso (a little faster than Andante, with grace), which begins with an intimate dialogue between piano and strings. Its main idea is derived from a motive of the opening theme of the first movement. The Intermezzo is in a simple ternary form (**A-B-A**); the middle contrasting section features a broad cello line.

The Concerto

Multimovement work for solo instrument and orchestra
Normally 3 movements: fast–slow–fast

Standard Concerto Form

I. First movement: Allegro
    Sonata form, with double exposition
        Exposition: Themes 1 and 2—orchestra
        Themes 1 and 2—solo instrument
        Development
        Recapitulation
        Cadenza: Solo instrument alone
        Coda
II. Second movement: Slow, lyrical
    A-B-A form common
III. Third movement: Very fast
    Sonata or rondo forms popular

Third movement   The finale is an Allegro vivace (fast and lively) in 6/8 time, which creates a sense of vigorous movement that conjures up the outdoors. The movement abounds in elaborate passage work for the solo instrument that demands not only nimble fingers but also an impeccable sense of timing. (For a detailed analysis of the work, see Listening Guide 36.)

In this concerto Schumann achieved the perfect fusion of dramatic and lyric elements. The work is universally regarded as his masterpiece.

Listening Guide 36   6A/3   II/2/2

SCHUMANN: Piano Concerto in A minor

Date: 1841/45

Movements: 3

I. First movement: Allegro affettuoso, double exposition sonata-allegro form, 4/4 meter, A minor

2	EXPOSITION
	0:00 Orchestral introduction: Fast
	Theme 1—lyrical melody, in minor

3   0:00   Orchestral statement (oboe)
    0:00   Solo piano statement

4   Theme 2—derived from first theme, marked Animato (animated)

2:00   Solo piano introduces theme
2:25   Orchestra (clarinet)—in animated statement

       Closing—triumphal orchestral statement

5 DEVELOPMENT

4:20   Marked Andante espressivo. Features dialogue between piano and clarinet. Modulates, returns to A minor for Recapitulation

RECAPITULATION

6 7:17   Theme 1—orchestra (oboe), in A minor; solo piano

7 9:12   Theme 2—solo piano orchestra (clarinet)

8 11:20   CADENZA: Solo piano, unaccompanied, in improvised style

9 13:06   CODA: Marked Allegro molto
            Marchlike melody, based on Theme 1

II. Second movement: Intermezzo (Interlude), Andantino grazioso. Ternary (A-B-A) form, 2/4 meter, in F major

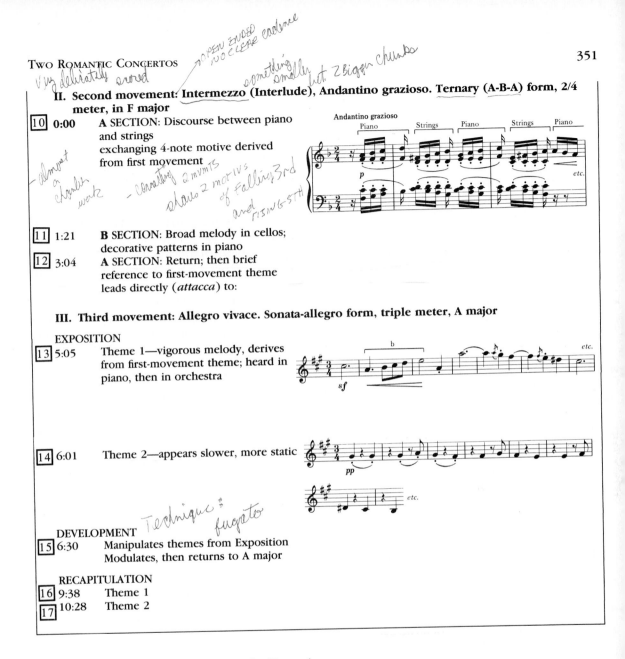

10	0:00	A SECTION: Discourse between piano and strings exchanging 4-note motive derived from first movement

11	1:21	B SECTION: Broad melody in cellos; decorative patterns in piano
12	3:04	A SECTION: Return; then brief reference to first-movement theme leads directly (*attacca*) to:

III. Third movement: Allegro vivace. Sonata-allegro form, triple meter, A major

EXPOSITION

13	5:05	Theme 1—vigorous melody, derives from first-movement theme; heard in piano, then in orchestra

14	6:01	Theme 2—appears slower, more static

DEVELOPMENT

15	6:30	Manipulates themes from Exposition Modulates, then returns to A major

RECAPITULATION

16	9:38	Theme 1
17	10:28	Theme 2

Tchaikovsky: Violin Concerto in D major

Composers of a concerto may write it with a particular artist in mind and may even consult him about the technical peculiarities of the instrument. Such was the case with Tchaikovsky, who wrote his Violin Concerto for the virtuoso Leopold Auer, remembered today as the teacher of Jascha Heifetz, Mischa Elman, and other great violinists. Tchaikovsky intended to dedicate the work to Auer, but when the latter rejected it, on the ground that it was unplayable, he rededicated it to another virtuoso, Adolf Brodsky, who gave the piece its first performance in Vienna in 1881. Tchaikovsky evidently went beyond the accepted notions of what a violin could or should do, for the leading Viennese critic, Eduard Hanslick, reported that in this work "the violin is no longer played, it is yanked about, it is torn asunder, it is beaten black and blue." To Auer's credit, he reconsidered his decision and ended by playing the piece with huge success all over Europe, thereby establishing its reputation as one of the most admired violin concertos of the nineteenth century, alongside those of Beethoven, Mendelssohn, and Brahms.

In the traditional concerto scheme most of the themes were introduced by orchestral tutti. In the first movement of this concerto, Tchaikovsky departs from the accepted pattern by letting the solo instrument introduce and develop the themes. A cadenza-like introduction leads into the memorable main ideas of the first movement. Here Tchaikovsky is the supreme melodist who exploits the violin's capacity for heartfelt song. Notable is the placement of the cadenza, which occurs not toward the end of the movement but slightly past the middle.

Second is the Canzonetta (little song), which the violin plays, a song marked by the gentle melancholy that was dear to Tchaikovsky's heart. This Andante serves as an area of relaxation that prepares the listener for the Finale, which is marked Allegro vivacissimo (fast, extremely lively). The music conjures up figures whirling through the air as they execute a rude peasant dance, arms akimbo and heels flying. Like several other nineteenth-century nationalists, Tchaikovsky only rarely used existing folksongs and dances. He was so identified with the soul of his people that what he created in the style of folksong and dance sounded utterly authentic. This brilliant Allegro invariably "brings down the house."

S3B/3

S3/22

UNIT XX

■

Choral and Dramatic Music in the Nineteenth Century

59

The Nature of Romantic Choral Music

"In a sense no one is ignorant of the material from which choral music springs. For this material is, in large measure, the epitomized thought, feeling, aspiration of a community rather than an individual."—PERCY M. YOUNG: THE CHORAL TRADITION

Amateur choral groups

The nineteenth century, we found, witnessed a broadening of the democratic ideal and an enormous expansion of the musical public. This climate was uniquely favorable to choral music, which flowered as an enjoyable group activity involving increasing numbers of music lovers. As a result, choral music came to play an important part in the musical life of the Romantic era.

Singing in a chorus required less skill than playing in an orchestra. It attracted many music lovers who had never learned to play an instrument, or who could not afford to buy one. With a modest amount of rehearsal (and a modest amount of voice), they could learn to take part in the performance of great choral works. The music they sang, being allied to words, was somewhat easier to understand than absolute music, both for the performers and the listeners. The members of the chorus not only enjoyed a pleasant social evening once or twice a week but also, if their group was good enough, became a source of pride to their community.

Choral music offered the masses an ideal outlet for their artistic energies. It served to alleviate the drabness of life in the English factory towns of the early Victorian period. And it had the solid support of the authorities, who felt that an interest in music would protect the lower orders from dangerous

In the nineteenth century, enormous choral and orchestral forces were the order of the day. A contemporary engraving depicting the opening concert at St. Martin's Hall, London, 1850.

new ideas that were floating around. This aspect of the situation is amusingly illustrated in the constitution of the Huddersfield Choral Society (1836), which stipulated that "No person shall be a member of this Society who frequents the 'Hall of Science' or any of the 'Socialist Meetings,' nor shall the Librarian be allowed to lend any copies of music (knowingly) belonging to this society to any Socialist, upon pain of expulsion." England was approaching the ferment of the Chartist uprisings over social and political reforms, and one had to be careful.

The repertory centered about the great choral heritage of the past. Nevertheless, if choral music was to remain a vital force, its literature had to be enriched by new works that would reflect the spirit of the time. The list of composers active in this area includes some of the most important names of the nineteenth century: Schubert, Berlioz, Mendelssohn, Schumann, Liszt, Verdi, Franck, Brahms, Dvořák. Out of their efforts came a body of choral music that forms a delightful enclave in the output of the Romantic period.

Choral forms

Among the main forms of choral music in the nineteenth century were the Mass, Requiem, and oratorio. We have seen that all three forms were originally intended to be performed in church, but by the nineteenth century they had found a wider audience in the concert hall. In addition, a vast literature sprang up of secular choral pieces. These were settings for chorus of lyric poems in a variety of moods and styles. They were known, we saw,

Partsongs

as *partsongs*—that is, songs in three or four voice parts. Most of them were short melodious works, not too difficult for amateurs. They gave pleasure both to the singers and their listeners, and played an important role in developing the new mass audience of the nineteenth century.

It is important to remember that in choral music the text is related to the music in a different way than in solo song. The words are not as easy to grasp when a multitude of voices project them. In addition, the four groups in the chorus may be singing different words at the same time. Most important of all, music needs more time to establish a mood than words do. For these reasons the practice arose of repeating a line, a phrase, or an individual word over and over again instead of introducing new words all the time. This principle is well illustrated by both choral works discussed in the next chapter.

Choral texts

60

Two Romantic Choral Works

Brahms: A German Requiem

"I had all humanity in mind."

A German Requiem was rooted in the Protestant tradition into which Brahms was born. Its aim was to console the living and lead them to a serene acceptance of death as an inevitable part of life. Hence its gentle lyricism. Brahms chose his text from the Old as well as New Testament, from the Psalms, Proverbs, Isaiah, and Ecclesiastes as well as from Paul, Matthew, Peter, John, and Revelation. He was not a religious man in the conventional sense, nor was he affiliated with any particular church; significantly, Christ's name is never mentioned. He was impelled to compose his requiem by the death, first of his benefactor and friend Robert Schumann, then of his mother, whom he idolized; but the piece transcends the personal and endures as a song of mourning for all mankind.

Written for soloists, four-part chorus, and orchestra, *A German Requiem* is in seven movements arranged in a formation resembling an arch. There are connections between the first and last movements, between the second and sixth, and between the third and fifth; this leaves the fourth movement, the widely sung chorus *How Lovely Is Thy Dwelling Place*, as the centerpiece of the arch.

The opening movement is marked *Ziemlich langsam und mit Ausdruk* (fairly slow and with expression). It is an **A-B-A** form that moves from despair to acceptance, from darkness to light. "Blessed are they that mourn, for they shall be comforted. They that sow in tears shall reap in joy."

First movement

Second movement

The second movement, marked *Langsam, marschmässig* (slow, in the manner of a march), in 3/4 time, begins in a special pianissimo, with the violins and violas muted. "Behold, all flesh is as the grass, and all the goodliness of man is as the flower of grass. For lo, the grass withers and the flower thereof decays." Here too, the movement moves from darkness to light, culminating in a mood of affirmation: "The redeemed of the Lord shall return, and come to Zion with shouts of joy." This is worked into a fortissimo climax with much repetition of the key words *Freude* (joy). But in the final passage Brahms allows this burst of energy to simmer down and brings the movement to a quiet ending.

Third movement

Third is an Andante moderato (the German marking is *Mässig bewegt*) for baritone solo. "Lord, teach me that my life has to end and I must leave it." Once again the music surges forward from doubt and entreaty to an affirmation of faith on the thought, "The souls of the righteous are in the hand of God, no pain nor grief shall touch them."

Fugue

These words introduce a *fugue*, a type of complex polyphonic texture. We saw earlier that the term suggests the flight of a basic theme from one voice to another in a polyphonic texture. In effect, the various voice parts take turns in presenting the basic idea or *subject* of the fugue. The subject of this particular fugue is presented by the tenors, while the orchestra presents a fugue of its own, so that we really hear a double fugue. Building to a triumphal close, this section represents a unique amalgam of technique and imagination. (For a detailed analysis see Listening Guide 37.)

Fourth movement

The fourth movement is the centerpiece of the Brahms Requiem. The verse is from Psalm 84: "How lovely is Thy dwelling place, O Lord of Hosts!" The first two lines of the Psalm are heard three times, separated by the two contrasting sections that present the other lines. The form, therefore, is **A-B-A-C-A**. The first two sections for the most part move in quarter notes, but the third section (**C**) moves more quickly in a vigorous rhythm, as befits the line "that praise Thee evermore," with much expansion on "evermore." With the final reappearance of the **A** section the quarter notes return. Marked piano and dolce (soft, sweet), this passage serves as a coda that brings the piece to its gentle close.

Fifth movement

The soprano's promise of solace in the fifth movement answers the baritone's outpouring of grief in the third. Added by the composer after his mother's death, this part contains a setting of the poignant line from Isaiah: "I will comfort you as one whom his mother comforts." The sixth movement

Sixth movement

sings the final victory over death. From its uncertain beginning the music advances inexorably to the promise that when the last trumpet sounds the dead will arise. "O death, where is your sting?" the chorus exults. "O grave, where is your victory?"

Seventh movement

The opening line of the seventh movement—"Blessed are the dead which die in the Lord henceforth"—is akin in mood to the opening line of the work. The music accordingly recaptures the gentle flow and serenity of the first movement. But the relationship of last to first goes deeper. In the final measures of *A German Requiem* Brahms returns to the passage that ended the first movement. Therewith the circle is closed, and the listener is left with a wonderful sense of completion.

Listening Guide 37

7A/2   II/3/9

BRAHMS: *A German Requiem*   *started on 1857*

Date: 1868

Genre: Requiem, for Protestant church

Medium: 4-part chorus, soloists, and orchestra

Movements: 7

Language: German

A/A

9 **Third movement:** baritone solo, followed by double fugue with chorus/orchestra

Text	*Translation*
Ich hoffe auf dich	My hope is in thee
Der Gerechten Seelen sind in Gottes Hand, und keine Qual rühret sie an.	But the righteous souls are in the hand of God, nor pain nor grief shall touch them.

o

Fugue subject (in tenors):

Der Ge-rech-ten See-len sind in Got-tes Hand, und kei-ne Qual rüh - ret sie an,

Opening order of fugal entries of subject: Tenors
Altos
Sopranos
Basses

4 voice
4 orch

Fugue subject (orchestral), based on vocal
subject (x's mark notes taken from vocal fugue subject):

x x   x x x x x x x   x x x   x x x

10 **Fourth movement: Mässig bewegt** — *BEGINS AS WALTZ.*

Text: Psalm 84

Form: Rondo **(A-B-A-C-A)**

Character: Lilting triple meter, marked Dolce (sweetly)

Opening melody: clarinets and flutes
begin in inversion of beginning phrase in
chorus:

Homophonic major key

Mässig bewegt
Cl.   Sop.
p dolce   p Wie lieb - lich sind dei - ne Woh - nun - gen,

melodic inversion

keine qual - feeling no pain
word painting - mel...

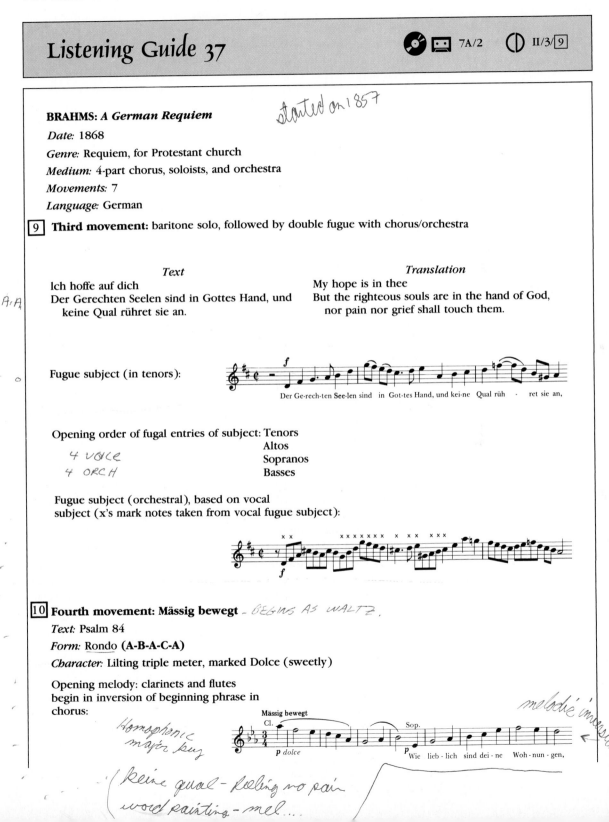

Form	Text	Translation	Description
A	Wie lieblich sind deine Wohnungen Herr Zebaoth!	How lovely is Thy dwelling place, O Lord of hosts!	flowing arch-shaped melody; sopranos begin; homophonic texture
B	Meine Seele verlanget und sehnet sich nach den Vorhöfen des Herrn: sein Lieb und Seele freuen sich in dem lebendigen Gott.	My soul longs and even faints for the courts of the Lord; my flesh and soul rejoice in the living God.	builds up through word repetition to "sehnet"; climax on "lebendigen"
A	Wie lieblich . . .	How lovely . . .	
C	Wohl denen, die in deinem Hause wohnen, die loben dich immerdar!	Blessed are they that live in Thy house, that praise Thee evermore!	martial quality; faster note movement in strings; more vitality
A	Wie lieblich . . .	How lovely . . .	coda-like; soft, gentle closing

TIME FOR MINOR & WORD PAINTING (handwritten annotation)

Berlioz: L'enfance du Christ

S3A/1

S3/[1]

Berlioz, we saw, was fond of huge forces and gigantic effects. This, however, represented only one side of his genius. The other side—a capacity for gentle lyricism of the most intimate kind—is well represented by his oratorio *L'enfance du Christ* (The Childhood of Christ, 1854), a splendid example of French choral music of the nineteenth century.

Written for soloists, chorus, and orchestra, the oratorio consists of three parts—Herod's Dream, The Flight into Egypt, and The Arrival at Saïs. In the first part Herod, terror-stricken by his recurrent dream of a child destined to end his power, consults with the soothsayers and decides upon the slaughter of the innocents. The second part opens with an Overture, a mood piece that creates an atmosphere of quiet devotion. This is followed by the shepherds' farewell to the Holy Family. In the third part Joseph and Mary, having arrived at the end of their journey, seek shelter for the Child.

The Farewell of the Shepherds, from Part II, is a chorus for sopranos, altos, tenors, and basses accompanied by orchestra. A pastoral mood is established by clarinets and oboes; the music unfolds in a lilting triple meter and in three symmetrical stanzas in strophic form. These are set off from one another by an interlude that repeats the four-measure introduction of the woodwinds. The Parisian audience that heard the first performance of *L'enfance du Christ* was enchanted by this work. For the better part of a century and a half, subsequent listeners have responded in the same way.

61

Romantic Op

"It is better to invent reality than to copy

For well over three hundred years the opera
alluring forms of musical entertainment. A sp
everything connected with it—its arias, singer
its opening nights.

At first glance opera would seem to make
credulity of the spectator. It presents us with
dramatic situations, who sing to each other in
sonable question is (and it was asked most poin
of opera by literary men): how can an art for
procedure be convincing? The question ignor
the fundamental aspiration of art: not to copy
awareness of it.

True enough, people in real life do not sin
they converse in blank verse, as Shakespeare'
rooms of which one wall is conveniently missi
look in. All the arts employ conventions that are
and the audience. The conventions of opera are
of poetry, painting, drama, or film, but they are
we have accepted the fact that the carpet car
that it can also carry the prince's luggage.

onizetti's Don Pasquale,

6), Gaetano Donizetti (1797– *Donizetti*
uding *Lucia di Lammermoor*
ose *Norma* (1831) is in the *Bellini*
s were all written in the *bel* *Bel canto style*
terized by florid melodic lines,
rity of tone. The consummate
erdi, who sought to develop

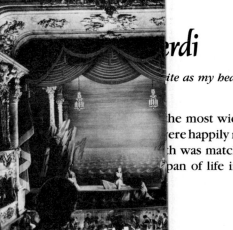

erdi

ite as my heart dictates!"

he most widely loved of op-
ere happily met. He inherited
h was matched by masterful
pan of life in which his gifts

ather kept a little inn, Verdi,
illage life. His talent attracted

Giuseppe Verdi

the attention of a prosperous merchant in the neighboring town of Busseto, a music lover who made it possible for the youth to pursue his studies. After two years in Milan he returned to Busseto to fill a post as organist. When he fell in love with his benefactor's daughter, the merchant in wholly untraditional fashion accepted the penniless young musician as his son-in-law. Verdi was twenty-three, Margherita sixteen.

Three years later he returned to the conquest of Milan with the manuscript of an opera. *Oberto, Count of San Bonifacio* was produced at La Scala in 1839 with fair success. The work brought him a commission to write three others. Shortly after, Verdi faced the first crisis of his career. He had lost his first child, a daughter, before coming to Milan. The second, a baby boy, was carried off by fever, a catastrophe followed several weeks later by the death of his young wife. "My family had been destroyed, and in the midst of these trials I had to fulfill my engagement and write a comic opera!" *Un giorno di regno* (King for a Day) failed miserably. "In a sudden moment of despondency I despaired of finding any comfort in my art and resolved to give up composing."

The months passed; the distraught young composer adhered to his decision. One night he happened to meet the impresario of La Scala, who forced him to take home the libretto of *Nabucco* (Nebuchadnezzar, King of Babylon). "I came into my room and, throwing the manuscript angrily on the writing table, I stood for a moment motionless before it. The book opened as I threw it down. My eyes fell on the page and I read the line *Va pensiero sull' ali dorate* (Go, my thought, on golden wings—first line of the chorus of captive Jews who by the waters of Babylon mourn their ravished land). Resolved as I was never to write again, I stifled my emotion, shut the book, went to bed, and put out the candle. I tried to sleep, but *Nabucco* was running a mad course through my brain." In this fashion the musician was restored to his art. *Nabucco*, presented at La Scala in 1842, was a triumph for the twenty-nine-year-old composer and launched him on a spectacular career.

Verdi the nationalist   Italy at this time was in the process of birth as a nation. The patriotic party aimed at liberation from the Hapsburg yoke and the establishment of a united kingdom under the House of Savoy. Verdi from the beginning identified himself with the national cause. "I am first of all an Italian!" In this charged atmosphere his works took on special meaning for his countrymen. No matter in what time or place the opera was laid, they interpreted it as an allegory of their plight. The chorus of exiled Jews from *Nabucco* became a patriotic song. As the revolutionary year 1848 approached, Verdi's works—despite the precautions of the Austrian censor—continued to nourish the zeal of the nationalists. In *Attila* the line of the Roman envoy to the leader of the Huns, "Take thou the universe—but leave me Italy!" provoked frenzied demonstrations. When, in *The Battle of Legnano*, a chorus of medieval Italian knights vowed to drive the German invaders beyond the Alps, audiences were aroused to indescribable enthusiasm.

But the impact of Verdi's operas went deeper than the implications of the plot. The music itself had a dynamic force, a virility that was new in the

Verdi visiting baritone Victor Maurel, who created the role of Iago in Otello, *backstage at the Paris Opéra, 1894.*

Italian theater. This was truly, as one writer called it, "agitator's music." It happened too that the letters of Verdi's name coincided with the initials of the nationalist slogan—*Vittorio Emanuele, Re d'Italia* (Victor Emmanuel, King of Italy). The cries of *Viva Verdi* that rang through Italian theaters not only hailed the composer but voiced the national dream. Rarely has a musician more ideally filled the role of a people's artist.

Although he was now a world-renowned figure, Verdi retained the simplicity that was at the core both of the artist and man. He returned to his roots, acquiring an estate at Busseto where he settled with his second wife, the singer Giuseppina Strepponi. She was a sensitive and intelligent woman who had created the leading roles in his early operas and who was his devoted companion for half a century. After Italy had won independence, he was urged to stand for election to the first parliament because of the prestige his name would bring the new state. The task conformed neither to his talents nor inclinations, but he accepted and sat in the chamber of deputies for some years.

The outer activities of this upright man framed an inner life of extraordinary richness. It was this that enabled him to move with unflagging creativity from one masterpiece to the next. He was fifty-seven when he wrote *Aïda*. At seventy-three he completed *Otello*, his greatest lyric tragedy. In 1893, on the threshold of eighty, he astonished the world with *Falstaff*. Such sustained productivity invites comparison with the old masters, with a Monteverdi, Michelangelo, or Titian.

His death at eighty-seven was mourned throughout the world. He bequeathed the bulk of his fortune to a home for aged musicians founded by him in Milan. Italy accorded him the rites reserved for a national hero. From the thousands who followed his funeral bier there sprang up a melody—"Va pensiero sull' ali dorate." It was the chorus from *Nabucco* that he had given his countrymen as a song of solace sixty years before.

His Music

Verdi's music struck his contemporaries as the epitome of dramatic energy and passion. Endowed with an imagination that saw all emotion in terms of action and conflict, he was able to imbue a dramatic situation with shattering expressiveness. True Italian that he was, he based his art on melody, which to him was the most immediate expression of human feeling. "Art without spontaneity, naturalness, and simplicity," he maintained, "is no art."

Early years

Of his first fifteen operas the most important is *Macbeth*, in which for the first time he derived his story material from Shakespeare. There followed in close succession *Rigoletto*, based on Victor Hugo's drama *Le Roi s'amuse* (The King Is Amused); *Il trovatore*, derived from a fanciful Spanish play; and *La traviata*, which we will discuss. In these works of sustained pathos the musical dramatist stands before us all in full stature.

Middle period

The operas of the middle period are on a more ambitious scale, showing Verdi's attempt to assimilate elements of the French grand opera. The three most important are *Un ballo in maschera*, *La forza del destino*, and *Don Carlos*. "After *La traviata*," he declared, "I could have taken things easy and written an opera every year on the tried and true model. But I had other artistic aims."

Final period

These aims came to fruition in *Aïda*, the work that ushers in his final period (1870–93). *Aïda* was commissioned in 1870 by the Khedive of Egypt to mark the opening of the Suez Canal. Delayed by the outbreak of the Franco-Prussian War, the production was mounted with great splendor in Cairo the following year. In 1874 came the Requiem, in memory of Alessandro Manzoni, the novelist and patriot whom Verdi revered as a national artist.

Verdi and Boito

Verdi found his ideal librettist in Arrigo Boito (1842–1918). For their first collaboration they turned to Shakespeare's *Otello*, the apex of three hundred years of Italian lyric tragedy. After its opening night the seventy-four-year-old composer declared, "I feel as if I had fired my last cartridge.

Principal Works

28 operas, including *Macbeth* (1847), *Rigoletto* (1851), *Il trovatore* (The Troubadour, 1853), *La traviata* (The Lost One, 1853), *Un ballo in maschera* (A Masked Ball, 1859), *La forza del destino* (The Force of Destiny, 1862), *Don Carlos* (1867), *Aïda* (1871), *Otello* (1887), *Falstaff* (1893)

Vocal music, including a Requiem Mass (1874)

Chamber music, including 1 string quartet and piano works

Music needs youthfulness of the senses, impetuous blood, fullness of life." He disproved his words when six years later, again with Boito, he completed *Falstaff* in 1893. Fitting crown to the labors of a lifetime, this luminous comic opera ranks with Mozart's *Figaro*, Rossini's *Barber of Seville*, and Wagner's *Meistersinger*.

Verdi: La traviata

La dame aux camélias—The Lady of the Camellias, known on the English stage simply as *Camille*—by the younger Alexandre Dumas, was a revolutionary play in its time, for it contrasted the noble character of a courtesan—a so-called fallen woman—with the rigidly bourgeois code of morals that ends by destroying her. With a libretto by Francesco Piave based on Dumas's play, the opera—under the title *La traviata* (The Lost One)—quickly won a worldwide audience. It is a work suffused with intimate lyricism and emotion.

The heroine is Violetta Valéry, one of the reigning beauties of Paris, who already is suffering from the first ravages of consumption when the drama begins. She lives for the pleasure of the moment until Alfredo Germont, a young man of good Provençal family, falls in love with her and offers to take her away from the fast life that is killing her. They go off to a country villa; but their idyllic existence is interrupted by Alfredo's father, a dignified gentleman who appeals to Violetta not to lead his son to ruin and disgrace the family name. She reveals to him that, far from taking money from Alfredo, she has been supporting them herself. The elder Germont is amazed, as the interview progresses, by the dignity of her bearing. All the same, her past is against her, and he points out to her the futility of a liaison that can never win the approval of God or society. Violetta makes the agonizing decision to leave Alfredo and returns to Baron Douphol, whose mistress she has been.

Unaware of his father's intervention, Alfredo breaks into a festive party at the home of Violetta's friend Flora. Mad with jealousy and rage, he accuses Violetta of having betrayed him, insults her in the presence of her friends, and is challenged to a duel by the Baron. The last act takes place in Violetta's bedroom. Her doctor friend comes to cheer her up but confides to her maid Annina that she is dying. Left alone, Violetta reads a letter from the elder Germont informing her that the duel has taken place. He has told his son of her great sacrifice; both are coming to ask for her forgiveness. Alfredo arrives. He is followed by his father who realizes how blind he has been and, filled with admiration for Violetta, welcomes her as his daughter. It is too late. Violetta dies in Alfredo's arms.

We hear the finale of the second act, at Flora's party. Alfredo, at the gambling table, has played for huge stakes against the Baron and won a great deal of money. When the guests go to the next room for supper, Violetta remains behind to wait for him. Their scene unfolds against a tense, repetitive rhythm in the orchestra that betrays their agitation. She begs him to leave the party at once; she is terrified of the Baron and fears that Alfredo will come to harm. Their dialogue exemplifies Verdi's uncanny ability to find

Act II, Scene 2 in the Opera Theatre of Saint Louis production of La traviata *with Sheri Greenawald as Violetta and Jon Frederic West as Alfredo.* (Photo by Ken Howard)

the right music for a suspenseful dramatic situation. Unable to reveal to Alfredo that she left him at his father's bidding, Violetta lets him believe that she threw him over because she loved the Baron. (See Listening Guide 38 for the Italian-English text.)

At this point Alfredo, beside himself, throws open the door and summons the guests into the room. Violetta, he tells them, squandered all she possessed upon him and he was deluded enough to allow her to do so because he thought she loved him. Now he wants to repay her. With the utmost contempt he hurls at her feet the purse containing his winnings. Violetta faints in Flora's arms, and the guests react with horror at Alfredo's behavior. Germont arrives in time to witness his son's outburst and is thoroughly ashamed of him.

We hear the great ensemble that crowns the act, with the voices of the principal characters intermingling as each expresses his feelings. Alfredo is overwhelmed with remorse, Germont is horrified, the Baron decides that only a duel can wipe out the insult. Flora and her guests (the chorus) sympathize with Violetta, whose voice soars above them in a beautiful passage. Some day, she hopes, Alfredo will learn the truth and understand.

Such an ensemble depends upon an outstanding melody that will guide the ear through the intricate maze of vocal lines. Verdi's great theme soars in a broad curve that imprints itself indelibly upon the mind and—more important—the heart.

Listening Guide 38

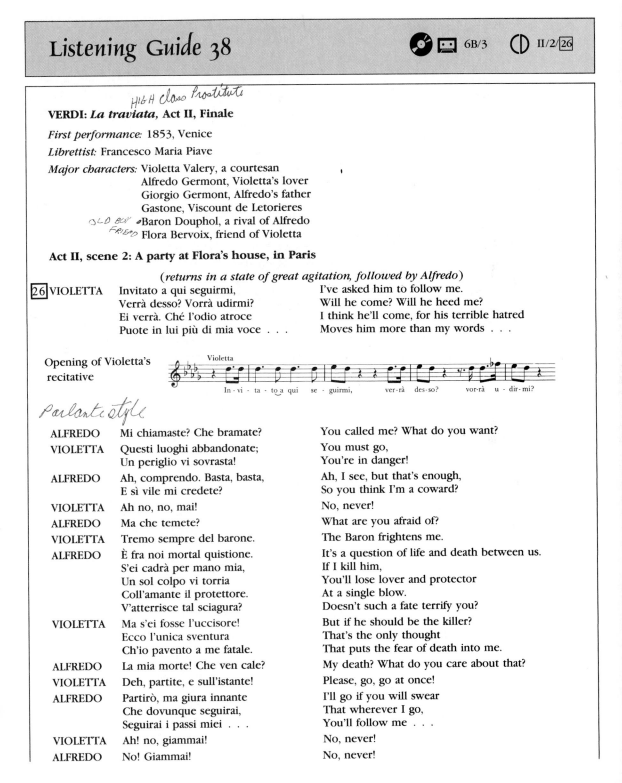

6B/3   II/2/26

HIGH Class Prostitute

VERDI: *La traviata,* **Act II, Finale**

First performance: 1853, Venice

Librettist: Francesco Maria Piave

Major characters: Violetta Valery, a courtesan
Alfredo Germont, Violetta's lover
Giorgio Germont, Alfredo's father
Gastone, Viscount de Letorieres
OLD BOY Baron Douphol, a rival of Alfredo
FRIEND Flora Bervoix, friend of Violetta

Act II, scene 2: A party at Flora's house, in Paris

(returns in a state of great agitation, followed by Alfredo)

26 VIOLETTA	Invitato a qui seguirmi,	I've asked him to follow me.
	Verrà desso? Vorrà udirmi?	Will he come? Will he heed me?
	Ei verrà. Ché l'odio atroce	I think he'll come, for his terrible hatred
	Puote in lui più di mia voce . . .	Moves him more than my words . . .

Opening of Violetta's recitative

In-vi-ta-to a qui se-guirmi, ver-rà des-so? vor-rà u-dir-mi?

Parlanti style

ALFREDO	Mi chiamaste? Che bramate?	You called me? What do you want?
VIOLETTA	Questi luoghi abbandonate;	You must go,
	Un periglio vi sovrasta!	You're in danger!
ALFREDO	Ah, comprendo. Basta, basta,	Ah, I see, but that's enough,
	E sì vile mi credete?	So you think I'm a coward?
VIOLETTA	Ah no, no, mai!	No, never!
ALFREDO	Ma che temete?	What are you afraid of?
VIOLETTA	Tremo sempre del barone.	The Baron frightens me.
ALFREDO	È fra noi mortal quistione.	It's a question of life and death between us.
	S'ei cadrà per mano mia,	If I kill him,
	Un sol colpo vi torria	You'll lose lover and protector
	Coll'amante il protettore.	At a single blow.
	V'atterrisce tal sciagura?	Doesn't such a fate terrify you?
VIOLETTA	Ma s'ei fosse l'uccisore!	But if he should be the killer?
	Ecco l'unica sventura	That's the only thought
	Ch'io pavento a me fatale.	That puts the fear of death into me.
ALFREDO	La mia morte! Che ven cale?	My death? What do you care about that?
VIOLETTA	Deh, partite, e sull'istante!	Please, go, go at once!
ALFREDO	Partirò, ma giura innante	I'll go if you will swear
	Che dovunque seguirai,	That wherever I go,
	Seguirai i passi miei . . .	You'll follow me . . .
VIOLETTA	Ah! no, giammai!	No, never!
ALFREDO	No! Giammai!	No, never!

VIOLETTA	Va, sciagurato!	Go, you are wicked!
	Scorda un nome ch'è infamato!	Forget a name that's without honour!
	Va, mi lascia sul momento	Go, leave me this minute.
	Di fuggirti un giuramento	I've made a solemn vow
	Sacro io feci.	To fly from you.
ALFREDO	A chi? Dillo, chi potea?	Who to? Tell me, who could make you?
VIOLETTA	A chi dritto pien n'avea.	One who had every right.
ALFREDO	Fua Douphol?	Was it Douphol?

(with great force)

VIOLETTA	Si.	Yes.
ALFREDO	Dunque l'ami?	Then you love him?
VIOLETTA	Ebben . . . l'amo . . .	Yes . . . I love him . . .

(running to the door and shouting)

| ALFREDO | Or tutti a me. | Come here, all of you! |

(The rest of the company rush in.)

| ALL | Ne appellaste? Che volete? | You called us? What do you want? |

(pointing to Violetta, who leans feebly against a table)

ALFREDO	Questa donna conoscete?	You know this lady?
ALL	Chi? Violetta?	You mean Violetta?
ALFREDO	Che facesse non sapete?	But you don't know what she's done.
VIOLETTA	Ah! taci!	Oh, don't!
ALL	No.	No.

[27] ALFREDO — *dominant 7 chord of E maj tonic*

	Ogni suo aver tal femmina	For me this woman lost all she possessed. *lut, C major*
	Per amor mio sperdea.	I was blind.
	Io cieco, vile, misero,	A wretched coward,
	Tutto accettar potea.	I accepted it all.
	Ma è tempo ancora!	But it's time now for me
	Tergermi da tanta macchia bramo.	To clear myself from debt.
	Qui testimon vi chiamo,	I call you all to witness here
	Che qui pagata io l'ho.	That I've paid her back!

Opening of Alfredo's solo,
expressing anger and
bitterness

(Contemptuously, he throws his winnings at Violetta's feet. She swoons in Flora's arms. Alfredo's father arrives suddenly.)

ALL	Oh, infamia orribile	What you have done is shameful!
	Tu commettesti!	So to strike down a tender heart!
	Un cor sensibile	You have insulted a woman!
	Così uccidesti!	Get out of here!
	Di donne ignobile insultatore,	We've no use for you!
	Di qua allontanati,	We've no use for such as you!
	Ne desti orror! Va!	Go!

Choral response to
Alfredo's charges against
Violetta, sung in unison,
delivered forcefully

28 GERMONT *(dignified in his anger)*

Di sprezzo degno sé stesso rende	A man who offends a woman, even in anger,
Chi pur nell'ira la donna offende.	Merits nothing but scorn.
Dov'è mio figlio?	Where is my son?
Pitù non io vedo;	I see him no more
In te più Alfredo	In you, Afredo,
Trovar non so.	No more in you.

(to himself)

ALFREDO

Ah sì! Chi feci! Ne sento orrore!	What have I done? Yes, I despise myself!
Gelosa smania, deluso amore	Jealous madness, love deceived,
Mi strazian l'alma, più non ragiono . . .	Ravaged my soul, destroyed my reason.
Da lei perdono più non avrò.	How can I ever gain her pardon?
Volea fuggirla, non ho potuto.	I would have left her, but I couldn't;
Dall'ira spinto son qui venuto!	I came here to vent my anger,
Or che Io sdegno ho disfogato,	But now I've done so, wretch that I am,
Me sciagurato, rimorso n'ho!	I feel nothing but a deep remorse!

Opening of Alfredo's remorseful solo, in response to his father (Germont) and the crowd

(to Violetta)

FLORA, GASTON, THE DOCTOR, THE MARQUIS, THE CHORUS

O, quanto peni!	Yes, you have suffered,
Ma pur fa cor!	But take heart!
Qui soffre ognuno del tuo dolor;	Each one of us has shared your pain;
Fra cari amici qui sei soltanto	Friends are about you to dry the tears
Rasciuga il pianto che t'inondò.	You have shed.

(to himself)

GERMONT

Io sol fra tanti so qual virtude	Alone I known the true devotion
Di quella misera il sen racchiude	This poor girl hides within her breast;
Io so che l'ama, che gli è fedele;	I know her faithful heart
Eppur crudele tacer dovrò!	That's vowed so cruelly to silence.

	(softly to Alfredo)	
BARON	A questa donna l'atroce insulto	Your deadly insult to this lady
	Qui tutti offese, ma non inulto	Offends us all, but such an outrage
	Fia tanto oltraggio, provar vi voglio	Shall not go unavenged!
	Che il vostro orgoglio fiaccar saprò!	I shall find a way to humble your pride!
ALFREDO	Che feci! Ohimè!	Alas, what have I done?
	Ohimè, che feci!	What have I done?
	Ne sento orrore!	How can I ever
	Da lei perdono più non avrò.	Gain her pardon?

	(coming to herself)	
29 VIOLETTA	Alfredo, Alfredo, di questo core	Alfredo, how should you understand
	Non puoi comprendere tutto l'amore,	All the love that's in my heart?
	Tu non conosci che fino a prezzo	How should you known that I have proved it,
	Del tuo disprezzo provato io l'ho.	Even at the price of your contempt?
	Ma verrà tempo, in che il saprai	But the time will come when you will know,
	Come t'amassi, confesserai . . .	When you'll admit how much I loved you.
	Dio dai rimorsi ti salvi allora!	God save you then from all remorse!
	Ah! Io spenta ancora t'amerò.	Even after death I shall still love you.

(Germont leads his son away with him; the Baron follows. Flora and the Doctor take Violetta into the other room as the rest of the company disperses.)

Violetta's melody, vowing
her love to Alfredo

Al-fre-do, Al-fre - do, di que-sto co - re non puoi com-pren-de-re tut-to l'a - mo - re,

---

63

Richard Wagner

"The error in the art genre of opera consists in the fact that a means of expression—music—has been made the object, while the object of expression—the drama—has been made the means."

Richard Wagner

Richard Wagner (1813–83) looms as probably the single most important phenomenon in the artistic life of the latter half of the nineteenth century. Historians, not without justice, divide the period into "Before" and "After" Wagner. The course of post-Romantic music is unthinkable without the impact of this complex and fascinating figure.

His Life

Wagner was born in Leipzig, son of a minor police official who died when Richard was still an infant. A year later the widow married Ludwig Geyer, a talented actor, playwright, and painter, who encouraged the artistic inclinations of his little stepson. The future composer was almost entirely self-taught; he had in all about six months of instruction in music theory. At twenty he abandoned his academic studies at the University of Leipzig and obtained a post as chorus master in a small opera house. In the next six years he gained practical experience conducting in provincial theaters. He married the actress Minna Planer when he was twenty-three, and produced his first operas. As with all his later works, he wrote the librettos himself. He was in this way able to achieve unity of the musical-dramatic conception beyond anything that had been known before.

Early years

While conducting at the theater in Riga he began a grand opera based on Bulwer-Lytton's historical novel *Rienzi, Last of the Tribunes*. This dealt with the heroic figure who in the fourteenth century led the Roman populace against the tyrannical nobles and perished in the struggle. With the first two acts of *Rienzi* under his arm he set out with Minna to conquer the world. His destination was Paris. But the world, then as now, was not easily conquered; Wagner failed to gain a foothold at the Paris Opéra.

The two and a half years spent in Paris (1839–42) were fruitful nevertheless. He completed *Rienzi* and produced *A Faust Overture*, the first works that bear the imprint of his genius. To keep alive he did hack work such as arranging popular arias for the cornet, and turned out a number of articles, essays, and semifictional sketches. He also wrote the poem and music of *The Flying Dutchman*. All this despite poverty and daily discouragement.

Just as the harassed young musician was beginning to lose heart, a lucky turn rescued him from his plight: *Rienzi* was accepted by the Dresden Opera. Suddenly his native land was wreathed in the same rosy mist as had formerly enveloped Paris. He started for Dresden, gazed on the Rhine for the first time, and "with great tears in his eyes swore eternal fidelity to the German fatherland." *Rienzi*, which satisfied the taste of the public for historical grand opera, was extremely successful. As a result, its composer in his thirtieth year found himself appointed conductor to the King of Saxony.

With *The Flying Dutchman* Wagner had taken an important step from the drama of historical intrigue to the idealized folk legend. He continued on this path with the two dramas of the Dresden period—*Tannhäuser* and *Lohengrin*—which bring to its peak the German Romantic opera as established by his revered model, Carl Maria von Weber (1786–1826). The operas use subjects derived from medieval German epics, display a profound feeling for nature, employ the supernatural as an element of the drama, and glorify the German land and people. But the Dresden public was not prepared for *Tannhäuser*. They had come to see another *Rienzi* and were disappointed.

A dedicated artist who made no concessions to popular taste, Wagner dreamed of achieving for opera something of the grandeur that had characterized ancient Greek tragedy. To this task he addressed himself with the fanaticism of the born reformer. He was increasingly alienated from a frivolous court that regarded opera as an amusement; from the bureaucrats in control of the royal theaters, who thwarted his plans; and from Minna, his wife, who was delighted with their social position in Dresden and had no patience with what she considered his utopian schemes. He was persuaded that the theater was corrupt because the society around it was corrupt. His beliefs as an artist led him into the camp of those who, as the fateful year 1848 approached, dreamed of a revolution in Europe that would end the power of the reactionary rulers. With reckless disregard of the consequences, Wagner appeared as speaker at a club of radical workingmen, and published two articles in an anarchist journal: "Man and Existing Society" and "The Revolution." "The present old world is crumbling to ruin. A new world will be born from it!"

Wagner the revolutionary

The revolution broke out in Dresden in 1849. King and court fled. Troops dispatched by the King of Prussia crushed the insurrection. Wagner escaped to his friend Liszt at Weimar, where he learned that a warrant had been issued for his arrest. With the aid of Liszt he was spirited across the border and found refuge in Switzerland.

In the eyes of the world—and of Minna—he was a ruined man; but Wagner did not in the least share this opinion. "It is impossible to describe my delight when I felt free at last—free from the world of torturing and ever unsatisfied desires, free from the distressing surroundings that had called forth such desires." He settled in Zurich and entered on the most productive period of his career. He had first to clarify his ideas to himself, and to prepare the public for the novel conceptions toward which he was finding his way. For four years he wrote no music, producing instead his most important literary works, *Art and Revolution, The Art Work of the Future*, and the two-volume *Opera and Drama*, which sets forth his theories of the *music drama*, as he named his type of opera. He next proceeded to put theory into practice in the cycle of four music dramas called *The Ring of the Nibelung*. When he reached the second act of *Siegfried* (the third opera in the cycle), he grew tired, "of heaping one silent score upon the other," and laid aside the gigantic task. There followed two of his finest works—*Tristan und Isolde* and *Die Meistersinger von Nürnberg*.

The Zurich years

The Ring

The years following the completion of *Tristan* were the darkest of his life. The mighty scores accumulated in his drawer without hope of performance: Europe contained neither theater nor singers capable of presenting them. Wagner succumbed to Schopenhauer's philosophy of pessimism and renunciation—he who could never renounce anything. He was estranged from Minna, who failed utterly to understand his artistic aims. His involvement with a series of women who did understand him—but whose husbands objected—obtruded the *Tristan* situation into his own life and catapulted him into lonely despair. As he passed his fiftieth year, his indomitable will was broken at last. He contemplated in turn suicide, emigration to America, escape to the East.

At this juncture intervened a miraculous turn of events. An eighteen-year-old boy who was a passionate admirer of his music ascended the throne of Bavaria as Ludwig II. One of the young monarch's first acts was to summon the composer to Munich, where *Tristan* and *Meistersinger* were performed at last. The King commissioned him to complete the *Ring*, and Wagner took up the second act of *Siegfried* where he had left off a number of years before. A theater was planned especially for the presentation of his music dramas,

Bayreuth

Richard Wagner at home in Bayreuth, *painting by* **W. Beckmann,** *1882. To Wagner's left is his wife, Cosima; to his right, Franz Liszt and Hans von Wolzogen.*

which ultimately resulted in the festival playhouse at Bayreuth. And to crown his happiness he found, to share his empire, a woman equal to him in will and courage—Cosima, the daughter of his old friend Liszt. For the last time the *Tristan* pattern thrust itself upon him. Cosima was the wife of his fervent disciple, the conductor Hans von Bülow. She left her husband and children in order to join her life with Wagner's. They were married some years later, after Minna's death.

The Wagnerian gospel spread across Europe, a new art-religion. Wagner societies throughout the world gathered funds to raise the temple at Bayreuth. The radical of 1848 found himself, after the Franco-Prussian War, the national artist of Bismarck's German Empire. The *Ring* cycle was completed in 1874, and the four dramas were presented to worshipful audiences at the first Bayreuth festival in 1876.

One task remained. To make good the financial deficit of the festival the master undertook his last work, *Parsifal* (1877–82), a "consecrational festival drama" based on the legend of the Holy Grail. He finished it as he approached seventy. He died shortly after, in every sense a conqueror, and was buried at Bayreuth.

His Music

Wagner did away with the old "number" opera with its arias, duets, ensembles, choruses, and ballets. His aim was a continuous tissue of melody that would never allow the emotions to cool. He therefore evolved an "endless melody" that was molded to the natural inflections of the German language, more melodious than traditional recitative, more flexible and free than traditional aria.

Endless melody

The focal point of Wagnerian music drama is the orchestra. He developed

Principal Works

13 music dramas (operas), including *Rienzi* (1842), *Der fliegende Holländer* (The Flying Dutchman, 1843), *Tannhäuser* (*1845*), *Lohengrin* (1850), *Tristan und Isolde* (1865), *Die Meistersinger von Nürnberg* (The Mastersingers of Nuremberg, 1868), *Der Ring des Nibelungen* (The Ring of the Nibelung, 1869–76) consisting of *Das Rheingold* (The Rhine Gold, 1869), *Die Walküre* (The Valkyrie, 1856), *Siegfried* (1876), and *Götterdämmerung* (The Twilight of the Gods, 1876); and *Parsifal* (1882)

Orchestral music, including *Siegfried Idyll* (1870)

Piano music; vocal music; choral music

a type of symphonic opera as native to the German genius as vocal opera is to the Italian. The orchestra is the unifying principle of his music drama. It floods the action, the characters, and the audience in a torrent of sound that incarnates the sensuous ideal of the Romantic era.

Leitmotifs   The orchestral tissue is fashioned out of concise themes, the *leitmotifs*, or "leading motives"—Wagner called them basic themes—that recur throughout the work, undergoing variation and development even as the themes and motives of a symphony. The leitmotifs carry specific meanings, like the "fixed idea" of Berlioz or the river theme in Smetana's symphonic poem. They have an uncanny power of suggesting in a few strokes a person, an emotion, or an idea; an object—the gold, the ring, the sword; or a landscape—the Rhine, Valhalla, the lonely shore of Tristan's home. Through a process of continual transformation the leitmotifs trace the course of the drama, the changes in the characters, their experiences and memories, their thoughts and hidden desires. As the leitmotifs accumulate layer upon layer of meaning, they themselves become characters in the drama, symbols of the relentless process of growth and decay that rules the destinies of gods and heroes.

Harmonic innovations   Wagner's musical language was based on chromatic harmony, which he pushed to its then farthermost limits. Chromatic dissonance imparts to Wagner's music its restless, intensely emotional quality. Never before had the unstable tone combinations been used so eloquently to portray states of soul. The active chord (the dominant, built on the fifth scale degree) seeking resolution in the chord of rest (the tonic, on the first scale degree) became in Wagner's hands the most romantic of symbols: the lonely man—Flying Dutchman, Lohengrin, Siegmund, Tristan—seeking redemption through love, the love of the ideal woman, whether Senta or Elsa, Sieglinde or Isolde.

Wagner: Die Walküre

The Ring of the Nibelung centers on the treasure of gold that lies hidden in the depths of the Rhine, guarded by three Rhine Maidens. The world is young and knows not the power of gold. Only he who renounces love can gain that power. Alberich the Nibelung, of the hideous race of dwarfs who inhabit the dark regions below the earth, tries to make love to each of the maidens. When they repulse him, he renounces love, steals the treasure, and fashions from it a ring that brings unlimited power to its owner. Wotan, father of the gods (for whom our Wednesday or *Wotan's Day* is named) compromises his honor by obtaining the ring through trickery. Whereupon Alberich pronounces a terrible curse upon it. May it destroy the peace of mind of all who gain possession of it, may it bring them misfortune and death.

Thus begins the cycle of four dramas—the Tetrology, as it is known—that ends only when the curse-bearing ring is returned to the Rhine Maidens. Gods and heroes, mortals and Nibelungs intermingle freely in this tale of betrayed love, broken promises, magic spells, and general corruption engendered by the lust for power. Wagner freely adapted the story from the myths of the Norse sagas and the legends associated with a medieval German epic, the *Nibelungenlied*.

He wrote the four librettos in reverse order. First came his poem on the death of the hero Siegfried. This became the final opera, *Götterdämmerung*, in the course of which Siegfried, now possessor of the ring, betrays Brünnhilde, to whom he has sworn his love, and is in turn betrayed by her. Wagner then realized that the events in Siegfried's life were shaped by what had happened to him in his youth; the poem of *Siegfried* explained the forces that shaped the young hero. Aware that these in turn were determined by forces set in motion before the hero was born, Wagner wrote the poem about Siegfried's parents, Siegmund and Sieglinde, that became *Die Walküre*. Finally, this trilogy was prefaced by *Das Rheingold*, the drama that unleashed the workings of fate and the curse of gold out of which the entire action stemmed. Wagner composed the music in sequence, interrupting the gigantic task, as we saw, to write *Tristan* and *Die Meistersinger*. Thus twenty-six years elapsed (1848–74) from the time he began the epic to its completion.

First performed in Munich in 1870, *Die Walküre* revolves around the twin brother and sister who are the offspring of Wotan by a mortal. (In Norse as in Greek-Roman mythology, kings and heroes were the children of gods.) The ill-fated love of Siegmund and Sieglinde is not only incestuous but also adulterous, for she has been forced into a loveless marriage with the grim chieftain Hunding. During a violent thunderstorm Siegmund, a fugitive from his enemies, finds refuge in Hunding's dwelling. He has lost his sword, he is utterly exhausted. Sieglinde does her best to revive him, but he does not wish to stay. Touched by her kindness, he does. When Hunding returns, Siegmund tells his story. One day long past, returning from the hunt with his father, they found their dwelling burned, his mother slain and his sister gone. His father disappeared soon after, so that he has remained alone ever since. It now turns out that the enemies he was fleeing are kinsmen of Hunding, who tells Siegmund he can stay the night but will have to fight him in the morning. Hunding thereupon orders his wife out of the room and follows her.

Act I

Flames leap up around the rock, as Wotan, sung by James Morris in this Metropolitan Opera production of Die Walküre, *is silhouetted against the sky.* (Photograph courtesy Winnie Klotz)

Siegmund despairs. His father had promised that he would have a sword in his hour of need. Where is it now? Sieglinde joins him; she has poured a sleeping potion into her husband's drink. In the ensuing love scene between them, one of the most eloquent that Wagner ever wrote, each recognizes in the other the long-lost playmate of childhood. Sieglinde reveals that during the feast at her luckless marriage a stranger entered the hall and drove a sword deep into the ash tree in the center of Hunding's hut. The warriors tried to pull the sword out but none was able to do so. Now she knows: the stranger was their father, and the sword was intended for him, her hero. The outer door swings open, revealing the beautiful spring night that has followed the storm. Siegmund, enraptured, sings his spring song in which the awakening of the earth after the storms of winter is identified with the awakening of love after the despair of loneliness. He draws out the sword and claims his sister and bride. In a transport of passion the lovers rush into the night.

Act II   The second act opens with a scene between Wotan and Brünnhilde. She is one of the Valkyries, the nine daughters of Wotan whose task it is to circle the battlefield on their winged horses, swooping down to gather up the fallen heroes, whom they bear away to Valhalla, where they will sit forever feasting with the gods. Wotan tells his favorite daughter that, in the ensuing combat between Siegmund and Hunding, he wants her to protect his son. He has raised Siegmund as an ally in his struggle to regain the ring, since he alone knows what evil will befall if it should remain in the hands of his enemies. After Brünnhilde leaves him, he turns to face Fricka, his wife, the stern goddess of marriage and the sacredness of the home. Siegmund's love for his sister, Fricka insists, flouted the most sacred law of the universe. Therefore, in the ensuing combat, he must die. Although he argues with her, Wotan sadly realizes that even he, father of the gods, must obey the law. He summons Brünnhilde to contravene his previous command; she is to see to it that Hunding is the victor. When she comes to Siegmund to reveal to him his fate, she yields to pity and decides to disobey her father. The two heroes fight, and Brünnhilde tries to shield Siegmund. At the decisive moment Wotan appears and holds out his spear, upon which Siegmund's sword is shattered. Hunding buries his sword in Siegmund's breast. Wotan, overcome by his son's death, turns a ferocious look upon Hunding, who falls dead. Then the god rouses himself and hurries off in pursuit of the daughter who dared to defy his command.

Act III

The prelude to Act III is the famous Ride of the Valkyries, a vivid tone picture of the Amazon-like goddesses whirling through the storm on their chargers. On the Valkyries' rock Brünnhilde rushes in with Sieglinde, whom she has carried off from the scene of battle. Sieglinde wants to die, but Brünnhilde hands her the two fragments of Siegmund's sword and tells her she must live to bear his son, who will become the world's mightiest hero. Sieglinde thereupon seeks refuge in the forest while Brünnhilde remains to face her father's wrath. Her punishment is severe. She is to be deprived of her godhood, Wotan tells her, and become a mortal woman. No more will she sit with the gods, no more bear heroes to Valhalla. He will put her to sleep on the rock and she will fall prey to the first one who finds her. Brünnhilde defends herself. In trying to protect Siegmund was she not carrying out her father's innermost desire? She begs him to mitigate her punishment. Let him at least surround the rock with flames, so that only a fearless hero will be able to penetrate the wall of fire. Wotan relents and grants her request.

He kisses her on both eyes, which at once close. Wagner's stage directions are explicit: "She sinks gently unconscious in his arms. He bears her tenderly to a low mossy bank shaded by a great fir tree. Again he gazes on her features, closes her helmet and sorrowfully covers her with the Valkyrie shield. Then he stalks with solemn determination to the center of the stage and turns the point of his spear toward a mighty rock." Striking the rock three times, he invokes Loge, the god of fire. Flames spring up around the rock—and in the music, as the tall figure of the god in his black cloak is silhouetted against the red sky, "He who fears the point of my spear shall never step through the fire," he intones as the orchestra announces the theme of Siegfried, the fearless hero who in the next music drama will force his way through the flames and awaken Brünnhilde with a kiss. (See Listening Guide 39 for text and an analysis.) The curtain falls on as poetic a version of the sleeping-beauty legend as any artist ever penned.

Listening Guide 39

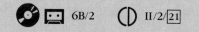 6B/2   II/2/21

WAGNER: *Die Walküre,* **Act III, scene 3**

Date: 1856; first performed 1870, Munich

Genre: Opera, second in a cycle of four, *The Ring of the Nibelung*

Characters: Wotan, father of the Gods
            Brünnhilde, one of the Valkyries, the favorite of the nine daughters of Wotan

Closing of scene: Orchestra, with "slumber" motive,
Langsam (slow)

21 Opening melody of Wotan's farewell

Text

Der Augen leuchtendes Paar,
das oft ich lächelnd gekost,
wenn Kampfeslust ein Kuss dir lohnte,
wenn kindisch lallend der Helden Lob
von holden Lippen dir floss:
dieser Augen strahlendes Paar,
das oft im Sturm mir geglänzt,
wenn Hoffnungssehnen das Herz mir sengte,
nach Welten wonne mein Wunsch verlangte
aus wild webendem Bangen:
zum letztenmal
letz' es mich heut
mit des Lebewohles letztem Kuss!
Dem glücklichern Manne
glänze sein Stern:
dem unseligen Ew'gen
muss es scheidend sich schliessen.
Denn so kehrt der Gott sich dir ab,
so küsst er die Gottheit von dir!

Translation

That bright pair of eyes
that often I fondled with smiles,
when lust of battle won you a kiss,
when childlike chatter in praise of heroes
flowed from your dear lips:
that radiant pair of eyes
that often in tempests blazed at me,
when hopeful yearning burned up my heart,
when for worldly joy my desires longed
amid wild weaving fear:
for the last time
let them delight me today
with farewell's last kiss!
May their star shine
for that happier man:
for the luckless immortal
they must close in parting.
For thus the God departs from you,
thus he kisses your godhead away!

*Wotan holds Brünnhilde's head in both hands. He kisses her long on the eyes. She sinks with eyes closed;
he carries her to a mossy mound.*

22 Accompanied by "magic sleep" motive, in woodwinds
and harp

The "slumber" motive is heard again. Wotan walks to center stage and points his spear at a rock.

23 Accompanied by forceful trombone passage

Wotan summons Loge, the God of Fire, accompanied by string tremolos.

Loge, hör! Lausche hieher!
Wie zuerst ich dich fand, als feurige Glut,
wie dann einst du mir schwandest,
als schweifende Lohe;
wie ich dich band, bann ich dich heut!
Herauf, wabernde Lohe,
umlodre mir feurig den Fels!
Loge! Loge! Hieher!

Loge, listen! Harken here!
As I found you first, a fiery blaze,
as once you vanished from me,
a random fire;
as I allied with you, so today I conjure you!
Arise, magic flame,
girdle the rock with fire for me!
Loge! Loge! Come here!

Flames flash out from the rock, and it begins to glow like fire.

24 "Magic fire music" is heard in full orchestra

Wotan points his spear as if casting a spell, and sings:

Wer meines Speeres Spitze fürchtet,
durchschreite das Feurer nie!

Whosoever fears the tip of my spear
shall never pass through the fire!

25 Brass announce the "Siegfried" motive,
of hero to come

Wotan looks back at Brünnhilde with sorrow, to accompaniment of "magic fire" and "slumber" motives.
He looks back again, then disappears through the fire, as "magic fire" music dies out.

64

Two Other Romantic Operas

"The composer gives the best of himself to the making of a work. He believes, doubts, enthuses, despairs, rejoices, and suffers in turn."—
GEORGES BIZET

Georges Bizet

Blazing with color and passion, Bizet's opera *Carmen* is one of those rare works that enjoys the admiration of musicians no less than that of a worldwide public. It exemplifies the Gallic genius at its best.

Georges Bizet: His Life and Music

Georges Bizet (1838–75) was born and raised in Paris. A student at the Conservatoire, in his twentieth year he won the highest award of the school, the Prix de Rome, which made possible a three-year stay in the Italian capital. The rest of his career was passed in his native city. The works of his youth were followed by three operas that display the composer's power of evoking exotic atmosphere. *The Pearl Fishers* is a drama of love and ritual in Ceylon. Four years later came *The Fair Maid of Perth* (after Walter Scott's novel), which takes place in a romanticized Scotland, and *Djamileh*, which is set in Cairo. Although none of these was an overwhelming success, they established Bizet's reputation as a composer to be reckoned with.

Bizet was then offered the libretto that Meilhac and Halévy had fashioned from Prosper Mérimée's celebrated story of Gypsy life and love. He was ready for his appointed task. There resulted the greatest French opera of the century.

Mérimée's tale belonged to a new type of literature that tried to get closer to the realities of life. His Gypsies, smugglers, and brigands were depicted with an honesty that heralded the new realism. The opera softened the naked fury of the original story. But enough remained to disturb the audience that assembled for the opening night on the third of March, 1875. The Opéra-Comique was a "family theater" where the bourgeois of Paris brought their wives and marriageable daughters. Passion on the stage was acceptable if it concerned kings and duchesses long dead; Carmen and her unsavory companions were too close for comfort.

The opera was not the fiasco that popular legend makes it out to have been. It did fail, incomprehensibly, to conquer its first audience. However, the rumor that the piece was not quite respectable helped give it a run of thirty-seven performances in the next three months, an average of three a week. In addition the manager offered the composer and his librettists a contract for their next work. *Carmen* was a failure only in Bizet's mind. He had put every ounce of his genius into the score. Its reception was a bitter disappointment. His delicate constitution, worn out by months of rehearsals and by the emotional tension that had attended the production, was ill

Principal Works

Orchestral music, including incidental music for *L'Arlésienne* (The Woman of Arles, 1872) and the Symphony in C (1855)

Operas, including *Les pêcheurs de perles* (The Pearl Fishers, 1863), *La jolie fille de Perth* (The Fair Maid of Perth, 1867), *Djamileh* (1872), and *Carmen* (1875)

Piano music; vocal music

prepared to take the blow. Exactly three months after the premiere he succumbed to a heart attack, at the age of thirty-seven. His death came just when he had found his mature style.

The work was immediately dropped by the Opéra-Comique. Yet within three years it had made its way to Vienna and Brussels, London and New York. Five years later it returned to Paris, was received rapturously, and embarked on its fabulously successful career. Today it is one of the best-loved operas of the world.

Bizet: Carmen

The power of this lyric drama stems from the impact with which it projects love, hate, desire. The story line follows one of the most compelling themes literature has to offer—the disintegration of a personality. The action is swift and unfaltering as the characters are carried step by step to their doom. The action centers around a beautiful, tempestuous Gypsy girl who works in a cigarette factory in Seville, and the simple soldier who falls in love with her. Don José had been planning to marry his childhood sweetheart Micaela, but his desire for Carmen grips him with the force of an obsession. She tries to lure him into the band of Gypsy smugglers to which she belongs, but he cannot possibly abandon the respectable life he has known. However, when his superior officer, Lieutenant Zuniga, tries to make love to Carmen, José, mad with jealousy, attacks him. The die is cast; he can no longer return to the barracks. The Gypsies welcome the deserter into their midst with a rousing chorus that hails the freedom of their lawless life.

Acts I and II

In a deserted mountain pass that serves as the hideout of the smugglers José gloomily reflects on his life. His happiness with Carmen was short-lived. As fickle as she is willful, she has tired of him and transferred her affection to the handsome bullfighter Escamillo. She suggests to José that he had perhaps better return to his village. They quarrel. Carmen's friends, Frasquita and Mercedes, open a deck of cards and tell their fortunes. The cards promise to each what her heart desires—to Frasquita a handsome young lover, to Mercedes a rich old husband who will die and leave her his money. Carmen cuts the cards and draws the ace of spades. "Death! I've read it well. First I, then he." Micaela comes looking for José, hoping still to rescue him from his madness. Then Escamillo arrives, eager to join Carmen. A fight develops between him and the jealous José; they draw knives but are separated. José

The chorus of the street children from Act I of Carmen *in a New York City Opera production.* (© Beth Bergman, 1989)

learns from Micaela that his mother is dying and is persuaded to leave with her. "We will meet again!" he warns Carmen, as the orchestra intones the motive of Fate that has run like a dark thread through the score.

Act III   The final act takes place outside the bullring in Seville. A festive crowd hails the bullfighters; finally Escamillo enters, with a radiant Carmen on his arm. The crowd accompanies him into the bullring; Carmen remains to face José. Their encounter is taut, volcanic. Each is driven by the basic law of his nature: José cannot relinquish his love, she cannot surrender her freedom. He entreats her to go with him; there is still time to begin anew. She refuses. "Then you love me no more?" "No, I love you no more." "But I, Carmen, I still love you!" He reaches the breaking point against the jubilant strains of the chorus in the arena. "For the last time, you fiend, will you come with me?" "No!" He stabs her as the "Toreador Song" rises from the crowd pouring out of the arena. José, dazed, kneels beside her body. The orchestra sounds the motive of Fate.

The libretto is a tightly knit affair revolving around a few key words—*l'amour* (love), *le sort* (Fate), *jamais* (never), *la morte* (death), all eminently singable. Bizet's brilliant orchestration and rhythmic vitality evoke all the warmth and color of Spain. The work remains one of the great examples of nineteenth century exoticism; its picturesque atmosphere is inescapably romantic. With its spoken dialogue, set to music after Bizet's death by his friend Ernest Guiraud, *Carmen* issued from the tradition of popular opéra comique. But it expanded that tradition, with its realism, sensuality, and tragic ending, in the same way that a century later *West Side Story* expanded the conventions of the Broadway musical. Bizet never actually saw Spain. It remained for him a symbol of that distant, unattainable land whose memory every artist carries in his heart.

Act I is set in a square in Seville in front of the cigarette factory. Soldiers loiter before the guard house. A trumpet offstage announces the changing of the guard; the relieving squad arrives, led by bugle and fife. The newcomers are hailed by a crowd of street boys who strut beside them, pretending to be soldiers, too. They sing a snappy march tune in high register, their *Ta ra ta ta ta* imitating a bugle call. The retiring squad marches offstage, followed by the youngsters, and the march tune dies away in the distance "as soft as possible."

The factory bell rings at noon, and the young men of the town gather to flirt with the girls who are about to come out. They express their anticipation in a short chorus sung in unison. The girls enter smoking cigarettes, which was quite a daring thing to do back in 1875. They blow smoke rings as they sing their chorus: "When our lovers swear to us how much they care, it's all smoke!" The gentle melody is in Bizet's suavest manner.

The mood changes as a few agitated measures prepare us for the entrance of Carmen. The scene is set for her aria in the graceful dotted rhythm of a Habanera, the Cuban dance-song that originated in Havana and was popular in the early nineteenth century. Based on a descending chromatic scale, the Habanera follows a "verse and chorus" form; at the choral verse, Carmen sings a seductive counter melody on the keyword "l'amour." Carmen's song establishes her character—capricious, tough, and dangerous. "Love is a wayward bird that none may hope to tame. When it suits him to refuse you, in vain you call his name . . . If you don't love me, I love you. And if I do, beware!" She throws Don José a flower. He doesn't know it yet, but she has already settled his fate.

It was a German philosopher who, awakening from the intoxication of Wagnerian music drama, discovered in *Carmen* the ideal lyric tragedy. "It is necessary to Mediterraneanize music!" Nietzsche declared in one of the most eloquent tributes ever penned to a work of art. "I envy Bizet for having had the courage of this sensitiveness—which hitherto in the music of European culture had found no means of expression. I know of no case in which the tragic irony that constitutes the kernel of love is expressed with such severity or in so terrible a formula as in the last cry of Don José: "Yes, it is I who killed her—Ah, my adored Carmen!"

Giacomo Puccini: His Life and Music

> *"Almighty God touched me with his little finger and said, 'Write for the theater—mind you, only for the theater!' And I have obeyed the supreme command."*

The Italian operatic tradition was carried on, in the post-Romantic era, by a group of composers led by Giacomo Puccini (1858–1924). His generation included Ruggiero Leoncavallo, remembered for *I pagliacci* (The Clowns, 1892), and Pietro Mascagni, whose reputation likewise rests on a single success, *Cavalleria rusticana* (Rustic Chivalry, 1890). These Italians were associated with the movement known as *verismo* (realism), which tried to bring into the lyric theater the naturalism of writers Zola, Ibsen, and their contemporaries. Instead of choosing historical or mythological themes, they picked subjects from everyday life and treated them in down-to-earth fashion. Puccini was strongly influenced by this trend toward operatic realism.

Giacomo Puccini

Principal Works

10 operas, including *Manon Lescaut* (1893), *La bohème* (The Bohemian, 1896), *Tosca* (1900), *Madama Butterfly* (1904), *La fanciulla del West* (The Girl of the Golden West, 1910), *Il trittico* (3 one-act operas: *Il tabarro, Suor Angelica, Gianni Schicchi*; 1918), and *Turandot* (1926)
Vocal music, including a Mass (1880)

Giacomo Puccini was born in 1858 in Lucca, Italy, son of a church organist in whose footsteps he expected to follow. It was at Milan, where he went to complete his studies, that his true bent came to the fore. He studied at the Conservatory with Amilcare Ponchielli, composer of *La gioconda*. The ambitious young musician did not have to wait long for success. *Manon Lescaut*, based on the novel of Abbé Prévost, established him as the most promising among the rising generation of Italian composers. In Luigi Illica and Giuseppe Giacosa he found an ideal pair of librettists, and with this writing team he produced the three most successful operas of the early twentieth century: *La bohème, Tosca,* and *Madama Butterfly*. The years separating these works should dispel the popular notion of Puccini as a facile melodist who tossed off one score after another. Each of his operas represented years of detailed work involving ceaseless changes until he was satisfied.

Handsome and magnetic, Puccini was idolized and feted wherever he went. His wife was jealous, not without reason. "I am always falling in love," he confessed. "When I no longer am, make my funeral." As he entered middle age this singer of youth and love began to feel that his time was running out. "I am growing old and that disgusts me. I am burning to start work but have no libretto and am in a state of torment. I need work just as I need food." After much seeking he found a story that released the music in him and embarked on his final task—*Turandot*. He labored for four years on this fairy-tale opera about the beautiful and cruel princess of China. A work of consummate artistry, it is his most polished score. Puccini, ill with cancer, pushed ahead with increasing urgency. "If I do not succeed in finishing the opera, someone will come to the front of the stage and say, 'Puccini composed as far as this, then he died.'"

He was sent to Brussels for treatment, accompanied by his son and the rough draft of the final scene. He died in 1924, following an operation, at the age of sixty-six. *Turandot* was completed from his sketches by his friend Franco Alfano. However, at the first performance at La Scala on April 25, 1926, the composer's wish was fulfilled. Arturo Toscanini, his greatest interpreter, laid down the baton during the lament over the body of Lì. Turning to the audience he said in a choking voice, "Here ends the master's work."

Puccini: La bohème

Puccini's best-loved work is based on Henri Murger's *Scènes de la vie de Bohème* (Scenes from Bohemian Life). The novel depicts the joys and sorrows of the young artists who flock to Paris in search of fame and fortune, congregating in the Latin Quarter on the Left Bank of the Seine River. "A gay life yet a terrible one," Murger called their precarious existence, woven of bold dreams and bitter realities. Puccini's music was peculiarly suited to this atmosphere of "laughter through tears." Remembering his own life as a struggling young musician in Milan, he recaptured its wistfulness and charm.

The first act takes place in the attic where live four penniless young *Act I* artists—Rodolfo the poet, Marcello the painter, Schaunard the musician, and Colline the philosopher. Rodolfo and Marcello are trying to work but they've run out of firewood and can think of nothing but the cold. They are joined first by Colline, then by Schaunard, who by a stroke of luck has come upon some money, which calls for a celebration. The landlord arrives with a nasty word—rent!—and is turned away. The young men go off to the Café Momus to celebrate Christmas Eve, Rodolfo staying behind to finish an article he is writing. Enter Mimi, and romance.

Her candle has gone out; will Rodolfo light it for her? He does. Mimi leaves, but soon returns. She has lost her key. A gust of wind extinguishes both their candles and, kneeling on the floor, they search for the key in the darkness. When Rodolfo finds it, he has the presence of mind to slip it into his pocket. Their hands touch, and it is time for an aria. (The dialogue up to this point has been carried on in a melodious recitative.) Rodolfo's aria, "Che gelida manina" (What a frozen little hand, let me warm it for you), flows into a scene of sheer magic as he describes his calling. "Who am I? A poet. What do I do? I write. How do I live? In dreams, hopes, and castles in the air. I'm as rich as a millionaire." (See Listening Guide 40 for the Italian-English text of this number and those that follow.) We have here the great Italian cantabile style, rising in a golden curve to its climax on a ringing

From the Metropolitan Opera production in 1981, the lovers' meeting in Act I of La bohème *by Giacomo Puccini. José Carreras is Rodolfo and Teresa Stratas is Mimi.* (© Beth Bergman, 1983)

high C. Three centuries of operatic tradition stand behind an aria such as this.

"Now that you know all about me, tell me who you are." She does, singing "Mi chiamano Mimi" (They call me Mimi). We learn that she is a shy, sensitive girl who earns her living by sewing and embroidering. This aria has given several generations of great primadonnas something to sing about.

Rodolfo's friends call up to him to join them. He tells them he soon will. There follows the duet that crowns the act, "O soave fanciulla" (O lovely girl). It would be impossible in a spoken drama for two young people to meet and, only fifteen minutes later, declare their love for each other. But music adds its own dimension to time. Or, better, it lifts time to its own dimension. The love that Rodolfo and Mimi welcome so ecstatically seems not only natural and convincing but altogether inevitable. Rodolfo invites her to accompany him to the cafe to lines that have become part of the Italian vocabulary of flirtation.

Act II   Act II, set on Christmas Eve in the Latin Quarter, opens with a festive street scene in which Puccini's Italian sensibility blends perfectly with the Parisian setting. Rodolfo, having bought his new flame a rose-colored bonnet, brings her to the table where his friends are waiting. The appearance of Musetta, Marcello's former sweetheart, causes a stir. She sends her elderly admirer on a fool's errand, whereupon a grand reconciliation takes place between her and Marcello. The act ends in a blaze of color and movement as the young people disappear in the crowd.

Act III   In dramatic contrast, Act III opens in a pallid wintry dawn near a toll gate outside Paris. To one side a tavern, from which sound the voices of the last carousers, including Musetta's. Mimi appears, seeking Marcello, and confides to him her difficulties with Rodolfo, who is insanely jealous and makes their life unbearable. When Rodolfo comes out of the tavern, Mimi hides to one side behind some trees to avoid a scene. Rodolfo pours out his heart to Marcello; he is helpless against this jealousy and fear. Mimi is ill, she is dying; he is too poor to provide her with the care she needs. Mimi's tears and coughing reveal her presence. She bids farewell to Rodolfo in a touching aria, "Addio, senza rancor" (Goodbye, without bitterness). The peak of this act is the Quartet—better, double duet—at the close. Mimi and Rodolfo melodiously resign themselves to the parting they dread, while Marcello and Musetta quarrel violently, he accusing her of flirting, she retaliating with lively epithets.

Act IV   With Act IV we are back in the attic. Marcello and Rodolfo try to work, as they did in the opening scene; but their thoughts revert to their lost loves. Schaunard and Colline arrive with four rolls and a herring for their scanty meal. The young men indulge in horseplay that comes to an abrupt halt with the entrance of Musetta. In great agitation she tells them that Mimi is below, too weak to climb the stairs. They help her in.

The friends depart on various errands to lighten Mimi's last moments. Now the lovers are alone. "Ah, my lovely Mimi" . . . "You still think me pretty" . . . "Lovely as the sunrise" . . . "You've made the wrong comparison; you should have said, 'Lovely as the sunset . . .'" The others return,

Marcello with medicine, Musetta with a muff to warm Mimi's hands. Rodolfo weeps. Mimi comforts him. "Why do you cry so? Here . . . love . . . always with you! My hands . . . warm . . . and . . . to sleep . . ." Musetta prays. Schaunard whispers to Marcello that Mimi is dead. Rodolfo's outcry, "Mimi . . . Mimi!" is heard against the brief and terrible postlude of the orchestra. Puccini wrote the final scene with tears in his eyes. The world has listened to it in like fashion.

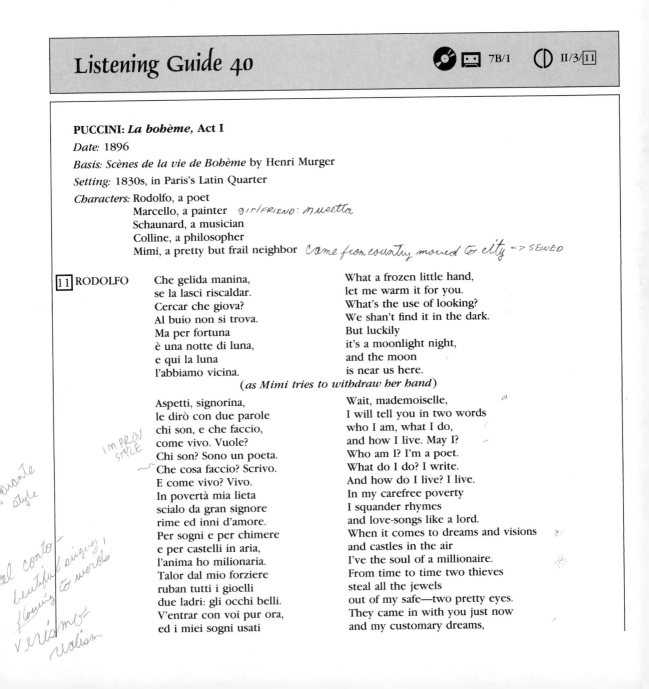

Listening Guide 40

7B/1   II/3/11

PUCCINI: *La bohème,* **Act I**

Date: 1896

Basis: Scènes de la vie de Bohème by Henri Murger

Setting: 1830s, in Paris's Latin Quarter

Characters: Rodolfo, a poet
Marcello, a painter *girlfriend: musetta*
Schaunard, a musician
Colline, a philosopher
Mimi, a pretty but frail neighbor *Came from country moved to city => sewed*

11	RODOLFO	Che gelida manina,	What a frozen little hand,
		se la lasci riscaldar.	let me warm it for you.
		Cercar che giova?	What's the use of looking?
		Al buio non si trova.	We shan't find it in the dark.
		Ma per fortuna	But luckily
		è una notte di luna,	it's a moonlight night,
		e qui la luna	and the moon
		l'abbiamo vicina.	is near us here.

(as Mimi tries to withdraw her hand)

IMPROV STYLE

Aspetti, signorina,
le dirò con due parole
chi son, e che faccio,
come vivo. Vuole?
Chi son? Sono un poeta.
Che cosa faccio? Scrivo.
E come vivo? Vivo.
In povertà mia lieta
scialo da gran signore
rime ed inni d'amore.
Per sogni e per chimere
e per castelli in aria,
l'anima ho milionaria.
Talor dal mio forziere
ruban tutti i gioielli
due ladri: gli occhi belli.
V'entrar con voi pur ora,
ed i miei sogni usati

Wait, mademoiselle,
I will tell you in two words
who I am, what I do,
and how I live. May I?
Who am I? I'm a poet.
What do I do? I write.
And how do I live? I live.
In my carefree poverty
I squander rhymes
and love-songs like a lord.
When it comes to dreams and visions
and castles in the air
I've the soul of a millionaire.
From time to time two thieves
steal all the jewels
out of my safe—two pretty eyes.
They came in with you just now
and my customary dreams,

bel canto—beautiful singing! flowing to words
verismo = realism
avante style

e i bei sogni miei	my lovely dreams,
tosto si dileguar!	melted at once into thin air.
Ma il furto non m'accora,	But the theft doesn't upset me,
poichè, poichè v'ha preso stanza	for their place has been taken
la speranza!	by hope.
Or che mi conoscete,	Now that you know all about me,
parlate voi, deh! parlate. Chi siete?	you tell me now who you are.
Vi piaccia dir!	Please do!

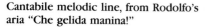

Cantabile melodic line, from Rodolfo's
aria "Che gelida manina!"

Aria

12 MIMÌ

Sì. Mi chiamano Mimì,	Yes. They call me Mimi,
ma il mio nome è Lucia.	but my name is Lucia.
La storia mia	My story
è breve: a tela o a seta	is brief: I embroider linen
ricamo in casa e fuori.	or silk, at home or outside.
Son tranquilla e lieta,	I'm contented and happy,
ed è mio svago	and it's my pleasure
far gigli e rose.	to make roses and lilies.
Mi piaccion quelle cose	I love those things
che han sì dolce malia,	which possess such sweet enchantment,
che parlano d'amor, di primavere;	which speak of love and springtime,
che parlano di sogni e di chimere,	of dreams and visions,
quelle cose che han nome poesia.	those things that people call poetic.
Lei m'intende?	Do you understand?

RODOLFO   Sì.   Yes.

MIMÌ

Mi chiamano Mimì,	They call me Mimi,
il perchè non so.	why, I don't know.
Sola mi fo	All alone
il pranzo de me stessa.	I make my own supper.
Non vado sempre a messa,	I don't always go to Mass,
ma prego assai il Signor.	but I pray diligently to God.
Vivo sola, soletta,	I live alone, quite alone
là in una bianca cameretta;	there in a little white room
guardo sui tetti e in cielo,	I overlook roofs and sky;
ma quando vien lo sgelo,	but when the thaw comes,
il primo sole è mio;	the first sunshine is mine,
il primo bacio dell'aprile è mio!	April's first kiss is mine!
Il primo sole è mio!	The first sunshine is mine!
Germoglia	In a vase
in un vaso una rosa;	a rose is coming into bloom;
foglia a foglia	petal by petal
la spio! Così gentil	I watch it! The scent
il profumo d'un fior.	of a flower is so sweet.
Ma i fior ch'io faccio, ahimè! . . .	But the flowers I make, alas,
i fior ch'io faccio, ahimè!	the flowers I make
non hanno odore!	have no smell!

	Altro di me non le saprei narrare:	There's no more I can tell you about myself.
	sono la sua vicina	I am your neighbour
	che la vien fuori d'ora	who comes to bother you
	a importunare.	at the wrong moment.

Opening of Mimi's aria "Mi chiamano Mimi"

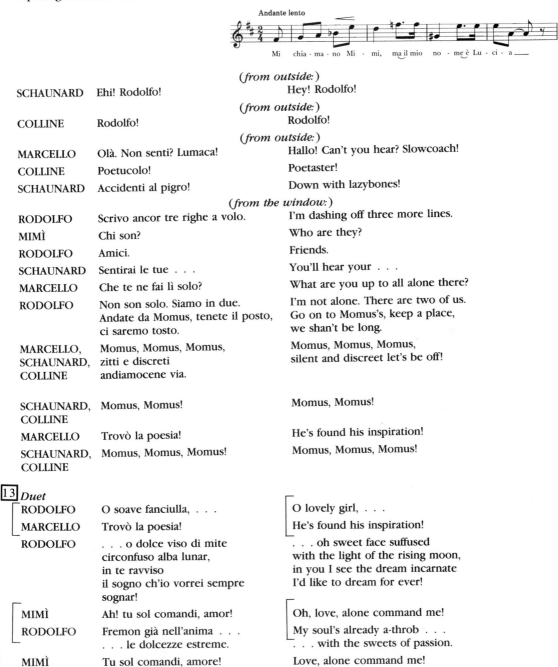

	(from outside:)	
SCHAUNARD	Ehi! Rodolfo!	Hey! Rodolfo!
	(from outside:)	
COLLINE	Rodolfo!	Rodolfo!
	(from outside:)	
MARCELLO	Olà. Non senti? Lumaca!	Hallo! Can't you hear? Slowcoach!
COLLINE	Poetucolo!	Poetaster!
SCHAUNARD	Accidenti al pigro!	Down with lazybones!
	(from the window:)	
RODOLFO	Scrivo ancor tre righe a volo.	I'm dashing off three more lines.
MIMÌ	Chi son?	Who are they?
RODOLFO	Amici.	Friends.
SCHAUNARD	Sentirai le tue . . .	You'll hear your . . .
MARCELLO	Che te ne fai lì solo?	What are you up to all alone there?
RODOLFO	Non son solo. Siamo in due.	I'm not alone. There are two of us.
	Andate da Momus, tenete il posto,	Go on to Momus's, keep a place,
	ci saremo tosto.	we shan't be long.
MARCELLO,	Momus, Momus, Momus,	Momus, Momus, Momus,
SCHAUNARD,	zitti e discreti	silent and discreet let's be off!
COLLINE	andiamocene via.	
SCHAUNARD,	Momus, Momus!	Momus, Momus!
COLLINE		
MARCELLO	Trovò la poesia!	He's found his inspiration!
SCHAUNARD,	Momus, Momus, Momus!	Momus, Momus, Momus!
COLLINE		

13 *Duet*

RODOLFO	O soave fanciulla, . . .	O lovely girl, . . .
MARCELLO	Trovò la poesia!	He's found his inspiration!
RODOLFO	. . . o dolce viso di mite	. . . oh sweet face suffused
	circonfuso alba lunar,	with the light of the rising moon,
	in te ravviso	in you I see the dream incarnate
	il sogno ch'io vorrei sempre	I'd like to dream for ever!
	sognar!	
MIMÌ	Ah! tu sol comandi, amor!	Oh, love, alone command me!
RODOLFO	Fremon già nell'anima . . .	My soul's already a-throb . . .
	. . . le dolcezze estreme.	. . . with the sweets of passion.
MIMÌ	Tu sol comandi, amore!	Love, alone command me!

| RODOLFO | Fremon nell'anima . . .
. . . dolcezze estreme, *ecc.*
Nel bacio freme amor! | My soul's a-throb already . . .
. . . with the sweets of passion, *etc.*
Love trembles in a kiss! |
| MIMÌ | Oh! come dolci scendono
le sue lusinghe al core,
tu sol comandi, amore! | Oh, how sweetly his flattery
falls upon my heart.
Love, alone command me! |

(as he tries to kiss her:)

No, per pietà!	No, please!

Example from Rodolfo's and Mimi's duet,
beginning "Fremon nell'anima"

RODOLFO	Sei mia!	You're mine!
MIMÌ	V'aspettan gli amici.	Your friends are waiting for you.
RODOLFO	Già mi mandi via?	Are you sending me away already?
MIMÌ	Vorrei dir . . . ma non oso . . .	I like to say . . . but dare not . . .
RODOLFO	Di'.	Say it!
MIMÌ	Se venissi con voi?	Suppose I came with you?
RODOLFO	Che? Mimì! Sarebbe così dolce restar qui. C'è freddo fuori.	What? . . . Mimì! It would be lovely to stay here. It's cold outside.
MIMÌ	Vi starò vicina!	I shall be near you!
RODOLFO	E al ritorno?	And when we return?
MIMÌ	Curioso!	Wait and see!
RODOLFO	Dammi il braccio, mia piccina.	Give me your arm, my sweet.
MIMÌ	Obbedisco, signor!	I obey, Monsieur!
RODOLFO	Che m'ami di'.	Say you love me.
MIMÌ	Io t'amo!	I love you!

(as they go out:)

MIMÌ, RODOLFO	Amor! Amor! Amor!	Ah, love, love, love!

65

Tchaikovsky and the Ballet

"Dancing is the lustiest, the most moving, the most beautiful of the arts, because it is no mere translation or abstraction from life; it is life itself."—HAVELOCK ELLIS

Ballet—Past and Present

Ballet has been an adornment of European culture for centuries. Ever since the Renaissance it has graced lavish festivals and theatrical entertainments presented at the courts of kings and dukes. Royal weddings and similar celebrations were accompanied by spectacles with scenery, costumes, and staged dancing. This continued during the Baroque with the *intermedio* in Italy, the *masque* in England, and the *ballet de cour* in France. Louis XIV even took part himself in one as the Sun King. Elaborate ballets were featured too in the operas of Lully and Rameau.

The eighteenth century saw the rise of ballet as an independent art. French ballet achieved pre-eminence in the early nineteenth century. Then Russian ballet came into its own, fostered by the patronage of the Tsar's court. A decisive event in this development was the arrival in 1847 at St. Petersburg of the great choreographer Marius Petipa, who left an indelible mark on the art of ballet. He created the dances for more than a hundred works, invented the structure of the classic *pas de deux* (dance for two), and brought the art of staging ballets to unprecedented heights.

The history of early twentieth-century ballet is indissolubly tied up with the career of Serge Diaghilev (1872–1929), whose genius lay in his ability to recognize genius. Diaghilev's dance company, the Ballets Russes, which he brought to Paris in the years before the First World War, opened up a new chapter in the cultural life of Europe. He surrounded his dancers—the greatest were Vaslav Nijinsky and Tamara Karsavina—with productions worthy of them. He invited such artists as Picasso, Léger, and Braque to paint the scenery, and commissioned the three ballets—*The Firebird*, *Petrushka*, and *The Rite of Spring*—that catapulted the composer Igor Stravinsky to fame. His ballets have served as models for the composers and choreographers who came after.

Ballet is the most physical of the arts depending as it does upon the leaps and turns of the human body. Out of this material it weaves an enchantment all its own. We watch with amazement as the ballerinas in their white tutus and their male partners float through the air, seeming to triumph over the laws of gravity. A special glamour attaches to the great dancers—Nureyev, d'Amboise, Baryshnikov, Makarova, and their peers—as they hold a world-wide public in thrall. Yet theirs is a demanding art based on an inhumanely demanding discipline. Their bodies are their instruments, which they must keep in top shape in order to perform the gymnastics required of them. They create moments of elusive beauty, but the basis of these is their total control of their muscles. It is this combination of physical and emotional factors that marks the distinctive power of ballet. The dancer transforms the body into a work of art, and it is this transformation that the world eagerly witnesses.

As our century approaches its end we see ballet becoming more and more popular in the United States. Regional groups thrive throughout the country, their activities supplemented by visits from the famous European companies—the Bolshoi from Moscow, the Royal Ballet from London, the Paris Opéra Ballet, Stuttgart and Danish Ballets, among others. This is a many-faceted art, and the number of its devotees is steadily growing. One has only to watch a good performance to understand why.

Peter Ilyich Tchaikovsky: His Life and Music

"Truly there would be reason to go mad were it not for music."

Peter Ilyich Tchaikovsky

Few composers typify the end-of-the-century mood as does Peter Ilyich Tchaikovsky (1840–93). He belonged to a generation that saw its truths crumbling and found none to replace them. He expressed as did none other the pessimism that attended the final phase of the Romantic movement.

Tchaikovsky was born at Votkinsk in a distant province of Russia, son of a government official. His family intended him for a career in the government. He graduated at nineteen from the aristocratic School of Jurisprudence in St. Petersburg and obtained a minor post in the Ministry of Justice. Not until he was twenty-three did he reach the decision to resign his post and enter the newly founded Conservatory of St. Petersburg. "To be a good musician and earn my daily bread"—his was a modest goal.

He completed the course in three years and was immediately recommended by Anton Rubinstein, director of the school, for a teaching post in the new Conservatory of Moscow. Despite the long hours and large classes, the young professor of harmony applied himself assiduously to composition. His twelve years at Moscow saw the production of some of his most successful works.

Extremely sensitive by nature, Tchaikovsky was subject to attacks of depression aggravated by his guilt over his homosexuality. In the hope of achieving some degree of stability, he entered into an ill-starred marriage with a student of the Conservatory, Antonina Miliukov, who was hopelessly in love with him. His sympathy for Antonina soon turned into uncontrollable aversion, and in a fit of despair he wandered into the icy waters of the Moscow River. Some days later he fled, on the verge of a serious breakdown, to his brothers in St. Petersburg.

In this desperate hour, there appeared the kind benefactress who enabled him to go abroad until he had recovered his health, freed him from the demands of a teaching post, and launched him on the most productive period of his career. Nadezhda von Meck, widow of an industrialist, was an imperious and emotional woman. She lived the life of a recluse in her mansion in Moscow, from which she ran her railroads, her estates, and the lives of her eleven children. Her passion was music, especially Tchaikovsky's. Bound by the rigid conventions of her time and her class, she had to be certain that her enthusiasm was for the artist, not the man; hence she stipulated that she was never to meet the recipient of her bounty.

Thus began the famous friendship by letter that soon assumed a tone of passionate attachment. For the next thirteen years Mme. von Meck made Tchaikovsky's career the focal point of her life, providing for his needs with exquisite devotion and tact. Save for an accidental glimpse of one another at the opera or during a drive, they never met.

The correspondence gives us an insight into Tchaikovsky's method of work. "You ask me how I manage the instrumentation. I never compose in the abstract. I invent the musical idea and its instrumentation simultaneously." Mme. von Meck inquires if the Fourth Symphony (which he dedicated to her) has a definite meaning. Tchaikovsky replies, "How can one express the indefinable sensations that one experiences while writing an instrumental composition that has no definite subject? It is a purely lyrical process. It is a musical confession of the soul, which unburdens itself through sounds just as a lyric poet expresses himself through poetry. . . . As Heine said, 'Where words leave off music begins.'"

The years covered by the correspondence saw the spread of Tchaikovsky's fame. He was the first Russian whose music appealed to Western tastes, and in 1891 he was invited to come to America to participate in the ceremonies that marked the opening of Carnegie Hall. From New York he wrote, "These Americans strike me as very remarkable. In this country the honesty, sincerity, generosity, cordiality, and readiness to help you without a second thought are extremely pleasant. . . . The houses downtown are simply colossal. I cannot understand how anyone can live on the thirteenth floor. I went out on the roof of one such house. The view was splendid, but I felt quite giddy when I looked down on Broadway. . . . I am convinced that I am ten times more famous in America than in Europe."

The letters of his final years breathe disenchantment and the suspicion that he had nothing more to say. "Is it possible that I have completely written myself out? I have neither ideas nor inclinations!" But ahead of him lay his two finest symphonies.

Principal Works

8 operas, including *Eugene Onegin* (1879) and *Pique Dame* (The Queen of Spades, 1890)

3 ballets: *Swan Lake* (1877), *The Sleeping Beauty* (1890), and *The Nutcracker* (1892)

Orchestral music, including 7 symphonies (No. 1, 1866; No. 2, 1872; No. 3, 1875; No. 4, 1878; No. 5, 1888; and No. 6, *Pathétique*, 1893; *Manfred*, 1885); 3 piano concertos, 1 violin concerto (1878); symphonic poems and overtures (*Romeo and Juliet,* 1870)

Chamber and keyboard music; Choral music and songs

Immediately after finishing his Sixth Symphony, the *Pathétique*, he went to St. Petersburg to conduct it. The work met with a lukewarm reception, due in part to the fact that Tchaikovsky, painfully shy in public, conducted his music without any semblance of conviction. Some days later, although he had been warned of the prevalence of cholera in the capital, he carelessly drank a glass of unboiled water and contracted the disease. He died within the week, at the age of fifty-three. The suddenness of his death and the tragic tone of his last work led to rumors that he had committed suicide. Almost immediately there accrued to the *Symphonie pathétique* the sensational popularity it has enjoyed ever since.

"He was the most Russian of us all!" said Stravinsky. In the eyes of his countrymen Tchaikovsky is a national artist. He himself laid great weight on the Russian element in his music. "I am Russian through and through!" At the same time, in the putting together of his music Tchaikovsky was a cosmopolite. He came under the spell of Italian opera, French ballet, German symphony and song. These he assimilated to the strain of folk melody that was his heritage as a Russian, setting upon the mixture the stamp of a sharply defined personality.

Tchaikovsky: The Nutcracker

Tchaikovsky had a natural affinity for the ballet. Dances, especially waltzes, are scattered throughout his works, from the rousing waltz of the opera *Eugene Onegin* to the exquisite one of the *Serenade for Strings*. His three ballets—*Swan Lake*, *Sleeping Beauty*, and *The Nutcracker*—were not immediate successes with the dancers. They complained at first that the rhythms were too complicated to be danced to. Within a few years, however, they had changed their view, and these three ballets established themselves as basic works of the Russian repertoire.

The Nutcracker was based on a fanciful story by E. T. A. Hoffmann (the Romantic writer from whom the composer Offenbach derived his opera *Tales of Hoffmann*). An expanded version by Alexandre Dumas père served as the basis for Petipa's scenario, which was offered to Tchaikovsky when he returned from his visit to the United States in 1891.

Act I takes place at a Christmas party during which two children, Clara and Fritz, help decorate the tree. Their godfather arrives with gifts, among which is a nutcracker. (Russian nutcrackers are often shaped like a human head or a whole person, which makes it quite logical for little Clara to dream that this one was transformed into a handsome prince.) The children go to bed but Clara returns to gaze at her gift. The dreams begin: she is terrified to see mice scampering around the tree. Then, the dolls she has received come alive and fight a battle with the mice, which comes to a climax in the combat between the Nutcracker and the Mouse King. Clara helps her beloved Nutcracker by throwing a slipper at the Mouse King, who is vanquished. The Nutcracker then becomes the prince who takes Clara away with him.

*Mikhail Baryshnikov in
an American Ballet
Theater production of*
The Nutcracker.
(© Martha Swope)

Act II takes place in Confiturembourg, the land of sweets, that is ruled by the Sugar Plum Fairy. The prince presents Clara to his family and a celebration follows, with a series of dances that reveal all the attractions of this magic realm.

The mood is set by the Overture, whose light, airy effect Tchaikovsky achieved by omitting most of the brass instruments. The March is played as the guests arrive for the party, and a snappy little march it is. "I have discovered a new instrument in Paris . . ." Tchaikovsky wrote his publisher, "something between a piano and a glockenspiel, with a divinely beautiful tone, and I want to introduce it into the ballet." The instrument was the *celesta*, whose ethereal timbre perfectly suits the Sugar Plum Fairy and her veils. In the "Trepak" or "Russian Dance," the orchestral sound is enlivened by a tambourine. Coffee dances the muted "Arab Dance," while Tea responds with the "Chinese Dance," in which bassoons set up an ostinato that bobs up and down against the shrill melody of flute and piccolo. The "Dance of the Toy Flutes" is extraordinarily graceful, which is as it should be. And the climax of the ballet comes with the "Waltz of the Flowers," which has delighted audiences for a century. With its suggestion of swirling ballerinas, this finale conjures up everything we have come to associate with the Romantic ballet.

PART EIGHT

■

The
Twentieth Century

"The century of aeroplanes has a right to its own music. As there are no precedents, I must create anew."—CLAUDE DEBUSSY

Nicolas de Stael (*1914–55*) Le Grand concert (*The Big Concert*) (Musée Picasso, Antibes)

TRANSITION V

■

The Post-Romantic Era

"I came into a very young world in a very old time."—ERIK SATIE

The post-Romantic era, overlapping the Romantic period, extended from around 1890 to 1910. This generation of composers included radicals, conservatives, and those in between. Some continued in the traditional path; others struck out in new directions; still others tried to steer a middle course between the old and the new. During these years several newcomers appeared on the musical horizon. And there emerged the movement that more than any other ushered in the twentieth century—Impressionism.

Gustav Mahler: His Life and Music

"To write a symphony is, for me, to construct a world."

One of the striking phenomena of the current musical scene has been the upsurge of Gustav Mahler's popularity. For whatever reason, his troubled spirit seems to reach our musical public in a most persuasive way. "My time will come," he used to say. It has.

Gustav Mahler (1860–1911) was born and raised in Bohemia. His father, owner of a small distillery, was not slow in recognizing the boy's talent. Piano lessons began when Gustav was six. He was sent to Vienna and entered the Conservatory at fifteen, the University three years later. His professional career began modestly enough: at the age of twenty, he was engaged to conduct operettas at a third-rate summer theater. A dynamic conductor who found his natural habitat in the opera house, Mahler soon achieved a reputation that brought him ever more important posts, until at twenty-eight he was director of the Royal Opera at Budapest. From Budapest Mahler went to Hamburg. Then, at thirty-seven, he was offered the most important musical position in the Austrian Empire—the directorship, with absolute powers, of the Vienna Opera. His ten years there (1897–1907) made history. He brought to his duties a fiery temperament, unwavering devotion to ideals, and the inflexible will of the zealot. When he took over, Massenet was the chief drawing card. By the time his rule ended, he had taught a frivolous public

Gustav Mahler

Vienna Opera

399

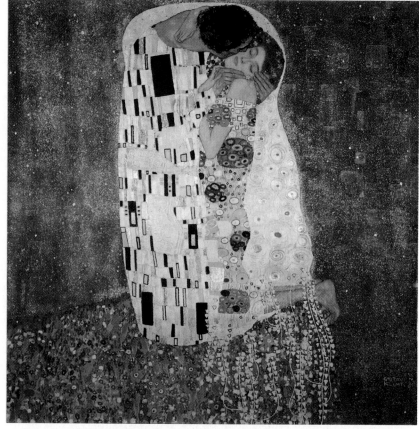

Gustav Klimt (*1862– 1918*), *like Mahler a product of the post-Romantic era in Vienna, has created in* The Kiss (*1907–08*), *an illusion of rich beauty and deeply-felt emotion.* (Osterreichische Gallerie, Vienna)

to revere Mozart, Beethoven, and Gluck, and made them listen to uncut versions of Wagner's operas.

Conversion to Catholicism

Shortly before he was appointed to Vienna, Mahler became a convert to Catholicism. This step was motivated in the first instance by the desire to smooth his way in a city where anti-Semitism was rampant. Beyond that, Mahler belonged to a generation of Jewish intellectuals who had lost identification with their religious heritage and who sought roots in the Austro-German culture of which they felt themselves to be a part. "I am thrice homeless," he remarked. "As a Bohemian born in Austria. As an Austrian among Germans. And as a Jew throughout the world."

"Humanly I make every concession, artistically—none!" Such intransigence was bound to create powerful enemies. Mahler's final years in Vienna were embittered by the intrigues against him, which flourished despite the fact that he had transformed the Imperial Opera into the premier lyric theater of Europe. The death of a little daughter left him grief-stricken. A second disaster followed soon after: he was found to have a heart ailment. When he finally was forced to resign his post, the blow was not unexpected. Mahler, now almost forty-eight (he had only three more years to live), accepted an engagement at New York's Metropolitan Opera. He hoped to earn enough to be able to retire at fifty, so that he finally might compose with the peace of mind that had never been granted him. His three years in New York were not free of the storms that his tempestuous personality inevitably provoked. In 1909 he assumed direction of the New York Philharmonic Orchestra. When the ladies of the Board made it plain to Alma Mahler that her husband had flouted their wishes, she expostulated, "But in Vienna the Emperor himself did not dare to interfere!"

New York Philharmonic

In the middle of a taxing concert season with the Philharmonic he fell ill with a streptococcus infection. It was decided to bring him to Paris, where a new serum treatment had been developed. In Paris, he took a turn for the worse. Thus he set forth on his last journey, back to the scene of his greatest triumphs—the enchanting, exasperating Vienna he both loved and detested. On his deathbed he conducted with one finger on the quilt, uttering a single word: "Mozart. . . ." He was buried, as he had requested, beside his daughter in a cemetery outside Vienna. At last that unquiet heart was at rest.

"The act of creation in me is so closely bound up with all my experience that when my mind and spirit are at rest I can compose nothing." In this identification of art with personal emotion Mahler was entirely the Romantic.

The spirit of song permeates Mahler's art. He followed Schubert and Schumann in cultivating the song cycle. *Songs of a Wayfarer*, composed in 1885, is a set of four songs suffused with Schubertian longing. Mahler wrote the texts himself, roused by an image that appealed strongly to his imagination: the rejected lover wandering alone over the face of the earth. His next cycle was inspired by a famous collection of German folk poetry, *The Youth's Magic Horn*. The moving *Songs on the Death of Children* is a cycle for voice and orchestra to the grief-laden poems of Rückert. The peak of his achievement in this direction is the cycle of six songs with orchestra that make up *The Song of the Earth*.

Vocal music

Mahler was the last in the illustrious line of Viennese symphonists that extended from Haydn, Mozart, Beethoven, and Schubert to Bruckner and Brahms. His tonal imagery was permeated by the jovial spirit of Austrian popular song and dance. His nine symphonies abound in lyricism, with melodies long of line and richly expressive harmonies. (The Tenth Symphony was left unfinished at his death, but recently has been edited and made available for performance.) In his sense of color Mahler ranks with the great masters of the art of orchestration. He contrasts solo instruments in the manner of chamber music, achieving his color effects through clarity of line

Symphonies

Principal Works

Orchestral music, including 10 symphonies

Song cycles with orchestra, including *Lieder eines fahrenden Gesellen* (Songs of a Wayfarer, 1885), *Das knaben Wunderhorn* (The Youth's Magic Horn, 1888), *Kindertotenlieder* (Songs on the Death of Children, 1904), *Das Lied von der Erde* (The Song of the Earth, 1908); Lieder

rather than massed sonorities. It was in the matter of texture that Mahler made his most important contribution to contemporary technique. Basing his orchestral style on counterpoint, he caused two or more melodies to unfold simultaneously, each setting off the other. Mahler never abandoned the principle of tonality; he needed the key as a framework for his vast design.

Mahler: Symphony No. 4

First movement

The Fourth Symphony, completed in 1900, is one of Mahler's least problematical works. The mood of the first movement is one of heartwarming lyricism; its melodies have about them a folklike simplicity.

Second movement

Second is the Scherzo, which Mahler described as "mystical, bewildering, and weird." Here, he wrote in a sketchbook, "Death plays the music." The figure of Death as a fiddler has haunted the imagination of Europe's artists since the Middle Ages. Mahler in this movement heightens the fantastic element by writing a solo for a violin tuned a full step higher than usual, giving it a shriller, tauter sound, and directs that the instrument be played "like a street fiddle" (as opposed to the more elegant violin).

Third movement

Third is the slow movement, a lyric meditation descended from the serene Andantes of Schubert. Like the slow movement of Beethoven's Fifth, which we studied earlier, it is cast in the form of a set of variations on two themes.

Like many with sophisticated, complex natures, Mahler longed for the innocence and trust of childhood. Something of this he found in the folk poems of *The Youth's Magic Horn*, which furnished texts for his songs

Fourth movement

S3A/6

S3/28

throughout his career. From this set came the poem that inspired the final movement of the Fourth Symphony, a child's view of Heaven that Mahler transformed into an enchanting song for soprano and orchestra. The anonymous poet depicts the joys of the celestial abode in artless terms. There is much dancing and singing, encouraged by an endless supply of fresh fruit, vegetables, free wine, and bread baked by the angels. The opening clarinet melody recalls the flute theme from the first movement's Development, and the sleigh-bell motive recurs as a ritornello or refrain between the stanzas. The opening phrase of the vocal part sets the tone of childlike innocence. The mood is sustained until the end, when the English horn plays in longer notes the jingling grace-note figure, now becalmed, with which the work began.

Mahler engaged in a gigantic effort to breathe vitality into the Romantic world of thought and feeling that was in process of disintegration. This circumstance imparts to his music its fevered unrest, his nostalgia. His intensely personal vision of life and art has made him one of the major prophets of the twentieth century.

UNIT XXI

■

The Impressionist and Post-Impressionist Eras

66

Debussy and Impressionism

"For we desire above all—nuance,
Not color but half-shades!
Ah! nuance alone unites
Dream with dream and flute with horn."—PAUL VERLAINE

The Impressionist Painters

In 1867 Claude Monet, rebuffed by the academic salons, exhibited under less conventional auspices a painting called *Impression: Sun Rising*. Before long "impressionism" had become a term of derision to describe the hazy, luminous paintings of this artist (1840–1926) and his school. A distinctly Parisian style, Impressionism counted among its exponents Camille Pissarro (1830–1903), Edouard Manet (1832–83), Edgar Degas (1834–1917), and Auguste Renoir (1841–1919). Discarding those elements of the Romantic tradition that had hardened into academic formulas, they strove to retain on canvas the freshness of their first impressions. They took painting out of the studio into the open air. What fascinated them was the continuous change in the appearance of things. They painted water lilies, a haystack, or clouds again and again at different hours of the day. Instead of mixing their pigments on the palette, they juxtaposed brush-strokes of pure color on the canvas, leaving it to the eye of the beholder to do the mixing. An iridescent sheen bathes their painting. Outlines shimmer and melt in a luminous haze.

The Impressionists abandoned the grandiose subjects of Romanticism. The hero of their painting is not man but light. Not for them the pathos,

The Impressionists took painting out of the studio into the open air; their subject was light. **Claude Monet** (*1840–1926*), Impression: Sun Rising (Musée Marmottan, Paris.)

the drama-packed themes that had inspired centuries of European art. They preferred "unimportant" material: still life, dancing girls, nudes; everyday scenes of middle-class life, picnics, boating and café scenes; nature in all her aspects, Paris in all her moods. Ridiculed at first—"Whoever saw grass that's pink and yellow and blue?"—they ended by imposing their vision upon the age.

The Symbolist Poets

A parallel revolt against traditional modes of expression took place in poetry under the leadership of the Symbolists, who strove for direct poetic experience unspoiled by intellectual elements. They sought to suggest rather than describe, to present the symbol rather than state the thing. Symbolism as a literary movement came to the fore in the work of Charles Baudelaire (1821–67), Stéphane Mallarmé (1842–98), Paul Verlaine (1844–96), and Arthur Rimbaud (1854–91). These poets were strongly influenced by Edgar Allan Poe (1809–49), whose writings were introduced into France by his admirer, Baudelaire. They used a word for its color and its music rather than its proper meaning, evoking poetic images "that sooner or later would be accessible to all the senses."

The Symbolists experimented in free verse forms that opened new territories to their art. They achieved in language an indefiniteness that had hitherto been the privilege of music alone. Characteristic was Verlaine's pronouncement: "Music above all!" The essentially musical approach of the Symbolists was not lost upon the musicians. According to the composer Paul Dukas, it was the writers, not the musicians, who exerted the strongest influence on the greatest of the musical Impressionists, Claude Debussy.

Impressionism in Music

Impressionism came to the fore at a crucial moment in the history of European music. The major-minor system had served the art since the seventeenth century. Composers were beginning to feel that its possibilities had been exhausted. Debussy and his followers were attracted to other scales, such as the church modes of the Middle Ages, which imparted an archaic flavor to their music. They began to emphasize the primary intervals—octaves, fourths, fifths, and the parallel movement of chords in the manner of Medieval organum. They were sympathetic to the novel scales introduced by nationalists such as the Russian composers Borodin and Musorgsky, or the Norwegian nationalist Edvard Grieg. Especially they responded to the influence of non-Western music: the Moorish strain in the songs and dances of Spain, and the Javanese and Chinese orchestras that were heard in Paris during the World Exposition of 1889. Here they found a new world of sonority: rhythms, scales, and color that offered a bewitching contrast to the traditional forms of Western music.

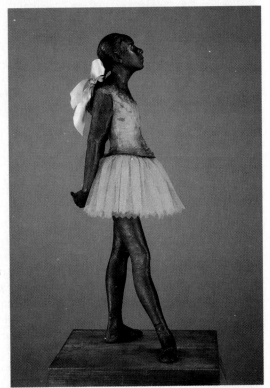

Music and ballet provided **Edgar Degas** (*1834–1917*) *with many themes, as in this sculpture,* Grande danseuse habillée (*Dressed Ballerina*). (Musée d'Orsay, Paris)

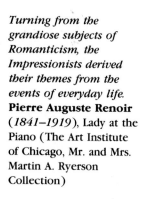

Turning from the grandiose subjects of Romanticism, the Impressionists derived their themes from the events of everyday life. **Pierre Auguste Renoir** (*1841–1919*), Lady at the Piano (The Art Institute of Chicago, Mr. and Mrs. Martin A. Ryerson Collection)

The major-minor system, as we saw, is based on the pull of the active tones to the tonic or rest tone. Impressionist composers regarded this as a formula that had become too obvious. We do not hear in their works the triumphal final cadence of the Classic-Romantic period, in which the dominant chord is resolved to the tonic with the greatest possible emphasis. The time was ripe for more subtle harmonic relationships. Classical harmony looked upon dissonance as a momentary disturbance that found its resolution *Use of dissonance* in the consonance. Composers now began to use dissonance as a value in itself, freeing it from the need to resolve. They taught their contemporaries to accept tone combinations that had hitherto been regarded as inadmissible, even as the Impressionist painters taught them to see colors in sky, grass, and water that had never been seen there before.

Whole-tone scale The *whole-tone scale* that figures prominently in Impressionist music derives from non-Western sources. This is a pattern built entirely of whole-tone intervals. It cannot be formed from the white or black keys alone on a piano keyboard, but by a combination of both (the sequence C-D-E-F♯-G♯-A♯-C provides an example). This scale does not have the pull of the seventh tone to the eighth, the tonic that is a major force in Western music, as the interval is not the usual half step but a whole step instead. There results a fluid scale pattern whose charm can be gauged only from hearing it played.

Several other procedures came to be associated with musical Impressionism. One of the most important is the use of parallel or "gliding" chords, in which a chord built on one tone is duplicated immediately on a higher or lower tone. Such parallel motion was prohibited in the Classical system of harmony, but it was precisely these forbidden progressions that Impressionist composers found fascinating.

Parallel chords

The harmonic innovations inseparable from Impressionism led to the formation of daring new tone combinations. Characteristic was the use of the five-tone combinations known as *ninth chords* (from the interval of a ninth between the lowest and highest tones of the chord). These played so prominent a part in Debussy's opera *Pelléas et Mélisande* that the work came to be known as "the land of ninths." As a result of the procedures just outlined, Impressionist music wavered between major and minor without adhering to either. It floated in a borderland between keys, creating elusive effects that might be compared to the misty outlines of Impressionist painting.

Ninth chords

An iridescent sheen bathes this late Impressionist painting as outlines shimmer and melt in a luminous haze. Dated thirty years after Impression: Sun Rising, *but also by* **Claude Monet,** Water Lilies. (Photograph by Lee Boltin)

Orchestral color

These evanescent harmonies demanded colors no less subtle. No room here for the thunderous climaxes of the Romantic orchestra. Instead, there was a veiled blending of hues, an impalpable shimmer of pictorial quality: flutes and clarinets in their dark lower register, violins in their lustrous upper range, trumpets and horns discreetly muted; and over the whole a silvery gossamer of harp, celesta, and triangle, glockenspiel, muffled drum, and cymbal brushed with a drumstick. One instrumental color flows into another close to it, as from oboe to clarinet to flute, in the same way that Impressionist painting flows from one color to another close to it in the spectrum, as from yellow to green to blue.

Rhythm

Impressionist rhythm, too, shows the influence of non-Western music. The metrical patterns of the Classic-Romantic era were marked by a recurrent accent on the first beat of the measure. Such emphasis was hardly appropriate for the new dreamlike style. In many a work of the Impressionist school the music glides from one measure to the next in a floating rhythm that discreetly veils the pulse.

Small forms

The Impressionists turned away from the large forms of the Austro-German tradition, such as symphony and concerto. They preferred short lyric forms— preludes, nocturnes, arabesques—whose titles suggested intimate lyricism or Impressionist painting. Characteristic are Debussy's *Clair de lune* (Moonlight), *Nuages* (Clouds), *Jardins sous la pluie* (Gardens in the Rain). The question arises: Was Impressionism a revolt against the Romantic tradition or simply its final manifestation? Beyond question, Debussy and his followers rebelled against certain aspects of Romanticism, especially the symphony of Beethoven and the music drama of Wagner. Yet in a number of ways Impressionism continued the fundamental tendencies of the Romantic movement: in its love of beautiful sound, its emphasis on program music, its tone painting and nature worship, its addiction to lyricism; its striving to unite music, painting, and poetry; and its emphasis on mood and atmosphere. In effect, the Impressionists substituted a thoroughly French brand of Romanticism for the Austro-German variety.

Claude Debussy: His Life and Music

> *"I love music passionately. And because I love it I try to free it from barren traditions that stifle it. It is a free art gushing forth, an open-air art boundless as the elements, the wind, the sky, the sea. It must never be shut in and become an academic art."*

Claude Debussy

The most important French composer of the early twentieth century, Claude Debussy (1862–1918) was born near Paris in the town of St. Germain-en-Laye, where his parents kept a china shop. He entered the Paris Conservatoire when he was eleven. Within a few years he shocked his professors with bizarre harmonies that defied the sacred rules. "What rules then do you observe?" inquired one of his teachers. "None—only my own pleasure!" "That's all very well," retorted the professor, "provided you're a genius." It became increasingly apparent that the daring young man was.

He was twenty-two when his cantata *L'enfant prodigue* (The Prodigal

Musical Impressionism

1. Whole-tone scale (beginning on C)

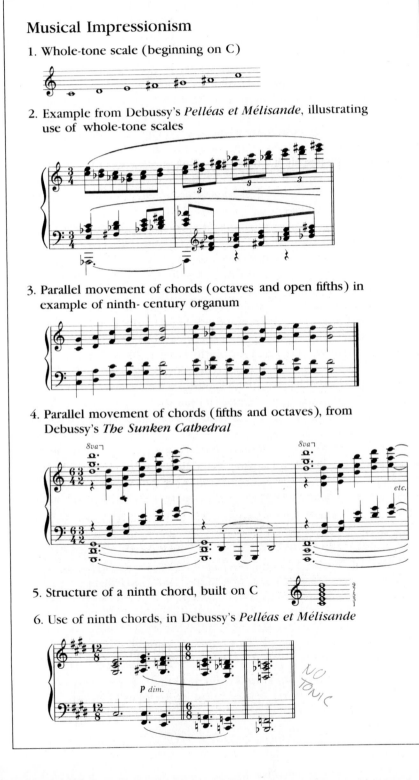

2. Example from Debussy's *Pelléas et Mélisande*, illustrating use of whole-tone scales

3. Parallel movement of chords (octaves and open fifths) in example of ninth- century organum

4. Parallel movement of chords (fifths and octaves), from Debussy's *The Sunken Cathedral*

5. Structure of a ninth chord, built on C

6. Use of ninth chords, in Debussy's *Pelléas et Mélisande*

Early years   Son) won the Prix de Rome. Like Berlioz before him, he looked upon his stay in the Italian capital as a dreary exile from the boulevards and cafés that made up his world. Already he discerned his future bent. "The music I desire," he wrote a friend, "must be supple enough to adapt itself to the lyrical effusions of the soul and the fantasy of dreams."

The 1890s, the most productive decade of Debussy's career, culminated in the writing of *Pelléas et Mélisande*. Based on the symbolist drama by the Belgian poet Maurice Maeterlinck, this opera occupied him for the better part of ten years. He continued to revise the score up to the opening night, which took place on April 30, 1902, at the Opéra-Comique. *Pelléas* was attacked as being decadent, precious, lacking in melody, form, and substance. Nevertheless, its quiet intensity and subtlety of nuance made a profound impression upon the musical intelligentsia. It caught on and embarked on an international career.

After *Pelléas* Debussy was famous. He appeared in the capitals of Europe as conductor of his works and wrote the articles that established his reputation as one of the wittiest critics of his time. In the first years of the century he exhausted the Impressionist vein and found his way to a new and tightly controlled idiom, a kind of distillation of Impressionism.

Later years   His energies sapped by the ravages of cancer, he worked on with remarkable fortitude. The outbreak of war in 1914 rendered him for a time incapable of all interest in music. France, he felt, "can neither laugh nor weep while so many of our men heroically face death." After a year of silence he realized that he must contribute to the struggle in the only way he could, "by creating to the best of my ability a little of that beauty which the enemy is attacking with such fury." His last letters speak of his "life of waiting— my waiting-room existence, I might call it—for I am a poor traveler waiting for a train that will never come any more."

Debussy died in March 1918 during the bombardment of Paris. The funeral procession made its way through deserted streets as the shells of the German guns ripped into his beloved city. It was just eight months before the victory of the nation whose culture found in him one of its most distinguished representatives.

Principal Works

Orchestral music, including *Prélude à "L'après-midi d'un faune"* (Prelude to "The Afternoon of a Faun," 1894), Nocturnes (1899), *La mer* (The Sea, 1905), *Images* (1912), incidental music

Dramatic works, including the opera *Pelléas et Mélisande* (1902) and the ballet *Jeux* (Games, 1913)

Chamber music, including a string quartet (1893) and various sonatas (cello, 1915; violin, 1917; flute, viola, and harp, 1915)

Piano music, including *Pour le piano* (Suite, For the Piano, 1901), *Estampes* (1903), and 2 books of Préludes (1909–10, 1912–13)

Songs and choral music, including cantatas

For Debussy, as for Monet and Verlaine, art was primarily a sensuous experience. The epic themes of Romanticism were distasteful to his temperament both as man and artist. "French music," he declared, "is clearness, elegance, simple and natural declamation. French music aims first of all to give pleasure."

Upholding the genius of his race, he turned against the grand form that was the supreme achievement of the Germans. Exposition-Development-Restatement he regarded as an outmoded formula. At a concert he whispered to a friend, "Let's go—he's beginning to develop!" But the Viennese sonata-cycle was not the only form alien to the Gallic spirit. A greater threat was posed by the Wagnerian music drama, which at that time attracted the intellectuals of France. The French, he points out, are too easily influenced by the "tedious and ponderous Teuton." Wagner's grandiose *Ring* he found especially tedious. "The idea of spreading one drama over four evenings! Is this admissible, especially when in these four evenings you always hear the same thing? . . . My God! how unbearable these people in skins and helmets become by the fourth night." In the end, however, he paid moving tribute to the master whose fascination he had had to shake off before he could find his own way. Wagner "can never quite die," he writes, and calls him "a beautiful sunset that was mistaken for a dawn."

From the Romantic exuberance that left nothing unsaid Debussy sought refuge in an art of indirection, subtle and discreet. He substituted for the sonata structure those short flexible forms that he handled with such distinction. Mood pieces, they evoked the favorite images of Impressionist painting: gardens in the rain, sunlight through the leaves, clouds, moonlight, sea, mist.

Debussy worked slowly, and his fame rests on a comparatively small output; his opera, *Pelléas et Mélisande*, is viewed by many as his greatest achievement. Among the orchestral compositions the *Prelude to "The Afternoon of a Faun"* is firmly established in public favor, as are the three Nocturnes (*Clouds, Festivals, Sirens*) and *La mer*. His handling of the orchestra has the French sensibility. He causes individual instruments to stand out against the mass. In his scores the lines are widely spaced, the texture light and airy.

Orchestral works

One of the important piano composers, he created a distinctive new style of writing for the instrument. The widely spaced chords with their parallel successions of seconds, fourths, and fifths create a sonorous halo. He exploits the resources of the instrument with infinite finesse—the contrast of low and high registers, the blending of sonorities through the use of pedal, the clash of overtones. His piano pieces form an essential part of the modern repertory. Among the best known are *Clair de lune* (Moonlight), the most popular piece he ever wrote; *Evening in Granada, Reflections in the Water*, and *The Sunken Cathedral*.

Piano pieces

Debussy was one of the most influential among the group of composers who established the French song as a national art form independent of the Lied. His settings of Baudelaire, Verlaine, and Mallarmé—to mention three poets for whom he had a particular fondness—are marked by exquisite

Vocal music

Chamber music   refinement. In chamber music he achieved an unqualified success with his String Quartet in G minor. The three sonatas of his last years—for cello and piano; flute, viola, and harp; violin and piano—reveal him as moving toward a more abstract, more concentrated style.

Debussy: Prelude to "The Afternoon of a Faun"

Debussy's best-known orchestral work was inspired by a pastoral of Stéphane Mallarmé that evokes the landscape of pagan antiquity. The poem centers on the mythological creature of the forest, half man, half goat. The faun, "a simple sensuous passionate being," in Edmund Gosse's phrase, awakes in the woods and tries to remember. Was he visited by three lovely nymphs or was this but a dream? He will never know. The sun is warm, the earth fragrant. He curls himself up and falls into a wine-drugged sleep.

The piece opens with a flute solo in the velvety lower register. The melody glides along the chromatic scale, narrow in range, languorous. (See Listening Guide 41 for themes and an excerpt from the poem.) Glissandos on the harp usher in a brief dialogue of the horns. Of these sounds it may be said that their like had never been heard before.

The work is in sections that follow the familiar pattern of statement-departure-return. Yet the movement is fluid, rhapsodic. Almost every fragment of melody is repeated forthwith, a trait that the composer carries to the length of mannerism. Characteristic is the relaxed rhythm which flows across the barline in a continuous stream. By weakening and even wiping out the accent Debussy achieved that dreamlike fluidity which is a prime trait of Impressionist music.

A more decisive motive emerges, marked *en animant* (growing lively). The third theme is marked *même movement et très soutenu* (same tempo and very sustained). It is an ardent melody that carries the composition to

A contemporary photograph of the legendary dancers Vaclav Nijinsky and Tamara Karsavina as they appeared in the ballet L'après-midi d'un faune *in Paris, 1912.*

an emotional crest. The first melody returns in an altered guise. At the close, antique cymbals are heard, pianissimo. (*Antique cymbals* are small disks of brass, held by the player one in each hand; the rims are struck together gently and allowed to vibrate.) "Blue" chords sound on the muted horns and violins, infinitely remote. The work dissolves in silence. It takes nine minutes to play. Rarely has so much been said so briefly.

Listening Guide 41

7A/4 II/3/14

NYMPHS ARE FEMALE COUNTER PART OF A FAUN

DEBUSSY: *Prelude to "The Afternoon of a Faun"* *poem published in 1886*

Date: 1894

½ GOAT ½ MAN

Genre: Orchestral tone poem

Orchestra: Strings, with two harps, flute, oboes, English horn, clarinets, French horns, and antique cymbals

Basis: Symbolist poem by Stéphane Mallarmé

Form: Free ternary (**A-B-A′**)

Style: Impressionistic, interest in timbre; subtle, floating rhythms, free form

Opening of poem

Ces nymphes, je les veux perpétuer.
    Si clair,
Leur incarnat léger, qu'il voltige dans l'air
Assoupi de sommeils touffus.
    Amais-je un rêve?
Mon doute, amas de nuit ancienne, s'achève

En maint rameau subtil, qui, de meuré les vrais
Bois mèmes, prouve, hélas! que bien seul je
    m'offrais
Pour triomphe la faute idéale de roses

Réfléchissons . . . ou si les femmes dont tu
    gloses
Figurent un souhait de tes sens fabuleux!

These nymphs I would perpetuate.
    So light
their gossamer embodiment, floating on the air
inert with heavy slumber.
    Was it a dream I loved?
My doubting harvest of the bygone night,
    concludes
in countless tiny branches; together remaining
a whole forest they prove, alas, that since I am
    alone,
my fancied triumph was but the ideal
    imperfection of roses
let us reflect . . . or suppose those women that
    you idolize
were but imaginings of your fantastic lust!

A SECTION

Time		
14 0:00	Opening chromatic melody in flute; passes, from one instrument to another, accompanied by muted strings and vague beat	*Très modere*
15 3:20	New theme, more animated rhythmically, in solo oboe, builds in crescendo	*Solo*

B SECTION

16 4:32	Contrasting theme in woodwinds, then strings, with syncopated rhythms, builds to climax	

A′ SECTION

17 6:10	Abridged return, in varied setting

67

Ravel and
Post-Impressionism

"I did my work slowly, drop by drop. I tore it out of me by pieces."

Maurice Ravel (1875–1937) stands to Debussy somewhat as Matisse does to Monet: he was a post-Impressionist. His instinctive need for order and clarity of organization impelled him to return—as did the painter—to basic conceptions of form. (See illustrations on pages 5 and 197.) Thus, his art unfolded between the twin goals of Impressionism and neo-Classicism.

His Life and Music

Maurice Ravel

Ravel was born in Ciboure, near Saint-Jean-de-Luz, in the Basses-Pyrénées region at the southwestern tip of France. The family moved to Paris shortly after Maurice was born. His father, a mining engineer who had aspired to be a musician, was sympathetic to the son's artistic proclivities. Maurice entered the Conservatoire when he was fourteen, and remained there for sixteen years—an unusually long apprenticeship.

Early years

Ravel's artistic development was greatly stimulated by his friendship with a group of avant-garde poets, painters, and musicians who believed in his gifts long before those were recognized by the world at large. Youthful enthusiasts, they called themselves the "Apaches." In this rarefied atmosphere the young composer found the necessary intellectual companionship. Ravel's career followed the same course, more or less, as that of almost all the leaders of the modern movement in art. At first his music was hissed by the multitude and cried down by the critics. Only a few discerned the special quality of his work, but their number steadily grew. Ultimately the tide turned, and he found himself famous.

In the years after the First World War Ravel came into his own. He was acknowledged to be the foremost composer of France and was much in demand to conduct his works throughout Europe. In 1928 he was invited to tour the United States. Before he would consider the offer he had to be assured of a steady supply of his favorite French wines and cigarettes. Ravel and America took to one another, although he tired first. "I am seeing magnificent cities, enchanting country," he wrote home, "but the triumphs are fatiguing. Besides, I was dying of hunger."

American trip

Toward the end of his life Ravel was tormented by restlessness and insomnia. He sought surcease in the hectic atmosphere of the Parisian nightclubs, where he would listen for hours to American jazz. As he approached sixty, he fell victim to a rare brain disease that left his faculties unimpaired but attacked the centers of speech and motor coordination. It gradually became impossible for him to read notes, to remember tunes, or to write.

Last years

414

Once, after a performance of *Daphnis et Chloé*, he began to weep, exclaiming: "I have still so much music in my head!" His companion tried to comfort him by pointing out that he had finished his work. "I have said nothing," he replied in anguish. "I have still everything to say."

So as not to watch himself "go piece by piece," as he put it, he decided to submit to a dangerous operation. This was performed toward the end of 1937. He never regained consciousness.

Like Debussy, Ravel was so thoroughly French that he did not need to aspire to a conscious nationalism. He was a national artist to the very core of his being. He was drawn, along with Debussy, to the images that fascinated the Impressionist painters: daybreak, the sea, the interplay of water and light. He too exploited Spanish dance rhythms, worshiped the old French harpsichordists, and was attracted to the scales of Medieval as well as exotic music.

Comparison with Debussy

But the differences between him and Debussy were as pronounced as the similarities. His music has an enameled brightness that contrasts with the twilight softness of Debussy's. His rhythms are more incisive and have a drive that Debussy rarely strives for. His sense of key is firmer, his harmony is more dissonant, and his melodies are broader in span. His orchestration derives, as Debussy's did not, from the nineteenth-century masters: he stands in the line of descent from Berlioz, Rimsky-Korsakov, and Richard Strauss. Where Debussy aimed to "decongest" sound, Ravel handled the huge orchestra of the post-Romantic period with brilliant virtuosity. And he was drawn to the Classical forms much earlier in his career than Debussy, who turned to them only toward the end.

One of the outstanding piano composers of the twentieth century, Ravel extended the heritage of Liszt even as Debussy became the disciple of Chopin.

Principal Works

Orchestral music, including *Rapsodie espagnole* (Spanish Rhapsody, 1908), *Pavane pour une infante défunte* (Pavane for a Dead Princess, 1910), *Le tombeau de Couperin* (1919), Piano Concerto for the Left Hand (1930), Piano Concerto in G (1931)

Ballets, including *Ma mère l'oye* (Mother Goose, 1911), *Daphnis et Chloé* (1912), *La valse* (1920), *Boléro* (1928)

2 operas: *L'heure espagnole* (The Spanish Hour, 1911) and *L'enfant et les sortilèges* (The Child and the Spells, 1925)

Chamber music, including a string quartet (1903) and sonatas (violin and violin/cello)

Piano music, including *Pavane pour une infante défunte* (1908), *Jeux d'eau* (Water Games, 1901), *Gaspard de le nuit* (Gaspard of the Night, 1908), *Ma mère d'oye* (four-hands, 1910, later orchestrated), *Le tombeau de Couperin* (1917, later orchestrated)

Songs, with instruments, including *Schéhérazade* (1903); songs with piano

The French art song found in him one of its masters. But it was through his orchestral works that he won the international public. The *Spanish Rhapsody*, *Mother Goose*, the two concert suites from the ballet *Daphnis et Chloé*, *La Valse*, and *Boléro* have remained among the most frequently performed works of our century. Widely admired too are the Classically oriented Piano Concerto in G and the dramatic Concerto for the Left Hand, a masterpiece.

Ravel, like Debussy, became immensely popular in the United States. His harmonies and orchestration exercised a particular attraction for jazz arrangers and Hollywood composers. As a result, his idiom—somewhat altered, to be sure—became part of the daily listening experience of millions of Americans.

Ravel: Le tombeau de Couperin

A *tombeau*—the French word for tomb—was a Baroque form consisting of a group of instrumental pieces that commemorated the death of someone; hence it was a gesture of homage. Ravel's piece represents a twentieth-century revival of the form. It was meant as a tribute to the great French Baroque harpsichord composer François Couperin, and in a larger sense to the eighteenth-century tradition of French art that he so ably represented. It thus combined a nationalist gesture with the revival of old forms dear to the neo-Classicist.

Ravel, like Debussy, was profoundly shaken by the outbreak of war in 1914. After making a vain attempt to join the army—he was almost forty—he was accepted in the air force, became a driver in the motor transport, and was sent to the Verdun sector. After a year of service he was discharged because of ill health and returned to Paris just before the death of his mother. In a mood of severe depression he resumed his work with *Le tombeau de Couperin*, his grief transformed into a set of six serenely graceful dance pieces for piano, each dedicated to the memory of a fallen comrade. He completed the work in 1917. *Le tombeau* was one of several piano pieces of his that he subsequently orchestrated.

S4A/4

S4/12

The final number of *Le tombeau*, the Rigaudon, is a lively dance in duple meter that was popular at the French court under Louis XIV and figured as well in the ballets and keyboard suites of Lully, Rameau, and their contemporaries. Ravel's Rigaudon is a stylized dance movement in which the duple meter of the old form is retained, but with irregular phrasing not typical of Baroque dance pieces. It is in three-part form (**A-B-A**), with a slow middle section, and does not repeat each section as Baroque dance forms usually did.

Ravel held up an ideal of sonorous beauty that incarnated the sensibility, elegance, and esprit of French art. And he was one of the composers who opened wide the door to the twentieth century.

The Early Twentieth Century

68

Main Currents in Early Twentieth-Century Music

"The entire history of modern music may be said to be a history of the gradual pull-away from the German musical tradition of the past century."—AARON COPLAND

The Reaction Against Romanticism

As the quotation from Aaron Copland makes clear, the first quarter of the twentieth century was impelled before all else to throw off the oppressive heritage of the nineteenth. The new generation of composers had to fight not only the Romantic past but the Romanticism in themselves.

Non-Western Influences

The new attitudes took shape just before the First World War. European art sought to escape its overrefinement. There was a desire to capture the spontaneity, the freedom from inhibition that was supposed to characterize primitive life. Music turned to the dynamism of non-Western rhythm even as the fine arts discovered the abstraction of African sculpture and the monumental simplicity that shaped the exotic paintings of Paul Gauguin and Henri Rousseau. Composers ranged from Africa to Asia and Eastern Europe in their search for fresh rhythmic concepts. Out of the unspoiled, vigorous

The powerful abstraction of African sculpture helped European art escape its overrefinement. A bronze musician from Nigeria. (Photograph by Lee Boltin)

The transition from nineteenth-century Romanticism to twentieth-century fantasy was epitomized in the exotic painting by **Henri Rousseau** (*1844–1910*), *entitled* The Repast of the Lion. (Metropolitan Museum of Art. Bequest of Sam. A. Lewisohn, 1951)

folk music in these areas came powerful rhythms of an elemental fury that tapped fresh sources of feeling and imagination, as in Bartók's *Allegro barbaro* (1911), Stravinsky's *The Rite of Spring* (1913), and Prokofiev's *Scythian Suite* (1914). We will take up this merger of styles in more detail in a later chapter.

Expressionism

Expressionist values

Expressionism was the German answer to French Impressionism. Whereas the French genius rejoiced in luminous impressions of the outer world, the Germanic temperament preferred digging down to the subterranean regions of the soul. Through the symbolism of dreams expressionism released the primitive impulses suppressed by the intellect.

As with Impressionism, the impulse for the movement came from painting. Wassily Kandinsky (1866–1944), Paul Klee (1879–1940), Oskar Kokoschka (1886–1980), and Franz Marc (1880–1916) influenced Schoenberg and his disciples even as the Impressionist painters influenced Debussy. The distorted images of their canvases issued from the realm of the unconscious— hallucinated visions that defied conventional notions of beauty in order to achieve the most powerful expression of the artist's inner self.

Expressionism in music triumphed first in the central European area that lies within the orbit of Germanic culture. The movement reached its peak in the period of the Weimar Republic. It is familiar to Americans through the paintings of Kandinsky and Klee, the writings of Franz Kafka (1883–1924), the dancing of Mary Wigman (made familiar in the United States through the art of Martha Graham), the acting of Conrad Veidt, and through such films as *The Cabinet of Dr. Caligari*. Expressionist tendencies entered European opera through Richard Strauss's *Salome* and *Elektra*, and reached their full tide in the dramatic works of Schoenberg and his disciple Alban Berg. Within the orbit of our own culture, Expressionistic elements are to be discerned in the work of such dissimilar artists as James Joyce, William Faulkner, and Tennessee Williams.

The musical language of Expressionism favored a hyperexpressive harmonic language linked to inordinately wide leaps in the melody and to the use of instruments in their extreme registers. In its preoccupation with states of soul, Expressionist music sought ever more powerful means of communicating emotion, and soon reached the boundaries of what was possible within the major-minor system. Inevitably, it had to push beyond.

The New Classicism

One way of rejecting the nineteenth century was to return to the eighteenth. The movement "back to Bach" assumed impressive proportions in the early

The images on the canvases of Expressionist painters issued from the realm of the unconscious: hallucinated visions that defied the traditional notions of beauty in order to express the artist's inner self. **Wassily Kandinsky** (*1886–1944*), Painting No. 199 (The Museum of Modern Art, New York. Nelson A. Rockefeller Fund)

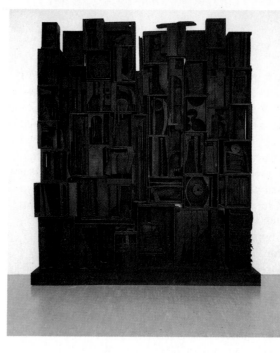

Constructivists, like **Louise Nevelson** (*1900–89*), *exalt the virtues of order, balance, and proportion, as exemplified in her* Sky Cathedral. (The Museum of Modern Art, New York. Gift of Mr. and Mrs. Ben Mildwoff)

1920s. There was no question here of duplicating the accents of the Baroque master; the slogan implied rather a revival of certain principles that appeared to have been best understood in his time. Instead of worshiping at the shrine of Beethoven and Wagner, as the Romantics had done, composers began to emulate the great musicians of the eighteenth century—Bach, Handel, Scarlatti, Couperin, Vivaldi—and the detached, objective style that was supposed to characterize their music.

Each age recreates the past in its own image. To the nineteenth century, Bach was a visionary and mystic. For the twentieth he became the model for an amiable counterpoint that jogged along as crisply as ever did a piece of dinner music for a German prince. Basic to the new aesthetic was the notion that the composer's function is not to express emotions but to manipulate abstract combinations of sound. This view found its spokesman in Igor Stravinsky. "I evoke neither human joy nor human sadness," he declared. "I move toward a greater abstraction." Music, he maintained, "is given to us with the sole purpose of establishing an order among things." This order, to be realized, requires a construction. "Once the construction is made and the order achieved, everything is said." A similar goal animated constructivist painters such as Mondrian and Léger, and Louise Nevelson, one of the great sculptors of our time.

Absolute music　　Neoclassicism tried to rid the art of the story-and-picture meanings with which the nineteenth century had endowed it. The new Classicists turned away from the symphonic poem and the Romantic attempt to bring music closer to poetry and painting; they preferred absolute to program music. They focused attention on craftsmanship, elegance, and taste, and concentrated on technique rather than content. Future generations will find it significant that in a period of social, political, and artistic upheaval there should have been affirmed so positively the Classical virtues of objectivity, poise, and control.

69

New Elements of Musical Style

*"Music is now so foolish that I am amazed. Everything that is wrong
is permitted, and no attention is paid to what the old generation
wrote as composition."*—SAMUEL SCHEIDT *(1651)*

The Revitalization of Rhythm

Europe after the First World War found an outlet for its shattered nerves
in athletics and sports. The body itself came to be viewed as a rhythmic
machine. Thus ballet came to provide an important platform for the new
music, and some of the foremost composers of the twentieth century won
success in this field.

This physicality—along with primitivism, the hectic pace of urban life,
the surge and clatter of a highly industrialized society—found a musical
outlet in increasingly complex rhythms. Twentieth-century music turned
away from the standard patterns of duple, triple, or quadruple meter. Composers explored the possibilities of nonsymmetrical patterns based on odd
numbers: five, seven, eleven, thirteen beats to the measure.

In nineteenth-century music a single meter customarily prevailed through
an entire movement or section. Now the metrical flow shifted constantly,
sometimes with each measure, as we shall see in Stravinsky's *The Rite of
Spring*. Formerly, music presented to the ear one rhythmic pattern at a time,
sometimes two. Now composers turned to *polyrhythm*—the use of several
rhythmic patterns simultaneously. As a result of these innovations, Western
music achieved something of the complexity and suppleness of Asiatic and
African rhythms.

Polyrhythm

The new generation of composers preferred freer rhythms that are flexible
in the highest degree, of an almost physical power and drive. Indeed, the
revitalization of rhythm is one of the major achievements of early twentieth-
century music.

Music has also been vitalized through materials drawn from popular styles.
The ragtime piano style, with its sprightly syncopations, traveled across the
Atlantic to Europe. The rhythmic freedom of jazz captured the ears of many
composers, who strove to achieve something of the spontaneity of the popular style. (We will look into the origins of jazz and its influence on other
styles in a later chapter.)

The New Melody

Rhythm was not the only element in which symmetrical structure was abandoned. Melody was affected, too. Twentieth-century composers do not develop the neatly balanced repetitions that prevailed formerly. Their ideal is
a direct forward-driving melody from which all nonessentials have been cut

Instrumental melody

away. They assume a quicker perception on the part of the hearer than did composers in the past.

Nineteenth-century melody was fundamentally vocal in character; composers tried to make the instruments "sing." Twentieth-century melody is neither unvocal nor antivocal; it is simply not conceived in relation to the voice. It abounds in wide leaps and dissonant intervals. Besides, much twentieth century music lacks a melodic orientation. Sometimes no melody is to be found because the composer had other goals in mind.

Twentieth-century composers have enormously expanded our notion of what is a melody. As a result, many a pattern is accepted as a melody today that would hardly have been considered one a century ago.

The New Harmony

Polychords and polyharmony

No single factor sets off the music of our time more decisively from that of the past than the new conceptions of harmony that emerged in the twentieth century. The triads of traditional harmony, we saw, were formed by combining three tones, on every other degree of the scale, or in thirds: 1–3–5 (for example, C–E–G), 2–4–6 (D–F–A), and so on. Traditional harmony also employed four-note combinations, with another third piled on top of the triad, known as *seventh chords* (steps 1–3–5–7), and, as we saw in the music of the Impressionists, five-note combinations known as *ninth chords* (steps 1–3–5–7–9). Twentieth-century composers added more "stories" to such chords, forming highly dissonant combinations of six and seven tones. The emergence of these complex "skyscraper" chords brought greater tension to music than had existed before, and allowed the composer to play two or more streams of harmony against each other, creating *polyharmony.*

Quartal harmony

To some composers, the interval of the third was associated with the music of the past. To free themselves from the sound of the eighteenth and nineteenth centuries, they cast about for new methods of chord construction; for example, they began to base chords on the interval of the fourth. This turning from *tertial* to *quartal harmony* constitutes one of the important differences between nineteenth- and twentieth-century music.

New Conceptions of Tonality

The new sounds of twentieth-century music necessarily burst the confines of traditional tonality and called for new means of organization, extending or replacing the major-minor system. These approaches, in general, followed four principal paths—expanded tonality, polytonality, atonality, and twelve-tone music.

Expanded Tonality

The widespread use of chromatic harmony in the late nineteenth century led, in the early twentieth century, to the free use of all twelve tones around a center. Although this approach retained the basic principle of traditional tonality—gravitation to the tonic—it wiped out the distinction between diatonic and chromatic and between major and minor modes.

In general, a key no longer defined an area in musical space as strongly as it had, and the shift from one key center to another was made with a speed that put to shame the most exuberant modulations of the Wagner era. Transitional passages were often dispensed with; one tonality was simply displaced by another, in a way that kept both the music and the listener on the move.

We will see that the expansion of tonality was encouraged by an increased interest in the music of non-Western cultures as well as in the Medieval church modes.

Polytonality

From the development of polyharmony, which we discussed earlier, a further step followed logically: to heighten the contrast of two keys by presenting them simultaneously. Confronting the ear with two keys at the same time meant a radical departure from the basic principle of traditional harmony, a single central key. *Polytonality*—the use of two or more keys together— came to the fore in the music of Stravinsky and Milhaud, whence it entered the vocabulary of the age. Toward the end of a piece, one key was generally permitted to assert itself over the others. In this way the impression was restored of orderly progression toward a central point.

Atonality

The concept of total abandonment of tonality is associated with the composer Arnold Schoenberg, whom we shall discuss later. He advocated doing away with the tonic by treating the twelve tones as of equal importance.

The music of Schoenberg and his school came to be known as *atonal*. Atonality was much more of an innovation than polytonality, for it entirely rejected the framework of key. Consonance, according to Schoenberg, was no longer capable of making an impression; atonal music moved from one level of dissonance to another, functioning always at maximum tension, without areas of relaxation. Dissonance resolving to consonance had been, symbolically, an optimistic act, affirming the triumph of rest over tension, of order over chaos. Atonal music, significantly, appeared at a time in European culture when belief in that triumph was sorely shaken.

The Twelve-Tone Method

Having accepted the necessity of moving beyond the existing tonal system, Schoenberg sought a unifying principle that would take the place of the system of tonality. He found this in a strict technique that he had worked out by the early 1920s. He named it "the method of composing with twelve tones"—that is, with twelve equal tones, no one of which is more important than any other. Each composition that uses Schoenberg's method is based

Serialism

The tone row   on an arrangement of the twelve chromatic tones called a *tone row*. This row is the unifying idea for that particular composition, and serves as the source of all the musical events that take place in it. (The term *dodecaphonic*, the Greek equivalent of *twelve-tone*, is sometimes also used for Schoenberg's method, while *serial music*, an allusion to the series of twelve tones, has come to refer, in more recent decades, to postwar extensions of the technique.)

A tone row thus establishes a series of pitches from which a composer builds themes, harmonies, and counterpoints. Schoenberg provided flexibility and variety in this seemingly confining system through alternative forms of the tone row, based on its *transposition* (beginning on other notes),
Forms of the row   its *inversion* (with the intervals moving in the opposite direction), its *retrograde* (or pitches in reverse order), or even the combination of the last two, in *retrograde inversion*. (You will remember we saw these same techniques or contrapuntal devices in earlier music, especially in the Baroque fugue.)

The adherents of the twelve-tone method gained worldwide influence in the years following the Second World War. In the 1950s and '60s, serial thinking emerged as the most advanced line of thought in musical aesthetics, and profoundly influenced the course of contemporary music.

The Emancipation of Dissonance

The history of music, we have seen, has been the history of a steadily increasing tolerance on the part of listeners. Throughout this long evolution, one factor remained constant: a clear distinction was drawn between dissonance, the element of tension, and consonance, the element of rest. Consonance was the norm, dissonance the temporary disturbance. In many contemporary works, however, tension becomes the norm. Therefore, a dissonance can serve even as a final cadence, provided it is less dissonant than the chord that came before. In relation to the greater dissonance, it is judged to be consonant.

Twentieth-century composers emancipated the dissonance by freeing it from the obligation to resolve to consonance. Their music taught listeners to accept tone combinations whose like had never been heard before.

Texture: Dissonant Counterpoint

The nineteenth century was preoccupied with harmony; the early twentieth emphasized counterpoint. The new style swept away both the Romantic cloudburst and Impressionistic haze. In their stead was installed an airy linear texture that fit the Neoclassical ideal of craftsmanship, order, and detachment.

Consonance unites the constituent tones of harmony or counterpoint; dissonance separates them and makes them stand out against each other. Composers began to use dissonance to set off one line against another. Instead of basing their counterpoint on the euphonious intervals of the third and sixth, they turned to astringent seconds and sevenths. Or the independence of the voices might be heightened by putting them in different keys. Thus came into being a linear texture based on dissonant counterpoint.

Orchestration

The rich sonorities of nineteenth-century orchestration were alien to the temper of the 1920s and '30s. The trend was toward a smaller orchestra and a leaner sound, one that was hard, bright, sober.

The decisive factor in the handling of the orchestra was the change to a linear texture. Color came to be used in the new music not so much for atmosphere or enchantment as for bringing out the lines of counterpoint and of form. Whereas the nineteenth-century orchestrator made his colors swim together, the Neoclassicist desired each to stand out against the mass. Instruments were used in their unusual registers. The emotional crescendo and diminuendo of Romantic music gave way to even levels of soft or loud. This less expressive scheme revived the solid areas of light and shade of the age of Bach. The string section lost its traditional role as the heart of the orchestra. Its tone was felt to be too personal. Attention was focused on the more objective winds. There was a movement away from brilliancy of sound. The darker instruments came to the fore—viola, bassoon, trombone. The emphasis on rhythm brought the percussion group into greater prominence than ever before and the piano, which in the Romantic era was preeminently a solo instrument, found a place for itself in the orchestral ensemble.

New Conceptions of Form

The first quarter of the century saw the final expansion of traditional form in the gigantic symphonies of Mahler and Strauss. What had been a concise, twenty-five-minute form in the hands of Haydn and Mozart now took over an hour and a half to play. Music could hardly go farther in this direction. A reaction took shape as composers began to move toward the Classical ideals of tight organization and succinctness.

The Neoclassicists took over from their Romantic predecessors the large forms of absolute music—symphony and concerto, solo sonata, string quartet, and other types of chamber music—which they adapted to their own aesthetic. Their attitude was summed up in Prokofiev's observation, "I want nothing better than sonata form, which contains everything necessary for my needs." In addition, they revived a number of older forms: toccata, fugue, passacaglia and chaconne, concerto grosso, theme and variations, suite, and the social forms of the Viennese period—divertimento and serenade.

The tendency to elevate formal above expressive values is known as *formalism*. The New Classicism, like the old, strove for purity of line and proportion. Characteristic of this goal was Stravinsky's emphasis on formal beauty rather than emotional expression: "One could not better define the sensation produced by music than by saying that it is identical with that evoked by contemplating the interplay of architectural forms. Goethe thoroughly understood this when he called architecture frozen music."

Formalism

70

Igor Stravinsky

"I hold that it was a mistake to consider me a revolutionary. If one only need break habit in order to be labeled a revolutionary, then every artist who has something to say and who in order to say it steps outside the bounds of established convention could be considered revolutionary."

Igor Stravinsky

It is granted to certain artists to embody the most significant impulses of their time and to affect its artistic life in the most powerful fashion. Such an artist was Igor Stravinsky (1882–1971), the Russian composer who for half a century gave impetus to the main currents in twentieth-century music.

His Life

Stravinsky was born in Oranienbaum, a summer resort not far from St. Petersburg (now Leningrad), where his parents lived. He grew up in a musical environment; his father was the leading bass at the Imperial Opera. Although he was taught to play the piano, his musical education was kept on the amateur level; his parents wanted him to study law. He matriculated at the University of St. Petersburg and embarked on a legal career, meanwhile continuing his musical studies. At twenty he submitted his work to Rimsky-Korsakov, with whom he subsequently worked for three years.

Success came early to Stravinsky. His music attracted the notice of Serge Diaghilev, the legendary impresario of the Paris-based Russian Ballet, who commissioned Stravinsky to write the score for *The Firebird*, which was produced in 1910. Stravinsky was twenty-eight when he arrived in Paris to attend the rehearsals. Diaghilev pointed him out to the ballerina Tamara Karsavina with the words, "Mark him well—he is a man on the eve of fame."

Diaghilev

The Firebird was followed a year later by *Petrushka*. Presented with Nijinsky and Karsavina in the leading roles, this production secured Stravinsky's position in the forefront of the modern movement in art. In the spring of 1913 was presented the third and most spectacular of the ballets Stravinsky wrote for Diaghilev, *The Rite of Spring*. The opening night was one of the most scandalous in modern musical history; the revolutionary score touched off a near riot. People hooted, screamed, slapped each other, and were convinced that what they were hearing "constituted a blasphemous attempt to destroy music as an art." A year later the composer was vindicated when the work, presented at a symphony concert under Pierre Monteux, was received with enthusiasm and established itself as a masterpiece of the new music.

The outbreak of war in 1914 brought to an end the whole way of life on which Diaghilev's sumptuous dance spectacles depended. Stravinsky, with his wife and children, took refuge in Switzerland, their home for the next six years. The difficulty of assembling large bodies of performers during the war worked hand in hand with his inner evolution as an artist: he moved away from the grand scale of the first three ballets to works more intimate in spirit and modest in dimension.

The Russian Revolution had severed Stravinsky's ties with his homeland. In 1920 he settled in France, where he remained until 1939. During these years Stravinsky concertized extensively throughout Europe, performing his own music as pianist and conductor. He also paid two visits to the United States. In 1939 he was invited to deliver the Charles Eliot Norton lectures at Harvard University. He was there when the Second World War broke out, *American years* and decided to live in this country. He settled in California, outside Los Angeles, and in 1945 became an American citizen. In his later years, Stravinsky's worldwide concert tours made him the most celebrated figure in twentieth-century music, and his caustically witty books of "conversations" with his disciple Robert Craft are full of musical wisdom and footnotes to history. He died in New York on April 6, 1971.

His Music

Stravinsky showed a continuous development throughout his career. This evolution led from the post-Impressionism of *The Firebird* and the audacities of *The Rite of Spring* to the austerely controlled classicism of his maturity.

Stravinsky, we noted, was a leader in the revitalization of European rhythm. *Early works* His first success was won as a composer of ballet, where rhythm is allied with body movement and expressive gesture. His is a rhythm of unparalleled dynamic power, furious yet controlled. In harmony Stravinsky reacted against the restless chromaticism of the Romantic period, but no matter how daring his harmony, he retained a robust sense of key. Stravinsky's subtle sense of sound makes him one of the great orchestrators. Unmistakably his is that enameled brightness of sonority, and a texture so clear that, as Diaghilev remarked, "One can see through it with one's ears."

The national element predominates in his early works, as in *The Firebird*

Principal Works

Orchestral music, including Symphonies of Wind Instruments (1920), Concerto for Piano and Winds (1924), *Dumbarton Oaks Concerto* (1938), Symphony in C (1940), Symphony in Three Movements (1945), *Ebony Concerto* (1945)

Ballets, including *L'oiseau de feu* (The Firebird, 1910), *Petrushka* (1911), *Le sacre du printemps* (The Rite of Spring, 1913), *Les noces* (The Wedding, 1923), *Agon* (1957)

Operas, including *Oedipus rex* (1927) and *The Rake's Progress* (1951)

Choral music, including *Symphony of Psalms* (1930), *Canticum sacrum* (1955), *Threni* (1958), and *Requiem Canticles* (1966)

Chamber music; piano music (solo and for two pianos); songs

and *Petrushka*, in which he found his personal style. *The Rite of Spring* recreates the rites of pagan Russia. The decade of the First World War saw the turn toward simplification of means. *The Soldier's Tale*, a dance-drama for four characters, is an intimate theater work accompanied by a seven-piece band. The most important work of the years that followed is *The Wedding*, a stylization of a Russian peasant wedding.

Neoclassical period

Stravinsky's Neoclassical period culminated in several major composi-tions. *Oedipus Rex* is an "opera-oratorio"; the text is a translation into Latin of Cocteau's adaptation of the Greek tragedy. The *Symphony of Psalms*, for chorus and orchestra, is regarded by many as the chief work of Stravinsky's maturity; it was composed, according to the composer, "for the glory of God." Equally admired is *The Rake's Progress*, an opera on a libretto by W. H. Auden and Chester Kallman, after Hogarth's celebrated series of en-gravings. Written as the composer was approaching seventy, this radiantly melodious score, which uses the set forms of the Mozartean opera, is the quintessence of Neoclassicism.

Stravinsky, imperturbably pursuing his own growth as an artist, had still another surprise in store for his public. In the works written after he was seventy, he showed himself increasingly receptive to the serial procedures of the twelve-tone style, which in earlier years he had opposed. This pre-occupation came to the fore in a number of works dating from the middle 1950s, of which the most important is the ballet *Agon* and *Threni: Lam-entations of the Prophet Jeremiah*.

Twelve-tone works

Stravinsky: The Rite of Spring

The Rite of Spring—"Scenes of Pagan Russia"—not only embodies the cult of primitivism that so startled its first-night audience; it also sets forth the lineaments of a new tonal language—the percussive use of dissonance, polyrhythms, and polytonality. The work is scored for a large orchestra, including an exceptionally varied percussion group.

Part I

Part I: "The Adoration of the Earth." The Introduction is intended to evoke the birth of spring. A long-limbed melody is introduced by the bassoon, taking on a curious remoteness from the circumstance that it lies in the instrument's uppermost register. (See Listening Guide 42 on page 430.) The awakening of the earth is suggested in the orchestra. On stage, a group of young girls is discovered before the sacred mound, holding a long garland. The Sage appears and leads them toward the mound. The orchestra erupts into a climax, after which the bassoon melody returns.

"Dance of the Youths and Maidens." Dissonant chords in the lower register of the strings exemplify Stravinsky's "elemental pounding"; their percussive quality is heightened by the use of polytonal harmonies. A physical excite-ment attends the dislocation of the accent, which is underlined by syncopated chords hurled out by eight horns. The main theme of the movement, a more endearing melody in folk style, is introduced by the horns.

"Game of Abduction." The youths and maidens on the stage form into two phalanxes which in turn approach and withdraw from one another. Fanfares on the woodwinds and brass add a luminous quality to the sound.

Valentine Hugo's *sketches of the* Danse Sacrale *for the original production of the ballet* Le Sacre du Printemps (*1913*), *choreographed by Nijinsky.*

Listening Guide 42   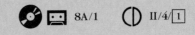 8A/1   II/4/1

STRAVINSKY: *The Rite of Spring*

Date: 1913

Genre: Ballet (also concert work for orchestra)

Basis: Scenes of pagan Russia; use of folksongs

OVERALL STRUCTURE:

PART I: THE ADORATION OF THE EARTH

Introduction
Dance of the Youths and Maidens
Game of Abduction
Spring Rounds
Games of the Rival Tribes
Procession of the Sage
Adoration of the Earth
Dance of the Earth

PART II: THE SACRIFICE

Introduction
Mystical Circle of the Adolescents
Glorification of the Chosen One
Evocation of the Ancestors
Sacrifical Dance of the Chosen One

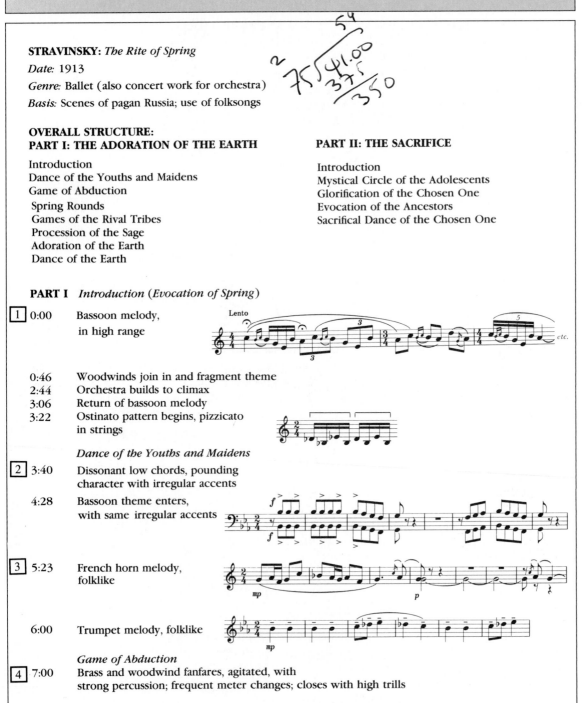

PART I   *Introduction (Evocation of Spring)*

1 0:00   Bassoon melody,
              in high range

0:46   Woodwinds join in and fragment theme
2:44   Orchestra builds to climax
3:06   Return of bassoon melody
3:22   Ostinato pattern begins, pizzicato
           in strings

Dance of the Youths and Maidens

2 3:40   Dissonant low chords, pounding
              character with irregular accents

4:28   Bassoon theme enters,
           with same irregular accents

3 5:23   French horn melody,
              folklike

6:00   Trumpet melody, folklike

Game of Abduction

4 7:00   Brass and woodwind fanfares, agitated, with
              strong percussion; frequent meter changes; closes with high trills

In the numbers that follow, modal harmonies create an archaic atmosphere. Part I ends with the "Dance of the Earth," performed to music of the sheerest physicality.

In Part II, "The Sacrifice," the Sage must choose the Elect One who will be sacrificed to ensure the fertility of the earth. Tension builds steadily through the numbers that follow. In the "Evocation of the Ancestors—Ritual Act of the Old Men," the movement settles down, after a violent opening, to a kind of languorous "blues" that carries a suggestion of swaying bodies and shuffling feet. The climax of the ballet comes with the final number, the "Sacrificial Dance of the Chosen One." The music mounts in fury as the chosen maiden dances until she falls dead. The men in wild excitement bear her body to the foot of the mound. With an ascending run on flutes and piccolos and a fortissimo growl in the orchestra, this vibrant score comes to an end.

Part II

71

Arnold Schoenberg

"I personally hate to be called a revolutionist, which I am not. What I did was neither revolution nor anarchy."

It is worthy of note that, like Stravinsky, the other great innovator of our time, Arnold Schoenberg (1874–1951) disclaimed revolutionary intent. Quite the contrary, his disciples regard him as having brought to its culmination the thousand-year-old tradition of European polyphony.

Arnold Schoenberg

His Life

Schoenberg was born in Vienna. He began to study the violin at the age of eight, and soon afterward made his initial attempts at composing. Having decided to devote his life to music, he left school while in his teens. For a time he earned his living working in a bank, and meanwhile continued to compose, working entirely by himself. Presently he became acquainted with a young musician, Alexander von Zemlinsky, who for a few months gave him lessons in counterpoint. This was the only musical instruction he ever had.

Through Zemlinsky young Schoenberg was introduced to the advanced musical circles of Vienna, which at that time were under the spell of Wagner's *Tristan* and *Parsifal*. In 1899, when he was twenty-five, Schoenberg wrote the string sextet *Transfigured Night*, which he later orchestrated. The following year several of Schoenberg's songs were performed in Vienna and precipitated a scene. "And ever since that day," he once remarked with a smile, "the scandal has never ceased."

Early years

In 1901, after his marriage to Zemlinsky's sister, he moved to Berlin and obtained a post in a theater, conducting operettas and music-hall songs. Schoenberg's early music already displayed certain traits of his later style. A publisher to whom he brought a quartet observed, "You must think that if the second theme is a retrograde inversion of the first theme, that automatically makes it good!"

Return to Vienna

Upon his return to Vienna Schoenberg became active as a teacher and soon gathered about him a band of disciples, of whom the most gifted were Alban Berg and Anton Webern. The devotion of these advanced young musicians sustained him in the fierce battle for recognition that still lay ahead. With each new work Schoenberg moved closer to as bold a step as any artist has ever taken—the rejection of tonality.

The First World War interrupted Schoenberg's creative activity. Although he was past forty, he was called up for military service in the Vienna garrison. He had reached a critical point in his development. There followed a silence of seven years, between 1915 and 1923, during which he clarified his position in his own mind and evolved a set of structural procedures to replace tonality. The goal once set, Schoenberg pursued it with that tenacity of purpose without which no prophet can prevail. His "method of composing with twelve tones" caused great bewilderment in the musical world. All the same, he was now firmly established as a leader of contemporary musical thought. On his fiftieth birthday the chorus of the Vienna Opera performed his cantata *Peace on Earth*, which he had written almost two decades before. The next year he was appointed to succeed Ferruccio Busoni as professor of composition at the Berlin Academy of Arts.

This period in Schoenberg's life ended with the coming to power of Hitler in 1933. Like many Austrian-Jewish intellectuals of his generation, he had grown away from his Jewish origins and ultimately converted to Catholicism. After he left Germany, he found it spiritually necessary to return to the

Move to the United States

Hebrew faith. He arrived in the United States in the fall of 1933. After a short period of teaching in Boston, he joined the faculty of the University of Southern California, and shortly afterward was appointed professor of composition at the University of California in Los Angeles. In 1940 he became an American citizen. He taught until his retirement at the age of seventy, and continued his musical activities until his death in 1951. A seeker after truth until the end, to no one more than to himself could be applied the injunction he had written in the text of his cantata *Jacob's Ladder*: "One must go on without asking what lies before or behind."

His Music

Post-Wagnerian Romanticism

Schoenberg's first period may be described as one of post-Wagnerian Romanticism; he still used key signatures and remained within the boundaries of tonality. The best-known work of this period is *Transfigured Night*, Opus 4. Schoenberg's second period, the atonal-Expressionist, got under way with the Three Piano Pieces, Opus 11, in which he abolished the distinction between consonance and dissonance as well as the sense of a home key.

Atonal Expressionism

Principal Works

Orchestral music, including Five Pieces for Orchestra (1909), *Verklärte Nacht* (Transfigured Night, 1917), Variations for Orchestra (1928), concertos for violin (1936) and piano (1942)

Operas, including *Die glückliche Hand* (The Blessed Hand, 1913), *Moses und Aron* (incomplete, 1932)

Choral music, including *Gurrelieder* (1911), *Die Jacobsleiter* (Jacob's Ladder, 1922), *A Survivor from Warsaw* (1941); smaller choral works, including *Friede auf Erden* (Peace on Earth, 1907)

Chamber music, including 4 string quartets, serenade, wind quintet, string trio

Vocal music, including *Pierrot Lunaire* (1912)

Piano music, including Three Piano Pieces, Op. 11 (1909)

The high points of this period are the Five Pieces for Orchestra, Opus 16, and *Pierrot lunaire*, Opus 21, which we shall discuss.

Schoenberg's third period, that of the twelve-tone method, reached its climax in the Variations for Orchestra, Opus 31, one of his most powerful works. In the fourth and last period of his career—the American phase—he carried the twelve-tone technique to further stages of refinement. Several among the late works present the twelve-tone style in a manner markedly more accessible than earlier pieces, often with tonal implications. Among those are the brilliant Piano Concerto and the cantata *A Survivor from Warsaw*.

Twelve-tone period

American period

Schoenberg was a tireless propagandist for his ideas. Essays and articles flowed from his pen, conveying his views in a trenchant style which, late in life, he transferred from German to English. The following observations are characteristic: "Genius learns only from itself, talent chiefly from others. . . . Creation to an artist should be as natural and inescapable as the growth of apples to an apple tree. . . . The twelve tones will not invent for you. . . . An apostle who does not glow preaches heresy. . . . The laws of nature manifested in a man of genius are but the laws of the future."

Schoenberg: Pierrot lunaire

One of Schoenberg's preoccupations was the attempt to bring spoken word and music as close together as possible. He solved the problem through *Sprechstimme* (spoken voice), a new style in which the vocal melody is spoken rather than sung on exact pitches and in strict rhythm. As Schoenberg explained it, the reciter sounded the written note at first but abandoned it by rising or falling in pitch immediately after. The result was a weird, strangely effective vocal line which he brought to perfection in his most celebrated work, *Pierrot lunaire*.

Sprechstimme

In 1884 the Belgian poet Albert Giraud, a disciple of the Symbolists—he was especially influenced by Verlaine—published a cycle of fifty short poems

Schoenberg conducting a performance of Pierrot lunaire *with soprano Erica Stiedry-Wagner at Town Hall, New York on November 17, 1940. A sketch by* **Benedict Fred Dolbin** (*1883–1971*).

under the title that Schoenberg later adopted. His Pierrot was the poet-rascal-clown whose chalk-white face, passing abruptly from laughter to tears, enlivened every puppet show and pantomime in Europe. (In Russia he was Petrushka, in Italy Pagliaccio.) Giraud's poems were liberally spiced with those elements of the macabre and the bizarre that suited the end-of-century taste for "decadence." Translated into German by Otto Erich Hartleben, the poems, with their abrupt changes of mood from guilt and depression to atonement and playfulness, fired Schoenberg's imagination. He picked twenty-one, arranged them in three groups of seven, and set them for a female reciter and a chamber-music ensemble of five players using eight instruments: piano, flute–piccolo, clarinet–bass clarinet, violin–viola, and cello. The work, he explained, was conceived "in a light, ironical, satirical tone."

Giraud's short poems enabled Schoenberg to create a series of miniatures for which Sprechstimme served as a unifying element. This unity was balanced by the utmost variety from one piece to the next of structure, texture—from dense to sparse—and instrumentation. The result was a perfect musical expression of the bizarre images in the text. Schoenberg also experimented *Klangfarbenmelodie* with what he called *Klangfarbenmelodie* (tone-color melody), in which each note of a melody is played by another instrument, giving a shifting effect that well evoked the moonbeams of which the poet spoke. Each of the poems is a *rondeau*, a French verse form of thirteen lines in which the first and second lines are repeated as the seventh and eighth, and the first reappears again as the last.

No. 18 We hear two of the poems. No. 18 is "Der Mondfleck" (The Moonfleck; see Listening Guide 43 for the text). Pierrot, out for fun, is disturbed by a white spot—a patch of moonlight—on the collar of his jet-black jacket. He rubs and rubs but cannot get rid of it. His predicament inspired Schoenberg to contrapuntal complexities of a spectacular kind. The piano presents a three-voice fugue while the other instruments unfold such devices as strict canons in diminution (smaller note values) and retrograde (backwards). Schoenberg was obviously fascinated by such constructions, which recall the wizardry of the Renaissance contrapuntists.

The last poem, No. 21, is "O alter Duft" (O Scent of Fabled Yesteryear), in which Schoenberg brings in all eight instruments. Pierrot revels in the fragrant memories of old times, looking out serenely on a world bathed in sunlight. This return to an earlier, more innocent time leads Schoenberg to sound the gentle thirds and consonant triads of the harmonic system he had abandoned. Pierrot's Sprechstimme dies away in a pianissimo. Thus ends the work that Stravinsky called "the solar plexus as well as the mind of early twentieth-century music."

No. 21

It is given to certain creative spirits to capture the mood of their time and place. Rarely has an artist done so as completely as Schoenberg did in his *Pierrot lunaire*.

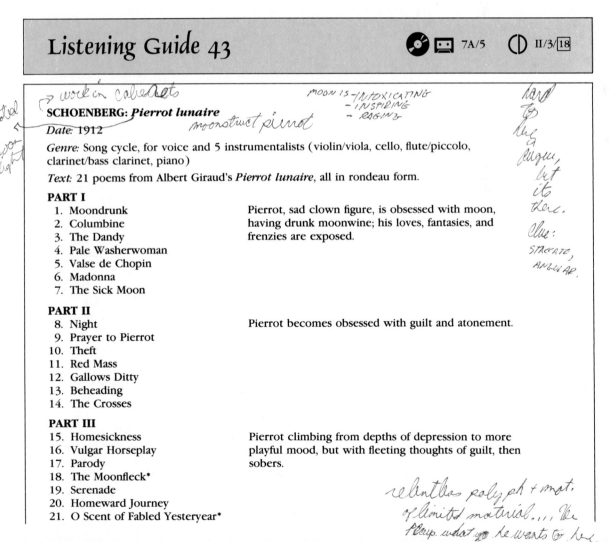

Listening Guide 43

7A/5   II/3/18

work in cabarets

dominated by mystic light

MOON IS — INTOXICATING
— INSPIRING
— RAGING

moonstruct pierrot

SCHOENBERG: *Pierrot lunaire*

Date: 1912

Genre: Song cycle, for voice and 5 instrumentalists (violin/viola, cello, flute/piccolo, clarinet/bass clarinet, piano)

Text: 21 poems from Albert Giraud's *Pierrot lunaire*, all in rondeau form.

hard to hear a fugue, but it's there.

Clue: STACATTE, ANGULAR.

PART I
1. Moondrunk
2. Columbine
3. The Dandy
4. Pale Washerwoman
5. Valse de Chopin
6. Madonna
7. The Sick Moon

Pierrot, sad clown figure, is obsessed with moon, having drunk moonwine; his loves, fantasies, and frenzies are exposed.

PART II
8. Night
9. Prayer to Pierrot
10. Theft
11. Red Mass
12. Gallows Ditty
13. Beheading
14. The Crosses

Pierrot becomes obsessed with guilt and atonement.

PART III
15. Homesickness
16. Vulgar Horseplay
17. Parody
18. The Moonfleck*
19. Serenade
20. Homeward Journey
21. O Scent of Fabled Yesteryear*

Pierrot climbing from depths of depression to more playful mood, but with fleeting thoughts of guilt, then sobers.

relentless polyph + mat. of limited material.... the sleep what you he wants to hear

18 *18. "DER MONDFLECK"*   18 "THE MOONFLECK"

(*Piccolo, clarinet in B♭, violin, cello, piano*)
Slow piano introduction, then fast, intense, and dissonant; canonic treatment veiled
in flickering effect of instruments. Italics indicate repeated text of rondo form.

Einen weißen Fleck des hellen Mondes   *With a fleck of white—from the bright moon—*
Auf dem Rücken seines schwarzen Rockes,   *On the back of his black jacket,*
So spaziert Pierrot im lauen Abend,   Pierrot strolls about in the mild evening
Aufzusuchen Glück und Abenteuer.   To seek his fortune and to find adventure.

Plötzlich stört ihn was an seinem Anzug,   Suddenly something strikes him as wrong,
Er beschaut sich rings und findet richtig–   He checks his clothes over and sure enough finds
Einen weißen Fleck des hellen Mondes   *A fleck of white—from the bright moon.*
Auf dem Rücken seines schwarzen Rockes.   *On the back of his black jacket.*

Warte! denkt er: das ist so ein Gipsfleck!   Damn! he thinks: there's a spot of plaster!
Wischt und wischt, doch—   Rubs and rubs, but—he can't get it off.
     bringt ihn nicht herunter!
Und so geht er, giftgeschwollen, weiter,   And so goes on his way, his pleasure poisoned,
Reibt und reibt bis an den fruhen Morgen—   Rubs and rubs till the early morning—
Einen weißen Fleck des heilen Mondes.   *A fleck from the bright moon.*

Opening, for voice
and instruments

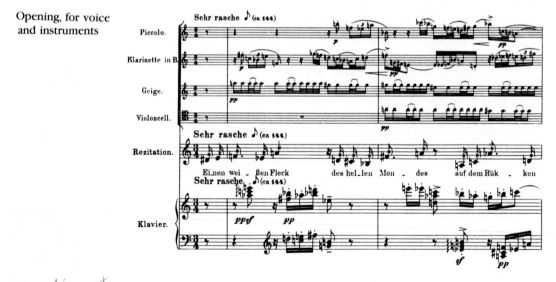

Not as dissonant

19 *21. "O ALTER DUFT"*   21. "O SCENT OF FABLED YESTERYEAR"

(*Flute, piccolo, clarinet in A, bass clarinet in B♭, violin, viola, cello, piano*)
Melancholy mood in simpler setting, dissonant, with musical refrain on words "O alter Duft aus
Märchenzeit" (O scent of fabled yesteryear).

O alter Duft aus Märchenzeit.   *O scent of fabled yesteryear,*
Berauschest wieder meine Sinne: *Intoxicating my senses once again!*
Ein närrisch Heer von Scheimerein   A foolish swarm of idle fancies
Durchschwirrt die leichte Luft.   Pervades the gentle air.

Ein glückhaft Wunschen macht mich froh   A happy desire makes me yearn for
Nach Freuden, die ich lang verachtet: Joys that I have long scorned:
O alter Duft aus Märchenzeit,   O scent of fabled yesteryear,
Berauschest wieder mich!   Intoxicating me again!

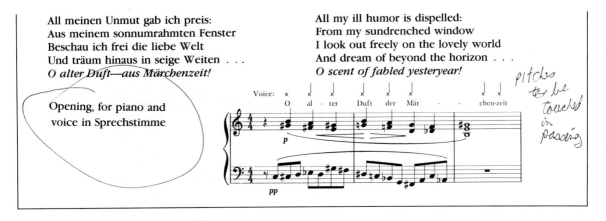

All meinen Unmut gab ich preis:	All my ill humor is dispelled:
Aus meinem sonnumrahmten Fenster	From my sundrenched window
Beschau ich frei die liebe Welt	I look out freely on the lovely world
Und träum hinaus in seige Weiten . . .	And dream of beyond the horizon . . .
O alter Duft—aus Märchenzeit!	O scent of fabled yesteryear!

Opening, for piano and voice in Sprechstimme

pitches to be touched in passing

72

Alban Berg

"When I decided to write an opera, my only intention was to give to the theater what belongs to the theater. The music was to be so formed that at each moment it would fulfill its duty of serving the action."

It was the unique achievement of Alban Berg (1885–1935) to humanize the abstract procedures of the Schoenbergian technique, and to reconcile them with the expression of feeling. Upon a new and difficult idiom he imprinted the stamp of a lyric imagination of the first order.

His Life

Berg was born in Vienna. He came of a well-to-do family and grew up in an environment that fostered his artistic interests. At nineteen he made the acquaintance of Arnold Schoenberg, who was sufficiently impressed with the youth's manuscripts to accept him as a pupil. During his six years with Schoenberg (1904–09) he acquired the consummate mastery of technique that characterizes his later work. Schoenberg was not only an exacting master, but also a devoted friend and mentor who shaped Berg's whole outlook on art.

The outbreak of war in 1914 hurled Berg into a period of depression. "The urge 'to be in on it,'" he wrote to Schoenberg, "the feeling of helplessness at being unable to serve my country, prevented any concentration on work." A few months later he was called up for military service, despite his uncertain health (he suffered from asthma and attacks of nervous debility). He was presently transferred to the War Ministry in Vienna. Already *Wozzeck*

Alban Berg

occupied his thoughts, but he could not begin writing the music until the war was over. In December 1925 *Wozzeck* was presented at the Berlin State Opera. At one stroke Berg was lifted from comparative obscurity to international fame.

In the decade that remained to him he produced only a handful of works, but each was a significant contribution to his total output. During these years he was active as a teacher. He also wrote about music, propagandizing tirelessly on behalf of Schoenberg and his school. With the coming to power of Hitler, the works of the twelve-tone composers were banned in Germany as alien to the spirit of the Third Reich. The resulting loss of income was a source of worry to Berg, as was, in far greater degree, the rapid Nazification of Austria. Schoenberg's enforced emigration to the United States was a bitter blow.

Exhausted and ailing after the completion of his Violin Concerto, Berg went to the country for a short rest before resuming work on his opera *Lulu*. An insect bite brought on an abscess that caused infection. Upon his return to Vienna he was stricken with blood poisoning. He died on Christmas Eve 1935, seven weeks before his fifty-first birthday.

His Music

Berg's art issued from the world of German Romanticism—the world of Schumann, Brahms, Wagner, Richard Strauss, and Mahler. The Romantic streak in his temperament bound him to this heritage even after he had embraced the twelve-tone style. Berg's was the imagination of the musical dramatist. For him the musical gesture was bound up with character and action, mood and atmosphere. Yet, like his teacher, he leaned toward the formal patterns of the past—fugue and invention, passacaglia, variations, sonata, and suite.

Berg's most widely known composition, after *Wozzeck*, is the *Lyric Suite*. The work is in six movements. The first and last follow strictly "the method of composing with twelve tones." Originally written for string quartet, the *Lyric Suite* achieved such popularity that the composer arranged the three middle movements for string orchestra.

Principal Works

2 operas: *Wozzeck* (1917–22) and *Lulu* (unfinished, 1935)

Orchestral music, including Three Orchestral Pieces, Op. 6 (1915), Chamber Concerto (1925), Three Pieces from *Lyric Suite* (1928), Violin Concerto (1935)

Chamber music, including String Quartet (1910) and *Lyric Suite* (1926)

Piano music, including Piano Sonata, Op. 1 (1908)

Songs, including Four Songs, Op. 2 (1910)

Berg spent the last seven years of his life on the opera *Lulu*. The work is based on a single twelve-tone row. The composer fashioned the libretto himself from two dramas by Frank Wedekind—*Earth Spirit* (1893) and *Pandora's Box* (1901). Lulu is the eternal type of *femme fatale* "who destroys everyone because she is destroyed by everyone." Berg was in the midst of orchestrating *Lulu* when he interrupted the task to write the Violin Concerto. The opera remained unfinished for many years, but recently the orchestration was completed by the Austrian composer Friedrich Cerha, and now *Lulu* has taken its place alongside *Wozzeck* as one of the challenging works of the modern lyric theater.

Alban Berg is probably the most widely admired master of the twelve-tone school. His premature death robbed contemporary music of a major figure.

Berg: Wozzeck

In 1914 Berg saw the play that impelled him to the composition of *Wozzeck*. The author, Georg Büchner (1813–37), belonged to the generation of intellectuals stifled by the political repressions of Metternich's Europe. In the stolid infantryman Wozzeck he created an archetype of "the insulted and injured" of the earth.

Berg's libretto tightened the original play. He shaped the material into three acts, each containing five scenes. These were linked by brief orchestral interludes whose motivic structure serves to round off what has preceded as well as to introduce what follows. As a result, Berg's "opera of protest and compassion" has astonishing unity of texture and mood.

The action centers on Wozzeck's unhappy love for Marie, by whom he has had an illegitimate child. Wozzeck is the victim of the sadistic Captain and of the Doctor, a coldly scientific gentleman who uses Wozzeck for his experiments—to which the soldier submits because he needs the money. (Wozzeck is given to hallucinations. The Doctor is bent on proving his theory that mental disorder is related to diet.) Marie cannot resist her infatuation with the handsome Drum Major. Wozzeck slowly realizes that she has been unfaithful to him. Ultimately he kills her. Driven back to the death-scene by guilt and remorse, he drowns himself.

Harmonically, the greater part of the opera is cast in an atonal-Expressionist idiom. Berg anticipates certain twelve-tone procedures; he also looks back to the tonal tradition, puts a number of passages in major and minor keys, and uses leitmotifs in the Wagnerian manner.

We hear the final two scenes of the opera. In scene 4 of Act III Wozzeck comes back to the path near the pond where he has killed Marie, and stumbles against her body. How poignant is his "Marie, what's that red cord around your neck?" (See Listening Guide 44 for the text.) He finds the knife with which he committed the murder, throws it into the pond and, driven by his delusions, follows it into the water. His last words as he drowns—"I wash myself in blood—the water is blood . . . blood!"—usher in a series of ascending chromatic scales that pass in a ghostly pianissimo from strings

Act III, Scene 4

The final, heart-breaking moment of **Alban Berg's** Wozzeck *in the Metropolitan Opera production.* (© Beth Bergman, 1983)

to woodwinds to brass. The Doctor appears, followed by the Captain. We see the haunted scene through their eyes as, terrified, they run away.

Act III, Scene 5   The final scene opens with a symphonic interlude in D minor, a passionate lament for the life and death of Wozzeck. This inspired fantasy indicates how richly Berg's art was nourished by the Romanticism of Mahler. The final scene takes place in the morning in front of Marie's house. Children are playing. Marie's little boy rides a hobbyhorse. Other children rush in with news of the murder, but Marie's son does not understand. The children run off as he continues to ride and sing. Then, noticing that he has been left alone, he calls "Hop, hop" and rides off on his hobbyhorse, to the sound of clarinet, drum, xylophone, and strings playing pianissimo. For sheer heartbreak, the final curtain has few to equal it in the contemporary lyric theater.

Wozzeck envelops the listener in a hallucinated world in which the hunters are as driven as the hunted. It could have come only out of *mittel Europa* in the 1920s. But its characters reach out beyond time and place to become eternal symbols of the human condition.

Listening Guide 44

BERG: *Wozzeck*

Date: 1917–22

Genre: Opera, in three acts

Basis: Expressionist play by Büchner

ACT III, scene 4, By the pond

Characters: Wozzeck, Doctor, Captain

WOZZECK

Das Messer? Wo ist das Messer? Ich hab's dagelassen.	The knife? Where is the knife? I left it there. Around
Näher, noch näher. Mir graut's . . . da regt sich was.	here somewhere. I'm terrified . . . something's moving.
Still! Alles still und tot.	Silence. Everything silent and dead.

(*shouting*)

Mörder! Mörder!	Murderer! Murderer!

(*whispering again*)

Ha! Da ruft's. Nein, ich selbst.	Ah! Someone called. No, it was only me.

(*still looking, he staggers a few steps further and stumbles against the corpse*)

Marie! Marie! Was hast Du für eine rote Schnur um den Hals?	Marie! Marie! What's that red cord around your neck!
Hast Dir das rote Halsband verdient, wie die	Was the red necklace payment for your sins, like the
Ohrringlein, mit Deiner Sünde! Was hängen Dir die	ear-rings? Why's your dark hair so wild about you?
schwarzen Haare so wild? Mörder! Mörder! Sie werden	Murderer! Murderer! They will come and look for me.
nach mir suchen. Das Messer verrät mich!	The knife will betray me!

(*looks for it in a frenzy*)

Da, da ist's!	Here! Here it is!

(*at the pond*)

So! Da hinunter!	There! Sink to the bottom!

(*throws the knife into the pond*)

Es taucht ins dunkle Wasser wie ein Stein.	It plunges into the dark water like a stone.

(*The moon appears, blood-red, from behind the clouds. Wozzeck looks up.*)

Aber der Mond verrät mich, der Mond ist blutig.	But the moon will betray me: the moon is blood-stained.
Will denn die ganze Welt es ausplaudern?	Is the whole world going to incriminate me?
Das Messer, es liegt zu weit vorn, sie finden's beim	The knife is too near the edge: they'll find it when they're
Baden oder wenn sie nach Muscheln tauchen.	swimming or diving for snails.

(wades into the pond)

Ich find's nicht. Aber ich muss mich waschen.	I can't find it. But I must wash myself.
Ich bin blutig. Da ein Fleck—und noch einer.	There's blood on me. There's a spot here—and there's
Weh! Weh! Ich wasche mich mit Blut—das Wasser ist	another. Oh, God! I am washing myself in blood—the
Blut . . . Blut . . .	water is blood . . . blood . . .

(drowns)

Wozzeck's last words before drowning, accompanied by very soft ascending chromatic scales in strings:

9   *(The doctor appears, followed by the captain.)*

CAPTAIN

Halt!	Wait!

DOCTOR *(stops)*

Hören Sie? Dort!	Can you hear? There!

CAPTAIN

Jesus! Das war ein Ton!	Jesus! What a ghastly sound!

(stops as well)

DOCTOR *(pointing to the pond)*

Ja, dort!	Yes, there!

CAPTAIN

Es ist das Wasser im Teich. Das Wasser ruft.	It's the water in the pond. The water is calling.
Es ist schon lange Niemand ertrunken.	It's been a long time since anyone drowned.
Kommen Sie Doktor!	Come away, Doctor.
Es ist nicht gut zu hören.	It's not good for us to be hearing it.

(tries to drag the doctor away)

DOCTOR *(resisting, and continuing to listen)*

Das stöhnt, als stürbe ein Mensch.	There's a groan, as though someone were dying.
Da ertrinkt Jemand!	Somebody's drowning!

CAPTAIN

Unheimlich! Der Mond rot, und die Nebel grau.	It's eerie! The moon is red, and the mist is grey.
Hören Sie? . . .	Can you hear? . . .
Jetzt wieder das Ächzen.	That moaning again.

DOCTOR

Stiller, . . . jetzt ganz still.	It's getter quieter . . . now it's stopped altogether.

CAPTAIN

Kommen Sie! Kommen Sie schnell!	Come! Come quickly!

(He rushes off, pulling the doctor along with him.)

10 **Orchestral Interlude in D minor**

11 Act III, Scene 5, Children playing in front of Marie's house

Melody of children's
song, distorted

Rin - gel, Rin - gel, Ro - sen-kranz, Rin - gel-reih'n! Rin - gel, Rin - gel, Ro - sen-kranz, Rin -

CHILDREN

Ringel, Ringel, Rosenkranz, Ringelreih'n.   Ring-a-ring-a-roses.
Ringel, Ringel, Rosenkranz, Ring . . .   A pocket full of . . .

(Their song and game are interrupted by other children
bursting in.)

ONE OF THE NEWCOMERS

Du, Käthe! Die Marie!   Hey, Katie! Have you heard about Marie?

SECOND CHILD

Was ist?   What's happened?

FIRST CHILD

Weisst' es nit? Sie sind schon Alle 'naus. Don't you know? They've all gone out there.

THIRD CHILD *(to Marie's little boy)*

Du! Dein' Mutter ist tot!   Hey! Your mother's dead!

MARIE'S SON *(still riding)*

Hopp, hopp! Hopp, hopp! Hopp, hopp! Hop hop! Hop hop! Hop hop!

SECOND CHILD

Wo ist sie denn?   Where is she then?

FIRST CHILD

Drauss' liegt sie, am Weg, neben dem Teich. She's lying out there, on the path near the pond.

THIRD CHILD

Kommt, anschaun!   Come and have a look!

(All the children run off.)

MARIE'S SON *(continuing to ride)*

Hopp, hopp! Hopp, hopp! Hopp, hopp! Hop hop! Hop hop! Hop hop!

(He hesitates for a moment and then rides after the other children.)

TR. BY SARAH E. SOULSBY

Child on hobbyhorse, with
pianissimo accompaniment

73

Anton Webern and
Olivier Messiaen

Two other European composers, neither very well known to the public at large, were nevertheless highly influential in shaping the musical thinking of our time: Anton von Webern (he dropped the prefix of nobility in later life) and Olivier Messiaen.

Webern: His Life and Music

"With me, things never turn out as I wish, but only as is ordained for me—as I must."

Anton Webern

Anton Webern (1883–1945) was born in Vienna. His musical gifts asserted themselves at an early age. He was twenty-one when he met Schoenberg and, with Alban Berg, formed the nucleus of the band of disciples who gathered around the master. He also studied musicology, and received his doctorate in this field.

After leaving the university, Webern conducted at various German provincial theaters and in Prague. But Vienna was the hub of his world. He directed the Vienna Workers' Symphony Concerts organized by the authorities of the then socialist city, but as the years passed he found public activity less and less congenial to his retiring disposition. After the First World War he settled in Mödling, a suburb of Vienna, where he lived quietly, devoting himself to composition and teaching.

Webern suffered great hardship after Austria became part of the Third Reich. The Nazis regarded his music as *Kulturbolshevismus* (cultural Bolshevism), forbade its performance, and burned his writings. He was permitted to teach only a few pupils, and had to give his lectures—in which he expounded the Schoenbergian point of view—in secret. In order to avoid forced labor during the war, he worked as proofreader for a Viennese publisher. To escape the Allied bombings of Vienna, Webern and his wife sought refuge at the home of their son-in-law in Mittersill, a small town near Salzburg. But fate awaited him there. On September 15, 1945, as he stepped out of his house in the evening to smoke a cigarette (the war had ended five months before, but Mittersill was still under a curfew), he failed to understand an order to halt and was shot by a trigger-happy sentry of the American occupying forces. "The day of Anton Webern's death," wrote his most celebrated admirer, Igor Stravinsky, "should be a day of mourning for any receptive musician. We must hail not only this great composer but also a real hero. Doomed to total failure in a deaf world of ignorance and indifference, he inexorably kept on cutting his dazzling diamonds, of whose mines he had such a perfect knowledge."

Principal Works

Orchestral music, including Passacaglia, Op. 1 (1908), Five Pieces for Orchestra, Op. 10 (1913), Symphony, Op. 21 (1928), Variations, Op. 30 (1940)

Chamber music, including Five Movements for String Quartet (1909), string quartets

Choral music, including cantatas; many songs
Piano music, including Variations, Op. 27 (1936)

Webern responded to the radical portion of Schoenbergian doctrine, just as Berg exploited its more conservative elements. Of the three masters of the modern Viennese school, he was the one who cut himself off most completely from the tonal past. The Schoenbergians, we saw, favored the short forms. Webern carried this urge for brevity much further than either of his comrades. Hardly less novel is the musical fabric in which he clothed his ideas. His scores call for the most unusual combinations of instruments. Each tone is assigned its specific function in the overall scheme. The instruments are often used in their extreme registers; they not infrequently play one at a time, and very little. This technique confers upon the individual sound an importance it never had before.

In the works of Webern's maturity the twelve-tone technique was used with unprecedented strictness. Schoenberg had contented himself with an organization based upon fixed series of pitches. Webern extended this concept to include timbres and rhythms. Therewith he moved toward complete control of the sonorous material—in other words, total serialization. His disciples carried the implications of Webern's music still further. As a result, Webern emerged as the dominant influence on the dodecaphonic thinking of the mid-twentieth century.

Webern: Symphony, Opus 21

The Symphony, Opus 21—for clarinet, bass clarinet, two horns, two harps, violins, violas, and cellos—ushered in the most important phase of Webern's career, when his desire for absolute purity of language led him to his own completely original style. With this work he became the first of the modern Viennese school to undertake the grand form of the Classical period. (As we saw, neither Schoenberg nor Berg cultivated the symphony.) It goes without saying that Webern's piece is far removed from the expansion-and-development techniques traditionally associated with symphonic style. It is equally far from the tonic-dominant opposition that made the symphony the embodiment of tonal thinking.

S4B/1
S4/15

Webern's Symphony takes just under ten minutes to play, and shows the same concentration of thought and sparseness of writing as do his other scores. In the matter of color, Webern expanded Schoenberg's device of

In this pointillistic drawing, **Georges-Pierre Seurat** (*1859–91*) *used black crayon to suggest all of the nuances of light and form normally accorded to color.* At the "Concert Européen" (The Museum of Modern Art, New York. Lillie P. Bliss Collection)

Klangfarbenmelodie (tone-color melody), in which each note of a melodic line was played by another instrument; he assigned two, three, or four notes to each. There resulted the exact tonal equivalent of *pointillism* in painting, in which dots of pure color were juxtaposed to create a shimmering effect.

The Symphony abounds in those complex contrapuntal procedures, such as double canon and retrograde (backward) motion that fascinated composers from the late Middle Ages to the Baroque era. It is in two movements. The first, based on a tone row, is in a sonata form with canonic structures; the second is a theme with seven variations and a coda, all derived from the tone row of the first movement. The symmetrical organization shows the workings of Webern's mind: Variations 1 and 7 are double canons, 2 and 6 are trios, 3 and 5 are pointillistic in effect, and the fourth variation occupies the central position and serves as the turning point of the movement.

The creator of this remarkable music was content to go his way, overshadowed by those who made a bigger noise in the world. He had no way of knowing that little over a decade after his death, many avant-garde musicians in Europe and America would think of themselves as belonging to "the Age of Webern."

Messiaen: His Life and Music

"I consider rhythm the prime and perhaps the essential part of music."

Olivier Messiaen (1908–), who was born in Avignon, received his musical training at the Paris Conservatoire, where he won most of the available prizes. At twenty-three he became organist of the Church of the Trinity and five years later professor at both the Ecole Normale de Musique and the Schola Cantorum. He was drafted into the army shortly after the outbreak of war, was captured by the Germans in June 1940, and for two years was a prisoner of war. On his release he was appointed to the faculty of the Paris Conservatoire. He subsequently taught at the summer schools at Tanglewood, Massachusetts, at Darmstadt, and at various centers of contemporary music in North and South America.

Olivier Messiaen

Messiaen has steadfastly adhered to his conception of art as the ideal expression of religious faith. A mystic and a visionary, he considers his religious feeling to be the most important aspect of his art, "the only one perhaps that I will not regret at the hour of my death." Works inspired by religious mysticism occupy a central position in his list, from *Hymn to the Holy Sacrament* for orchestra to *The Transfiguration of Our Lord Jesus Christ* for chamber group, chorus and orchestra, completed in 1969. Such religious dedication on the part of a musician is uncommon in our time.

Many streams commingle in Messiaen's music. His love of nature has centered on his interest in bird songs, in which he has found an inexhaustible source of melody. He has also been strongly influenced by the undulating melodic line of Gregorian chant, the quiet remoteness of the Medieval modes, the subtle nonsymmetrical rhythms of India, and the delicate bell sounds

Principal Works

Orchestral music, including *Hymne au Saint Sacrement* (Hymn to the Holy Sacrament, 1932), *Turangalîla-symphonie* (1948), *Oiseaux exotiques* (Exotic Birds, 1956), *Chronochromie* (1960)

Chamber music, including *Quatuor pour la fin du temps* (Quartet for the End of Time, 1941)

Choral music, including *La transfiguration de Notre Seigneur Jésus-Christ* (1969)

Vocal music, including *Poèmes pour Mi* (1936), song cycle *Harawi* (1945); one opera, *St. François d'Assise* (1983)

Piano music, including *Vingt regards sur l'enfant Jésus* (Twenty Glances at the Infant Jesus, 1944)

Organ music, including *Le nativité du Seigneur* (The Lord's Nativity, 1935)

Theoretical works including *La technique de mon langage musical* (1944)

of the Javanese gamelan. All these strands are woven into the colorful tapestry of his *Turangalîla-Symphony*, a monumental orchestral work in ten movements. He has also made a contribution of unparalleled importance to the twentieth-century literature of the organ and the piano.

Messiaen: Vingt regards sur l'enfant Jésus

S4B/3

S4/26

Vingt regards sur l'enfant Jésus is a difficult work that illustrates Messiaen's attempt to discover novel, almost orchestral sonorities on the piano. It consists of twenty miniatures based on three principal themes: the Theme of God, the Theme of the Star and the Cross (symbolizing the beginning and end of Jesus's life), and the Theme of Unity. We hear the second number, *Regard de l'étoile* (Glance of the Star), which is based on two main ideas that alternate throughout. The first rushes upward to birdlike figurations in high register, followed by dissonant chords divided between high register and low. The second is the theme of the Star and the Cross, a sinuously chromatic idea that follows an irregular pattern of beats, heard in distant octaves in the extreme registers of the piano. Upon its return this theme is played fortissimo in the middle register with high figurations above it. It recurs at the end of the piece in dissonant octaves before dying away.

Messiaen has been a pathfinder on many levels. But perhaps his most important role was to reaffirm the power of music to express human emotion and to embody our profoundest aspirations. This needed doing in our time, and Messiaen did it boldly, imaginatively, with unshakeable conviction.

UNIT XXIII

◼

The Nationalism of the Twentieth Century

74

The European Scene

"The art of music above all other arts is the expression of the soul of a nation. The composer must love the tunes of his country and they must become an integral part of him." —RALPH VAUGHAN WILLIAMS

Twentieth-century nationalism differed from its nineteenth-century counterpart in one important respect. It approached the old folksongs in a scientific spirit, prizing the ancient tunes precisely because they departed from the conventional mold. By this time the phonograph had been invented. The new students of folklore took recording equipment with them into the field in order to preserve the songs exactly as the village folk sang them, and the composers who used them in their works respected and tried to retain their antique flavor.

Comparison with nineteenth century

National Schools

French composers in the generation after Debussy and Ravel tried to recapture the wit and *esprit* that are part of their national heritage. They were disciples of Erik Satie (1866–1925) in their attempt to develop a style that combined that composer's objectivity and understatement with Neoclassicism and new concepts of tonality. Darius Milhaud (1892–1975) is remembered in this country mainly for his ballet *The Creation of the World* (1923) and as a leader in the development of polytonality. Arthur Honegger (1892–1955), born in France of Swiss parents, shocked the world with *Pacific 231*, a symphonic poem glorifying the locomotive.

French school

Francis Poulenc (1899–1962) has emerged as the most significant figure of this group. He was one of the outstanding song composers of our time, and his piano pieces, urbane and thoroughly Parisian, constitute a twentieth-century brand of salon music. His two operas—*Dialogues of the Carmelites*,

449

on a libretto by Georges Bernanos (1953–55) and *The Human Voice*, based on a one-act play by Jean Cocteau—found a wide audience in the United States in English versions by the present writer.

Russian school   In the post-Romantic period the Russian school produced two composers of international fame. The piano works of Sergei Rachmaninoff (1873–1953) are enormously popular with the American public, especially his Second Piano Concerto and Variations on a Theme of Paganini. Alexander Scriabin (1872–1915), a visionary artist whose music is wreathed in a subtle lyricism, was one of the leaders in the twentieth-century search for new harmonies. In the next generation we find two important figures in Sergei Prokofiev (1891–1953), whom we shall discuss in a later chapter, and Dmitri Shostakovitch (1906–1975), the first Russian composer of international repute who was wholly a product of Soviet musical culture. Shostakovitch was trained at the Leningrad Conservatory.

English school   England had produced no major composer for two hundred years before the post-Romantic period, until Sir Edward Elgar (1857–1934) appeared upon the scene. He and Frederick Delius (1862–1934) marked their country's return to the concert of nations. They were followed by two figures who were of prime importance in establishing the modern English school— Ralph Vaughan Williams (1872–1958), whom we shall discuss, and Benjamin Britten (1913–76), whose works for the stage have established his reputation as one of the foremost opera composers of our time. Among them are *Peter Grimes* (1945), an opera about an English fishing village based on George Crabbe's poem *The Borough,* and *Billy Budd* (1952), after Herman Melville's story. Widely admired too are the lovely Serenade for tenor solo, horn, and string orchestra (1953) and the deeply moving *War Requiem* (1961). You will recall that we discussed Britten's *Young Person's Guide to the Orchestra* earlier in the book.

German school   Among the composers who came into prominence in Germany in the years after the First World War, Paul Hindemith (1895–1963) was the most substantial figure. He left Germany when Hitler came to power—his music was banned from the Third Reich as "cultural Bolshevism"—and he spent two decades in the United States, during which he taught at Yale University and at Tanglewood, Massachusetts, where many young Americans came under his influence.

Carl Orff (1895–1982) took his point of departure from the clear-cut melodies and vigorous rhythms of Bavarian folk song. He is best known in this country for his "dramatic cantata" *Carmina burana* (1936). Kurt Weill (1900–50) was one of the most arresting figures to emerge in Germany in the 1920s. For the international public his name is indissolubly linked with *The Three-Penny Opera* (1928) which he and the poet Berthold Brecht adapted from John Gay's *The Beggar's Opera*. Frequent revivals have made this one of the century's best-known theater pieces.

Other nationalists   Hungarian nationalism found two major representatives in Béla Bartók (1881–1945), whom we shall discuss, and Zoltán Kodály (1882–1967), who was associated with Bartók in the collection and study of peasant songs. The folklore element is prominent in his music. Czechoslovakia is well represented by Leoš Janáček (1854–1928), whose operas *Jenufa* (1916) and *The*

Cunning Little Vixen (1926) have found great favor with the American public. Spain contributed two attractive nationalists of the post-Romantic era—Isaac Albéniz (1860–1919) and Enrique Granados (1867–1916), who paved the way for the major figure of the modern Spanish school, Manuel de Falla (1876–1936).

Jean Sibelius (1865–1957) cut an important figure during the '20s and '30s, especially in England and the United States. His Second Symphony, Violin Concerto, and *Finlandia* retain their popularity. Carl Nielsen (1865–1931) is a Danish composer whose six symphonies have slowly established themselves in our concert life. Ernest Bloch (1880–1959), a native of Switzerland, was one of the few composers of Jewish background who consciously identified himself with his heritage. In *Schelomo*—the Biblical name of King Solomon—he produced a "Hebrew Rhapsody" for cello and orchestra that gave eloquent expression to his nationalism.

The English School: Ralph Vaughan Williams

"The greatest artist belongs to his country as much as the humblest singer in a remote village."

The English renaissance in music was heralded by an awakening of interest in native folksong and dance. The movement toward a national school was also strengthened by the revival of interest in the masters of Tudor church music, the madrigal composers of the Elizabethan age, and the art of Purcell. Out of this ferment came a generation of composers, the most important of whom was Ralph Vaughan Williams (1872–1958).

Ralph Vaughan Williams

His Life and Music

Vaughan Williams was born in Gloucestershire, the son of a well-to-do clergyman, and at the age of eighteen entered the Royal College of Music. He subsequently attended Trinity College at Cambridge. After a short stay abroad, during which he studied in Berlin with Max Bruch, a composer in the Romantic tradition, he returned to Cambridge and in 1901 received his doctorate in music, the most respectable appendage a British musician can acquire.

A decisive influence was Vaughan Williams's involvement with the folksong revival. He later wrote that "this revival gave a point to our imagination; far from fettering us, it freed us from foreign influences which weighed on us." In spite of this statement he went to acquire some foreign influence in Paris, where he studied briefly with Maurice Ravel.

The outbreak of war in 1914 relegated music to a secondary place in his life. Although he was forty-two he enlisted, was commissioned as a lieutenant in the Royal Garrison Artillery, and saw combat duty in France throughout 1918. The war over, he resumed his career. He became professor of composition at the Royal College of Music, in which post he helped train many musicians of the new generation, and was the most active of the so-called

Principal Works

Orchestral music, including 9 symphonies (No. 1, *A Sea Symphony*, 1909; No. 2, *A London Symphony*, 1913; No. 3, *A Pastoral Symphony*, 1921; *Sinfonia antartica*,1952); *Fantasia on a Theme by Thomas Tallis* (1910), *Fantasia on "Greensleeves"* (1934)

Operas, including *Sir John in Love* (1929) and *The Pilgrim's Progress* (1951)

Choral music, including *Dona nobis pacem* (1936), *Serenade to Music* (1938)

Vocal music, including song cycle *On Wenlock Edge* (1909); folksong arrangements

Chamber music; 1 ballet, *Job* (1931); piano music; film scores

folksong school of composers. In the last years of his life Vaughan Williams was the unofficial composer laureate of his native land. At the coronation of Queen Elizabeth II, the Credo and Sanctus of his Mass in G minor were performed in Westminster Abbey. He completed his Ninth Symphony at the age of eighty-five and died a year later.

Vaughan Williams stood at the farthest possible remove from the "art for art's sake" doctrine that prevailed at the end of the century. "The composer," he wrote, "must not shut himself up and think about art; he must live with his fellows and make his art an expression of the whole life of the community."

In the ancient tunes of the peasantry Vaughan Williams found the living expression of the English spirit. Having assimilated the character of popular melody to his personal thinking, he wrote music that sounded English whether he quoted actual folksongs or not. His style derived from the polyphonic masters of the Tudor era and the Elizabethan madrigalists. His interest in the golden age of English music inspired one of his most successful works, the *Fantasia on a Theme by Thomas Tallis*, in which he paid homage to the great composer of the reign of Henry VIII.

Vaughan Williams was essentially a melodist. His harmony was either diatonic or, because of his interest in old music, modal. He favored older forms such as fugue, passacaglia, and concerto grosso. His study of the Elizabethan madrigal liberated him from the regular rhythms of the Classic-Romantic period. He also adopted the Elizabethan *fantasia*, with its flowing counterpoint.

Vaughan Williams: Fantasia on "Greensleeves"

S4A/3

S4/10

The *Fantasia on "Greensleeves"* was originally part of the opera *Sir John in Love*, based on Shakespeare's *The Merry Wives of Windsor*, which was written in 1921. Some years later Vaughan Williams transformed it into an independent concert piece.

Greensleeves, one of the most beautiful of English folksongs, was already popular in Shakespeare's time and is mentioned in several of his plays. Vaughan Williams's Fantasia is modeled after an Elizabethan form of string music in contrapuntal texture. It is an **A-B-A** form with an introduction for solo flute and harp, in a flowing meter. The lower strings enter with the *Greensleeves* tune. The **B** section introduces another old English song, *Lovely Joan*, after which the **A** section is repeated, including the flute and harp introduction.

One senses the manly personality and the warm heart behind this music. "He looks like a farmer," Stephen Williams wrote of him, "A big, heavy, lumbering figure, usually dressed in rough tweeds, who looks as though he is on his way to judge the shorthorns at an agricultural fair." Vaughan Williams perfectly met the needs of his time and place. He was, as one of his compatriots called him, "the most English of English composers."

The Russian School: Sergei Prokofiev

> *"The cardinal virtue (or, if you like, vice) of my life has always been the search for originality. I hate imitation. I hate hackneyed methods. I do not want to wear anyone else's mask. I want always to be myself."*

His Life and Music

Sergei Prokofiev (1891–1953) was one of those fortunate composers who achieved popularity with the general public and with musicians alike. He appeared at a twilight moment in the history of Russian music, imbuing it with a fresh but traditional air. Prokofiev entered the St. Petersburg Conservatory at the age of thirteen, arriving for the entrance examination armed with the manuscripts of four operas, two sonatas, a symphony, and a number of piano pieces. Rimsky-Korsakov, who was one of the examiners, exclaimed, "Here is a pupil after my own heart!"

Sergei Prokofiev

At nineteen Prokofiev made his first public appearance in St. Petersburg with a group of his piano pieces, among them *Suggestion Diabolique*. The dynamism of this music at once revealed a distinctive personal style. The works that followed—especially the Second Piano Concerto, the Second Piano Sonata, and the *Sarcasms* for piano—established the young composer as the *enfant terrible* of Russian music, a role he thoroughly enjoyed.

The Revolution of 1917 caught Prokofiev unaware, since politics lay outside his sphere of interest. As the conditions of life grew ever more difficult, he decided to emigrate to the United States, where he would be able to work in peace. It became clear, however, that the conquest of the New World was not going to be as easy as he had imagined. "I wandered through the enormous park in the center of New York and, looking up at the skyscrapers that bordered it, thought with cold fury of the marvelous American orchestras that cared nothing for my music, of the critics who balked so violently at anything new, of the managers who arranged long tours for artists playing the same old hackneyed programs fifty times over." There was nothing for it but to admit defeat and look elsewhere.

For the next ten years Prokofiev made Paris his home, with frequent journeys to the musical centers of Europe and the United States to perform his music. Yet the sense of being uprooted grew within him. "I've got to talk to people who are of my own flesh and blood, so that they can give me back something I lack here—their songs, my songs," he wrote a friend.

The years of wandering were followed by nineteen years in Russia (except for professional trips abroad). During this period he consolidated his position as the leading composer of the Soviet school. As one who had voluntarily rejoined the Soviets when he might have made a career in the West, he was sought out by the regime, laden with honors and financial rewards. In 1943 he received the Stalin Prize for his Seventh Piano Sonata. The following year he was awarded the Order of the Red Banner of Labor for outstanding service in the development of Soviet music.

At the same time, of all the Soviet composers he was the one who, because of his long residence abroad, was most closely associated with the Western influences that the regime considered inimical to socialist art. When the Central Committee of the Communist Party in 1948 accused the leading Soviet composers of "bourgeois formalism"— the conventional term for non-Soviet trends in art—Prokofiev was one of the principal targets. The government showed its displeasure by ordering his works to be removed from the repertory, along with those of Shostakovich, Khachaturian, and Miaskovsky. However as these men happened to be the Big Four of Soviet music, the prohibition could not very well be maintained. After a few months Prokofiev's works—first his ballets, then his symphonies—began to be performed again.

He died five months later, at the age of sixty-two. His death came one day after that of Joseph Stalin. The Soviet Government withheld the news for forty-eight hours,presumably so that the one event would not overshadow the other.

Principal Works

Orchestral works, including 7 symphonies (No. 1, *Classical*, 1917); *Scythian Suite* (1915); *Peter and the Wolf* (with narrator, 1936); 5 piano concertos; 2 violin concertos; 1 cello concerto

Operas, including *The Love for Three Oranges* (1921), *The Flaming Angel* (1923), and *War and Peace* (1943)

Ballets, including *The Prodigal Son* (1929), *Romeo and Juliet* (1938), and *Cinderella* (1945)

Choral music, including *Alexander Nevsky* (1939, cantata adapted from film score)

Chamber music, including string quartets and sonatas
Piano music, including 9 sonatas

Film music, including *Lieutenant Kijé* (1933) and *Alexander Nevsky* (1938); incidental music; songs

Prokofiev himself has provided us with the best analysis of the elements of *Classical elements*
his style. "The first is Classical, originating in my early childhood when I
heard my mother play Beethoven sonatas. It assumes a Neo-classical aspect
in my sonatas or concertos, or imitates the Classical style of the eighteenth
century." In the *Classical Symphony*, composed "as Haydn might have written it had he lived in our day," Prokofiev came as close as anyone in the
twentieth century to recapturing the spirit of Haydn's effortless Allegros.
The second element in his style he identified as the search for innovation. *Search for innovation*
"At first this consisted in the quest for an individual harmonic language but
was later transformed into a medium for the expression of strong emotions."

"The third is the element of the toccata, or motor element, probably *Motor elements*
influenced by Schumann's Toccata, which impressed me greatly at one time."
The toccata is associated with a strong rhythmic drive, generally of the
"perpetual motion" type that is much to the fore in the music of our century.
"The fourth element is lyrical. Since my lyricism has for a long time been *Lyrical elements*
denied appreciation, it has grown but slowly. But at later stages I paid more
and more attention to lyrical expression." This element understandably
dominated his final phase in the Soviet Union.

"I should like to limit myself to these four elements, and to regard the
fifth, that of the grotesque which some critics try to foist on me, as merely *The comic and the*
a variation of the others. In application to my music, I should like to replace *mischievous*
the word *grotesque* by 'Scherzo-ness' or by the three words giving its gradations: *jest, laughter, mockery*." Prokofiev stood in the forefront of those
who attempted to broaden musical expression to include the comic and
the mischievous. In his later years the grotesquerie mellowed into a com-
passionate humor.

Prokofiev became one of the most popular of twentieth-century composers, and a number of his works have become "classics." In his later
symphonies he sought to recapture the heroic affirmation of the Beethovenian symphony. Of his operas, two in particular found favor outside his
homeland: *The Love for Three Oranges* and *The Duenna*, a sprightly work
based on Sheridan's comedy. Two other operas are especially impressive—
The Flaming Angel and *War and Peace*, based on Tolstoy's novel. Both
works were introduced to this country in English versions by the present
writer, the first by the New York City Opera in 1966 and the second in a
television performance by the NBC Opera Theater in 1957. *War and Peace*
is Prokofiev's masterpiece in the lyric theater.

Prokofiev: Alexander Nevsky

The decade preceding the outbreak of World War II was a period of mounting
tension throughout Europe as the Soviet Union felt increasingly threatened
by Hitler's Germany. Thus a film based on the life of a folk hero who defeated
the Germans was bound to have a morale-raising effect on the Russian people.
Such a film was produced by the great director Sergei Eisenstein, about
Alexander Nevsky, the Grand Duke of Novgorod who in 1240 defeated an
attacking Swedish army on the river Neva, and in 1242 defeated the German

The opposing armies face each other across the river Neva in this scene from Sergei Eisenstein's great film, Alexander Nevsky. (The Museum of Modern Art/ Film Stills Archive)

attackers in a battle on the frozen surface of Lake Chudskoye. Prokofiev wrote the film score, which he later shaped into a cantata. That the project had the full backing of the Soviet government is indicated by the fact that members of the Russian army served as extras for the film.

The cantata, for chorus, mezzo-soprano, and orchestra, is in seven movements. (See Listening Guide 45 for their titles.) We hear the final movement, *Alexander's Entry into Pskov*. The Grand Duke and his troops return triumphant from the decisive battle. The folksong-like tune of the fourth movement reappears against brilliant orchestration. Throughout the movement, percussion punctuates the choral parts, which often separate into women's and men's voices. Prokofiev here anticipated the mood of the final scene of *War and Peace*, in which Marshall Kutuzov and his soldiers celebrate their victory over Napoleon's invading army.

Despite his difficulties with the Soviet government and its official doctrine of "socialist realism" (as opposed to the "bourgeois formalism" of the West), Prokofiev appears to have remained faithful to the aesthetic he espoused upon his return to Russia. A year before his death he wrote the following lines, which may be taken as a final affirmation of his creed: "When I was in the United States and England I often heard discussions on the subject of whom music ought to serve, for whom a composer ought to write, and to whom his music should be addressed. In my view the composer, just as the poet, the sculptor, or the painter, is in duty bound to serve man, the people. He must beautify human life and defend it. He must be a citizen first and foremost, so that his art may consciously extol human life and lead man to a radiant future. Such, as I see it, is the immutable goal of art."

Listening Guide 45

8A/4 II/4/12

PROKOFIEV: *Alexander Nevsky*

Date: 1939

Genre: Cantata for chorus, mezzo-soprano, and orchestra, in 7 movements

Basis: Film score for *Alexander Nevsky* (1938), directed by Sergei Eisenstein

I. Russia Beneath the Yoke of the Mongols
(Orchestral prelude). Portrays the desolation of the country under the foreign invaders.

II. Song About Alexander Nevsky. Celebrates Alexander's earlier victory over the Swedes.

III. The Crusaders in Pskov (Chorus). Depicts the brutal treatment of the people of Pskov by the Germans.

IV. Arise, People of Russia (Chorale). Rallies the people to rise up and defend the motherland.

V. The Battle on the Ice. Spectacular orchestral movement, with choral chants. Depicts the victory of the Russians as the Germans sink under the cracking ice.

VI. The Field of the Dead (mezzo-soprano solo). Laments the fate of a fallen knight.

VII. Alexander's Entry into Pskov

Text	*Translation*	*Description*
12 *Chorus of Russians:*		
Na vyliki boi vykhodila Rus'.	Russia marched out to mighty battle.	stately chorus
Voroga pobyedila Rus'.	Russia overcame the enemy.	punctuated with
Na rodnoi zyemlye nye byvat' vragu.	On our native soil, let no foe exist.	percussion
Kto pridyot, budyet nasmyert' bit.	Whoever invades, will be killed.	
Women:		
Vyesyelisya, poi, mat'rodnaya Rus'!	Be merry, sing, mother Russia!	bells begin
Na rodnoi Rusi nye byvat' vragu.	In our native Russia, let no foe exist.	folk-like, quicker
Nye vidat' vragu nashikh russikh syol.	Let no foe see our native villages.	women's voices
Kto pridyol na Rus', budyet nasmert' bit.	Whoever invades Russia, will be killed.	

Sopranos

Altos Vye-sye - lis - ya, poi   mat' rod - na - ya Rus'!   Na rod - noi Ru - si   nye by - vat' vra - gu.

Men:		
Nye vidat' vragu nashikh russikh syol.	Let no foe see our native villages.	bells continue
Kto pridyot na Rus', budyet nasmert' bit.	Whoever invades Russia, will be killed.	men's voices imitate women countermelody in violins
13 Na Rusi rodnoi, na Rusi bol'shoi nye byvat' vragu.	In our native Russia, in great Russia, let no foe exist.	Motherland Russia theme. Lower voices sing

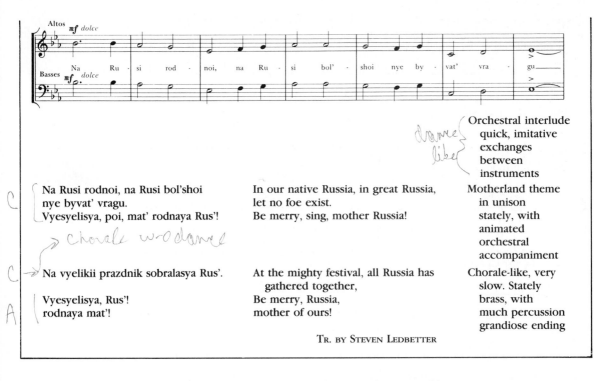

| Na Rusi rodnoi, na Rusi bol'shoi nye byvat' vragu. Vyesyelisya, poi, mat' rodnaya Rus'! | In our native Russia, in great Russia, let no foe exist. Be merry, sing, mother Russia! | Motherland theme in unison stately, with animated orchestral accompaniment |
| Na vyelikii prazdnik sobralasya Rus'. Vyesyelisya, Rus'! rodnaya mat'! | At the mighty festival, all Russia has gathered together, Be merry, Russia, mother of ours! | Chorale-like, very slow. Stately brass, with much percussion grandiose ending |

TR. BY STEVEN LEDBETTER

The East European School: Béla Bartók

"What is the best way for a composer to reap the full benefits of his studies in peasant music? It is to assimilate the idiom of peasant music so completely that he is able to forget all about it and use it as his musical mother tongue."

Béla Bartók

It was the mission of Béla Bartók (1881–1945) to reconcile the folk melody of his native Hungary with the main currents of European music. In the process he created an entirely personal language and revealed himself as one of the major artists of our century.

His Life and Music

Bartók was born in a small Hungarian town where his father was director of an agricultural school. He studied at the Royal Academy in Budapest, where he came in contact with the nationalist movement aimed at shaking off the domination of German musical culture. His interest in folklore led him to realize that what passed for Hungarian in the eyes of the world— the idiom romanticized by Liszt and Brahms and kept alive by café musicians—was really the music of Gypsies. The true Hungarian folk idiom, he decided, was to be found only among the peasants. In company with his fellow composer Zoltán Kodály he toured the remote villages of the country, determined to collect the native songs before they died out forever. "Those days I spent in the villages among the peasants," he wrote later, "were among

Béla Bartók as a young man recording folksongs in a Transylvanian mountain village. (The photograph was taken in the 1900s by fellow-composer Zoltán Kodály. (Collection of G. D. Hackett)

bag pipes

the happiest of my life. In order to feel the vitality of this music one must, so to speak, have lived it. And this is possible only when one comes to know it by direct contact with the peasants."

With the performance at the Budapest Opera of his ballet *The Wooden Prince*, Bartók came into his own. The fall of the Hapsburg monarchy in 1918 released a surge of national fervor that created a favorable climate for his music. In the ensuing decade Bartók became a leading figure in the musical life of his country.

The alliance between Admiral Horthy's regime and Nazi Germany on the eve of the Second World War confronted the composer with issues that he faced squarely. He protested the performances of his music on the Berlin radio and at every opportunity took an anti-Fascist stand. To go into exile meant surrendering the position he enjoyed in Hungary. But he would not compromise. "He who stays on when he could leave may be said to acquiesce tacitly in everything that is happening here." Bartók's friends, fearing for his safety, prevailed upon him to leave the country while there was still time. He came to the United States in 1940 and settled in New York City.

Emigration to the U.S.

The last five years of his life yielded little in the way of happiness. Sensitive and retiring, he felt uprooted, isolated in his new surroundings. He made some public appearances, playing his music for two pianos with his wife and onetime pupil, Ditta Pásztory-Bartók. These did not suffice to relieve his financial straits.

Last years

In his last years he suffered from leukemia and was no longer able to appear in public. Friends appealed for aid to ASCAP (American Society of Composers, Authors, and Publishers). Funds were made available that provided the composer with proper care in nursing homes and enabled him to continue writing to the end. A series of commissions from various sources spurred him to the composition of his last works. They rank among his finest.

"The trouble is," he remarked to his doctor shortly before the end, "that I have to go with so much still to say." He died in the West Side Hospital in New York City.

The tale of the composer who spends his last days in poverty and embitterment only to be acclaimed after his death would seem to belong to the Romantic past, to the legend of Mozart and Schubert. Yet it happened in our time. Bartók had to die in order to make his success in the United States. Almost immediately there was an upsurge of interest in his music.

Like Stravinsky, Bartók was careful to disclaim the role of revolutionary. "In art there are only fast or slow developments. Essentially it is a matter of evolution, not revolution." Despite the newness of his language he was rooted in the Classical heritage. "In my youth my ideal was not so much the art of Bach or Mozart as that of Beethoven." He adhered to the logic and beauty of Classical form, and to Beethoven's vision of music as an embodiment of human emotion.

Melody and harmony

Bartók found authentic Hungarian folk music to be based on ancient modes, unfamiliar scales, and nonsymmetrical rhythms. These freed him from what he called "the tyrannical rule of the major and minor keys," and brought him to new concepts of melody, harmony, and rhythm.

Classical and Romantic elements intermingle in Bartók's art. His Classicism shows itself in his emphasis on construction. His harmony can be bitingly dissonant. Polytonality abounds in his work; but, despite an occasional leaning toward atonality, he never wholly abandoned the principle of key. Bartók's is one of the great rhythmic imaginations of modern times. His pounding,

Rhythmic innovation

stabbing rhythms constitute the primitive aspect of his art. Passages in his scores have a Stravinskyan look, the meter changing almost at every bar. Like the Russian master, he is fond of syncopation and repeated patterns (ostinatos). Bartók played a major role in the revitalization of European rhythm, infusing it with earthy vitality and tension.

Principal Works

Orchestral works, including *Music for Strings, Percussion, and Celesta* (1936), Concerto for Orchestra (1943); 2 violin concertos (1908, 1938), 3 piano concertos (1926, 1931, 1945)

1 opera: *Bluebeard's Castle* (1918)

2 ballets: *The Wooden Prince* (1917) and *The Miraculous Mandarin* (1926)

Chamber music, including 6 string quartets (1908–39); *Contrasts* (for violin, clarinet, and piano, 1938); sonatas, duos

Piano music, including *Allegro barbaro* (1911) and *Mikrokosmos* (6 books, 1926–39)

Choral music, including *Cantata profana* (1930); folksong arrangements

Songs, including folksong arrangements

He was more traditional in respect to form. His model was the sonata of Beethoven. In his middle years he came under the influence of pre-Bach music and turned increasingly from harmony to linear thinking. His complex texture is a masterly example of modern dissonant counterpoint. It sets forth his development toward greater abstraction, tightness of structure, and purity of style.

Form

From the orchestra of Richard Strauss and Debussy, Bartók found his way to a palette all his own. His orchestration ranges from brilliant mixtures to threads of pure color that bring out the intertwining melody lines; from a hard, bright glitter to a luminous haze. A virtuoso pianist himself, Bartók is one of the masters of modern piano writing. He typifies the twentieth-century use of the piano as an instrument of percussion and rhythm. His six string quartets may very well rank among the finest achievements of our century. Bartók is best known to the public by the three major works of his last period. The *Music for Strings, Percussion and Celesta* is regarded by many as his masterpiece. Tonal opulence and warmth characterize the Concerto for Orchestra, a favorite with American audiences. The master's final statement, the Third Piano Concerto, is an impassioned and broadly conceived work.

Orchestration

String quartets

Bartók's music encompasses the diverse trends of his time, polytonality and atonality, Expressionism and Neoclassicism, folk dance and machine music, the lyric and the dynamic. It reaches from the primitive to the intellectual, from program music to the abstract, from nationalism to the universal. Into all these he infused the high aim of a former age: to touch the heart.

Bartók: Music for Strings, Percussion and Celesta

This work was a landmark in the twentieth-century cultivation of chamber music textures. Bartók's conception called for two string groups to frame the percussion and celesta. He carefully specified the arrangement of the players on the stage:

	Double Bass I	Double Bass II	
Cello I	Timpani	Bass Drum	Cello II
Viola I	Side Drums	Cymbals	Viola II
Violin II	Celesta	Xylophone	Violin IV
Violin I	Piano	Harp	Violin III

The first movement, marked Andante tranquillo, is a fugue based on a single crescendo that grows inexorably from pianissimo to a fortissimo climax and then works back to a softer pianississimo (*ppp*). The second movement is an Allegro. The main idea of this closely knit sonata form is a taut, imperious subject whose chromatic character relates it to the subject of the preceding movement. The third movement, an Adagio, is a "night piece" that reveals Bartók's gift for evoking a magical nocturnal landscape through instrumental color. The movement is an "arch form," proceeding to a high point and then retracing its path back to the beginning.

First movement

Middle movements

We hear the fourth movement, an Allegro molto in rondo form, that combines the passionate abandon of Magyar folk dance and contrapuntal processes tossed off with true virtuosity. The assymetrical dance-like rhythm of the central idea alternates with the propulsive, jazzy animation in the contrasting sections. Each recurrence of the rondo theme brings fresh variation. (See Listening Guide 46 for analysis.)

Listening Guide 46

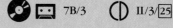 7B/3   II/3/25

BARTÓK: *Music for Strings, Percussion, and Celesta*

Date: 1936

Medium: double string orchestra, percussion, piano, and celesta

I.   Andante tranquillo: Fugue

II. Allegro: Sonata form

III. Adagio: "Night Music"

IV. Allegro molto
Form: Rondo
Basis: folk dance tunes, the first a transformed version of the opening movement fugue subject

Pizzicato chords in strings, resembling folk instruments, and timpani

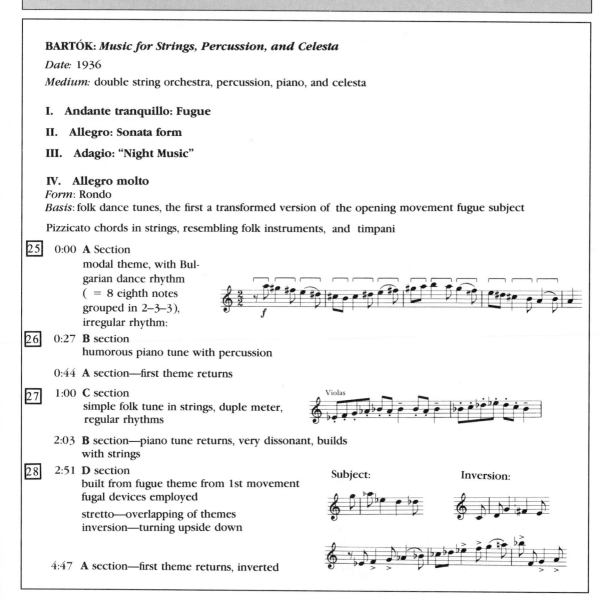

|25| 0:00 **A Section**
modal theme, with Bulgarian dance rhythm (= 8 eighth notes grouped in 2–3–3), irregular rhythm:

|26| 0:27 **B section**
humorous piano tune with percussion

0:44 **A section—first theme returns**

|27| 1:00 **C section**
simple folk tune in strings, duple meter, regular rhythms

Violas

2:03 **B section—piano tune returns, very dissonant, builds with strings**

|28| 2:51 **D section**
built from fugue theme from 1st movement fugal devices employed

Subject: Inversion:

stretto—overlapping of themes
inversion—turning upside down

4:47 **A section—first theme returns, inverted**

Bartók's prime characteristic both as musician and man was the uncompromising integrity that informed his every act—what a compatriot of his has called "the proud morality of the mind." He was one of the great spirits of our time.

75

The American Scene: Art Music

"Music. . . the favorite passion of my soul"—THOMAS JEFFERSON

The American quality in music is not a single thing. It is the great achievement of our nation to have created, out of elements inherited from the past, entirely new and fresh kinds of music.

The Development of an American Style

Until the end of the nineteenth century, the music of the native American Indians remained an isolated oral tradition, ignored by those who arrived here later. Immigrant groups—the Spanish who came to seek gold and preach Catholicism, the Dutch who came to trade, the British and French and Germans who came to escape religious or political persecution, and the Africans who were brought as slaves—carried their own music with them from their homelands. This was the mélange that provided the initial ingredients for America's musical melting pot.

Early history

In the Atlantic colonies, English music dominated. The Puritans of New England sang psalms from their Protestant tradition, and their *Bay Psalm Book* (1638) was the first book printed in the British colonies of North America. The ballads of England and Scotland continued to be sung in colonial America, gradually changing as they were handed down from generation to generation. As cities became more populous in the eighteenth century, theatrical entertainments—primarily successful ballad operas from London—flourished.

The Revolutionary War made little difference to musical life, for in the early nineteenth century American society continued to model itself to a considerable extent on its English counterpart. The Handelian choral tradition soon took root in such organizations as the Boston Handel and Haydn Society, founded in 1815 to perform *Messiah, The Creation*, and other oratorios. Even opera first came to American via London, in the form of English-language adaptations such as *The Libertine*, a version of Mozart's *Don Giovanni* introduced to New York in 1817.

19th-century concert life

Frontispiece of The New England Psalm-Singer (*1770*), *featuring a canon by William Billings engraved by Paul Revere.*

But music from other sources found an audience as well. As early as 1825, Rossini's *Barber of Seville* was performed in New York in Italian, by a touring company under Manuel García, the Spanish tenor who had sung in the opera's first performance. New Orleans became a center of French opera. The increasing flow of German immigrants, especially after the failure of the 1848 revolutions, included many musicians, and Germans were important figures in the founding of the Philharmonic Society of New York in 1842, America's first permanent orchestra.

The beginning of American nationalism

That, perhaps, is the crucial point in defining American music: when did it become something that could not have happened anywhere else? Already in the eighteenth century, William Billings (1746–1800) of New England composed highly individual hymns, anthems, and "fuging tunes," of a directness quite unlike the more genteel work of his English forebears. Later and in another style came Stephen Foster (1826–64), whose universally loved songs drew on sources as diverse as Italian opera, English ballads, Irish popular songs, and the music of the minstrel show (a theatrical entertainment performed by whites in blackface). African slaves, taught to sing Protestant hymns when they were converted to Christianity, absorbed this idiom into the tradition they had brought from Africa, developing what came to be known as the "spiritual," with a rhythmic pulse and melodic colorings not known in the churches of their masters. All of these were new kinds of music, unique to America.

By 1850, a substantial concert life had grown up in our major cities, but it continued to be dominated by Europe. German music and musicians ruled the concert halls, while opera was principally supplied by the Italians. Young Americans who were attracted to a musical career, whether as composers

or performers, went abroad to complete their studies. When they returned home they brought the European traditions with them. One of the first to use native song and dance as a source of inspiration was Louis Gottschalk (1829–69), a charismatic pianist and composer born in New Orleans and trained in Paris, who made his American debut in 1853. Some of Gottschalk's original piano pieces, such as *The Banjo* and *Bamboula*, incorporated features of an Afro-American musical idiom. It was only gradually that American musicians shook off the influence of German music. This development was consummated with Charles Tomlinson Griffes (1884–1920), who turned for inspiration to France and the music of the Impressionists rather than to Germany, where he was trained. Meanwhile an unknown New Englander was working in isolation to find a vital way of expressing the American spirit in music—Charles Ives, whom the perspective of history reveals as the first major prophet of our musical coming of age.

In this century American composers of art music, beginning with Ives, have found their own voices, drawing upon the youthful traditions of which, as Americans, they are inheritors—not hewing to any one style, but distilling their own innovative, personal, national syntheses from among the available possibilities. The extraordinary emigration of composers and other musicians from Europe on the eve of the Second World War added a further element to the mix, and their teaching has been assimilated as well. Since World War II, the United States has been the birthplace of many of the most significant new developments in art music. After a long period in search of "American music," we have discovered that there is no such thing, but many different American musics—every one of them impossible to imagine as the product of any other culture.

Under P. T. Barnum's management, the Swedish soprano Jenny Lind took American audiences by storm. A contemporary engraving depicts her first appearance in America, at Castle Garden on September 11, 1850.

Charles Ives

Charles Ives

"Beauty in music is too often confused with something that lets the ears lie back in an easy chair. Many sounds that we used to do not bother us, and for that reason we are inclined to call them beautiful. Frequently, when a new or unfamiliar work is accepted as beautiful on its first hearing, its fundamental quality is one that tends to put the mind to sleep."

Charles Edward Ives (1874–1954) waited many years for recognition. Today he stands revealed as the first great American composer of the twentieth century, and one of the most original spirits of his time.

His Life and Music

Ives was born in Danbury, Connecticut. His father had been a bandmaster in the Civil War, and continued his calling in civilian life. Charles at thirteen held a job as church organist and already was arranging music for the various ensembles conducted by his father. At twenty he entered Yale, where he studied composition with Horatio Parker. Ives's talent for music asserted itself throughout his four years at Yale; yet when he had to choose a career he decided against a professional life in music. He suspected that society would not pay him for the kind of music he wanted to compose. He was right.

He therefore entered the business world. Two decades later he was head of the largest insurance agency in the country. The years it took him to achieve this success—roughly from the time he was twenty-one to forty-two—were the years when he wrote his music. He composed at night, on weekends, and during vacations, working in isolation, concerned only to set down the sounds he heard in his head.

The few conductors and performers whom he tried to interest in his compositions pronounced them unplayable. After a number of these rebuffs Ives gave up showing his manuscripts. When he felt the need to hear how his music sounded, he hired a few musicians to run through a work. Save for these rare and quite inadequate performances, Ives heard his music only in his imagination. He pursued his way undeflected and alone, piling up one score after another in his barn in Connecticut. When well-meaning friends suggested that he try to write music that people would like, he could only retort, "I can't do it—I hear something else!"

Ives's double life as a business executive by day and composer by night finally took its toll. In 1918, when he was forty-four, he suffered a physical breakdown that left his heart damaged. The years of unrewarded effort had taken more out of him emotionally than he had suspected. Although he lived almost forty years longer, he produced nothing further of importance.

When he recovered he faced the realization that the world of professional musicians was irrevocably closed to his ideas. He felt that he owed it to his music to make it available to those who might be less hidebound. He therefore had the *Concord Sonata* for piano privately printed, also the *Essays Before a Sonata*—a kind of elaborate program note that presented the essence of his views on life and art. These were followed by the *114 Songs*. The three volumes, which were distributed free of charge to libraries, music critics, and whoever else asked for them, caused not a ripple as far as the public was concerned. But they gained Ives the support of other experimental composers who were struggling to make their way in an unheeding world. The tide finally turned in this country when the American pianist John Kirkpatrick, at a recital in Town Hall in January 1939, played the *Concord Sonata*. Ives was then sixty-five. The piece was repeated several weeks later by Kirkpatrick and scored a triumph. The next morning Lawrence Gilman hailed the *Concord Sonata* as "the greatest music composed by an American."

Ives had already begun to exert a salutary influence upon the younger generation of composers, who found in his art a realization of their own ideals. Now he was "discovered" by the general public and hailed as the grand old man of American music. In 1947 his Third Symphony achieved performance and won a Pulitzer Prize. This story of belated recognition was an item to capture the imagination, and was carried by newspapers through-out the country. Ives awoke at seventy-three to find himself famous. He died in New York City at the age of eighty.

Charles Ives, both as man and artist, was rooted in the New England heritage, in the tradition of plain living and high thinking that came to flower in the idealism of Hawthorne and the Alcotts, Emerson and Thoreau. The sources of his tonal imagery are to be found in the living music of his childhood: hymn tunes and popular songs, the town band at holiday parades, the fiddlers at Saturday night dances, patriotic songs and sentimental parlor ballads, the melodies of Stephen Foster, and the medleys heard at country fairs and in small theaters.

This wealth of American music had attracted other musicians besides Ives. But they, subservient to European canons of taste, had proceeded to smooth out and "correct" these popular tunes according to the rules they had absorbed in Leipzig or Munich. Ives was as free from subservience to the European tradition as Walt Whitman. His keen ear caught the sound of untutored voices singing a hymn together, some in their eagerness straining and sharpening the pitch, others just missing it and flatting; so that in place of the single tone there was a cluster of tones that made a deliciously dissonant

Principal Works

Orchestral music, including 4 symphonies (1898, 1902, 1904, 1916), *Three Places in New England* (1914), *The Unanswered Question* (1908), and *The Fourth of July* (1913)

Chamber music, including 2 string quartets and 4 violin sonatas

Piano music, including 2 sonatas (No. 2, *Concord*, 1915)

Choral music and many songs, including *General William Booth Enters into Heaven* (1914)

Ives's music was as firmly rooted in uniquely American traditions as the cowboy bronzes of **Frederic Remington** (*1861– 1909*), *such as* The Bronco Buster (Amon Carter Museum, Fort Worth, Texas)

chord. Some were a trifle ahead of the beat, others lagged behind; consequently the rhythm sagged and turned into a welter of polyrhythms. He heard the pungent clash of dissonance when two bands in a parade, each playing a different tune in a different key, came close enough together to overlap; he heard the effect of quarter tones (an interval half the size of a half step) when fiddlers at a country dance brought excitement into their playing by going a mite off pitch. He remembered the wheezy harmonium at church accompanying the hymns a trifle out of tune. All these, he realized,

Ives's polytonality and polyrhythm

were not departures from the norm. They *were* the norm of popular American musical speech. Thus he found his way to such conceptions as polytonality, atonality, polyharmony, cluster chords based on intervals of a second, and polyrhythms. All this in the last years of the nineteenth century, when Schoenberg was still writing in a post-Wagnerian idiom, when neither Stravinsky nor Bartók had begun their careers. All the more honor then to this singular musician who, isolated from the public and his fellow composers, was so advanced in his conceptions and so accurate in his forecast of the paths that twentieth century music would follow.

Orchestral works

The central position in his orchestral music is held by the four symphonies. Among his other orchestral works are *Three Places in New England* and *The Unanswered Question*. The Sonata No. 2 for piano—"Concord, Mass., 1840–1860"—which occupied him from 1909 to 1915, reflects various aspects of the flowering of New England; its four movements are entitled "Emerson," "Hawthorne," "The Alcotts," and "Thoreau." Ives also wrote a variety of songs, as well as chamber, choral, and piano compositions.

Ives: Symphony No. 2

Ives completed his Symphony No. 2 in 1902, although parts of the last movement were sketched earlier. The work had to wait a long time for its first performance. Walter Damrosch, the conductor of the New York Philharmonic, asked to see the score and never returned it. In 1951, fifty-four years after Ives wrote it, Leonard Bernstein presented the symphony at four concerts of the New York Philharmonic. The prospect of finally hearing the work agitated the composer, who was now seventy-seven; he attended neither the rehearsals nor the performance. But he was one of the millions who listened to the Sunday afternoon radio broadcast.

The piece includes quotations of the American tunes that Ives loved in his youth, such as *Turkey in the Straw, Old Black Joe*, and *America the Beautiful*. These and similar allusions firmly relate Ives to his heritage. He also included snatches of the European composers who influenced him— Brahms, Wagner, Beethoven, Dvořák. The Symphony No. 2, consequently, is a kind of spiritual odyssey of an American musician seeking to find himself at the turn of the nineteenth century, as he weaves elements of the past into the texture of his own language. The symphony has five movements arranged in an unusual order, as both the third and fourth movements are in slow tempo.

We hear the last two movements. The fourth is a short, majestic work that makes a musical reference to the first movement, as well as to *Columbia, the Gem of the Ocean.* It seems less a separate movement than a prelude to the Finale. This movement opens with a lively, dancelike melody that is interrupted by allusions to tunes such as *Camptown Races* in the horns and a patriotic fife-and-drum motive. (See Listening Guide 47.) The second theme is a lovely melody reminiscent of Stephen Foster, which is treated contrapuntally against a violin countermelody. This is interrupted by the flute, later the oboe, with *Long, Long Ago*. The return of the first theme brings with it another quotation of *Camptown Races*, followed by *Columbia, the Gem of the Ocean* in the brass, and finally the bugle call *Reveille* in the trumpet. One can truly say that this music is as American as apple pie.

Fourth and Fifth movements

The works of Charles Ives are now firmly established in our concert life. Like the writers he admired most—Emerson, Hawthorne, Thoreau—he has become an American classic.

Listening Guide 47   🔴 📼 7B/2   ◐ II/3/20

IVES: Symphony No. 2
Date: 1902
Movements: 5

I. Andante moderato. Baroque-like theme in strings; free melody in oboe leads into second movement.

II. Allegro. Musical citations of *Bringing in the Sheaves* and Beethoven's Fifth Symphony.

III. Adagio cantabile. Musical citation of Brahms's First Symphony, and *America the Beautiful*

20 **IV. Lento maestoso.** Solemn character; citations in the brass to first movement theme and *Columbia, the Gem of the Ocean;* leads directly to Finale.

V. Allegro molto vivace

21 Theme 1, dancelike, from second
movement

Interrupted by *Camptown Races*
in horns

Fife/drum motive, in piccolo and
percussion

22 Theme 2, from *The American Woods*
Melancholy horn melody (Stephen Foster-
like), with countermelody in violin

23 Flute with *Long, Long Ago*

Animated section, leads to Theme 1 dance
tune with *Camptown Races* in horns

24 *Columbia, the Gem of the Ocean* heard in
trombones and trumpets

Cello melody with flute countermelody.
Oboe introduces *Long, Long Ago*. More
animated and contrapuntal, each family of
orchestra going in different direction

Columbia, the Gem of the Ocean heard
complete in trombones, interrupted by
Reveille (bugle call) in trumpets

Leads up to final, raucous chord

Aaron Copland

Aaron Copland

"I no longer feel the need of seeking out conscious Americanisms. Because we live here and work here, we can be certain that when our music is mature it will also be American in quality."

Aaron Copland (1900–90) has been generally recognized as the representative figure among present-day American composers. He manifested the serenity, clarity, and sense of balance that we regard as the essence of the Classical temperament.

His Life and Music

Copland was born "on a street in Brooklyn that can only be described as drab. . . . Music was the last thing anyone would have connected with it." During his early twenties he studied in Paris with Nadia Boulanger, her first full-time American pupil. When Boulanger was invited to give concerts in America, she asked Copland to write a work for her. This was the Symphony for Organ and Orchestra. Contemporary American music was still an exotic dish to New York audiences. After the first performance (1925) Walter Damrosch found it necessary to assuage the feelings of his subscribers. "If a young man at the age of twenty-five," he announced from the stage of Carnegie Hall, "can write a symphony like that, in five years he will be ready to commit murder." Damrosch's prophecy, as far as is known, has not been fulfilled.

In his growth as a composer Copland mirrored the dominant trends of his time. After his return from Paris he turned to the jazz idiom, a phase that culminated in his brilliant Piano Concerto. There followed a period during which the Neoclassicist experimented with the abstract materials of his art; he produced his Piano Variations, *Short Symphony,* and *Statements for Orchestra.* "During these years I began to feel an increasing dissatisfaction with the relations of the music-loving public and the living composer. It seemed to me that we composers were in danger of working in a vacuum."

Jazz idiom

Neoclassical period

Principal Works

Orchestral music, including 3 symphonies, Piano Concerto (1927), *Short Symphony* (1933), *Statements for Orchestra* (1933–35), *El Salon México* (1936), *A Lincoln Portrait* (1942), *Fanfare for the Common Man* (1942), and *Connotations for Orchestra* (1962)

3 ballets: *Billy the Kid* (1938), *Rodeo* (1942), and *Appalachian Spring* (1944)

Film scores, including *The Quiet City* (1939), *Of Mice and Men* (1939), *Our Town* (1940), *The Red Pony* (1948), and *The Heiress* (1949)

Piano music, including Piano Variations (1930)

Chamber music; choral music and songs

He realized that a new public for contemporary music was being created by the radio, phonograph, and film scores. "It made no sense to ignore them and to continue writing as if they did not exist. I felt that it was worth the effort to see if I couldn't say what I had to say in the simplest possible terms." In this fashion Copland was led to what became a most significant development after the 1930s: the attempt to simplify the new music so that it would communicate to a large public.

The "new" music

The decade that followed saw the production of the scores that established Copland's popularity. Almost all the works listed above have become classics, especially the three ballets, *Billy the Kid, Rodeo*, and *Appalachian Spring*, which continue to delight an international audience.

Copland: "Hoe-Down" from Rodeo

The second of Copland's American ballets, *Rodeo*, boasts one of his freshest scores. The choreographer was Agnes de Mille, whose innovations opened a new era in the American dance theater. It was she who gave Copland the idea for the ballet. "Throughout the American Southwest," de Mille explained, "the Saturday afternoon rodeo is a tradition. On the remote ranches, as well as in the trading centers and the towns, the 'hands' get together to show off their skill in roping, riding, branding, and throwing. The afternoon's exhibition is usually followed by a Saturday night dance at the Ranch House."

The action of the ballet is a cowboy version of the Cinderella/Ugly Duckling story. The Cowgirl, awkward and tomboyish, is in love with the Head Wrangler and tries to impress him by competing with the cowboys; but she makes no headway with the object of her affections, for he has eyes only for the Rancher's daughter. During the afternoon rodeo she is thrown by a bucking bronco and is ridiculed by all. Later, at the Saturday night dance, still dressed in her mannish outfit of pants and shirt, she is very much the wallflower. The sight of the Head Wrangler dancing cheek to cheek with her rival is too much for her. She runs off, disconsolate. When she returns she is completely transformed: the trousers have been replaced by a pretty dress, the boots by slippers, she has a bow in her hair, is the epitome of feminine allure, and quickly becomes the belle of the ball.

The concert suite that Copland arranged from the ballet consists of four "dance episodes." (See Listening Guide 48 for titles and analysis.) We hear the fourth, "Hoe-Down," a sprightly Allegro for which Copland borrowed two square-dance tunes, *Bonyparte* and *McLeod's Reel*. The music vividly suggests the traditional stance—head up, chest out, elbows raised, knees bobbing up and down—that we associate with the more vigorous forms of square dancing. Copland repeats and alternates the tunes, pits snatches of solo against the full orchestra, contrasts "vamps" (repeated passages) in the bass with melodies in the upper register of winds and strings, and manages in an unforgettable way to convey the boundless energy and zest for life that animated the generations who built our country.

Perhaps a psychologist could explain how it happened that the son of Russian-Jewish immigrants, growing up on that drab street in Brooklyn,

A scene from the American Ballet Theater production of Rodeo. (Photo © 1983 by Martha Swope)

Listening Guide 48

8B/1   II/4/20

COPLAND: *Rodeo*

Date: 1942

Genre: Ballet, arranged as orchestral suite

I. "Buckaroo Holiday"
2 cowboy songs: *Sis Joe* and *If He'd Be a Buckaroo*

II. "Corral Nocturne"

III. "Saturday Night Waltz"

IV. "Hoe-Down"
2 square-dance tunes

Bonyparte

McLeod's Reel

20   0:00   Opening: animated, fast triplet pattern.

          Strings sound as if they are tuning up. Piano and woodblock set up syncopated rhythms with pizzicato strings

   0:40   Tune 1: *Bonyparte*—fast, in strings and xylophone. Brass with syncopated rhythm

21   1:40   Tune 2: *McLeod's Reel*—lighter, sprightly dance heard first in trumpet, passed to various instruments, violins, oboes

   2:38   Piano and pizzicato string rhythm, as above. Slows down and comes to stop on long chord with celesta (bells)

   2:57   Tune 1 returns—interspersed with short references to Tune 2

created the sound by which the cowboy is best known in the ballet houses and concert halls of the world. Whatever the mystery of the artist's imagination, Copland was able to capture in his music the poetic image of the prairie and, in so doing, became the most American of our composers.

76

The American Scene: Popular Styles

"Jazz I regard as an American folk music; not the only one, but a very powerful one, which is probably in the blood and feeling of the American people more than any other style of folk music. I believe that it can be made the basis of serious symphonic works of lasting value."—GEORGE GERSHWIN

Music in American Popular Culture

We saw that a diversity of cultures met in the great melting pot that is America. Out of those our country developed distinctive musical styles quite outside the classical idiom. The marches of John Philip Sousa (1855–1932) came to be internationally recognized as a peculiarly American contribution. So too jazz, rooted in spirituals, blues, and ragtime, which were part and parcel of the American scene, captured the imagination of the world. Around the turn of the twentieth century the insistent rhythms of Afro-American music began to infuse new life into our popular musical theater. The songs of Jerome Kern, Irving Berlin, and George Gershwin transformed Broadway, and later Hollywood, into world musical centers of popular music. In the ensuing decades American folk and popular idioms came to be loved everywhere.

These styles thrived side by side with the growing tradition of American art music that we discussed in the last chapter. They not only coexisted with so-called serious music but profoundly influenced it as well. It is this synthesis of styles that we will examine in the following pages.

Scott Joplin: Treemonisha

Scott Joplin (1868–1917), known as "the King of Ragtime," was one of the first black Americans to become an important composer. He was born in Texarkana, Texas, to a musical family. His father, an ex-slave, played violin, his mother sang and played banjo, as did his brothers. Joplin began his musical career by playing guitar and bugle, but soon showed such a gift for improvisation that he was given free piano lessons on a neighbor's instrument. He left home when he was fourteen, after the death of his mother, and traveled throughout the Mississippi Valley, playing in honky-tonks and piano bars where he absorbed the current styles of folk and popular music. In 1885, he went to St. Louis, which had become the center of a growing ragtime tradition.

Ragtime, so called for its "ragged" rhythm, was originally a piano style marked by highly syncopated melodies. It first gained public notice as a form of instrumental ensemble music when Joplin and his small orchestra performed at the World Columbian Exposition of 1893 in Chicago. Fame came to Joplin in 1899 with the publication of his *Maple Leaf Rag*, a piano piece that sold thousands of copies. All the same his first opera, *A Guest of Honor*, written in 1903, was never performed during his lifetime and is now lost. In 1906, he moved from St. Louis to Chicago and ultimately to New York, where he was active as a teacher, composer, and performer.

Scott Joplin

Ragtime up to that time had been mostly improvised. Joplin saw its possibilities as a serious art form on a level with European art music, which could be used as the basis for large forms such as opera and symphony. He realized that he must lead the way toward this merger of styles, and began work on his opera *Treemonisha,* which he finally finished in 1911. Unable to obtain financial backing for the work, Joplin produced a scaled-down performance that met with little approval. The setback brought on a severe depression from which he never recovered. He entered Manhattan State Hospital a year later, and died there on April 1, 1917. *Treemonisha* remained virtually unknown until its extremely successful revival in 1972 by the Houston Grand Opera. In 1976, almost sixty years after his death, Joplin was awarded the Pulitzer Prize for his masterpiece.

Joplin is best remembered today for his approximately fifty piano rags, which have now been recorded in their original form as well as in arrangements for various instruments. Several, including *The Entertainer,* gained popularity in the movie *The Sting.* These pieces reflect Joplin's preoccupation with classical forms. They exhibit balanced phrasing and key structures, together with melodies that are catchy and imaginative. Like earlier dance music, they unfold in clear-cut sections, their patterns of repetition and reprise reminiscent of those heard in the marches of Sousa.

Treemonisha presents the story of an abandoned black child who is found

Principal Works

2 operas: *A Guest of Honor* (1903, now lost) and *Treemonisha* (1911)

Ballet: *Ragtime Dance* (1902)

Piano music, mostly rags, including *The Maple Leaf Rag* (1899) and *The Entertainer* (1902)

Songs, including *A Picture of Her Face* (1895) and *Please Say You Will* (1895)

476

The Finale of the Houston Grand Opera production of Treemonisha *in March, 1982.* (Photograph by Ann Jean Mears)

under a tree by a childless couple. They take her into their home to raise and educate her. Treemonisha in time tries to help her people by teaching them to fight off the superstitions that bedevil their thinking. She is accepted as their leader and shows them that the way to freedom is through education.

Act III

The opera, in three acts, is modestly scored for eleven voices and orchestra. The work is replete with dance sequences, choruses, recitatives, and memorable arias. We hear the last two numbers of the score. Treemonisha and the full chorus join in singing "We Will Trust You as Our Leader," an inspirational melody heard against a rich harmonic background. The sweeping lines of the chorus are interrupted by declamation on the words "We feel blue, dear, we feel blue," which unfold against increasingly chromatic harmonies punctuated by chords in the orchestra. Treemonisha's vocal line soars above the chorus as she accepts her role as leader.

S4A/2

S4/7

The grand finale of the opera is a dance number. Entitled "A Real Slow Drag," the music presents a pastiche of dance steps that include the slow drag, the marchlike dude walk, and the schottische, a round dance with the feel of a slow polka. The composer indicates the choreography in the score and the dances are "called"—in the time-honored manner of group dancing—by the vocal part, which is first sung by Treemonisha, then as a duet with Lucy against a choral refrain. Treemonisha delivers her high vocal line with crystalline clarity and the typical syncopations of ragtime are presented with the utmost conviction.

Joplin was not alone in his attempt to merge ragtime with classical styles. Stravinsky, fascinated with the piano rag, incorporated its rhythmic vitality and syncopations in his *Ragtime for Eleven Instruments* (1918), his *Piano-Rag-Music* (1919), and in one dance number from *The Soldier's Tale* (1918). Debussy too captured the spirit of ragtime in the strutting rhythm of *Golliwog's Cake-walk*. The composer whose lead they followed is acknowledged today as a truly innovative musician. Joplin has been well described as "the central figure and prime creative spirit of ragtime, a composer from whom a large segment of twentieth-century American music derived its shape and spirit."

Louis Armstrong: West End Blues

By *jazz* we mean a music created mainly by black Americans in the early twentieth century as they blended elements drawn from African musics with the popular and art traditions of the West. By examining the basics of jazz and blues we come to appreciate the impact these styles have had on our art music.

Jazz

Blues is a truly American form of folk music based on a simple, repetitive poetic-musical structure. A blues text typically has a three-line stanza of which the first two are identical. The vocal style of blues was derived from the work songs of Southern blacks. The term *blues* refers to a mood as well as a harmonic progression, usually twelve or sixteen bars (measures) in length. Characteristic is the *blue note*, which represents a slight drop in pitch on the third, fifth, or seventh tone of the scale. One of the greatest of blues singers was Bessie Smith, whose performances were profoundly emotional and expressive.

Blues

Blues form

Blues was a fundamental form in jazz. The music we call jazz was born in New Orleans through the fusion of such black elements as ragtime and blues with other traditional styles—spirituals, work songs, and shouts. Basic to these elements was the art of improvisation. Performers made up their parts as they went along, often with a number of them improvising at once. They were able to do this because all the players knew the basic conditions— the tempo, the form, the harmonic progression, and the order in which instruments were to be featured. A twelve-bar blues progression followed the standard pattern given below.

New Orleans jazz

New Orleans jazz depended upon multiple improvisations by the players, which created a polyphonic texture. Each instrument had its role. The trumpet or cornet played the melody proper or an embellished version of it; the

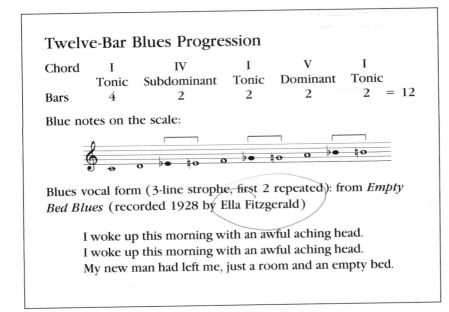

Twelve-Bar Blues Progression

Chord	I	IV	I	V	I	
	Tonic	Subdominant	Tonic	Dominant	Tonic	
Bars	4	2	2	2	2	= 12

Blue notes on the scale:

Blues vocal form (3-line strophe, first 2 repeated): from *Empty Bed Blues* (recorded 1928 by Ella Fitzgerald)

> I woke up this morning with an awful aching head.
> I woke up this morning with an awful aching head.
> My new man had left me, just a room and an empty bed.

King Oliver's Jazz Band in 1923. The young Louis Armstrong may be seen kneeling in front playing a slide trumpet. (William Ransom Hogan Jazz Archive, Tulane University)

clarinet was often featured in a countermelody above the main tune; the trombone improvised below the trumpet and signaled the chord changes; and the rhythm section—consisting of string bass or tuba, guitar or banjo, and drums—provided rhythmic and harmonic support. Among the "greats" of New Orleans jazz were Joseph "King" Oliver on cornet, Sidney Bechet on soprano saxophone, Ferdinand "Jelly Roll" Morton on piano, and Louis "Satchmo" Armstrong on trumpet.

In the early 1920s, many New Orleans musicians went up the Mississippi River to Chicago, where "King" Oliver had a New Orleans style ensemble. Louis "Satchmo" Armstrong (c. 1898–1971), a native of New Orleans, joined this band in 1922, at a time when King Oliver's Creole Jazz Band had ten players. The young Armstrong, playing cornet, made his first recordings in 1923 with this ensemble, and went on to revolutionize jazz.

Armstrong was unquestionably the most important single force in the development of early jazz styles. He was a great improviser who expanded the capacities of his instrument in range and tone colors through the use of various mutes. His was a unique melodic-rhythmic style of performance for which his admirers coined the term "swing," which became a standard description of jazz. His 1926 recording of *Heebie Jeebies* introduced *scat singing*, a jazz style that sets nonsense syllables (vocables) to an improvised vocal line. Ella Fitzgerald later brought this technique to a truly virtuosic level.

Swing

Scat singing

Armstrong's style of jazz introduced a number of new features: stop-time choruses (solos accompanied by spaced staccato chords); double-time choruses in which each beat of each measure was subdivided; a flat two- or four-beat meter based on evenly accented pulses; and solo rather than ensemble choruses. Through these innovations, jazz was transformed into a solo art that presented fantasias on chord changes rather than on a repeated melody.

West End Blues is a twelve-bar blues recorded in 1922 by Armstrong and the Savoy Ballroom Five. It features "Satchmo" on trumpet and in a vocal along with Fred Robinson on trombone, Jimmy Strong on clarinet, Mancy Cara on banjo, Zutty Singleton on drums, and the great Earl "Fatha" Hines on piano. This number opens with an unaccompanied trumpet solo by Armstrong in double time. There follow five choruses on the tune over the repeating twelve-bar progression we mentioned earlier. (See analysis in Listening Guide 49 on page 480.) In the first chorus, we hear a solo trumpet melody set to a fairly simple chordal accompaniment. The second chorus brings in the mellow voice of the trombone, supported by a percussive accompaniment. The third chorus features clarinet against Satchmo's scat singing in a call-and-response pattern, while the fourth highlights Hines's so-called trumpet-style piano playing. In the last chorus, a trumpet and clarinet duet is heard over the insistent chords, beginning with a sustained note—a high B flat—on the trumpet, followed by a double-time melody. This chorus is extended with a brief tag (the jazz term for a short coda). Throughout the selection, we hear many "blue" or bent notes.

Louis Armstrong's sound summed up an era. It has remained one of the high points of the American jazz style.

Duke Ellington: Ko-Ko

From the inspired, improvisational style of Louis Armstrong, we turn to the brilliantly composed jazz of Duke Ellington and the big-band era. Edward Kennedy "Duke" Ellington (1899–1974) was born in Washington, D.C., and was playing in New York jazz clubs in the 1920s. He became famous as a composer in the following decade. With the advent of the big bands, the need was greater for music to be arranged or written down. Ellington played a major role in this development. Himself a fine pianist, he was even better as an orchestrator. As one of his collaborators remarked, "He plays piano, but his real instrument is the orchestra."

Ellington's orchestral palette was much richer than that of the New Orleans band. It included two trumpets, one cornet, three trombones, four saxophones (some doubling on clarinet), two string basses, guitar, drum, vibraphone, and piano.

One of Ellington's best-known and most unpretentious works is *Ko-Ko*, originally written for his unfinished opera *Boola*. First recorded in 1940, *Ko-Ko*, like Armstrong's *West End Blues*, is a twelve-bar blues, expressively set in a minor key. In this work, Ellington drew inspiration from the drum ceremonies based on African religious rites that used to take place in New Orleans's Congo Square.

Ko-Ko opens with a distinctive rhythmic pattern in the tom-tom and baritone saxophone that is persistent throughout the score. In both form

Duke Ellington

S4B/2

S4/18

Listening Guide 49   8A/5   II/4/14

West End Blues, 1928, Louis Armstrong and the Savoy Ballroom Five

Louis "Satchmo" Armstrong, trumpet and vocal
Fred Robinson, trombone
Jimmy Strong, clarinet   Zutty Singleton, drums
Mancy Cara, banjo   Earl "Fatha" Hines, piano

Form: 12–bar blues (Introduction and 5 choruses)

14 Introduction (9 bars—double time)

Trumpet solo: rhythmically
complex and varied; opens
with descending, then
ascending line

15 Chorus 1: Trumpet solo over
chords; simple, homophonic
setting (12 bars)

16 Chorus 2: Trombone solo over chords, with percussion accompaniment (12 bars)

17 Chorus 3: Clarinet and vocal solos (scat singing); motives exchanged in imitation (12 bars)

18 Chorus 4: Piano solo; simple chordal accompaniment (12 bars)

19 Chorus 5: Trumpet and clarinet duet
(8 bars); polyphonic texture begins
with high held note for 4 bars, then
trumpet with double-time movement

Piano solo (4 bars)

Tag (2-bar coda): full ensemble

and content, this is an accomplished jazz "composition." Throughout its seven choruses, it continually builds in dynamic, harmonic, and textural intensity. Solo choruses feature valve trombonist Juan Tizol, backed by the orchestra in a call-and-response exchange; trombonist Joe Nanton, with his characteristic plunger-mute style; Ellington on piano, with imaginative figurations that superimpose dissonant harmonies over the established E♭-minor tonality; and bassist Jimmy Blanton, heard against the full ensemble divided into choirs of varying tone colors. The final chorus features a fullness of orchestration that suggests more instruments than are actually playing. A rounded binary form of **A-B-A** is alluded to by a Coda that recapitulates the opening.

Ellington made a many-faceted contribution to the world of jazz. As a composer, he brought his art to new heights and a new-found legitimacy; as an arranger, he left a rich legacy of works for a wide range of jazz groups; as a band leader, he served as teacher and model to a whole generation of jazz musicians. He occupies a special place in our cultural heritage.

John Lewis: Sketch

By the end of the 1940s, musicians had become disenchanted with big-band jazz and its limited possibilities. Their rebellion took shape in bop, bebop, and cool-style jazz. *Bop* was a contraction of *bebop*, an invented word whose two syllables suggest the two-note phrase that was the trademark of this style. Dizzie Gillespie, Charlie Parker, Bud Powell, and Thelonius Monk developed bebop in the 1940s. In the next two decades the term came to include a number of substyles such as cool jazz (the "cool" suggesting its restrained, unemotional manner), West Coast jazz, hard bop, and soul jazz. Bebop also featured much scat singing.

John Lewis

In 1957 the composer Gunther Schuller, in a lecture delivered at Brandeis University, promulgated the doctrine that any kind of music could profit by being combined with another kind; art music could learn from jazz and vice versa. He coined the term *third stream*, holding that classical music was the first stream, jazz the second, and the third combined the other two. Although the designation referred mainly to the instruments used, it was soon extended to include other elements as well: the adoption of classical forms and tonal devices.

The third stream

Schuller's idea was taken over by a number of jazz musicians, among them John Lewis (1920–   ). He formed his Modern Jazz Quartet in answer to the growing demand for jazz on college campuses across the country. The ensemble played concerts that "swung" but also featured serious, composed works. Lewis's *Sketch,* a work recorded in 1959, combined the foursome of his jazz ensemble with the Beaux Arts Quartet, one of the finest string quartets in the country. His string writing in this composition is reminiscent of Haydn's. The instruments of the Modern Jazz Quartet—piano, vibraphone, drums, and string bass—continually exchange their material with the string quartet. (A *vibraphone* is a percussion instrument that originated in the United States, with metal bars and electrically driven rotating propellors

Modern Jazz Quartet

S4B/7

S4/33

under each bar that produces an attractive vibrato sound.) The piece presents two basic ideas. A disjunct, leaping motive of two quarter notes (the two-note phrase, we saw, was typical of bebop) is followed by a rhythmic call of three eighth notes and an eighth rest. Both ideas are manipulated according to the classical procedures of augmentation (motive repeated in longer notes), diminution (repeated in shorter notes), and inversion (motive upside down). Lewis handles the motives subtly in his first piano solo, and then provides a supportive motivic accompaniment to the vibraphone solo played by Milt Jackson.

Influence of jazz   We noted earlier the influence of ragtime on several contemporary European composers. So too some of them fell under the spell of jazz. They were fascinated by the vigorous syncopations of jazz rhythms and the chamber music sonorities that resulted when an ensemble of soloists on woodwind and brass played against a rhythmic-harmonic background of piano, string bass, banjo or guitar, and drums. The untrammeled counterpoint of group improvisation introduced them to a new kind of texture, while the minute off-key inflections of blues musicians intrigued ears accustomed to more "correct" intonation. Although European composers did not adopt the improvisational procedures that are basic to jazz, they did capture something of its spontaneity and rhythmic freedom. Stravinsky wrote his *Ebony Concerto* (1945) for jazz clarinetist Woody Herman. Ernst Krenek's opera *Jonny spielt auf* (Johnny Plays, 1926), with a jazz violinist as hero, won an international success. The dry textures and snappy rhythms of jazz also resonate through such typically European works as Maurice Ravel's Piano Concerto in G, and Darius Milhaud's ballet *La création du monde* (The Creation of the World, 1923), the operas of Kurt Weill—*The Three-Penny Opera* (1928) and *Mahagonny* (1929)—as well as Alban Berg's *Lulu*.

The American Musical Theater

The American musical theater of today developed from the comic opera or *operetta* tradition of Johann Strauss, Jacques Offenbach, and other Europeans. It was acclimated to the American taste through a number of composers, chief among them Victor Herbert (1850–1924), whose works include such charming items as *Babes in Toyland* (1903), *Mlle. Modeste* (1905), and *Early musicals*   *Naughty Marietta* (1910). The Broadway musical came to maturity in the 1920s, with such works as Sigmund Romberg's *The Student Prince* (1924), set in a glamorized Old Heidelberg, and Jerome Kern's *Show Boat* (1927). In the ensuing decades, the musical established itself as America's unique contribution to world theater.

The genre was dependent on romantic plots in picturesque settings enlivened by comedy, appealing melodies, choruses, and dances. Within the framework of a thoroughly commercial theater a group of talented composers and writers created a body of works that not only enchanted their time but lasted well beyond it. Among these may be mentioned Burton Lane's *Finian's Rainbow* (1947), Cole Porter's *Kiss Me, Kate* (1948), Frank Loesser's *Guys and Dolls* (1950), Harold Rome's *Fanny* (1954), and Lerner and Loewe's *My Fair Lady* (1956).

The musical had begun as a form with a contrived, often silly plot whose main function was to serve as scaffolding for the songs and dances. It moved steadily toward maturity through a more convincing treatment of character and situation. Decisive in this regard was the fact that composers began to derive their plots from sophisticated literary sources. *Show Boat* was based on an Edna Ferber novel, *Kiss Me, Kate* on *The Taming of the Shrew*, *Guys and Dolls* on the stories of Damon Runyon, *Fanny* on Marcel Pagnol's trilogy, and *My Fair Lady* on George Bernard Shaw's *Pygmalian*. As their approach grew more serious the genre outgrew its original limitations. This had already happened with what became the most enduring work of our lyric theater, George Gershwin's masterpiece *Porgy and Bess* (1935), based on the novel and play by DuBose and Dorothy Hayward. This "American folk opera," as Gershwin called it, was so far ahead of its time that, despite its focus on Afro-American folk idioms, it did not establish itself with any degree of success until its European tour in the 1950s. This work paved the way for such musicals as Leonard Bernstein's *West Side Story* (1957), one of the first to have a tragic ending, and Jerry Bock's *Fiddler on the Roof* (1964), with lyrics by Sheldon Harnick, based on the stories about Tevyah the Milkman by the great Jewish humorist Sholem Aleichem. Both works won worldwide success, and both would have been unthinkable twenty years earlier.

Sources of plots

In this climate the collaboration of Richard Rodgers and Oscar Hammerstein II produced a series of memorable works: *Oklahoma!* (1943), *Carousel* (1945), *South Pacific* (1949), *The King and I* (1951), and *The Sound of Music* (1959). Here too the literary sources were of high order. *Carousel* was based on Ferenc Molnár's *Liliom*, *Oklahoma!* on Lynn Riggs's *Green Grow the Lilacs*, *South Pacific* on the stories of James Michener, *The King and I* on *Anna and the King of Siam* by Margaret Landon, and *The Sound of Music* on the moving memoir of Baroness von Trapp.

Rodgers and Hammerstein

In the '70s and '80s Stephen Sondheim brought the genre to new levels of sophistication in a series of works that included *A Little Night Music* (1973), *Sweeney Todd* (1979), *Sunday in the Park with George* (1983), and *Into the Woods* (1988). A new era opened with two rock musicals— Gale MacDermot's *Hair* (1968) and Andrew Lloyd Webber's *Jesus Christ Superstar* (1971). Suddenly the romantic show tunes to which millions of young Americans had learned to dance and to flirt went completely out of fashion. After a while, however, melody returned. The British Webber conquered the international stage with *Evita* (1978), *Cats* (1981), and *The Phantom of the Opera* (1986)—works in which, as in the court operas of the Baroque, song and dance were combined with dazzling scenic effects. Together with Claude-Michel Schönberg's *Les Misérables* (1987), these pieces represented a new phenomenon. What had been almost exclusively an American product was now taken over by Europeans.

Stephen Sondheim

Andrew Lloyd Webber

Leonard Bernstein

Leonard Bernstein: His Life and Music

As a composer, conductor, educator, pianist, and television personality, Leonard Bernstein (1918–90) had one of the most spectacular careers of our time. He was born in Lawrence, Massachusetts, the son of Russian-Jewish immigrants. At thirteen he was playing with a jazz band. He entered Harvard when he was seventeen and studied composition with Walter Piston. He attended the Curtis Institute in Philadelphia, then became one of the band of disciples whom the conductor Serge Koussevitzky gathered around him in Tanglewood. In 1943, when he was twenty-five, Bernstein was appointed Artur Rodzinski's assistant at the New York Philharmonic. A few weeks later, Bruno Walter, the guest conductor, was suddenly taken ill; Rodzinski was out of town. Bernstein, at a few hours' notice, took over the Sunday afternoon concert and coast-to-coast broadcast, and gave a spectacular performance. Overnight he was famous. Thereafter his career proceeded apace until, in 1958, at the age of forty, he was appointed director of the New York Philharmonic, the first American-born conductor (and the youngest) to occupy the post.

As a composer Bernstein straddled the worlds of serious and popular music. He was thus able to bring to the Broadway musical a compositional technique and knowledge of music that few of its practitioners had possessed. In his concert works he spoke the language of contemporary music with enormous fluency, not as an experimenter, but as one who, having inherited the great tradition, set upon it the stamp of his own personality. He had a genuine flair for orchestration; the balance and spacing of sonorities, the use of the brass in the high register, the idiomatic writing that shows off each instrument to its best advantage—all these bespeak a master. His harmonic idiom is spicily dissonant, his jazzy rhythms have great vitality; he had the gift of melody as well.

Bernstein's feeling for the urban scene—specifically the New York scene—is vividly projected in his theater music. In *On the Town*, a full-length version of his ballet *Fancy Free*, *Wonderful Town*, and *West Side Story*, he achieved

Principal Works

Orchestral works, including the *Jeremiah Symphony* (1942), Symphony No. 2, *The Age of Anxiety* (piano and orchestra, 1949), Serenade (violin, strings, and percussion, 1954), Symphony No. 3, *Kaddish* (1963)

Works for chorus and orchestra, including *Chichester Psalms* (1965) and *Songfest* (1977)

Operas, including *A Quiet Place* (1983)

Musicals, including *On the Town* (1944), *Wonderful Town* (1953), *Candide* (1956), and *West Side Story* (1957)

Other dramatic music, including the ballet *Fancy Free* (1944), the film score *On the Waterfront* (1954), and Mass (1971)

Chamber and instrumental music; solo vocal music

Riff (center) leads the Jets in the "Cool" fugue from West Side Story, *one of the highlights of the 1989 stage hit,* Jerome Robbins' Broadway. (Photo © 1989 Martha Swope)

a sophisticated kind of musical theater that explodes with movement, energy, and sentiment. These works capture "the hectic quality, the lonely quality, and the athletic quality" that the composer regards as constituting the special character of American music.

Bernstein: *Symphonic Dances from* West Side Story

West Side Story, with book and lyrics by Stephen Sondheim, updated the Romeo and Juliet saga to a modern-day setting of rival gangs of youths on the streets of New York. The hostility between the Jets and the Sharks becomes the modern counterpart of the feud of the Capulets and the Montagues in Shakespeare's play. Tony, one of the Jets, falls in love with Maria, whose brother leads the Sharks. The tale of the star-crossed lovers unfolds in scenes of great tenderness, whence come memorable songs like "Tonight" and "Maria," alternating with electrifying dances choreographed by Jerome Robbins, as the tale mounts inexorably to Tony's tragic death. Bernstein subsequently adapted their music in a set of Symphonic Dances in eight episodes. (See Listening Guide 50.) These are based on motives drawn from the chief songs, especially "Maria" and "There's a Place for Us," which here receive the kind of symphonic expansion not possible in the theater. The score displays the composer's colorful orchestration as well as his imaginative handling of jazz and Latin American rhythms. It calls for an expanded woodwind and percussion section, including the piano. The music of the "Cool" Fugue builds to several climaxes with fugal textures that become increasingly dense and polyphonic before they grow gentle and relaxed. This section of the score is from a dance sequence by the Jets, prior to the final fight, or Rumble, with the Sharks. Fleeting references to the lyrical ballads of the play resonate through the score, which demands much of our ears, especially our tolerance of high levels of dissonance. It was Bernstein's intent to bring the mood and atmosphere of the drama into the concert hall. He succeeded.

Listening Guide 50

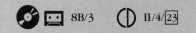

BERNSTEIN: Symphonic Dances from *West Side Story*

Date: 1961

Basis: Dance sequences from musical *West Side Story* (1957)

OVERVIEW OF SYMPHONIC DANCES

Prologue (Allegro moderato)
The growing rivalry between the two teen-age gangs, the Jets and the Sharks.

"Somewhere" (Adagio)
In a visionary dance sequence, the two gangs are united in friendship.

Scherzo (Vivace leggiero)
In the same dream, they break through the city walls, and suddenly find themselves in a world of space, air, and sun.

Mambo (Presto)
Reality again; competitive dance between the two gangs.

Cha-cha (Andantino con grazia)
The star-crossed lovers see each other for the first time and dance together.

"Cool," Fugue (Allegretto)
An elaborate dance sequence in which the Jets practice controlling their hostility.

Rumble (Molto allegro)
Climactic gang battle during which the two gang leaders are killed.

Finale (Adagio)
Love music developing into a procession, which recalls, in tragic reality, the vision of "Somewhere"

"Cool," Fugue

Based largely on several short rhythmic motives

Melody of above drawn from opening of "Maria" (rising augmented fourth, music going to a fifth)

23 0:00   Allegretto: grows out of rhythmic patterns above, adding instruments and increasingly syncopated; alternating woodwinds and strings

0:41   Muted trumpet solo, with regular brush pattern on cymbals, punctuated by 3-note motive (vibraphone, piano)

24 1:00   Fugue subject, with dotted rhythms, begins in flute, against constant brush in cymbals; then heard in clarinet and piano, marked "with jazz feel"

1:30	3-note dotted pattern returns and builds, against long notes in string
2:12	Solo percussion break followed by homophonic syncopated chords
	Second solo percussion break followed by unison section based on 3-note motive
25 2:38	Brass featured in syncopated jazz section, with shakes on high notes, accompanied by syncopated patterns in strings and woodwinds

| 3:03 | Rhythmic pattern from opening returns, builds to climax |

Rumble, Molto allegro

| 26 3:42 | Syncopations, rhythmic vitality, and complexity build to loud, homophonic chords in orchestra, irregularly spaced |
| 4:28 | Fugal section grows out of 3-note pattern, instruments added, building to regular pulse on eighth notes; marked crescendo on rising chromatic pattern leads to final glissando and closing chords. |

Leonard Bernstein was not only one of our foremost American conductors, but a composer whose creative activity extended over an unusually wide spectrum. Beyond that, he is remembered as one of the extraordinary musical personalities of our century.

UNIT XXIV

◼

The New Music

77

New Directions

"From Schoenberg I learned that tradition is a home we must love and forgo."—LUKAS FOSS

We have seen that the term "new music" has been used throughout history. Has not every generation of creative musicians produced sounds and styles that had never been heard before? All the same, the years since World War II have seen such far-reaching innovations in the art that we are perhaps more justified than any previous generation in applying the label to the music of the present. In effect, we have witnessed nothing less than the birth of a new world of sound.

New Trends in the Arts

Only rarely does an important movement in art come into being without precursors. It should therefore not surprise us that several elements of avant-garde art can be traced back to earlier developments. For example, the Dada movement grew up in Zurich during the war and after 1918 spread to other major art centers. The Dadaists, in reaction to the horrors of the blood bath that engulfed Europe, rejected the concept of Art with a capital A—that is, something to be put on a pedestal and reverently admired. To make their point, they produced works of manifest absurdity. They also reacted against the excessive complexity of Western art and tried to recapture the simple, unfettered way in which a child views the world. Erik Satie led the way toward a simple, "everyday" music, and exerted an important influence in the 1920s—along with the writer Jean Cocteau—on the generation of Milhaud, Honegger, and Poulenc. Several decades later this influence came to the fore in the work of the American composer John Cage. The Dada group,

Futurism

Dadaism

488

decades later this influence came to the fore in the work of the American composer John Cage, whom we shall discuss in a later chapter. The Dada group, which included artists like Hans Arp, Marcel Duchamp, and Kurt Schwitters, subsequently merged into the school of Surrealists, who exploited the symbolism of dreams. The best-known Surrealists, such as the writers Guillaume Apollinaire and André Breton, the painters Giorgio de Chirico, Max Ernst, and Salvador Dali, organized the indiscipline of Dada into a visionary art based on the distorted images of the world of dreams. Other elements entering into the family tree of contemporary art were Cubism, the Paris-based style of painting embodied in the work of Pablo Picasso, Georges Braque, and Juan Gris, which encouraged the painter to construct a visual world in terms of geometric patterns; and Expressionism, which we discussed in Chapter 68. (See illustrations on pages 418 and 419.)

Surrealism

Cubism

Art since the Second World War has unfolded against a background of unceasing social turmoil. This restlessness of spirit is inevitably reflected in the arts, which are passing through a period of violent experimentation with

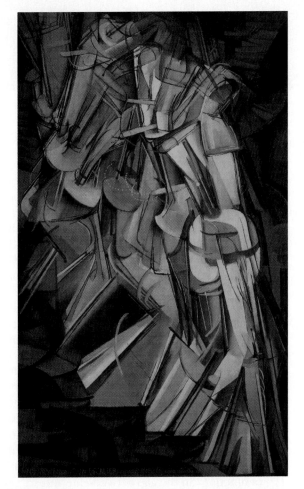

Marcel Duchamp (*1887–1968*), *in his* Nude Descending a Staircase, No. 2, *organized the indiscipline of Dada into a visionary art.* (The Philadelphia Museum of Art. Louise and Walter Arensberg Collection 50-134-59)

Pablo Picasso (*1881–1974*) *constructs a visual world of Cubist patterns in his* Three Musicians (The Philadelphia Museum of Art. A. E. Gallatin Collection 52-61-96)

new media, new materials, new techniques. Artists are freeing themselves from every vestige of the past in order to explore new areas of thought and feeling. Some even prefer to reject thought and feeling altogether.

Since the human eye responds more readily to fresh impressions than does the ear, contemporary painting and sculpture have reached a wider public than has contemporary music. The trend away from objective painting *Abstract expressionism* guaranteed the supremacy of Abstract Expressionism in this country during the 1950s and '60s. In the canvases of such men as Robert Motherwell, Jackson Pollock, Willem de Kooning, Franz Kline, and Philip Guston, space, mass, and color are freed from the need to imitate objects in the real world; they become values in the autonomous realm of painting. In other words, the Abstract Expressionists strengthened the tradition of "pure" painting— pure, that is, in its independence of external reality. The urge toward abstraction has been felt equally in contemporary sculpture, as is evident in the work of such artists as Henry Moore, Isamu Noguchi, and David Smith. (see illustration on page 492.)

At the same time, a new kind of realism has come into being in the art of Jasper Johns, Robert Rauschenberg, and their fellows, who owe some of their inspiration to the Dadaists of four decades earlier. Rauschenberg's aim, as he put it, was to work "in the gap between life and art." This trend culminated in Pop Art, which draws its themes and techniques from modern *Pop art* urban life: machines, advertisements, comic strips, movies, commercial photography, and familiar objects connected with everyday living. The desire to function "in the gap between life and art" motivated Andy Warhol's *Four*

Campbell's Soup Cans and *Brillo Boxes*, Jim Dine's *Shovel* and *A Nice Pair of Boots*, Claes Oldenburg's monumental *Bacon, Lettuce and Tomato* and *Dual Hamburgers*. Pop Art has absorbed the literal vision of photography and the silk-screen techniques of reproducing photographs on canvas; also the Dada-like inclusion of incongruous objects into art works. For example, Rauschenberg has incorporated into his abstractions a quilt and pillow, a tire, Coke bottles, electric clocks, and fans. These impart to his paintings the three-dimensional quality of sculpture. In this respect he is one of an influential group that is determined to expand the resources of the painter's art.

New materials

Developments in music have paralleled these trends. A number of composers have been strongly influenced by their painter friends. The long association between Edgard Varèse and the painter Marcel Duchamp engendered a strikingly similar point of view in both artists. A like parallelism exists between Jackson Pollock's attempt to achieve an "indeterminate" kind of painting by allowing the colors to drip freely onto the canvas, and the attempt of John Cage and his followers to achieve an indeterminate music by using procedures based on chance. A similar desire for freedom inspired the mobiles of Alexander Calder (see illustration on page 494), the component parts of which shift with each current of air to create new relationships. Artists tend more and more to look upon form as the all-pervading element in art that flows directly out of the material, so that each individual work, instead of following a set pattern, must be allowed to create its own form. Significant in this respect is Cage's remark that "Form is what interests

Indeterminacy

In Abstract Expressionism, space and mass become independent values, liberated from the need to express reality. Elegy to the Spanish Republic No. 18 *by* **Robert Motherwell** (*b. 1915*). (The Museum of Modern Art, New York. Charles Mergentime Fund)

492

The urge toward abstraction has been felt by sculptors such as **Henry Moore** (*b. 1898*) *in his* Lincoln Center Reclining Figure *located in the reflecting pool on New York's Lincoln Center Plaza North.* (Photo © Susanne Faulkner Stavens)

everyone and fortunately it is wherever you are and there is no place where it is not."

Other arts, too, have been subject to wide experimentation. The dance, traditionally chained to specific anecdote and gesture, found itself liberated from storytelling (in the work of George Balanchine) and from traditional patterns of movement (in the work of Martha Graham). Since the Second World War the trend toward abstraction has grown apace. The most important choreographer of the avant-garde, Merce Cunningham, has worked closely throughout his career with John Cage, introducing elements of chance and indeterminacy into his dance compositions. His object, he states, is "to make a space in which anything can happen."

Poetry

In the field of literature, poetry has, understandably, been the most experimental genre. Many of our poets face the world of today with a profound sense of alienation. They reflect their disjointed epoch in the fragmentation of their syntax and the violence of their imagery. Contemporary American poetry ranges over a wide gamut from the elegant intellectualism of a John Hollander or a Richard Wilbur to the Whitmanesque exuberance of the two leading poets of the "Beat Generation"—Allen Ginsberg and Gregory Corso. The utmost freedom of verse forms and a sardonic wit tinged with bitterness characterize many of the younger poets, such as the two best-known members of the so-called New York group: Kenneth Koch and John Ashbery.

Theater of the Absurd

Although the forms of drama and novel are by their very nature based on an imitation of life, they have not remained indifferent to the new trends. The theater has moved away from the social and psychological concerns that permeated the work of Arthur Miller and Tennessee Williams in the 1950s. It has turned instead to the "theater of the absurd," whose leading European proponents—Samuel Beckett, Eugene Ionesco, and Jean Genêt—view the world with a vast disillusionment, placing metaphysical absurdity at the core of human existence. No less pervasive has been the influence of the English dramatist Harold Pinter, whose plays transform the realities of human relationship into unpredictable patterns. The spirit of the absurd has also penetrated the novel—witness such works as Joseph Heller's *Catch 22* and John Barth's *Giles Goat-Boy*, to name only two of a considerable number of novels that have captured the pulse of our time.

Finally, the cinema—of all the arts the one most securely chained to storytelling of a popular kind—has also responded to the twin impulses of experimentation and abstraction. Among the "new wave" directors may be mentioned Michelangelo Antonioni, Jean-Luc Godard, and Federico Fellini. In films like Alain Resnais' *Last Year at Marienbad* and Ingmar Bergman's *Persona*, the Abstract Expressionist urge found perhaps its most successful cinematic realization to date.

"New wave" in cinema

We have mentioned only a few landmarks on the contemporary scene, but these are enough to indicate that art today has become increasingly intellectual, experimental, and abstract.

Toward Greater Organization in Music

When Schoenberg based his twelve-tone method on the use of tone rows, he was obviously moving toward a much stricter organization of the sound material. This desire was even more clearly manifest in the music of Webern.

The themes and techniques of Pop Art are drawn from modern urban life while incorporating incongruities into each work. A construction by **Robert Rauschenberg** (*b. 1925*), First Landing Jump. (The Museum of Modern Art, New York. Gift of Philip Johnson)

However, it remained for their disciples to extend the implications of the tone-row principle to the elements of music other than pitch. The arrangement of the twelve tones in a series might be paralleled by similar groupings of twelve durations (time values), twelve dynamic values (degrees of loudness), or twelve timbres. Other factors, too, might be brought under serial organization: the disposition of registers and densities, of types of attack, or sizes of intervals. By extending the serial principle in all possible directions a composer could achieve a totally organized fabric, controlled by the basic premise: the generating power of the series.

Extension of serial principle

This move toward *total serialism* resulted, in the decades after the war, in an extremely complex, ultrarational music. The composers who embraced total serialism, such as Pierre Boulez and Karlheinz Stockhausen, pushed to the farthermost limits some of the new ways of hearing and experiencing music.

Total serialism

Toward Greater Freedom in Music

The urge toward a totally controlled music had its counterpart in the desire for greater—even total—freedom from all predetermined forms and procedures. Music of this type emphasizes the antirational element in artistic experience: intuition, chance, the spur of the moment. Composers who wish to avoid the rational ordering of musical sound may rely on the element of chance and allow, let us say, a throw of dice to determine the selection of their material, or may perhaps build their pieces around a series of random numbers generated by a computer. They may allow the performer to choose the order in which the sections are to be played; or indicate the general course of events in regard to pitches, durations, registers, but leave it up to the performer to fill in the details. The performance thus becomes a musical "happening" in the course of which the piece is recreated afresh each time it is played.

Antirationalism

Such indeterminate music is known as *aleatory* (from *alea*, the Latin word for "dice," which from ancient times have symbolized the whims of chance). In aleatory music the overall form may be clearly indicated but the details are left to choice or chance. On the other hand, some composers, among them John Cage will indicate the details of a composition clearly

Aleatory music

enough, but leave its overall shape to choice or chance; this type of flexible structure is known as *open form*.

Related to these tendencies is the increased reliance on improvisation— *Use of improvisation* a technique common enough in music of the Baroque and earlier eras, but so long dormant that it has had to be reintroduced, in the 1950s and '60s, from the domain of jazz. Traditionally improvisation consists of spontaneous invention within a framework and a style that have been clearly established, so that player and listener have fairly well-defined ideas of what is "good" and what is "bad." In the more extreme types of aleatory music no such criteria are envisaged; anything that happens is acceptable to the composer.

A representative figure of this new freedom is Lukas Foss (1922–), whose *Lukas Foss* *Time Cycle* (1960) and *Echoi* (1961–63) established his place in the forefront of those who were experimenting with indeterminacy, group improvisation, and fresh approaches to sound. Foss was also a leader in the trend toward *collage*, whereby contemporary composers use for their own purpose material borrowed from the past. This orientation is manifest in the *Baroque Variations for Orchestra* (1967). In the ensuing decades he consistently maintained his position as one of the leaders of the avant-garde, the compositions of his later period for the most part employing aleatoric procedures.

The Internationalism of the New Music

The links between Europe and America were forged before World War II, when such leaders of European music as Stravinsky, Schoenberg, Bartók, Hindemith, and Krenek came to the United States. The war and the events leading up to it disrupted musical life on the Continent much more than in this country, with the result that the United States forged ahead in certain areas. For example, the first composer to apply serial organization to dimensions other than pitch was the American Milton Babbitt. The experiments of John Cage anticipated and influenced similar attempts abroad. Earle Brown was the first to use open form; Morton Feldman was the first to write works that gave the performer a choice. Once the war was over the Europeans quickly made up for lost time. Intense experimentation went on in Italy, Germany, France, England, Holland, and Scandinavia. This has gradually spread eastward into the Communist world: serial and electronic music have also taken root in Japan, while the music of the East has in turn influenced Western composers.

A number of Europeans have achieved international reputations. Pierre *Pierre Boulez* Boulez (1925–), the most important French composer of the avant-garde, is widely known because of his activities as a conductor. For five years he was music director of the New York Philharmonic. At the head of IRCAM (the French government's institute of composition and acoustics), he is the official leader of French musical life today. A pupil of Messiaen, he took over the plastic rhythms of his teacher and applied them to his own use within the twelve-tone technique. He also extended Schoenberg's serialism to include not only pitch but the other elements of music as well. His best-known work, *Le marteau sans maître* (The Hammer Without a Master, 1953–54)—

a suite of nine movements on three short poems of René Char—represents the chief traits of his style within a compact frame.

Luciano Berio

Luciano Berio (1925–) is a leading figure among the radicals of the post-Webern generation in Italy. He was one of the founders of the electronic studio in Milan that became a center of avant-garde activity, and for several years taught composition at the Juilliard School in New York. Berio's music exemplifies three major trends in the contemporary scene—serialism, electronic technology, and indeterminacy. His interest in linguistics has led him to a highly original treatment of language sounds; he also experimented with combining live music and tape. Characteristic is his homage to Martin Luther King, Junior, in his best-known work, *Sinfonia* for orchestra, organ, harps, piano, chorus, and reciters (1968).

Iannis Xenakis

The Greek composer Iannis Xenakis (1922–) exemplifies the close ties between music and science characteristic of our time; he was trained as an engineer. Caught up in the anti-Nazi Resistance, he sustained severe face injuries, imprisonment, and a sentence of death. He studied with Messiaen in Paris and worked with the architect Le Corbusier. Xenakis's music derives its very special sound from massed sonorities, prominent use of glissandos, and a texture woven out of individual parts for each instrument in the orchestra.

Krzysztof Penderecki

Krzysztof Penderecki (1933–) is an outstanding Polish composer. His search for new sonorities and new ways of producing them has impelled him to include in his scores such noises as the sawing of wood and the clicking of typewriters. His choral music includes special effects such as hissing, shouting, whistling, articulating rapid consonants, and the like. In this area he has been much influenced by Iannis Xenakis.

Other Aspects of the New Music

New concepts of form

Whether it is serial or aleatory, live or electronic, most new music reflects the conviction that each composition is based upon a set of premises that are unique to it. The function of the piece is to realize fully what is implicit in these premises. Each work is regarded as a self-contained structure independent of all other structures, whose form springs from and is determined by conditions peculiar to itself. Ours obviously is no longer a time when thousands of pieces can be written in sonata, rondo, or **A-B-A** form. These forms ultimately had to degenerate into formulas, in spite of the infinite ingenuity with which the great masters handled them, because their rationale was based on the harmonic system of the Classic-Romantic era. The concept of predetermined form is completely alien to the spirit of the new music. The force that holds a piece together is not superimposed from without but flows directly out of the material. Since the material is unique to the piece, so is the form.

Contemporary attitudes, it need hardly be said, have liberated all the elements of music from the restrictions of the past. The concept of a music based on the twelve pitches of the chromatic (tempered) scale has obviously been left far behind. Electronic instruments make possible the use of sound

Microtonal intervals

"in the cracks of the piano keys"—the *microtonal* intervals, such as quarter or third tones, that are smaller than the traditional semitone—and very skilled string and wind players have begun to master these novel scales. In addition, the notion of what is acceptable sonorous material has been broadened to include sounds that in earlier times would have been relegated to the domain of noise.

Stravinsky, Bartók, Schoenberg, and their disciples developed a musical rhythm no longer based on equal measures and the regular recurrence of accent. Their concepts have been immensely refined in the past quarter century. Many composers today try to focus the listener's attention on a texture in which each sonority or density stands almost by itself, detached from its surroundings. Their music may unfold as a series of sonorous points, each of which is momentarily suspended in time, surrounded by plenty of "air pockets" of organized silence: great static blocks of sound juxtaposed in musical space, fashioned out of tiny cell-like clusters that spin, whirl, combine, and recombine with a kind of cumulative force.

New concepts of rhythm

We have mentioned several composers who have tried to reconcile serial procedures with tonality. None has played a more important role in this area than George Perle (1915–). In a language based on the twelve-tone scale he has retained the concept of tonal centers and the traditional differentiation between the vertical and horizontal dimensions of music. Several of his works do not use a tone row but combine various serial details with melodically generated tone centers, intervallic cells, symmetrical formations, and similar devices. Perle had to wait until his seventies to be recognized as one of the important composers of his generation. Official recognition came in 1986 when he won the Pulitzer Prize for his *Wind Quintet IV* and one of the "genius fellowships" of the MacArthur Foundation. Before that he was known chiefly for his books, including *Serial Composition and Atonality* (1962) and *Twelve-Tone Tonality* (1978).

George Perle

Charles Wuorinen (1938–) started out from the sound world of Stravinsky, Schoenberg, and Varèse, and found his way to the twelve-tone system in the 1960s. He freely adapts the procedures of the twelve-tone "system" to the needs of the particular piece he is writing. He is a prolific composer in all areas of music, has received his share of awards and honors, among them a Pulitzer Prize and a MacArthur Fellowship, and is acknowledged to be one of the leading figures of his generation.

Charles Wuorinen

Ralph Shapey (1921–) directs the Contemporary Chamber Players at the University of Chicago. The disciple of Varèse speaks in Shapey's definition of music as "an object in Time and Space: aggregate sounds structured into concrete sculptural forms." His output is mostly instrumental; but he was one of the first American composers to view the voice as an instrument "using syllables in organized sound-structures." *Rituals*, for symphony orchestra (1959), serves as a good introduction to Shapey's style.

Ralph Shapey

Women in Contemporary Music

Women have played a much more prominent role in the contemporary music scene than they did in the past. They have distinguished themselves not only as performers, a role in which they always excelled, but also as composers, teachers, and conductors. The Paris Conservatoire, for example,

Nadia Boulanger

has long stood out for the caliber of the women musicians it has produced. Germaine Tailleferre (1892–1983) was an active member of the group of young composers known as *Les Six* who came out of the Conservatoire in the 1920s and became leaders of the modern movement in France. In the '20s too Nadia Boulanger (1887–1979) emerged as one of the great teachers of the time. She stood very close to Stravinsky and became one of the leading advocates of the Neoclassical aesthetic. Her students included Copland, Virgil Thomson, Walter Piston, Elliott Carter, Philip Glass, Thea Musgrave, and many others; she was also active as a conductor and did much to promulgate the new interest in music of the French Baroque and Renaissance.

Ruth Crawford

Women took their place in the modern American school from its very beginnings. The best known among the first generation of modern American composers is Ruth Crawford (1901–53), who made her reputation as an avant-garde composer during the 1920s. She was the first woman awarded a Guggenheim fellowship to study composition in Europe. Her String Quartet (1931) foreshadows in remarkable ways the compositional techniques that preoccupied composers a quarter century later. The last movement is totally organized in regard to pitch, dynamics, tempo, instrumentation, and form. She became the wife of the musicologist Charles Seeger and took an active interest in American folksongs, an area in which her stepson Pete was pre-eminent.

Louise Talma

Among the women composers active today, Louise Talma (1906–) stands out for her expert craftsmanship and refinement. She started out from the sound-world of Stravinskian Neoclassicism, her thinking shaped by a long personal association with Nadia Boulanger. In the '50s she embraced serial techniques. Pieces for solo voice and chorus occupy a prominent place in her output; those for piano show her profound knowledge of that instrument. (She began her career as a pianist.) Her list also includes orchestral works and an opera, *The Alcestiade*, on a libretto by Thornton Wilder (1955–58).

Miriam Gideon

Miriam Gideon (1906–) was influenced by the aesthetic of atonal Expressionism, but molded its vocabulary to her own expressive ends. She has a marked affinity for vocal music, but has also produced a variety of chamber works and the *Symphonia brevis* (1953). Her mature style is well illustrated by *Rhymes from the Hill*, for voice, clarinet, cello, and marimba (1968).

Jean Eichelberger Ivey

Jean Eichelberger Ivey (1923–) is one of several composers who are striving to achieve a synthesis of the diverse influences playing upon our time. She is much concerned with combining tape and live performers, which seems to her "to offer the best of both worlds, plus a dimension which neither live performer nor tape can reach alone."

Joan Tower

Joan Tower (1938–) has been strongly influenced by Stravinsky and Beethoven. She has moved from the twelve-tone virtuosity of the '60s to a more accessible, lyrical style that does not exclude tonal elements. A typical work is *Breakfast Rhythms I and II* for clarinet and five instruments (1975).

Ellen Taaffe Zwilich

Ellen Taaffe Zwilich (1939–) is the first woman composer to have been awarded a Pulitzer Prize, which she received for her Symphony No. 1 in 1983. She has produced a series of works in various instrumental combinations, as well as a song cycle for soprano and chamber group called *Passages* (1981), based on poems of A. B. Ammons.

The first American woman to win the prestigious Prix de Rome, Barbara Kolb (1939–), emerged in the '70s as one of our most widely performed composers. Her music bespeaks a sonic imagination of the first order. A number of her works are recorded, including *Rebuttal* for two clarinets (1964), *Trobar Clus* for chamber ensemble (1970), *Solitaire* for piano, vibraphone, and tape (1972), and *Yet That Things Go Round* (1987) for chamber orchestra. *Barbara Kolb*

Lucia Dlugoszewski (1934–) was a pupil of Edgard Varèse. As in his case, her studies included work in physics and mathematics. She also absorbed his abiding interest in pure sound textures and has developed over a hundred pitched and unpitched percussion instruments, which she herself plays. Like John Cage, she has been profoundly influenced by Oriental philosophy. *Lucia Dlugoszewski*

Betsy Jolas (1926–) is one of a group of French composers who turned from serialism to aleatory procedures. She has also experimented with spatial effects based on the physical separation of instrumental groups; her closely woven polyphonic textures derive their clarity from her skillful exploitation of the chamber-orchestra sound. Her music is becoming increasingly well known in the United States. *Betsy Jolas*

It is apparent that these composers represent a diversity of techniques and styles. Their work establishes the importance of women today, and augurs well for the future.

78

Non-Western Music and the Contemporary Scene

Unlike Europe, the continents of Asia and Africa do not constitute single cultural units. On the contrary, their societies represent the utmost diversity, from ancient civilizations such as China and India, whose artistic instincts have been refined through thousands of years, to societies like the Pygmies of Africa or the Aborigines of Australia, whose development has not kept pace with the modern world. All these societies have music, but their musical languages differ from one another as much as they differ from the language of Beethoven or Chopin.

But this barrier between musical languages is not an impassable one. Until recently, the Western public had little opportunity to hear music of other cultures. The Second World War brought these disparate worlds closer. The success in the West of such artists as Ravi Shankar introduced European and

The internationally renowned Ravi Shankar playing the sitar.

American audiences to the exquisitely subtle art of India. Authentic recordings of Asian and African music have become increasingly available, making it possible for Western listeners to expand their ears by hearing musics based on totally different assumptions, and performing groups from all over the world are much in demand by Western audiences.

Conversely, Western music has begun to make inroads in Japan, Korea, Indonesia, China, and other countries of Asia. Today symphony orchestras perform works of Beethoven in Beijing and Tokyo, Delhi and Seoul. Their conservatories are teaching Western music, and students from the Far East are coming to study music at the Juilliard School and similar institutions. In addition, artists such as the conductors Zubin Mehta and Seiji Ozawa, the cellist Yo Yo Ma, composers like Toru Takemitsu, Yuji Takahashi, and Chou Wen-Chung are playing an ever more important part in Western musical life. But perhaps the greatest impact that Western music has had worldwide is through the immense popularity of rock music with the world's youth. Thus, in spite of Rudyard Kipling's famous poem—"Oh, East is East, and West is West, and never the twain shall meet,"— East and West are steadily drawing closer.

Music in Society

In every culture, music is intricately woven into the lives and beliefs of its people. Just as in the West, the "classical" exists alongside the "popular," both nourished from the unbelievably rich store of folk music that is intimately interwoven with daily living. Music serves different functions in different societies, though some basic roles are universal: accompanying ceremonial acts, religious or civic; accompanying work to pass the time;

entertaining through singing and dancing. The social organization of any particular culture has much to do with the resulting music of its people. In some cultures, only a few people are involved with the actual performance of music, while in others, such as that of the African Pygmies, cooperative work is so much a part of their society that they sing as a group, with each person weaving a separate part to build a complex whole. Music exists for every conceivable type of occasion, but the specific occasions celebrated vary from culture to culture. Thus, musical genres, or categories of repertory, do not transfer from one culture to the next.

Not all music is written down and learned from books or formal lessons. In some cultures, music is transmitted through a master-apprentice relationship that lasts many years, while in others there is no formal instruction; rather, the aspiring musician must learn from watching and listening. Music of most cultures of the world, including some styles of Western popular music, is transmitted by example or imitation and is performed from memory. This music is said to exist in *oral tradition*.

Oral tradition

The Languages of Non-Western Musics

We have seen that Western music is largely a melody-oriented art based on a particular musical system from which underlying harmonies are also built. Relatively speaking, rhythm and meter in Western music are based on simpler principles than are melody and harmony. Musics of other cultures sound completely foreign to our ears, sometimes "out of tune," because they are based on entirely different musical systems. Strange as it may seem to Westerners, the music of many cultures does not involve harmony to any great extent. Rather, the construction of melody and the organization of musical time are central to their differing musical languages.

One important factor in these differing languages of music is the way in which the octave is divided. We have seen that in Western music the octave is divided into twelve semitones, from which seven are chosen to form the major scale while a slightly different group of seven comprises the minor scale. These two scales have constituted the basis of the Western musical language for nearly four hundred years.

But the musical languages of other cultures divide the octave differently, producing different scale patterns. Among the most common is the *pentatonic*, or five-note, scale, used in some African, Far Eastern, and American Indian musics. There are a number of different patterns possible in fashioning a pentatonic scale, each with its own unique quality of sound. Thus the scales heard in Japan and China, although both pentatonic, sound quite different. Other scale types include *tritonic*, a three-note pattern found in the music of some South African cultures, and *heptatonic*, or seven-note scales fashioned from a different combination of intervals than major and minor scales.

Pentatonic scale

Tritonic and heptatonic scales

Some scales are not playable on Western instruments because they employ microtonal intervals that sound "off-key" to Western ears. One manner of producing microtonal music involves an inflection of a pitch, or a brief

In their tribal rituals, African dancers may create their own rhythmic accompaniment with gourd rattles strapped to their legs.

microtonal dip from the original pitch; this technique, similar to that of the *blue note* in jazz discussed earlier, makes possible a host of subtle inflections unknown in the melody of the West.

We have seen that rhythm is the element that organizes music through time. Since all sounds and silences have duration, all musics have a rhythmic basis. But the regular pulse of Western music, and the organization of these beats into patterns of two, three, and four, are not universal features of music. Indeed, the music of many cultures is far more varied and complex, using patterns and combinations of patterns that are unknown in Western music. Repetitive patterns, often with an obsessive insistence, are a feature of some African musics; these patterns unfold in a web of cross-rhythms and poly-rhythms that amaze and confuse the Western ear. Some musics are based on changing meters. On the other hand, a musical selection from southern *Tala* India depends on a fixed time cycle known as a *tala*, built from uneven groupings of beats (such as 4 + 2 + 2). In the latter music, a drum first marks the cycle, then divides the tala into smaller and smaller rhythmic cells, building a complex arabesque of sound.

Musical performance practices vary radically from one culture to the next. In musics where a single melodic line is prevalent, instruments may accompany the line with elaborations on it, so that the result remains basically monophonic in texture. Many musics depend on the simple accompaniment of one or several repeated tones for harmonic support. This device, known *Drone* as a *drone*, is heard in Western music as well. (You will remember that we heard a drone as a part of the improvised accompaniment to the Medieval saltarello.) The *bagpipe,* for example, is a drone instrument that has been popular for centuries both in Eastern and Western Europe. It has several tubes, one of which plays the melody while the others sound the drones, or sustained notes.

Simple harmonies and polyphonic textures are typical of some musics of Central and Western Africa. Polyphony can arise from the singing or playing of parallel intervals, such as thirds, fourths, or fifths, much as we heard in medieval organum. It can take the form of a simple round with a leader and chorus singing the same melody at different times, or it may result from the use of an ostinato, or repeated pattern, sounded in accompaniment to a melody. One formal practice that can be found throughout much of the world is *call-and-response* or *responsorial* singing. Heard in the musics of the Pan-Islamic region of North Africa, the North American Indians, and the New World Negro, to mention only a few, this style of performance is based on a social structure that recognizes a singing leader who is imitated by a chorus of followers. This simple procedure is fundamental to much folk music and to jazz performance as well.

Responsorial singing

Musical Instruments of the World

The diversity of musical instruments around the world defies the imagination. Every conceivable method of sound production is used; every possible raw material employed. It would be impossible to list or catalog them here. Nor do they all conveniently fit into the standard families of Western instruments (strings, woodwinds, brass, percussion). Thus, specialists have devised an alternate method for classifying instruments, one based solely on the manner in which they generate sounds. There are four categories in this classification system. *Aerophones* produce sound by using air as the primary vibrating means. Common instruments in this grouping are flutes, whistles, and horns. *Chordophones* are instruments that produce sound from a vibrating string stretched between two points. The string may be set in motion by bowing, striking, or plucking. *Idiophones* produce the sound from the substance of the instrument itself. They may be struck, blown, shaken, scraped, or rubbed. Examples of idiophones are bells, rattles, xylophones, and cymbals. The fourth category is *membranophones,* referring to any instrument sounded from tightly stretched membranes. These drum-type instruments can be struck, plucked, rubbed, or even sung into, thus setting the skin in vibration. This method works conveniently as an alternate classification for Western instruments as well.

Aerophones

Chordophones

Idiophones

Membranophones

Cross-Cultural Exchanges of Music

Throughout the course of history, the West has felt the influence of other cultures. We have already noted the nineteenth-century fascination with exoticism that spurred interest in the Orient and its arts. Composers of the Russian school were particularly intrigued with the East. The music of Spanish Gypsies is suggested in Bizet's opera *Carmen,* the splendor of ancient Egypt

In this performance of a Balinese Topeng (Masked Dance), part of the gamelan—a double-headed drum and three metallophones—may be seen behind the dancer. (Photograph by Thomas Haar, courtesy of The Asia Society)

is captured in Verdi's *Aida*, and the spirit of the so-called "dark continent" is evinced in Saint-Saën's fantasy for piano and orchestra *Afrique* (Africa). Since these composers were writing works based on Western harmonies to be played on Western instruments, they naturally made no attempt to use the authentic scales of Asia or Africa. They contented themselves with writing works which to their imaginations resembled the sound of musics of distant lands. We have also discussed the more sustained efforts at exoticism of the

Exoticism Post-Romantics, especially Debussy who, we saw, fell under the spell of the Javanese gamelan and the whole-tone scale.

Twentieth-century composers, we noted earlier, found inspiration not only in African music but also in the strong rhythmic features of the songs and dances of the borderlands of Western culture—southeastern Europe, Asiatic Russia, and the Near East. Notable among these were Bartók, Stravinsky, and Prokofiev. We have also encountered the strong impetus toward

Primitivism primitivism that came from the Afro-American styles developed by black American musicians, which combined the powerful rhythmic impulse of their heritage with the major-minor tonality of their new home. Out of this amalgam grew the rich literature of Negro spirituals, work songs and shouts, and ultimately ragtime, blues and jazz, swing and rock.

The musics of Africa and Asia constitute a rich literature that has had a profound influence on contemporary composers. A number of them have responded to the philosophy of the Far East, especially Zen Buddhism and Indian thought. Among them are three Californians whose work has attracted much notice: Henry Cowell, Harry Partch, and especially John Cage, whose name has been associated with the avant-garde scene for over fifty years.

Henry Cowell Henry Cowell (1897–1965), was drawn toward a variety of non-Western musics. His studies of the music of Japan, India, Iran, and rural Ireland and America led him to combine Asian instruments with traditional Western ensembles, as in his two koto concertos (1962 and 1965). (The *koto* is a Japanese zither with thirteen strings stretched over bridges and tuned to one of a variety of pentatonic scales.) He also experimented with the use of exotic scales, which he harmonized with Western triadic chords. The piano provided Cowell with an outlet for a number of his innovations: these include tone clusters (groups of adjacent notes) that are sounded with the fist, palm, or forearm, and the playing of the piano strings with the fingers rather than the keys.

The piano also lent itself to experiments with new tuning systems. One of the first to attempt microtonal music for the piano was Charles Ives, who wrote for pianos tuned a quarter tone apart. But perhaps the most serious proponent of this technique was Harry Partch (1901–74), who single-mindedly pursued the goal of a microtonal music. In the 1920s he evolved a scale of forty-three microtones to the octave and built instruments with this tuning, adapting Hindu and African instruments to meet his purpose. Among his idiophones are cloud-chamber bowls (made of glass), cone gongs (made of metal), diamond marimba (made of wood), and tree gourd. His performance group, called the Gate 5 ensemble, played his works from memory, producing a music whose interest lay not in harmony but in melody and in timbre. One work that espouses his vision is *The Delusion of Fury* (1969), a large-scale ceremonial piece that employs elements of Eastern Noh drama in its first part, "On a Japanese Theme," and demands that its instrumentalists make choral-voice sounds in its second part, entitled "On an African Theme."

Harry Partch

John Cage: His Life and Music

"I am more like a hunter or inventor than a lawmaker."

John Cage (1912–) represents the type of eternally questing artist who no sooner solves one problem than he presses forward to another. Born in Los Angeles and educated at Pomona College, Cage left school to travel in Europe. He exhibited an early interest in non-Western scales, which he learned from his mentor Henry Cowell. As a student of Arnold Schoenberg, Cage explored for a time compositions with fixed tone rows, but was eventually persuaded that the path of advance lay through rhythm rather than pitch. This abiding interest in rhythm led him to explore the possibilities of percussion instruments. Cage soon realized that the traditional dichotomy between consonance and dissonance had given way to a new opposition between music and noise, as a result of which the boundaries of the one were extended to include more of the other. In 1937, Cage prophesied that "the use of noise to make music will continue and increase until we reach a music produced through the aid of electrical instruments, which will make available for musical purposes any and all sounds that can be heard."

John Cage

Cage's exploration of percussive rhythm led him to invent, in 1938, what he christened the "prepared piano." The preparation consisted of inserting nails, bolts, nuts, screws, and bits of rubber, wood, or leather at crucial points between the strings of an ordinary grand piano. There resulted a myriad of sounds whose overall effect resembled that of a Javanese gamelan (an ensemble made up of various kinds of gongs, xylophones, drums, bowed and

Prepared piano

plucked strings, cymbals, and sometimes singers). Cage wrote a number of works for the prepared piano, notably the set of *Sonatas and Interludes* (1946–48). The music reflects the composer's preoccupation with Oriental philosophy. "After reading the work of Ananda K. Coomaraswamy, I decided to attempt the expression in music of the 'permanent emotions' of Indian tradition: the heroic, the erotic, the wondrous, the mirthful, sorrow, fear, anger, the odious, and their common tendency toward tranquility." The striving for tranquility was to become a pervasive element in Cage's life and work.

Cage's interest in indeterminacy led to compositions with choices made by throwing dice. He has also relied on the *I Ching* (Book of Changes), an ancient Chinese method of throwing coins or marked sticks for chance numbers, from which he derived a system of charts and graphs governing the series of events that could happen within a given structural space. One final frontier conquered by Cage was the transfer of indeterminacy to tape. This problem he solved in his *Fontana Mix* (1958), which became the first taped work to establish conditions whose outcome could not be foreseen. These experiments established John Cage as a seminal force in the artistic life of our time.

Cage: Sonatas and Interludes

Sonatas and Interludes represents Cage's crowning achievement in this non-traditional category of works for prepared piano. In these he approx-imates most imaginatively the veiled, subtle sound of the Javanese gamelan. Notable is the static effect of a music that seems to float above time, free from the accents and dynamism of the West: a motionless music that suggests the meditative character of so much Oriental thought.

There are sixteen sonatas in the set, ordered in four groups of four sep-arated by Interludes. Cage provides detailed instructions at the beginning of the score, indicating that forty-five of the piano's eighty-eight notes were to be prepared by the insertion of various types of screws, bolts, and bits of rubber and plastic between the strings, at distances carefully specified by the composer. He further explains that "mutes of various materials are placed between the strings of the keys used, thus effecting transformations of the piano sounds with respect to all of their characteristics." The effect achieved varied, depending upon the material inserted, its position, and whether the soft pedal was used. Some strings produce a nonpitched per-cussive thump while others produce tones whose pitch and timbre are altered. This music is not concerned with the simultaneous sounding of pitches, but with timbre and rhythmic groupings of sounds.

Sonata V from the set is a short but highly structured work whose overall shape is binary, with each section repeated (**A-A-B-B**). Here the sonority of the prepared piano, almost ethereal in quality, is remarkably like that of the gamelan orchestra of pitched and nonpitched percussion instruments. Certainly, the effect is far removed from the timbre we generally associate with the piano. Cage's piece is made up of wholly original sounds to delight

S4B/5

S4/30

the ears. This is music that, as the composer described it, "sets the soul in operation."

The infusion of non-Western sounds into Western music was not reserved for the classical idiom. In jazz and rock, too, Eastern influences were felt. The saxophonist John Coltrane wrote music that was freed of the rhythmic and harmonic traditions of jazz; rather it employed drones and unusual scales reflecting his interest in Indian and Arabian music. The popularity of meditation drew many jazz performers to Far Eastern ways, as it did Beatles George Harrison and John Lennon in the 1960s. In all these endeavors, we find a fusion of Eastern and Western music that cannot fail to enrich us.

79
New Sounds on Traditional Instruments

The New Virtuosity

Musical styles so different from all that went before need a new breed of instrumentalists and vocalists to cope with their technical difficulties. One has only to attend a concert of avant-garde music to realize how far the art of piano playing or singing has moved from the world of Chopin or Verdi. The piano keyboard may be brushed or slammed with fingers, palm, or fist; or the player may reach inside to hit, scratch, or pluck the strings directly. A violinist may tap, stroke, and even slap the instrument. Vocal music runs the gamut from whispering to shouting, including all manner of groaning, moaning, or hissing on the way. Wind players have learned to produce a variety of double-stops, subtle changes of color, and microtonal progressions; and the percussion section has been enriched by an astonishing variety of noisemakers and special effects. In each of the important musical centers groups of players and singers are springing up who have a genuine affinity with the new music. Singers like Bethany Beardslee, Phyllis Bryn-Julson, and Jan DeGaetani, pianists like David Burge, Robert Helps, Gilbert Kalish, Ursula Oppens, and Charles Rosen, violinists like Matthew Raimondi and Paul Zukofsky, to mention only a few, are masters of a new kind of virtuosity that cannot fail to amaze those who were brought up on the old. They are performing an invaluable service for the new music, and it is an encouraging sign that their numbers are growing.

Elliott Carter (© Photo
by Malcolm Crowthers)

Elliott Carter: Eight Etudes and a Fantasy

*"I like music to be beautiful, ordered, and expressive of the more
important aspects of life."*

Of the composers who have come into prominence in recent years, none
is more widely admired by musicians than Elliott Carter (1908–). His works
are not of the kind that achieve easy popularity; but their profundity of
thought and maturity of workmanship bespeak a musical intellect of the first
order.

Carter started out with a musical idiom rooted in diatonic-modal harmony,
but gradually assimilated a dissonant chromaticism that places him (if one
must attach a label) among the Abstract Expressionists. He employs fluc-
tuating tempo as a form-building element, through the use of a novel technique that he calls "metrical modulation," whereby the speed of the rhythmic
pulse is subtly modified. When several instruments are playing together,
each with its own pulse and each changing that pulse independently in a
different direction, there results an original and powerful kind of texture.

The works of Carter's maturity explore the possibilities of this technique
in a variety of ways. The three string quartets are bold, uncompromising
works that constitute the most significant contribution to this medium since
Bartók; both the Second and Third brought the composer Pulitzer Prizes.

S4B/4

S4/28

Fifth etude

Carter's impeccable craftsmanship is manifest in Eight Etudes and a Fantasy
(1950), which offers a fine introduction to his art. The piece grew directly
out of his activity as a teacher. He had asked his students to bring in examples
illustrating the use of woodwind instruments, and had invited four woodwind
players to class to perform them. Disappointed in what the class had written,
he sketched some passages on the blackboard for the woodwind players to
try. These he later developed into the Eight Etudes and a Fantasy, a work
that explores the possibilities of flute, oboe, clarinet, and bassoon in imaginative ways.

The fifth etude explores the expressive capacities of pure woodwind
sound. These are utilized to create the kind of emotional lyricism we generally
associate with the string instruments. The music takes on an almost tragic
intensity, and reveals anew how completely the vocabulary of atonality is
attuned to the aesthetic goals of Expressionism.

Principal Works

Orchestral works, including Variations for Orchestra (1955),
Double Concerto (harpsichord and piano, 1961), Concerto for
Orchestra (1969), and A Symphony of Three Orchestras (1976)

Chamber works, including 3 string quartets (1951, 1960, 1971);
Eight Etudes and a Fantasy (1950); various sonatas and quintets

Vocal music, including *A Mirror on Which to Dwell* (1976) and
Syringa (1978)

2 ballets

The eighth etude is a *perpetuum mobile* (continuous motion) whose forward drive never lets up. The rapid sixteenth notes are heard against single quarter notes in high or low register that seem to comment on the main action. These quarter notes make an effective contrast, in rhythm as well as register, with the running passages.

Carter's works, oriented toward the most serious aspects of musical art, offer a continual challenge to the listener. They confirm his position as one of the most important composers in America.

Eighth etude

György Ligeti: Atmosphères

György Ligeti (1923–) a native Hungarian who established himself first in Vienna, then in Stockholm, belongs to the circle of composers who have tried to broaden the heritage of Schoenberg by making it responsive to more recent currents. He found ways to achieve with traditional instruments the finer gradations of sound made familiar by electronic music. Through tone clusters and amalgams of sound that create a flow of shifting densities and colors, Ligeti has gone beyond focusing on fixed, recognizable pitches to working with large clusters of tones.

György Ligeti

One of Ligeti's major preoccupations has been the interweaving of many separate strands into a complex polyphonic fabric, deriving the shape and momentum of the music from barely perceptible changes in timbre, dynamics, density, and texture rather than from more easily recognized external events. The result is a shimmering current of sound, to which he applied the term *micropolyphony*. This phase of Ligeti's development reached its fullest expression in his works of the early 1960s. He subsequently moved toward a style with more transparent textures and more clear-cut melodic, harmonic, and rhythmic contours.

Atmosphères, "for large orchestra without percussion," establishes Ligeti's position as a leader of the European avant-garde. Together with his choral work *Lux aeterna,* it was included in the sound track of the film *2001: A Space Odyssey,* making the composer's name familiar to an international public. In *Atmosphères,* he explored the region that lies between instrumental and electronic music. Although the score interweaves more than sixty individual lines, what the listener hears is a murmurous continuum. As he put it, he was composing with blocks of sound—except that the blocks all merged into a continuous flow. At certain points the composer's minutely notated score takes on the appearance of a geometric pattern.

The piece opens with a massive yet gentle cluster chord containing every

S4B/8

S4/37

Principal Works

Orchestral works, including *Apparitions* (1958–59), *Atmosphères* (1961), and *Lontano* (1967)

Chamber works, including Chamber Concerto (1970)

Theater works, including *Aventures* (1962), *Nouvelles aventures* (1962–65), and *Le grand macabre* (1976)

semitone within a span of nearly five octaves. The winds and violins fade out, leaving only the lower strings, among which individual notes briefly swell and project from the sonic blanket. Wind and string chords alternate, intermix, and then begin to vibrate. At the end, everything fades into an amorphous vibration, made by sweeping across the strings of a piano with the brushes used by jazz drummers. Then this, too, evaporates "as it were into nothingness."

There is a dreamlike, otherworldly quality to this piece. It belongs to a group of works that in the 1960s pointed the way to new worlds of sound. As such, it constitutes an important addition to the present-day repertory.

Witold Lutosławski: Venetian Games

The Polish composer Witold Lutosławski (1913–) is one of the most prominent members of the avant-garde. Yet he has found ways to combine contemporary procedures with elements drawn from more traditional styles.

His serial period began with *Funeral Music* (1958), in a unique style that blended twelve-tone elements with chromatic harmony in elaborately contrapuntal textures abounding in canonic devices. He next fell under the influence of John Cage. While listening to Cage's Concerto for Piano and Orchestra (1960), "I suddenly realized," Lutosławski wrote, "that I could compose music different from that of my past. I could progress toward the whole not from the small detail but the other way around—I could start out from chance and create order in it gradually." Lutosławski coined the term "aleatoric counterpoint" to indicate a type of music in which the pitches for all the parts are written out but the rhythms are improvised within given rules.

Venetian Games derives its title from the Festival of Contemporary Music in Venice, for which it was written. We hear the first movement, which has a distinct architectural structure in which aleatoric sections alternate with notated ones. The orchestra is divided into two groups, winds and percussion pitted against the strings, one group alternating with the other. The wind sections are written out; they often begin and end with a loud percussion chord. The music is very active rhythmically, with a piano part added to the winds towards the end of the movement. The string sections throughout are aleatoric; in these the composer strives for maximum freedom of choice.

Witold Lutosławski
(© Photo by Malcolm Crowthers)

First movement

Principal Works

Orchestral works, including 3 symphonies (1947, 1967, 1983), Concerto for Orchestra (1954), *Funeral Music* (1958), *Jeux vénitiens* (Venetian Games, 1961)

Vocal music, including *Three Poems of Henri Michaux* (with orchestra, 1963)

Chamber music, including String Quartet (1964)
Piano music, including *Bucolics* (1952)

They feature dissonant chord clusters, with loud entries on particular pitches, some pizzicato. There are eight sections, labeled from A to H in the score. The woodwind-and-percussion sound at the beginning of the movement is balanced by string sound at the end. Four percussion chords shape the final cadence, each softer than the one before. (See Listening Guide 51.)

The second movement ends with a passage for piano *ad libitum* (an indication that gives the performer the liberty to include or omit that particular part). The third movement includes a free solo part for flute, with the entries of the other instruments decided by the conductor. There are fixed time frames for passages which are otherwise free. In the fourth movement the opening and closing sections are notated while the middle part is aleatoric.

Remaining movements

Lutosławski's music shows how avant-garde elements can commingle with older styles. He has established himself as one of the most interesting personalities on the contemporary scene.

Listening Guide 51

          8B/2   II/4/22

LUTOSŁAWSKI: *Venetian Games*

Date: 1961

Movements: 4

First movement—Alternates winds/percussion with strings
Timed sections (A–H), given in seconds (")
Strings very free (aleatoric); winds notated more precisely

	Sections	Length	Description
0:00	A	(13")	woodwinds and percussion; closes with percussive chord
0:13	B	(33")	strings—individual entries on pitches; closes with high violin pitch
0:46	C	(21")	woodwind, percussion, with timpani added; percussive chord begins and ends section
1:07	D	(28")	strings—high repeated notes, dissonant clusters
1:35	E	(7")	woodwind, percussion, timpani, with brass added begins with percussive chord
1:42	F	(2")	strings
1:44	G	(28")	woodwinds, brass, percussion, timpani, with piano added, begins with percussive chord
2:12	H	(64")	strings; closes with 4 percussion chords, each softer

George Crumb: Ancient Voices of Children

George Crumb

In recent years George Crumb (1929–) has forged ahead to a notable position among the composers of his generation. He owes this pre-eminence partly to the emotional character of his music, allied to a highly developed sense of the dramatic. His kind of romanticism is most unusual among the advanced composers of his generation. Crumb uses contemporary techniques for expressive ends that make an enormous impact in the concert hall. He has won numerous honors and awards, and is currently professor of composition at the University of Pennsylvania.

Crumb has shown an extraordinary affinity for the poetry of Federico García Lorca, the great poet who was killed by the Fascists during the Spanish Civil War. Besides his *Ancient Voices of Children*, his Lorca cycle includes four other works: *Night Music I*; four books of madrigals; *Songs, Drones and Refrains of Death*; and *Night of the Four Moons*. "In *Ancient Voices of Children*, as in my earlier Lorca settings," the composer states, "I have sought musical images that enhance and reinforce the powerful yet strangely haunting imagery of Lorca's poetry. I feel that the essential meaning of this poetry is concerned with the most primary things: Life, death, love, the smell of the earth, the sounds of the wind and the sea." These concepts, Crumb goes on to explain, "are embodied in a language which is primitive and stark, but which is capable of infinitely subtle nuance."

Ancient Voices of Children is a cycle of songs for mezzo-soprano, boy soprano, oboe, mandolin, harp, electric piano, and percussion. Endowed with an aural imagination of remarkable vividness, Crumb tirelessly explores new ways of using voice and instruments. Like many contemporary composers he uses the voice like an instrument, in a vocal style which he describes as ranging "from the virtuosic to the intimately lyrical." He has found his ideal interpreter in the mezzo-soprano Jan DeGaetani, whose recording of the work remains as an example for all other interpreters.

Vocalise

The score abounds with unusual effects. The soprano opens with a fanciful *vocalise* (a wordless melody, in this case based on purely phonetic sounds) which she directs at the strings of an electrically amplified piano, arousing a shimmering cloud of sympathetic vibrations. The pitch is "bent" to produce quarter tones. Included in the score are a toy piano, harmonica, and musical

Principal Works

Orchestral music, including *Echoes of Time and the River* (1967)

Vocal music based on Lorca poetry, including *Night Music I* (1963); four books of madrigals (1965–69); *Songs, Drones and Refrains of Death* (1968); *Night of the Four Moons* (1969) and *Ancient Voices of Children* (1970)

Music for amplified piano, including 2 volumes of *Makrokosmos* (1972, 1973) and *Music for a Summer Evening* (1974)

saw. The percussion players use all kinds of drums, gongs, and cymbals, Tibetan prayer stones, Japanese temple bells, and tuned tom-toms (high-pitched drums of African origin); also a marimba, vibraphone, sleigh bells, glockenspiel plates, and tubular bells.

The first song from this cycle, *El niño busca su voz* (The little boy is looking for his voice), is very free and fantastic in character. The soprano part offers a virtuoso exhibition of what the voice can do in the way of cries, sighs, whispers, buzzings, trills, and percussive clicks. There are even passages marked "fluttertongue"—an effect we have hitherto associated only with instruments. Throughout Crumb captures the rapturous, improvisational spirit of flamenco song. The passion is here, the sense of mystery and wonder—but in a thoroughly twentieth-century setting.

In *Ancient Voices* Crumb has found the right music for the dark intimations of Lorca's poetry. (See Listening Guide 52 for text.) The work has justly established itself as a prime example of contemporary imagination and feeling.

Listening Guide 52

8B/5   II/4/32

CRUMB: *Ancient Voices of Children*

Date: 1970

Genre: Song cycle (5 songs and 2 instrumental interludes), based on poetry of Federico García Lorca

1. *El niño busca su voz* (The little boy is looking for his voice)

Text	Translation	Description
		Opens with elaborate vocalise for soprano—cries, trills, other vocal gymnastics Sings into piano with pedal down for resonance
32 El niño busca su voz.	The little boy is looking for his voice.	Strophe 1—sung by soprano alone with turns, trills, hisses
(La tenía el rey de los grillos.)	(The king of the crickets had it.)	Continues with low-pitched recitation
En una gota de agua buscaba su voz el niño.	In a drop of water the little boy was looking for his voice.	
33 No la quiero para hablar; me haré con ella un anillo que llevará mi silencio en su dedo penqueñito.	I do not want it to speak with; I will make a ring of it so that he may wear my silence on his little finger. Tr. by W. S. MERWIN	Strophe 2—overlaps Strophe 1 Boy soprano sings offstage through cardboard tube Folklike character to melody

80

Electronic Music

"I have been waiting a long time for electronics to free music from the tempered scale and the limitations of musical instruments. Electronic instruments are the portentous first step toward the liberation of music."—EDGARD VARÈSE

Perhaps the single most important musical development of the 1950s and '60s was the emergence of electronic music. This was foreshadowed, during the earlier part of the century, by the invention of a variety of electronic instruments of limited scope. From such instruments as the electronic organ and the *ondes Martenot* (Martenot's waves)—an instrument producing sounds by means of an electronic oscillator—a future was pointed that was quickly realized by the booming revolution of technology.

The Technological Revolution

The postwar emergence of electronic music falls into three stages. The first stage came with the use of magnetic tape recording, which was much more flexible as a medium for storing sounds than the flat-disk recording that had been used previously. Around 1947 a group of technicians at a Paris radio station, led by Peter Schaeffer, had already begun to experiment with what they called *musique concrète*, a music made up of natural sounds and sound effects that were recorded and then altered and manipulated electronically. Their activities took on a new impetus when they began to use tape, which gave them a vastly wider range of possibilities in altering the sounds they used as source material, and also enabled them to cut and splice the sounds into new combinations.

Musique concrète

The possibility of using not only natural but also artificially generated sounds soon presented itself. A wide variety of equipment for generating and altering sounds came into use. Significant in this regard were the experiments carried on by Otto Luening and Vladimir Ussachevsky at Columbia University, and by Herbert Eimert and Karlheinz Stockhausen in Cologne. These men began their work around 1951. Within a few years there were studios for the production of tape music in many of the chief musical centers of Europe and America. With the raw sound (either naturally or electronically produced) as a starting point, the composer could isolate its components, alter its pitch, volume, or other dimensions, play it backward, add reverberation (echo), filter out some of the overtones, or add additional components by splicing and overdubbing. Even though all these operations were laborious and time-consuming—it might take many hours to process only a minute of finished music—composers hastened to avail themselves of the new medium.

The second step in the technological revolution came with the development of *synthesizers*, which are essentially devices combining sound

Synthesizers

The RCA Electronic Music Synthesizer at the Columbia-Princeton Music Center, New York

generators and sound modifiers in one package with a unified control system. The first and most elaborate of these devices was the RCA Electronic Music Synthesizer, first unveiled in 1955; a more sophisticated model was installed four years later at the Columbia-Princeton studio in New York City. This immense and elaborate machine is capable of generating any imaginable sound or combination of sounds, with an infinite variety of pitches, durations, timbres, dynamics, and rhythmic patterns far beyond the capabilities of conventional instruments. The synthesizer represented an enormous step forward, since the composer was now able to control all the characteristics beforehand, and thus could bypass some of the time-consuming manual techniques associated with tape-recorder music. The German composer Karlheinz Stockhausen (1928–), working in the Cologne studio, wrote two *Electronic Studies* (1953–54), built entirely from electronic sounds devoid of overtones, and later produced his electronic masterpiece *Gesang der Jünglinge* (Song of the Youths, 1956) for vocal and synthesized sounds on tape.

Karlheinz Stockhausen

Because of its size and cost the RCA machine at Columbia has remained unique; but various smaller synthesizers have been devised that bring most of the resources of electronic music within the reach of a small studio. The best known of these were the Moog, Buchla, and ARP. Today, the Synclavier is the standard machine in many electronic studios. One advantage of these smaller machines is that they can be played directly, thus making "live" electronic performance a possibility.

The third stage of electronic development involves the use of the electronic computer as a sound generator. The basic principle here is the fact that the shape of any sound wave can be represented by a graph, and this graph can in turn be described by a series of numbers, each of which will represent a point on the graph. Such a series of numbers can be translated, by a device known as a digital-to-analog converter, into a sound tape that

Computer-generated music

can be played on a tape recorder. In theory, then, all that a composer has to do is to write down a series of numbers representing the sound desired, feed them into the converter, and play the tape. But composers do not traditionally think in terms of the shape of sound waves, so it was necessary to devise a computer program that would translate musical specifications—pitches, durations, timbres, dynamics, and the like—into numbers. There are now many such programs, and the wide availability of home computers has made them readily accessible. Computer sound-generation is the most flexible of all electronic media, and is likely to dominate the field in years to come.

Electronic music has two aspects of novelty. The most immediately obvious one is the creation of "new sounds," and this has impelled many musicians to use the new medium. Equally important, perhaps, is the fact that the composer of electronic music is able to work directly with the sounds, and can produce a finished work without the help of an intermediary—the performer.

However, the combination of electronic sounds with live music has also proved to be a fertile field, especially since many younger composers have been working in both media. Works for soloist and recorded tape have become common, even "concertos" for tape recorder (or live-performance synthesizer) and orchestra. One important composer working in this mixed medium is Mario Davidovsky, a professor of composition at Columbia University and director of the Columbia-Princeton Electronic Center. Among his works for tape and live performer is a series known as *Synchronisms* (1963–74). These are dialogues for solo instruments and prerecorded tape; No. 1, for flute and tape, is particularly effective due to the flute's purity of tone, wide range of dynamics, and agility in pitch and articulation. "The attempt here has been made," he writes, "to preserve the typical characteristics of the conventional instruments of the electronic medium respectively—yet to achieve integration of both into a coherent musical texture."

Mario Davidovsky

Electronic music has permeated the commercial world of music making in a big way. Much of the music we hear today as movie and TV sound tracks is electronically generated, although some effects are so like conventional instruments that we are not always aware of the new technology. Popular music groups have been "electrified" for some years, but now regularly feature synthesizers which simulate conventional rock band instruments as well as altogether new sounds.

Edgard Varèse: His Life and Music

"I refuse to submit myself only to sounds that have already been heard."

Edgard Varèse (1883–1965) was one of the truly original spirits in the music of our time. The innovations of Stravinsky, Schoenberg, and Bartók unfolded within the framework of the traditional elements of their art, but Varèse went a step further: he rejected certain of those elements altogether.

Varèse was born in Paris in 1883, of Italian-French parentage. He studied mathematics and science at school, since his father intended for him an engineering career. But at eighteen he entered the Schola Cantorum, and subsequently studied at the Paris Conservatoire. With the outbreak of the war in 1914 Varèse was mobilized into the French army, but was discharged the following year after a serious illness. He came to the United States in 1915, when he was thirty-two, and lost no time in making a place for himself in the musical life of his adopted land.

The greater part of Varèse's music was written during the 1920s and early '30s. He found a champion in the conductor Leopold Stokowski, who performed his scores despite the violent opposition they aroused in conventional-minded concertgoers. Then, like his colleague Ives, Varèse fell silent when he should have been at the height of his powers. During the next twenty years he followed the new scientific developments in the field of electronic instruments, and resumed composing in 1949, when he began work on his *Déserts*.

Edgard Varèse

By that time the scene had changed; there existed a public receptive to electronic music. When an enterprising recording company made available four of his works, Varèse was enabled to reach an audience that had never before heard his music. He was invited by the State Department to conduct master classes in composition in Darmstadt, Germany. The younger generation of European composers who were experimenting with taped music suddenly discovered him as one whose works had been prophetic of theirs. Their long-neglected master finally came into his own. He died in New York City.

The abstract images that brood over Varèse's music are derived from the life of the big city: the rumble of motors, the clang of hammers, the shriek and hiss and shrilling of factory whistles, turbines, steam drills. His stabbing, pounding rhythms conjure up the throb and hum of the metropolis. It follows that his attention is focused on the percussion instruments, which he handles with inexhaustible invention. His music unfolds in geometrical patterns based on the opposition of sonorous planes and volumes—patterns which, in their abstraction, are the counterpart in sound of the designs of Cubist painting. Varèse's music was utterly revolutionary in its day. It sounded like nothing that had ever been heard before. As you can see from the list of his works, the fanciful names he gave them indicated the connection in the composer's mind between his music and scientific process.

Principal Works

Orchestral music, including *Arcana* (1927–28)

Chamber music, including *Hyperprism* (woodwinds, brass, and percussion, 1923), *Octandre* (8 instruments, 1923), *Intégrales* (winds and percussion, 1925), and *Ionisation* (percussion ensemble, 1931)

Works with tape, including *Déserts* (orchestra with tape, 1954) and *Poème électronique* (1958)

The Philips Pavilion at the 1958 Brussels World Fair, designed by architect Le Corbusier, had music written for it by Edgard Varèse.

Varèse: Poème électronique

In 1958 the Philips Corporation, a Dutch electrical company, commissioned the famous architect Le Corbusier to design a pavilion at the Brussels World Fair. Le Corbusier invited Varèse to write the music for an eight-minute fantasy of light, color, rhythm, and tone designed to put its audience "in the presence of the genesis of the world." For this occasion Varèse produced his only work that is entirely in the electronic medium. Varèse's music was played over four hundred speakers, so arranged as to create a continuous sonority, and with it a sense of spatial dimension. The music was accompanied by projections of images chosen by Le Corbusier: photographs, written and printed script, paintings, and montages. No matter when the spectator arrived he heard the piece in its entirety as he passed through the pavilion. Although no attempt was made to synchronize the images with the sounds, the visual and aural elements worked together to engender a total environment that was seen and heard by thousands of people a day.

The music was composed on three channels, most of it created directly on tape. Varèse combined sounds of the human voice, treated electronically, with percussion and synthetic sounds. He used an oscillator and several filters. Some of the drum sounds were produced by a pulse generator. These, together with sirens and bell sounds in persistent rhythmic patterns, unfold in a continuum whose curiously depersonalized quality grips the imagination and conjures up visions of a strange new world. The human quality is represented by a wailing female voice. We hear a poem of organized sounds that is unified by a recurring motive consisting of a high-pitched figure of

Harriet, the Woman Called Moses (1985, based on the life of Harriet Tubman, the black Civil War heroine). Her output also includes two full-length ballets and a number of orchestral, chamber, and choral works.

As a leading exponent of the New Romanticism, Musgrave was one of a long line of dramatists and composers who were attracted to the sad tale of the legendary Mary of Scotland. Besides, a composer born in Scotland cannot but view Mary's tangled career as a nationalist theme. Mary, the young widowed Queen of France, returns to Scotland on the death of her father and ascends the throne. Her half brother James, the ambitious Earl of Moray, aspires to replace her and is thwarted when Mary takes an English nobleman, Lord Darnley, as her lover and advisor. She eventually marries Darnley, and becomes pregnant with his child; James finally turns against her. Weak and ill after the birth of her son, Mary takes refuge in Stirling Castle and asks her friend, the Earl of Bothwell, for help. Bothwell joins her at the castle and eventually seduces her. They are discovered; Bothwell and Darnley are murdered; and James demands that Mary, hopelessly compromised in the eyes of the nation, abdicate in favor of her infant son. She flees. James is murdered, and the boy ascends the throne of Scotland as James VI.

The opera ends here but Mary's subsequent fate is well known. She went to England to seek the protection of her cousin Queen Elizabeth, who kept her imprisoned for some twenty years, after which she was accused of plotting against Elizabeth and ultimately condemned to her death. Elizabeth is said to have signed the death warrant with the remark, "There is room for only one queen in England." After Elizabeth's death Mary's hope was realized: her son became James I of England.

In the first scene of Act III, in which Mary, attended by her lady-in-waiting Mary Seton, sings a lullaby to her baby. Musgrave is meticulous in her setting of the English language. The words float on the music and are never sub-

Thea Musgrave

Act III, scene 1 of the Virginia Opera production of Mary, Queen of Scots *in 1977. Ashley Putnam sang the leading role.*

merged in it. (See Listening Guide 54 for text.) The dialogue between Mary and her servant is transformed into a melodious recitative to which the orchestral underpinning adds drama. Also dramatic is the contrast between the lullaby, a song of innocence that mirrors Mary's feeling for her child, and the tumultuous events surrounding it. The melody is in a lilting 6/8, a meter traditionally associated with cradle songs. It first appears as a duet between the two women in which their voices intertwine mellifluously. When it reappears, sung by Mary alone, it is heard against a countermelody in the lower strings. There follows a passage of dialogue between Mary and Gordon to which the orchestra adds excitement, which leaves the voices free to sing the words against discreetly dissonant harmonies. Mary and Gordon express their conflicting reactions to her decision to send for Bothwell. The lullaby returns as Mary warns the sleeping child of the dangers that await him. The scene is notable for the variety of emotions packed within its frame and illustrates how readily our language lends itself to opera when handled well.

Listening Guide 54

8B/4   II/4/27

MUSGRAVE: *Mary, Queen of Scots*, Act III, scene 1

Date: 1977

Genre: Opera in three acts

Librettist: the composer, after a play by Amalia Elguera

27 (*Orchestral prelude incorporates the distant sounds of a battle before it melts into the music of a lullaby. It is evening. Mary's supper room: a solitary lamp lights the set. Mary lies sleeping on a couch; she is still very weak and ill from the birth of her son. Enter Mary Seton on tiptoe, bringing the baby to her. Mary wakes.*)

28 MARY	Where is Darnley? Why does he not come to see his son?
MARY SETON	Oh Madam! He is, as usual, Playing cards and drinking.
MARY	He does not care! Neither the recollection Of our early friendship Nor any hope for the future Can make me forget the wrong. I have so sore a heart That I . . . (*she weeps*)
MARY SETON	Oh Madam! (*she consoles Mary.*) Why do you not send him away To France or England? Divorce him!

MARY

(*weak but* firm)
No! That I cannot do.
I must protect my honor
And safeguard the succession
For the sake of my son.
No more tears!
A Kingdom to be ruled!
And you, my son,
You shall be the one to unite
The Kingdoms of Scotland and
England.
You shall be King!

29 MARY & MARY SETON

Lullaby, sung as duet

Sleep little child, sleep
Till you wake to be King.
Sleep in the cradle of gold
Till you wake to earth and stone
To the wind and the sea.
Sleep little child
Till you wake to be King.

MARY

Mary, go and see if Bothwell has
come!

MARY SETON

Bothwell! You have sent for
Bothwell?

MARY

Yes! He is loyal
And he will protect me and my
son.
I fear my brother . . .

MARY SETON

And you do not fear Bothwell?

MARY

Go! Do as I say!
Send him to me at once!
(*Mary Seton exits.*)

MARY

Lullaby

Sleep little child, sleep
Till you wake to be King.
Sleep in the cradle of gold
Till you wake to mountain and
moor
To the lochs and the bens.
Sleep little child
Till you wake to be King.

30

(*Gordon rushes in, distraught and out of breath.*)

MARY

Gordon, what is it?
You are pale and trembling.

GORDON

It is James . . .

MARY

James? What do you mean?

GORDON

James has returned
With an army behind him.
The people have turned to him;

	And now they march on
	Edinburgh
	To demand that you restore him
	to power.
MARY	I, restore him to power?
GORDON	Go, go to Stirling!
	There take refuge!
	Be decisive!
	Stand firm!
	But stand alone and the people
	Will again turn to you.
	Go, you must go now!
MARY	Ah no!
	Fear not, Gordon! I foresaw this.
	I have mended my quarrel with Bothwell;
	I have sent for him to protect me from James.
GORDON	Bothwell! People fear him!
	They turn to James
	Because of him. Do not trust him!
	He will overpower you!
MARY	No! I will stand my ground.
GORDON	Go, go to Stirling;
	There lies your strength and safety.
MARY	No! I will stand my ground.
GORDON	I beg you Mary!
	Do not trust Bothwell!
MARY	Leave me Gordon! My mind is made.
GORDON	Your Majesty . . .
MARY	Go, search out what plans
	James may have in hand.
	(*Gestures ineffectually and she turns impatiently away from him.*)
GORDON	I fear this night,
	What calamity it will bring.
	I am alone to warn
	And she will not heed my words.
	I tremble, I tremble for my
	Queen.
MARY	These are an old man's fears!
	I will tame Bothwell. Yes!
	And I will shape his desires
	To my own purposes!
	(*She goes over to her son.*)

31 Reprise of lullaby, sung by   Sleep little child, sleep
    Mary alone   till you wake . . .

                                         Then you must be strong
                                         To face the world
                                         In all its cunning;
                                         When bitter experience
                                          Will line your face
                                          And cause the innocence
                                          To fade from your smile.

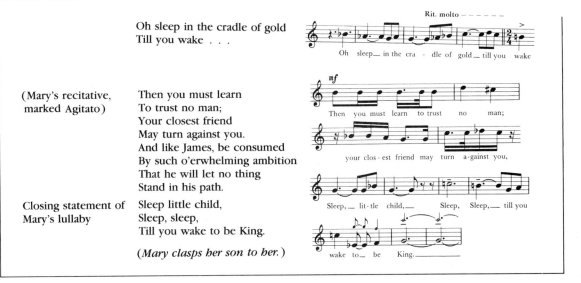

Oh sleep in the cradle of gold
Till you wake . . .

(Mary's recitative,
marked Agitato)

Then you must learn
To trust no man;
Your closest friend
May turn against you.
And like James, be consumed
By such o'erwhelming ambition
That he will let no thing
Stand in his path.

Closing statement of
Mary's lullaby

Sleep little child,
Sleep, sleep,
Till you wake to be King.

(*Mary clasps her son to her.*)

Tobias Picker: Old and Lost Rivers

Tobias Picker (1954–) is the youngest of the composers discussed in this book. He is thus a voice of the rising generation of American composers. A native New Yorker, Picker studied at the Manhattan School of Music, at the Juilliard School, and at Princeton University with what one critic called "the grand trio of American academic rationalists"—Charles Wuorinen, Elliott Carter, and Milton Babbitt. His starting point, consequently, was the serial technique that was the prevailing mode of musical thought in the decades after the Second World War. He soon took his place among the composers who were attempting to adapt that technique to broader levels of expressivity. "My training," he has written, "is as a serial composer; I was steeped in it. But I'm very flexible. Basically I'm a twelve-tone composer who writes anything he feels like writing."

Picker belongs to that fortunate breed of artists to whom success comes early enough to be enjoyed. His First Symphony (1982) was commissioned by the San Francisco Symphony Orchestra under conductor Edo de Waart. His Second Symphony was given its premiere by the Houston Symphony Orchestra in 1986, to be followed by his Third in 1989. *Keys to the City* (1982, really his Second Piano Concerto) was written for the one hundredth anniversary of the Brooklyn Bridge and, with the composer as soloist, was broadcast on national television. In these works Picker unfolds a style of grand gesture, sweeping melodies, expressive harmonies, and virtuoso instrumental writing that ranks him with the New Romantics.

Tobias Picker

Old and Lost Rivers is one of a number of works commissioned by the Houston Symphony as part of the celebration of the Texas Sesquicentennial. (Picker has been composer-in-residence with the orchestra since 1985.) The title refers to the wetlands "near the great Trinity River," the composer explains, "which snakes down from Houston to the Gulf. These Old and Lost Rivers are the traces that the Trinity River has left upon the land when it shifted—as rivers do—over time."

S4B/9

S4/40

A mood piece that evokes the nostalgia in its title, *Old and Lost Rivers* unfolds its delicate orchestral colors and gentle melodies with impressionistic subtlety. Its D-flat major tonality eschews serial complexities in favor of pure lyricism. One might define Picker's Romanticism as an infinite longing wrapped up in the sound of the French horn. These rivers flow through a landscape as remote as it is solitary: the unrecapturable landscape of lost dreams.

The composer of this evocative tone poem is the perfect example of a young artist who has found his own voice and is encouraged to do his best because he knows there is a public waiting for it. He is, as the critic Andrew Porter called him, " a genuine creator with a fertile, unforced vein of invention."

Minimalism

Independently of the New Romantics, a group of young composers found their way to simplification of the musical language. They stripped their compositions down to the barest essentials in order to concentrate the listener's attention on a few basic details. This urge toward a minimal art first found expression in painting and sculpture. It became a significant force in contemporary music during the 1970s.

The salient feature of *minimalist music*, as it has come to be known, is the repetition of melodic, rhythmic, and harmonic patterns with very little variation. The music changes so slowly that the listener is forced to focus a maximum of attention on a minimum of detail. Such concentration can have a hypnotic effect, and indeed the term "trance music" has attached itself to some works of the minimalists. But it is a label they reject because, as they point out, their material is selected most carefully and worked out in highly disciplined procedures. One can say, however, that in their music—as in the great novel by Marcel Proust—time moves at a different pace from what most of us are accustomed to.

By simplifying melody, rhythm, and harmony within an unwavering tonality, the minimalists represent a turning away from the complex, highly intellectual style of the serialists. They reject the heritage of Schoenberg and Webern just as they do the cerebral preoccupations of Boulez and Babbitt. Instead, they open themselves to modes of thought emanating from the Third World, especially the contemplative art of India and the quasi-obsessive rhythms of Africa, as well as jazz, pop, and rock. Although influenced by the early ideas of John Cage, for the most part they reject his interest in

In this untitled, minimalist sculpture dated 1971, **Donald Judd** (*b. 1928*) *strips his work down to a simple circle of hot-rolled steel.* (The Solomon R. Guggenheim Museum, New York)

indeterminacy and chance. They prefer to control their sounds.

There are several kinds of minimalist music. In some works the pulse is repeated with numbing regularity. Others are very busy on the surface, though the harmonies and timbres change very slowly. Terry Riley (1935–) introduced the element of pulse and the concept of tiny motivic cells that repeat in his ninety-minute work entitled *In C* (1964). Influenced by the music of the Far East, by ragtime and jazz, and by the theories of John Cage, Riley has introduced elements of performer choice into electronic music, along with improvisation. The music of Steve Reich (1936–) moves so slowly that it seems to come out of a time sense all his own; this is particularly true of his works on tape. Reich describes his sense of time as "a musical process happening so gradually that listening resembles watching the minute hand of a watch—you perceive it moving only after you stay with it for a while." This contemplative quality is his answer to the pace of our overly competitive society.

Terry Riley

Steve Reich

The most widely known minimalist is Philip Glass (1937–), whose career began conventionally enough with attendance at the University of Chicago and the Juilliard School, after which he went off to Paris on a Fulbright scholarship to study with Nadia Boulanger. It was she who imparted to him, as he put it, "the skills that make music go." Even more decisive was his contact with the Indian sitar player Ravi Shankar. Glass was fascinated with non-Western music. "And, of course, I was also hearing the music of Miles Davis, of John Coltrane, and the Beatles." When he returned to New York he became convinced that "modern music had become truly decadent, stagnant, uncommunicative. Composers were writing for each other and the public didn't seem to care." It was out of this conviction that he evolved his own style, drawing upon the musical traditions of India and Africa as well as the techniques of rock and progressive jazz.

Philip Glass

John Adams: Short Ride in a Fast Machine

Although both minimalism and the New Romanticism sought above all to escape the overly intellectual world of serialism, they did so by completely different paths. There was bound to appear a composer who, by seeking to expand the expressive gamut of minimalist music, would respond to the emotional impulses emanating from the New Romantics. Such a one was John Adams (1947–), the best known among the second generation of minimalists, who was educated at Harvard and in 1972 began teaching at the San Francisco Conservatory of Music. Strongly influenced by Steve Reich, Adams's is a subtle music marked by warm sonorities and much energy. At the same time he presents a more personal approach to music than do either Glass or Reich.

John Adams

Adams attracted much attention with his opera *Nixon in China* (1987), which takes place in Beijing during the three days of former President Nixon's visit. The works that followed show Adams increasingly receptive to the sumptuous orchestral palette and expressive harmonies of the New Romanticism. They fully justify his description of himself as "a very emotional composer, one who experiences music on a very physical level. My music is erotic and Dionysian, and I never try to obscure those feelings when I compose."

Short Ride in a Fast Machine is an exuberant work for large orchestra and two synthesizers that stems from the extrovert side of Adams's personality. When asked about the title, Adams replied, "You know how it is when someone asks you to ride in a terrific sports car, and then you wish you hadn't." *Short Ride in a Fast Machine* features a persistent ostinato that with repetition takes on an almost hypnotic power. The steady pulse in the woodblock is so insistent as to be, in the composer's words, "almost sadistic." (See Listening Guide 55 for analysis.) One is reminded of Arthur Honegger's ode to the locomotive, *Pacific 231* (1923), except that Adams's machine is both more propulsive and more lively as it careens along the narrow road between music and organized sound. Although Adams was almost forty when he wrote it, this is youthful music in its physical vitality and devil-may-care optimism. It serves as a fine introduction to a composer whose work encompasses a variety of moods.

Listening Guide 55   8B/6   II/4/34

ADAMS: *Short Ride in a Fast Machine*

Date: 1986, for the Great Woods Festival in Mansfield, Mass., first performed by the Pittsburgh Symphony.

Medium: Orchestra and two synthesizers

Genre: Fanfare

Basis: Repetition of rhythmic motives

34 0:00   Delirando (frenzied), in 3/2 meter
               Insistent rhythm in woodblock
               Synthesizers and woodwinds join with faster pattern
               Brass enter with highly syncopated pattern that continually evolves

               Woodwinds punctuate activity with fast figure

     0:35   Brass pattern now even, then grows uneven and builds into dissonance again

     1:05   Strings enter, with uneven rhythmic pattern punctuated by bass drum

     1:45   Secco section, spaced notes in strings and woodwinds; lighter texture, builds again

35 3:00   Trumpet solo emerges in section marked "slightly slower"; half-note movement in brass against faster rhythms in other parts

     4:03   Tempo I, fast, syncopated nonmelodious pattern, until end

Coda

We have included in these pages a variety of facts—historical, biographical, and technical—that have entered into the making of music and that must enter into an intelligent listening to music. For those who desire to explore the subject further we include a list of books that will guide music lovers in their reading. But books belong to the domain of words, and words have no power over the domain of sound. They are helpful only insofar as they lead us to enjoy the music.

The enjoyment of music depends upon perceptive listening. And perceptive listening (like perceptive anything) is something that we achieve gradually, with practice and effort. By acquiring a knowledge of the circumstances out of which a musical work issued, we prepare ourselves for its multiple meanings; we lay ourselves open to that exercise of mind and heart, sensibility and imagination that makes listening to music so unique an experience. But in the building up of our musical perceptions—that is, of our listening enjoyment—let us always remember that the ultimate wisdom resides neither in dates nor in facts. It is to be found in one place only—the sounds themselves.

Appendix I

Musical Notation

Our musical notation is the result of an evolution that reaches back to antiquity. It has adapted itself to successive systems of musical thought, and continues to do so. It is by no means a perfect tool, but it has proved adequate to the constantly new demands made upon it.

The Notation of Pitch

Musical notation presents a kind of graph of the sounds with regard to their duration and pitch. These are indicated by symbols called *notes,* which are written on the *staff,* a series of five parallel lines with four spaces between: *Staff*

The position of the notes on the staff indicates the pitches, each line and space representing a different degree of pitch.

A symbol known as a *clef* is placed at the left end of the staff, and determines the group of pitches to which that staff refers. The *treble clef* (𝄞) is used for pitches within the range of the female singing voices, and the *bass clef* (𝄢) for a lower group of pitches, within the range of the male singing voices. *Clefs*

Pitches are named after the first seven letters of the alphabet, from A to G; the lines and spaces are named accordingly. (From one note named A to the next is the interval of an octave, which—as we have seen—is the distance from one *do* to the next in the *do-re-mi-fa-sol-la-ti-do* scale). The pitches on the treble staff are named as follows: *Pitch names*

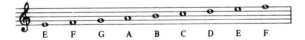

And those on the bass staff:

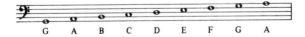

For pitches above and below these, short extra lines called *ledger lines* can be added:

Middle C—the C that, on the piano, is situated approximately in the center of the keyboard—comes between the treble and bass staffs. It is represented by either the

533

first ledger line above the bass staff or the first ledger line below the treble staff, as the following example makes clear. This combination of the two staffs is called the *great staff* or *grand staff*:

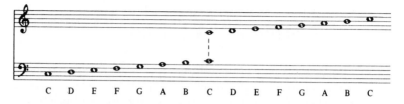

C   D   E   F   G   A   B   C   D   E   F   G   A   B   C

Accidentals

There are also signs known as *accidentals,* which are used to alter the pitch of a written note. A *sharp* (♯) before the note indicates the pitch a semitone above; a *flat* (♭) indicates the pitch a semitone below. A *natural* (♮) cancels a sharp or flat. Also used are the *double sharp* (×) and *double flat* (♭♭), which respectively raise and lower the pitch by two half-tones—that is, a whole tone.

In many pieces of music, where certain sharped or flatted notes are used consistently throughout the piece, the necessary sharps or flats are written at the beginning of each line of music, in order to save repetition. This may be seen in the following example of piano music. Notice that piano music is written on the great staff, with the right hand usually playing the notes written on the upper staff and the left hand usually playing the notes written on the lower:

etc.

The Notation of Rhythm

Note values

The duration of tones is indicated by the appearance of the notes placed on the staff. These use a system of relative values. For example, in the following table each note represents a duration half as long as the preceding one:

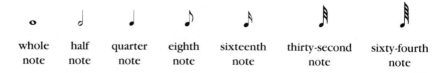

| whole note | half note | quarter note | eighth note | sixteenth note | thirty-second note | sixty-fourth note |

In any particular piece of music, these note values are related to the beat of the music. If the quarter note represents one beat, then a half note lasts for two beats, a whole note for four, with two eighth notes on one beat, or four sixteenths. The following chart makes this clear:

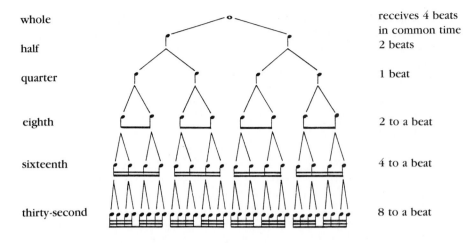

whole	receives 4 beats in common time
half	2 beats
quarter	1 beat
eighth	2 to a beat
sixteenth	4 to a beat
thirty-second	8 to a beat

When a group of three notes is to be played in the time normally taken up by only two of the same kind, we have a *triplet:*

Triplet

It is possible to combine successive notes of the same pitch, using a curved line known as a *tie:*

Tie

beats: 4 + 4 = 8   2 + 4 = 6   1 + ½ = 1½

A *dot* after a note extends its value by half:

Augmentation dot

beats: 4 + 2 = 6   2 + 1 = 3   1 + ½ = 1½   ½ + ¼ = ¾

Time never stops in music, even when there is no sound. Silence is indicated by symbols known as *rests,* which correspond in time value to the notes:

Rests

whole rest	half rest	quarter rest	eighth rest	sixteenth rest	thirty-second rest	sixty-fourth rest

The metrical organization of a piece of music is indicated by the *time signature,* which specifies the meter. This consists of two numbers, written one above the other. The upper numeral indicates the number of beats within the measure; the lower one shows which unit of value equals one beat. Thus, the time signature ¾ means that there are three beats to a measure, with the quarter note equal to one beat. In ⁶⁄₈ time there are six beats in the measure, each eighth note receiving one beat. Following are the most frequently encountered time signatures:

Time signature

duple meter	$\frac{2}{2}$	$\frac{2}{4}$	
triple meter	$\frac{3}{2}$	$\frac{3}{4}$	$\frac{3}{8}$
quadruple meter		$\frac{4}{4}$	
sextuple meter		$\frac{6}{4}$	$\frac{6}{8}$

The following examples show how the system works. It will be noticed that the measures are separated by a vertical line known as a *barline;* hence a measure is sometimes referred to as a *bar.* As a rule, the barline is followed by the most strongly accented beat, the ONE.

Appendix II

Suggested Reading

The following list is merely a starting point, with emphasis on recent and easily available books. Those desiring to pursue the subject further will find specialized bibliographies in many of the works listed below. An asterisk (*) denotes a book available in a paperback edition.

On the Nature of Art

*Dewey, John. *Art as Experience.* New York: Putnam, 1958.

*Fleming, William. *Arts and Ideas.* New brief ed. New York: Holt, Rinehart & Winston, 1974.

Meyer, Leonard B. *Music, the Arts and Ideas: Patterns and Predictions in 20th-Century Culture.* Chicago: U. of Chicago, 1969.

*———— *Emotion and Meaning in Music.* Chicago: U. of Chicago, 1956.

*Read, Herbert. *Art and Society.* Rev. ed. New York: Schocken, 1966.

Dictionaries

*Apel, Willi, and Don Michael Randel. *The Harvard Brief Dictionary of Music.* Cambridge: Harvard, 1978.

Baker's Biographical Dictionary of Musicians. 7th ed. (ed. Nicolas Slonimsky). New York: Schirmer, 1984. Concise version, 1988.

Cohen, Aaron I. *International Encyclopedia of Women Composers.* 2nd rev. ed., 2 vols. New York: Books & Music, 1987.

The New Grove Dictionary of Music and Musicians (ed. Stanley Sadie), 20 vols. New York: Macmillan, 1980.

The New Harvard Dictionary of Music (ed. Don Michael Randel). Cambridge: Harvard, 1986.

The Norton/Grove Concise Encyclopedia of Music (ed. Stanley Sadie). New York: Norton, 1988.

Scholes, Percy A. *Concise Oxford Dictionary of Music.* 3rd ed. (ed. Michael Kennedy). New York: Oxford, 1980.

Thompson, Oscar. *The International Cyclopedia of Music and Musicians.* 10th rev. ed. (ed. Bruce Bohle). New York: Dodd, Mead, 1975.

*Westrup, J. A. and F. L. Harrison. *The New College Encyclopedia of Music.* Rev. ed. (ed. Conrad Wilson). New York: Norton, 1977.

The Materials of Music

*Bekker, Paul. *The Orchestra.* New York: Norton, 1963.

*Bernstein, Leonard. *The Joy of Music.* New York: New American Library, 1967.

*Clough, John, and Joyce Conley. *Scales, Intervals, Keys, Triads, Rhythm, and Meter.* New York: Norton, 1983.

*Cooper, Grosvenor W., and Leonard Meyer. *The Rhythmic Structure of Music.* Chicago: U. of Chicago, 1960.

*Copland, Aaron. *What to Listen for in Music.* New York: Mentor, 1964.

*Manoff, Tom. *The Music Kit.* 2nd ed. New York: Norton, 1984.

Ratner, Leonard G. *Music: The Listener's Art.* 3rd ed. New York: McGraw-Hill, 1977.

*Tovey, Donald F. *The Forms of Music.* New York: Meridian, 1956.

Music History (One-Volume Works)

Abraham, Gerald. *The Concise Oxford History of Music.* New York: Oxford, 1979.

Borroff, Edith. *Music in Europe and the United States: A History.* Englewood Cliffs, N.J.: Prentice-Hall, 1971.

*Einstein, Alfred. *A Short History of Music.* New York: Random House, 1954.

Grout, Donald J., and Claude V. Palisca. *A History of Western Music.* 4th ed. New York: Norton, 1988.

*Janson, H. W., and Joseph Kerman. *A History of Art and Music.* New York: Abrams, 1968.

Lang, Paul Henry. *Music in Western Civilization.* New York: Norton, 1941.

Rosenstiel, Léonie, *et al.* (eds.). *Schirmer History of Music.* New York: Schirmer, 1982.

Musical Instruments

Baines, Anthony (ed.). *Musical Instruments through the Ages.* New York: Walker, 1975.

*Belt, Philip R., *et al. The Piano.* New York: Norton, 1988.

*Boyden, David, *et al. Violin Family.* New York: Norton, 1989.

Gill, Dominic (ed.). *The Book of the Piano.* Ithaca: Cornell, 1981.

*Ripin, Edwin R., *et al. Early Keyboard Instruments.* New York: Norton, 1989.

*Williams, Peter and Barbara Owen. *The Organ.* New York: Norton, 1988.

Styles and Periods

Antiquity and Medieval

Hoppin, Richard H. *Medieval Music.* New York: Norton, 1978.
Reese, Gustave. *Music in the Middle Ages.* New York: Norton, 1940.
*Seay, Albert. *Music in the Medieval World.* 2nd. ed. Englewood Cliffs, N.J.: Prentice-Hall, 1975.
*Strunk, Oliver (ed.). *Source Readings in Music History: Antiquity and the Middle Ages.* New York: Norton, 1965.

Renaissance and Baroque

*Anthony, James, *et al. The New Grove French Baroque Masters.* New York: Norton, 1986.
*Arnold, Denis, *et al. The New Grove Italian Baroque Masters.* New York: Norton, 1984.
*Blume, Friedrich. *Renaissance and Baroque Music* (tr. M. D. Herter Norton). New York: Norton, 1967.
*Brown, Howard M. *Music in the Renaissance.* Englewood Cliffs, N.J.: Prentice-Hall, 1976.
Bukofzer, Manfred F. *Music in the Baroque Era.* New York: Norton, 1947.
*Donington, Robert. *Baroque Music: Style and Performance.* New York: Norton, 1982.
*Palisca, Claude V. *Baroque Music.* Englewood Cliffs, N.J.: Prentice-Hall, 1968.
Reese, Gustave. *Music in the Renaissance.* Rev. ed. New York: Norton, 1959.
*Reese, Gustave, *et al. The New Grove High Renaissance Masters.* New York: Norton, 1984.
*Rifkin, Joshua, *et al. The New Grove North European Baroque Masters.* New York: Norton, 1985.
*Strunk, Oliver (ed.). *Source Readings in Music History: The Baroque Era.* New York: Norton, 1965.
*——— *Source Readings in Music History: The Renaissance.* New York: Norton, 1965.

Classic and Romantic

*Brown, David, *et al. The New Grove Russian Masters 1.* New York: Norton, 1986.
*Blume, Friedrich. *Classic and Romantic Music* (tr. M. D. Herter Norton). New York: Norton, 1970.
*Cooke, Deryck, *et al. The New Grove Late Romantic Masters.* New York: Norton, 1985.
Dahlhaus, Carl. *Nineteenth-Century Music* (tr. J. Bradford Robinson). Berkeley: U. of California, 1989.
Einstein, Alfred. *Music in the Romantic Era.* New York: Norton, 1947.
*Longyear, Rey M. *Nineteenth-Century Romanticism in Music.* 2nd ed. Englewood Cliffs, N.J.: Prentice-Hall, 1973.
*Pauly, Reinhard G. *Music in the Classic Period.* 2nd ed. Englewood Cliffs, N.J.: Prentice-Hall, 1973.

Plantinga, Leon. *Romantic Music.* New York: Norton, 1984.
*Praz, Mario. *The Romantic Agony.* New York: Oxford, 1970.
*Ratner, Leonard. *Classic Music: Expression, Form, and Style.* New York: Schirmer, 1980.
*Rosen, Charles. *The Classical Style.* New York: Norton, 1972.
*Strunk, Oliver (ed.). *Source Readings in Music History: The Classic Era.* New York: Norton, 1965.
*——— *Source Readings in Music History: The Romantic Era.* New York: Norton, 1965.
*Temperly, Nicholas, Gerald Abraham, and Humphrey Searle. *The New Grove Early Romantic Masters 1.* New York: Norton, 1985.
*Warrack, John, Hugh MacDonald, and Karl-Heinz Köhler. *The New Grove Early Romantic Masters 2.* New York: Norton, 1985.

Contemporary

*Abraham, Gerald, *et al. The New Grove Russian Masters 2.* New York: Norton, 1989.
Austin, William. *Music in the Twentieth Century.* New York: Norton, 1966.
*Austin, William, *et al. The New Grove Twentieth-Century American Masters.* New York: Norton, 1988.
*Copland, Aaron. *The New Music, 1900–1960.* New York: Norton, 1968.
*Cowell, Henry. *American Composers on American Music.* New York: Ungar, 1962.
Griffiths, Paul. *Modern Music: the Avant-Garde Since 1945.* London: Dent, 1981.
Machlis, Joseph. *Introduction to Contemporary Music.* 2nd ed. New York: Norton, 1979.
*McVeagh, Diana, *et al. The New Grove Twentieth-Century English Masters.* New York: Norton, 1986.
Morgan, Robert. *Twentieth-Century Music.* New York: Norton, 1990.
*Nectoux, Jean-Michel, *et al. The New Grove Twentieth-Century French Masters.* New York: Norton, 1986.
*Neighbour, Oliver, Paul Griffiths, and George Perle. *The New Grove Second Viennese School.* New York: Norton, 1983.
*Salzman, Eric. *Twentieth-Century Music: An Introduction.* 3rd ed. Englewood Cliffs, N.J.: Prentice-Hall, 1988.
Simms, Bryan R. *Music of the Twentieth Century: Style and Structure.* New York: Schirmer, 1986.
Slonimsky, Nicolas. *Music Since 1900.* 4th ed. New York: Scribner, 1971. Supplement 1986.
*Somfai, László, *et al. The New Grove Modern Masters.* New York: Norton, 1984.
*Tyrrell, John, Hugh MacDonald, and Karl-Heinz Köhler. *The New Grove Turn-of-the-Century Masters.* New York: Norton, 1985.
Watkins, Glenn. *Soundings: Music in the Twentieth Century.* New York: Schirmer, 1988.

Genres

*Gossett, Philip, *et al. The New Grove Masters of Italian Opera.* New York: Norton, 1983.

Griffiths, Paul. *The String Quartet.* London: Thames and Hudson, 1983.

Grout, Donald. *A Short History of Opera.* 2nd ed. New York: Columbia, 1965.

*Kerman, Joseph. *Opera as Drama.* New revised edition, Berkeley: U. of California, 1988.

*Lang, Paul Henry. *The Experience of Opera.* New York: Norton, 1973.

Meister, Barbara. *An Introduction to the Art Song.* New York: Taplinger, 1980.

Newman, William S. *A History of the Sonata Idea,* 3 vols. Rev. ed. New York: Norton, 1983.

*Oliver, Paul, *et al. The New Grove Gospel, Blues, and Jazz.* New York: Norton, 1986.

*Rosen, Charles. *Sonata Forms.* 2nd ed. New York: Norton, 1988.

Sadie, Stanley (ed.) *History of Opera.* New York: Norton, 1990.

*Simpson, Robert (ed.). *The Symphony,* 2 vols. London: David and Charles, 1972.

Ulrich, Homer. *Chamber Music.* 2nd ed. New York: Columbia, 1966.

*Veinus, Abraham. *The Concerto.* New York: Dover, 1964.

American Music

Chase, Gilbert. *America's Music, from the Pilgrims to the Present,* 2nd rev. ed. Westport, Conn.: Greenwood, 1981 (repr. of 1966 ed.).

Hamm, Charles. *Music in the New World.* New York: Norton, 1982.

*———. *Yesterdays: Popular Song in America.* New York: Norton, 1979.

*Hitchcock, H. Wiley. *Music in the United States: A Historical Introduction.* 2nd ed. Englewood Cliffs, N.J.: Prentice-Hall, 1974.

Howard, John Tasker. *Our American Music.* 4th ed. New York: Crowell, 1965.

*Mellers, Wilfred. *Music in a New Found Land.* New York: Oxford, 1987.

Rockwell, John. *All American Music: Composition in the Late Twentieth Century.* New York: Knopf, 1983.

*Schuller, Gunther. *Early Jazz.* New York: Oxford, 1968.

*———. *The Swing Era: The Development of Jazz, 1930–1945.* New York: Oxford, 1989.

*Southern, Eileen. *The Music of Black Americans.* 2nd ed. New York: Norton, 1983.

*———. *Readings in Black American Music.* 2nd ed. New York: Norton, 1982.

*Thomson, Virgil. *American Music Since 1910.* New York: Holt, Rinehart & Winston, 1971.

Tirro, Frank. *Jazz: A History.* New York: Norton, 1977.

Tischler, Barbara. *An American Music: The Search for an American Musical Identity.* New York: Oxford, 1986.

Non-Western Music

*Malm, William. *Music Cultures of the Pacific, the Near East and Asia.* Englewood Cliffs, N.J.: Prentice-Hall, 1967.

*Nettl, Bruno, Gerard Béhague, and Valerie Goertlen. *Folk and Traditional Music of the Western Continents.* 3rd ed. Englewood Cliffs, N.J.: Prentice-Hall, 1990.

Titon, Jeff Todd (gen. ed.) *Worlds of Music: An Introduction to the Music of the World's People.* New York: Schirmer, 1984.

Women Composers

*Ammer, Christine. *Unsung: A History of Women in American Music.* Westport, Conn.: Greenwood, 1980.

*Bowers, Jane and Judith Tick, eds. *Women Making Music: The Western Art Tradition, 1150–1950.* Urbana: University of Illinois, 1986.

*Jezic, Diane Peacock. *Women Composers: The Lost Tradition Found.* New York: The Feminist Press at CUNY, 1988.

Composers (By and On)

BABBITT

Babbitt, Milton. *Words About Music.* Madison: U. of Wisconsin, 1987.

BACH, J. S.

*David, Hans T., and Arthur Mendel (eds.). *The Bach Reader.* Rev. ed. New York: Norton, 1966.

Felix, Werner. *Johann Sebastian Bach.* New York: Norton, 1985.

Geiringer, Karl, with Irene Geiringer. *Johann Sebastian Bach: The Culmination of an Era.* New York: Oxford, 1966.

*Wolff, Christoph, *et al. The New Grove Bach Family.* New York: Norton, 1983.

BARTÓK

*Stevens, Halsey. *The Life and Music of Béla Bartók.* Rev. ed. New York: Oxford, 1967.

*Lampert, Vera and László Somfai. *Béla Bartók* in *The New Grove Modern Masters.* New York: Norton, 1984.

BEETHOVEN

*Anderson, Emily (ed. and tr.). *The Letters of Beethoven.* New York: Norton, 1985.

*Forbes, Elliot (ed.). *Thayer's Life of Beethoven.* Rev. ed. Princeton: Princeton U., 1967.

*Kerman, Joseph. *The Beethoven Quartets.* New York: Knopf, 1967.

*Schindler, Anton. *Beethoven as I Knew Him.* New York: Norton, 1972.

*Solomon, Maynard. *Beethoven.* New York: Schirmer, 1979.

*Sonneck, O. G. (ed.). *Beethoven: Impressions by His Contemporaries.* New York: Dover, 1967.

*Tyson, Alan, and Joseph Kerman. *The New Grove Beethoven.* New York: Norton, 1983.

BERG

Jarman, Douglas. *The Music of Alban Berg.* Berkeley: U. of California, 1978.

*Perle, George. *Alban Berg* in *The New Grove Second Viennese School.* New York: Norton, 1983.
Reich, Willi. *The Life and Works of Alban Berg.* New York: Da Capo, 1982.

BERLIOZ

*Barzun, Jacques. *Berlioz and His Century: An Introduction to the Age of Romanticism.* Chicago: U. of Chicago, 1982.
———. *Berlioz and the Romantic Century.* 2 vols. 3rd ed. New York: Columbia, 1969.
Holoman, D. Kern. *Berlioz.* Cambridge: Harvard, 1989.
*Macdonald, Hugh. *Berlioz* in *The New Grove Early Romantic Masters 2,* New York: Norton, 1985.
Primmer, Brian. *The Berlioz Style.* New York: Oxford, 1973.

BIZET

Curtiss, Mina. *Bizet and His World.* Westport, Conn.: Greenwood, 1977 (repr. of 1958 ed.).

BOULEZ

Boulez, Pierre. *Orientations.* Cambridge: Harvard, 1986.
*Hopkins, G. W. *Pierre Boulez* in *The New Grove Twentieth-Century French Masters.* New York: Norton, 1986.

BRAHMS

*Becker, Heinz. *Johannes Brahms* in *The New Grove Late Romantic Masters.* New York: Norton, 1985.
Geiringer, Karl. *Brahms: His Life and Works.* 3rd ed. New York: Da Capo, 1981 (repr. of 1948 ed.).
Jacobson, Bernard. *The Music of Johannes Brahms.* London: Tantivy, 1977.

BYRD

Holst, Imogen. *Byrd.* New York: Praeger, 1972.

CAGE

*Cage, John. *A Year From Monday; New Lectures and Writings.* Middletown, Conn.: Wesleyan U., 1969.
*———. *Silence.* Middletown, Conn.: Wesleyan U., 1961.
———. *Themes and Variations.* Barrytown, N.Y.: Station Hill, 1982.
*Hamm, Charles. *John Cage* in *The New Grove Twentieth-Century American Masters.* New York: Norton, 1988.

CARTER

Edwards, Allen. *Flawed Words and Stubborn Sounds: A Conversation with Elliott Carter.* New York: Norton, 1971.
*Northcott, Bayan. *Elliott Carter* in *The New Grove Twentieth-Century American Masters.* New York: Norton, 1988.
Schiff, Elliott. *The Music of Elliott Carter.* New York: Da Capo, 1983.
Stone, E., and K. Stone (eds.). *The Writings of Elliott Carter: An American Composer Looks at Modern Music.* Bloomington, Ind.: Indiana U., 1977.

CHOPIN

*Temperley, Nicholas. *Fryderyk Chopin* in *The New Grove Early Romantic Masters I.* New York: Norton, 1985.
*Walker, Alan. *The Chopin Companion: Profiles of The Man and the Musician,* New York: Norton, 1973.

COPLAND

*Austin, William W. *Aaron Copland* in *The New Grove Twentieth-Century American Masters.* New York: Norton, 1988.

*Copland, Aaron. *Copland on Music.* New York: Norton, 1963.
*Copland, Aaron and Vivian Perlis. *Copland: 1900 through 1942.* New York: St. Martin's, 1984.

DEBUSSY

*Debussy, Claude. "Monsieur Croche," in *Three Classics in the Esthetics of Music.* New York: Dover, 1962.
*Lesure, François (ed.) *Debussy on Music.* Ithaca: Cornell, 1977.
Lockspeiser, Edward. *Debussy.* Rev. 5th ed. London: Dent, 1980.
*Nichols, Roger. *Claude Debussy* in *The New Grove Twentieth-Century Masters.* New York: Norton, 1986.
*Vallas, Leon. *Claude Debussy: His Life and Works.* New York: Dover, 1973.

DVOŘÁK

Clapham, John. *Dvořák.* New York: Norton, 1979.

GABRIELI

*Arnold, Denis. *Giovanni Gabrieli and the Music of the High Renaissance.* New York: Oxford, 1979.

GLUCK

*Einstein, Alfred. *Gluck.* New York: McGraw-Hill, 1972.

HANDEL

Abraham, Gerald (ed.). *Handel, A Symposium.* London: Oxford, 1954.
Dean, Winton. *Handel's Dramatic Oratorios and Masques.* London: Oxford, 1959.
*Dean, Winton, with Anthony Hicks. *The New Grove Handel.* New York: Norton, 1983.
Hogwood, Christopher. *Handel.* London: Thames and Hudson, 1984.
*Lang, Paul Henry. *George Frideric Handel.* New York: Norton, 1966.
Robbins Landon, H. C. *Handel and His World.* Boston: Little, Brown and Co., 1984.

HAYDN

Geiringer, Karl. *Haydn: A Creative Life in Music.* 2nd rev. and exp. ed. Berkeley: U. of California, 1982.
*Larsen, Jens Peter, with Georg Feder. *The New Grove Haydn.* New York: Norton, 1983.
Robbins Landon, H. C. and David Wyn Jones. *Haydn: His Life and Music.* Bloomington, Ind.: Indiana U., 1988.

IVES

Kirkpatrick, John. *Charles Ives* in *The New Grove Twentieth-Century American Masters.* New York: Norton, 1988.
*Perlis, Vivian. *Charles Ives Remembered: An Oral History.* New York: Norton, 1976.
Rossiter, Frank. *Charles Ives and His America.* New York: Liveright, 1975.

LISZT

Perenyi, Eleanor. *Liszt: The Artist as Romantic Hero.* New York: Little, Brown, 1974.
*Searle, Humphrey. *Franz Liszt* in *The New Grove Early Romantic Masters 1.* New York: Norton, 1985.
*Walker, Alan. *Franz Liszt: The Virtuoso Years, 1811–47.* Ithaca: Cornell, 1987.
———. *Franz Liszt: The Weimar Years, 1848–61.* New York: Knopf, 1989.

MAHLER

Blaukopf, Kurt. *Mahler: A Documentary Study*. New York: Oxford University Press, 1976.

Banks, Paul and Donald Mitchell. *Gustav Mahler* in *The New Grove Turn-of-the-Century Masters*. New York: Norton, 1985.

Cooke, Deryck. *Gustav Mahler: An Introduction to His Music*. London: Faber and Faber, 1980.

Lebrecht, Norman (ed.). *Mahler Remembered*. New York: Norton, 1987.

*Mahler, Alma Schindler. *Gustav Mahler: Memories and Letters* (ed. Donald Mitchell). Rev. and enlarged. Seattle: U. of Washington, 1971.

Mitchell, Donald. *Gustav Mahler: The Early Years*. rev. P. Banks and D. Matthews. Berkeley: U. of California, 1980.

*————. *Gustav Mahler: The Wunderhorn Years*. Berkeley: U. of California, 1980.

MENDELSSOHN

Köhler, Karl-Heinz. *Felix Mendelssohn* in *The New Grove Early Romantic Masters 1*. New York: Norton, 1985.

MESSIAEN

*Griffiths, Paul. *Olivier Messiaen* in *The New Grove Twentieth-Century French Masters*. New York: Norton, 1986.

*Johnson, Robert Shelaw. *Messiaen*. New ed. Berkeley: U. of California, 1989.

MONTEVERDI

Arnold, Denis. *Monteverdi* (rev. ed.). London: J. M. Dent, 1978.

*Arnold, Denis, and Nigel Fortune (eds.). *The New Monteverdi Companion*. London: Faber and Faber, 1985.

Redlich, H. F. *Claudio Monteverdi: Life and Works* (tr. Kathleen Dale). Westport, Conn.: Greenwood, n.d. (repr. of 1952 ed.).

MOZART

Anderson, Emily (ed.). *The Letters of Mozart and His Family*. New York: Norton, 1985.

*Blom, Eric. *Mozart*. New York: Macmillan, 1966.

Deutsch, Otto Erich. *Mozart: A Documentary Biography*. 2nd ed. Stanford, Cal.: Stanford U., 1966.

*Landon, H. C. Robbins, and Donald Mitchell (eds.). *The Mozart Companion*. New York: Norton, 1969.

*Lang, Paul Henry (ed.). *The Creative World of Mozart*. New York: Norton, 1963.

*Sadie, Stanley. *The New Grove Mozart*. New York: Norton, 1983.

PROKOFIEV

Nestyev, Israel V. *Prokofiev* (tr. Florence Jonas). Stanford, Cal.: Stanford U., 1960.

PUCCINI

Ashbrook, William. *The Operas of Puccini*. New York: Oxford, 1968.

*Carner, Mosco. *Giacomo Puccini*, in *The New Grove Masters of Italian Opera*. New York: Norton, 1983.

PURCELL

Westrup, Jack. *Henry Purcell* in *The New Grove North European Baroque Masters*. New York: Norton, 1985.

RAVEL

Nichols, Roger (ed.). *Ravel Remembered*. New York: Norton, 1988.

Orenstein, Arbie. *Ravel: Man and Musician*. New York: Columbia, 1975.

SCARLATTI, D.

Boyd, Malcolm. *Domenico Scarlatti*. New York: Schirmer, 1987.

*Kirkpatrick, Ralph. *Domenico Scarlatti*. New York: Apollo, 1968.

SCHOENBERG

*Neighbour, Oliver. *Arnold Schoenberg* in *The New Grove Second Viennese School*. New York: Norton, 1983.

Rosen, Charles. *Arnold Schoenberg*. New York: Viking, 1975.

Schoenberg, Arnold. *Style and Ideas: Selected Writings of Arnold Schoenberg* (ed. Leonard Stein). New York: Faber and Faber, 1982.

SCHUBERT

*Brown, Maurice J. E., with Eric Sams. *The New Grove Schubert*. New York: Norton, 1983.

Deutsch, Otto Erich. *Schubert: Memoirs by His Friends*. New York: Humanities, 1958.

Gál, Hans. *Franz Schubert and the Essence of Melody*. New York: Crescendo, 1977.

Hilmar, Ernst. *Franz Schubert in His Time* (tr. Reinhard G. Pauly). Portland, Or.: Amadeus, 1989.

SCHUMANN, CLARA

Reich, Nancy B. *Clara Schumann: The Artist and The Woman*. Ithaca: Cornell, 1985.

SCHUMANN, ROBERT

*Abraham, Gerald. *Robert Schumann* in *The New Grove Early Romantic Masters 1*, New York: Norton, 1985.

*Walker, Alan (ed.). *Robert Schumann: The Man and His Music*. London: Barrie and Jenkins, 1976.

STRAUSS, R.

Del Mar, Norman. *Richard Strauss: A Critical Commentary on His Life and Work*. 3 vols. Philadelphia: Chilton, 1978.

*Kennedy, Michael. *Richard Strauss* in *The New Grove Turn-of-the-Century Masters*. New York: Norton, 1985.

Strauss, Richard. *Recollections and Reflections* (ed. Willi Schuh, tr. L. J. Lawrence). Westport, Conn.: Greenwood, 1974 (repr. of 1953 ed.).

STRAVINSKY

*Stravinsky, Igor. *An Autobiography*. New York: Norton, 1962.

*————. *Poetics of Music*. Cambridge: Harvard, 1970.

*————, with Robert Craft. *Conversations with Igor Stravinsky*. Berkeley: U. of California, 1980.

*————, with Robert Craft. *Dialogues*. Berkeley: U. of California, 1980.

*————, with Robert Craft. *Expositions and Developments*. Berkeley: U. of California, 1981.

*————, with Robert Craft. *Memories and Commentaries*. Berkeley: U. of California, 1981.

*————. *Themes and Conclusions*. Berkeley: U. of California, 1982.

White, Eric Walter. *Stravinsky, the Composer and His Works.* 2nd ed. Berkeley: U. of California, 1980.

*————. *Igor Stravinsky* in *The New Grove Modern Masters.* New York: Norton, 1984.

TCHAIKOVSKY

*Abraham, Gerald. *The Music of Tchaikovsky.* New York: Norton, 1974.

Brown, David. *Tchaikovsky: The Early Years, 1840–1874.* New York: Norton, 1978.

————. *Tchaikovsky: The Crisis Years, 1874–1878.* New York: Norton, 1983.

————. *Tchaikovsky: The Years of Wandering, 1878–1885.* New York: Norton, 1986.

*Garden, Edward. *Tchaikovsky.* London: J. M. Dent, 1973.

VARÈSE

Varèse, Louise. *Varèse: A Looking Glass Diary.* New York: Norton, 1972.

VAUGHAN WILLIAMS

*Ottaway, Hugh. *Ralph Vaughan Williams* in *The New Grove Twentieth-Century English Masters.* New York: Norton, 1986.

VERDI

*Budden, Julian. *The Operas of Verdi.* 3 vols. New York: Oxford, 1984.

*Porter, Andrew. *Giuseppe Verdi,* in *The New Grove Masters of Italian Opera.* New York: Norton, 1983.

*Walker, Frank. *The Man Verdi.* Chicago: U. of Chicago, 1982.

*Weaver, William, and Martin Chusid (eds.). *The Verdi Companion.* New York: Norton, 1989.

VIVALDI

*Pincherle, Marc. *Vivaldi.* New York: Norton, 1962.

WAGNER

Cosima Wagner's Diaries (ed. Martin Gregor-Dellin and Dietrich Mack, tr. Geoffrey Skelton), 2 vols. New York: Harcourt Brace Jovanovich, 1976–77.

*Deathridge, John, and Carl Dahlhaus. *The New Grove Wagner.* New York: Norton, 1983.

*Gutman, Robert. *Richard Wagner: The Man, His Mind, and His Music.* New York: Harcourt Brace Jovanovich, 1974.

*Millington, Barry. *Wagner.* New York: Vintage, 1987.

*Newman, Ernest. *The Life of Richard Wagner.* 4 vols. New York: Cambridge, 1976.

————. *The Wagner Operas.* New York: Knopf, 1972.

WEBERN

*Griffiths, Paul. *Anton Webern* in *The New Grove Second Viennese School.* New York: Norton, 1983.

Kolneder, Walter. *Anton Webern: An Introduction to His Works* (tr. Humphrey Searle). Berkeley: U. of California, 1968.

Appendix III

Glossary

absolute music Music that has no literary, dramatic, or pictorial program. Also *pure music*.

a cappella Choral music performed without instrumental accompaniment.

accelerando Quickening or getting faster.

accent The emphasis on a beat resulting in one louder or longer than another in a measure.

accompagnato Accompanied; also a recitative which is accompanied by orchestra.

adagio Quite slow.

aerophone Instrument that produces sound by using air as the primary vibrating means, such as flute, whistle, and horn.

agitato Agitated or restless.

aleatory Indeterminate music in which certain elements of performance (such as pitch, rhythm, or form) are left to choice or chance.

allegro Fast, cheerful.

allemande German dance in moderate duple time, popular during the Renaissance and Baroque periods; often the first movement of a Baroque suite.

alto Up until the 18th century, a high vocal part; thereafter the lowest of the female voices. Also *contralto*.

andante Moderately slow or walking pace.

answer Second entry of the subject in a fugue, usually pitched a 4th below or a 5th above the subject.

anthem Choral setting of a religious text in English, similar to the motet.

antiphonal Performance style in which an ensemble is divided into two or more groups, performing in alternation and then together.

antique cymbals Small disks of brass, held by the player one in each hand, that are struck together gently and allowed to vibrate.

aria Lyric song for solo voice with orchestral accompaniment, generally expressing intense emotion; found in opera, cantata, and oratorio.

arioso Short, aria-like passage.

arpeggio Broken chord in which the individual tones are sounded one after another instead of simultaneously.

Ars Antiqua French sacred polyphonic musical style from the period c. 1160–1320.

Ars Nova 14th-century French polyphonic musical style that transformed the art increasingly from religious to secular themes.

a tempo Return to the previous tempo.

atonality Total abandonment of tonality (centering in a key). Atonal music moves from one level of dissonance to another, without areas of relaxation.

augmentation Statement of a melody in longer note values, often twice as slow as the original.

bagpipe Wind instrument popular in Eastern and Western Europe that has several tubes, one of which plays the melody while the others sound the drones, or sustained notes.

ballade French poetic form and chanson type of the Middle Ages and Renaissance with courtly love texts. Also a Romantic genre, especially a lyric piano piece.

ballad opera English comic opera, usually featuring spoken dialogue alternating with songs set to popular tunes.

ballet A dance form featuring a staged presentation of group or solo dancing with music, costumes, and scenery.

baritone Male voice of moderately low range.

bass Male voice of low range.

bass clarinet Woodwind instrument of the clarinet family with the lowest range.

bass drum Percussion instrument that is played with a large soft-headed stick; the largest orchestral drum.

basse danse Graceful court dance of the early Renaissance; an older version of the pavane.

basso continuo Italian for "continuous bass." See *figured bass*. Also refers to performance group playing the bass, consisting of one chordal instrument (harpsichord, organ) and one bass melody instrument (cello, bassoon).

bassoon Double-reed woodwind instrument with a low range.

bass viol See *double bass*.

beat Regular pulsation; a basic unit of length in musical time.

bebop Complex jazz style developed in the 1940s. Also *bop*.

bel canto "Beautiful singing"; elegant Italian vocal style characterized by florid melodic lines delivered by voices of great agility, smoothness, and purity of tone.

bent pitch See *blue note*.

binary form Two-part (**A-B**) form with each section normally repeated. Also *two-part form*.

blue note A slight drop of pitch on the third, fifth, or seventh tone of the scale, common in blues and jazz. Also *bent pitch*.

blues American form of secular black folk music, related to jazz, that is based on a simple, repetitive poetic-musical structure.

bop See *bebop*.

bourrée Lively French Baroque dance type in duple meter.

branle Quick French group dance of the Renaissance, related to the *ronde*.

brass instrument Wind instrument with a cup-shaped mouthpiece, a tube that flares into a bell, and slides or valves to vary the pitch. Most often made of brass or silver.

bridge Transitional passage connecting two sections of a composition.

bugle Brass instrument that evolved from the earlier military or field trumpet.

Burgundian chanson Fifteenth-century French composition, usually for three voices, some or all of which may be played by instruments. Also *chanson.*

cadence Resting place in a musical phrase; music punctuation.

cadenza Virtuosic solo passage in the manner of an improvisation, performed near the end of an aria or a movement of a concerto.

call and response Performance style with a singing leader who is imitated by a chorus of followers. Also *responsorial singing.*

canon Type of polyphonic composition in which one musical line imitates another at a fixed distance throughout.

cantabile Songful, in a singing style.

cantata Vocal genre for solo singers, chorus, and instrumentalists based on a lyric or dramatic poetic narrative. It generally consists of several movements including recitatives, arias, and ensemble numbers.

cantus firmus "Fixed melody," usually of very long notes and based on a fragment of Gregorian chant that served as the structural basis for a polyphonic composition, particularly in the Renaissance.

capriccio Short lyric piece of a free nature, often for piano.

carol English medieval strophic song with a refrain (burden) repeated after each stanza; now associated with Christmas.

cassation Classical instrumental genre related to the serenade or divertimento and often performed outdoors.

castanets Percussion instruments consisting of small wooden clappers that are struck together. They are widely used to accompany Spanish dancing.

castrato Male singer who was castrated during boyhood to preserve the soprano or alto vocal register, prominent in seventeenth- and early eighteenth-century opera.

celesta Percussion instrument resembling a miniature upright piano, with metal plates struck by hammers that are operated by a keyboard.

cello See *violoncello.*

chaconne Baroque form similar to the *passacaglia,* in which the variations are based on a repeated chord progression.

chamber choir Small group of up to about twenty-four singers, who usually perform *a cappella* or with piano accompaniment.

chamber music Ensemble music for up to about ten players, with one player to a part.

chamber sonata See *sonata da camera.*

chanson French polyphonic song of the Middle Ages and Renaissance, set both to courtly and popular poetry. See also *Burgundian chanson.*

chimes Percussion instrument of definite pitch that consists of a set of tuned metal tubes of various lengths suspended from a frame and struck with a hammer. Also *tubular bells.*

choir A group of singers who perform together, usually in parts, with several on each part; often associated with a church.

chorale Baroque congregational hymn of the German Lutheran church.

chorale prelude Short Baroque organ piece in which a traditional chorale melody is embellished.

chorale variations Baroque organ piece in which a chorale is the basis for a set of variations.

chord Simultaneous combination of two or more typically three tones that constitutes a single block of harmony.

chordophone Instrument that produces sound from a vibrating string stretched between two points; the string may be set in motion by bowing, striking, or plucking.

chorus Fairly large group of singers who perform together, usually in parts with several on each part.

chromatic Melody or harmony built from many if not all twelve semitones of the octave. A *chromatic scale* consists of an ascending or descending sequence of semitones.

church sonata See *sonata da chiesa.*

clarinet Single-reed woodwind instrument with a wide range of sizes.

clausula Short medieval composition in discant style, sung to one or two words or a single syllable, based on a fragment of Gregorian chant.

clavecin French word for harpsichord. See *harpsichord.*

clavichord Stringed keyboard instrument popular in the Renaissance and Baroque that is capable of unique expressive devices not possible on the harpsichord.

clavier Generic word for keyboard instruments, including harpsichord, clavichord, piano, and organ.

coda The last part of a piece, usually added to a standard form to bring it to a close.

codetta In sonata form, the concluding section of the Exposition.

collegium musicum An association of amateur musicians, popular in the Baroque era. A modern University ensemble dedicated to the performance of early music.

comic opera See *opéra comique.*

common time See *quadruple meter.*

compound meter Meter in which each beat is divisible by three, rather than two.

con amore With love, tenderly.

concertante Style based on the principle of opposition between two dissimilar masses of sound; concerto-like.

concert band Instrumental ensemble ranging from forty to eighty members or more, consisting of wind and percussion instruments.

concertino Solo group of instruments in the Baroque *concerto grosso.*

concerto Instrumental genre in several movements for solo instrument (or instrumental group) and orchestra.

concerto grosso Baroque concerto type based on the opposition between a small group of solo instruments (the concertino) and orchestra (the ripieno).

concert overture Single-movement concert piece for orchestra, typically from the Romantic period and often based on a literary program.

conductor Person who, by means of gestures, leads performances of musical ensembles, especially orchestras, bands, or choruses.

con fuoco With fire.

conjunct Smooth, connected melody that moves principally in stepwise motion.

con passione With passion.

consonance Concordant or harmonious combination of tones that provides a sense of relaxation and stability in music.

continuous imitation Renaissance polyphonic style in which the motives move from line to line within the texture, often overlapping one another.

contrabass See *double bass.*

contrabassoon Double-reed woodwind instrument with the lowest range in the woodwind family. Also *double bassoon.*

contralto See *alto.*

cornet Valved brass instrument similar to the trumpet but more mellow in sound.

cornetto Early instrument of the brass family with woodwind-like fingerholes. It developed from the cow horn, but was made of wood.

counterpoint The art of combining in a single texture two or more melodic lines.

countersubject In a fugue, a secondary theme heard against the subject; a countertheme.

courante French Baroque dance, a standard movement of the suite, in triple meter at a moderate tempo.

crescendo Growing louder.

crumhorn Early woodwind instrument, whose sound is produced by blowing into a capped double reed and whose lower body is curved.

cymbals Percussion instruments consisting of two large circular brass plates of equal size that are struck sidewise against each other.

da capo An indication to return to the beginning of a piece.

da capo aria Lyric song in ternary or **A-B-A** form, commonly found in operas, cantatas, and oratorios.

decrescendo Growing softer.

Development Structural reshaping of thematic material; second section of sonata-allegro form that moves through a series of foreign keys while themes from the exposition are manipulated.

diatonic Melody or harmony built from the seven tones of a major or minor scale. A *diatonic scale* encompasses patterns of seven whole tones and semitones.

diminuendo Growing softer.

diminution Statement of a melody in shorter note intervals, often twice as fast as the original.

discant Medieval polyphony in which all voices move at approximately the same speed; the movement of the lower part (the chant) parallels the movement of the newly composed upper voice.

disjunct Disjointed or disconnected melody with many leaps.

dissonance Combination of tones that sounds discordant and unstable.

divertimento Classical instrumental genre for chamber ensemble or soloist, often performed as light entertainment. Related to *serenade* and *cassation.*

doctrine of the affections Belief during the Baroque period that the aim of music is to excite or move the passions.

dodecaphonic Greek for twelve-tone; see *twelve-tone music.*

dolce Sweetly.

dolente Sad, weeping.

dominant The fifth scale step, *sol.*

dominant chord Chord built on the fifth scale step, the V chord.

double bass Largest and lowest pitched member of the bowed string family. Also called *contrabass* or *bass viol.*

double bassoon See *contrabassoon.*

double exposition In the concerto, twofold statement of the themes, once by the orchestra and once by the soloist.

double-stop Playing two notes simultaneously on a string instrument.

downbeat First beat of the measure, the strongest in any meter.

drone Sustained sounding of one or several tones for harmonic support, a common feature of folk music.

dulcimer Early folk instrument that resembles the psaltery; its strings are struck with hammers instead of being plucked.

duple meter Basic metrical pattern of two beats to a measure.

duplum Second voice of a polyphonic work, especially the Medieval motet.

duration Length of time something lasts, e.g. the vibration of a musical sound.

dynamics Element of musical expression relating to the degree of loudness or softness or volume of a sound.

embellishment Melodic decoration, either impovised or indicated through *ornamentation* signs in the music.

embouchure The placement of the lips, lower facial muscles, and jaws in playing a wind instrument.

English horn Tenor-range double-reed woodwind instrument, larger and lower in range than the oboe.

episode Interlude or intermediate section in the Baroque fugue, which serves as an area of relaxation between statements of the subject.

espressivo Expressively.

euphonium Tenor-range brass instrument resembling the tuba.

exoticism Romantic musical style in which rhythms, melodies, or instruments evoke the color and atmosphere of far-off lands.

Exposition Opening section; in the fugue, the first section in which the voices enter in turn with the subject; in sonata-allegro form, the first section in which the major thematic material is stated. Also *Statement.*

fantasia Free instrumental piece of fairly large dimensions in an improvisational style; in the Baroque, it often served as introductory piece to a fugue.

figured bass Baroque practice consisting of an independent bass line, which continues throughout a piece and often includes numerals indicating the harmony required of the performer. Also *thorough-bass.*

first-movement form See **sonata-allegro form.**

flat sign Musical symbol (♭) which indicates lowering a pitch by a semitone.

fluegelhorn Valved brass instrument resembling a bugle with a wide bell, used in jazz and commercial music.

flute Soprano-range woodwind instrument, usually made of metal and held horizontally.

form Structure and design in music, based on repetition, contrast, and variation; the organizing principle of music.

formalism Tendency to elevate formal above expressive value in music, as in Neoclassical music.

forte (f) Loud.

fortissimo (ff)   Very loud.

French horn   Medium-range valved brass instrument that can be played "stopped" with the hand as well as open. Also *horn*.

French overture   Baroque instrumental introduction to an opera, ballet, or suite, in two sections: a slow opening followed by an Allegro, often with a brief return to the opening.

fugato   A fugal passage in a nonfugal piece, such as in the Development section of a sonata-allegro form.

fugue   Polyphonic form popular in the Baroque era in which one or more themes are developed by imitative counterpoint.

full anthem   Anglican devotional work similar to the motet of the Catholic Church, performed by choir throughout.

galliard   Lively, triple-meter French court dance.

gavotte   Duple-meter Baroque dance type of a pastoral character.

gigue   Popular English Baroque dance type, a standard movement of the Baroque suite, in a lively compound meter.

gioioso   Joyous.

glee club   Specialized vocal ensemble that performs popular music, college songs, and more serious works.

glissando   Rapid slide through pitches of a scale.

glockenspiel   Percussion instrument with horizontal tuned steel bars of various sizes that are struck with mallets and produce a bright metallic sound.

gong   Percussion instrument consisting of a broad circular disk of metal, suspended in a frame and struck with a heavy drumstick. Also *tam-tam*.

Gradual   Fourth item of the Proper of the Mass, sung in a melismatic style, and performed in a responsorial manner in which soloists alternate with a choir.

grand opera   Style of Romantic opera developed in Paris, focusing on serious, historical plots with huge choruses, crowd scenes, elaborate dance episodes, ornate costumes, and spectacular scenery.

grave   Solemn; very, very slow.

Gregorian chant   Monophonic melody with a freely flowing, unmeasured vocal line; liturgical chant of the Roman Catholic church. Also *plainchant* or *plainsong*.

ground bass   A repeating melody, usually in the bass, throughout a vocal or instrumental composition.

guitar   Plucked string instrument originally made of wood with a hollow resonating body and a fretted fingerboard.

harmonics   Individual pure sounds that are part of any musical tone; in string instruments, crystalline tones in the very high register, produced by lightly touching a vibrating string at a certain point.

harmony   The simultaneous combination of notes and the ensuing relationships of intervals and chords.

harp   Plucked string instrument, triangular in shape with strings perpendicular to the soundboard.

harpsichord   Early Baroque keyboard instrument in which the strings are plucked by quills instead of being struck with hammers like the piano.

heptatonic scale   Seven-note scale; in non-Western musics, often fashioned from a different combination of intervals than major and minor scales.

homophonic   Texture with principal melody and accompanying harmony, as distinct from *polyphony*.

horn   See *French horn*.

idiophone   Instrument that produces sound from the substance of the instrument itself by being struck, blown, shaken, scraped, or rubbed. Examples include bells, rattles, xylophones, and cymbals.

imitation   Subject or motive presented in one voice and then restated in another, each part continuing as others enter.

improvisation   Creation of a musical composition while it is being performed, seen in Baroque ornamentation, cadenzas of concertos, jazz, and non-Western music. See also *embellishment*.

incidental music   Music written to accompany dramatic works.

instrument   Mechanism that generates musical vibrations and transmits them into the air.

intermezzo   Short, lyric piece or movement, often for piano; also a comic interlude performed between acts of an eighteenth-century *opera seria*.

interval   Distance and relationship between two pitches.

inversion   Mirror image of a melody or pattern, found in fugues and twelve-tone composition.

isorhythmic motet   Medieval and early Renaissance motet based on a repeating rhythmic pattern throughout one or more voices.

Italian overture   Baroque overture consisting of three sections: fast-slow-fast.

jazz   A musical style created mainly by black Americans in the early twentieth century that blended elements drawn from African musics with the popular and art traditions of the West.

jazz band   Instrumental ensemble made up of reed (saxophones and clarinets), brass (trumpets and trombones), and rhythm sections (percussion, piano, double bass, and sometimes guitar).

jig   Vigorous English Renaissance dance that may be the predecessor of the Baroque *gigue*.

jongleurs   Medieval wandering entertainers who played instruments, sang and danced, juggled, and performed plays.

kettledrums   See *timpani*.

key   Defines the relationship of tones with a common center or tonic; also a lever on a keyboard or woodwind instrument.

keyboard instrument   Instrument sounded by means of a keyboard (a series of keys played with the fingers).

keynote   See *tonic*.

key signature   Sharps or flats placed at the beginning of a piece to show the key of a work.

Klangfarbenmelodie   Twentieth-century technique in which the notes of a melody are distributed among different instruments, giving a pointillistic texture.

lamentoso   Like a lament.

largo   Broad; very slow.

legato   Smooth and connected; opposite of staccato.

leitmotif   "Leading motive" or basic recurring theme representing a person, object, or idea, commonly used in Richard Wagner's operas.

libretto   Text of an opera.

lied   German for "song"; most commonly associated with the solo art song of the nineteenth century, usually accompanied by piano.

lute   Plucked string instrument, of Middle Eastern origin, popular in Western Europe from the late Middle Ages to the eighteenth century.

lyric opera Hybrid form combining elements of *grand opera* and *opéra comique,* and featuring appealing melodies and romantic drama.

madrigal Renaissance secular work originating in Italy for voices, with or without instruments, set to a short, lyric love poem; also popular in England.

madrigal choir Small vocal ensemble that specializes in *a cappella* secular works.

maestoso Majestic.

Magnificat Biblical text on the words of the Virgin Mary, sung polyphonically in church from the Renaissance on.

major scale Scale consisting of seven different tones that comprises a specific pattern of whole and half steps. It differs from a minor scale primarily in that its third degree is raised half a step.

march A style incorporating characteristics of military music, including strongly accented duple meter in simple, repetitive rhythmic patterns.

marching band Instrumental ensemble of American origin; a popular group for entertainment at sports events and parades, consisting of wind and percussion instruments, drum majors/majorettes, and baton twirlers.

marimba Percussion instrument that is a mellower version of the xylophone; of African and Latin American origins.

masque English genre of aristocratic entertainment that combined vocal and instrumental music with poetry and dance, developed during the sixteenth and seventeenth centuries.

Mass Central service of the Roman Catholic Church.

mazurka Type of Polish folk dance in triple meter.

measure Rhythmic group or metrical unit that contains a fixed number of beats, divided on the musical staff by barlines.

melismatic Melodic style characterized by many notes sung to a single text syllable.

melody Succession of single tones or pitches perceived by the mind as a unity.

membranophone Any instrument that produces sound from tightly stretched membranes that can be struck, plucked, rubbed, or sung into (setting the skin in vibration).

meno Less.

mesto Sad.

metallophone Percussion instrument consisting of tuned metal bars, usually struck with a mallet.

meter Organization of rhythm in time; the grouping of beats into larger, regular patterns, notated as *measures.*

mezzo forte (mf) Moderately loud.

mezzo piano (mp) Moderately soft.

mezzo-soprano Female voice of middle range.

micropolyphony Twentieth-century technique encompassing the complex interweaving of all musical elements.

microtone Musical interval that is smaller than a semitone, prevalent in non-Western music and in some twentieth-century music.

minimalist music Contemporary musical style featuring the repetition of short melodic, rhythmic, and harmonic patterns with little variation.

minnesingers Late Medieval German poet-musicians.

minor scale Scale consisting of seven different tones that comprises a specific pattern of whole and half steps. It differs from the major scale primarily in that its third degree is lowered half a step.

minuet and trio An A-B-A form (A = minuet; B = trio) in a moderate triple meter that is often the third movement of the Classical sonata cycle.

misterioso Mysteriously.

modal Characterizes music that is based on modes other than major and minor, especially the early church modes.

mode Scale or sequence of notes used as the basis for a composition; major and minor are modes.

moderato Moderate.

modulation The process of changing from one key to another.

molto Very.

monody Vocal type, established in the Baroque, in which a single melody predominates.

monophonic Single line or melody without accompaniment.

monothematic Work or movement based on a single theme.

motet Polyphonic vocal genre, secular in the Middle Ages, but sacred or devotional thereafter.

motive Short melodic or rhythmic idea; the smallest fragment of a theme that forms a melodic-harmonic-rhythmic unit.

movement Complete, self-contained part within a larger musical work.

music drama Wagner's term for his operas.

musique concrète Music made up of natural sounds and sound effects that are recorded and then manipulated electronically.

mute Mechanical device used to muffle the sound of an instrument.

nakers Medieval percussion instruments resembling small kettledrums.

neumatic Plainchant melodic style with two to four notes set to each syllable.

neumes Early musical notation signs; square notes on a four-line staff.

ninth chord Five-tone chord spanning a ninth between its lowest and highest tones.

non troppo Not too much.

notturno "Night piece"; a serenade-type composition that combines elements of chamber music and symphony.

oboe Soprano-range double-reed woodwind instrument.

oboe da caccia Alto-range Baroque oboe.

oboe d'amore Mezzo-soprano range Baroque oboe, pitched somewhat below the ordinary oboe.

octave Interval between two tones seven diatonic pitches apart; the lower note vibrates half as fast as the upper and sounds an octave lower.

offbeat A weak beat or any pulse between the beats in a measured rhythmic pattern.

ondes Martenot Electronic instrument that produces sounds by means of an oscillator.

open form Indeterminate contemporary music in which some details of a composition are clearly indicated, but the overall structure is left to choice or chance.

opera Music drama that is generally sung throughout, combining the resources of vocal and instrumental music with poetry and drama, acting and pantomime, scenery and costumes.

opera buffa Italian comic opera, sung throughout.

opéra comique French comic opera, with some spoken dialogue.

opera seria Tragic Italian opera.

oral tradition Music that is transmitted by example or imitation and performed from memory.

oratorio Large-scale dramatic genre originating in the Baroque, based on a text of religious or serious character, performed by solo voices, chorus, and orchestra; it is similar to opera but without scenery, costumes, or action.

Ordinary Chants from the Roman Catholic Mass and other services that remain the same from day to day throughout the church year.

organ Wind instrument in which air is fed to the pipes by mechanical means; the pipes are controlled by two or more keyboards and a set of pedals.

organal style Organum in which the tenor sings the melody (original chant) in very long notes while the upper voices move freely and rapidly above it.

organum Earliest kind of polyphonic music that developed from the custom of adding voices above a plainchant; they first ran parallel to it at the interval of a fifth or fourth, and later moved more freely.

ornamentation See *embellishment.*

ostinato A short melodic, rhythmic, or harmonic pattern that is repeated throughout a work or a section of one.

overture An introductory movement for orchestra, as in an opera or oratorio, often presenting melodies from arias to come; also orchestral work for concert performance.

part song Vocal secular composition, unaccompanied, in three, four, or more parts.

pas de deux In ballet, a dance for two that is an established feature of classical ballet.

passacaglia Baroque form in moderately slow triple meter, based on a short, repeated bass-line melody that serves as the basis for continuous variation in the other voices.

passepied French Baroque court dance type; a faster version of the minuet.

pastorale Pastoral, country-like.

pavane Stately Renaissance court dance in duple meter.

pentatonic scale Five-note pattern used in some African, Far Eastern, and American Indian musics; can also be found in Western music as examples of exoticism.

percussion instrument Instrument made of metal, wood, stretched skin, or other material that is made to sound by striking, shaking, scraping, or plucking.

phrase Musical unit; often a component of a melody.

pianissimo (pp) Very soft.

piano (p) Soft.

piano Keyboard instrument whose strings are struck with hammers controlled by a keyboard mechanism; pedals control dampers in the strings that stop the sound when the finger releases the key.

pianoforte Original name for the piano.

piccolo Smallest woodwind instrument, similar to the flute, but sounding an octave higher.

pitch Location of a tone in relation to highness or lowness.

pizzicato Performance direction to pluck a string of a bowed instrument with the finger.

plainchant See *Gregorian chant.*

plainsong See *Gregorian chant.*

poco A little.

polka Lively Bohemian dance; also a short, lyric piano piece.

polonaise Stately Polish processional dance in triple meter.

polychoral Performance style developed in the late sixteenth century involving the use of two or more choirs that answer each other or sing together.

polyharmony Two or more streams of harmony played against each other, common in twentieth-century music.

polyphonic Two or more melodic lines combined into a multi-voiced texture, as distinct from *monophonic.*

polyrhythm The use of several rhythmic patterns or meters simultaneously, common in twentieth-century music.

polytonality The use of two or more keys simultaneously, common in twentieth-century music.

portative organ Medieval organ small enough to be carried or set on a table, usually with only one set of pipes.

positive organ Small single-manual organ, popular in the Renaissance and Baroque eras.

prelude Instrumental work intended to precede a larger work.

presto Very fast.

program music Instrumental music endowed with literary or pictorial associations, especially popular in the nineteenth century.

program symphony Multi-movement programmatic orchestral work, typically from the nineteenth century.

Proper Chants from the mass and other services that vary from day to day throughout the church year according to the particular liturgical occasion, as distinct from the *Ordinary,* which remain the same.

psaltery Medieval plucked string instrument similar to the modern zither, consisting of a soundbox over which strings were stretched.

pure music See *absolute music.*

quadruple meter Basic metrical pattern of four beats to a measure. Also *common time.*

quadruple stop Playing four notes simultaneously on a string instrument.

Quadruplum Fourth part of a polyphonic work.

quartal harmony Harmony that is based on the interval of the fourth as opposed to a third; used in twentieth-century music.

range Distance between the lowest and highest tones of a melody, an instrument, or a voice.

rebec Medieval bowed, string instrument, often with a pear-shaped body.

Recapitulation Third section of sonata-allegro form in which the thematic material of the Exposition is restated, generally in the tonic. Also *Restatement.*

recitative Solo vocal declamation which follows the inflections of the text, often resulting in a disjunct vocal style; found in the opera, cantata, and oratorio.

recorder End-blown woodwind instrument with a whistle mouthpiece, generally associated with early music.

regal Small Medieval reed organ.

register Specific area in the range of an instrument or voice.

relative key The major or minor key that shares the same key signature; for example, D minor is the relative minor of F major, both having one flat.

repeat sign   Musical symbol (:‖) that indicates repetition of a passage in a composition.

Requiem Mass   Roman Catholic Mass for the Dead.

resolution   Conclusion of a musical idea, as in the progression from an active chord to a rest chord.

response   Short choral answer to a solo verse; an element of liturgical dialogue.

responsorial singing   Singing, especially in Gregorian chant, in which a soloist or a group of soloists alternates with the choir. See also *call and response.*

Restatement   See *Recapitulation.*

retrograde   Backward statement of melody.

retrograde inversion   Mirror image and backward statement of a melody.

rhythm   The controlled movement of music in time.

ripieno   The larger of the two ensembles in the Baroque concerto grosso. Also *tutti.*

ritardando   Holding back, getting slower.

ritornello   Short recurring instrumental passage found both in the aria and the Baroque concerto.

romance   Originally a ballad; in the Romantic era, a lyric, instrumental work.

ronde   Lively Renaissance "round dance," associated with the outdoors, in which the participants danced in a circle or a line.

rondeau   Medieval and Renaissance poetic form and chanson type with courtly love texts.

rondo   Musical form in which the first section recurs, usually in the tonic. In the Classical sonata cycle, it appears as the last movement in various forms, including **A-B-A-B-A, A-B-A-C-A,** and **A-B-A-C-A-B-A.**

round   Perpetual canon at the unison in which each voice enters in succession with the same melody (for example, *Row, Row, Row Your Boat*).

rubato   "Borrowed time," common in Romantic music, in which the performer hesitates here or hurries forward there, imparting flexibility to the written note values. Also *tempo rubato.*

sackbut   Early brass instrument, ancestor of the trombone.

saltarello   Italian "jumping dance" characterized by triplets in a rapid 4/4 time.

sarabande   Stately Spanish Baroque dance type in triple meter, a standard movement of the Baroque suite.

saxophone   Family of single-reed woodwind instruments commonly used in the concert and jazz band.

scale   Series of tones in ascending or descending order that presents the notes of a key.

scat singing   A jazz style that sets nonsense syllables (vocables) to an improvised vocal line.

scherzo   Composition in **A-B-A** form, usually in triple meter.

secco   Operatic recitative which features a sparse accompaniment and moves with great freedom.

semitone   Also known as a half step, the smallest interval of the Western musical system.

sequence   Restatement of an idea or motive at a different pitch level.

serenade   Classical instrumental genre that combines ele-

ments of chamber music and symphony, often performed in the evening or at social functions. Related to *divertimento* and *cassation.*

serialism   Method of composition in which various musical elements (pitch, rhythm, dynamics, tone color) may be ordered in a fixed series. See also *total serialism.*

service   Anglican church term that denoted music for the unchanging Morning and Evening Prayers and for Communion.

seventh chord   Four-note combination consisting of a triad with another third added on top.

sextuple meter   Compound metrical pattern of six beats to a measure.

sforzando (sf)   Sudden stress or accent on a single note or chord.

sharp sign   Musical symbol (♯) which indicates raising a pitch by a semitone.

shawm   Medieval wind instrument that was the ancestor of the oboe.

side drum   See *snare drum.*

sinfonia   Short instrumental work, found in Baroque opera, to facilitate scene changes.

Singspiel   Comic German drama with spoken dialogue; the immediate predecessor of Romantic German opera.

slide trumpet   Medieval brass instrument of the trumpet family.

snare drum   Small cylindrical drum with two heads stretched over a metal shell, the lower head having strings across it; it is played with two drumsticks. Also *side drum.*

sonata   Instrumental genre in several movements for soloist or small ensemble.

sonata-allegro form   The opening movement of the sonata cycle, consisting of themes that are stated in the first section (Exposition), developed in the second section (Development), and restated in the third section (Recapitulation). Also *sonata form* or *first-movement form.*

sonata cycle   General term describing the multi-movement structure found in sonatas, string quartets, symphonies, concertos, and large-scale works of the eighteenth and nineteenth centuries.

sonata da camera   Baroque chamber sonata, usually a suite of stylized dances. Also *chamber sonata.*

sonata da chiesa   Baroque instrumental work intended for performance in church; in four movements frequently arranged slow-fast-slow-fast. Also *church sonata.*

sonata form   See *sonata-allegro form.*

sonatina   Short, modified sonata form, often consisting of an Exposition and Recapitulation without a Development.

soprano   Highest-ranged voice, normally possessed by women or boys.

sousaphone   Brass instrument adapted from the tuba with a forward bell that is coiled to rest over the player's shoulder for ease of carrying while marching.

Sprechstimme   A vocal style in which the melody is spoken at approximate pitches rather than sung on exact pitches; developed by Arnold Schoenberg.

staccato   Short, detached notes, marked with a dot.

Statement   See *Exposition.*

stile concitato   Baroque style developed by Monteverdi, which introduced novel effects such as rapid repeated notes as symbols of passion.

stile rappresentativo A dramatic recitative style of the Baroque period in which melodies moved freely over a foundation of simple chords.

stopping On a string instrument, altering the string length by pressing it on the fingerboard; on a horn, playing with the bell closed by the hand or a mute.

string instruments Bowed and plucked instruments whose sound is produced by the vibration of one or more strings; also *chordophone.*

string quartet Chamber music ensemble consisting of two violins, viola, and cello. Also, a multi-movement composition for this ensemble.

strophic form Song structure in which the same music is repeated with every stanza (strophe) of the poem.

style Characteristic manner of presentation of musical elements (melody, rhythm, harmony, dynamics, form, etc.).

subdominant Fourth scale step, *fa.*

subdominant chord Chord built on the fourth scale step, the IV chord.

subject Main idea or theme of a work, as in a fugue.

syllabic Plainchant melodic style with one note to each syllable of text.

symphonic poem One-movement orchestral form which develops a poetic idea, suggests a scene, or creates a mood, generally associated with the Romantic era. Also *tone poem.*

symphony Large work for orchestra, generally in three or four movements.

syncopation Deliberate upsetting of the meter or pulse through a temporary shifting of the accent to a weak beat or an offbeat.

synthesizer Electronic instrument that produces a wide variety of sounds by combining sound generators and sound modifiers in one package with a unified control system.

tabor Cylindrical Medieval drum.

taille French term for "tenor," as in a Baroque tenor oboe.

tala Fixed time cycle or meter in Indian music, built from uneven groupings of beats.

tambourine Percussion instrument consisting of a small round drum with metal plates inserted in its rim; it is played by striking or shaking.

tam-tam See *gong.*

tempo Rate of speed or pace of music.

tempo rubato See *rubato.*

tenor Male voice of high range; also, a part, often structural, in polyphony.

tenor drum Percussion instrument that is a larger version of the snare drum with a wooden shell.

ternary form Three-part (**A-B-A**) form based on a statement (**A**), a contrast or departure (**B**), and repetition (**A**). Also *three-part form.*

terraced dynamics Expressive style typical of Baroque music in which volume levels shift abruptly from soft to loud and back without gradual crescendos or decrescendos.

tertian harmony Harmony based on the interval of the third, particularly predominant from the Baroque through the nineteenth century.

texture The interweaving of melodic (horizontal) and harmonic (vertical) elements in the musical fabric.

thematic development Musical expansion of a theme by varying its melodic outline, harmony, or rhythm. Also *thematic transformation.*

thematic transformation See *thematic development.*

theme Melodic idea used as a basic building block in the construction of a composition; also *subject.*

theme and variations Compositional procedure in which a theme is stated and then altered in successive statements; occurs as an independent piece or as a movement of a sonata cycle.

theme group Several themes in the same key that function as a unit within a section of a form, particularly in sonata-allegro form.

third Interval between two notes that are two diatonic scale degrees apart.

third stream Jazz style that synthesizes characteristics and techniques of classical music and jazz; term coined by Gunther Schuller.

thorough-bass See *figured bass.*

three-part form See *ternary form.*

through-composed Song structure that is composed from beginning to end, without repetitions of large sections.

timbre The quality of a sound that distinguishes one voice or instrument from another. Also *tone color.*

timpani Percussion instrument consisting of a hemispheric copper shell with a head of plastic or calfskin, held in place by a metal ring and played with soft or hard padded sticks. A pedal mechanism changes the tension of the head, and with it the pitch. Also *kettledrums.*

toccata Virtuoso composition, generally for organ or harpsichord, in a free and rhapsodic style; in the Baroque, it often served as introduction to a fugue.

tombeau An instrumental piece or group of pieces that commemorate someone's death.

tom-tom Cylindrical drum without snares.

tonal Based on principles of major-minor tonality, as distinct from *modal.*

tonality Principle of organization around a tonic or home pitch, based on a major or minor scale.

tone color See *timbre.*

tone poem See *symphonic poem.*

tone row An arrangement of the twelve chromatic tones that serves as the basis of a twelve-tone composition.

tonic The first note of the scale or key, *do.* Also *keynote.*

tonic chord Triad built on the first scale tone, the I chord.

total serialism Extremely complex, totally controlled music in which the twelve-tone principle is extended to elements of music other than pitch.

transposition Shifting a piece of music to a different pitch level.

tremolo Rapid repetition of a tone; can be achieved instrumentally or vocally.

triad Common chord type, consisting of three pitches built on alternate tones of the scale (e.g. steps 1–3–5 or *do-mi-sol*).

triangle Percussion instrument consisting of a slender rod of steel bent in the shape of a triangle that is struck with a steel beater.

trill Ornament consisting of the rapid alternation between one tone and the next above it.

trio sonata   Baroque chamber sonata type written in three parts: two melody lines and the *basso continuo,* requiring four players to perform.

triple meter   Basic metrical pattern of three beats to a measure.

triple-stop   Playing three notes simultaneously on a string instrument.

triplum   Third part in early polyphony.

tritonic   Three-note scale pattern, used in the music of some Southern African cultures.

trombone   Tenor-range brass instrument that changes pitch by means of a moveable double slide. There is also a bass version.

troubadour   Medieval poet-musicians in southern France.

trouvère   Medieval poet-musicians in northern France.

trumpet   Highest-pitched brass instrument that changes pitch through valves.

tuba   Bass-range brass instrument that changes pitch by means of valves.

tubular bells   See *chimes.*

tutti   "All"; the opposite of solo. See also *ripieno.*

twelve-tone music   Compositional procedure of the twentieth century based on a free use of all twelve chromatic tones without a central tone or "tonic."

two-part form   See *binary form.*

unison   Interval between two notes of the same pitch; the simultaneous playing of the same notes.

upbeat   Last beat of the measure, a weak beat, that anticipates the downbeat.

verismo   Operatic "realism," a style popular in Italy in the 1890s which tried to bring naturalism into the lyric theater.

verse   Solo passage from the Gradual which precedes the response (choral answer). In poetry, a group of lines constituting a unit; in liturgical music for the Catholic Church, a phrase from the Scriptures that alternates with the *response.*

verse anthem   Anglican devotional work similar to the motet of the Catholic Church, for solo voices with a choral refrain.

vibraphone   A percussion instrument with metal bars and electrically-driven rotating propellors under each bar that produces an attractive vibrato sound, much used in jazz.

vibrato   Small fluctuation of pitch used as an expressive device to intensify a sound.

vielle   Medieval bowed instrument that was primarily cultivated by the privileged classes and was the ancestor of the violin.

viola   Bowed string instrument of middle range; the second highest member of the violin family.

viola da gamba   Family of Renaissance bowed string instruments that had six or more strings, was fretted like a guitar, and played held between the legs like a modern cello.

violin   Soprano or highest-ranged member of the bowed string instrument family.

violoncello   Bowed string instrument with a middle-to-low range and dark, rich sonority; lower than a viola. Also *cello.*

virelai   Medieval and Renaissance poetic form and chanson type with French courtly texts.

vivace   Lively.

vocalise   A textless vocal melody, as in an exercise or concert piece.

volume   Degree of loudness or softness of a sound. See also *dynamics.*

waltz   Ballroom dance type in triple meter; in the Romantic era, a short, stylized piano piece.

whole-tone scale   Scale pattern built entirely of whole-tone intervals, common in the music of the French impressionists.

woodwind   Instrumental family made of wood or metal whose tone is produced by a column of air vibrating within a pipe that has holes along its length.

word painting   Musical pictorialization of words from the text as an expressive device; a prominent feature of the Renaissance madrigal.

xylophone   Percussion instrument consisting of blocks of wood suspended on a frame, laid out in the shape of a keyboard and struck with hard mallets.

Appendix IV

Attending Concerts

Despite the many ways now available to hear fine quality recorded music, nothing can equal the excitement of a live concert. The crowded hall, the visual as well as aural stimulation of a perfomance, even the element of unpredictability—of what might happen on a particular night—all contribute to the unique, communicative powers of people making music. There are, however, certain traditions surrounding concerts and concert-going—how to chose seats, the way performers dress, the appropriate moment to applaud, are but a few. Understanding these traditions can contribute to your increased enjoyment of the musical event.

Choosing Concerts, Tickets, and Seats

Widely diversified musical events, performed by groups ranging from professional orchestras and college ensembles to church choirs, can be found in most parts of the country. It may take some ingenuity and research to discover the full gamut of concerts available in your area. Both city and college newspapers usually publish a calendar of upcoming events; these are often announced as well on the local radio stations. Bulletin boards on campus and in public buildings and stores are good places to find concert announcements. Often a music or fine arts department of a college will post a printed list of future events featuring both professional and student performers.

Ticket prices will vary considerably, depending on the nature of the event and the geographical location of the theater. Many fine performances can be heard for a small admission price, especially at college and civic auditoriums. For an orchestra concert or an opera in a major metropolitan area, you can expect to pay anywhere from $20 to $75 for a reserved seat. The first rows of the orchestra section, located at stage level, and of the first balcony or loge are usually the most expensive. Although many consider it desirable to sit as close as possible to the performers, these are often not the best seats for acoustical reasons. To hear a proper balance, especially of a large ensemble, you are better off sitting in the middle of the hall. Today, most new concert halls are constructed so that virtually all seats are satisfactory. For the opera, many people bring opera glasses or binoculars if they are sitting some distance from the stage.

Concert tickets may be reserved in advance as well as purchased at the door. Often, reduced prices are available for students and senior citizens. Tickets reserved by telephone, or charged to a credit card, are generally not refundable; they are held at the box office in your name.

Preparing for the Concert

You may want to find out what specific works will be performed at an upcoming concert so that you can read about them and their composers in advance. If this

WORLD EVENTS	COMPOSERS	PRINCIPAL FIGURES
1776 *Adam Smith's* The Wealth of Nations.	LUDWIG VAN BEETHOVEN (1770–1827)	J. M. W. Turner (1775–1851) English painter
1778 *La Scala Opera opened in Milan.*	GASPARO SPONTINI (1774–1851)	
1787 *Constitutional Convention.*	NICCOLÒ PAGANINI (1782–1840)	Jean Ingres (1780–1867) French painter
1789 *French Revolution begins.*	TIMOTHY SWAN (1785–1842)	Lord Byron (1788–1824) English poet
1791 *Bill of Rights.*	CARL MARIA VON WEBER (1786–1826)	Percy Bysshe Shelley (1792–1822), English poet
1793 *Eli Whitney's cotton gin.*	GIACOMO MEYERBEER (1791–1864)	Jean Baptiste Corot (1796–1875) French landscape painter
1796 *Jenner introduces vaccination.*	GIOACCHINO ROSSINI (1792–1868)	Alexander Pushkin (1799–1837) Russian poet and novelist
1800 *Laplace's mechanistic view of the universe.*		Honoré de Balzac (1799–1850) French novelist
1803 *Louisiana Purchase.*	LOWELL MASON (1792–1872) GAETANO DONIZETTI (1797–1848)	Ralph Waldo Emerson (1803–82) American poet and philosopher
1812 *Napoleon invades Russia.*		
1815 *Battle of Waterloo. Congress of Vienna.*	FRANZ SCHUBERT (1797–1828) VINCENZO BELLINI (1801–35)	Honoré Daumier (1808–79) French painter
1819 *First steamship to cross Atlantic.*	HECTOR BERLIOZ (1803–69) JOHANN STRAUSS (The Father) (1804–49)	Edgar Allan Poe (1809–49) American poet and writer
1823 *Monroe Doctrine.*	MIKHAIL GLINKA (1804–57) FELIX MENDELSSOHN (1809–47)	Nikolai Gogol (1809–52) Russian novelist
1824 *Bolivar liberates South America.*	FRÉDÉRIC CHOPIN (1810–49) ROBERT SCHUMANN (1810–56)	Charlotte Brontë (1816–55) English novelist
1829 *Independence of Greece.*	FRANZ LISZT (1811–86) RICHARD WAGNER (1813–83)	
1830 *First railroad, Liverpool-Manchester. July Revolution in France.*	GIUSEPPE VERDI (1813–1901) WILLIAM HENRY FRY (1815–64)	Henry David Thoreau (1817–62) American naturalist and poet
1832 *Morse invents telegraph.*	CHARLES GOUNOD (1818–93) JACQUES OFFENBACH (1819–80)	Ivan Turgenev (1818–83) Russian novelist
1833 *Slavery outlawed in British Empire.*	CLARA SCHUMANN (1819–96) CÉSAR FRANCK (1822–90)	Walt Whitman (1819–92) American poet
1834 *McCormick patents mechanical reaper.*	ÉDOUARD LALO (1823–92)	Charles Baudelaire (1821–67) French poet Feodor Dostoevsky (1821–81) Russian novelist
1837 *Queen Victoria ascends the throne.*	BEDŘICH SMETANA (1824–84)	Henrik Ibsen (1828–1906) Norwegian poet and playwright
1839 *Daguerrotype invented. New York Philharmonic Society and Vienna Philharmonic founded*	JOHANN STRAUSS (The Son) (1825–99)	Leo Tolstoi (1828–1910) Russian novelist
1846 *Repeal of Corn Laws. Famine in Ireland.*	GEORGE FREDERICK BRISTOW (1825–98) STEPHEN COLLINS FOSTER (1826–64)	Emily Dickinson (1830–86) American poet
1848 *Revolutions throughout Europe. Gold Rush in California. Marx's* Communist Manifesto.	WILLIAM MASON (1829–1908)	Camille Pissarro (1830–1903) French painter
1852 *Second Empire under Napoleon III. Stowe's* Uncle Tom's Cabin.	LOUIS MOREAU GOTTSCHALK (1829–69) JOHANNES BRAHMS (1833–97)	Edouard Manet (1832–83) French painter
1854 *Commodore Perry opens Japan to the West. Crimean War.*	ALEXANDER BORODIN (1834–87)	James Whistler (1834–1903) American painter
1855 *Charge of the Light Brigade.*	CAMILLE SAINT-SAËNS (1835–1921) LÉO DELIBES (1836–91)	Mark Twain (1835–1910) American author Algernon Swinburne (1837–1909) English poet

WORLD EVENTS	COMPOSERS	PRINCIPAL FIGURES
1857 *Dred Scott decision.*	MILY BALAKIREV (1837–1910)	
	GEORGES BIZET (1838–75)	H. H. Richardson (1838–86)
1858 *Covent Garden opened as opera house.*	MODEST MUSORGSKY (1839–81)	American architect
	JOHN KNOWLES PAINE	
	(1839–1906)	Paul Cézanne (1839–1906)
1859 *Darwin's* Origin of Species. *John Brown raids Harper's Ferry.*		French painter
	PETER ILYICH TCHAIKOVSKY	Auguste Rodin (1840–1917)
	(1840–93)	French sculptor
1861 *Serfs emancipated in Russia. American Civil War begins.*		Thomas Hardy (1840–1928)
	EMMANUEL CHABRIER (1841–94)	English novelist and poet
	ANTONÍN DVOŘÁK (1841–1904)	Pierre Renoir (1841–1919)
1863 *Emancipation Proclamation.*	JULES MASSENET (1842–1912)	French painter
	EDVARD GRIEG (1843–1907)	Henry James (1843–1916)
1865 *Civil War ends. Lincoln assassinated.*	NIKOLAI RIMSKY-KORSAKOV	American novelist
	(1844–1908)	Paul Verlaine (1844–96)
1866 *Transatlantic cable completed.*		French poet
	GABRIEL FAURÉ (1845–1924)	Friedrich Nietzsche (1844–1900)
1867 *Marx's* Das Kapital *(Vol. I). Alaska purchased.*	HENRI DUPARC (1848–1933)	German philosopher
	VINCENT D'INDY (1851–1931)	Mary Cassatt (1845–1926)
	ARTHUR FOOTE (1853–1937)	American painter
		Paul Gauguin (1848–1903)
1870 *Franco-Prussian War. Vatican Council proclaims papal infallibility.*	LEOŠ JANÁČEK (1854–1928)	French painter
		Vincent Van Gogh (1853–90)
	GEORGE CHADWICK (1854–1931)	Dutch painter
1871 *William I of Hohenzollern becomes German Emperor. Paris Commune. Unification of Italy. Stanley and Livingston in Africa.*	ERNEST CHAUSSON (1855–99)	Louis H. Sullivan (1856–1924)
		American architect
	EDWARD ELGAR (1857–1934)	George Bernard Shaw (1856–1950)
	RUGGIERO LEONCAVALLO	Irish dramatist and critic
	(1858–1919)	
1873 *Dynamo developed.*	GIACOMO PUCCINI (1858–1924)	Anton Chekhov (1860–1904)
	HUGO WOLF (1860–1903)	Russian writer
1875 *New Paris Opera House opened.*	ISAAC ALBÉNIZ (1860–1909)	Maurice Maeterlinck (1862–1949)
	GUSTAV MAHLER (1860–1911)	Belgian poet and dramatist
1876 *Telephone invented. Bayreuth theater opened.*	EDWARD MACDOWELL	Gabriele D'Annunzio (1862–1938)
	(1861–1908)	Italian poet and dramatist
	CHARLES MARTIN LOEFFLER	Henri de Toulouse-Lautrec
1877 *Phonograph invented.*	(1861–1935)	(1864–1901) French painter
	CLAUDE DEBUSSY (1862–1918)	Rudyard Kipling (1865–1936)
1880 *Irish Insurrection.*	FREDERICK DELIUS (1862–1934)	English novelist and poet
	HORATIO PARKER (1863–1919)	Wassily Kandinsky (1866–1944)
1881 *Tsar Alexander II assassinated. President Garfield shot. Panama Canal begun. Boston Symphony founded.*	PIETRO MASCAGNI (1863–1945)	Russian painter
	RICHARD STRAUSS (1864–1949)	H. G. Wells (1866–1946)
	ALEXANDER GRECHANINOV	English novelist
	(1864–1956)	Luigi Pirandello (1867–1936)
	PAUL DUKAS (1865–1935)	Italian dramatist
1882 *Koch discovers tuberculosis germ. Berlin Philharmonic founded.*	ALEXANDER GLAZUNOV	Maxim Gorky (1868–1936)
	(1865–1936)	Russian writer
	JEAN SIBELIUS (1865–1957)	Henri Matisse (1869–1954)
1883 *Brooklyn Bridge opened. Metropolitan Opera opened. Amsterdam Concertgebouw founded.*	FERRUCIO BUSONI (1866–1924)	French painter
	ERIK SATIE (1866–1925)	John Marin (1870–1953)
	MRS. H. H. A. BEACH	American painter
	(1867–1944)	Marcel Proust (1871–1922)
1884 *Pasteur discovers inoculation against rabies.*	SCOTT JOPLIN (1868–1917)	French novelist
	ALBERT ROUSSEL (1869–1937)	Theodore Dreiser (1871–1945)
	ARTHUR FARWELL (1872–1951)	American novelist
1886 *Statue of Liberty unveiled in New York harbor.*	RALPH VAUGHAN WILLIAMS	Sergei Diaghilev (1872–1929)
	(1872–1958)	Russian impressario
	MAX REGER (1873–1916)	Piet Mondrian (1872–1946)
1887 *Daimler patents high-speed internal combustion machine.*	SERGEI RACHMANINOFF	Dutch painter
	(1873–1943)	Willa Cather (1873–1947)
	DANIEL GREGORY MASON	American novelist
	(1873–1953)	Gertrude Stein (1874–1946)
1880 *Eiffel Tower. Brazil becomes a republic.*	ARNOLD SCHOENBERG	American poet
	(1874–1951)	
1890 *Journey around world completed in 72 days.*	CHARLES IVES (1874–1954)	W. Somerset Maugham (1874–
	MAURICE RAVEL (1875–1937)	1965), English novelist
	MANUEL DE FALLA (1876–1946)	and playwright

WORLD EVENTS	COMPOSERS	PRINCIPAL FIGURES
1892 *Duryea makes first American gas buggy.*	CARL RUGGLES (1876–1971)	Rainer Maria Rilke (1875–1926) German poet
	OTTORINO RESPIGHI (1879–1936)	
1894 *Nicholas II, last Tsar, ascends throne.*	ERNEST BLOCH (1880–1959) ILDEBRANDO PIZZETTI (1880–1968)	Constantine Brancusi (1876–1958) Rumanian sculptor Isadora Duncan (1878–1927)
1895 *Roentgen discovers X-rays. Marconi's wireless telegraphy.*	BÉLA BARTÓK (1881–1945) GEORGES ENESCO (1881–1955) GERMAINE TAILLEFERRE (1892–1983)	American dancer Paul Klee (1879–1940) Swiss painter
1897 *Queen Victoria's Diamond Jubilee.*	IGOR STRAVINSKY (1882–1971) ZOLTAN KODALY (1882–1967)	Pablo Picasso (1881–1973) Spanish artist
1898 *The Curies discover radium. Spanish-American War.*	GIAN FRANCESCO MALIPIERO (1882–1973) EDGARD VARÈSE (1883–1965)	Virginia Woolf (1882–1941) English novelist Franz Kafka (1883–1924)
1899 *Boer War. First International Peace Conference at the Hague.*	ANTON WEBERN (1883–1945) CHARLES T. GRIFFES (1884–1920)	Bohemian writer
1990 *Boxer Insurrection in China.*	ALBAN BERG (1885–1935) JELLY ROLL MORTON	Amadeo Modigliani (1884–1920) Italian painter and sculptor
1901 *Queen Victoria dies. Edward VII succeeds.*	(1885–1941) WALLINGFORD RIEGGER (1885–1961)	Sinclair Lewis (1885–1951) American novelist Diego Rivera (1886–1951)
1903 *Wrights' first successful airplane flight.*	HEITOR VILLA-LOBOS (1887–1959)	Mexican painter Juan Gris (1887–1927) Spanish painter
1905 *Sigmund Freud founds psychoanalysis. First Russian Revolution.*	BOHUSLAV MARTINU (1890–1959) JACQUES IBERT (1890–1963)	Georgia O'Keefe (1887–1986) American painter
1906 *San Francisco earthquake and fire.*	SERGE PROKOFIEV (1891–1952)	Giorgio di Chirico (1888–1978) Italian painter
1908 *Model-T Ford produced.*	ARTHUR HONEGGER (1892–1955)	Karel Čapek (1890–1938) Czech dramatist
1909 *Peary reaches North Pole.*	DARIUS MILHAUD (1892–1974)	Joan Miró (1893–1983) Spanish painter Martha Graham (1894–) American choreographer
1911 *Amundsen reaches South Pole.*	DOUGLAS MOORE (1893–1969)	Aldous Huxley (1894–1963) English novelist
1912 *China becomes republic. Titanic sinks.*	BESSIE SMITH (1894–1937)	Robert Graves (1895–1985) English poet
1914 *Panama Canal begins. World War I begins.*	WALTER PISTON (1894–1976) KAROL RATHAUS (1895–1954) PAUL HINDEMITH (1895–1963) WILLIAM GRANT STILL	F. Scott Fitzgerald (1896–1940) American novelist Louis Aragon (1897–) French novelist and poet
1917 *U.S. enters World War I. Russian Revolution. Prohibition Amendment.*	(1895–1978) CARL ORFF (1895–1982) HOWARD HANSON (1896–1981) ROGER SESSIONS (1898–1985)	Sergei Eisenstein (1898–1948) Russian film director Ernest Hemingway (1898–1961) American novelist
1918 *Kaiser abdicates. World War I ends in armistice.*	VIRGIL THOMSON (1896–1989) HENRY COWELL (1897–1965) GEORGE GERSHWIN (1898–1937)	Henry Moore (1989–) English sculptor
1919 *Treaty of Versailles. Mussolini founds Italian Fascist Party.*	ROY HARRIS (1898–1979) E. K. ("DUKE") ELLINGTON (1899–1974)	Federico García Lorca (1899–1936) Spanish poet and playwright
1920 *Women's suffrage: Nineteenth Amendment passed.*	RANDALL THOMPSON (1899–1984)	Thomas Wolfe (1900–38) American novelist
1922 *Discovery of insulin.*	FRANCIS POULENC (1899–1963) AARON COPLAND (1900–)	Ignazio Silone (1901–78) Italian novelist
1923 *U.S.S.R. established.*	ERNST KRENEK (1900–) KURT WEILL (1900–50)	André Malraux (1901–76) French novelist and critic
1927 *Lindbergh solo flight across Atlantic.*	LOUIS ARMSTRONG (1900–71) RUTH CRAWFORD (1901–53) WILLIAM WALTON	John Steinbeck (1902–68) American novelist Langston Hughes (1902–67)
1930 *The planet Pluto discovered*	(1902–83) STEFAN WOLPE (1902–71)	American poet and playwright

WORLD EVENTS	COMPOSERS	PRINCIPAL FIGURES
1931 *Japan invades Manchuria. Empire State Building is completed.*	LUIGI DALLAPICCOLA (1904–75) MARC BLITZSTEIN (1905–64)	Salvador Dali (1904–89) Spanish painter
1933 *Franklin D. Roosevelt inaugurated. Hitler takes over German government.*	LOUISE TALMA (1906–) DMITRI SHOSTAKOVICH (1906–75)	George Balanchine (1904–83) Russian choreographer
1936 *Spanish Civil War. Sulfa drugs introduced in the U.S.*	MIRIAM GIDEON (1906–) ELLIOTT CARTER (1908–) OLIVIER MESSIAEN (1908–)	Jean-Paul Sartre (1905–80) French philosopher and novelist
1937 *Japan invades China.*	HOWARD SWANSON (1909–78) SAMUEL BARBER (1910–82)	W. H. Auden (1907–73) English poet and dramatist
1939 *World War II starts. Germany invades Poland, Britain and France declare war on Germany, Russia invades Finland.*	WILLIAM SCHUMAN (1910–) GIAN CARLO MENOTTI (1911–) VLADIMIR USSACHEVSKY (1911–)	Richard Wright (1908–60) American novelist
1940 *Roosevelt elected to third term. Churchill becomes British prime minister.*	ARTHUR BERGER (1912–) JOHN CAGE (1912–) HUGO WEISGALL (1912–)	Eugene Ionesco (1912–) Rumanian-born French dramatist
1941 *U.S. attacked by Japan, declares war on Japan, Germany, Italy.*	WITOLD LUTOSŁAWSKI (1913–) BENJAMIN BRITTEN (1913–76) BILLIE HOLIDAY (1915–59)	Dylan Thomas (1914–53) Welsh poet and playwright
1943 *Germans defeated at Stalingrad and in North Africa. Italy surrenders.*	DAVID DIAMOND (1915–) GEORGE PERLE (1915–)	Tennessee Williams (1914–83) American playwright
1944 *D-Day. Invasion of France.*	MILTON BABBITT (1916–) ALBERTO GINASTERA (1916–83)	Arthur Miller (1915–) American playwright
1945 *Germany surrenders. Atom bomb dropped on Hiroshima. Japan surrenders. Roosevelt dies.*	ULYSSES KAY (1917–) LEONARD BERNSTEIN (1918–)	Ingmar Bergman (1918–) Swedish filmmaker
1948 *Gandhi assassinated.*	GEORGE ROCHBERG (1918–) LEON KIRCHNER (1919–)	J. D. Salinger (1919–) American novelist
1949 *Communist defeat Chang Kai-shek in China. U.S.S.R. explodes atom bomb.*	CHARLIE PARKER (1920–55) RALPH SHAPEY (1921–)	Federico Fellini (1920–) Italian filmmaker Richard Wilbur (1921–) American poet
1950 *North Korea invades South Korea.*	LUKAS FOSS (1922–) IANNIS XENAKIS (1922–)	
1952 *Eisenhower elected President.*	GYÖRGY LIGETI (1923–) JEAN EICHELBERGER IVEY (1923–)	Denise Levertov (1923–) American poet
1955 *Warsaw Pact signed. Salk serum for infantile paralysis.*	JOAN TOWER (1923–) PETER MENNIN (1923–83)	Norman Mailer (1923–) American novelist
1957 *First underground atomic explosion.*	MEL POWELL (1923–) NED ROREM (1923–)	James Baldwin (1924–87) American novelist
1959 *Alaska becomes 49th state. Castro victorious in Cuba. Hawaii becomes 50th state.*	LUIGI NONO (1924–) JULIA PERRY (1924–79)	Kenneth Koch (1925–) American poet
1960 *Kennedy elected President.*	LUCIANO BERIO (1925–)	Robert Rauschenberg (1925–) American artist
1963 *Cuban missile crisis. Algeria declared independent of France.* **1963** *Kennedy assassinated. Lyndon Johnson becomes President.*	PIERRE BOULEZ (1925–) GUNTHER SCHULLER (1925–) EARLE BROWN (1926–)	John Ashbery (1927–) American poet Günter Grass (1927–) German novelist
1965 *First walk in space. Alabama Civil Rights March.*	MORTON FELDMAN (1926–87)	John Hollander (1929–) American poet
1967 *Israeli-Arab "Six-Day War." First successful heart transplant.*	BEN JOHNSTON (1926–) BETSY JOLAS (1926–)	Adrienne Rich (1929–) American poet

WORLD EVENTS	COMPOSERS	PRINCIPAL FIGURES
1968 *Richard M. Nixon elected President. Martin Luther King and Robert F. Kennedy assassinated.*	HANS WERNER HENSE (1926–) SALVATORE MARTIRANO (1927–)	Claes Oldenburg (1929–) American artist
1970 *U.S. intervention in Cambodia. Nobel Prize in Literature to Solzhenitsyn.*	JACOB DRUCKMAN (1928–) THEA MUSGRAVE (1928–)	Jean-Luc Godard (1930–) French filmmaker
1972 *Richard Nixon reelected.*	KARLHEINZ STOCKHAUSEN (1928–)	Jasper Johns (1930–) American painter
1973 *Vietnam War ends. "Watergate Affair" begins. Vice President Agnew resigns.*	GEORGE CRUMB (1929–) DAVID BAKER (1931–)	Harold Pinter (1930–) English dramatist
1974 *President Nixon resigns.*	LUCIA DLUGOSZEWSKI (1931–)	Andy Warhol (1931–87) American artist
1975 *Francisco Franco dies.*		
1976 *Viking spacecraft lands on Mars. Mao Zedong dies. Jimmy Carter elected President.*	KRZYSZTOF PENDERECKI (1933–) MARIO DAVIDOVSKY (1934–) PETER MAXWELL DAVIES (1934–)	Yevgeny Yevtushenko (1933–) Soviet poet Inamu Amiri Baraka (Le Roi Jones) (1934–) American poet
1977 *New Panama Canal Treaty signed. Menachem Begin named Israeli Prime Minister.*	ALFRED SCHNITTKE (1934–) JOHN EATON (1935–) ARVO PÄRT (1935–)	Frank Stella (1936–) American artist
1978 *First Polish Pope (John Paul II).*	STEVE REICH (1936–)	Tom Stoppard (1937–) Czech-born English playwright
1979 *Shah of Iran deposed. Major nuclear accident at Three-Mile Island.*	DAVID DEL TREDICI (1937–)	Lanford Wilson (1937–) American playwright
1980 *Ronald Reagan elected President.*	PHILIP GLASS (1937–)	David Hockney (1937–) British painter
1981 *First woman appointed to Supreme Court. Egyptian President Sadat assassinated.*	WILLIAM BOLCOM (1938–) CHARLES WUORINEN (1938–)	Alan Ayckbourn (1939–) British dramatist
1983 *First woman astronaut into space. U.S. invades Grenada.*	ELLEN TAAFFE ZWILICH (1939–) BARBARA KOLB (1939–)	Sam Shepard (1943–) American playwright and actor
1984 *Reagan reelected President. AIDS virus identified. Bishop Tutu wins Nobel peace prize.*	LAURIE ANDERSON (1947–)	Rainer Werner Fassbinder (1946–82) German film and stage director
1985 *Reagan-Gorbachev summit meeting.*	JOHN ADAMS (1947–)	
1986 *Space shuttle Challenger crew dies in launching disaster. Iran-Contra scandal revealed.*	OLIVER KNUSSEN (1952–)	Wendy Wasserstein (1950–) American playwright
1988 *George Bush elected U. S. President. Mikhail Gorbachev named Soviet President.*	TOBIAS PICKER (1954–)	
1989 *Polish Solidarity trade union legalized. Pro-democracy demonstrations in China.*		Peter Sellars (1958–) American stage director

Index

Definitions of terms appear on the pages indicated in **bold** type.
Illustrations are indicated by *italic* numbers.